Samoan & Tonga

Paul Smitz
Susannah Farfor

WALLIS & FUTUNA (FRANCE)

SAMOA

TONGA

MT MATAVANU CRATER (p95)
Follow your nose through enigmatic plantations and up the side of a once-destructive volcano

AFU AAU FALLS (p99)
Visit a sublime, secretive waterhole fed by the cool overflow of a jungle waterfall

THE NIUAS (p265)
Be among the handful of visitors that venture this far

ELEVATION
2000m
1000m
500m
200m
0

LEGEND
Primary
Secondary
Unsealed

0 — 100 km
0 — 60 miles
Atolls not to scale

OFU BEACH (p127)
Relax on the gorgeous, coral-fringed jewel in the crown of Pacific beaches

AMERICAN SAMOA (USA)

PAGO PAGO

See Tutuila Enlargement

NATIONAL PARK OF AMERICAN SAMOA, TA'U (p129)
Hike through the rainforest in one of the most remote places on Earth

See 'Upolu Enlargement

PALOLO DEEP MARINE RESERVE (p64)
Check out the magical coral crevices, technicolour fish and some monster clams

ROBERT LOUIS STEVENSON MUSEUM (p74)
Wander through the immaculate grounds and history-soaked rooms of a famous author's villa

'Upolu

APIA

0 — 20 km
0 — 12 miles

Tutuila

MT ALAVA (p108)
Take the high road
to a razor-sharp ridge
with Pacific-wide views

Mt Alava (491m)
Matafao Peak (653m)
Mt Olotele (493m)
Mt Loalila'alava (354m)

PAGO PAGO

Pola Tai
Vatia
Onenoa
Amalau Valley
Masefau
Afono
Sa'ilele
Amouli
Rainmaker Mountain (523m)
Alofau
Aua
Lauli'ituai
Ma'a
Kamela
Faga'alu
Faganeanea
Utulei
Nu'uuli
Fagasa
Tafuna
Masepa
Airport
Hirili
Vaitogi
Avaoudou
Pava'ia'i
Taputimu
Vailoa
Nua
Asili
Leone
Fagamalo
Amanave
Fagali'i
Poloa

Aunu'u
Mt Olomoana (327m)
Nuusetoga

10 km
6 miles

Tongatapu

'Eue'iki
Nuku Fukave
Velitoa
'Oneval
'Onevao
Motutapu
Eafa
Makaha'a
Manuka
Pangaimotu
Manima
'Onealo
Afa
Kolonga
Niutoua
Lapaha Archaeological Area
Haveluliku
Fatumu
Lavengatonga
Hamula
Fua'amotu
Nuku'alofa
Hoi
Mua
Malapo
Pelehake
Ha'asini
Nukuleka
Nukunukumotu
Foladha
Vaini
Vietongo
'Utulau
Ha'akame
Airport
Tofoa
Pe'a
Kanatea
Puke
Fatai
Matahau
Houma
Vaotu'u
Mapu'a 'a
Vaca blowholes
Takoke
Tufaka
Alakipeau
Polo'a
Ha'atafu
Neiafu
Ha'akili
Kolovai
Fo'ui
Nukunuku
Ha'utu
Kala'au

Pita Passage

10 km
6 miles

International Date Line

VAVA'U (p243)
Swim, sail or dive in one
of the world's prime destinations
for watching humpback whales

Vava'u Group

TOFUA (p239)
Clamber up remote volcanic
Tofua and peer into its glowing
and rumbling caldera

LIFUKA GROUP (p228)
Immerse yourself in traditional
culture on Ha'ano, then watch
time float by your *fale* in paradise

Ha'apai Group
Lifuka Group

'EUA (p215)
Hike through rainforest,
descend into massive sinkholes
and monkey-climb a banyan
tree back out again

TONGATAPU (p179)
Marvel at the South Pacific's
Stonehenge, explore pyramidal tombs
and applaud the spurting blowholes

See Tongatapu
Enlargement

NUKU'ALOFA

Tongatapu
Group

Destination
Samoan Islands & Tonga

If beauty is in the eye of the beholder, then the inhabitants of the Samoan islands and Tonga must have the most beautiful eyes in the world.

The idyllic norm in all three of the small nations that are anchored to the bottom of the South Pacific involves lush, reef-fringed islands with sandy foreshores that almost glow in the tropical sunshine. Even when it rains, the sense of verdancy is so strong you can almost hear the *heilala*, *teuila* and hibiscus flowers stretching upwards. The pristine oceanic depths that thread through this Pacific enclave host thousands of species of marine life, from kaleidoscopic coral to the flukes of humpbacks that come to spawn their young in the warm waters.

Human life in the region is so passionately idiosyncratic that almost every local encounter yields a memorable moment. Local women and men break into loud, spontaneous song in restaurants and in bus station throngs. Villagers casually swing intimidating bush knives by their sides as they walk along the roadsides. Kids sit on the scuffed tombs of relatives in their front yards as if they were outdoor furniture, and have a habit of yelling 'bye bye'. Games of rugby and volleyball are played with gladiatorial intensity on sports grounds and fields.

While snorkelling, diving, sailing, swimming, hiking, drinking, whale-watching, feasting on seafood and talking about nothing in particular with loquacious locals, visitors to these islands quickly learn how to release their inner tensions and replace them with a paradisal calm.

PETER HENDR

Highlights

Catch some impressive wave action at Alofaaga Blowholes (p100), Savai'i, Samoa

MICHELLE BENNETT

PETER HENDRIE

Watch a traditional firedancer at Aggie Greys Hotel (p73), Apia, Samoa

Shop day or night at the Maketi Fou (p64), Apia, Samoa

MARK DAFFEY

OTHER HIGHLIGHTS

- Snorkel in the colourful depths of the Palolo Deep Marine Reserve (p64), 'Upolu, Samoa.
- Experience some magical fog when you swim into Mariner's Cave (p262), Nuapapu, Vava'u Group, Tonga.
- Visit the dramatic island of Tofua (p240) with its active volcano and impressive crater lake, Ha'apai Group, Tonga.

MARK DAFFE

Take a tour of the beautifully restored Villa Vailima, now the Robert Louis Stevenson Museum (p74), 'Upolu, Samoa

PETER HENDRIE

The ceiling of the Hotel Kitano Samoa (p69), 'Upolu, Samoa, borrows from traditional Samoan *fale* architecture

Look out for traditional Samoan tattoos (p38), Savai'i, Samoa

PETER HENDRIE

MICHELLE BENNETT

Local children form a welcoming committee, Olosega village, Olosega (p128), Manu'a Islands, American Samoa

Rain clouds approach the secluded Ofu Beach (p127), Ofu, Manu'a Islands, American Samoa

PETER HENDRIE

8

Swim with humpback whales (p248) in the waters off Vava'u Group, Tonga

Ponder the mysteries of the South Pacific's Stonehenge: Ha'amonga 'a Maui Trilithon (p209), Tongatapu Group, Tonga

Hike through pristine rainforest (p220) on 'Eua, Tongatapu Group, Tonga

Contents

Regional Map Contents

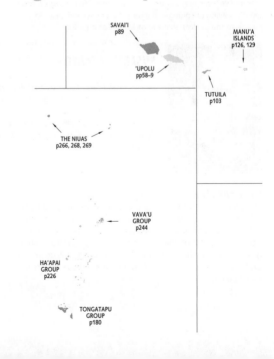

SAVAI'I
p89

MANU'A
ISLANDS
p126, 129

'UPOLU
pp58–9

TUTUILA
p103

THE NIUAS
p266, 268, 269

VAVA'U
GROUP
p244

HA'APAI
GROUP
p226

TONGATAPU
GROUP
p180

The Authors

PAUL SMITZ   Coordinating Author, Samoa & American Samoa

Paul has believed the South Pacific to be an adventurous place ever since a ship he was on caught fire off Fiji – OK, he was six years old at the time, but the memory has stayed with him. He has tackled several other Pacific destinations for Lonely Planet, including Australia and New Zealand, but he found his research on 'Upolu, Savai'i and Tutuila, plus numerous smaller islands such as Apolima, Ofu and Aunu'u, was as exhilarating as a tropical high-seas field trip gets. The spectacular terrain, the oceanic vistas and the warmth of the locals have entrenched the word 'paradisal' in his otherwise limited vocabulary.

The Coordinating Author's Favourite Trip

My trip across the Samoan islands contained numerous special moments, but swooping down on the minuscule airstrip on Ofu (p126) in the Manu'a Islands was the highlight. I stepped from the plane and straight into the warm hospitality of Va'oto Lodge (p128), then lunged across the airstrip and into the waters of the island's sublime lagoon. I caught a lift to Ofu village (p127), where I was greeted by local families and territorial dogs, before walking past the hidden, mystical To'aga site (p127) and plunging straight off deserted Ofu Beach (p127) to snorkel in the most magical waters I've ever seen. Later, I crossed the Ofu-Olosega bridge (p128) (leaving the plunge off it for another day) and past Olosega village to the perfect solitude of Maga Point (p128).

SUSANNAH FARFOR   Tonga

Susannah is an Australian-based writer and editor whose work regularly appears in food- and adventure-related travel publications. She has explored many of the South Pacific's gems since donning her first grass skirt in Tahiti at age seven, and has also researched and written on the Cook Islands and Australia series guides for Lonely Planet. For this title she got a taste for Tonga while sailing, snorkelling, kayaking, delving into caves and sinking her toes into the sand on long stretches of uninhabited beach.

My Favourite Trip

On Tonga's main island, Tongatapu, some of my happiest hours were spent discovering for myself the ancient, overgrown archaeological sites of Mu'a and Lapaha (p199) and chilling out near the magnificent edifice of the Ha'amonga 'a Maui trilithon (p209). Offshore, I had trouble leaving the luxury of Pangaimotu (p213) and loved the quiet tropical jungles of 'Eua and its national park (p215).

CONTRIBUTING AUTHORS

Martin Robinson wrote the Samoan islands Snapshots chapter. Martin lived on Samoa for a year getting to know the islands from the grassroots by staying with hospitable families in small villages on all the main islands. From his experiences and other research he has written numerous articles on Samoan culture and history for Pacific island magazines. He currently lives in Auckland, on another Polynesian island that he has written about for Lonely Planet.

Michael Sorokin wrote the Health chapter. Dr Sorokin has extensive experience as a physician and GP in South Africa, the UK, the Pacific islands and rural South Australia. He has special interests in rheumatology, infectious diseases and preventative medicine. He was recently awarded the Order of Fiji in recognition of his services to health care in Fiji. Dr Sorokin is partly responsible for the maintenance of the Traveller's Medical & Vaccination Centre (TMVC) Database and helps with reference material for the continuing education of TMVC medical staff.

Miranda Tetlow wrote and updated the Tonga Snapshots chapter. Miranda is a columnist, freelance writer and broadcaster, currently working in Australia for the *Canberra Times* and Triple J. In 2003 she was lucky enough to spend 12 months in Nuku'alofa. Most of this time was spent working as a Media Advisor for a Tongan NGO and learning the much maligned art of cooking *sipi* (mutton flaps). Despite a series of unfortunate events that involved dengue fever, tinned corned beef and an amorous taxi driver, Miranda has been passionate about Tonga and its people ever since.

LONELY PLANET AUTHORS

Why is our travel information the best in the world? It's simple: our authors are independent, dedicated travellers. They don't research using just the Internet or phone, and they don't take freebies in exchange for positive coverage. They travel widely, to all the popular spots and off the beaten track. They personally visit thousands of hotels, restaurants, cafés, bars, galleries, palaces, museums and more – and they take pride in getting all the details right, and telling it how it is. For more, see the authors section on www.lonelyplanet.com.

Getting Started

Figuring out how much time to allow for a trip is the main issue confronting travellers to Samoa, American Samoa and/or Tonga. Think carefully about your priorities before settling on an itinerary. Are you happy to sit on a single beach for a few weeks? Do you have an irresistible urge to explore every hiking trail in one particular island group? Or are you interested in combining relaxed tours of the main islands with brief excursions to smaller, outlying places that take more time and flexibility to reach?

As with any Pacific destination, it seems a shame to take a relatively expensive flight direct from Europe or North America to either Samoa, American Samoa or Tonga and straight back again, unless your travel agent has unearthed a spectacular deal for you or your midnight fare-searching sessions on the Internet have proved fruitful. Instead, consider stopping elsewhere in the Pacific in addition to your primary destination.

See Climate Charts (Samoan islands p139; Tonga p277) for more information.

WHEN TO GO

For the majority of the year, the climate in the Samoan islands and Tonga encourages visitors. Both Samoas lie near the equator, so conditions are almost perpetually hot and humid – the average annual temperature is 26.5°C in coastal areas, with a decrease in temperature as the land rises inland. Despite its great latitudinal range, Tonga does not experience dramatically diverse climatic conditions either, although Vava'u and the Niuas are noticeably warmer than Tongatapu, and 'Eua is noticeably cooler (for different reasons). It's when the wet season and the odd tropical cyclone have to be factored in that things get a little less straightforward.

The most comfortable time to visit the region is during the dry season between May and October. Not surprisingly, this is when most of the major Samoan and Tongan festivals are held. This is basically considered to be the region's high season, though there isn't necessarily much dif-

---

DON'T LEAVE HOME WITHOUT...

- Double-checking the visa situation (Samoan islands p146; Tonga p284).
- Hogwarts-strength anti-insect potion (ie bug repellent) to discourage mosquitoes (p297).
- Sunscreen, sunglasses and a hat to deflect fierce UV rays (p302).
- A travel insurance policy specifically covering you for diving, surfing, hiking and other high-risk activities (Samoan islands p141; Tonga p280).
- Knowing what your local embassy/consulate can and can't do to help you if you're in trouble (Samoan islands p140; Tonga p279).
- Your own snorkelling equipment (Samoan islands p136; Tonga p273), because it will often not be available for hire or, if it is, the quality may be poor.
- The ability to ask open-ended questions, particularly across Samoa. (Ask 'Where is the beach?'. Don't ask 'Is the beach over there?', to which the answer will always be a resounding 'Yes!', even if this is completely incorrect.)
- An inexhaustible supply of patience. You'll need it while waiting for objects to appear (buses, people etc).

FAVOURITE FESTIVALS & EVENTS

- Heilala Festival (p279; July) – the Tongan king has a week-long birthday bash
- Miss Galaxy Pageant (p279; July) – Tongan men get dressed up to party
- Teuila Festival (p141; September; www.teuilafestival.ws) – Samoa's major tourism-focused celebration
- White Sunday (p141; October) – when children run the show in both Samoas
- Tisa's Tattoo Festival (p141; October; www.tisasbarefootbar.com/eventstattoo.htm) – entrepreneurial spirit meets traditional art in American Samoa

---

ference between prices charged during this time and those charged over the rest of the year.

The region's wet season (ostensibly its low season) lasts from November to April. December and January are normally the wettest months across Samoa, while in Tonga, March tends to be the wettest month, especially in Vava'u. Remember, though, that most precipitation occurs at night and the main discomfort will be caused by a rise in the lethargy-inducing heat and humidity. The exception is the harbour area of Tutuila (American Samoa), where the famous Rainmaker Mountain ensures that the region receives over 5000mm of precipitation annually.

Both the Samoan islands and Tonga unfortunately lie squarely within the South Pacific's notorious cyclone belt. The season for tropical storms and cyclones is between November and March. Cyclones seem to occur, on average, every 10 to 15 years. However, in the early 1990s the Samoas were devastated in quick succession by two of the strongest and most destructive storms on record: cyclones Ofa and Val. The last big storm to hit the region was Olaf, which blew across the islands in early 2005.

If you plan to come during the December–January holiday period, when huge numbers of Samoans and Tongans return for the holidays (mostly from New Zealand, Australia and the USA), it's wise to book flights well in advance.

COSTS & MONEY

Your daily expenses will be affected markedly by how you travel, the type of accommodation you seek out, the sorts of eateries you frequent and how often you end up clutching a cold beer/wine/cocktail. Your choice of activities will also dramatically alter your budget – sitting on a beach costs nothing (except perhaps a small day access fee), but going on a diving trip or a surf safari obviously requires significant expenditure.

In Samoa, if you stay in midrange hotels interspersed with the occasional night in a standard beachside *fale*, buy all your meals from restaurants and hire a car to get around, you'll probably pay a minimum of ST160 per day (per person travelling as a couple). If, however, you stay almost exclusively in *fale* (particularly those that include two or more meals in the overnight rate), do at least some self-catering and bus it around the islands, you'll pay considerably less.

Due to American Samoa's reliance on the greenback, the costs here are higher than in Samoa. Using the same rough formula applied to Samoa – mainly midrange hotel or motel accommodation, restaurant meals and a hire car – you can expect to pay at least US$130 per person per day. In Tonga, for the same array of daily expenses you'll be looking at a minimum of T$125 per person per day.

While travelling anywhere within this region, always carry a supply of small-denomination notes. Bus drivers, kiosk and café proprietors, and villagers accepting payment for beach use can't be expected to change big bills.

Taxes

Samoa applies a 12.5% VAGST (Value Added Goods & Services Tax) to most commodities and to hotel and restaurant prices. This is almost always included in marked prices, though some top-end accommodation and eateries will add it to your bill.

All such prices in Tonga include a recently introduced 15% GST. All prices given in this book include these taxes.

READING UP
Books

Gavin Bell's *In Search of Tusitala – Travels in the Pacific after Robert Louis Stevenson* retraces the principal South Sea voyages of the Scottish writer, who settled on 'Upolu during the final four years of his life.

An entertaining account of travel through the South Seas is *Slow Boats Home* by Gavin Young, the sequel to *Slow Boats to China*. Combined, they recount the author's 1979 around-the-world boat-hop on vessels large and small. A good part of his journey is aboard a Tongan boat, and there's a well-observed Samoa chapter.

Transit of Venus – Travels in the Pacific, by Julian Evans, is a well-written account of the author's shoestring travels around the Pacific by boat and ship. It includes very entertaining chapters on the Samoas and Tonga.

A book travellers love to hate is *The Happy Isles of Oceania: Paddling the Pacific* by Paul Theroux, in which the perpetually miserable author kayaks around South Pacific islands. Cynics will love the amusingly downbeat prose; he is particularly hard on Nuku'alofa.

Friendly Isles: A Tale of Tonga; *'Utulei, My Tongan Home*; and *The Tongan Past* by Patricia Ledyard Matheson all relate anecdotes of Tongan life and make easy, interesting reading.

CONDUCT IN THE SAMOAN ISLANDS & TONGA

As a foreigner, you will be considered worthy of respect as long as you behave appropriately as far as the locals are concerned. This can be frustrating at times. Samoans and Tongans will often keep themselves at arm's length in order to avoid the possibility of making you unhappy. They will often answer your questions with the response they suppose you'd like to hear, rather than with the truth, which they believe may upset you. But the better you become acquainted with the people, of course, the more relaxed they will become.

It is perfectly normal in the Samoan islands and Tonga for members of the same sex to hold hands and display friendship in public, but open displays of affection between men and women, married or not, will be met with disapproval.

Be aware that Sunday is the traditional day of rest and quiet. This is the day when tourists are generally not welcome in villages or on local beaches.

A concept that causes breakdowns in communication between Samoans and foreigners is *musu*, which may be roughly translated as 'moodiness'. An otherwise pleasant and vivacious person may inexplicably become quiet and sullen. If this happens, don't worry – you haven't committed some unforgivable faux pas, so don't react with apologies or questions. Your friend is just experiencing *musu* and will usually get over it soon.

For more tips on how to get along with the locals, see the boxed texts on p35 and p160.

Tonga Islands: William Mariner's Account by Dr John Martin and *Tales of the Tikongs* by Epeli Hau'ofa should be mandatory companion reading for visits to Tonga. The former provides a fascinating historical background to many sights throughout the islands, while the latter is a collection of wry, satirical vignettes on life in 'Tiko'.

For a glimpse of American Samoan life in the mid-1970s through the eyes of a cynical American humorist, track down a copy of *Tales from the Margaret Mead Taproom* by Nicholas von Hoffman. It's illustrated by Garry Trudeau, the Doonesbury cartoonist.

My Samoan Chief by Fay G Calkins is a wonderfully entertaining account of how a young American woman deals with the often confounding customs of traditional Samoa after she moves there with her Samoan husband.

Websites

Lonely Planet (www.lonelyplanet.com) Get started with summaries on the Samoas and Tonga, links to island-related sites and travellers trading information on the Thorn Tree.

Matangitonga (www.matangitonga.to) Provides lots of Tongan news and current affairs.

Office of Tourism (www.amsamoa.com/tourism) Quite a good site on American Samoa, with information on history, language and customs, and a calendar of events.

Samoan Sensation (www.samoa.co.uk) Good general site about both Samoas. This website has the *Samoa Observer* and *Samoa News* online, a Q&A forum and a good selection of books about Samoa that can be ordered from the site.

Samoa Tourism Authority (www.visitsamoa.ws) Samoa's official website, with lots of useful info and links.

Tonga Visitors Bureau (www.tongaholiday.com) A good place to start looking for information, with lots of links that will be of interest to travellers.

RESPONSIBLE TRAVEL

If you enjoy snorkelling around reefs and getting glimpses of wildlife in their natural environments, then do your bit to protect them by not buying souvenirs made from endangered animals or plants – that means anything utilising coral (particularly black coral), shells (such as triton shells), turtles, sandalwood and the like. If you do buy such goods, it will probably be confiscated when you get back home anyway, due to international conventions banning trade in endangered species. Speaking of coral, avoid stepping on or otherwise damaging reefs while you're checking them out.

On the same theme, think carefully about visiting (and therefore supporting) any attractions that exploit wildlife, endangered or otherwise. For one such scenario in Savai'i, see Responsible Choices (p94).

The careful disposal of all nonbiodegradable rubbish should also be a priority for travellers. Anyone who has seen the rubbish that plagues beaches, parks and other public places across the Samoan islands and Tonga will need no further convincing of the importance of this. Also keep this in mind while you're quick-stepping it down a pristine walking trail. For further information, see p49 for the Samoan islands and p172 for Tonga.

Itineraries
CLASSIC ROUTES

The well-beaten Samoan path is lined with beautiful beaches, gorgeous snorkelling options, legendary sites and other natural trappings of tropical islands. Why come all the way to the Pacific to rush around? Take a few weeks to get into the Samoas' relaxed spirit.

SAMOAN ISLAND-HOPPING
Two Weeks / Apia to Pago Pago

In Samoa, experience the delightful **Palolo Deep Marine Reserve** (p64), then head inland to the charming **Robert Louis Stevenson Museum** (p74). Backtrack to Apia and head eastwards to the seductive sands of **Lalomanu Beach** (p83), with a pit-stop at **Fatumea Pool** (p78). Meander along **south coast beaches** (p79) to laze in more beachside *fale* before boating out to **Manono** (p84) to circumnavigate this peaceful islet.

Back on the 'mainland', catch the ferry to Savai'i (p148). Motor up the east coast, stopping for a dip at beautiful **Si'ufaga Beach** (p92). Now traverse the desolate **lava field** (p94) before depositing yourself on the sand at gregarious **Manase** (p96). Return down the east coast and continue west for the wave action at **Alofaaga Blowholes** (p100), then recross Apolima Strait and fly to American Samoa (p290).

Admire the beautiful harbour setting of **Pago Pago** (p105), then climb **Mount Alava** (p108) for spectacular views. Maroon yourself on **Alega Beach** (p116), detouring for a close-up of **Rainmaker Mountain** (p115). Wind along the coast to Au'asi for a small boat to **Aunu'u** (p121) to explore its wild nature, before taking a slow ride back to Pago Pago.

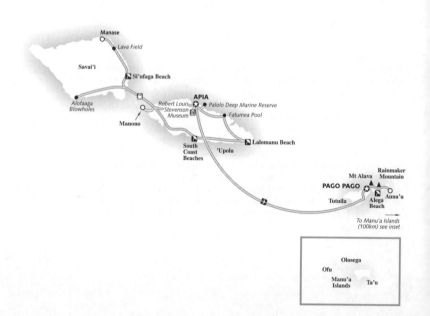

TONGAN SAILING TOUR

**10 Days to Two Weeks /
Nuku'alofa to the Vava'u Group**

One classic route taken in Tonga involves a thorough exploration of the vibrant jumble of islands that make up the ever-popular Vava'u Group, followed by an investigation of plantation-studded Tongatapu.

Head straight to the paradisal Vava'u Group, Tonga's activities playground. On **Vava'u Island** (p249), climb up to the peak of **Mount Talau** (p252) for some amazing island views and to map your path through the Port of Refuge. Then join a chartered or bare-boat yacht and sail around the islands of the group. Change your anchorage each night and jump off board each day to snorkel at the various sites. Stop at **Tapana** (p260) for a paella feast then make your next location **Hinakauea Beach** (p260) for a Tongan feast. Spend some time exploring the **Japanese Gardens** (p260) off Mala and swim into **Swallows' Cave** (p262) on Kapa. Experience the magical fog of **Mariner's Cave** (p262) on Nuapapu before moving on to lovely **Nuku** (p262), and then hike to the royal tomb on **'Euakafa** (p263). Arrange your charter to sail through the Ha'apai Group en route to Tongatapu, or catch a short flight.

On **Tongatapu** (p179), have a quick look around **Nuku'alofa** (p182) and then visit the island's fascinating archaeological excavations, including the **Lapaha archaeological site** (p199), followed by the energetic **Mapu'a 'a Vaca blowholes** (p211). Then get yourself in holiday mode by spending a day or two snorkelling, swimming or just being lazy on one of the resort islands to the north of Tongatapu, such as **Pangaimotu** (p213) or **Fafá** (p213).

See the relevant destination sections for information on transport options around each island grouping. For details of transport between Tongatapu and Vava'u, see p285.

> The Vava'u Group is an enticing cluster of islands – some topped with emerald green and with sheer basalt walls plunging into the protected waters, others ringed by idyllic swathes of sand and coral reefs. You'll want at least 10 days to let the wind fill your sails.

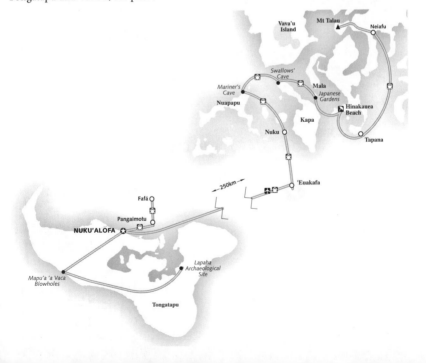

ROADS LESS TRAVELLED

INTO THE SAMOAN WILDS   One Month / Apia to Ta'u

To travel into the Samoan wilds is to weave your way between ancient Polynesian sites, quicksand lakes, collapsed calderas and some of the most beautiful beaches in the Pacific. Take two weeks, but a month would build in the flexibility required for trips to outlying islands such as Apolima and the Manu'a Group.

Most of the region's fascinating sites lie off the main coastal roads: in the middle of plantations, on the slopes of ruptured volcanoes, and on far-flung satellite islands. From **Apia** (p60), take the Cross-Island Rd to eerie **Lake Lanoto'o** (p77). On the north coast, rattle into the remote **Uafato Conservation Area** (p77). Peek into the sublime depths of the **To Sua Ocean Trench** (p81) and explore an overgrown trail in **O Le Pupu-Pu'e National Park** (p80). Then organise a visit to spectacular **Apolima** (p85) before sailing for Savai'i.

Delve into the **Tafua Peninsula Rainforest Preserve** (p92) before visiting the **Afu Aau Falls** (p99) and **Pulemelei Mound** (p100). Continue west to **Falealupo Peninsula** (p97) to trudge across the **Canopy Walkway** (p98). Head east to **Mount Matavanu** (p95). Relax at **Manase** (p96) before returning to 'Upolu.

On Tutuila, head for the **National Park of American Samoa** (p115). Go south to explore the pristine **Fagatele Bay National Marine Sanctuary** (p118), then travel beyond Leone at least as far as beautiful **Palagi Beach** (p119). Re-cross the island, stopping at **Alega Beach** (p116), then visit **Aunu'u** (p121). From Pago Pago, fly to Ofu to experience stunning **Ofu Beach** (p127) and **Maga Point** (p128). Your last stop is the remote rainforest grandeur of **Ta'u** (p129).

Getting Around sections fronting each destination chapter summarise travel around 'Upolu (p57), Savai'i (p90) and Tutuila (p104). For ferry info, see p148. For info on transport between Samoa and American Samoa, see p290. Transport between Tutuila and the Manu'a Islands is on p147.

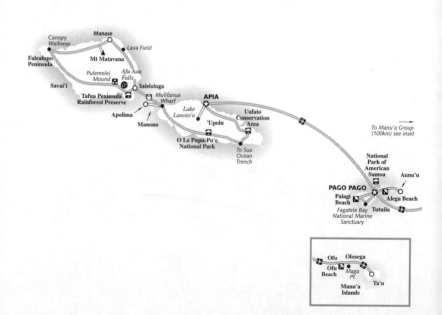

SLOW BOATS AROUND TONGA   One Month / Nuku'alofa to the Niuas

There's no better way of enjoying the peaceful solitude on Tonga's wonderfully isolated islands than to stow away on slow boats around the region, jumping off whenever the urge strikes you.

After spending a little time acclimatising to the tropics in **Nuku'alofa** (p182), head out to nearby **'Eua** (p215) and spend a few days (or why not a week?) hiking through the island's lush rainforests and exploring its caves and sinkholes, where you'll sometimes have to climb huge, tangled banyan trees to get out. From Nuku'alofa, clamber aboard a church boat headed for the coral charms and soothing serenity of the scattered, low-lying **Ha'apai Group** (p225). Visit remote **Nomuka** (p241) or **Ha'afeva** (p241) and immerse yourself in the culture and traditional lifestyle of Tonga – extra incentives to come out here are the amazing reefs and shallows you'll want to explore on snorkelling and diving trips. Spend some more time absorbing unexploited Tongan culture on friendly islands in the Lifuka Group, such as **Ha'ano** (p237) and **'Uiha** (p238), then shack up in a beachside *fale* on budget-oriented **Uoleva** (p237). Embark on a trip out to volcanic **Tofua** (p240) to hike up to the crater rim, and to nearby pyramidal **Kao** (p240) where you can scuba dive its blackened drop-offs.

If time is not your scarcest commodity, continue via the sundry physical distractions of the **Vava'u Group** (p243) to the remote **Niuas** (p265), three remote volcanic islands where you'll find lava fields, untrammelled ridges and languid locals.

See the relevant destination sections for information on transport options around each island grouping. For details of transport between Tongatapu, the Ha'apai Group and the Niuas, see p285.

Take as long as you can to get lost in the South Pacific of old. Discover 'Eua's tropical rainforest, the Ha'apai Group of stunning, far-flung and low-lying sand and reef islands, and the charm of slow-moving, unexploited Tongan culture.

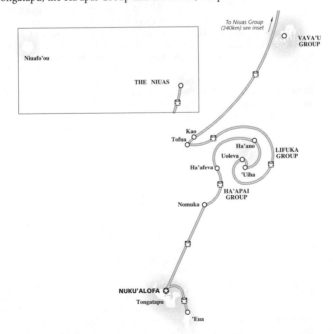

TAILORED TRIPS

WALK THIS WAY

If wandering along deserted trailways on remote Pacific islands with only a daypack, sunshine and local wildlife for company is your idea of paradise, then you'll find plenty of fulfilment waiting for you throughout the Samoan islands and Tonga.

On the main Samoan island of 'Upolu, tackle the challenging trek through overgrown terrain to the mysterious **Lake Lanoto'o** (p77), walk around the remote perimeter of **Fagaloa Bay** (p78) on the north coast, and disappear into the tangled flora of **O Le Pupu-Pu'e National Park** (p80). On the neighbouring island of Savai'i, scale some impressive ancient volcanic craters – namely the wonderful heights of **Mount Matavanu** (p95) and the **Tafua Savai'i crater** (p92) – before embarking on a hike through the lush undergrowth of a sprawling plantation to the ancient ambience of **Pulemelei Mound** (p100) and the magical sight of nearby **Afu Aau Falls** (p99), and then climbing up the beguiling slopes of **Mount Silisili** (p97).

In American Samoa, the serpentine island of Tutuila offers a ridge walk up to a derelict cable-car terminal on **Mount Alava** (p108) that continues down steep mountain slopes to idyllic **Vatia** (p116) and the strange contours of **Pola Tai** (p116) on the island's rugged north coast. Those with more energy to burn can then roam along the splendid **Massacre Bay walk** (p119) and prepare themselves for the challenging climb up **Matafao Peak** (p117). Meanwhile, in the deliriously secluded Manu'a Islands, you can march up **Mount Tumutumu** (p127) on the tiny island of Ofu and then fly over to the nearby enigmatic island of Ta'u to stumble through pristine rainforests and along some of the tallest sea cliffs in the world within the confines of the **National Park of American Samoa** (p129) on Ta'u.

The far-flung islands of Tonga also provide an abundance of other glorious trails to follow. The island of 'Eua in the midst of the Tongatapu Group has a myriad potential walks, such as the one through the beautiful **'Eua Plantation Forest** (p218). Walkers also devote themselves to exploring the pyramidal tombs and the South Pacific version of the famous **Stonehenge** (p209) on Tongatapu Island. In the Ha'apai Group, you can have the unique experience of scaling the active volcano on **Tofua** (p240), while the enormous cone of nearby **Kao** (p240) provides an even more strenuous climb for those with enough puff. For less of a physical workout but an absolutely brilliant view, take the short trail to **'Utula'aina Point** (p258) on the northern extremity of Vava'u Island. Then allow yourself to discover the queen's tomb on uninhabited '**Euakafa** (p263). The beautiful seashore of **Niuatoputapu** (p266) in the Niuas makes for a sublime circumnavigation, and from the imposing summit of **Tafahi** (p268) you can actually see across to the islands of neighbouring Samoa on a clear day. Finally, don't forget that the hundreds of kilometres of sandy beaches that garland the islands of Tonga make for superb soft walks – arguably the best of these can be experienced in **Ha'apai** (p225) and on **Niuatoputapu** (p266).

SPLASHING OUT

A bewildering array of water sports are available to travellers across this waterlogged region. The appealing options for immersing yourself in the stunning deep blue of the South Pacific range from plain old swimming – off sublime beaches and in sheltered and often secluded lagoons – to snorkelling, surfing, sailing, fishing and scuba diving.

Locations in the Samoan islands that regularly get a big thumbs up from travellers for the quality of the snorkelling and swimming on offer include the wonderful **Lalomanu Beach** (p83) and other fine watery spots within the Aleipata island district in the southeast corner of 'Upolu; the spectacular coral-encrusted hole at the centre of the **Palolo Deep Marine Reserve** (p64) off Apia; the superb freshwater swimming hole watered by **Afu Aau Falls** (p99) and surrounded by thick jungle on Savai'i; the marvellous swathe of **Alega Beach** (p116) on the southern coast of Tutuila; and, of course, glorious **Ofu Beach** (p127) in the Manu'a Islands, a place that easily rates as one of the best beaches and snorkelling locales in the entire South Pacific region. Keen surfers (you have to be not just keen but also very experienced to tackle the intimidating reef breaks in the region) head for the south coast of 'Upolu to well-known sites such as **Boulders** (p79), and to **Fagamalo** (p95) up on the far northern tip of wild Savai'i. The south coast of 'Upolu is also a great place for divers; with popular underwater features including **Sheer Wall** (p134) and **The Terraces** (p134). Samoa also offers **kayaking** (p136) around the peaceful satellite island of Manono and challenging **game fishing** (p135) in the deep waters off Tutuila.

In Tonga, there are few finer swims than the one into **Mariner's Cave** (p262) at Nuapapu in the Vava'u Group – those entering the cave will find themselves shrouded in a strange fog that materialises and then quickly dissipates with each new oceanic swell. Also located near Nuapapu is the superb snorkelling offered by the **Coral Gardens** (p262), which has earned the reputation for being the best snorkelling site in Vava'u. Needless to say, the opportunity to swim with the **humpback whales** (p248) around Vava'u between July and November, when the massive creatures slowly drift through, is reason in itself to cross the world to visit Tonga. The Ha'apai Group offers some

unforgettable diving, particularly around the hulking volcanic islands of
Tofua (p240) and **Kao** (p240), while easily accessible reef breaks tantalise
surfers just off **Ha'atafu Beach** (p212) on the island of Tongatapu. **Chartering a yacht** (p275) so that you can sail aimlessly around the outer islands
of the Ha'apai Group is another activity that's high on the list of things
to do for active travellers. Ha'apai also gives you the chance to camp out
and participate in organised **kayaking trips** (p228) around its outer islands.
Last, but not least, **game fishing** (p246) around Vava'u is another highly
pleasurable water sports drawcard in Tonga.

Samoan Islands

Samoan Islands

Lodged in the remote heart of the South Pacific, the beautiful Samoan islands offer much more than a chance to snooze in a *fale* (traditional thatched house) by the ocean, improve your snorkelling technique amidst gorgeous groves of coral, or try a new kind of beer – although as many travellers can attest to, each of these activities has plenty of individual merit. This is also your chance to learn much about a complex islander culture and to replace brochure depictions of tropical island life with memories collated after lengthy explorations of fabulously real island environments.

The nation known as Samoa and the neighbouring US territory known as American Samoa are separate political entities – they both belonged to the same Polynesian grouping until 1899, when the westernmost islands were handed over to Germany and those in the east were nabbed by America (for the full story behind these takeovers, see p30). But regardless of their political differences, Samoa and American Samoa still share essentially the same fascinating culture. So while travelling around 'Upolu and Savai'i, keep your eyes peeled for outrigger canoe races in Apia Harbour, watch the traditional carvers of Uafato fashion *'ava* bowls (p77), consider how long it took to arrange the stones that comprise Pulemelei Mound (p100) and learn the art of the *umu* (underground oven) while staying on the satellite isle of Manono (p85).

In American Samoa, note the weathered tombs adorning the front yards of family homes, compete with locals for breadfruit and freshly cooked *palusami* (taro leaves cooked in coconut cream) at Pago Pago's market (p108) and breathe in the atmosphere of legendary sites such as Ma'ama'a Cove (p122) on Aunu'u and the To'aga site (p127) on Ofu. And don't forget to squeeze yourself at least once into one of the raucous buses that rumble around Tutuila (p104).

Samoan Islands Snapshots

CURRENT EVENTS

SAMOA

New buildings and sports facilities are appearing in Apia, tourist resorts are sprouting up like coconut trees around the stunning coastline, and the modern world, in the shape of TV stations, mobile phones and Internet cafés, has arrived. But the microstate has become almost completely dependent on remittances (p32) and international aid agencies which fall over themselves to help. The Chinese government is loaning (gifting?) ST30 million to build a swimming pool complex. Australia hands over A$20 million a year with a big slice going to the police, New Zealand offers NZ$8 million a year for schoolbooks and scholarships, and Japan is renovating polytechnic buildings and wharf facilities (US$11.6 million). A Singapore charity has helped establish a kidney dialysis centre. Even the international rugby board recently handed over ST7 million.

Despite decades of this government-to-government aid, the islands are still mired in Third World poverty and most want to leave. The country also looks abroad for its heroes and feels proud when a Samoan in New Zealand becomes captain of the All Blacks (Tana Umaga), wins New Zealand Idol (Rosita Vai) or records a hit hip-hop CD (Scribe).

Although poor in money, the islands are rich in culture. Life has a very Polynesian flavour (p36), and the jungly rainforests, pristine beaches and dramatic waterfalls are being given legal protection (p46). Tropical, colourful Samoa stands out as somewhere special – remote, unspoilt islands where people still have time to be friendly.

Samoans love sport, especially their Manu Samoa rugby team. During August–September 2007, the South Pacific Games (p40) will take over Apia and thousands of visiting sportspeople and spectators will send the entire country into *fiafia* (party) mode.

AMERICAN SAMOA

Hot discussion topics always include the tuna canneries (p110) which provide thousands of jobs, but may move to a lower-wage country. LBJ hospital never has enough funds and patient fees keep rising, which is tough for those on low wages. Government corruption keeps popping up like an eel from a coral hole, and in 2005 four officials in different departments were sentenced by the courts, and the governor's office was raided by armed FBI agents.

However the territory does well for itself considering its total population of 59,000 is that of a small town. Unlike in America, the police are

FAST FACTS

Samoa
Population: 177,000
Minimum hourly wage: ST1.60
Unemployment rate: Very high
Annual inbound remittances: ST200 million
Emigration: 42,000 to New Zealand in 2005 alone

American Samoa
Population: 59,000
Minimum hourly wage: US$2.70-3.50
Obesity rate: Very high
Major employers: Government, tuna canneries
Wildlife off Ofu Beach: 300 species of fish and 150 species of coral

IN THE NAME OF CLARITY

The Samoan islands are divided into two political entities: Samoa and American Samoa. Samoa was formerly known as Independent Samoa (or Western Samoa), but in July 1997 the island nation officially adopted the name 'Samoa', which is how we refer to it throughout this book.

unarmed, and people live a relaxed 'don't worry, be happy' lifestyle. The unspoilt Manu'a Islands (p124) haven't changed much since anthropologist Margaret Mead researched the sex lives of teenagers there 80 years ago. Despite an epidemic of lifestyle diseases such as obesity, diabetes and hypertension, the islands have just about maintained their religion and culture, and are among the wealthiest in the South Pacific thanks to federal grants, remittances and the tuna canneries. Everyone could emigrate to America, but they prefer a Polynesian life on a tropical island.

Several thousand American Samoans serve in America's armed forces and by 2006 seven had been killed in Iraq, and 30 wounded.

HISTORY

The Samoan islands were traditionally divided into a dozen or so districts, each with their own high chiefs, with no overall political unity or king. In 1899 the islands were divided into Western Samoa (now known as Samoa) under German rule and American Samoa to the east.

Samoa is praying that their new no-frills airline, Polynesian Blue, loses less money than Polynesian Air (ST9 million a year) and generates a tourist boom.

PREHISTORY

Samoa is in the middle of Polynesia (Many Islands), which is spread over a vast watery triangle with its points at Hawai'i, Easter Island (off the west coast of South America) and New Zealand (Aotearoa).

Polynesians entered the Pacific from the west via the East Indies and the Malay peninsula. This idea is backed up by linguistic and DNA studies, archaeological evidence and oral histories. The first Polynesians are referred to as Lapita, after a site in New Caledonia where their distinctive pottery was first found.

The earliest known evidence of human occupation in the Samoan islands are the many pottery shards of a Lapita village found under the sea near Mulifanua on 'Upolu. Carbon tests have dated the site at 1000 BC. Undecorated pottery – known as Polynesian plainware – of a comparable age has been found at Aoa on Tutuila and at To'aga (p127) on Ofu. The art of pottery was later lost.

Thrill to epic tales of amazing ocean crossings in flimsy canoes following crude star maps in Man's Conquest of the Pacific by Peter Bellwood, the foremost authority on the subject.

Throughout the islands archaeologists have unearthed over a hundred star-shaped platforms (p116) which were almost certainly used to catch pigeons. The *matai* (chiefs) loved to catch wild pigeons, using tame decoy ones and a net. On Savai'i, near the village of Palauli, is the pyramid of Pulemelei (p100), the largest ancient platform structure in the Pacific. The site contains post holes, cairns, hearths and graves as well as basalt platforms, but its purpose is unknown.

Evidence suggests that in ancient times many more Samoan settlements were located inland in the valleys and on hillsides, and that the increase in coastal settlement was due to European influence and trade.

Around AD 950 warriors from Tonga established their rule on Savai'i, and then moved on to 'Upolu. But they were defeated by Savea, a Samoan chief, who was rewarded with the very high title Malietoa, derived from the parting words of the defeated Tongans: *malie toa* (brave warrior). The present nonagenarian head of state in Samoa bears this same proud title.

There was also contact with Fiji, from where legends say two girls brought the art of tattooing. But the Samoans never really trusted their neighbours – *togafiti* (literally 'tonga fiji') means a trick.

TIMELINE	1000 BC	AD 950
	Samoan islands inhabited by Lapita people, the first Polynesians, who made their way across the vast Pacific Ocean	Samoan warriors, led by Chief Savea, defeat the Tongan invaders; the chief rewarded with the title of *Malietoa*

Visit some of the museums (p65 and p109) to catch a glimpse of pre-European Samoa.

EUROPEAN CONTACT

In 1722 Dutchman Jacob Roggeveen sighted the Manu'a Islands, but sailed on without landing. In May 1768 the French explorer Louis-Antoine de Bougainville bartered with the inhabitants of the Manu'a Islands, but merely sighted the more westerly islands. He christened the archipelago les Îles des Navigateurs (the Navigator Islands).

Next to arrive was another Frenchman, La Pérouse, who landed at Fagasa on the north coast of Tutuila in 1787. The crew exchanged beads for pigs, chickens, fruit and the favours of Samoan women – brown-skinned Venuses clad in a grass skirt and nothing else. Word evidently spread about these *palagi* (foreigners, literally 'cloud bursters') because the following day, a big crowd gathered while the sailors were collecting water at A'asu (p119). When the Samoans tried to stop the sailors leaving, rocks were thrown, the sailors fired back, and in the ensuing battle 12 sailors were killed and 20 were badly injured, along with an estimated 39 Samoans killed. A'asu was named Massacre Bay and La Pérouse departed posthaste. Polynesia wasn't just sunshine and pretty girls.

By the 1820s a few Europeans had settled in the islands, most of them escaped convicts and retired whalers who were welcomed by the unsuspecting islanders because they knew the strange ways of the *palagi* and were willing to share their technological expertise. As elsewhere, the *palagi* also brought with them diseases to which the islanders had no immunity.

THE MISSIONARIES

In August 1830, missionaries John Williams and Charles Barff of the London Missionary Society (LMS) arrived at Sapapali'i on the eastern coast of Savai'i during a civil war. A monument (p91) commemorates the event. They were followed by Methodist and Catholic missionaries, and in 1888 Mormons added to the competition for souls. Tahitian and Rarotongan evangelists helped the *palagi* missionaries, just as Samoans later helped to convert other Pacific islands.

Given the similarity of Christian creation beliefs to Samoan legends and a prophecy by Nafanua, a legendary war goddess, that a new religion would take root in the islands, the Samoans were quite willing to accept Christianity. The wondrous possessions of the *palagi* were used as proof that the white man's God was more powerful and generous than the gods and *aitu* (spirits) of the Samoans.

The Christian gospel was widely accepted and it has remained an integral part of island life to the present day. Although interdistrict warfare was not abolished for another 70 years, schools and education were eagerly adopted. An early tourist, Frederick Walpole, reported in 1848: 'Samoans of all ages rush out on you, not armed with club and spear, but with slate and pencil; and thrusting them into your hands they make signs for you to finish their exercise or sum.' Polygamy was discontinued. When he first arrived, Rev John Williams reported that 'it is common for the young chiefs to have six, eight or ten wives, but the steady, respectable chiefs seldom have more than three'.

History buffs can dig up masses of archaeology reports at www.ashpo.org.

Read fascinating, first-hand history books by Robert Louis Stevenson, British consul William Churchward and missionary George Turner online at www.samoa.co.uk/history.

1787 — French explorer, La Pérouse, lands at Fagasa on the north coast of Tutuila; subsequent battle results in A'asu being renamed Massacre Bay

1830 — Arrival of London Missionary Society evangelist Rev John Williams on Savai'i during a civil war

EUROPEAN CONTROL OF APIA

A horde of settlers and transients – uncouth beachcombers, sailors, remittance men and drifters from Europe and America – had come in search of adventure and women and quick profits. All these *palagi* banded together and turned Apia into a bastion of *palagi* arrogance and greed, into a small Europe, notorious for its bars and political intrigues.

Albert Wendt

Both Pago Pago and Apia became major South Pacific ports. Some of the large wooden stores built along Beach Rd at this time are still standing. One Apia resident was American Bully Hayes, a notorious slaver or 'blackbirder', who kidnapped islanders to work on plantations in Fiji and Queensland (Australia), until he was killed by one of his own crew. The consuls in Apia had to deal with every kind of problem, but when one 'Blackguard' Brown complained to the British consul that his Samoan wife had run off back to her family, he was told that 'the British consulate is not a wife-retrieving bureau'.

A German trading company bought 300 sq km of land on 'Upolu and started a huge coconut plantation, which still stands today at Mulifanua, 40km west of Apia. But out in the villages, life carried on much as usual.

SQUABBLING SUPERPOWERS

There were (and still are) four paramount titles in the gift of four *'aiga* (extended families), equivalent to royal dynasties, in what is now Samoa: Malietoa, Tupua Tamasese, Mata'afa and Tu'imaleali'ifano. Tutuila was under the control of the Atua district of 'Upolu, and although Tui Manu'a was regarded as the most sacred title, it had more prestige than power. During the 1870s Samoa became embroiled in a civil war between two rival factions, led by Malietoa and Mata'afa, contending for supreme power. Samoans sold land to *palagi* to acquire guns to settle the matter.

The *palagi* were also divided as America, Britain and Germany appointed their own consuls in Apia. The Samoan civil war threatened to turn into a superpower war. By the late 1880s Apia Harbour was crowded with naval hardware as warships from Germany, Britain and America were sent there to back up their respective imperial interests. As one Samoan author put it, 'they were like three large dogs snarling over a very small bone'.

But on 16 March 1889 nature inflicted a terrible blow on the squabbling superpowers when Apia Harbour was hit by one of history's worst cyclones. The Germans and Americans both lost three warships each, while the British warship *Calliope* battled her way out of the harbour and escaped destruction. Ninety-two German and 54 American sailors were killed in the storm.

This disaster led to the Berlin Treaty of 1889, which stipulated that an independent Samoa would be established under the rule of a foreign-appointed Samoan king, and that the consuls of Britain, Germany and the USA would be given considerable advisory powers on 'Upolu. Malietoa was proclaimed 'king', but his hold on power proved to be tenuous, and

Read some brilliant analysis and descriptions of squabbling Samoans and *palagi* in Robert Louis Stevenson's very detailed *A Footnote to History: Eight Years of Trouble in Samoa.*

1889	1899
A cyclone sinks three American and three German warships cooped up in Apia Harbour – 146 sailors die	Tripartite Treaty gives Western Samoa to Germany and Eastern Samoa to America; Samoans hand in their guns

in the ten years that followed he was continually challenged by Mata'afa. 'I never saw such a place as Apia. You can be in a new conspiracy every day' was how one settler summed up this period to Robert Louis Stevenson, the great Scottish writer who lived with his family near Apia from 1889 until his untimely death in 1894.

In 1899, 12 *palagi* sailors were killed (a memorial to them stands in Mulinu'u) when they were caught up in the Samoan faction fighting. This was the final straw and later in the year the Tripartite Treaty was drawn up, giving control of Western Samoa to Germany and that of Eastern Samoa to America. All guns had to be handed in. Britain stepped out of the picture in exchange for renunciation of German claims to Tonga, the Solomon Islands and Niue. The German Flag Memorial (p66), erected in 1913, commemorates the takeover.

From this point, the histories of the Samoan islands diverged.

SAMOA
German Rule
In February 1900 Dr Wilhelm Solf was appointed governor and the German trading company DHPG (Deutsche Handels und Plantagen Gesellschaft der Südsee Inseln zu Hamburg) began to import thousands of Melanesians and Chinese to work on their huge plantations. Governor Solf confiscated all weapons that had been acquired during the long period of intermittent civil war. In 1903 he established a Lands & Titles Commission to determine land ownership, so that disputes could be resolved in a peaceful way without resorting to war. The governor then spoilt his good work by deposing the reigning king, Tupua Samoa, and placing Mata'afa (see p66 for his tomb) in the position of puppet paramount chief.

In 1905 Mt Matavanu erupted on Savai'i, destroying Sale'aula village. Fortunately no one was killed as the river of molten lava surged down from the mountain to the sea, leaving ruined churches (p94) in its wake.

Discontent with Mata'afa resulted in another type of eruption on Savai'i in 1908 when the Mau a Pule (Mau Movement) was organised by Namulau'ulu Lauaki Mamoe. In January 1909 he and his chief supporters were sent into exile.

Lagaga – A Short History of Samoa, edited by Malama Meleisea, is the definitive history and covers everything from legends and the infinite complexities of the *matai* (political representative) system to colonial rule and beyond from a Samoan perspective.

New Zealand Takes Over
In 1914, at the outbreak of WWI, New Zealand troops landed on German Samoa and the takeover was not resisted. But in 1918 disaster struck when SS *Tahune*, carrying passengers infected with Spanish influenza, was permitted to dock in Apia Harbour without being quarantined. In the dreadful months that followed, more than 7000 Western Samoans, 20% of the population, died of the disease, part of a worldwide epidemic worse than Europe's Black Death. American Samoa was not affected and their offers of medical help were refused. Anger at this mismanagement revived the Mau Movement, which used nonviolent tactics such as shop boycotts and refusing to pay taxes. The Mau slogan was '*Samoa o Samoa*' (Samoa for the Samoans) and leaders met secretly in a converted German bandstand (p66).

In February 1928, 400 Mau supporters were arrested, armed military police arrived and the New Zealand authorities continued the German

1905	1914
Mt Matavanu on Savai'i erupts; lava destroys a village, but no-one is killed	New Zealand troops occupy German-run Western Samoa without opposition at the beginning of WWI

policy of exiling Mau leaders. Then on 28 December 1929, Black Saturday, a big demonstration took place in Apia by Mau Movement members, who all wore purple *lava-lava* (sarong). Armed New Zealand police tried to arrest some wanted Mau members and a fight resulted. The police started firing into the crowd of unarmed people in Beach Rd, killing 11 protesters, including the movement's leader, Tupua Tamasese Lealofi III. His martyrdom and philosophy of nonviolence make him Samoa's Martin Luther King, and his tomb (p66) is near the German bandstand.

It was not until a Labour government came to power in New Zealand in 1935 that relations between Samoans and the New Zealand authorities improved.

Independence

Following WWII Western Samoa became a UN Trust Territory, administered by New Zealand. In 1947 an executive Council of State was established, consisting of the New Zealand High Commissioner and two Samoan high chiefs. A legislative assembly was also established. Finally, in 1962 independence arrived (see p66 for the Independence Memorial).

In 1962 Western Samoa became the first Pacific island colony to achieve independence.

Tupua Tamasese and Malietoa Tanumafili II became joint heads of state, but with very limited powers compared to the prime minister. The British-based parliamentary system reflected local custom and only *matai* were allowed to vote to fill the 49-seat Fono (Parliament). In 1990 everyone over 21 was given the vote, but only *matai* can be candidates, so the Fono is a kind of elected House of Lords.

The long-wished-for dream of independence raised hopes of rapid economic progress, but this was not to be. Samoa's exports to New Zealand at independence covered 60% of their imports from New Zealand, but this figure had declined to less than 2% by 2005.

Since Independence

The Human Rights Protection Party (HRPP) has been in power for most of the period since independence. Economic development has been excruciatingly slow or nonexistent, far below population growth, but at least the country has been politically stable, unlike neighbours Fiji and Tonga (p153). Fish and tropical produce such as cocoa, coffee, bananas, coconuts and taro were expected to become big export earners, but due to mismanagement, crop diseases and destructive cyclones, this has not happened. Nowadays container ships arrive piled up with imports, but leave almost empty. Only tourism provides a ray of hope for a brighter economic future.

Forty years of generous foreign aid have failed to create or inspire any economic growth, rather the opposite. The government bureaucracy has expanded out of all proportion to the population, while the real economy has declined due to a chronically weak private sector. The only major private employers are Vailima Brewery (p79), Aggie Grey's (see box, p69) and Yazaki which employs 2000 workers to assemble electrical components for cars. The nation desperately needs a dozen more Yazakis as it still has Least Developed Country Status. Tens of thousands have voted with their feet and emigrated to American Samoa and from

1918	1929
The New Zealand administration cops the blame for the Spanish influenza epidemic that kills 7000 people in Western Samoa	On 28 December, Black Saturday, armed New Zealand police gun down 11 Mau protesters on Beach Rd, Apia

there to America, and to New Zealand and from there to Australia. More Samoans now live outside the islands than on them, and they send back over ST200 million a year in remittances and bring back millions more on visits home.

The minimum wage is ST1.60 (US60¢) per hour, far below American Samoa (ST8.50 per hour) and New Zealand (ST18 per hour). Many workers are paid around ST5000 a year, less than ST100 a week, while families out in the villages depend on remittances and subsistence agriculture and fishing.

Hurricane damage is a regular occurrence in the South Pacific, and the damage to crops, buildings and infrastructure often amounts to millions of dollars. A stark example of the damage inflicted by hurricanes on the Samoan islands in the past 15 years can be seen on the Falealupo Peninsula on Savai'i (p98).

AMERICAN SAMOA
US Navy Rule

The formal annexation of Eastern Samoa by the USA took place on 17 April 1900, when a deed of cession was signed by the high chiefs, although the highest ranking chief, Tu'i Manu'a, didn't sign until 1904. The islands were run by the US Department of the Navy, which agreed to protect the traditional rights of the Samoans in exchange for the naval base and coaling station. The territory's inhabitants acquired the status of US nationals but were denied a vote or representation in Washington. Until the 1960s American Samoa retained its traditional social structure and subsistence economy, and the governor at the time warned against dragging the territory too quickly into the American version of the good life.

In 2005, 23 Samoans, including six from American Samoa, played in the NFL, America's top football league.

The Kennedy Effect

In the early 1960s an influential North American magazine published an article entitled 'America's Shame in the South Seas', which examined the simple subsistence lifestyle enjoyed by the American Samoans and determined it to be poverty by US standards. In response President Kennedy appointed Rex Lee to the governorship and instructed him to oversee the modernisation of the territory. Large funds were appropriated by Congress and, almost overnight, American Samoa became a Great Society construction project.

Development was fast-tracked – roads were built and European-style homes replaced traditional *fale* (*fah*-leh; a traditional thatched house), electrification and sewerage-treatment projects were implemented, and harbour facilities, schools and the Rainmaker Hotel (p112) were constructed. In addition, an international airport, a hospital, tuna canneries and TV broadcasts soon arrived. By the time Governor Lee left office in 1967, some American Samoan leaders were already lamenting the downfall of their society and the creation of a directionless welfare state.

Increasing Democracy & Prosperity

The territory's 1960 constitution established three branches of government: executive, legislative and judicial. Between 1951 and 1977 all of the territory's governors were appointed by the US Department of the

1962	1997
Ahead of the pack – Western Samoa celebrates becoming the first South Pacific island group to gain independence	Independent Samoa changes its name to Samoa

Interior, but they are now popularly elected. In 1980 American Samoans were allowed, for the first time, to elect a nonvoting delegate to serve in the US House of Representatives. The Fono (the legislative branch) is composed of a Senate which consists of 18 high chiefs elected by the county councils, and a House of Representatives with 20 popularly elected members. The two tuna canneries employ 5000 workers, but the rest of the territory's workforce is directly or indirectly employed by the government, which receives a generous amount (over US$100 million a year) from American taxpayers. A tiny population serviced by an enormous and expensive bureaucracy is a common South Pacific phenomenon.

American Samoa's territorial status has plenty of benefits besides the stack of multimillion-dollar federal grants: it allows all businesses based there, such as the tuna canneries and garment manufacturers, to export their goods duty-free to the US, yet the territory does not have to adhere to federal minimum-wage standards. Minimum-wage rates range from US$2.70 to $3.51, which are much lower than in the US, but far higher than in Samoa and other South Pacific islands. Even though American Samoans are American nationals, not citizens, they are free to move to America, where 130,000 Samoans already live.

Published in 1884, *Samoa – A Hundred Years Ago and Long Before* by George Turner is packed with myths, legends and stories that reveal the social structure and culture of the Samoan islands long before the onslaught of outside influences.

THE CULTURE

More than any other Polynesian people, Samoans have maintained their traditional way of life in their sauna of a climate, and still follow closely the social hierarchies, customs and courtesies established long before the arrival of Europeans. Like the coral reefs that protect the coasts, the *fa'a Samoa* (Samoan way) has protected the community, ensuring that life is orderly and meaningful. Many visitors sense that below the surface of the outwardly friendly and casual Samoan people lies a complex code of traditional etiquette. Beneath the light-heartedness, a strict and demanding code of behaviour is upheld with expectations that can stifle individuality and enterprise.

THE SAMOAN PSYCHE

The basis of the *matai* system is *'aiga* which gives life, culture, education, dignity and a purpose to individuals from the cradle to the grave and beyond. Every village contains a number of *'aiga*, which are often rivals as well as allies, and each includes as many relatives as can be claimed. The larger the *'aiga*, the stronger it becomes, and to be part of a powerful *'aiga* is the goal of every tradition-minded Samoan.

Each *'aiga* is headed by a senior *matai*, supported by junior *matai*, who represents the family on the *fono* (village council). The senior *matai* is normally elected by all adult members of the *'aiga*, but some inherit the title. In Samoa *'aiga* have created more and more junior titles, so there are now over 25,000 *matai*, and nearly every Sione and Sina has a title, but this dilution has not happened in American Samoa. More women are being given *matai* titles, but over 90% of *matai* are male.

The Samoan language has a special vocabulary of respectful words that are used at official *fono* meetings and any time when talking to a *matai*.

High chiefs have special privileges such as being allowed a two-storey house, a large tomb or a special seat in church. *Matai* are addressed by their title, so being given a title changes your name. Even today only *matai* can be elected to the national Fono in Samoa and to the Senate in American Samoa. You cannot pay your bills with a title, but *matai* are still respected and competition to acquire a high title can be intense. In the past opposing factions would go to war over a title.

TIPS ON MEETING LOCALS

Samoans believe that 'greeting a guest should be like the joy of the birds greeting the dawn'. But visits to villages can be disruptive and following a few guidelines can smooth the way.

- If you visit on a Sunday to go to church, it's best for men to wear long trousers and a shirt, while women should be well covered. Sunday is a day of rest and quiet, so doing any kind of work, swimming, drinking alcohol and even playing cards is forbidden in many villages.
- Public displays of affection between couples are taboo.
- If you stay with a village family, it's only fair to pay your way by buying a sack of rice or some tins of *pisupo* (corned beef) at the local store.
- Samoans eat with their fingers and the water that's passed round after the meal is to wash your hands with and not for drinking!
- Don't play Mother Teresa and hand out sweets or coins indiscriminately to village children.
- Falealupo is not the Costa Brava. Outside the resorts, visitors should show respect to the local culture and cover up. Women should avoid wearing swimsuits and other skimpy clothing away from the beach, no matter what the temperature. For men, knee-length shorts (or *lava-lava* – sarong) are best, and shirts or T-shirts should be worn.
- Shoes should always be removed when entering a *fale*. When invited in, always sit down to talk, and cross your legs. If this is uncomfortable throw a mat over your legs as it's rude for your feet to point at anyone. Wait outside until invited in. If you walk in front of anyone, especially an elder, murmur '*Tulou*' (Excuse me).
- If in a village around 6pm for *sa,* stop what you're doing and wait for the third bell, or perhaps consider joining a village family in evening prayers.
- If you want to swim at a village beach, climb a nearby mountain or take photos, ask first. Sometimes there's a small fee. Try to find a local to show you around the village rather than snooping around on your own.
- Mangy village dogs are a pain, but shouting '*Alu!*' (Go away!) usually works. If not, bending down and picking up a stone should scare them off.
- Don't be a *palagi* and ignore people who walk by; stop and chat.

Matai are divided into two types – *ali'i* and *tulafale*. While both are talking chiefs, it is the latter who delivers speeches at official ceremonies that are full of biblical references, traditional proverbs and poetic, flowery language. A wooden staff and a fly whisk are their symbols of office.

The village *fono* consists of *matai* from each *'aiga* associated with the village. All participants are seated according to their rank. The *fono* punishes such crimes as theft, violence and insubordination with fines, reparation or ostracism. Without the *matai* system a whole lot more policemen and judges would be needed. In extreme cases the miscreants can have their house and possessions burnt and suffer permanent exile from the village. Punishments by the local *fono* are taken into account if the case also comes before the *palagi*-style court system.

In Samoa, village *fono* build and maintain the local primary school and health clinic as well as housing and feeding the nurses and teachers, while the central government pays the wages. The village women's committees raise money through levies, bingo or putting on cultural shows. Traditionally Samoa was a nation of independent village republics with a weak central authority. One *matai* told anthropologist Margaret Mead, 'In the past we had two gods – Tagaloa and the village; the greater of these was the village.'

Ifoga is a traditional apology where the guilty person and family members sit down outside the victim's house with bowed heads until they're forgiven.

In theory, all wealth and property is owned communally by caring, sharing *'aiga*, and decisions about these matters are always made by the *matai*. You serve and give your wages to your *matai*, and in return your *matai* helps you if you become sick or need money for school fees or a trip to New Zealand. *'Aiga* members share their wealth and provide welfare services to needy family members. Children belong to the *'aiga*, not the biological parents, and are often adopted or borrowed by relatives.

Throughout the Samoas, individuals are subordinate to the extended family. There is no 'I', only 'we'. The lazy or incapable are looked after by their family rather than by taxpayers, and with such onerous family (plus village and church) obligations, it is a struggle for any individual to become wealthy. Life is not about individual advancement or achievement as in the *palagi* world, but about serving and raising up the status of your *'aiga*. Unfortunately the communal ownership of land and the lack of reward for individual effort cripples economic development.

LIFESTYLE – THE FA'A SAMOA
Family Life

Parents and other relatives treat babies very affectionately, but when they reach three years old, they are pushed away, and made the responsibility of an older sibling or cousin. *Fa'aaloalo* (respect for elders) is the most crucial aspect of the *fa'a Samoa*, and children are expected to obey not just their parents, grandparents, uncles and aunts, but all the *matai* and adults in the village as well as older siblings. It's tough to be at the beck and call of so many people! On the buses, you will see young people give up their seats to elders. Any disobedience or answering back is sternly punished. The Bible is often quoted to support this – 'the rod and reproof teach wisdom'. Samoans take a pessimistic view of human nature and believe that the devil never rests.

Children are taught the Samoan proverb, 'The path to power is through *tautua*' (service). But to young people this service can seem like a never-ending servitude to family, village and church. Most parents are strict and force their children to attend church, run errands and do household chores. School and homework are not the number-one priority.

Parents rarely hug, praise or encourage their children, so the youth often suffer from low self-esteem and lack confidence and ambition. Parents routinely resort to violence to punish their children, who have low status and often eat the leftovers after the adults have finished their meal. Fun family activities are few and far between – maybe only on White Sunday (p141) in October when children eat first, star in church services and are bought new clothes and toys. Some teenagers resort to *musu,* which is refusing to speak to anybody as a form of protest. For a desperate few the only escape is suicide, and the youth suicide rate remains tragically high despite all attempts to reduce it.

The best-selling anthropology book of all time is Margaret Mead's *Coming of Age in Samoa,* a brilliant but rose-tinted study that describes a Utopian society on Tau in the 1920s where casual attitudes to friendship and sex supposedly fostered a stress-free transition from childhood to adulthood.

Samoan Riddle: What roots go on for ever?

Answer on p43.

FA'AFAFINE

In general Samoans tend to share the attitude of other fundamental Christians and dislike gay men and women, but this is tempered by a tolerant but teasing attitude to *fa'afafine* – men who dress and behave like women. They see themselves as women trapped in a man's body, and have traditionally been outsiders who played the role of satirical jester and entertainer. Don't miss the boisterous Miss Tutti Frutti *fa'afafine* contest in Apia if you are around in September.

ALOFA

Alofa is love. Giving your entire pay packet to your parents is *alofa*. Beating your child so they learn right from wrong is *alofa*. Letting hungry relatives raid your fridge every night is *alofa*. Giving US$200 to the church every month is *alofa*. Forgiving a drunk driver who killed your daughter is *alofa*. Providing a weekly meal for the village schoolteachers is *alofa*. Giving up your free time to help others is *alofa*. Giving is never a loss, it raises your status and comes back one way or another. Don't give and you will die alone.

Fa'alavelave

Fa'alavelave (lavish gift-exchange ceremonies) are a fundamental part of the *fa'a Samoa*. It could be a wedding, funeral, title-installation or the opening of a new school or church; the basics are the same and can last all day. Everyone dresses up in dazzling colours as the *'aiga,* village or church shows off their wealth and status. This is measured in terms of *ie toga* (fine mats, p43) and money gifts as well as the feast of pork, taro, chop suey and cakes. An *'ava (kava)* ceremony (p38) involves the *matai* and honoured guests. Then the *tulafale* make long, poetic speeches and generous gifts of *ie toga*, food and money are exchanged by different groups. A careful note is made of all these exchanges and everything is done with a flourish. Afterwards youth groups may put on a *fiafia* with music and group dances.

It takes months to raise the money and weeks of hard work to organise these events. In American Samoa major ceremonies involve thousands of kilos of food, thousands of *ie toga* and tens of thousands of dollars. The large remittances sent back to their *'aiga* on the islands by Samoans abroad are another burdensome *fa'alavelave,* and are at the expense of their own, often struggling, families. Politics is also caught up in the system and before elections constituents receive *o'o* (gifts). Seven villages in one constituency received 20 cattle, 10 pigs, 150 boxes of salted beef, 400 cartons of herring and ST20,000 from one candidate. Democracy is more about *'aiga* alliances and *fa'alavelave* than a choice about policies.

Derek Freeman ignited a major controversy when in 1983 he published his look at the gloomy side of life in Samoa entitled *Margaret Mead and Samoa: The Making and Unmaking of an Anthropological Myth.*

The Gospel According to the Fa'a Samoa

Every village has at least one large church, and next to it is usually a church hall and a mansion for the pastor. Each village tries to build a bigger church than its neighbour. Churches don't just physically dominate the villages, they are a vital part of the social glue that holds everything together. Everyone from babes in arms to toothless grandmas dresses up in their Sunday best and goes to church at least once every Sunday. It's part religious belief, part social duty and part fashion show.

The *pese* (choirs) practice two or three times a week (with fines for being late or absent), church youth groups organise dance competitions and sports events, and church women's groups raise money by running bingo nights and aerobics classes in the church hall. Sunday school for the children is taken seriously with a panel of teachers and annual exams. The pastor is never a *matai* but as God's representative he has de facto *matai* status, and can mediate in disputes. Leading *matai* are church deacons. The church leaders sit down together for *to'ona'i* (Sunday lunch) and foreign guests may be invited too – a truly unique Samoan experience.

Families compete with each other to donate the most money to the church, and the amount given by each family is called out and written

Just outside the front door of some houses is a large concrete grave – be buried that close to home and you can't be forgotten.

down during the service. Families often give more than they can afford (up to 30% of their income) to maintain their social standing. Some give and expect to receive back good health and other blessings since God answers prayers, and the pastor's prayers are particularly powerful. Not all denominations do this – the Mormons pay a levy depending on their income.

Sa (which means 'sacred') are evening prayers, which still take place in some villages. Around 6pm a church bell (usually an empty propane tank that is hit with a stick) sounds and local *matai* patrol the village to make sure all activities cease. In one village a *palagi* jogger who refused to stop landed up in hospital. When the second bell is struck, *sa* begins and each family gathers together for DIY prayers and a hymn. After ten minutes a third bell is sounded and *sa* is over.

The 'Ava Ceremony

'Ava (or *kava* as it's known outside the Samoas) is the ceremonial *matai* drink. Made from the ground root of the pepper plant *(Piper methysti-cum)*, water is added to make a muddy-looking drink whose history goes back thousands of years.

The *matai* seat themselves in a *fale* meeting house with the wooden, multilegged *tanoa* ('ava bowl) at one end. The *taupou* (hostess) sits cross-legged behind the bowl, revealing her thigh tattoos if she has them, and maybe wearing *siapo* (p42) and a fancy headdress adorned with numerous mirrors and shells. She stirs the *'ava* and then the *tulafale* calls out the name of the person honoured with the first cup. The *taupou* dips a coconut shell into the *'ava* and passes it to a young server, who gives it to the recipient with a polite flourish. The recipient calls out *'Manuia lava'* (Cheers), spills a few drops on the ground (for the ancient Polynesian gods, as *'ava* drinking predates Christianity), and drinks it in one mouthful. This is repeated until everyone has been served in turn.

Tattooing

The missionaries tried to ban tattooing, but the tradition survived and a few young people, particularly in Samoa, still choose to suffer the painful ordeal as a mark of manhood and Samoan identity, or maybe to attract more girls.

The intricate protocol and burning agony of Samoan tattooing is caught on two documentary films – Micah Van der Ryn's excellent *Tatau: What One Must Do*, and *Skin Stories*, produced by PIC (Hawai'i) and KPBS (San Diego).

The male tattoo *(pe'a;* which also means 'bat') takes about 48 hours of work to complete, and is usually spread over two weeks to a month. It covers the body from the waist to the knees with such artistic density that it resembles a pair of dark trousers. The man receiving the tattoo lies on the floor while the *tufuga* (tattoo artist) works through the laborious process of incising the intricate design on his skin with a comb and small sticklike mallet. The process is a burning torture, a true test of guts and courage, which builds self-respect and pride. The female tattoo *(malu)* is lighter and covers only the thighs with small, decorative designs which take four to eight hours to complete.

Obtaining the tattoo involves a great deal of Samoan-style protocol, including gifts of food, money and *ie toga*. The skills and tools of the highly respected *tufuga* are traditionally passed from father to son, but it may be years before an apprentice is allowed to take charge of the tattoo combs and stick. Until then his main task is to stretch the skin tight so that the dye-filled lines of the tattoo remain straight.

Each *pe'a* is unique and the design of the geometric patterns and symbols incorporates images of fishing spears and nets, pandanus leaves, centipedes and shellfish. Circular flying patterns signify the cycles of life, and canoes signify the voyage through life.

Contact the Samoa Tourism Authority (p64) if you want to witness a tattooing session.

POPULATION

The population of Samoa is around 177,000, the vast majority of whom are Polynesian Samoans. The country has a high rate of emigration, particularly to American Samoa, New Zealand and Australia. The big island, Savai'i (population 42,000), is the most scenic and unspoilt, but a lack of jobs, good schools and medical facilities leads to migration to 'Upolu (population 110,000) and abroad. Although over 30% of the population lives in the one urban area, Apia, most still live in small seaside villages. A tiny ethnic minority is the Chinese Samoan community in Apia, which is prominent in the retail and restaurant sectors.

The population of American Samoa is much less at around 59,000, with nearly everybody living on the main island of Tutuila and less than 2000 living on the Manu'a Islands. The territory has a high population growth rate, but this is offset by emigration to Hawai'i and mainland America. Many Samoan citizens and some Tongans work in the two large tuna canneries in Pago Pago. In addition there are some 1500 foreigners who reside in American Samoa, most of whom are Koreans or Chinese involved in the tuna or garment industries. About one third of this number are *palagi* who hold government jobs usually in the teaching or health fields.

Samoan Riddle: What is round during the day and flat at night?

Answer on p46.

SPORT

On weekday afternoons after school or work, young Samoans gather on the *malae* (village green) to play rugby, volleyball and *kirikiti* (Samoan cricket) in Samoa, while American football, basketball and *kirikiti* are most popular in American Samoa. *Fautasi* (45-man canoe) races are held on special occasions. Samoa's biggest competitive sport is rugby (it's more like war than rugby), and the main stadium is at Apia Park (p73). Their team, Manu Samoa, travels the world playing matches, and Samoans play for rugby teams in many countries.

Among women, the most popular sport is netball, and many Samoans play for the world-beating New Zealand netball team.

New Zealand–based boxer David Tua, born in Samoa, won a bronze medal at the Barcelona Olympics in 1992 and fought for the world heavyweight title in 2000. Most Samoan heroes are tough sportsmen.

Both Samoas offer golf courses, gyms, snorkelling, scuba diving, surfing, game fishing, kayaking and rainforest treks.

IT'S JUST NOT CRICKET

Christianity, democracy and cricket have all been through the *fa'a Samoa* mangle. *Kirikiti* is so much more fun than the staid game of cricket. The balls are made of rubber and go much further when hit, and batters are armed with a three-sided war club adapted to a new use. Sport has replaced warfare, but the annual village *kirikiti* competition in both Samoas is still fiercely contested. The batter slogs every ball and tries to hit it into the sea, over the church or anywhere out of sight. In practice games any number can play, and men, women and children all join in the fun. The fielders don't just stand around, but usually pass the time singing and dancing, so *kirikiti* is a kind of *fiafia* (party). If you see a practice match going on, stop and watch and maybe you'll be invited to join in.

GAME ON

Apia is hosting the **South Pacific Games** (www.internationalgames.net/southpac.htm) for the second time in August–September 2007. First held in Suva, Fiji in 1963, the Games are held every four years and around 20 island nations take part. Competition is fierce as up to 4000 athletes battle it out in over 30 sports. New Caledonia usually tops the medal table, but Samoa hopes to improve on the 56 medals it won in the last games, and so does American Samoa which won only four medals.

MEDIA

Samoan newspapers have been feisty and independent ever since they first started up in the late 19th century. The *Observer* in Samoa has an outspoken editor, and the *Samoa Times* in American Samoa is a forum for virulent letters on every topic. Radio and TV tend to cast a less critical eye on social, economic and political issues. But the number one news media is beyond any government's control: coconut radio (village gossip) is a 3000-year-old South Pacific version of the Internet, which broadcasts all the latest news and rumours from one end of the islands to the other almost instantly. According to a proverb, even the lizards and grasshoppers know everything that goes on!

The Falealupo Rainforest, which the village agreed to preserve in return for ST55,000 towards a new primary school, has a tree-top canopy walkway.

RELIGION

The Christian missionaries did a thorough job of converting the islands to Christianity, although Samoans have done an equally impressive job of Samoanising Christianity. The national mottos of both countries mention God.

Churches still dominate life on the islands. Every village has a number of large churches, many of the best schools are run by churches, the Mormons run off-island universities, and Sunday is still the Sabbath and a day of rest. Church is not just a matter of Sunday worship and Sunday school – regular choir practices, women's meetings and youth sports and other activities can take up time on every day of the week.

About 40% of Samoans belong to the Congregational Church, originally the London Missionary Society (LMS). Another 20% are Catholics, while 15% are Methodists, 12% are Mormons, and the charismatic churches like the Seventh-Day Adventists and Assembly of God make up the remainder. The latter are more informal and democratic than the traditional churches. The figures are similar in both Samoas. There is a wonderful Bahá'í House of Worship (p77) in the middle of 'Upolu.

Despite the spread of Christianity, most Samoans still believe in *aitu* (spirits or ghosts) who swarm around at night and can jump inside you and make you sick. *Aitu* are believed to punish wrongdoing so be respectful to grandad or when he dies his vengeful *aitu* will really make you suffer. Two famous *aitu* are twin sisters with long blonde hair who lure men into the bush, while another, Nifoloa, has a long tooth. A legend recounts that *aitu* from Apolima stole a stream from Manono. Some Samoans turn their mirrors round to face the wall at night as they don't want to glimpse an *aitu* in it. In the old days every family had a protecting *aitu* as did almost every tree and rock.

WOMEN IN THE SAMOAN ISLANDS

A proverb states 'the women's row of thatch was completed but the men's was not' and it is still true. Samoan women don't usually hold the status positions, very few are in the *fono*, but behind the scenes they are the key organisers in village life. They run family, village and church events, raise funds, make handicrafts and sell produce in the markets as well as doing housework, looking after children and doing a million and one other things. Brothers were always taught to respect and guard their precious sisters. Equality does not exist yet, and domestic violence is all too common, but nowadays more women hold *matai* titles, and the pastor's wife often plays a key role in village life.

ARTS
Dance & Fiafia

A *fiafia* is a group music-and-dance presentation in which drummers keep the beat while the dancers, usually sitting on the floor, sing traditional songs illustrated by coordinated hand gestures. The slap dances are fun, but striptease dances haven't been seen since the missionaries arrived. A *fiafia* traditionally ends with the *siva*, a slow and fluid dance performed by the village *taupou* (usually the daughter of a high chief), dressed in *siapo* (decorated bark cloth) and with her body oiled seductively. Her beauty and grace is accentuated by male dancers who cavort around, climbing up house posts or rolling around on the floor. Larger hotels in Apia (p73) and Sadie's Thompson Inn (p114) in Pago Pago put on lavish *fiafia*, along with a hefty buffet dinner, which end with an exciting, but not traditional, fire dance.

Just to prove that Samoans don't only excel at sport, Neil Ieremia leads New Zealand's most original modern dance troupe, the all-male Black Grace.

Faleaitu

Faleaitu means 'House of Spirits' and is a traditional entertainment when the youth of the village are allowed to satirise and make fun of their seniors in a series of skits. It provides a safety valve and allows young people to let off steam and have a rare chance to express themselves freely. Samoan comics have made an impact in New Zealand, with successful comedy groups like the Naked Samoans, the Laughing Samoans and the TV cartoon series *bro'Town* carrying on the *faleaitu* tradition.

Literature

Albert Wendt is Samoa's (and the South Pacific's) most renowned novelist and scholar. His many novels deal with the *fa'a Samoa* coming up against *palagi* ideas and attitudes. His greatest novel, *Leaves of the Banyan Tree*, won the New Zealand Wattie Book of the Year Award. *Sons for the Return Home* is an earlier, best-selling novel, set in 1970s New Zealand and Samoa, that tells the story of two lovers (one white, one Samoan) and their families' response to their relationship.

Samoan performance poet and writer Sia Figiel uses traditional storytelling forms in her work. Her powerful first novel, *Where We Once Belonged*, tells the exuberant story of a young girl growing up and searching for identity in a traditional Samoan village. The in-your-face, episodic novel deromanticises Western perceptions of Pacific island women and tackles head-on issues such as domestic violence and youth suicide.

The Beach at Falesa by Robert Louis Stevenson is a brilliant story set in Samoa by a master stylist with inside knowledge of the South Pacific.

Music

Singing and dancing come as naturally to Samoans as talking and walking. Don't leave without hearing at least one church choir. Traditional

Since 2000 the South Pacific Business Development Bank has been providing small loans to female entrepreneurs to set up businesses such as jewellery making, bakeries and vegetable selling.

Race relations in 1970s New Zealand are neatly skewered in *Sons for the Return Home*, a film by Paul Maunder of Albert Wendt's no-holds-barred novel about two young Samoan-*palagi* lovers and their parents, who disapprove of their relationship.

music is normally sung in Samoan but can still be enjoyed by visitors. *We Are Samoa* by Jerome Grey is Samoa's unofficial national anthem.

A dozen villages in Samoa still maintain brass bands, which date back to German rule, but the top one is the Police Brass Band, which marches from the police station in Apia every weekday at 7.45am and performs as the national flag is raised in front of the new government offices (p66).

Buses in both Samoas are mobile discos that play the latest local and international hits. Head to the RSA Club (p73) in Apia to join the locals dancing to great live bands. Local songbirds Katrina, Random and Aniseto Falemoe have had success abroad, while in New Zealand Samoans King Kapisi and Scribe (www.samoanz.com) are the lords of hip-hop.

Mama by the Mt Vaea Band brings to life the infectious Samoan songs heard over the years at the legendary Apia nightspot, the Mt Vaea Club.

Architecture

The best example of traditional Samoan architecture is the *fale*. These Samoan homes or meeting halls have an oval structure without walls, which maximises the cool breezes inside. The thatched coconut-frond roof is lashed to wooden rafters with *sennit* (coconut-husk string) and supported by wooden posts. The floor consists of a platform of wood, coral rock or pebbles, covered with woven pandanus mats. The entire house is one room and without exterior or interior walls privacy is impossible, and chickens, dogs and even pigs sometimes have to be chased out. Palm-frond blinds, a Robinson Crusoe version of Venetian blinds, can be lowered when necessary to keep out wind and rain.

A superbly illustrated book, *Samoan Art & Artists* by Sean Mallon, covers every artistic genre from architecture to weaving, and contains interviews with contemporary Samoan artists on and off the islands.

Traditional *fale* are found throughout Samoa, but *palagi*-style square homes with walls, louvre windows and doors, though uncomfortably hot and requiring fans, have more status and are becoming more common. In American Samoa they have almost completely replaced the traditional *fale*.

Visit the Hotel Kitano Samoa (Tusitala) in Apia (p69) to see a fine modern *fale*. The many churches throughout the islands run the gamut of styles from Gothic to Wedding Cake to plain Mormon 'boilerhouses'. The iconic 19th-century wooden storefronts along Beach Rd in Apia deserve preservation. Inside the Catholic cathedral in Pago Pago is a carving of Christ wearing a *lava-lava* and holding an *'ava* bowl.

Handicrafts & Fashion

New materials are being incorporated into traditional designs, so plastic shopping bags are cut into strips and woven into pandanus bags or hats, while brightly coloured woollen playing card designs are woven into pandanus mats, and *lava-lava* have dollar bill designs on them as well as palm trees and hibiscus flowers. *Ula* (garlands) were traditionally made of flowers or seashells, but nowadays they are often made of plastic flowers or sweets. Visit the flea market (p65) for the best handicraft stalls.

Tapa of the Pacific by Neich and Pendergrast is a useful, illustrated booklet on *tapa* styles right across the Pacific from the Solomon islands to Tahiti.

SIAPO

The bark cloth known as *siapo*, or *tapa*, is made from the inner bark of *u'a* (the paper mulberry tree), and provides a medium for some of the loveliest artwork in the Samoas. The bark has to be soaked, scraped and flattened before being stamped with traditional patterns or painted on freehand. Geometric designs represent fishing nets, pandanus leaves, birds and starfish. Originally used as clothing, *siapo* is still used in customary gift exchanges. You can see *siapo* production in Palauli village (ask at the Samoan Tourism Authority for details) on the south coast of Savai'i, and don't miss the exquisite *siapo* wallpaper in Robert Louis Stevenson's former home (p74) overlooking Apia.

IE TOGA

Woven from pandanus leaves that have been split into very narrow widths, *ie toga* (fine mats) take months of painstaking work to complete. When finished they can have the look and feel of fine linen or silk. Nowadays they are only made in Samoa, and a few may be on sale in the market. They're never used as mats: *ie toga* are a traditional currency, and along with other woven mats, *siapo* and oils, make up the most important component of the 'gifts of the women' that must be exchanged at every *fa'alavelave*. Agricultural products comprise the 'gifts of the men'.

> Check out traditional *tapa* (bark cloth) artwork at www.siapo.com.

DRESS

Western T-shirts and shorts are common, but many Samoans (and visitors) wear the unisex *lava-lava*, a wraparound of brightly coloured cotton decorated with floral or geometric designs, and *aloha* (Hawaiian) shirts. Women also wear *puletasi*, a long skirt worn under a matching tunic, a cover-up fashion introduced by the early missionaries. Local designers in Apia are using Samoan-style fabrics and vibrant colours to make glamorous designer clothing. If a woman wears a flower over her left (or is it right?) ear, it means she's available. Fancy white hats appear on heads every Sunday when everyone dresses up for church.

> Riddle Answer: Family roots.

The Samoan equivalent of the business suit is the *ie faitaga*, an undecorated *lava-lava* of suit material worn with a plain shirt. This outfit is ideally accompanied by a briefcase, a chunky watch and a rotund physique, all of which denote high social status. Police wear a version of this with sandals. The kilt-like clothing helped make Robert Louis Stevenson feel at home in Apia despite being thousands of kilometres from his native Scotland.

ENVIRONMENT

THE LAND

The Samoan islands are made up of mostly high but very eroded volcanic islands with narrow coastal plains that lie in the heart of the vast South Pacific, 3700km southwest of Hawai'i. Tonga lies to the south, Fiji to the southwest, while Tuvalu is to the northwest, Tokelau to the north, and to the southeast are the Cook Islands and Tahiti.

> Meet Samoa's marine and terrestrial creatures in Meryl Rose Goldin's beautifully illustrated *Field Guide to the Samoan Archipelago* which also covers their habitats in the coral reefs, rainforests and protected areas.

Samoa, with a total land area of 2934 sq km, consists of two large islands, Savai'i (1700 sq km) and 'Upolu (1115 sq km), with two small inhabited islands, Manono and Apolima, lying in the 18km-wide strait that separates the two larger islands. All are of volcanic origin, and lava tubes (p98), lava blowholes (p100), lava tubes (p98) and lava fields (p94) can all be explored by the traveller. The highest peak, Mt Silisili on Savai'i, rises to an impressive 1866m and is often covered in cloud, which creates a special rainforest habitat.

American Samoa, 80km to the east, is made up of seven islands (six are inhabited) and a few rocky outcrops. Its land area is only 197 sq km. Tutuila (145 sq km) is a narrow, indented island 30km long and up to 6km wide, consisting of a sharp, winding ridge and plunging valleys. The highest peak is Mt Lata (966m). The island is nearly bisected by Pago Pago Harbor, a deep indentation in its eastern coast. The Manu'a Group, about 100km east, consists of three small islands, Ta'u, Ofu and Olosega, although the latter two are joined by a bridge. All are wildly steep and beautiful examples of volcanic remnants.

THE SEX LIFE OF CORAL

Sex is infrequent for coral as the mass spawning that creates new coral only takes place once a year – but when it happens, it's fireworks. The big event comes in late spring or early summer, beginning a night or two after a full moon and building to a crescendo on subsequent nights. Suddenly, right across the reef tiny bundles of eggs and sperm are released, and start floating upward towards the surface. Divers who have seen the event report that it looks like a fireworks display or an inverted snowstorm.

Amid the swarm, it's not easy for an individual sperm to find an egg of the same coral species, but biologists believe that spawning over a short period reduces the risk of being consumed by marine predators. Once fertilisation has occurred, the egg cells begin to divide, and within a day have become swimming coral larvae known as planulae. These are swept along by the current for several days before they sink to the bottom and, if the right spot is found, the tiny larvae become coral polyps, and a new coral colony is formed.

Darwin's theory about the life of a Pacific island can be traced by travelling west to east through the Samoan islands. Savai'i is a relatively young island and a volcano erupted there only a hundred years ago. Just to the east, the subtle peaks and ridges of 'Upolu show that it is still a fairly new island. But Tutuila and the Manu'a Group, further east, are heavily eroded and many of the volcanic craters they once contained are broken and submerged in the sea.

Swains Island is a tiny coral atoll – the coral has built up on top of an ancient, eroded volcano – that has been owned by the Jennings family since 1856. Uninhabited Rose Atoll, the easternmost island, is a bird and turtle sanctuary. Ultraprotected, it is easier to visit the moon than Rose Atoll.

WILDLIFE
Animals

The Samoan moss spider, *Patu marplesi*, is hard to spot because it measures 0.3mm and is the tiniest of the planet's 35,000 species of spider.

Because the Samoan islands are so remote, few animal species have managed to colonise them. Apart from the Polynesian rat, the sheath-tailed bat and two species of flying fox, mammals are limited to the marine varieties. The flying foxes (p115) are now protected throughout the islands after being hunted close to extinction. Whales, dolphins and porpoises migrate north and south through the Samoas, depending on the season. Most common are pilot whales, frequently seen in the open seas around the islands. Humpback whales may be seen in September and October.

Pili (skinks) and *mo'o* (geckos) can be seen in the bush, including on the hike up Mt Vaea to Stevenson's tomb (p76). The green house gecko patrols walls and ceilings, hunting for insects. The harmless *gata* (Pacific boa) snake is found only on Ta'u, and the green turtle and endangered hawksbill turtle are rare visitors. The hawksbill breeds on the Aleipata islands (off 'Upolu) and very occasionally on remote beaches on Savai'i, Tutuila and the Manu'a Islands. The green turtle nests on Rose Atoll, and tagged ones have been discovered as far away as Fiji and Tahiti. Other turtles occasionally visit American Samoa, where killing one can result in a US$10,000 fine. The cliffs at Vaitogi village (p118) are the best place to see a turtle and maybe a shark too.

For the lowdown on Samoa's colourful avian population pick up a copy of the classic *Field Guide to the Birds of Hawaii and the Tropical Pacific* by Pratt, Bruner and Berrett.

The only land creature to beware of (besides the unloved and unlovely dogs) is the giant centipede which packs a surprisingly nasty bite.

Over 50 species of birds can be seen or heard, including sea birds such as petrels, white-tailed tropicbirds, boobies, black noddies, curlews, frigate birds and terns. The most beautiful bird is the tiny, bright red cardinal honeyeater. Other species include the nearly flightless, endangered banded rails, the barn owl, seen occasionally in the Manu'a Islands, and the superb blue-crowned lory, which the Samoans call *sega*. While walking in the rainforests, listen for the haunting calls of the rare multicoloured fruit doves (maybe only 50 survive on Tutuila) and the beautiful green and white Pacific pigeons, found throughout the islands.

The coral reefs that ring the Samoan islands are home to brilliantly coloured tropical fish that look like they are on their way to a fancy-dress party, and countless species of shellfish, starfish and crustaceans. Over 200 species of coral and 900 species of fish have been identified, including several shark species which are generally small and remain outside the reefs and lagoons.

For a raise-a-smile blog about coconut trees and their cannonball-like seeds look at www .coconut.com/blog.

Plants

On all the islands, upland areas that haven't been altered by agriculture or logging are covered in green rainforest, predominately broadleaf evergreens, which are clothed in mosses, tree ferns and vines. Valleys, waterfalls and volcanic craters take on an otherworldly aspect in the jungle, and the highest peaks provide a unique cloud forest habitat as the sun rarely shines there.

The *aoa* (giant banyan tree) dominates the landscape of the higher areas, especially on Savai'i and 'Upolu. Known as the strangler fig, it grows in the upper reaches of a host tree, shoots out roots to the ground, and then slowly strangles its host to death. Other parts of the Samoas are covered by scrublands, marshes, pandanus forests and mangrove swamps. All round the islands brilliant tropical flowers, such as the *teuila* (red ginger), bloom all year round.

The Samoan rainforests are a natural pharmacy, containing some 75 plant species that are used by *fofo* (traditional healers) to treat many types

Cluny and La'avasa Macpherson interviewed 22 *fofo* (traditional Samoan healers) about their use of exorcism, psychology, medicinal herbs and massage in their pioneering study *Samoan Medical Belief*.

THE WORLD IN YOUR PALM

Samoans revere the tree of life, the coconut palm, a swaying South Seas icon with more uses than there are days in a year. The rich milk that is squeezed from the silky white flesh of the coconut is the soul of Samoan cuisine, and coconut water is a delicious, pure and refreshing drink. But there's a whole lot more to be gained from this 'milk bottle up a tree', so much so that it's difficult to imagine life on Samoa without it.

Copra is made by sun-drying the white coconut flesh, or placing it in a kiln and using the coconut shells as fuel. The copra is then pressed to produce coconut oil, which is made into margarine, soap, candles and cosmetics. Samoan women use it, together with *moso'oi* flower petals, to make a healing, scented massage oil which is sold in Apia market. The pressed flesh can be fed to cattle or pigs.

Coconut shells are used as drinking vessels in the 'ava ceremony and, when burned, make excellent charcoal. Polished shell is also fashioned into buttons and tourist souvenirs.

The stringy coconut husk is braided into string and used to make mats, fishing nets and to hold a *fale* together (in place of nails). In the villages you can still see old men rolling the strands on their knee to make it into string.

Coconut fronds are woven to make thatched roofs, blinds, baskets, hats, fans and food trays, while brooms are made from the frond spines. The trunk of the tree is used to make furniture, fences, firewood and posts for *fale*.

Coconut palms live for more than 70 years and produce about 60 coconuts a year. Climbing a coconut tree is an adventure sport rewarded with a refreshing drink.

NONU THE WONDER FRUIT

In need of a pick-me-up? Samoan *nonu* juice, a vile-tasting, olfactory-repulsing potion, made from the fruit of the *nonu* plant, has been hailed as a genuine cure-all. It's prescribed by some Samoan practitioners for ailments such as diabetes, digestive diseases, kidney disorders, high blood pressure, asthma and arthritis, to name just a few. Many Samoans swear by it, believing that a dose a day keeps the doctor away.

While this may be true, there's very little, if any, scientific evidence to prove its efficacy. Still, anything that tastes and smells this bad has to be good for you, right? At least the Samoans hope so, particularly as it's become a lucrative international export (marketed as the Tahitian *noni*). You can pick up a bottle in several shops around Apia for between ST10 and ST20 – or buy it for NZ$38 (473g) in New Zealand.

---

of illness. The bark of the *mamala* tree is being investigated for use as an AIDS medicine.

CONSERVATION AREAS
Samoa

On the southern shore of 'Upolu is O le Pupu-Pu'e National Park (p80), which contains a cross section of island habitats from the coastline up to the misty heights of Mt Fito (1100m) around the spine of the island. Togitogiga waterfall is nearby. Development in the park is limited but there are a couple of walking tracks, as well as opportunities to observe native forest and bird life. A drawback of building more paths is that some locals will use them to shoot flying foxes and pigeons, even though it is illegal. Apparently, barbecued flying fox tastes better than chicken.

Samoan Herbal Medicine, by Dr W Arthur Whistler, is an overview of the plants used and the ailments treated by traditional Samoan healers.

Lake Lanoto'o (p77) is a large crater lake that is designated to become a national park, but is difficult to access. Legends say it was filled by the tears of To'o after he heard about the death of his brother in one of Samoa's all-too-common wars.

The Uafato Conservation Area (p77), the Sataoa and Sa'anapu Conservation Area (p80) and the Aleipata Islands Conservation Area (p83) are also protected. In the Apia area, conservation areas include Palolo Deep Marine Reserve (p64) and Mt Vaea Scenic Reserve (p74).

A couple of villages have established their own protected areas – the Falealupo Rainforest Preserve (p97) and the Tafua Peninsula Rainforest Preserve (p92), which contains two tree-filled volcanic craters.

American Samoa

American Samoa's major contribution to nature conservation is the 4000-hectare National Park of American Samoa, which consists of three separate areas: firstly a large chunk of the upland forest, wild coastline and offshore waters of northern Tutuila (p115); secondly a magnificent stretch of beach and coral along the southern shore of Ofu (p127); thirdly the offshore waters, rugged cliffs and rainforested volcanic highlands of southern Ta'u (p129). Combined, these areas cover the largest tract of wilderness in the Samoas, with most of the island ecosystems represented.

Riddle Answer: Sleeping mats.

Currently there is just one major walking trail – the track leading to the top of Mt Alava on Tutuila. Future plans for the park include establishing hiking trails, basic camp sites and a rainforest canopy walkway in the Ta'u section of the park. Contact the National Park Visitor Information Centre (p108) for more information.

Other protected areas are the Fagatele Bay National Marine Sanctuary (p118; www.fbnms.nos.noaa.gov) on Tutuila, and isolated Rose Atoll (p123), a vital wildlife sanctuary for nesting turtles and seabirds. Pago Pago Harbor, Nu'uuli Pala Lagoon and the Leone wetlands are special management areas.

ENVIRONMENTAL ISSUES
Samoa
Deforestation is probably the most serious environmental challenge facing the country. Population pressures, and demand for wood both locally and to generate much-needed export revenue are the major threats. Much of the lowland rainforest has already been cleared and the rainforest now covers less than 37% of the land area. The current rate of forest depletion is about 3000 hectares per year – 80% due to agriculture and other activities, 20% the result of logging. The protection of Samoa's forests is crucial for the conservation of water and soil resources as well as to ensure the survival of flying foxes and unique island ecosystems.

Several key areas on 'Upolu and Savai'i have been declared protected areas, and visitors can help conservation efforts by only visiting and staying in villages that operate 'ecofriendly' activities and have pledged to protect the environment. Ask at the Samoa Tourism Authority (p64) for more details.

Unfortunately Samoan marine resources are under serious pressure as overfishing combined with modern, nonselective fishing techniques have resulted in declining fish stocks. Coastal habitats have been damaged by the illegal use of dynamite and poisons to catch fish as well as by an increase in siltation and pollution. Coral has been seriously reduced by cyclone damage and outbreaks of crown-of-thorns starfish (which may be the result of unnaturally high volumes of nutrients feeding the young starfish).

Mangrove swamps and wetland areas, which provide vital feeding and breeding grounds for fish and other sea creatures, are being reduced by land reclamation schemes. Vaiusu Bay, the largest mangrove area in eastern Polynesia, was used for many years as Apia's rubbish dump. The mangroves there are still being reclaimed, and leachate from the disused dump remains a threat to the marine environment.

Waste disposal is a growing problem, but the introduction of a waste pick-up service for many villages on 'Upolu and a few on Savai'i, where the rubbish is taken to designated land-fill areas, has helped. In 2005 a can-recycling plant was established and a new incinerator was built for hospital waste. Many houses are surrounded by litter-free gardens of

Mouse-click your way to the best Samoan environmental database at www.mnre.gov.ws /biodiversity.

www.nps.gov/npsa is a brilliant site with a comprehensive guide to the terrestrial and marine environment of American Samoa.

SUSTAINABLE TOURISM

Much of Samoa is relatively unspoiled and the government wants to keep it that way. As tourist numbers increase, so too does the need to ensure that this growth does not wreck the environment or damage social structures, both of which can be fragile. While 'ecotourism' (whether genuine or simply tours wrapped in green packaging) is a buzz word, 'sustainable tourism' is much broader in its approach. It involves improving or reducing waste disposal, increasing the proportion of the tourists' *tala* (money) that is spent on locally grown or made goods, and increasing the share that trickles down to the ordinary workers or local landowners.

The aim is to reduce the negative impacts that have been felt on other South Pacific islands like Fiji and Tahiti, where small villages have been swamped by mega resorts, and the fishermen have all become waiters and barmen, so that their families now live on tinned fish. A string of small, ecofriendly beach *fale* homestays have been developed around the islands which provide an authentic Samoan experience and put the philosophy into practice.

flowers and fruit trees, and Tidy Village competitions help make villages in Samoa less messy than in American Samoa.

Another waste-disposal problem is the contamination of groundwater and lagoons resulting from inadequate sewerage systems in private homes, which range from septic tanks to drains into the sea. The government and conservation groups, such as the O le Siosiomaga Society, work hard to persuade people to recycle waste and build composting toilets.

Detailed mapping has been carried out of coastal areas that are most at risk from rising sea levels associated with global warming. Around 75% of Samoa's coastline has been identified as highly vulnerable to coastal erosion, and 93% of the narrow coastal strip, the flat area where most of the population lives, is expected to be in a flood hazard zone in 50 years. Hazard maps have been presented to each village for discussion about the need to build new sea walls and shift roads and power lines inland.

A lack of town planning in Apia has resulted in traffic congestion, overcrowding, poor segregation of industry and dwellings, and some very ugly buildings. Pressure is mounting on the limited urban infrastructure as more people crowd into the capital from Savai'i and remote villages.

The government of Samoa has plans to outlaw plastic bags in shops as well as plastic containers and even disposable nappies.

American Samoa

The biggest issues affecting the environment in American Samoa are a high population growth rate, the increased generation of waste, greater demand for treated water and the development of the limited land available for homes and other uses.

The main source of industrial waste are the two tuna canneries that operate inside Pago Pago Harbor. For many years, cannery waste was discharged directly into the harbour in front of the canneries, and sludge was disposed of in pits on the island. Since the US Environmental Protection Agency (EPA) brought in strict waste-disposal requirements, the canneries have installed a pipeline to the outer harbour, and now transport most of the waste to an ocean dump site 9km from the harbour. An upgraded filtering system has reduced the smells coming from the canneries.

WHEN IT'S RAINING CATS AND DOGS

Jan Allen is about to face another day of desexing. She and her colleagues wait in a remote Samoan village for their clients to arrive. A small boy carries in a dog almost as big as himself. A young family brings a litter of female puppies. A man arrives on a bicycle carrying three cats in a rice sack. Jan whips out a scalpel and gets to work.

Jan is a veterinarian with the **Animal Protection Society of Samoa** (APS; www.samoa.ws/aps), placed by **Australian Volunteers International** (www.australianvolunteers.com). Her role is to provide animal health services in remote areas.

Samoa has large numbers of unwanted and unclaimed dogs and cats. These animals pose a significant health risk, especially in poor or rural areas, so the APS has embarked on a nationwide desexing programme to reduce the population. The programme includes regular village visits, where APS vets examine and desex animals, and humanely euthanise sick or neglected animals.

Jan reports that the programme is slowly but steadily making progress. 'The village visits are always successful in the numbers of animals treated, and also provide a wealth of community education. We have returned to villages five times because it's become the 'cool' thing to get your dog desexed.'

As the sun sets, Jan and her colleagues pack up and head back to the truck. They've picked up some extra cargo – the female puppies, for whom they'll find a home in Apia. Another day is over, and the rain of cats and dogs has slightly eased.

RESPONSIBLE TRAVEL

■ The Samoan islands have limited facilities for waste, so try to minimise the amount of packaging you buy.

■ Most land in the Samoas belongs to someone, so ensure you ask permission before you create your own tracks.

■ Don't purchase items or souvenirs made out of endangered resources like black coral or sandalwood.

■ Never fish, collect shells or other specimens in any of the marine reserves or national parks in the Samoan islands.

One study found the fish in Pago Pago Harbor to be contaminated with heavy metals and organochlorine compounds, probably related to waste disposal practices of the ship repair yards and power generation plants. Further action is required to reduce harbour pollution.

Solid waste collection on Tutuila is inadequate and garbage on the streets is an eyesore. After heavy rain (almost a daily occurrence), Pago Pago Harbor is ringed with floating rubbish carried there by streams and land drains. Litter task forces have been reintroduced and people caught littering can be fined US$50. The recycling programme deals only with aluminium cans and Vailima beer bottles, but any profit from recycling other materials during previous trials was cancelled out by shipping costs.

Increased land clearance for development is causing erosion and a degradation of water quality. Less than 28% of the native rainforest remains on Tutuila, but the National Park of American Samoa protects key remaining areas, and conservation group Le Tausagi is campaigning to protect the lowland Ottoville rainforest.

Many coastal mangrove swamps, inland freshwater marshes and some cultivated taro fields have been lost to development. In recent years up to 5% of the wetlands have been lost each year. To try to halt this decline, a village-based programme has been designed to make the public aware of their economic value and environmental significance.

FOOD & DRINK

Samoans love food, glorious food, and skinny Samoans are as rare as hawksbill turtles. Traditional Samoan meals consist of root vegetables, particularly *talo* (taro), *niu* (coconut products), *fuata* (breadfruit), *pua'a* (pork), *moa* (chicken), *i'a* (fish) and other seafood such as shellfish, octopus and lobster. Young coconuts have delicious coconut water and a little jelly-like white flesh, mature ones have coconut water and firm white flesh, while sprouting ones are full of a spongy white substance called *popo*, Samoan ice cream.

View www.samoa.co.uk for a worthwhile site on all things Samoan, including food 'n' drink.

STAPLES & SPECIALITIES

The best way to sample the local cuisine is to stay in a village, be invited into a Samoan home or take part in an *umu* feast. An *umu* is a traditional Polynesian oven that uses hot rocks to cook the food, and is much better than a microwave. *To'ona'i* (Sunday lunch) is usually cooked in an *umu*. A few hotels in Apia offer excellent *to'ona'i,* including the Pasefika Inn (p68).

Feasts are held in honour of every festive event, such as a wedding, birthday, investiture of title, the opening of a building or the arrival of VIPs. Typical foods offered include the ubiquitous chicken and fish, and the more prestigious roast suckling pig; cooked green bananas, taro and yams; *pisupo* (corned beef), which is surprisingly tasty when fried up with onions; dishes utilising coconut cream, such as scrummy *palusami* (young taro leaves baked in coconut cream); *oka* (marinated raw fish); *supo esi* (papaya pudding); *fa'ausi talo* (taro in coconut cream); s*upasui* (chop suey noodles), which is now part of the *fa'a Samoa*; and cakes or fresh fruit salad which make up dessert. Garlands of fresh flowers and wrapped sweets are hung round the necks of the more important guests.

For an *umu* meal, wrap taro, breadfruit, pork and *palusami* in leaves, put them on rocks heated in a fire and pile more leaves on top.

TASTES OF SAMOA

Oka
500g fresh skipjack or yellowfin tuna (or other reef fish, such as mullet)
1 cup lemon or lime juice
½ cup coconut cream
½ cup finely chopped onion
½ cup finely chopped tomatoes
½ cup diced cucumber
1 tsp chopped chilli peppers
salt to taste

Cut fish into cubes and rinse with cold water. Marinate in lemon or lime juice for at least two hours, or overnight in the fridge. Drain the juice and set aside. Mix together remaining ingredients, add some of the juice to taste and pour over fish. Serve chilled.

Palusami or Lu'au
12 young taro leaves
250g corned beef, shelled prawns or sweet potato
1 tin coconut cream
1 finely diced onion
salt to taste

Mix the meat, prawns or sweet potato with the coconut cream, onion and salt. Divide the mixture into 12 portions and wrap each in a taro leaf. Wrap each parcel in foil, place in a baking dish and bake in a medium oven for one hour.

Supo Esi
papayas
sago
coconut cream
lime leaf
sugar to taste

This refreshing and not-too-sweet dish can be enjoyed any time of the day, but is often eaten for breakfast. Take as many papayas as required, remove seeds, scoop out the flesh and place in a saucepan. Add water to the level of the fruit and ½ tsp of sago to every cup of water. Simmer the mixture until the sago is cooked (the sago will turn clear). Add ½ cup of coconut cream for every cup of water, sugar to taste if required, and one lime leaf. Cover the pan and simmer for five minutes. Remove lime leaf and allow mixture to cool.

TRAVEL YOUR TASTE BUDS

Dancing Spaghetti

Some time in October or early November, usually on the seventh night after a full moon, the *palolo* reef worm suddenly shifts into reproduction mode. Over the course of a few hours millions of the segmented coral worms break into two, and the back half – sacks of eggs and sperm – float up to the surface of the sea and indulge in a reproductive frenzy. The blue-green, vermicelli-like *palolo*, rich in calcium, iron and protein, taste like creamy caviar and are said to be a great aphrodisiac.

On the night when the *palolo* rise, hundreds of excited Samoans gather on beaches that have reefs just offshore, and then wade into the sea armed with lanterns, makeshift nets and buckets to scoop up the once-a-year delicacy. Some gatherers eat them raw, but others fry them up and serve them on toast, or cook them with coconut cream and onions. A big plateful costs ST15 to ST35 in the market.

We Dare You

▪ Sea cucumber innards in a murky liquid are sold in soft-drink bottles at Apia market.

▪ Raw sea urchins look disgusting and taste worse.

Food from the sea includes tuna, shark and other open-sea fish as well as lagoon fish, such as parrotfish and perch, lobster, squid, octopus, crabs and *limu* (a crunchy seaweed). Popular with Asian visitors is *sea* (sea cucumber), a turd-like creature that hoovers up detritus from the reef floor.

Tropical fruits grown locally include bananas, papayas, guavas, passionfruit, pineapples and *vi* (Tahitian apples). Mangoes are available from late September.

Unfortunately most food is now imported – for instance tins of fish have largely replaced fresh fish – and unless you spend time at a homestay out in a village, you can have a hard time finding traditional foods. Apia and Pago Pago both have more Asian than Polynesian restaurants.

Local people, especially in American Samoa, are experiencing severe health problems, such as obesity, diabetes and heart disease, as junk food, fatty meats and imported supermarket items replace the healthier diet to which Samoans have long been accustomed. Small village stores are often a nutrition nightmare, stocked with crisps, *pisupo,* instant noodles, processed white bread and fizzy drinks as well as cigarettes and Vailima beer. A diet of sausages, mutton flaps (belly meat), turkey tails and corned beef would soon supersize even Kate Moss.

Corned beef is called *pisupo* because early missionaries brought tins of pea soup to the islands and *pisupo* became the word for any tinned food.

Tuck into your Pasifica faves such as *panipopo* (coconut buns) and *koko araisa* (cocoa rice) with help from www.samoa.as/recipe.htm.

DRINKS
Nonalcoholic Drinks

The most refreshing drink available is the water inside an immature coconut, which is naturally carbonated and absolutely delicious. After cutting off the fibre surrounding the coconut, the top of the nut is taken off with a machete and a straw put in. Drinking coconuts are cheap and available year-round just about everywhere, although climbing up a tree to get one is not as easy as it looks.

Another delicious drink is *koko Samoa*, a chocolate bevy made with locally grown and roasted cocoa beans, sugar and water. Because they lack the bitterness of beans produced elsewhere, Samoan cocoa beans are considered to be the best in the world.

'AVA

'*Ava* is a time-honoured South Pacific drink made from the dried root of the kava plant. Traditionally mixed by the virgin daughter of the highest chief, '*ava* is the ceremonial drink imbibed at all important Samoan ceremonies and meetings (see p38). It has a muddy colour and a peppery taste. Although not alcoholic, it can have a mild sleep-inducing and numbing effect. Drunk in large quantities, it's a sedative, muscle relaxant and diuretic. In recent years the beverage has become controversial with some touting it (in pill form) as a New-Age cure-all, recommended for treatment of stress, anxiety and depression. It had become a small but growing export earner for Samoa, until in 2001 medical researchers linked '*ava* with liver failure, and exports collapsed. Although usually reserved for special occasions and restricted to *matai*, a big wooden bowl of '*ava* is often available at the market in Apia.

Real brewed coffee, some of it locally produced, can be found in quite a few places around the islands, though it's often made very weak. Tea is generally served black with lots of sugar.

A drink you might come across is *vaisalo*, made from coconut milk and flesh that is thickened with starch. Rich and nourishing, it is traditionally the first food offered to women after they have given birth. You may see people drinking it early in the morning at the markets.

Despite the variety of fruit on hand, fresh juices aren't always easy to come by. You're more likely to be served a sugary cordial or fizzy drink than freshly squeezed juice. Soft drinks and locally produced bottled water can be bought everywhere. Most of the milk available is the imported long-life variety.

Written by an experienced restaurateur, Sue Chambers, *The Flame Tree Cookbook* serves up heaps of Asian/South Pacific flavours with a tropical twist.

Alcoholic Drinks

Samoa's locally brewed lager, Vailima, is available just about everywhere in both Samoas, and is popular with visitors and locals alike. *Manuia*! (Cheers!) Apia's restaurants and bars stock a range of imported alcoholic drinks, including wines and beers from Australia and New Zealand. In American Samoa you can choose from American and other imported beers such as Budweiser, Coors, Miller's and Steinlager (although you'd have to be *mad* to turn down a Vailima for a Bud!).

CELEBRATIONS

Every celebration is accompanied by a splendid *umu* feast which includes whole roasted pigs, baked fish, lobsters for VIP guests, chicken, leaf-wrapped *palusami*, big platters of corned beef, taro, breadfruit and chop suey, a coconut drink, sweet black tea, and is finished off with fruit salad and coconut milk. Guests take home what they cannot finish.

Two hundred island-inspired recipes can be found in *Taste of the Pacific* by Parkinson, Stacy and Mattinson, including such delights as breadfruit bread, coconut egg curry and taro cakes.

WHERE TO EAT & DRINK

Apia and, to a lesser extent, Pago Pago have a range of restaurants, but outside these towns, options are very limited for eating out. Samoans don't eat out much, so most menus cater for Western tastes with seafood, steaks, pizzas and pasta, though some Apia hotels put on island-style buffets. Chinese restaurants in Apia are a good bet, while reasonable Mexican and Korean food and excellent Japanese food is available in American Samoa. Sometimes the more ordinary-looking places offer better food.

In Samoa a cheap main meal costs from around ST8, an upmarket feed from ST25. In American Samoa you'll pay US$5 for a cheap meal or takeaway, US$30 for a splurge.

Out of town, travellers have to rely on hotel restaurants or home-cooked food provided by the proprietors of beachside *fale*. Apia has a small fish market (go as early as possible), but elsewhere it's difficult to buy fresh fish and seafood to cook up yourself.

Supermarkets in Apia and Pago Pago are well-stocked, but high transport costs to the islands can make some items more expensive than you might expect. Every village has a store but they only stock the basics.

Quick Eats

The cheapest quick eats are in the markets in Apia, Salelologa on Savai'i, and Pago Pago, where a few *tala* or dollars will buy doughnuts (called pancakes) and hot cocoa, or a plate of fish and vegetables. Bakeries are best for a quick snack – try *panipopo* (buns dripping in coconut cream). Locally made breadfruit chips are healthier than crisps. *Masi* (cabin biscuits, a 19th-century seaman's staple), *sua fa'i* (banana porridge) or *koko araisa* are breakfast possibilities, while fresh fruit and coconuts are good bets. Fast food establishments can be found in both Apia and Pago Pago.

VEGETARIANS & VEGANS

It's tough. In Apia you can buy *palusami* and fresh fruit in the market, veggie burgers at Gourmet Seafood, vegetarian pizzas at Giordano's, a salad at McDonald's or a tofu dish in a Chinese restaurant. A few restaurants such as Sails will cook up something vegetarian if asked.

In Pago Pago, Hong Kong House has the best range of vegetarian meals, while Mom's Place has pancakes, Matai's has vegetarian pizzas, and Good Food Bakery has tempting snacks.

EATING WITH KIDS

Both Apia and Pago Pago have fast-food joints that sell burgers, chips, pizzas, fried chicken and fried fish, as well as Asian takeaways and restaurants, bakeries and ice cream shops, while the markets have piles of fresh tropical fruit.

Families eating out are unlikely to face any problems. Children may even be adopted by restaurant staff and given a free reign, although up-market restaurants may be less tolerant.

Kava, the Pacific Elixir by Lebot, Merlin and Lindstrom is an exhaustive New Age study of the South Pacific's oldest beverage.

Fans of the wonder root kava should head to www.kavaroot.com.

Samoan Riddle: What small boat floats on a brown sea?

Answer p54.

SAMOA'S TOP FIVE RESTAURANTS

- Bistro Tatau (p71)
- Aggie Grey's Fale Restaurant (p71)
- Gourmet Seafood (p70)
- Sails (p71)
- Lusia's Lagoon Chalets (p92)

AMERICAN SAMOA'S TOP FIVE RESTAURANTS

- Tisa's Barefoot Bar (p117)
- Sook's Sushi Restaurant (p113)
- DDW (p112)
- Rubble's Tavern (p120)
- Sadie's Restaurant (p113)

DOS & DON'TS

If invited home to a *fale* for a meal:

- Sit cross-legged on a floor mat to eat.
- Eat with your fingers and wash them after the meal.
- Reciprocate by buying some groceries or bringing a present.
- Guests often eat first so don't scoff the lot (probably impossible anyway) as what you leave will be shared by the family.
- Don't tuck in immediately as grace is sometimes said before a meal.
- Don't bring alcohol as the family may have religious objections to booze .

HABITS & CUSTOMS

Food, like everything else, is seen as something to be shared. So don't be surprised if someone on the bus gives you some fruit or a bun. Village families are hospitable and may invite you home for a meal, which is an opportunity to experience Samoan family life at first hand.

FOOD GLOSSARY

ai – eat
'ava – ceremonial drink made from *kava* roots
'ava malosi – liquor
esi – papaya
fa'i – banana
fala'oa – bread
fale'aiga – restaurant
fasi povi – meat
fuala'auaina – fruit
fuata – breadfruit
i'a – fish
kofe – coffee
koko Samoa – local cocoa drink
limu – edible seaweed
maketi – market
masi – cabin biscuits
mea taumafa – food
moa – chicken
niu – young coconut
nonu – native fruit marketed as *noni*, a cure-all
oka – raw fish marinated in coconut cream, lemon juice and onion
palolo – coral worm that provides a feast once a year
palusami – young taro leaves cooked in coconut cream
panipopo – buns in coconut cream
pia – beer
pisupo – tinned corned beef
popo – sprouting coconut
povi masima – salt beef
pua'a – pig
supasui – Samoan chop suey
supo esi – papaya pudding
susu – milk
ta'amu – giant taro
talo – taro, the staple root vegetable

Riddle answer: An *'ava* cup.

ti – tea
to'onai – Sunday lunch
uaina – wine
umu – oven made with hot rocks
vai – water
vai mama – mineral water
vaisalo – drink made with coconut and starch

'Upolu

Samoa's second-largest and most populated island outdoes itself with tropical grandeur. The main road that winds casually – almost sleepily – around the coast takes you past sublime beaches that are so pristine you feel guilty for putting footprints on them; outcrops of offshore coral that are just pieces of a much larger, more dazzling marine ecosystem; craggy lava cliffs that drop suddenly into a boiling ocean; and verdant plantations and conservation areas that sweep into the island's hilly, rainforested interior. Lined up between the natural spectacles are small villages where a wave and the flash of a smile are as commonplace as sunshine. Even in the crowded confines of the capital, Apia, you'll be warmly besieged by local greetings.

This is not the sort of place where you arrive in the morning, dash around on a manic day tour, and then rush back to the airport to catch a flight to somewhere else. This is a place for cruising around at your leisure. While away the hours bathing in ocean-fed pools or snorkelling amongst living reefs. Spend a day or two (why not a week?) snoozing in *fale* (traditional thatched house), overfeeding yourself on *palusami* (coconut cream wrapped in taro leaves), or unearthing star mounds on smaller islands such as Manono. Completely lose track of time inside beautiful colonial mansions or striding along bushy trails deep within a national park. Whatever you do, make sure you slow yourself down, pack away your watch and submit completely to island time.

HIGHLIGHTS

- Eyeballing technicolour coral and fish in the dreamy depths of **Palolo Deep Marine Reserve** (p64)
- Floundering in the gorgeous waters off pristine **Lalomanu Beach** (p83)
- Letting an ocean current swirl you around the superb **To Sua Ocean Trench** (p81)
- Breathing in the literary history of the charming **Robert Louis Stevenson Museum** (p74)
- Setting off on an early morning circumnavigation of idyllic **Manono** (p84)

- POPULATION: 110,000
- AREA: 1115 SQ KM

LONELY PLANET INDEX

- **Litre of unleaded petrol** ST2.15
- **Litre of bottled water** ST3.50-5
- **Bottle (355ml) of Vailima beer** ST3-4
- **Souvenir T-shirt** ST12
- **Street treat (palusami)** ST1

HISTORY

Early Polynesians are believed to have established their first village in Samoa on 'Upolu at Mulifanua, probably around 1000 BC. Europeans began fully acquainting themselves with 'Upolu in the early 19th century. Among these visitors were Christian missionaries such as John Williams, who began spreading his holy words in 1830, and Peter Turner, who landed on Manono in 1835. European traders began flooding into 'Upolu after 1850 and for the next 50 years the island became the centre of a territorial dispute between Germany, Britain and the USA, who at one stage all dispatched warships to Apia's harbour – six of these sunk during a massive cyclone in 1889. Germany triumphed but during WWI was relieved of control by New Zealand, which administered Samoa up until the country's independence in 1962.

'Upolu has had a habit of being battered by tropical cyclones in the past two decades, beginning with cyclone Ofa in February 1990 and cyclone Val in December 1991 – the latter caused 13 deaths and economic devastation. The most recent storm to hit the island was Olaf in February 2005, though damage on 'Upolu was much less than at first feared.

GETTING AROUND

Travelling around 'Upolu by car is easy, but getting around by bus is time-consuming. If travelling on public transport, don't try to visit too many places in a single day. A good rule of thumb is to allow an entire day for each excursion to a point of interest beyond the environs of Apia.

See under Manono (p85) and Apolima (p85) for details of transport to each of those islands.

For info on travelling to Savai'i by plane, see p147. For details of the ferry between 'Upolu and Savai'i, see p148.

Bus

Buses connect Apia with almost every other part of 'Upolu. They leave from Maketi Fou (the main market) and from the bus area behind the Flea Market. Bus terminals are quite a sight in the late afternoon when their perimeters are jammed with Samoans waiting for a ride home. Just because the bus has left the market, however, doesn't mean you're on your way. Buses will travel between the main market areas and around central Apia as many times as the driver deems necessary to fill the bus, or until he realises that it's no longer economically feasible to waste fuel making the circuit. If he decides that he hasn't inspired sufficient interest in the trip, it is cancelled altogether. Keep in mind that buses tend to begin running early but can stop in the early afternoon, according to the whim of the driver. If you'd like to visit a remote spot (say the Aleipata district) and return the same day, you'll need to get an early start.

All buses prominently display the name of their destination in the front window. To stop a bus, wave your hand and arm, palm down, as the bus approaches. To signal that you'd like to get off the bus, either knock on the ceiling or clap loudly. Fares are paid to the driver. A bus schedule that includes fare information is available from the Samoa Tourism Authority (p64).

Any bus with the sign 'Pasi o le Va'a' or 'Faleolo' in the window will be passing Faleolo Airport and going on to Mulifanua Wharf. If it also says 'Manono-uta' or 'Falelatai', it will be continuing to the Manono ferry dock or to the southwestern end of the island.

In order to reach the Aleipata district at the eastern end of the island, catch the Lalomanu bus, which takes Richardson Rd. If you're heading east along the north coast, take the Falefa, Fagaloa or Lotofaga bus. For any point along the main Cross Island Rd, take either the Si'umu or Salani bus. To get to Togitogiga and O Le Pupu-Pu'e National Park, you'll need to take the Falealili or Salani bus.

Sample fares from Apia include to Robert Louis Stevenson Museum (ST1.20), Falefa (ST2), Faleolo Airport (ST2), Mulifanua Wharf (ST2), Virgin Cove (ST2.30) and Lalomanu (ST4).

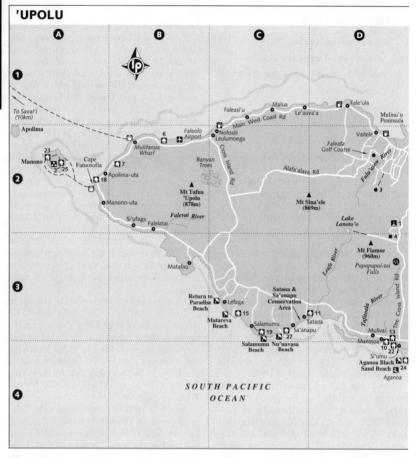

Car

The sealed Main Coast Rd follows the coast all the way around the island of 'Upolu. Three good cross-island roads pass over the east-west central ridge and divide the island roughly into quarters. The central one begins in Apia at Falealili St before becoming The Cross Island Rd further south. There's another Cross Island Rd to the west and the steeper, picturesque Le Mafa Pass Rd in the east. The general quality of these and other roads outside Apia has improved a lot in recent years, but they're still generally narrow with crumbling verges, and lined with dogs, pigs and pedestrians. Some of the side roads to beaches are rough and can get boggy after heavy rain, but in dry weather they can

almost all be negotiated in a high-clearance 2WD. If unsure, check with locals regarding road conditions before setting out.

Petrol availability is limited on 'Upolu. We only found one petrol station away from the north coast – it's just north of Lalomanu. For information on getting a temporary driving licence, see p149.

There are numerous car-hire agencies in Apia, so ring around to find the best deal. Prices start at around ST120 per day, with discounts offered for longer-term rentals. Hiring a car in Samoa means being subject to a ST2500 insurance excess (nonreduceable) in the event of any accident that's your fault. Most outfits allow you to put their vehicles on the ferry to Savai'i; but

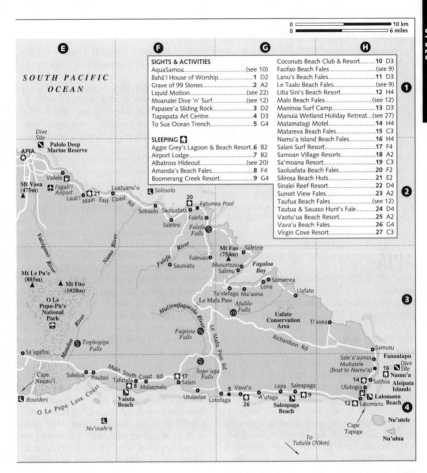

Map legend:

SIGHTS & ACTIVITIES
AquaSamoa	(see 10)
Bahá'í House of Worship	1 D2
Grave of 99 Stones	2 A2
Liquid Motion	(see 22)
Moanalei Dive 'n' Surf	(see 12)
Papasee'a Sliding Rock	3 D2
Tiapapata Art Centre	4 D3
To Sua Ocean Trench	5 G4

SLEEPING
Aggie Grey's Lagoon & Beach Resort	6 B2
Airport Lodge	7 B2
Albatross Hideout	(see 20)
Amanda's Beach Fales	8 F4
Boomerang Creek Resort	9 G4
Coconuts Beach Club & Resort	10 D3
Faofao Beach Fales	(see 9)
Lanu's Beach Fales	11 D3
Le Taalo Beach Fales	(see 9)
Litia Sini's Beach Resort	12 H4
Malo Beach Fales	(see 12)
Maninoa Surf Camp	13 D3
Manuia Wetland Holiday Retreat	(see 27)
Matamatagi Motel	14 H4
Matareva Beach Fales	15 C3
Namu'a Island Beach Fales	16 H4
Salani Surf Resort	17 F4
Samoan Village Resorts	18 A2
Sa'moana Resort	19 C3
Saoluafata Beach Fales	20 F2
Silirosa Beach Huts	21 E2
Sinalei Reef Resort	22 D4
Sunset View Fales	23 A2
Taufua Beach Fales	(see 12)
Tautua & Sauaso Hunt's Fale	24 D4
Vaotu'ua Beach Resort	25 A2
Vava'u Beach Fales	26 C3
Virgin Cove Resort	27 C3

double-check this if you plan to head over there.

Some recommended car-hire companies are as follows:

Blue Pacific Car Hire (☎ 22668; bluepacific@lesamoa .net) It doesn't have a depot as such, but offers free delivery to all Apia hotels and the airport.

Budget Car Rental (Map pp62-3; ☎ 20561, 22191; www.budget.com; ground fl, NPF Bldg, Beach Rd)

Funway Rent-A-Car (Map pp62-3; ☎ 22045; www .funwayrentals.ws; Beach Rd)

Juliana's Car Rentals (Map pp62-3; ☎ 23009; Mata'utu St)

Taxi

Taxis can be convenient for day-tripping around 'Upolu; you'll pay around ST30 an hour or ST150 for a full day of sightseeing. Some drivers still submit to a temptation to overcharge, so it pays to know the correct fare. Always agree on a price with the driver before climbing in.

At the time of writing, some sample fares to popular destinations were as follows. From Apia, a taxi to the Robert Louis Stevenson Museum costs ST6, while to the Bahá'í House of Worship costs ST14, to the Manono-uta wharf costs ST42, to Mulifanua Wharf costs ST45 and to Lalomanu costs ST65.

The following taxi companies in Apia are recommended.

City Central Taxis (☎ 23600)
Radio Taxi (☎ 24432)

HOW A LAZY LAD PUT 'UPOLU ON THE MAP

There are a number of ancient stories about the origin of the name 'Upolu. The most interesting one tells of the marriage of an earthly chief called Beginning to Timuateatea, a daughter of the god Tagaloa.

The couple had a son called Polu, who grew bored and lazy during his teenage years. Beginning thought his son ought to get a job and, looking over towards nearby Savai'i, he realised that it might be a good idea to send Polu over there to see if the island had any inhabitants. So he instructed Polu to pay a visit to his heavenly grandfather, who would provide carpenters to build a canoe for the journey. Polu initially refused but Beginning insisted and the boy finally agreed to do the job.

Up in heaven, the god Tagaloa looked down and noted that the initially reticent Polu had found the carpenters uninterested and lazy, but he had nevertheless managed to urge them to build his canoe. Thus, Tagalao decided to honour his grandson and name his island 'Upolu (The Urging of Polu).

In distant New Zealand, the Maori remember an island in their people's ancient past named Kuporu. Drop the 'k' and roll the 'r' into an 'l'…

APIA

pop 40,000

Samoa's capital is a small-town sprawl of low, modern buildings interspersed with dilapidated colonial architecture, old churches and smaller dilapidated structures that have long defied the imperatives of renovation. The brickwork is occasionally leavened by big old *pulu* (banyan) trees, and this is all wrapped around a charming little harbour that glows serenely at dusk.

Travellers rarely respond enthusiastically to Apia. The narrow streets can be choked with fume-belching cars and litter, the mixture of the traditional and the new doesn't sit easily side by side – such as when a jet ski buzzes noisily around a traditional canoe – and it's simply not the beachfront paradise that most people have come to see. But it's still worth spending a few days here, particularly for the Samoan streetlife. Plunge into the markets, elbow your way into a crowded bar and practice hopping on and off the manic local buses. Then dive into Palolo Deep and remember that Polynesia proper is only a slow ride away.

ORIENTATION

Apia is less a city and more an agglomeration of urbanised villages. From the centre, Apia's villages spread west along the coastal area and climb up into nearby valleys. The main drag is Beach Rd, which follows the curve of the harbour. At the eastern end of Beach Rd is the ferry wharf and Palolo Deep, while the western end becomes the peninsular Mulinu'u Rd. Most of Apia's activity is centred along Beach Rd between Aggie Grey's Hotel and the Flea Market, with the business district spreading south from the clock tower. The Maketi Fou and bus station are a few blocks south of the clock tower.

Maps

Hema publishes the detailed *Samoa* map (ST10) including a plan of Apia, but it hasn't been updated since 1999. Jasons offers a basic fold-out *Samoa Visitor Map* (free), with Apia's street grid, which is widely distributed in local hotels. Both maps are available from the Samoa Tourism Authority.

INFORMATION
Bookshops

CCK Store (Map pp62-3; Convent St) There are several shelves of used paperbacks upstairs.

Ia Malamalama (Map pp62-3; ☎ 24424; Beach Rd) Primarily stocks religious reading matter, but is also one of the few places that sells a Samoan dictionary – the 4th edition of Pratts, published in 1911 no less.

Le Tusi Faitau (Map pp62-3; ☎ 31626; Level 2, Wesley Arcade, Methodist Church Bldg, Beach Rd) Has a great supply of second-hand pulp fiction to see you through endless days lazing on the beach. Best range in town.

Emergency
Ambulance (☎ 996)
Fire (☎ 994)
Police (Map pp62-3; ☎ 995, 22222; Ifiifi St)

Internet Access

Apia's Internet cafés charge between ST2.50 and ST4 per 15 minutes.

iPasifika (Map p62-3; ☎ 29919; www.ipasifika.net; Beach Rd; ☺ 8.30am-5pm Mon-Fri, 8.30am-2pm Sat)

LeSamoa.net (Map p62-3; ☎ 21016; lesa@lesamoa .net; Lotemau Centre, cnr Convent & Mt Vaea Sts; ☺ 7.30am-6pm Mon-Wed & Fri, 7.30am-8.30pm Thu, 7.30am-1pm Sat)

Travellers' Lounge (Map pp62-3; ☎ 22144; Beach Rd; ☺ 7am-10pm Mon-Sat, 7am-8pm Sun) A café here serves meals and ice cream.

www.samoa.ws (Map pp62-3; ☎ 24159; www.samoa .ws; cnr Convent & Mt Vaea Sts; ☺ 8am-5pm Mon-Fri, 8am-noon Sat)

Laundry

Most laundries charge ST4/5 to wash/dry one load. A scoop of washing powder will cost ST2.

Cleanmaid Laundromat (Map pp62-3; Mata'utu St; ☺ 7am-8pm Mon-Sat)

Three Corners Laundromat (Map pp62-3; Mt Vaea St; ☺ 7am-9pm Mon-Sat) Charges slightly more per load than Cleanmaid.

Libraries

Nelson Memorial Public Library (Map pp62-3; Beach Rd; ☺ 9am-4.30pm Mon-Thu, 8am-4pm Fri, 8.30am-noon Sat) Has a good collection of Pacific titles. Visitors need to present a photo ID to peruse these books. Borrowing books requires temporary membership (ST20, of which ST5 is refunded when you leave Apia).

Medical Services

MedCen Hospital (Map p75; ☎ 26519, 26323; medcen@ipasifika.net; The Cross Island Road; ☺ 24hr) The best option for medical assistance is this private hospital, based at Vailima. A doctor is on site from 9am to 10pm Monday to Friday and from 9am to noon Saturday and Sunday; outside these times doctors are on call. A consultation costs ST55.

Samoa Pharmacy (Map pp62-3; ☎ 20355; Mulinu'u Rd; ☺ 8am-noon, 1.30-4.30pm & 6-10pm Mon-Fri, 8am-noon & 6-10pm Sat, 10am-noon & 6-10pm Sun) A little way out of town but well stocked.

Money

ANZ Bank (Map pp62-3; ☎ 69999; Beach Rd; ☺ 9am-3pm Mon-Wed, 9am-4pm Thu & Fri) The Beach Rd branch has a pair of ATMs. There's also an ANZ ATM at Faleolo Airport.

National Bank of Samoa (Map pp62-3; ☎ 23076; Beach Rd; ☺ 9am-3pm Mon-Fri) Also has a branch at the Maketi Fou which is open on Saturday from 8.30am to 12.30pm.

Westpac Bank (Map pp62-3; ☎ 20000; Beach Rd; ☺ 8.30am-3pm Mon-Wed, 8.30am-4pm Thu & Fri) Has an ATM out front.

Post

Main post office (Map pp62-3; Post Office St; ☺ 8.30am-4.30pm Mon-Fri, 8am-noon Sat) Apia's main post office has been incorporated into the head office of the country's telecommunications provider, SamoaTel. The counter at the far right sells postcards, phonecards and souvenir envelopes.

APIA IN...

One Day

Take an early-morning stroll around the harbourfront and treat yourself to breakfast on the balcony at **Sails** (p71). If it's high tide, head straight out to **Palolo Deep Marine Reserve** (p64). If it's not, lose yourself amidst the good-natured commercial mayhem of **Maketi Fou** (p64), then take a long walk past Mulinu'u Peninsula's tumble-down **monuments** (p66). Travel up The Cross Island Rd to the captivating **Robert Louis Stevenson Museum** (p74), perhaps stopping off en route at the **Curry House** (p70) for some takeaway, then double back to Beach Rd for a late-afternoon Vailima at **Paddles** (p71) or the **RSA Club** (also known as the Rosa; p73) before tackling a late dinner.

Two Days

Expand the one-day itinerary by allowing more time at Villa Vailima to wander the surrounding **Mount Vaea Scenic Reserve** (p74), followed by a quick peek at the nearby **Bahá'í House of Worship** (p77). Eat cheap seafood at **Gourmet Seafood** (p70), see a **fiafia** (celebration; p73) if at all possible, browse the **Museum of Samoa** (p65) and have a Bloody Mary at **Aggie Grey's** (p69) in honour of the hotel's namesake. Any extra time between these activities should be spent furthering your explorations of **Palolo Deep Marine Reserve** (p64).

'UPOLU

APIA

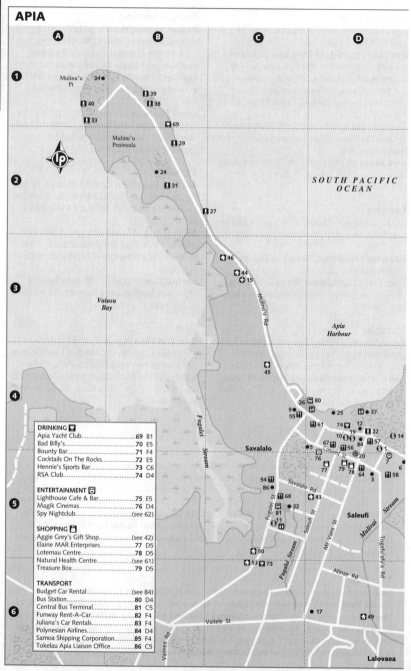

A   **B**   **C**   **D**

1

Mulinu'u Pt   34

39
38
69
40
33

Mulinu'u Peninsula

29

24

2

31

SOUTH PACIFIC OCEAN

27

46

44
15

3

Vaiusu Bay

Apia Harbour

45

Mulinu'u Rd

4

26   80
9   55
25   37
61   74   12
19   22
10   57
67   84
Convent St   14
5   56
76   @20
1
7
6
77   79   64
78
3
58

Fugalei Stream

Savalalo

54
86
68
81
43
32
11

5

Fugalei St
Savalalo Rd
Saleufi St
Mt Vaea St

Saleufi
Mulivai
Togafuafua Rd
Mulivai Stream

50
53   73

DRINKING ⬛
Apia Yacht Club.....................**69** B1
Bad Billy's.............................**70** E5
Bounty Bar............................**71** F4
Cocktails On The Rocks............**72** E5
Hennie's Sports Bar.................**73** C6
RSA Club...............................**74** D4

ENTERTAINMENT ⬛
Lighthouse Cafe & Bar..............**75** E5
Magik Cinemas.......................**76** D4
Spy Nightclub........................(see 62)

SHOPPING ⬛
Aggie Grey's Gift Shop..............(see 42)
Elaine MAR Enterprises.............**77** D5
Lotemau Centre......................**78** D5
Natural Health Centre..............(see 61)
Treasure Box.........................**79** D5

TRANSPORT
Budget Car Rental...................(see 84)
Bus Station...........................**80** D4
Central Bus Terminal................**81** C5
Funway Rent-A-Car..................**82** F4
Juliana's Car Rentals................**83** F4
Polynesian Airlines..................**84** D4
Samoa Shipping Corporation.......**85** F4
Tokelau Apia Liaison Office.........**86** C5

6

17
49

Vaitele St
Vaimea Rd
Atinae Rd

Lalovaea

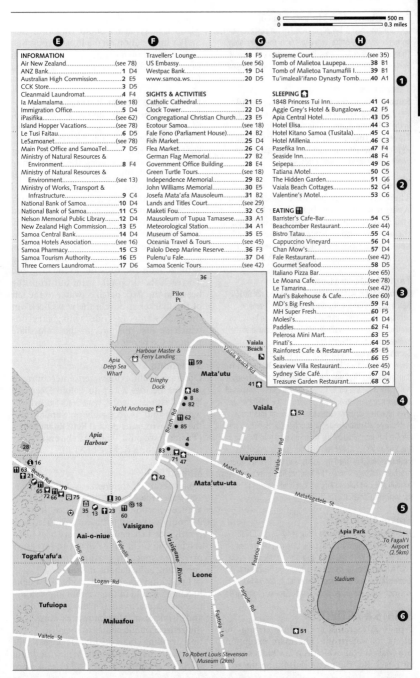

INFORMATION
Air New Zealand...........................(see 78)
ANZ Bank..................................**1** D4
Australian High Commission..........**2** E5
CCK Store..................................**3** D5
Cleanmaid Laundromat................**4** F4
Ia Malamalama..........................(see 18)
Immigration Office......................**5** D4
iPasifika....................................(see 62)
Island Hopper Vacations.............(see 78)
Le Tusi Faitau............................**6** D5
LeSamoanet...............................(see 78)
Main Post Office and SamoaTel.....**7** D5
Ministry of Natural Resources &
  Environment............................**8** F4
Ministry of Natural Resources &
  Environment............................(see 13)
Ministry of Works, Transport &
  Infrastructure...........................**9** C4
National Bank of Samoa...............**10** D4
National Bank of Samoa...............**11** C5
Nelson Memorial Public Library.....**12** D4
New Zealand High Commission.....**13** E5
Samoa Central Bank....................**14** D4
Samoa Hotels Association............(see 16)
Samoa Pharmacy........................**15** C3
Samoa Tourism Authority............**16** E5
Three Corners Laundromat...........**17** D6

Travellers' Lounge.......................**18** F5
US Embassy...............................(see 56)
Westpac Bank............................**19** D4
www.samoa.ws...........................**20** D5

SIGHTS & ACTIVITIES
Catholic Cathedral......................**21** E5
Clock Tower...............................**22** D4
Congregational Christian Church....**23** E5
Ecotour Samoa...........................(see 18)
Fale Fono (Parliament House)........**24** B2
Fish Market................................**25** D4
Flea Market................................**26** C4
German Flag Memorial.................**27** B2
Government Office Building...........**28** E4
Green Turtle Tours......................(see 18)
Independence Memorial................**29** B2
John Williams Memorial................**30** E5
Josefa Mata'afa Mausoleum..........**31** B2
Lands and Titles Court.................(see 29)
Maketi Fou................................**32** C5
Mausoleum of Tupua Tamasese......**33** A1
Meteorological Station.................**34** A1
Museum of Samoa.......................**35** E5
Oceania Travel & Tours................(see 45)
Palolo Deep Marine Reserve.........**36** F3
Pulenu'u Fale.............................**37** D4
Samoa Scenic Tours.....................(see 42)

Supreme Court............................(see 35)
Tomb of Malietoa Laupepa............**38** B1
Tomb of Malietoa Tanumafili I.......**39** B1
Tu'imaleali'ifano Dynasty Tomb.....**40** A1

SLEEPING
1848 Princess Tui Inn...................**41** G4
Aggie Grey's Hotel & Bungalows.....**42** F5
Apia Central Hotel.......................**43** D5
Hotel Elisa.................................**44** C3
Hotel Kitano Samoa (Tusitala)........**45** C4
Hotel Millenia.............................**46** C3
Pasefika Inn...............................**47** F4
Seaside Inn................................**48** F4
Seipepa.....................................**49** D6
Tatiana Motel.............................**50** C5
The Hidden Garden......................**51** G6
Vaiala Beach Cottages.................**52** G4
Valentine's Motel........................**53** C6

EATING
Barrister's Cafe-Bar.....................**54** C5
Beachcomber Restaurant.............(see 44)
Bistro Tatau...............................**55** C4
Cappuccino Vineyard...................**56** D4
Chan Mow's..............................**57** D4
Fale Restaurant..........................(see 42)
Gourmet Seafood.......................**58** D5
Italiano Pizza Bar.......................(see 65)
Le Moana Cafe...........................(see 78)
Le Tamarina..............................(see 42)
Mari's Bakehouse & Cafe.............(see 60)
MD's Big Fresh...........................**59** F4
MH Super Fresh.........................**60** F5
Molesi's....................................**61** D4
Paddles....................................**62** F4
Pelerosa Mini Mart.....................**63** E5
Pinati's.....................................**64** D5
Rainforest Cafe & Restaurant.......**65** E5
Sails..**66** E5
Seaview Villa Restaurant.............(see 45)
Sydney Side Café.......................**67** D4
Treasure Garden Restaurant.........**68** C5

'UPOLU

Poste restante office (Map pp62-3; Post Office St; 8.30am-noon & 1-4.30pm Mon-Fri) For poste restante, go to the separate office, two doors from the main lobby. To receive mail in Apia, have it addressed to you, care of: Poste Restante, Chief Post Office, SamoaTel, Apia, Samoa.

Telephone

SamoaTel (Map pp62-3; www.samoatel.ws; Beach Rd; 7.30am-4pm Mon-Fri) International calls can be made in the call centre located within the SamoaTel office.

Travellers' Lounge (Map pp62-3; ☎ 22144; Beach Rd; 7am-10pm Mon-Sat, 7am-8pm Sun) Make international calls here using phonecards.

Toilets

There are a few public toilet blocks around Apia, not all in the best shape but OK if you're desperate. Most are concentrated at the western end of town: near the Flea Market bus station, next to the Pulenu'u Fale, and at the southern side of the Maketi Fou.

Tourist Information

Samoa Hotels Association (Map pp62-3; ☎ 30160; Beach Rd; 8am-4.30pm Mon-Fri) This extremely helpful organisation can make accommodation bookings around 'Upolu and Savai'i. Its office is located within the Samoa Tourism Authority *fale*.

Samoa Tourism Authority (Map pp62-3; ☎ 63500; www.visitsamoa.ws; Beach Rd; 8am-4.30pm Mon-Fri, 8am-noon Sat) The large *fale* housing the Samoa Tourism Authority was built on reclaimed land atop the remains of the German warship *Adler*, destroyed in the 1889 cyclone. Over repeated visits we unfortunately found Tourism Authority staff disinterested and unhelpful. Hopefully their service has improved by the time you read this. Pick up the *Samoa Visitor Guide* and fold-out *Samoa Visitor Map*, both free and published by Jasons, and the free self-tour brochure *Discover Samoa*. The Tourism Authority also keeps a small office at Faleolo Airport, but it only seems to open for incoming international flights.

Travel Agencies

Island Hopper Vacations (Map pp62-3; ☎ 23388; www.islandhoppervacations.com; Lotemau Centre, cnr Convent & Mt Vaea Sts) Also has a desk at Faleolo Airport (☎ 42938), though its opening hours are haphazard.

Oceania Travel & Tours (Map pp62-3; ☎ 24443; www.oceania-travel.ws; Hotel Kitano Samoa, Mulinu'u Rd)

SIGHTS & ACTIVITIES

Apia's attractions are mainly strung out along its waterfront. The main exceptions are Maketi Fou, which is a few blocks south of Beach Rd, the memorials lining the road

leading to the tip of Mulinu'u Peninsula, and Madd Gallery, at the southern end of Ifiifi St. For information on the Robert Louis Stevenson Museum and other attractions south of town, see The Cross Island Road section (p74).

Palolo Deep Marine Reserve

Past the wharf, near the *palagi* (white people) enclaves of Mata'utu and Vaiala, is the sublime **Palolo Deep Marine Reserve** (Map pp62-3; Vaiala Beach Rd; adult/child ST2/1; 8am-6pm). After lazing or picnicking along the beach, strap on your snorkelling gear (two-hour rentals of snorkels/flippers/masks cost ST2/4/4) and head out to where the shallow reef suddenly drops away into a deep blue hole flanked by walls of coral and densely populated by colourful species of fish.

Palolo Deep is best visited at high tide, otherwise you'll find yourself belly dancing with coral on your way out to the drop-off. To reach the drop-off, swim out from the beach to the dark patch of water to the left of the marker stick. On the way check out the underwater cages filled with giant clams which lie just offshore, to the immediate right of the beach.

Swimming

Other possibilities for watery entertainment in Apia besides a trip to Palolo Deep are **Vaiala Beach** (Map pp62-3; Vaiala Beach Rd), which, we were told, is accessible on Sunday, and the fine swimming pool at **Hotel Kitano Samoa** (Tusitala; see p69), which can be enjoyed by nonguests for a day fee of ST20.

Maketi Fou

Apia's centre of commerce is its main market, **Maketi Fou** (Map pp62-3; Fugalei St), which has a huge selection of fresh produce. It hums 24 hours a day and to have a stall there is so prestigious that family members take turns staying the night in order not to lose their privileged spots. Its bustling atmosphere is enlivening at just about any time.

Every kind of meat and produce available in Samoa is sold in this vibrant and colourful place. Here, *matai* (chiefs) gather to chat and drink *'ava* (also known as *kava*) and the general public comes to socialise. You'll find drinking coconuts for sale, kiosks selling ready-made *palusami*, *fa'ausi* pudding (taro in coconut cream), cakes and *koko*

'UPOLU

Samoa (locally grown cocoa served hot and black with lots of sugar).

Also on sale here are craft goods such as *siapo* (bark cloth), wood carvings and an amazing variety of coconut-shell jewellery, items woven from coconut fronds, *kirikiti* (cricket) bats and balls, *lava-lava* (sarongs) and printed T-shirts.

At the back of the main market are shops selling tinned foods, bread and other dry goods. Right next to the market is the **central bus terminal** (Map pp62-3; near Fugalei St), serving the entire island of 'Upolu, where colourfully painted wooden buses blast Samoan pop music and compete for passengers on their seemingly endless cycles around the market square. This is also a popular hangout for local pool sharks, who congregate at the pool halls alongside the terminal.

Flea Market

Apia's **flea market** (Map pp62-3; off Beach Rd; ⊙ 8am-4pm Mon-Fri, 8am-noon Sat) is housed in the old central market building. Here you'll find stalls selling everything from cheap clothing (the range here is bigger than at Maketi Fou), tubs of styling gel and wooden writing tablets to coconut-shell jewellery, *siapo* and *'ava* bowls. Most stalls sell exactly the same things, so it's puzzling how they all make enough money to survive. Tucked away beyond the craft stalls, on the northern side of the market, is a row of cheap food stalls selling greasy fried fare.

Fish Market

Sunday morning is the busiest time at the **fish market** (Map pp62-3; off Beach Rd; ⊙ 7am-2pm), with everyone rushing in to buy seafood for the end-of-week *umu* (stone oven) before hurrying off to attend church services. Regardless what day you visit, get there early before the best of the catches is snapped up. Look out for Coca-Cola bottles full of sea-slug innards (a Samoan delicacy) and the bright-green seaweed that looks like bunches of tiny grapes. Battered fishing boats bob away behind the market building.

Churches & Religious Services

On Sunday, masses of Apians dress in sparkling white to attend morning church services. Most churches have several services on this day, usually lasting an hour and some conducted in English. Visitors are welcome

to attend, but make sure you dress modestly and in light colours.

A landmark of the city's waterfront is the impressive **Catholic Cathedral** (Map pp62-3; Beach Rd), which sports a quartet of recessed statues on its façade and a statue of Madonna and child up top between two small turrets. The cathedral, completed in 1905 and coloured a blazing white, could be seen from up to 20km out to sea before the government building and the Samoa Central Bank were constructed in front of it.

The **Anglican Church** (Map p75; Ifiifi St) is a lovely, unassuming building, the only such church in Samoa. Although not an old building, it has some beautiful stained-glasswork in the windows. The cornerstone inscription states that it was laid on '3 December 1944, the 50th anniversary of the falling asleep of Tusitala', referring to the anniversary of Robert Louis Stevenson's death.

When the Reverend John Williams of the London Missionary Society (LMS) was killed on 20 November 1839, on Erromanga in Vanuatu, he was subjected to the cannibalistic traditions of the Melanesians of the day. His bones were recovered, however, and buried on the site where the simple wood and stone architecture of the disused **Congregational Christian Church** (Map pp62-3; cnr Beach Rd & Falealili St) now stands. Across the street is a **monument to Williams** (Map pp62-3; Beach Rd) and his 'martyrdom', a surprisingly underwhelming structure considering the reverend's influence. It was erected in 1930, commemorating 'the first hundred years of Christianity in Samoa'.

Museum of Samoa

The **Museum of Samoa** (Map pp62-3; Beach Rd; admission free; ⊙ noon-3.30pm Mon-Fri) has a small but interesting display on Samoan history and culture. The collection includes examples of *siapo* and *lalaga* (weaving), a parliamentary meeting table that involved some impressive carpentry, a rather cumbersome traditional costume prepared for Miss Samoa 1998, enlightening old photographs and some great traditional carvings, some in the form of model outrigger canoes. Unfortunately, the potted history of the islands only goes as far as the year 2000. The museum is upstairs in the same building as the Justice Department and the Supreme Court (p66).

Madd Gallery

One of Samoa's best-known contemporary painters, Momoe von Reiche, set up the **Madd Gallery** (Map p75; ☎ 28533; Ifiifi St; admission free; ⏱ 9am-3pm Mon-Fri) in 1984 to encourage local interest in the arts. Madd (which stands for Motivational Art, Dance and Drama) displays paintings and *siapo*, and hosts occasional poetry readings, dance performances and visiting exhibitions. The onsite shop sells a small array of craftwork.

Clock Tower

Located in the town centre, the **clock tower** (Map pp62-3; Beach Rd) was constructed in memory of those who fought and were killed in WWI, and sits on the site of an old bandstand where sailors from incoming warships were serenaded by their compatriots. Its clock and chimes were a gift to the city from one of Samoa's most successful early businesspeople, Mr Olaf Frederick Nelson. It was donated in memory of Olaf's only son, Ta'isi, who died in the influenza epidemic brought to the islands by the New Zealand ship SS *Talune* in 1918.

Government Buildings & Monuments

The seven-storey **government office building** (Map pp62-3; off Beach Rd), a product of Chinese benevolence, sits astride an area reclaimed from the sea. Built in 1993, its universally unpopular design was only slightly improved by the addition of a *fale* – a last-minute concession to *fa'a Samoa* (Samoan customs and traditions) – which forms its top floor. Sharing this reclaimed area is the **Pulenu'u Fale** (Map pp62-3; off Beach Rd) where *pulenu'u* (village mayors) meet.

A two-storey knocked-about colonial building is home to the **Supreme Court** (Map pp62-3; Beach Rd). It was on the street here that the bloody clash between the formerly peaceful Mau Movement ('Samoa for Samoans') and the New Zealand police brought about the deaths of 11 Samoans, including the Mau leader, Tupua Tamasese Lealofi III, on 28 December 1929.

At 7.45am every weekday, the Police Band of Samoa marches from the **police station** (Map pp62-3; Ifiifi St) to the government building. Vehicle and pedestrian traffic is stopped and the national anthem is played while the flag is raised. It's a great way to start the day, especially in 'winter', when the sun is low

and casts a serene morning glow over the harbour.

Near the gleaming new **Mormon temple** (Map p75; Vaitele St) is the **German bandstand** (Map p75; Vaitele St) that was used as the headquarters of the Mau Movement. Near to the bandstand is the **tomb of Tupua Tamasese Lealofi III** (Map p75; Vaitele St).

WALKING TOUR

This walking tour takes you up and around the Mulinu'u Peninsula, which stretches out into the South Pacific Ocean to the northwest of central Apia. The peninsula seems to serve as a repository for political monuments and memorials, though most of these are now rather derelict.

Start from outside Apia's lively **Flea Market (1**; p65). The first monument you encounter while ambling along the sea wall that buttresses the peninsula's eastern shore is the **German Flag Memorial (2)**, which was erected in 1913 to commemorate the raising of the German flag over the islands on 1 March 1900. Nowadays, it registers as little more than a small pile of stones surrounded by a rusty fence.

On the lawn in front of the Fale Fono is the **Josefa Mata'afa Mausoleum (3)**. Josefa Mata'afa was the puppet paramount chief supported by the Germans after they annexed Western Samoa in 1899. The grave is not of Samoan design and it seems that the Germans constructed it hoping to undermine the pride the locals had in their leaders by altering their age-old burial customs.

The **Fale Fono (4)** itself, Samoa's parliament house, resembles a large beehive and was opened on 31 May 1972. Nearby is the **Lands and Titles Court (5)**, the entity that settles land-rights cases. In case you had any doubts about Samoa's Christian leanings, have a look at the **Independence Memorial (6)** in front of the court building. It was built to mark the independence of Western Samoa, granted on 1 January 1962, and bears the inscription 'Samoa was founded on God'.

Further up the peninsula are the **tombs of Malietoa Laupepa (7)** and **Malietoa Tanumafili I (8)**, the grandfather and father, respectively, of the present ceremonial head of state. Small tended gardens surround the tombs but the tombs themselves look forlorn. To see something a bit cheerier, continue to the **meteorological station** on the tip of the peninsula and skirt it via the shoreline embankment, which offers a nice vista of Vaisua Bay.

Coming around the northwestern edge of the peninsula, you'll find two more tombs: the seven-tiered **tomb of the Tu'imaleali'ifano dynasty (9)** and the **mausoleum of Tupua Tamasese (10)**. Having had enough of old monuments by now, and probably getting a bit thirsty too, you should head back to Mulinu'u Rd

---

WALK FACTS

Start Flea Market
Finish Apia Yacht Club
Distance 2km
Duration 1 hour

APIA WALKING TOUR

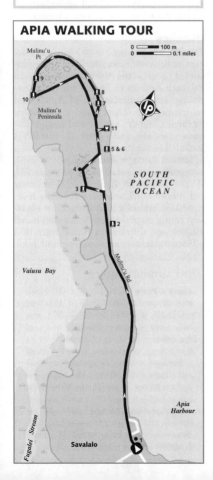

and down to the **Apia Yacht Club (11**; p72) for a well-earned drink – if the timing of your walk doesn't coincide with the club's opening hours, just stroll into a bar in one of the peninsula's well-appointed hotels.

APIA FOR CHILDREN

There are lots of distractions for children in Apia, which is fitting for a country that lavishes so much attention upon its own young. Kids will be fascinated by offerings in the **Maketi Fou** (p64) and the **Flea Market** (p65). They'll also love snorkelling at **Palolo Deep** (p64) – even if your child isn't a confident swimmer, you can still lead them only a short distance offshore to where the giant clams lie. The traditional Samoan **fiafia** (p73) is a memorable experience for families, as is a ride in one of the colourful local **buses**. Only a short distance from Apia is the **Robert Louis Stevenson Museum** (p74) and its beautiful grounds (perfect for a picnic), the **Tiapapata Art Centre** (p77) with its great art workshops for children, and the challenging **Papasee'a Sliding Rock** (p78).

TOURS

The following Apia-based companies conduct assorted tours of 'Upolu and Savai'i; for more info on Savai'i tours, see p90. Tours are usually not staged on Sunday.

Ecotour Samoa (Map pp62-3; ☎ 22144; www.eco toursamoa.com) Offers all-inclusive ecotours encompassing culture, nature, adventure and education around the various Samoan islands. Tours include 4WD trips in air-conditioned comfort; seven-day bird-watching, sea-kayaking or 'safari' trips; or, for the hard core, the three- to 30-day 'Samoan Survival', where guests learn to survive on uninhabited Nu'utele island, off 'Upolu's southeast coast. The majority of tours cost US$190 per person per day.

Green Turtle Tours (Map pp62-3; ☎ 22144, 29229; www.greenturtletours.com) Travellers have mixed opinions about this tour outfit. True, the guide-accompanied hop-on, hop-off bus services conveniently circle 'Upolu and Savai'i daily. But the company's attempts to get you to prebook with its favoured accommodation doesn't work in favour of travellers seeking true flexibility, and budget travellers can easily find better deals than its ST90-per-night accommodation vouchers. A one-month pass costs ST170 per island, not including accommodation and many of the daily activities. Green Turtle also offers day tours of 'Upolu and Savai'i (each ST90).

Oceania Travel & Tours (Map pp62-3; ☎ 24443; http://www.oceania-travel.ws; Hotel Kitano Samoa, Mulinu'u Rd) Among the day tours offered by Oceania is one taking in eastern 'Upolu (US$40), including Lalomanu and Piula Cave, and one of Manono (US$40).

Samoa Scenic Tours (Map pp62-3; ☎ 26981, 22880; www.samoascenictours.com) Runs half- and full-day scenic, cultural and ecotours around Apia, 'Upolu and Savai'i from ST60 (half-day) or ST120 (full day) per person. Tailor-made itineraries are also offered. Has a desk at Aggie Grey's Hotel.

FESTIVALS & EVENTS

The city's most prominent celebration is the Teuila Festival, a week of festivities which has become Samoa's key cultural event. See p141 for details.

SLEEPING

Some of Apia's accommodation is arranged along the harbour, including the peaceful foreshore of the Mulinu'u Peninsula. But most hotels, motels, modern homestays and budget *fale* are scattered throughout the villages to the south of the centre – several of these lie 1km from the harbour along the route to The Cross Island Rd.

Budget

Hidden Garden (Map pp62-3; ☎ 25416, 31252; gar denvi@lesamoa.net; Vini Rd; fale per person ST35-45) *Fale* set on stilts and small shacks, all scattered throughout a naturally overgrown garden, are the hallmarks of this excellent, restful place. Guests share toilets, a kitchen and the environmental knowledge of the owner, Eti, who conducts foot-powered explorations of the island in the guise of SamoaOnFoot (see p136). Ask about kayaking trips around nearby Taumeasina.

Seipepa (Map pp62-3; ☎ 25447; seipepa@samoa -experience.com; off Vaitele St; dm/s/d ST45/75/90; ▯) Lovely, intimate place tucked away among village houses. Accommodation is available either in *fale*, which are squeezed together and don't offer much privacy, or in four comfortable, nicely decorated rooms in the main house (only one has a double bed). Bathrooms are shared and there's a communal kitchen (prices include breakfast).

Valentine's Motel (Map pp62-3; ☎ 22158; valen tine@samoa.ws; Fugalei St; s/d from ST40/60; 🕸 ▯ 🗙) This friendly place feels more like a big family home than a motel, with a neat lawn out back, a breezy downstairs lounge and a minimum of fuss from the lovely owner. Budget rooms have shared bathrooms and are nothing flash, but are well-priced. Air-

conditioned rooms with en suites are available for ST100. Breakfast is included in the room price.

Seaside Inn (Map pp62-3; ☎ 22578; seasideinn@ ipasifika.net; Beach Rd; dm ST30, s ST65-70, d ST75-85) The rooms at this appealingly low-key place are a little scuffed and dreary but are otherwise in reasonable condition. Breakfast is included in the price and there's a kitchen and a laundry service. Commanding the patio out front is a small café-bar where travellers swap apocryphal stories over beer and burgers.

Tatiana Motel (Map pp62-3; ☎ 26829; www.tati ana-motel.com; Fugalei St; dm ST30, r ST50-120; 🕸 ▯ 🗙) Tatiana offers mostly no-frills rooms on a barren roadside plot. But it is a friendly place and backpackers will appreciate the 'dorm' price (one bed in a twin room).

Midrange

Pasefika Inn (Map pp62-3; ☎ 20971; www.pasefi kainn.ws; Mata'utu St; r from ST90; 🕸 🗙) The fan-cooled rooms at the Pasefika, just off Beach Rd, each have an en suite, fridge and telephone, and comprise one of Apia's best midrange deals. There's also a communal kitchen, a laundry service and a large veranda to exploit, and a tropical breakfast is included in the price.

Samoan Outrigger Hotel (Map p75; ☎ 20042; outrigger@samoa.ws; Falealili St; fale per person ST45, s ST100-140, d ST110-160; 🕸 ▯ 🔊 🗙) This lovely old timber hotel, shaded a soothing blue, is nestled behind a high hedge. It's a low-key, restful place that provides a communal kitchen and distractions in the form of a billiard table and an above-ground pool.

THE AUTHOR'S CHOICE

Aniva's Place (Map p75; ☎ 23431, 20501; anivas@lesamoa.net; off Falealili St, Moto'otua; s ST95-115, d ST115-135; 🕸 🔊 🗙) This two-storey 'suburban' dwelling offers all the creature comforts of someone else's home and is an excellent place to repose in-between making excursions into Apia and 'Upolu's hinterland. Flake out in the upstairs lounge, make full use of the guest bar, and refresh yourself in a pool swaddled in a broad deck. The nine rooms here are homely and the price includes breakfast; dinners can also be arranged. This place doubtless garners much return custom.

THERE'S SOMETHING ABOUT BLOODY MARY

Agnes Genevieve Swann was the daughter of William Swann, a Lincolnshire chemist who had migrated to Samoa in 1889, and Pele, a Samoan girl from Toamua village. In 1917 she married Gordon Hay-Mackenzie, the recently arrived manager of the Union Steamship Company. They had four children before Gordon died eight years later. Soon afterwards, Aggie married Charlie Grey, who was, unfortunately, a compulsive gambler. Charlie lost everything they had and Aggie had to look for some new means of supporting the family.

In 1942 American soldiers arrived in Apia carrying 'unimaginable wealth', and Aggie saw an opportunity to earn a little money. She borrowed US$180, bought the site of a former hotel and began selling hamburgers and coffee to US servicemen. Response to her business was overwhelming and, although supplies were difficult to come by during WWII, Aggie built up an institution that became famous Pacific-wide as a social gathering place for war-weary soldiers. She even succeeded in getting through the New Zealand–imposed prohibition of alcoholic beverages.

When James Michener published his enormously successful *Tales of the South Pacific*, Aggie Grey was so well known throughout that realm that it was widely assumed she was the prototype for the character of Michener's Tonkinese madam, Bloody Mary. Michener has said that he did visit Aggie's place whenever he could, to get away from 'unutterably dull and militarily stuffy' Pago Pago, where he was frequently stationed. However, he denies that anything but the good bits of Bloody Mary were inspired by Aggie Grey.

Over the next few decades, the snack bar expanded into a hotel where numerous celebrities stayed while filming or travelling in the area. (Many of the *fale* rooms are named after these famous people.) If you'd like to read more about Aggie Grey, who died in June 1988 at the age of 91, pick up a copy of her biography, *Aggie Grey of Samoa*, by Nelson Eustis.

Besides the restful rooms, you can also hire one of the four *fale* out back.

Vaiala Beach Cottages (Map pp62-3; ☎ 22202; www.samoana.org/vaiala; Vaiala-vini Rd; s/d/tr US$45/70/80; ⊠) The attractive fan-cooled timber cottages here have plenty of furniture and facilities squeezed into them, including a stove and fridge, bathroom, one double bed and two single beds. They're set in a nice garden and are ideal for families, with discounts offered for longer stays. Walk a little further down the street to see an unusual turreted church.

Hotel Millenia (Map pp62-3; ☎ 28284; www.hotel milleniasamoa.com; Mulinu'u Rd; r from ST180; ⊠ ⊠) This three-storey hotel is perched halfway up Mulinu'u Peninsula, where it's regularly swept by ocean breezes. It's worth paying about ST30 more for an upper-level room as some of the lower-floor rooms are disquietingly close to the adjacent nightclub. Rates should include breakfast, which (along with afternoon cocktails) should ideally be taken out on the upper deck.

Other possibilities:

Samoa Holiday Hotel (Map p75; ☎ 28016, 28017; samoaholiday@lesamoa.net; Moamoa Rd; s/d ST160/175; ⊠ ⊠) Plain white-brick block offering good self-contained accommodation, but it's away from the centre.

Apia Central Hotel (Map pp62-3; ☎ 20782; http://www.samoahotels.ws/apiacentral.htm; Savalalo Rd; s/d ST140/170; ⊠) Overpriced considering its lack of character but centrally located and worth considering if other places are full.

1848 Princess Tui Inn (Map pp62-3; ☎ 23342; www.princesstui.ws; Vaiala Beach Rd; dm/s/d from ST40/90/110; ⊠ ⊠ ⊠) Not all facilities are up to scratch in this attractive old house, but you can't argue with the superb location opposite Vaiala Beach.

Top End

Hotel Kitano Samoa (Tusitala; Map pp62-3; ☎ 211 22; www.kitano.ws; Mulinu'u Rd; s US$95-175, d US$105-180, tr US$125-195; ⊠ ⊠ ⊠ ⊠) This luxury hotel on Mulinu'u Peninsula looks squat and motel-like from the outside, but rooms are spacious and very well-equipped. The tiered pool area is marvellous, while the 5.5 hectares of landscaping eschews the overgrown style of other hotels for an open feel. In true Samoan style, the reception area is not garnished by a fountain but by a dugout canoe. There's also a children's playground and the excellent Seaview Villa Restaurant (p71).

Aggie Grey's Hotel & Bungalows (Map pp62-3; ☎ 22880; www.aggiegreys.com; Beach Rd; s US$120-170, d & tw US$125-175, ste US$280-340; ⊠ ⊠ ⊠ ⊠)

'UPOLU

Aggie Grey's was founded as a club in 1942 by a woman who became a Pacific celebrity (for more on Aggie Grey, see box, p69) and is now an iconic four-star hotel. It's set in appealing tropical gardens and has some excellent facilities. There's 24-hour room service, a playground and good eateries, including the cavernous Fale Restaurant (opposite). The bungalows and poolside rooms, however, lack Pacific flavour, so get a harbour-facing room. Several rooms have disabled access. Try to catch the Wednesday night *fiafia* (p73). In 2005 Aggie Grey's opened a resort near the airport (p79).

Hotel Insel Fehmarn (Map p75; ☎ 23301; www .inselfehmarnsamoa.com; Falealili St; s/d from ST220/250; 🛇 🖳 🕿 🗶) This modern three-storey block has airy and well-equipped (though somewhat bland) rooms, and good facilities, including a pool, tennis courts and a shuttle service into town. It's frequently booked out by conferences and other events. It's named after an island in the Baltic Sea; see their brochure for the full story.

Hotel Elisa (Map pp62-3; ☎ 21116; www.hotel elisa .ws; Mulinu'u Rd; r ST290-320, ste ST750; 🛇 🖳 🗶) Hotel Elisa is peacefully sited on Mulinu'u Peninsula. It has an austerity in its modern décor that gives it a lack of overall character, but you'll forget about this when standing on your private balcony and gazing out at the sea or the silhouette of 'Upolu's mountainous interior. On the ground floor is the formal Beachcomber Restaurant (p72).

EATING

Apia's extensive eating scene has a bit of everything, from fried food emporiums and international cuisines like Chinese and Indian, to top-notch restaurants and an embryonic café culture. There's plenty of good food and value for money on offer all around town.

Cafés & Quick Eats

Sydney Side Café (Map pp62-3; ☎ 779 0495; Gold Star Bldg, Convent St; meals ST10-22; 🕑 breakfast & lunch Tue-Sun; 🗶) Imported direct from Sydney (or at least its coffee and its prices are) is this accomplished modern café, which is very popular with *palagi* who are yearning for a authentic cuppa – everything from a flat white to an *affogato* (short black poured over ice cream) – and perhaps the illusion of being back home. It makes excellent gourmet sandwiches and salads.

Gourmet Seafood (Map pp62-3; ☎ 24625; Togafu'afu'a Rd; meals ST5-8; 🕑 breakfast, lunch & dinner Mon-Sat) Very popular with both locals and *palagi*, this eatery has a pleasant *fale*-style dining area draped with fishing nets. Lots of seafood, burgers, steaks and toasted sandwiches are served up here. The fish and chips are reliably tasty.

Cappuccino Vineyard (Map pp62-3; ☎ 22049; ACB Bldg; meals ST7-16; 🕑 breakfast, lunch & dinner) There's not much to look at inside this busy café except for people crowded on stools around the bar, but the umbrella-shaded tables lining the mall outside make for a nice retreat. Situated on a pedestrian mall off Convent St, it does a range of good breakfasts, burgers and salads (try the swordfish version), plus decent coffee and smoothies. At night it turns into a popular wine bar (p73).

Curry House (Map p75; ☎ 26815; The Cross Island Rd; meals ST4-20; 🕑 lunch & dinner Mon-Sat) This popular Indian café serves its butter chicken and lamb korma curries, plus smaller dishes like dhal and *baigan* (spiced eggplant), on a small deck that has views down to the sea. It also does a roaring trade in takeaway. Makes a nice change from steak or eggs.

Le Moana Cafe (Map pp62-3; ☎ 24828; Lotemau Centre, cnr Convent & Mt Vaea Sts; meals ST7-18; 🕑 breakfast, lunch & dinner Mon-Sat; 🗶) Simple, well-patronised café with a small fan-cooled courtyard and a menu of sizeable egg and pancake breakfasts, burgers, toasted sandwiches, salads, steaks and other filling fare. Every Wednesday night it dusts off a Weber and cooks up an all-you-can-eat barbecue (ST37) which is accompanied by live music. Some international wines are also available here.

Pinati's (Map pp62-3; ☎ 24248; Convent St; mains ST2-5; 🕑 breakfast & lunch Mon-Fri) Pinati's is one of the few remaining places in town selling cheap nosh with a Samoan influence. It's a cavernous, unsigned eatery that's always full of Samoan workers and serves up huge meals, including chow mein, chop suey and curry.

Mari's Bakehouse & Cafe (Map pp62-3; ☎ 30658; Beach Rd; meals ST12-19; 🕑 breakfast & lunch Mon-Fri; 🗶) This humble café, adjacent to MH Super Fresh supermarket, dutifully services local office workers and quickly fills at lunchtime. It's not the cheapest café around but you won't go hungry here. There's the usual array of high-calorie breakfasts and fried lunches, plus tasty burritos, enchiladas, soups and pastries (think blueberry turnover).

Barrister's Cafe-Bar (Map pp62-3; ☎ 29136; Ministry of Communications & Information Technology Bldg, Fugalei St; meals ST9-15; ☺ breakfast & lunch Mon-Sat; ☒) No-frills place tucked away at the end of an arcade. Its steak sandwiches and big breakfasts will get the cholesterol oozing through your veins, or you can choose a cheap seafood platter. The plastic seats are doubled up to support those large Samoan bodies.

One of the best places for a cheap meal, particularly for breakfast, is the **Maketi Fou** (p64), or try the food stalls behind the **Flea Market** (p65).

Restaurants

Sails (Map pp62-3; ☎ 20628; Beach Rd; breakfast & lunch ST15-25, dinner ST30-45; ☺ breakfast, lunch & dinner Mon-Sat, dinner Sun; ☒) Sails is housed upstairs in a cosy 140-year-old colonial building that was Robert Louis Stevenson's first Samoan home. Its balcony overlooks the harbour and is a superb place to dine. The service here is assured and the good-quality food includes big breakfasts and plenty of seafood – try the megaplatter that costs ST80 for two people. Disappointingly, vegetarian meals aren't standard menu inclusions and usually have to be requested.

Seaview Villa Restaurant (Map pp62-3; ☎ 21122; Hotel Kitano Samoa, Mulinu'u Rd; mains ST30-45; ☺ dinner Mon-Sat; ☒) This accomplished restaurant dishes up fine Japanese cuisine and seafood in the building to the immediate right as you turn in to Hotel Kitano Samoa (Tusitala). Nibble lobster thermidor, sushi and donburi-style meals (served on rice in bowls) and sip international wines in the restaurant's intimate interior or on the ocean-facing balcony.

THE AUTHOR'S CHOICE

Bistro Tatau (Map pp62-3; ☎ 22727; Beach Rd; mains ST25-50; ☺ lunch & dinner Mon-Sat; ☒) Eggs Benedict, laksa and calamari salad round out the lunch menu at this suave fine-dining establishment, while double-baked soufflés, huge steaks and vegetable crêpes headline the dinners. The rich mains are complemented by ultrarich desserts. Come here for a special occasion, even if you have to make one up.

Italiano Pizza Bar (Map pp62-3; ☎ 24330; Beach Rd; small/medium/large pizzas from ST15/25/27; ☺ lunch & dinner Mon-Sat, dinner Sun) A sociable pizza joint handily located in the heart of town. Doesn't have much character inside but there's almost always a small crowd eating and drinking (usually smoking too) on the front deck, and the pizzas are very tasty. They do free deliveries to hotels in central Apia.

Paddles (Map pp62-3; ☎ 20194; Beach Rd; mains ST16-38; ☺ lunch & dinner Mon-Fri, dinner Sat) The balcony of this fine restaurant-bar is one of the best places in town to have a meal or late-afternoon drink accompanied by a harbour view, but bring your sunglasses. The varied (mostly meaty) menu includes seared tuna steak, seafood crêpes, creamy pastas and several salad variations. Later in the evening it becomes Spy Nightclub (p73).

Giordano's Pizzeria (Map pp62-3; ☎ 25985; Falealili St; small/large pizzas from ST15/20, pasta ST18; ☺ lunch & dinner Tue-Sat, dinner Sun) Serves some of Apia's tastiest pizzas, which can be taken away or eaten in the inviting candle-lit courtyard. Also serves good salads and pasta. It's a bit of a hike from downtown but worth the trip.

Treasure Garden Restaurant (Map pp62-3; ☎ 22586; Fugalei St; mains ST13-30; ☺ lunch & dinner Mon-Fri, dinner Sat; ☒) This cavernous restaurant takes up the entire ground floor of the Treasure Garden Hotel and offers arguably the best Chinese food in town. Steel pillars, plastic plants and a sea of red table cloths all battle for your attention, but it's the extensive menu (takeaway available) centred on chicken, pork, beef and seafood, plus a handful of vegetarian and tofu meals, that will inevitably occupy you.

Fale Restaurant (Map pp62-3; ☎ 22880; Aggie Grey's Hotel, Beach Rd; breakfast & lunch from ST15, dinner from ST19; ☺ breakfast, lunch & dinner; ☒) This informal restaurant sits within an enormous *fale* beside Aggie Grey's pool and serves up lots of Western-style meals at the tables scattered between the enormous carved pillars. A *fiafia* (ST55/15 with/without buffet) is staged each Wednesday night.

Le Tamarina (Map pp62-3; ☎ 22880; Aggie Grey's Hotel, Beach Rd; lunch/dinner from ST35/50; ☺ lunch & dinner Tue-Sat, dinner Mon; ☒) Fortunately for this upmarket eatery, its encircling windows ameliorate what would otherwise have been a stiffly formal ambience. Don't turn up here in shorts though; formal attire is requested. The restaurant serves highly rated meat meals like beef Wellington and rack of lamb, but no vegetarian pleasures appear on the menu.

Rainforest Cafe & Restaurant (Map pp62-3; ☎ 25736; Beach Rd; lunch ST8-16, dinner ST14-26; ⏱ 9am-3pm & 6pm-late Mon-Fri; ✗) If the Swiss Family Robinson built a restaurant, it would look like this: wood shavings on the floor, pandanus-woven walls screened by lots of greenery, and *siapo* hangings. Despite the overdone tropical theme, this BYO restaurant has a laidback feel and serves curries and other hearty meals, including several vegetarian options. Book ahead for a table on the small front porch.

Beachcomber Restaurant (Map pp62-3; ☎ 21116; Hotel Elisa, Mulinu'u Rd; mains ST20-55; ⏱ breakfast, lunch & dinner; ✗) The windows that ringing this one-room restaurant open up to admit the sea breeze, or you can sample the salt air while clutching an aperitif on the front veranda. The wine list has some good international choices and the menu, though not adventurous, should satisfy. For some pointless reason, men are required to wear a collar.

Self-Catering

The best places for fresh produce are **Maketi Fou** (see p64) and the **Fish Market** (p65). Central supermarkets with reasonable selections include **Chan Mow's** (Map pp62-3; ☎ 22616; Beach Rd; ⏱ 8am-5pm), **Molesi's** (Map pp62-3; Beach Rd; ⏱ 6am-5.30pm Mon-Sat) and **MH Super Fresh** (Map pp62-3; Beach Rd; ⏱ 6am-7pm). The ramshackle **Pelerosa Mini Mart** (Map pp62-3; ☎ 26042; Beach Rd; ⏱ 8am-8pm Mon-Sat) has a bakery selling bread, muffins, pies and donuts.

Imported food is sold at **Lynn's Supermarket** (Map p75; ☎ 20275; Salenesa Rd; ⏱ 5.30am-10pm). Another good option is **MD's Big Fresh** (Map pp62-3; Beach Rd; ⏱ 7am-7pm); head to the fruit and vegetables section to find a rack of Australian and New Zealand wines.

DRINKING

For a smallish place, Apia has a rather large number of bars. The waterfront is where the vast majority of the drinking action is, and most large hotels have an area reserved for barflies. Most places open in the early afternoon and close at the stroke of midnight. The Apia Yacht Club is one of the few places serving alcohol on a Sunday.

Hennie's Sports Bar (Map pp62-3; ☎ 22221; Fugalei St) Hennie's is an appealingly boisterous place hung with fairy lights and filled with the strains of Polynesian dance music. An older crowd of locals and expats gather in this convivial rumpus room of a bar to play darts and pool, or just to cheer on those who are. Several small-screen televisions show a variety of sports, but the commentary is lost in the drinkers' chatter.

Cocktails on the Rocks (Map pp62-3; ☎ 20736; Beach Rd) This teensy but busy bar concocts a dozen standard cocktails (ST8/20 per glass/jug), including a potent Bloody Mary. There's almost always a row of *palagi* seated out front, staring across the road at nothing in particular.

RSA Club (Returned Services Association; Map pp62-3; ☎ 20171; Beach Rd) Don't be fooled by the billboard advertising Wondersoft toilet paper at the entrance. Nicknamed 'The Rosa', this place is anything but soft: the standard drink is a 750ml Vailima, the floor has possibly the oldest, most scarred linoleum on the planet, and you don't want to be here when a fight breaks out (usually around the pool tables at closing time). That said, you see all types in here and the atmosphere is always lively, especially when bands play (opposite).

Apia Yacht Club (Map pp62-3; ☎ 21313; Mulinu'u Rd; ⏱ 4pm-midnight Tue-Sat, 2pm-midnight Sun) The local yacht club is a welcoming place up near the tip of Mulinu'u Peninsula, where it enjoys ocean views and is untroubled by the traffic noise of the town centre. Sip a drink or devour a cheap meal while allowing your hair (assuming you have any) to be ruffled by a sea breeze.

Bad Billy's (Map pp62-3; ☎ 30298; Beach Rd) This rousing saloon-style bar has a cracked concrete floor, an unusually tall timber-plank bar and surfboards stuck on the wall for decoration. It's usually bereft of foreigners but loquacious locals make up for the shortfall in noise. The pool tables shut down at 10pm so everyone can concentrate on drinking.

Bounty Bar (Map pp62-3; ☎ 28506; Mata'utu St) Bounty is a one-room bar filled with what appears to be garden furniture and cheerfully devoted to playing rousing feel-good ballads as loudly as possible. While you're enjoying the cold, cheap beer, spare a thought for those attempting to sleep in the upstairs motel.

ENTERTAINMENT

The possibilities for entertaining yourself in the evening in Apia include a handful of nightclubs, the DJs and bands that play at some of the local bars and cafés, and the high-spirited *fiafia* staged at some hotels. Like bars, nightclubs tend to close at midnight.

Nightclubs

Lighthouse Cafe & Bar (Map pp62-3; ☎ 26669; Beach Rd; admission Wed-Sat night ST5; ⏲ noon-midnight Mon-Sat) This high-ceilinged place looks like an enormous open-fronted barn. It functions primarily as an entertaining bar-club, with lounges and chairs to sprawl in, Vailima in hand, as you listen to the click of pool balls colliding and to live and recorded Polynesian rap and dance music. It also moonlights as a reasonable **café** (meals ST7-19; ⏲ lunch & dinner Mon-Fri, dinner Sat) serving kebabs, pastas and grilled meats.

Spy Nightclub (Map pp62-3; ☎ 20194; Beach Rd; admission Thu & Fri ST5, Sat ST6, dinner guests free; ⏲ 9pm-midnight Thu-Sat) The upstairs space of Paddles restaurant (p71) is taken over by a DJ for a few hours on most nights after the kitchen starts winding down. It's usually low-key and friendly, and in-between songs you can chill to the harbour view from the balcony.

Live Music

Cappuccino Vineyard (Map pp62-3; ☎ 22049; ACB Bldg; meals ST7-16) By day Cappuccino Vineyard is a mild-mannered café but at night it transforms itself into an exuberant wine bar, where the drinkers crowded around the tables outside the front door are serenaded for free several nights a week by local musicians. It's a relaxing venue where striking up a conversation is as easy as lifting a glass.

RSA Club (Map pp62-3; ☎ 20171; Beach Rd) Samoan bands regularly brave the Rosa's intimidating reputation. Gigs are often free but occasionally there's a cover charge (around ST4 to ST5), particularly if two bands are playing on the same night.

Fiafia

Spectacular Samoan dance performances called *fiafia* are staged regularly at various hotels. You'll need to book ahead to get decent seats. A buffet dinner usually accompanies the performance, though you can choose to see the show only. There's a *fiafia* at **Aggie Grey's Hotel & Bungalows** (Map pp62-3; ☎ 22880; Beach Rd; show ST15, dinner & show ST55) every Wednesday evening, while an equally lavish production is staged just out of town at **Aggie Grey's Lagoon & Beach Resort** (Map pp58-9; ☎ 22880; Main West Coast Rd; show ST15, dinner & show ST55) every Thursday. **Hotel Kitano Samoa** (Tusitala Map pp62-3; ☎ 21122; Mulinu'u Rd; show ST15, dinner & show ST50) has its *fiafia* on Friday night. Children are often charged half-price for these shows.

Cinemas

Magik Cinemas (Map pp62-3; ☎ 28126; Convent St; adult/child ST5/3.50) The pair of theatres here is devoted to mainstream movie releases and gets insanely busy on the weekend of a first release.

Sport

Apia Park (☎ 21400; off Faatoia Rd) The big national and international rugby tournaments are held here. It's also where the athletics events and opening and closing ceremonies of the 2007 South Pacific Games will be staged.

SHOPPING

Lots of businesses have moved out of Apia's centre in recent years due to large increases in rent, but you'll still find plenty of shops crowded together in the streets running off Beach Rd.

Elaine MAR Enterprises (Map pp62-3; ☎ 25891; Saleufi St) This shop is just one of many places around Apia where you can buy *lava-lava* machine-printed with traditional designs for ST9 or have one made up for you – the hand-printed material costs around ST10 per yard. It's worth visiting just to be mesmerised by the array of colourful fabric.

Aggie Grey's Gift Shop (Map pp62-3; ☎ 22880; Beach Rd) This retail offshoot of the luxury hotel has a good selection of locally produced crafts and artwork, especially reasonably priced 'ava bowls and wooden models of traditional outrigger canoes, as well as roll upon roll of printed fabric.

Treasure Box (Map pp62-3; ☎ 20470; Convent St) It has lots of upmarket Samoan jewellery but this shop specialises in black pearls that are imported and then matched with locally designed settings. Pop inside just to see the dark lustre of the pearls.

'UPOLU

'UPOLU

Plantation House (Map p75; ☎ 22839; Lotopa Rd) Beautiful, high-quality, Samoan-made *lava-lava*, prints, tailored shirts, jewellery, lacquer-ware and other crafts line the walls of this fine boutique, situated at the front of the owner's house.

Caffeine fans might want to hunt down some yummy *koko Samoa* and Samoan coffee in the larger supermarkets; for details of these, see p72. If you're on a health kick, you might be interested in purchasing some *nonu* juice, Samoa's popular cure-all (see Nonu the Wonder Fruit; p46). You can buy a litre bottle of this bitter stuff for ST20 at the **Natural Health Centre** (Map pp62-3; ☎ 21317; Beach Rd).

A treasure trove of crafts is yours for the browsing in the **Maketi Fou** (p64) and the **Flea Market** (p65).

GETTING THERE & AWAY

For information about transport between Apia and other parts of 'Upolu, see Getting Around (p57) at the start of this chapter. For information on the cargo ship route between Apia and Tokelau, see p294. For details of ferry services between Apia and Pago Pago (American Samoa), see p294. Information on international flights to Apia can be found on p290.

GETTING AROUND

All major international flights (including those servicing American Samoa) use Faleolo Airport, 35km west of Apia. Fagali'i Airport, a few kilometres east of Apia, is used mainly for flights to Savai'i, but nearly all travellers head across on the ferry. To get to Faleolo from Apia, take any bus marked 'Pasi o le Va'a' or 'Faleolo' (ST2); note that the last bus leaves Apia at 2.30pm. Alternatively, a seat on the airport shuttle that primarily services guests of Aggie Grey's Hotel can be organised through **Samoa Scenic Tours** (Map pp62-3; ☎ 22880; Aggie Grey's Hotel, Beach Rd), which has a desk down the stairs from the hotel's reception. Tickets (ST15) must be prebooked and the shuttle picks up from any central Apia hotel. This shuttle does not meet incoming flights and won't service flights departing for American Samoa unless there are at least three passengers. Taxis between Apia and Faleolo Airport cost ST40 each way.

Taxis in Apia are cheap and plentiful. Most trips around downtown cost between ST2 and ST3.

THE CROSS ISLAND ROAD

The main road that leads from Apia in the north to Si'umu in the south is one of 'Upolu's three cross-island roads. It links the Samoan capital with several key attractions, including the Robert Louis Stevenson Museum and mysterious Lake Lanoto'o.

ROBERT LOUIS STEVENSON MUSEUM & MOUNT VAEA SCENIC RESERVE

Only a short drive inland from Apia is the **Robert Louis Stevenson Museum** (Map p75; ☎ 20798; adult/child ST15/5; ⏲ 9am-3.30pm Mon-Fri, 8am-noon Sat), set in the famous Scottish author's beautifully restored former residence, Villa Vailima. Stevenson spent the last four years of his life here and after he died, Vailima was occupied in turn by a wealthy German philanthropist, a Kiwi official during the New Zealand administration and then, after Samoan independence, by the country's head of state. This fine mansion, which now sports a creamy paint job but was originally painted peacock blue, opened as a museum in 1994 on the centenary of Stevenson's death. From the benches on the front porch you look across a vast expanse of lawn to a low horizon of manicured plants, below which is the ocean. It's a fascinating, wonderfully restful place.

Guided tours last 30 to 45 minutes and begin when enough people arrive. While strolling around on polished wooden floors you'll see a collection of early musical instruments, including a Gem roller organ that still works; the Smoking Room, papered in a beautiful copy of the original *siapo* wallpaper and complete with a rather redundant fireplace Stevenson installed to remind him of home; the author's library and bedroom, where some of his favourite books and his own original editions are displayed; and his wife Fanny's bedroom, lined with polished Californian redwood.

Stevenson and Fanny are buried in the adjacent **Mount Vaea Scenic Reserve** (Map p75; admission free), the central feature of which overlooks Apia and the surrounding mountains. To get to the tombs, which are on a plateau just below the summit, take the path on the western side of the house (the guide

GREATER APIA

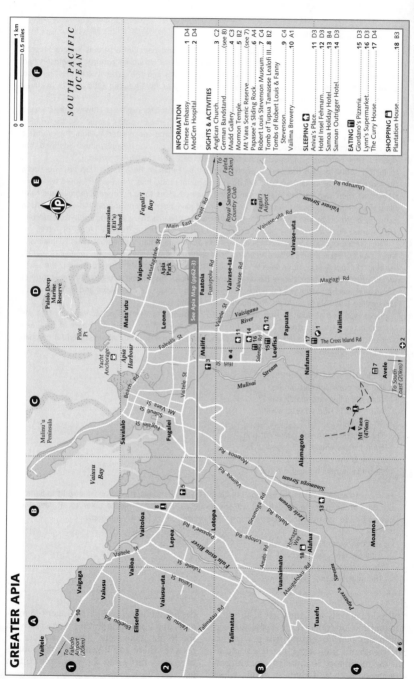

0	1 km
0	0.5 miles

INFORMATION
Chinese Embassy	1 D4
MedCen Hospital	2 D4

SIGHTS & ACTIVITIES
Anglican Church	3 C2
German Bandstand	(see 8)
Madd Gallery	4 C3
Mormon Temple	5 B2
Mt Vaea Scenic Reserve	(see 7)
Papasee'a Sliding Rock	6 A4
Robert Louis Stevenson Museum	7 C4
Tomb of Tupua Tamasese Lealofi III	8 B2
Tombs of Robert Louis & Fanny	
Stevenson	9 C4
Vailima Brewery	10 A1

SLEEPING 🛏
Aniva's Place	11 D3
Hotel Insel Fehmarn	12 D3
Samoa Holiday Hotel	13 B4
Samoan Outrigger Hotel	14 D3

EATING 🍴
Giordano's Pizzeria	15 D3
Lynn's Supermarket	16 D3
The Curry House	17 D4

SHOPPING 🛍
Plantation House	18 B3

SOUTH PACIFIC OCEAN

'UPOLU

HERE HE LIES WHERE HE LONGED TO BE

In December 1889 the already famous Scottish author and poet Robert Louis Balfour Stevenson and his wife Fanny Osborne arrived in Apia aboard the schooner *Equator*. Stevenson had left Europe in search of relief from worsening tuberculosis and the general sickliness that had plagued him all his life. He was enchanted by Samoa and in 1890 he paid £200 for 126 hectares of land in the hills above Apia.

Stevenson's health improved and, with his family, he set sail for Australia. However, he became ill again in Sydney and it was decided that the climate of Samoa would be much better for him. The Stevenson family returned to Apia in September 1890 and constructed Vailima, the grandest home ever seen on the island. They imported furniture from Stevenson's native Scotland and dressed their Samoan employees in *lava-lava* patterned with the Stuart tartan.

In the 1890s, during the period of strife in Samoa between Britain, the USA and Germany, Stevenson became an activist for Samoan rights, maintaining that the people should be left to determine their own destiny in accordance with their customs. Most Europeans there would have liked to see him deported at the time, but this would have been very unpopular indeed; Stevenson came to be loved by the Samoans for his friendliness towards them and his ability to entertain with stories. They respectfully and affectionately referred to him as Tusitala (Teller of Tales).

On 3 December 1894 Stevenson died of a stroke at Vailima. When the Samoan chief Tu'imaleali'ifano spoke of Stevenson's death, he echoed the sentiments of many Samoans: *'Talofa e i lo matou Tusitala. Ua tagi le fatu ma le 'ele'ele,'* he said. ('Our beloved Tusitala. The stones and the earth weep'.) Just two months before his death, in gratitude for his kindness to them, a delegation of Samoan chiefs had arranged for a hand-dug road to be made between Apia and Vailima, which they called O Le Ala O Le Alofa, the Road of the Loving Heart.

Stevenson had stipulated that he wished to be buried at the top of Mt Vaea, part of the Vailima estate. And so, after a Christian burial service, the coffin was laid on a base of coral and volcanic pebbles and the grave lined with black stones, a practice normally reserved for Samoan royalty. His epitaph reads:

Under the wide and starry sky,
Dig the grave and let me lie.
Glad did I live and gladly die,
And I laid me down with a will.

This be the verse you grave for me:
Here he lies where he longed to be;
Home is the sailor, home from the sea,
And the hunter home from the hill.

Fanny, who was known as Aolele (Floating Cloud) by the Samoans, stayed on for a while in Samoa but died in California in 1914. In her will she requested that her ashes be taken to Mt Vaea and buried beside her husband's. Her epitaph, also composed by Stevenson, reads:

Teacher, tender comrade, wife,
A fellow farer, true through life,
Heart whole and soul free,
The august father gave to me.

will point it out) and turn left at the first intersection of trails. After a short, steep climb this path forks into two new paths: the righthand trail is the shortest route to the mountain top (30 minutes), entailing an extremely steep and slippery climb, while the lefthand trail is slightly longer (45 minutes) and less taxing. Even if you don't visit the tombs, take some time to wander the reserve where you'll hear only the sounds of insects, birds and the odd Apia church bell.

A taxi from Apia to Vailima should cost ST6. To go by bus (ST1.20), take the Vaoala or Siumu bus.

BAHÁ'Í HOUSE OF WORSHIP

Near the highest point of The Cross Island Rd is the elegant 19m-high tiled dome of the **Bahá'í House of Worship** (Map pp58-9; ☎ 24192; ☯ information centre 6am-6pm). Designed by Iranian Husain Amanat and dedicated in 1984, this beautiful structure is one of only eight Bahá'í houses of worship in the world. All these buildings are architecturally different except for the fact that all are domed and have nine sides and entrances, which reflects the faith's central tenet of a basic unity of religions and peoples under one 'Creator'.

The Bahá'í faith, which has no professional clergy or priesthood, originated in Persia in 1844. Services are held on Sunday at 10am and consist of prayers, meditations and readings from the scriptures of the faith, as well as from other religions.

Visitors are welcome and attendants in the adjoining information centre will happily answer any questions. Nature lovers will appreciate the beautifully manicured gardens, criss-crossed by paths lined with pink tea plants.

A taxi from Apia will cost around ST14.

TIAPAPATA ART CENTRE

Signposted off the main road just south of the Bahá'í House of Worship is located the lovely **Tiapapata Art Centre** (Map pp58-9; ☎ 23524, 29272; percival@lesamoa.net; ☯ 9am-4pm Mon-Fri). The accomplished artists responsible for the two small rooms of purchasable ceramics, paintings and prints live right next door and will pop out to greet visitors. Excellent art workshops for children are usually held two afternoons a week; call ahead for exact times. The two-hour lessons costs ST15 which includes all materials, but there's an extra charge (rarely more than ST10) for using the oven due to the high cost of electricity. Adults get their two-hours lessons (ST20) in things such as pottery and *siapo* making two mornings a week.

The road in is very bumpy but you can exit along a smoother road running alongside the Bahá'í House of Worship. A taxi from Apia will cost around ST15.

LAKE LANOTO'O

Lake Lanoto'o is an eerie, pea-green crater lake in the central highlands and makes for an adventurous excursion. It's full of wild goldfish which locals used to collect as pets until the government banned it, and so is also known as Goldfish Lake. During the German occupation a basic resort was established here and in 1919 local traders suggested that a road be built to the lake to allow easy access for holiday-makers, but proponents of 'controlled tourism' prevented such development. The Samoan government has proposed creating a national park around the lake, but this is yet to be formalised.

The lake is an excellent place for a swim but also a little spooky because of alternating warm and cold currents. The trail leading in to the lake from the car park – located 3km along a very rough road branching off The Cross Island Rd – is steep, overgrown and slippery, and forks and multiplies the further in you get. We heard of more than a few hikers getting lost trying to find the lake. For these reasons, walkers are strongly advised to hire a guide. A dependable and knowledgeable outfit is **SamoaOnFoot** (Map pp62-3; ☎ 21529, 25416; samoaonfoot@hotmail.com), which organises half-day trips to the lake (ST55, including gumboot hire).

PAPAPAPAI-TAI FALLS

About 3.5km south of the Bahá'í House of Worship is the parking area for **Papapapai-tai Falls** (Map pp58-9; ☯ 9.30am-4pm Tue-Sat). It's only a few steps to the lookout for this spectacular 100m waterfall that plunges into a dramatic, forested gorge.

NORTHEASTERN 'UPOLU

The northeastern corner of 'Upolu contains one of the island's wildest, least-visited areas: the Uafato Conservation Area. On the way there, stop off to refresh yourself at Fatumea Pool or to overnight in some splendidly isolated *fale*.

UAFATO CONSERVATION AREA

The Uafato region is blessed with some magnificent scenery. A rough track follows the rugged coastline as far as the picturesque village of **Uafato**, where 14 sq km of the surrounding rainforest and coastal waters have been declared a conservation area. This is one of the few remaining areas in Samoa where an intact band of rainforest stretches from the sea to the interior uplands. The area also contains a rare stand of *ifilele* (the tree used for carving *'ava* bowls), as well as many bat and bird species, including the rare *manumea* (tooth-billed pigeon). **Traditional carvers** live in Uafato and are usually willing to demonstrate their art to visitors.

You can take a 15km guided walk (ST90) around Fagaloa Bay with **SamoaOnFoot** (Map pp62-3; ☎ 21529, 25416; samoaonfoot@hotmail.com). Pay a bit more to include a wood-carving and *'ava* session in Uafato in this tour (ST120).

Although there's no formal accommodation at Uafato, it may be possible to stay here overnight. Ask to speak to the *pulenu'u* (mayor) when you arrive, or contact SamoaOnFoot about the possibility of tying in an overnight stay with one of their tours.

You can reach Uafato via the rough track that winds all the way around Fagaloa Bay – the turn-off is at the powerful Falefa Falls. This track offers beautiful views through the rainforest down to the sea, but we wouldn't advise going past Saletele without a high-clearance vehicle. Another option is the road (4WD only, about 10km) signposted off Le Mafa Pass Rd to the village of Ta'elefaga.

FATUMEA POOL

Also known as Piula Cave Pool, **Fatumea Pool** (Main East Coast Rd; admission ST2; ⏲ 8am-4pm Mon-Sat) lies beneath Piula Methodist Theological College. It's a wonderful spot to spend a few hours picnicking, swimming in the clear springs and exploring the water-filled caves.

This freshwater pool is separated from salt water by black lava rock. At the rear of the first cave you'll be able to see light through the wall under the water. A 3m swim through the opening will take you to the second cave pool. If you don't fancy a James Bond–type swim, the opening to the second cave is about 20m northeast of the first cave. Beware when you climb down into the second cave: there's a moss-covered concrete platform that gets very slippery.

SLEEPING & EATING

Albatross Hideout (☎ 40375; Saoluafata; fale per person ST30, r ST70) This excellent accommodation in Saoluafata is easy to miss – look for the

sign reading 'Dal Mart' on its top half. It has five modern *fale* equipped with lighting and decks that jut out over a lovely shallow bay, or you can stay in a pleasant room in the main house. Tiny Albatross Island is only a short wade away. The onsite restaurant (breakfast ST10, lunch & dinner ST18-45; ⏲ lunch & dinner Mon-Sat) does yummy soups and Thai-style curries, served direct to your *fale*.

Silirosa Beach Huts (☎ 40656; Lauli'i; r per person ST30) Set up by a former minister for the sheer love of it, this is an overgrown little beachfront sanctuary that will suit self-sufficient travellers. It has a couple of cheerfully ramshackle huts that have been cobbled together from driftwood and other odds and ends but will keep you snug and dry. You can cook your own food on a wood stove, surf some convenient offshore breaks and learn traditional weaving.

Saoluafata Beach Fales (☎ 778 0769; Saoluafata; fale & r per person from ST50) The *fale* here are a little the worse for wear but are slowly being revamped, and you can also hire a room in the family house. Prices include breakfast and dinner. Guests access the beach for free but day trippers pay ST2.

NORTHWESTERN 'UPOLU

There are a couple of worthwhile attractions between Apia and Faleolo Airport, namely some very slippery rocks and a site that's regarded as a national monument by thirsty Samoans.

PAPASEE'A SLIDING ROCK

A trip to the **Papasee'a Sliding Rock** (Map p75; off Maugafolau Rd; adult/child ST2/1; ⏲ 6am-6pm), accessed via 200-odd steep and slippery stone steps, is obligatory for every visitor to Apia. The ritual involves a 5m slide down a waterfall into a jungle pool. If the big slide puts you off, there are three smaller ones to choose from. The best time to visit is between December and June; at other times the water levels may be low and the slide not as fun (or safe).

To get to the rock, take the Se'ese'e bus (ST1.30) from the Maketi Fou and ask to be dropped off at the turnoff for Papasee'a.

VAILIMA BREWERY

Several million litres of the national beer, Vailima, are brewed by **Samoa Breweries** (Map p75; ☎ 20200, 20201; www.vailima.ws; Main West Coast Rd) annually. The brewery opened in 1978 and is now owned by Carlton & United Breweries. Free one- to two-hour tours of the brewing operation are run at 9.30am Tuesday and Thursday. Just turn up at reception, which is in the low white building to the right of the entry gate. Wear enclosed shoes.

SLEEPING & EATING

Aggie Grey's Lagoon & Beach Resort (Map pp58-9; ☎ 22880; www.aggiegreys.com; Main West Coast Rd; s/d/ste US$180/190/400; ✿ 🖵 ☀ ✗) This new addition to the Aggie Grey empire occupies a 90-hectare plot of land. At the time of research it had over 140 rooms, with more still to be added. Practice your swing on an 18-hole golf course, play tennis, go snorkelling and watch planes swoop overhead on their way to the nearby airport. It's already a favourite of package tours and lavish weddings.

Airport Lodge (Map pp58-9; ☎ 45584; www.samoahotels.ws/airportlodge.htm; Main West Coast Rd; s ST110-140, d ST125-170; ✿) The plane-shaped sign in mid-take off out front is a dead giveaway for Airport Lodge, which occupies a pleasant site opposite the ocean. Its bungalows have plain décor but admit plenty of sunlight, and each comes with an en suite and small outdoor deck. You can order breakfast (ST18) and a set-menu communal dinner (ST35).

Samoan Village Resorts (Map pp58-9; ☎ 46028; www.samoanvillageresorts.com; Main West Coast Rd; fale d from US$125; ☀) This was being upgraded at the time of research, with new *fale* being built, the bar area being revamped and a Chinese restaurant being established, all of which should be ready by the time you read this. Its location on Cape Fatuosofia provides good ocean views, but the swimming and snorkelling here isn't great.

SOUTH COAST & SURROUNDS

Along with the Aleipata Islands district and Manono, the south coast of 'Upolu offers plenty of beautiful palm-fringed beaches where it wouldn't be difficult to pass a week or two in sandy bliss. The region's hinterland has some stunning waterfalls and waterholes to visit, as well as the rugged environs of Samoa's sole national park.

SOUTH COAST BEACHES & REEFS

At Lefaga village is the idyllic **Return to Paradise Beach** (day access per person/bicycle/car ST2/3/10; ☯ Mon-Sat), made famous in the 1951 Gary Cooper film based on the James Michener novel, *Return to Paradise*. While the setting lives up to its name, the beach isn't ideal for swimming due to shallow reefs, volcanic boulders and heavy surf. It's a popular spot for Saturday barbecues and has toilets and showers.

Follow the narrow, winding and quite beautiful road west from Return to Paradise Beach to the sizeable settlement of **Falelatai**. At times you'll be hemmed in by village life, while the final descent into Falelatai yields superb views of the reefs and waters off 'Upolu's western nub.

Down a 3km access road east of Return to Paradise Beach is **Matareva** (day access person/bicycle/car ST2/3/10), a series of delightful coves with safe, shallow snorkelling areas and lots of rock pools to explore. A few kilometres east of Matareva is beautiful **Salamumu Beach** (day access bicycle/car ST3/6; ☯ Mon-Sat), reached via a potholed 5.5km track.

About 15km further east is **Aganoa Black Sand Beach** (day access car ST5). Unlike most 'Upolu beaches, the water here is deep enough for swimming. There is also a popular surf break called **Boulders**, just off Cape Niuato'i. The very rough 3km track to Aganoa isn't signposted off the main road. The turn-off (opposite a blue house) is 150m east of the one-lane stone bridge in Sa'agafou. Sand Beach is a 10-minute walk east of where this track terminates; locals told us to just ignore the 'Private Property' sign.

Accessed from the village of Tafatafa to the east of O Le Pupu-Pu'e National Park is **Vaiula Beach**, which has a good surf break and a castaway feel. Experienced board riders can go day surfing at **Salani Surf Resort** (p81); the ST150 fee covers guided surfing and a buffet lunch.

Liquid Motion (☎ 64381; www.liquidmotion.ws), based at Sinalei Reef Resort (p82), does various south-coast dives (ST150 for one dive, ST120 for each of one to five dives) and offers four- to five-day PADI courses (ST1200). Another recommended diving outfit is **AquaSamoa** (☎ 23805; www.aqua

'UPOLU

samoa.com), based at Coconuts Beach Club & Resort (p82).

SATAOA & SA'ANAPU CONSERVATION AREA

In an effort to preserve one of 'Upolu's most important coastal wetland areas, the mangrove forests around the villages of Sataoa and Sa'anapu were declared a conservation area. Mangroves provide a vital habitat for the breeding of fish and crabs, they help to keep erosion in check and the leaves and bark are used in traditional medicine.

At **Sataoa** there's a **nature trail** (per person ST5) but it's just a rough car track that skirts the mangroves before terminating at some wind-blown *fale*. A better option is to stop at Lanu's Beach Fales (see p83) and ask about organising a 90-minute **outrigger canoe trip** (per person ST20) through the mangroves.

Off the potholed road to **Sa'anapu** is a better **nature trail** (per car/motorcycle ST5/2), consisting of a boardwalk that winds through the mangroves for several kilometres. It begins at the sign detailing the car and motorcycle toll.

O LE PUPU-PU'E NATIONAL PARK

The name of Samoa's only national park, the 29-sq-km **O Le Pupu-Pu'e National Park** (☽ 6am-6pm), means 'From the Coast to the Mountain Top'. Created in 1978, the park's northern boundary is formed by a ridge between the volcanic 885m Mt Le Pu'e and 1028m Mt Fito, which is the island's highest peak. In the south is the rugged O Le Pupu Lava Coast. The park entrance is near the Togitogiga Recreation Reserve (opposite), which lies just outside the park to the east. The information building at the entrance has been closed for some time. A ranger lives onsite and usually appears when visitors arrive.

A hiking trail begins opposite the side road to O Le Pupu Lava Coast and heads through thick rainforest to **Pe'ape'a Cave** (six hours return). This large, pit-like cave (actually a lava tube) is full of circling *pe'ape'a* (swiftlets). You can explore the cave with a torch, but be careful climbing into the pit over mossy, slippery rocks. This walk is only recommended for people with hiking experience.

It's possible to continue beyond the cave to **Ofa Waterfall** (three days return). This track is infrequently tackled by government

scientists and is usually heavily overgrown, so a guide is advisable. If you're interested in doing this trek, visit the resource centre at the **Ministry of Natural Resources & Environment** (Map pp62-3; ☎ 23800; Beach Rd) office beside the New Zealand High Commission in Apia.

At the park's western boundary, a rough 3.5km **track** (☽ 6am-6pm) leads south from the main road to the magnificently rugged **O Le Pupu Lava Coast**. From the car park, a rock-strewn path heads east through coastal rainforest and along the coast. Go at least as far as the first lookout to see the sheer cliffs with their melted patterns of ancient lava flows, and the enormous waves that thump against them.

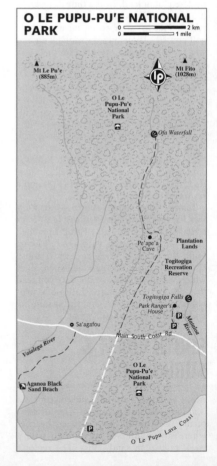

O LE PUPU-PU'E NATIONAL PARK

SamoaOnFoot (Map pp62-3; ☎ 21529, 25416; sa moaonfoot@hotmail.com) conducts a day tour of O Le Pupu-Pu'e (ST80) that includes a two-hour walk to Pe'ape'a Cave and a swim at Togitogiga Falls.

TOGITOGIGA FALLS & RECREATION RESERVE

The tongue-twisting **Togitogiga Recreation Reserve** (✆ 6am-6pm), with its gentle waterfalls, lies just east of O Le Pupu-Pu'e National Park. The reserve entrance is the same as for the national park; just drive on to the second parking area. Several levels of falls are separated by pools, all great for a cool swim, and the surrounding grounds make a gorgeous place for a picnic. The facilities here have deteriorated due to a lack of funding, however, and even the toilet block was boarded up when we visited.

SOPO'AGA FALLS

Just south of the turn-off to the Main South Coast Rd are the lovely, 54m-high **Sopo'aga Falls** (Le Mafa Pass Rd; adult/child ST3/free). The lookout to the waterfall and its immense gorge is accessed through a garden replete with tropical plants such as Indian mulberry, pineapple and *'ava*, all accompanied by signs detailing their Samoan, English and scientific names. Some traditional artefacts are also on display, including drums and an *umukuka* (cooking house). There's an honesty box for when the attendant's house is unattended.

FUIPISIA FALLS

A few kilometres north of Sopo'aga Falls is the 350m trail to **Fuipisia Falls** (Le Mafa Pass Rd; admission ST10; ✆ 8am-dusk), a 55m plunge off the Mulivaifagatola River. Standing on top of the falls is a heady, worthwhile experience. But the standard fee levied by the property owner to 'guide' you the short distance to the falls is way too high and we suggest you discourage such overcharging by negotiating a fairer price (around ST4).

TO SUA OCEAN TRENCH

The short, bumpy track to the fabulous **To Sua Ocean Trench** (South Coast Rd; adult/child ST4/2; ✆ 8am-5pm) is marked by a faded sign that's easy to miss if you're travelling westwards, due to the way it's angled. The trench consists of a pair of huge sunken waterholes

connected by a short rocky tunnel, all of it swept by an ocean current that enters through an underwater passageway. A 15m rope ladder allows you to descend into the southernmost waterhole, where you can gaze up at the sky far above the hole's rocky lip while letting the tenacious ocean current swirl you around – it's a magical experience.

Be warned, however, that most of the rope ladder swings freely because it's unattached to the rock face and so can be very difficult to ascend. We heard of several travellers who got stuck and needed help to climb back up. So don't enter the waterhole (certainly not without help at hand) unless you're absolutely sure you can climb out. Some travellers have also been encouraged by locals to swim out to the ocean through the underwater passage, but this is an extremely dangerous proposition and you'd be well advised not to try it.

Beyond the waterholes is a short track leading to views of the area's superb coastal cliffs, including an energetic blowhole.

SLEEPING & EATING

Virgin Cove Resort (☎ 777 5000; http://www.virgin-cove.ws/; Sa'anapu; fale per person ST70-90) If you turn right once you reach the beach at Sa'anapu, you'll soon find this superb resort. It has purpose-built *fale* strung out along a beautiful, gentle beach, disturbed only by fluttering herons, and uses ecologically friendly composting toilets and solar power. Prices include breakfast and dinner on the balcony of the main house, the latter accompanied by traditional Samoan music. Vegetarians can request nonmeat meals. Guided walks (ST10) are conducted from here along Sa'anapu's mangrove boardwalk.

Salani Surf Resort (☎ 41069; www.surfsamoa.com; Salani; surf package ST350, nonsurfer package ST275, B&B d ST150; ✖) This excellent resort's enclosed *fale*, each fan-cooled and with a private deck and two single beds (bathrooms are shared), is located at the mouth of the Fuipisia River. *Fale* numbers 4 and 5 look out beyond the river mouth to where a pair of reef breaks entertain surfing guests. Only very experienced surfers can book in (stitches and broken boards are regular occurrences here) and numbers are limited to 12 guests. Surf packages include transfers, accommodation, meals, tours and guided surfing. Nonsurfers can also sample the friendly, laidback atmosphere here, though their package only includes accommodation and meals. Samoan culture is emphasised at the resort, hence no surfing on Sunday.

Sinalei Reef Resort (☎ 25191; www.sinalei.com; off South Coast Rd; r US$190-600; 🚫 💻 🔁 🚫) This elegant adult retreat (children under 12 are not admitted) is spread out over 13 landscaped hectares. The refreshing swimming pool is complemented by tennis courts, a golf course, a Wednesday-night *fiafia* (ST65 for dinner and show) and a Saturday *umu* feast (ST40). Accommodation is in modern, porch-fronted units. The 'Garden View' unit is a comfy affair with an open-air bathroom; try for one opposite the pool. The most expensive units have superb sea views. Sinalei's **restaurant** (lunch ST18-30, dinner ST25-50; 🕑 lunch & dinner; 🚫), also open to nonguests, has an eclectic menu of seafood paella, Thai curries, pizzas and large burgers.

Vava'u Beach Fales (☎ 41306; Vava'u; fale ST180, extra adult/child ST20/10; 🚫) These upmarket enclosed *fale* are on an idyllic plot of land off serene Vava'u Beach. Each *fale* sleeps up to five people and has its own en suite, porch and views to the beach on one side and to a well-tended garden on the other. Ask for a *fale* at the property's western end, where the beach is shielded by a nearby islet. The varied menu of the onsite **restaurant** (mains ST14-28; 🕑 breakfast, lunch & dinner) includes chicken stir-fry and Polynesian *oka* (marinated raw fish).

Maninoa Surf Camp (☎ 31200; off South Coast Rd; fale per person ST70) Squeezed in between Sinalei Reef Resort and Coconuts is this modest surfie's haunt, a good option for a cheap sleep. Accommodation is in simple enclosed *fale* and prices include breakfast and dinner. There's a solitary pool table in a small shed, but thirsts can only be quenched at one of the neighbouring resort bars. Guided surfing trips (ST20 to ST40) can be arranged by telephoning ☎ 31175.

Tautua & Sauaso Hunt's Fale (☎ 778 3186, 779 6056; Aganoa Black Sand Beach; fale per person ST60) Travellers seeking isolation or surfers treating themselves to some waves at Boulders can consider sleeping at Aganoa Black Sand Beach. The sole *fale* here contains a couple of beds and a mattress and is run by a friendly family. The price includes all meals. For directions on how to get here, see p79.

Matareva Beach Fales (☎ 35139; Matareva Beach; fale per person ST40, with all meals ST70) The water off Matareva Beach is a beautiful turquoise colour and numerous rock pools line a serene swimming area, so it's a great spot to overnight. These attributes also make the beach very popular with locals. The accommodation prices we were quoted seem unusually high; try to negotiate a more reasonable fee. A shop here sells basic meals.

Sa'moana Resort (☎ 777 1460; www.samoanaresort.com; Salamumu Beach; 7-day all-inclusive package per person per night from US$115; 🚫 🔁 🚫) This splendid resort is on lovely Salamumu Beach. When you're not resting inside one of the A-frame bungalows, you can stroll into the large lounge to play pool, watch DVDs or fix yourself a drink. There's also a superb beachside saltwater pool and guided surfing trips can be organised. Children are well catered for. All the food is deliciously fresh, some of it imported from New Zealand. There are no walk-in bookings; book package in advance through their website.

Coconuts Beach Club & Resort (☎ 24849; www .coconutsbeachclub.com; Maninoa; r US$200-300; 🚫 💻 🔁 🚫) Cool your heels at this relaxed resort. Those feeling active should head for the pool-side *fale* to hire kayaks (guests/nonguests ST10/15) and surfboards (ST15/25) but, surprisingly, not snorkels. Inactive types should jump in the pool and point themselves towards the swim-up bar. There's a free Saturday night *fiafia*; book in advance. Accommodation includes beachside bungalows, over-the-water *fale* and balcony-equipped tree house rooms. Large *'matai' fale* were being built to accommodate families when we visited. Sieni's 3-Stool Bar & Restaurant (breakfast ST15-25, lunch ST22-30, dinner ST35-45; 🕑 breakfast, lunch & dinner) serves up good food like curried or flambéed *ula* (lobster).

Amanda's Beach Fales (☎ 41428; Tafatafa; fale per person ST30, with breakfast & dinner ST40) Amanda's place is on pretty, Vaiula Beach, which the proprietor refers to proprietorially as Amanda's Beach. There are four basic *fale* here, planted among coconut palms that lean out over the sea. The turn-off to the beach is beside the Mormon church in Tafatafa.

Manuia Wetland Holiday Retreat (☎ 28934, 779 8606; Sa'anapu; fale per person ST30, with all meals ST70, r ST100) This grouping of no-frills *fale* and self-contained bungalows is on a sandy, tree-shaded plot east of Sa'anapu, on the way to Virgin Cove. The old-fashioned, fan-cooled bungalows have a couch, electric stove and bathroom, and sleep up to six people (each extra person after the initial two people pays ST50). There are barbecue areas.

Lanu's Beach Fales (☎ 24300; Sataoa; fale per person ST70) You'll find a pair of wind-blown but cosy *fale* at the back of the shop in Sataoa with the Coca-Cola sign out front (on the left as you near the beach). One *fale* has a single bed and the other a double mattress, and the price includes all meals.

ALEIPATA DISTRICT

The reefs in the Aleipata district at the easternmost end of the island are 50m or so offshore, and the water is a remarkable turquoise blue, making for the loveliest beaches and the best swimming on 'Upolu. The centrepiece beach is Lalomanu, where several accommodation options shoulder each other on the crisp sand.

ALEIPATA BEACHES & REEFS

The snorkelling at Aleipata is excellent due to a remarkably well preserved reef system, but beware the numerous cone shells found here. Some are mildly poisonous, but the most beautiful ones can be deadly. Also beware the strong currents that prevail at high tide. Beautiful **Lalomanu** is where most travellers flop onto the sand. Other beaches in the district such as **Saleapaga** aren't quite as inviting as Lalomanu but are still very attractive. This area is overflowing with beach *fale*, particularly around Lalomanu and further west at Saleapaga.

The offshore islands **Nu'utele** and **Nu'ulua** also offer good snorkelling. Part of the **Aleipata Islands Conservation Area**, the islands are important sea-bird nesting grounds. Nu'utele served as a leper colony from 1916 to 1918, when the residents were relocated to Fiji.

Moanalei Dive 'n' Surf (☎ 777 7216), based at Taufua Beach Fales (right), conducts guided surfing (from ST50) and diving (from ST195) trips along 'Upolu's southeastern coast. Dive sites include Namu'a Island and 'Turtle Minefield', so named because of the high numbers of sea turtles consistently seen there.

The bus ride from Apia to either Lalomanu (ST4) or A'ufaga (ST4) can take up to 90 minutes.

SLEEPING & EATING

Litia Sini's Beach Resort (☎ 41050, 41388; www.litia sinibeach.ws; South Coast Rd, Lalomanu; fale per person ST70; 🖥) This superb place on pristine Lalomanu Beach has 17 enclosed *fale*, each with their own small deck and plenty of privacy. The beachside bar has an outside deck that's perfect for an evening guzzle, and you can hire snorkel gear (ST15, ST50 deposit) to investigate the offshore coral. Rates include breakfast and dinner, and the onsite **restaurant** (meals ST12-20) cooks up basic lunches.

Namu'a Island Beach Fales (☎ 20566; namuaisland@ hotmail.com; Namu'a; fale per person ST70) If you think 'Upolu's coastline is soporific, just wait until you sit on the beach of this tiny, inactive island. The seven beachfront *fale* are rudimentary but sturdy, and prices include all meals. Ask for one facing west, as those facing north bear the brunt of incoming wind. A steep, slippery track scales Namu'a's small peak (25 minutes), at the top of which a side trail (to the left) yields a spectacular vista of another offshore island and adjoining reef, and you can circumnavigate the island at low tide. You are run across by boat from Mutiatele, where you can have your car minded (ST10).

Taufua Beach Fales (☎ 41051; South Coast Rd, Lalomanu; fale per person ST55-60) This place offers good-standard accommodation beside Litia Sini's Beach Resort on wonderful Lalomanu Beach. Choose between a knot of enclosed *fale* and slightly cheaper open *fale* that sit closer to the water. The deck of the main building is a sociable gathering place at mealtimes. Prices include breakfast and dinner.

Faofao Beach Fales (☎ 41067; South Coast Rd, Lepa; fale per person ST20) Faofao is a truly hospitable, family-run place 1km west of Boomerang Creek Resort. It has a large clutch of basic *fale* on the beach, plus a hall across the road where Vailima and meals are served (breakfast ST10, lunch and dinner ST15) and a *fiafia* is held on Saturday night (guests/nonguests free/ST30).

Boomerang Creek Resort (☎ 40358; www.boo merangcreek.ws; South Coast Rd, Saleapaga; fale s ST25-50, d ST40-75) This inviting resort offers a choice between appealingly private hillside *fale*, set up on landscaped terraces with a backdrop of spectacular verdant cliffs, or more expensive beachside *fale*. All *fale* are fan-cooled and prices include breakfast. The resort's **Kangarama Restaurant** (meals ST10-40; ⊗ breakfast, lunch & dinner), which is occasionally swamped by tour groups, favours fried food like burgers but also dishes up seafood and vegetarian meals. You can also hire snorkels (ST5), get a Samoan massage (ST20), organise a day-long fishing trip (from ST600) and attend the Saturday-night *fiafia* (ST10/30 without/with food).

Other options:

Matamatagi Motel (☎ 47155, 47098; South Coast Rd, Satitoa; r ST80-100) Located opposite a safe swimming beach, this new motel wasn't yet open when we visited but will suit those wanting to swap windswept *fale* for a spacious room in an old family home.

Malo Beach Fales (☎ 47059; South Coast Rd, Lalomanu; fale per person ST25, with breakfast & dinner ST45) These basic but well-maintained *fale* are at the western end of the crowded Lalomanu strip. The beach is a bit rocky here but it's only a short walk east to smoother sands.

Le Taalo Beach Fales (☎ 41231; South Coast Rd, Saleapaga; fale per person ST30, with all meals ST60) This simple, reclusive grouping of *fale* is located on a fairly rough beach about 500m west of Boomerang Creek Resort.

APOLIMA STRAIT ISLANDS

The tiny islands of Manono and Apolima lie in the strait between 'Upolu and Savai'i. Though both islands have embraced modern conveniences, in many ways they are still well-preserved microcosms of traditional Samoan life and offer a different experience to the main islands.

MANONO
area 3 sq km / pop 1400

The small island of Manono offers a wonderful respite from some of Samoa's noisier modern-day features, its 3-sq-km mass untroubled by any cars or dogs. It's not always the peaceful haven it used to be: round-the-clock electricity was delivered here by submarine cable from 'Upolu several years ago and now music blares more frequently from out of local domiciles. But the pace is even slower than that of the main islands (which you wouldn't think was humanly

possible) and it's impossible not to relax while drifting above well-preserved coral in the tranquil surrounding waters.

The people living on Samoa's third-largest island are scattered across four villages and have a semisubsistence lifestyle.

Sights & Activities
The highlight of a visit to Manono is an early-morning walk around the island, which takes two to 2½ hours. The track circumnavigating the island often resembles a garden path. Sometimes only as wide as a footprint and edged with distinctive yellow *lautalotalo* (crinum lily), banana palms and hibiscus, it wends its way between the sea and the bottom of people's gardens. As you stroll around you'll see kids playing *lafo*, a game in which they compete to be the first to flick a coin into a hole in the dirt, and you may be approached by women selling traditional handicrafts such as *lava-lava* and woven baskets. Unfortunately, you'll also see a fair amount of rubbish lying around, a problem that's widespread in Samoa.

At Lepuia'i is the late-19th-century **Grave of 99 Stones**, a two-tiered edifice of black rocks. The story goes that high chief Vaovasa, who had 99 wives, was killed as he tried to escape from 'Upolu with his 100th wife. A grave was to be built on Manono with 100 stones, but remains unfinished. The large gap in the wall facing the beach was where the final stone was to be placed. Further east at Faleu is the **Peter Turner monument**, a

---

BEHAVING YOURSELF

Manono is a relatively traditional island, though the days when everyone lived in thatched *fale* are long gone and modernity is a growing presence. Nonetheless, visitors are requested to be particularly mindful of accepted village behaviour. Outside the two places to stay, which apply their own 'dress codes', women and men should wear either a *lava-lava* or knee-length shorts, including while swimming.

If you are walking through a village when the bell sounds for *sa* (evening prayer), stop and wait until another bell signals the end of the ritual (about 15 minutes later). Visitors are also requested not to give money or sweets to children.

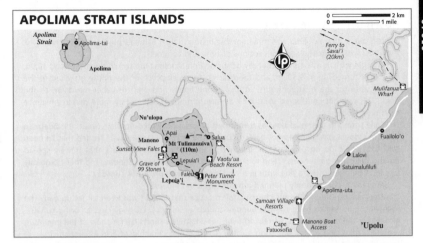

APOLIMA STRAIT ISLANDS

simple white structure commemorating the 1835 landing of the Methodist missionary on Manono. Also look out for the large **grave** with a muzzled cannon protruding from it, just south of Vaotu'ua Beach Resort.

On top of Mt Tulimanuiva (110m) is a large, 12-pointed **star mound** (see Star Mounds, p116). Nearby is the **grave of Afutiti**, who was buried standing up, to keep watch over the island. The best way up the mountain is via the path (90 minutes to two hours return) behind the women's committee building in Salua.

Guided tours of Manono (ST20) and various other activities, from canoe trips to instruction in traditional weaving and cooking, are offered by both of the island's places to stay. A seven-day sea-kayaking tour that takes in Manono is available with **EcoTour Samoa** (Map pp62-3; ☎ 22144; www.ecotoursamoa .com). It costs US$190 per day per person.

The surrounding **coral reefs** offer excellent snorkelling opportunities. Bring your own snorkelling gear.

Sleeping & Eating

Sunset View Fales (☎ 45640; Lepuia'i; fale per person ST90) Loquacious Leota runs this cosy accommodation where you stay in cute and colourful waterfront shacks; the two either side of the communal area have the least privacy. Leota will take you out in his boat to snorkel the reef, show you how to make *palusami* in an *umu*, and talk about all aspects of Samoan culture. The price includes all meals.

Vaotu'ua Beach Resort (☎ 46077; Faleu; fale per person ST45, with all meals ST90) Comprises a half-dozen open-sided *fale* in a shaded beach-side grove fenced in by foliage. Another two *fale* are reserved for the excellent communal meals and a pool table, respectively. The tiled sinks outside the shared showers are a nice touch. Meals can be purchased separately for ST15 each.

All accommodation prices include boat transfers from 'Upolu. There are a few kiosk-type shops in Faleu, including a well-stocked one opposite Vaotu'ua Beach Resort.

Getting There & Away

To visit Manono, head for the jetty at Cape Fatuosofia, just south of Samoan Village Resorts. To charter a boat for a return day trip should cost ST40 for the entire boat. Make sure to confirm which village you'll be picked up from.

Buses marked 'Manono-uta' or 'Falelatai' (ST2) will take you to the jetty from Apia. A taxi will cost ST42.

APOLIMA

area 1 sq km / pop 100

The minuscule island of Apolima looks impressive from a distance, but just wait until you see this lush gem close up. Apolima is the remnant of a volcanic crater and lies outside the reef encircling 'Upolu and Manono, which means sometimes braving sizeable swells to get there. It meets the sea in high, steep cliffs that are unbroken

'UPOLU

HOSPITALITY, SAMOAN STYLE *Paul Smitz*

My trip out to tiny Apolima was a memorable lesson in how Samoa's big-hearted hospitality is entwined with uniquely local conceptions of time and comfort.

To begin with, it was agreed that my boat ride from Apolima-uta would depart around 10am. I dutifully turned up at 9.50am, and then sat on the back porch of the house attached to the village store for the next six hours until someone finally appeared to usher me down to the dock. This was not considered unusual – departure times in Samoa rely more on circumstance than on a clock.

While sitting in the small boat as it motored across a becalmed Apolima Strait, the boatman asked me how I was going to get back to 'Upolu the next day (a Sunday). I replied that I'd been told this would be no problem. He laughed – an infectious ho-ho-hoing that quickly spread among the other passengers – and told me that no boats sailed on Sunday, and that I probably wouldn't be able to get a ride until late on Monday afternoon, if not Tuesday.

Samoans 1, painstakingly planned itinerary 0. Ho ho indeed.

After hearing the mellifluous church choir practice that night, I was keen to get up early the following morning to have the full Sunday church experience. I'd neglected to bring suitable clothes for the occasion (a dirt-streaked t-shirt and battered shorts fell far short of the minimum requirement), but a donor was soon located. I strode into church awash in a Samoan-size collared shirt and equally enormous *lava-lava* and settled happily on a pew to listen to beautiful harmonies and the preachings of a Barry White-sized pastor.

Church services were followed by the *to'ona'i*, the traditional Sunday lunch. As I'd found out the previous night, the Samoan mealtime means being buried alive in an avalanche of baked bananas and taro, *palusami*, stews, baked fish, coconut juice and pretty much every other edible substance within reach. It's customary for a guest to be served first and for the family to have the 'leftovers', and so I sat at a large table on my own, trying to make a respectable dent in the food around me. As I lay gurgling on the floor of a *fale* a short while later, my stomach the size of a tethered airship, one of my hosts walked up and announced that a boat had been organised to take me back across the Strait that day. She cheerfully added that it would leave in 10 minutes.

Feeling queasy with anticipation, I hefted my stomach down to the beach and climbed on a rocking boat, absolutely convinced that the motion of the vessel would have me redistributing my lunch within seconds of setting off. Surprisingly, I made it back to 'Upolu without losing my lunch or my pride, though with a much better understanding of the idiosyncrasies of Samoan generosity.

except for a single gap in the north. Sailing through the narrow heads and into the crater, right up to Apolima's only beach, makes a dramatic introduction to the island.

The name of the island is said to be derived from Apo i le Lima, meaning 'Poised in the Hand', in reference to the spear used by a prince to kill his brother. The wound the spear caused is the aforementioned crater entrance, which shelters the village and its harbour.

Someone will offer to guide you through overgrown backyards to the old, steep steps leading up to a small **lighthouse**. The view from here is simply spectacular. In the afternoon you might also take part in a game of volleyball. (Sporty types take note: these guys are good.)

If you're there on a Saturday, ask to go along to **choir practice** that night to hear wonderful voices echoing in harmony around a timber-roofed church. Another highlight is attending Sunday-morning **church services**, when parishioners are ablaze in white. You'll need to dress up for the occasion.

To visit Apolima, it's best to receive an invitation from a resident of the island. Drop into the shop in Apolima-uta with the Western Union sign out front, beside the primary school, and ask to speak to Sofia. There are no guarantees, but she may contact an islander on your behalf to arrange a visit – we stayed with Fipi and Puluseu, who provided great hospitality. Boats to the island depart from the wharf behind this shop. Accommodation providers on nearby

Manono (see p85) may also be able to arrange a visit.

To stay and be fed on Apolima should cost around ST50 per person per night. It is also much appreciated if you bring some food as a gift for the host family; about ST20 worth of chicken is a reliable choice. You should confirm that the cost of the return boat trip is included in the agreed price. If a boat has to be organised expressly for you (such as on Sunday, when Apolima's boats are normally high and dry on the beach) it will cost ST150 for a one-way trip.

Savai'i

The island of Savai'i offers a wilder experience of Pacific life than 'Upolu. Apart from being the largest island in Polynesia outside New Zealand and Hawai'i, it's also mostly uninhabited, which means there's more spectacular tropical terrain at hand and less signs of modern life to be encountered while you're exploring it. Most of the island's villages are speckled along the main coast road and, as you drive, bus or walk through these, you're liable to see locals dozing in large *fale* (traditional thatched house) and bathing in communal rock pools; a remarkable assortment of weathered churches; pigs scampering about, their tails swishing feverishly as they root around in the dirt or sand; and horses tethered by the roadside or being bathed in the sea, particularly along the island's east coast.

Away from the villages and their traditional ways is a wonderfully rough, legendary landscape awaiting discovery. Scattered across the island are numerous archaeological sites – fortifications, star mounds and ancient platforms – many of which have been swallowed up by the nearly impenetrable jungle. Savai'i is studded with about 450 craters, many of them along the island's central ridge, and the more accessible of these allow you to peer into the depths of a huge, silent, overgrown caldera. Violent eruptions a century ago coated much of the island's northeast with lava – pick your way through the fields of charred, broken rock and imagine what the heat must have been like. To top it all off, there are also magnificent waterfalls and hiking trails secreted within old plantations, untouched rainforests blanketing remote peninsulas, and furious blowholes making their presence felt along the stormy coast.

HIGHLIGHTS

- Plunging into the sublime pool beneath **Afu Aau Falls** (p99) before standing atop enigmatic **Pulemelei Mound** (p100)
- Watching coconuts shoot into the sky at **Alofaaga Blowholes** (p100)
- Imagining the volcanic fury that caused the desolate landscape of the **Lava Field** (p94)
- Climbing an ancient banyan tree and standing at the end of the world on the **Falealupo Peninsula** (p97)
- Staring into the eerie depths of the **Mount Matavanu Crater** (p95)

Falealupo Peninsula ★
Lava Field ★
★ Mt Matavanu Crater
Pulemelei Mound ★
★ Afu Aau Falls
★ Alofaaga Blowholes

POPULATION: 55,000	AREA: 1813 SQ KM

SAVAI'I

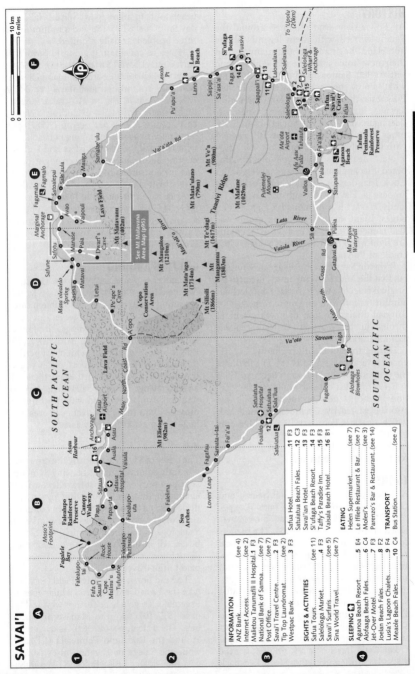

SAVAI'I

HISTORY

All Polynesians who migrated around the Pacific carried with them legends of the homeland they had left, and many named their new home after the old. Thus, when settlers left Samoa in about AD 300, for what is now the Society Islands in French Polynesia, they named an island there after Savai'i. Hundreds of years later, when settlers again departed the Society Islands for other parts of Polynesia, they still carried with them that ancient name.

New Zealand's Maori people remembered the ancient homeland as Hawaiki, Cook Islanders as 'Avaiki, and Society Islanders as Havai'i (though the Society Islands' Havai'i is now named Ra'iatea). The largest island of the Hawai'ian group was also named after it. So in a sense, Samoans are right when they claim that Savai'i is 'the cradle of Polynesia'.

It was on Savai'i, in the village of Safotulafai, that the Mau Movement was formed. Its original objective was to replace the German administration with one more respectful of Samoan affairs, an aim that was extended throughout the years of the New Zealand administration.

During the 20th century, Savai'i experienced several natural disasters. The first was the eruption of Mt Matavanu between 1905 and 1911, which caused wholesale devastation in the island's northeast. Savai'i was also devastated by Cyclones Ofa and Val, which struck in February 1990 and December 1991, respectively. Many of the villages in the northwestern corner of the island were completely destroyed.

TOURS

A good option for Savai'i sightseeing and cultural excursions is **Safua Tours** (Map p89; ☎ 51271; Safua Hotel, Main South Coast Rd, Lalomalava), based at the Safua Hotel (p93). The owners command an impressive knowledge of local geography and customs, and conduct separate day tours (ST125) of the island's south and north coasts. Sites visited include beautiful Afu Aau Falls, Pulemelei Mound, Tafua Savai'i crater and the Alofaaga Blowholes. They also organise village stays for around ST60 per person, which includes transport and meals. Rates are negotiable for groups.

Sina World Travel (Map p89; ☎ 51499; Blue Bird Mall, Salelologa) offers everything from laid-back beach tours to hikes up Mt Silisili. Half/full-day tours cost ST75/150 and a minimum of three people is usually required.

If you're considering going to Savai'i to surf, contact **Savai'i Surfaris** (Map p89; ☎ 58248; fax 58007 for local inquiries), based at Aganoa Beach. Bookings are through **Atoll Travel** (☎ 03-5682 1088; www.atolltravel.com) in Australia. Seven-night surfer packages, excluding airfares, cost around A$960 per person (A$870 per person for twin-share) staying in beach *fale*, with two daily meals, transfers and surf accommodation included. Seven-night packages for nonsurfers cost from A$660/570 for single/twin-share accommodation in *fale*.

Apia-based **Green Turtle Tours** (Map pp62-3; ☎ 22144, 29229; www.greenturtletours.com) operate a daily hop-on, hop-off bus service around Savai'i and also do day tours of the island. For more information, see p67.

GETTING AROUND

Whenever a plane arrives from 'Upolu at Ma'ota Airport, nearly every taxi on Savai'i is waiting for it, so there's no problem finding transport. The taxis, however, are relatively expensive. To Salelologa, the fare is ST7.80 and to Tuasivi (about 13km), ST22. Public buses are very convenient for getting to Salelologa from the airport, but if you're travelling to Tuasivi or further north, you'll have to change buses at Salelologa. Airport transfers can be arranged with most hotels, provided you book in advance. Buses and taxis also greet every ferry arrival.

Bus

The buses of Savai'i are mostly the crowded, vibrantly coloured affairs blasting Samoan-style pop music that most travellers usually encounter first on 'Upolu. But newer, generic buses are becoming a more common sight on the island's roads. The market in Salelologa is the main terminal for Savai'i buses. All buses display the name of their destination in the front window. Fares are paid to the driver.

To head north to the Lava Field (ST2.50), take the Lava Field Express, which goes to Fagamalo. To go a little further west to Manase (ST3.10), take the Manase or Sasina bus. The Falealupo bus will take you up around the Falealupo Peninsula (ST4.50), while the Salega or Fagafau buses trundle past the Alofaaga Blowholes (ST2) and Satuiatua Beach (ST3). The most you'll pay is for the bus ride to Asau (ST5). Ferry passengers will have the most luck connecting with buses to out-of-the-way destinations – that is, beyond the cluster of villages along the southeast coast – as such buses mostly depart as soon as the ferry comes in.

Car

It's a joy to motor along the sealed Main Coast Rd that winds around the island, but keep an eye out for stray children, pigs, dogs and chickens. Off the main road you'll encounter a few bumpy tracks where at the very least you'll need a high-clearance 2WD (or 4WD if there's been heavy rain). These include the steep, rocky climb up Mt Matavanu and the plantation tracks leading to Pulemelei Mound and through the Tafua Peninsula Rainforest Preserve.

There are several petrol stations along the east and north coasts.

Cars can be hired in Salelologa from several operators, including **Sina World Travel** (Map p89; ☎ 51499; Blue Bird Mall, Salelologa), from about ST150 per day. Note that a ST2500 insurance excess will apply if you cause an accident.

Taxi

Taxis are relatively expensive on Savai'i and useful only for short trips.

SOUTHEASTERN SAVAI'I

The southeastern chunk of Savai'i is where most of the island's business is conducted, namely in the banks, shops and marketplace of Salelologa. But once outside the shabby strip of commerce running north from the ferry terminal, you'll encounter some superb beaches and the lush wilds of the Tafua Peninsula Rainforest Preserve.

INFORMATION

Most of Savai'i's main facilities are in Salelologa and nearby in Tuasivi.

ANZ Bank (☎ 51213; Salelologa; 🕑 8am-3pm Mon-Fri) Situated beside the market, it has a 24-hour ATM.

Internet access (Salelologa; per 30min ST14; 🕑 8am-4pm Mon-Fri, 8am-noon Sat) In the same building as Savai'i Travel Centre.

Main post office (Blue Bird Mall, Salelologa; 🕑 8.30am-4.30pm Mon-Fri, 8.30-noon Sat) Doubles

as a call centre (using phonecards). There are also post offices at Tuasivi, Asau, Fagamalo and Sala'ilua (not open weekends).

Malietou Tanumafili II Hospital (☎ 53511; Main North Coast Rd, Tuasivi; 🕑 8.30am-11pm) Doctors are on call around the clock. There are other basic hospitals at Safotu, Sataua and Foailalo.

National Bank of Samoa (☎ 51398; Blue Bird Mall, Salelologa; 🕑 8.30am-3pm Mon-Fri, 8.30-11.30am Sat)

Savai'i Travel Centre (☎ 51206; savaiitravelcentre@lesamoa.net; Salelologa) Arranges travel around the island. Also an agent for Polynesian Airlines (☎ 22737, 22738).

Sina World Travel (☎ 51499; Blue Bird Mall, Salelologa) Also for travel around the island.

Tip Top Laundromat (Salelologa; wash/dry ST5/6; 🕑 8am-4pm Mon-Fri, 8am-noon Sat) Shares a building with Savai'i Travel Centre.

Westpac Bank (☎ 20000; Salelologa; 🕑 8.30am-3pm Mon-Wed, 8.30am-4pm Thu & Fri)

SALELOLOGA

Salelologa is a scrappy, ramshackle, heavily littered settlement strung out along the 1.5km road leading north from the ferry terminal to the junction with the Main South Coast Rd. Most travellers stop long enough to stock up on petrol and other supplies and grab a bite to eat, then move on.

The handicraft stalls at the **market** (🕑 early-late Mon-Sat) are worth a browse. At the rear a large group of men sit blearily around several large drums from which *'ava* (also known as *kava*) is continually ladled into small black cups.

JOHN WILLIAMS MONUMENT

In front of the London Missionary Society (LMS, or Congregational) church at Sapapali'i is a small stone monument commemorating the landing of the former British ironmonger turned missionary, Reverend John Williams, who arrived on his makeshift vessel, the *Messenger of Peace*, in 1830. He didn't stay long but succeeded in converting a powerful warrior chief, Malietoa Vainu'upo, to Christianity, which in turn encouraged other Savai'ians to convert.

There's a gorgeous **rock pool** beside the monument. Ask for permission before taking a plunge.

EAST-COAST BEACHES

Along the east coast between Salelologa and Pu'apu'a are nice beaches and good snorkelling spots. Many of the villages charge beach-access fees of ST2/5 per person/car. The best beaches are at **Si'ufaga**, which boasts a magnificent turquoise-coloured lagoon, and **Lano**. The area also has numerous freshwater pools and springs for bathing.

PU'APU'A

There are two freshwater **bathing pools** in Pu'apu'a village. The pool on the eastern side of the road is for women and the one on the western side is for men. If you'd like to swim here, the locals will be flattered that you chose their pool, but it's still best to ask villagers' permission before jumping in.

On Pu'apu'a's foreshore is an eye-catching *fale*-shaped **shrine** raised up above a three-pointed mound of black rock and framed by potted flowers, with a large statue of Madonna and child tucked inside. Further south in Lano is another creative **shrine** – a blue tiered structure with Madonna perched on top in a Pope-mobile-style plexiglass bubble.

TAFUA PENINSULA RAINFOREST PRESERVE

The **Tafua Peninsula Rainforest Preserve** (admission ST2) occupies much of the Tafua Peninsula. It's one of Samoa's most accessible and beautiful stands of rainforest and contains rugged stretches of lava coast studded with cliffs, sea arches and blowholes. A highlight of the preserve is the extinct **Tafua Savai'i crater**, which rises above the village of Tafua. The crater is choked with vegetation and has a lost world feel to it, enhanced by glimpses of the relatively rare Samoan flying fox circling the treetops. You may even see the definitely rare *manume'a* (Samoan tooth-billed pigeon).

To get here, take the road signposted off the Main South Coast Rd opposite Ma'ota Airport; you pay the custom fee about 50m down this road. About 2.6km from the main road turn left on to a pair of ruts (if you reach the Tafua village sign, you've gone too far). At this turn-off you may be accosted by a local family demanding another access payment, but politely refuse. Now drive for 650m along this bumpy track (OK for 2WDs except after heavy rain) to where there's a small, car-sized clearing on the right, opposite a large tree (if the road starts sloping downwards, you've gone too far). The trail to the crater (15 minutes) is easy to follow

from here. You can also approach a Tafua villager to guide you to this trail.

After reaching the crater's edge, the trail continues to the left around the rim. Follow it until you're on the southern side of the crater, from where you'll have the best view of the bats and a far-ranging view of the island's southern coastline and crater-studded highlands.

At the western end of Fa'a'ala village is a track leading to lovely **Aganoa Beach** (nonsurfer/surfer ST5/20), dotted with picnic *fale*. There are strong currents here so swim with care. Pay fees at Kahuna Bar & Grill (opposite).

SLEEPING & EATING
Salelologa

Jet-Over Motel (☎ 51565; Blue Bird Mall; r ST110-120; 🅿 ❌) This motel is located at the rear of Blue Bird Mall – reception is at the kiosk in the middle of the mall's downstairs concourse. Its rooms are pricey but big and well-equipped, with a fridge, TV and microwave. Cheaper rooms look out on an adjacent lumber yard, while the costliest have a marginally better view.

Taffy's Paradise Inn (☎ 51544; r per person ST35) This particular 'paradise', about 800m north of the wharf, unfortunately resembles a construction site, but it's OK as a budget option if you want a room as opposed to a *fale*. There are four no-frills rooms upstairs in the blue house, all of which get ample natural light and share a bathroom, sitting area and an antique fridge.

THE AUTHOR'S CHOICE

Lusia's Lagoon Chalets (☎ 51487, 25018; www.lusiaslagoonchalets.ws; fale per person ST35-45; ❌) Lusia's is located 1km southwest of Salelologa's wharf and is a superb place to stay. It's spread out over a small, bushy slice of land and has *fale* raised up over the waters of a sublime little cove sometimes visited by sea turtles. Hire a snorkel (ST5) or canoe (ST10) to explore offshore, sunbake on the waterfront deck, swim in a sea-fed rock pool, or slurp cocktails (ST15) at the bar. The onsite restaurant (mains ST8-25; 🕒 breakfast, lunch & dinner) utilises the freshest seafood wherever possible, without frying all the taste out of them, and does splendid home-baked desserts.

Le Ifilele Restaurant & Bar (☎ 51299; behind Blue Bird Mall; meals ST9-40; ☘ breakfast, lunch & dinner Mon-Fri, dinner Sat) Le Ifilele has a handful of tables on a small terrace beside a tiny bar and within several nearby waterside *fale*. The restaurant has a nice, open feel and a menu full of goodies not often served elsewhere on Savai'i, such as eggs Benedict and surf 'n' turf (New Zealand beef smothered in a seafood sauce). A traditional Samoan spread (ST12) is served on Friday.

Salelologa market (☘ early-late Mon-Sat) At the back of this market are food stalls serving cheap fried snacks and sweets, and behind it is a cluster of tiny general stores selling inexpensive staples.

Self-caterers can also stock up at:

Helen Supermarket (Blue Bird Mall; ☘ 7.30am-5pm Mon-Fri, 7.30am-1pm Sat)

Molesi's (Main South Coast Rd; ☘ 8am-4.30pm Mon-Fri, 8am-1pm Sat, 6am-8pm Sun)

Around Salelologa

Aganoa Beach Resort (☎ 50180; www.atolltravel.com /samoa/samoasavaii.htm; Fa'a'ala; nonsurfer/surfer ST80/100) This resort caters mainly to surfers keen to ride the reef breaks only a short paddle offshore. Accommodation is in two- to four-bed *fale* (the beds make a nice change from thin mattresses) and prices include breakfast and dinner. Day visitors pay ST5 and day surfers ST20; the surfing fee goes to the local conservation committee. Basic lunches are available at the Kahuna Bar & Grill (meals ST6-15; ☘ lunch).

Joelan Beach Fales (☎ 7781956; Main North Coast Rd, Lano; fale per person ST50) At Joelan's, eight simple *fale* are planted above the high tide mark on a great curve of beach at the northern end of Lano village. A volleyball net has been strung up and there's great snorkelling offshore. Price includes breakfast and dinner; other supplies can be purchased from the small village kiosks.

Savai'ian Hotel (☎ 51296; savaiian@lesamoa.net, Main South Coast Rd, Lalomalava; s ST45-125, d ST65-150; ⊠ ☙) The accommodation here is mainly in motel-style units (continental breakfast included) that look across a swathe of lawn to remote breakers and the hazy outline of 'Upolu. Behind the units are some *fale*, which are plain but have their own bathrooms and are protected from the wind.

Si'ufaga Beach Resort (☎ 53518; www.siufaga .com; Main North Coast Rd, Tuasivi; s ST70-320, d ST90-350;

⊠ ⊠) Located opposite palm tree–lined Si'ufaga Beach, this resort offers several types of units. The 'deluxe' models are closest to the glorious beach and have bathrooms, cable TV, fridge and hot water. Behind these are 'superior' units, some of which cater for disabled travellers, followed by relatively inexpensive 'standard' units that each have a bathroom and fridge. The picnic table at the end of the small spit opposite reception, which is at Parenzo's Bar & Restaurant, is a good place for your morning cuppa.

Safua Hotel (☎ 51271; fax 51272; safuahotel@yahoo .com; Main South Coast Rd, Lalomalava; fale s/d/f ST80/110/ 140) This hotel inhabits an overgrown compound well off the main road, away from the beach. It offers reasonable beds in distinctive enclosed *fale*-bungalows (breakfast included in price) but is looking a bit shabby these days and you should inspect the rooms before committing yourself. There's a nightly dinner buffet (ST38) and a small bar with a pool table that's usually commandeered by locals. The highly knowledgeable Safua Tours (p90) is based here.

Parenzo's Bar & Restaurant (☎ 53518; Si'ufaga Beach Resort, Main North Coast Rd, Tuasivi; mains ST25-40; ☘ lunch & dinner Mon-Sat, dinner Sun; ⊠) The outdoor terrace of stylish Parenzo's affords great views of beautiful Si'ufaga Beach and is perfect for an early evening meal and a glass of red. The pasta is tasty but nothing

---

SUNDAY LUNCH

On Sunday mornings you'll find the islands shrouded in smoke as villagers everywhere light fires to warm stones needed for the *umu* (ground ovens) used to bake *to'ona'i* (Sunday lunch). Visitors sometimes complain that nothing happens in Samoa on Sunday, but it's hardly true – after a small breakfast (on account of the looming lunch) Samoans go to church and sing their lungs out, at noon they eat an enormous roast dinner and in the afternoon they sleep.

You may be lucky enough to be invited to a family *to'ona'i*. A typical spread includes baked fish and other seafood (freshwater prawns, crabs, octopus cooked in coconut milk), suckling pig, baked breadfruit, bananas, *palusami* (coconut cream wrapped in taro leaves), salads and curry dishes.

to rave about, though they do take their garlic bread seriously – don't expect to be able to breathe on anyone for several days. Seafood dishes are also available and they brew a strong coffee.

NORTHEASTERN SAVAI'I

Neighbouring 'Upolu remains in distant view as the coastal road heads north from Pu'apu'a past the sun-baked lava that flooded over a large slice of Savai'i's northeast a century ago. This region gets the most attention from the island's visitors, who come here to scramble over the volcanic debris, swim with turtles, scale spectacular Mt Matavanu and mingle with fellow travellers at Manase.

Raci's Beach Club (RBC; ☎ 54003; Main North Coast Rd, Manase; ☟ 8.30-11am & 2-6.30pm Mon-Sat) provides Internet access (ST10 for the first 10 minutes, ST0.50 each subsequent minute) and also hires bikes (ST20/30 per half/full day), kayaks (ST25/35 per half/full day) and flippers (ST5 per day).

LAVA FIELD

The Mt Matavanu eruptions between 1905 and 1911 created a moonscape in Savai'i's northeastern corner as a flow of hot lava 10m to 150m thick rolled across plantations and villages, destroying everything in its path. The Main North Coast Rd between Samalae'ulu and Sale'aula crosses this **lava field**, a vast expanse of twisted dark rock peppered with green plants, and provides access to several fascinating sites.

The village of **Mauga** (Map p89), which means 'mountain', encircles a nearly perfect crater. This shallow crater is filled with banana palms (excepting the centre, which is occupied by a *kirikiti* – cricket – pitch) and ringed by modern *fale* with corrugated-iron roofs. A massive **Catholic church** looms over the village entrance, close to where Savai'i's first Catholic church was destroyed by lava in 1906. If you'd like to be shown around, most villagers will be happy to oblige. You get your first good look at the lava field about 1.5km north of Mauga: a desolate field of black stretching down to the sea.

In Sale'aula, 5km north of Mauga, are the remains of several **lava-ruined churches** (admission ST3). The local guides (from the Information Fale) can be quite disinterested, so it's often better to explore the site by yourself. To the left of the Information Fale (as you face it from the road) is a trail leading to the **LMS Church**, where 2m of lava flowed through the front door and was eerily imprinted by corrugated iron when the roof collapsed. A mango tree has now taken root inside the ruined walls. Beside the church is an old **cemetery**, many of its graves still marked by smooth, water-rounded boulders. Behind the LMS church, a short trail leads to a rest *fale* at the edge of the lava field – clamber over the rubble to your heart's content, but watch the kiddies on this deeply cracked

---

RESPONSIBLE CHOICES

Most of Savai'i's conservation initiatives are genuine efforts to safeguard fragile environments, including the animals that live there, and to empower local people to take responsibility for them. But occasionally ventures are established that look like conservation projects, but are in fact primarily money-raising schemes. It's hard to blame villagers for wanting to make more *tala*, but, in the interests of responsible tourism, travellers at the very least need to be aware of what they're supporting.

The turtle enclosure at Satoalepai (opposite), for instance, is undoubtedly a pleasant and well-maintained spot. But the family running this venture admit it's a business rather than a conservation effort. This, and the fact that the turtles have been removed from their natural environment, is worth remembering when deciding whether or not to visit it. We saw no sign of the animals being manhandled when we visited, but this would also be something to watch out for.

A far less salubrious case in point is the so-called turtle pond in the neighbouring village of Safa'i. It comprises three turtles that are trapped in a murky, wire-enclosed pool and are badly manhandled – when we visited, a boy yanked one of the animals out of the water and waved it upside down to show off its exposed underbelly. In the interests of animal welfare, we urge you not to support it.

terrain. A short walk north of the LMS church is the **Virgin's Grave**, the subject of a legend stating that a *taupo* (high chief's daughter) who died of tuberculosis was so pure that the lava flowed around her grave, leaving it untouched. Though venerated by some, to others this 2m-deep pit is not much more than an ill-defined strip of lime cement surrounded by colourful plants.

TURTLES

Signposted off the Main North Coast Rd in the village of Satoalepai is a **turtle enclosure** (Satoalepai; admission ST10; 8am-5pm); look for the sign 'Turtle Swimming'. At the end of a short side-road you'll find a purpose-built lagoon containing over 15 healthy-looking turtles in a clear mixture of fresh- and saltwater. The admission fee allows you to swim with these fascinating creatures. You can also hire snorkels (ST5), and the lagoon is surrounded by several *fale* in which to lounge.

For some issues you might want to consider before visiting this enclosure and similar wildlife-viewing places, see Responsible Choices, opposite.

FAGAMALO & AVAO

The waters off Fagamalo generate some fine **surf** when there's a swell coming from the north, usually between December and April. Scuba divers should check out **Dive Savai'i** (59622; www.divesavaii.com; Main North Coast Rd, Fagamalo), which conducts four-day PADI open-water courses (ST1000) and organises regional dives (one/two dives ST150/220).

At **Avao**, 3km west of Fagamalo, is the site where early missionaries began translating the Bible into Samoan in 1834, a task that took 11 years. The pulpit of the LMS church is carved from the stump of the tree that shaded the translators as they worked. There's also a monument to them at the site where the tree actually grew.

SAFOTU

The long, strung-out village of Safotu, west of Manase around several rocky headlands, has three large and prominent **churches** in a row. The medieval-looking one is the Sacred Heart Catholic Church – much of its original whiteness has now flaked off. Next door is the LMS church and further along, the Methodist – both new churches replacing older buildings. West of the churches

are a series of **freshwater pools** for bathing or swimming. Some are for men and some for women, so be sure to ask which ones are which.

MOUNT MATAVANU CRATER

Mt Matavanu is the culprit responsible for the volcanic rubble blanketing large swathes of northeastern Savai'i. The mountain's remote **crater** is a spectacular sight, an eerily silent pit cloaked in jungle and overseen by gliding swiftlets. The track leading here presents a great opportunity to experience some of Savai'i's wild interior.

From Safotu take the turn-off to Paia from where the signposted track to the mountain. Lots of people hike the 8km route from Paia, which leads through lush countryside and up over the ragged old lava flow. You can drive up the mountain in a high-clearance 2WD, but it's steep and rocky and a 4WD is recommended. You'll eventually reach a blue *fale* occupied by 'Da Craterman', a cheerful bush-knife–wielding local who maintains the **crater track** (admission ST15; 9am-4pm Mon-Sat) on behalf of Paia. He'll accompany you for

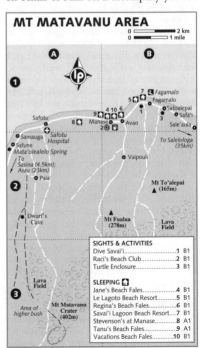

MT MATAVANU AREA

SIGHTS & ACTIVITIES	
Dive Savai'i	1 B1
Raci's Beach Club	2 B1
Turtle Enclosure	3 B1

SLEEPING	
Jane's Beach Fales	4 B1
Le Lagoto Beach Resort	5 B1
Regina's Beach Fales	6 B1
Savai'i Lagoon Beach Resort	7 B1
Stevenson's at Manase	8 A1
Tanu's Beach Fales	9 A1
Vacations Beach Fales	10 B1

SAVAI'I

the next kilometre to where the climb to the crater begins, at the sign reading 'Lemalola Aimasi Park' (which roughly translates as 'no rest, eat biscuit'). The crater track is lined with handmade signs – you can commission your own for ST35 – which, while raising more money for Paia, are an unfortunate eyesore. Up on the crater rim, a path winds along it to the left; don't get too close to the edge. If Da Craterman isn't at the *fale* when you arrive, just head up the track and you'll doubtless run into him soon.

The main track continues for another 3km from Mt Matavanu to Mt Maugaloa, but at the time of writing this part of the track still required clearing and was not open. Ask Da Craterman for an update.

DWARF'S CAVE

Legend has it that this cave, actually a lava tube, was a hide-out for a tribe of dwarfs with magical abilities. One man who stumbled upon them found that he was able to make food appear by simply wishing for it. When his wife questioned the source of this extraordinary ability, the man revealed the secret of the dwarfs' hide-out and instantly fell dead.

The turn-off to the cave is signposted off the Main North Coast Rd, just west of the Mt Matavanu turn-off. In Paia look for the faded red signpost on the right and wait outside the blue *fale* at this intersection. Someone should appear to guide you to the **Dwarf's Cave** (Paia; guide per group ST20; ☉ 9am-5pm Mon-Sat). You need a guide as the way to the cave involves several turn-offs (you can drive the 1.5km to the cave entrance) and the trail through the cave splits several times. Everyone should carry their own torch and reliable footwear, as the lava tube is slippery.

Throughout the cave are small pools (basically mixtures of bird droppings and water – not the best for swimming) and some underground waterfalls. Apparently some people have been invited to slide into a waterhole that marks the end of one of the side-trails, but this waterhole is deep and we'd recommend declining such an offer if it's made.

MATA'OLEALELO SPRING

This ample, bubbling **freshwater spring** (Safune; car ST5; ☉ 7am-5pm Mon-Sat) is officially claimed by Safune village, although it lies opposite the sign for Matavai village. From the road, head across the *kirikiti* pitch to indulge in a refreshing jet-bath type of swim.

PE'APE'A CAVE

It's easy to find **Pe'ape'a Cave** (Map p89; Main North Coast Rd; adult/child ST5/1; ☉ 8am-5pm), which is right beside the road just south of Letui. Fiu Pisimati or a family member will guide you through this short lava tube. The whole excursion takes only 10 minutes, but you'll see white-rumped Polynesian swiftlet nests up close, the birds chittering sharply as they swoop around you in the dark. Bring your own torch.

SLEEPING & EATING

A number of basic beach *fale* have sprung up along the northeast coast in recent years, most charging between ST40 and ST50 per person, including at least two meals. Manase has become crammed with accommodation in recent years and is now a certified resort area. Many travellers get off the 'Upolu ferry and head straight to its shallow, sandy beach. Many Manase accommodation providers will pick up from the ferry in Saleologa.

Regina's Beach Fales (☎ 596026; Main North Coast Rd, Manase; fale per person ST50) Regina's is overwhelmingly friendly, relaxing and great value for money, as the rate includes three delicious meals served up at a communal dining table. The *fale* have some colourful touches and are right on the beach, removed from the road by a strip of soft lawn. It's at the eastern end of the Manase strip.

Jane's Beach Fales (☎ 54066; Main North Coast Rd, Manase; fale per person ST50) Jane's has become one of the most popular places on the crowded Manase strip. There are lots of *fale* side by side here, each of them enclosed with and with a little deck, but somehow Jane's avoids feeling crowded – must be that soporific Manase Beach. Rates include breakfast and dinner. There's a bar here and canoes can be hired for ST10.

Le Lagoto Beach Resort (☎ 58189; lelagoto@samoa .ws; Main North Coast Rd, Fagamalo; s & d ST250-450, each extra person ST22; ✗) This resort's nice, low-key but expensive bungalows are fanned out along a wonderful little beach. Each can accommodate four people and is well-equipped with its own bathroom, kitchenette and TV. **Le Lagoto Restaurant** (breakfast &

lunch ST15, dinner ST30-40; ☽ breakfast, lunch & dinner) operates within a large *fale* and serves pastas, curries and fried meats, as well as a half-dozen vegetarian choices. Appended to it is a small bar fronting a calm, gorgeous cove.

Vacations Beach Fales (☎ 54024; www.pacific-resorts.com/samoa/vacations-resort; Main North Coast Rd, Manase; fale per person ST70) Vacations is pricey when compared to some of its neighbours, although you may decide this is justified by its long, comfortable *fale*, equipped with thick mattresses. Another temptation is the airy Jetty Bar, which has a beachfront deck and is the best place in the area for a drink.

Savai'i Lagoon Beach Resort (☎ 54168; savaii lagoon@samoa.ws; Main North Coast Rd, Fagamalo; s & d ST260, each extra person ST30; ✗) Next door to Le Lagoto is this friendly accommodation, with a half-dozen modern units painted a startling white inside and positioned to take advantage of any sea breeze. Rooms get lots of light and have good facilities, though they lack any real beachy character.

Tanu's Beach Fales (☎ /fax 54050; Main North Coast Rd, Manase; fale per person ST50) Tanu's has long dominated Manase's accommodation scene. It resembles a small village of *fale*, some spread along the beach and others arranged closer to the road. In the midst of this is a communal dining *fale* and a shop selling basic supplies. Tanu's has, however, grown so big that it lacks intimacy and seems increasingly impersonal. Rates include breakfast and dinner.

Stevenson's at Manase (☎ 58219; fax 24166; Main North Coast Rd, Manase; hotel d ST50, villa d ST250; ☒) The hotel rooms at Stevenson's are very cheap (they were being renovated when we visited and prices may rise) and the beachfront villas are spacious and attractive, but overall the place looks ragged and has a slightly barren atmosphere. It's an option if elsewhere in Manase is booked up, but check it out first.

NORTHWESTERN SAVAI'I

Western Savai'i ends at the remote Falealupo Peninsula, a snout-shaped piece of land where travellers can wobble across a rainforest swing bridge, acquaint themselves with some of Samoa's ancient legends and (technically) look into the future. Meanwhile, committed hikers can trek from A'opo up into the island's wild heart.

A'OPO CONSERVATION AREA & MOUNT SILISILI

It's possible to climb **Mount Silisili** (1866m), the Samoas' highest point, and at the same time experience the splendid natural confines of the **A'opo Conservation Area**. The peak itself is nondescript – really little more than a volcanic knob, much like scores of other little cinder cones in the area – but the two-day return trip takes you through some stunning and rarely visited rainforest. The lower part of the track is a plantation road; sections of the upper part are still covered by deadfall from the cyclones of the early '90s, which makes for slow going. Mt Silisili is part of the high Tuasivi Ridge, which affords great views from the road either side of A'opo.

Those interested in climbing Mt Silisili should speak to the *pulenu'u* (mayor) of A'opo (ask in the town's small shop for directions), who can arrange a guide for the trek. The charge is ST40 per person per day. You'll need to carry food and water for two (possibly three) days and provide supplies for the guide. It can be quite cold on the mountain at night, so also bring warm clothing, a sleeping bag and a tent. Sturdy walking boots are essential.

FALEALUPO PENINSULA

The wild and beautiful Falealupo Peninsula is where you'll find rock pools, caves, ancient star mounds and spectacular sunsets. **Cape Mulinu'u** is the most westerly land point on earth – the only place where you can see tomorrow. Take great care swimming around Cape Mulinu'u, though, or you could end up in the Solomons.

There's a good swimming beach at **Papa** on the northeastern side of the peninsula. Ask a local which track you should take off the main road to get here. Beach fees on the peninsula are usually ST5/2 per car/individual.

Falealupo Rainforest Preserve

Considered sacred by the villagers of Falealupo, this 1200-hectare area of lowland rainforest on the northern side of the peninsula became the first customary-owned conservation area in Samoa in 1989. This

SAVAI'I

GATEWAY TO THE UNDERWORLD

The Falealupo Peninsula figures prominently in local legend. The natural beauty
of the area belies the dark significance it
holds for Samoans, who believe that the
gateway to the underworld of the *aitu*
(spirits) is found here: the place where the
sun sets in the sea. According to tradition,
there are two entrances to the underworld,
one for chiefs and another for commoners.
One entrance is through a cave near Cape
Mulinu'u and the other is on the trail made
by the setting sun over the sea. During the
night, these spirits wander abroad, but at
daybreak they must return to their hell-
ish home or suffer the unpleasant consequences of being caught out by daylight.

was achieved thanks to the assistance of Dr
Paul Alan Cox, an American ethnobotanist
and founder of the conservation founda-
tion Seacology. Dr Cox was working with
indigenous healers in Falealupo when he
discovered that the *matai* (chief) of the
area had reluctantly signed a contract with
a Japanese logging firm in order to pay for
the construction of a primary school in the
village.

After watching the whole village weeping over the loss of their rainforest, Dr Cox
decided to personally guarantee the money
for the school. On learning of this, Chief
Fuiono Senio ran 9km through the forest
to stop the bulldozers toppling another tree.
Unfortunately, the reserve suffered serious
damage during the cyclones of the early '90s
(60% of the trees were destroyed, and bird
and bat numbers dropped significantly),
but it is slowly and surely recovering.

Canopy Walkway

The prime attraction on Falealupo Peninsula, besides its natural beauty, is the **Canopy
Walkway** (Falealupo Rd; admission ST20; ☉ 7am-6pm),
which allows you to scale a stately 225-year-
old banyan tree, and even sleep up there,
too. Technically it's not really a 'canopy
walkway' as there's no canopy as such, but
still, it's an impressive engineering feat and
well worth visiting.

The walkway consists of a 24m-long swing
bridge hoisted 9m above the rainforest floor
(it has a mean sway to it), and a 20m stair-

way that ends in the uppermost reaches of
the banyan tree. The tree house at the end of
the climb is really just a platform (no roof),
but the view is spectacular and it can be a
magical place to spend the night; for more
info, see opposite.

The fee for admission, which also covers
entry to the Rock House and Moso's Footprint (keep the receipt as proof), is payable
at the *fale*-kiosk off Falealupo Rd, beside the
primary school.

Moso's Footprint

The ancient 1m by 3m rock enclosure called
Moso's Footprint (Falealupo Rd; admission incl in Canopy
Walkway ticket; ☉ 7am-6pm) is easy to miss – look
for the red signpost beside a large white
church. Legend has it that the giant Moso
made the footprint – which is garlanded
by seashells and reveals that Moso had one
hell of a big toe – when he stepped from
Fiji to Samoa. There is said to be another
'footprint' on the Fijian island of Viti Levu
that marks his point of departure.

The scientific explanation is a bit more
complicated. When lava cools and contracts,
it breaks into blocks. These blocks are often
lifted and moved by tree roots growing down
into the joints. Once they're on the surface, a
cyclone could easily clear them away, leaving
various indentations in the crust.

Falealupo Ruins & Rock House

Cyclones Ofa and Val struck the peninsula
in 1990 and 1991, completely destroying the
village of Falealupo, which villagers have rebuilt slightly inland and renamed Falealupo-
uta; the original village is now known as
Falealupo-tai. The ruins of the old **Catholic
church** (Falealupo Rd) are eerie, particularly when
you stand amongst them, look out at the
ocean and imagine the winds and waves that
shattered the stonework.

About 300m southwest of the church are
the two closely associated lava tubes known
as the **Rock House** (Falealupo Rd; admission incl in Canopy
Walkway ticket; ☉ 7am-6pm). Inside is a crude
stone armchair and stone benches around
the sides. Legend has it that the Rock House
is the result of a competition between the
men and the women of Falealupo to find out
which sex was more adept at house building.
At the end of the first day of construction, the
men were winning so the women decided to
stay up and work through the night while the

men were asleep. The women won, of course, and the men were so angry about it that they never finished their house, leaving the obvious hole in the ceiling.

Fafa O Sauali'i

At Cape Mulinu'u you'll find **Fafa O Sauai'i** (Falealupo Rd; car ST10; 8.30am-5pm Mon-Sat). A guided tour takes you a few minutes inland to see the small, watery Vaatausili Cave and a mossy, near-empty pool mysteriously called Blood Well, before doubling back to the real attraction – a chance to scamper over large blocks of lava and stand on the tip of Cape Mulinu'u, the westernmost point of land in the world. A big white 'X' has been painted there for your convenience. While you're out here, take a swim in the lovely ocean pool created by the lava outflow.

The admission price isn't really worth it if you've driven here on your own, but is arguably reasonable for a group.

WEST-COAST BEACHES

There are pleasant beaches at **Fai'a'ai**, about 16km southeast of the Falealupo Peninsula, and nearby at **Foailalo** and **Satuiatua**. The custom fee for day use of any of these beaches is usually ST5/2 per car/person.

Satuiatua has an excellent left-hand surf break. Surfers pay a ST10 levy, which is used to support the local school. Unfortunately we found a disturbing amount of broken glass in the sand at the northern end of the beach.

SLEEPING & EATING

Vaisala Beach Hotel (58016; fax 58017; off Main North Coast Rd, Vaisala; s/d/tr/q/f from ST90/105/115/125/140;) Except for one budget room (single/double ST60/70), all rooms here face the ocean beyond an attractive little beach. The serene vistas from the first-floor balconies are highly recommended. The hotel restaurant (lunch ST6-15, dinner ST38; lunch & dinner) resembles a large dining hall and has a great outdoor deck. It does good set-menu dinners and guests are occasionally serenaded by local musicians, one of whom is a whiz on the 'Samoan cello' (a unique arrangement of overturned bucket, stick and twine). Breakfast is included in the price.

Banyan tree (per person ST50) The Canopy Walkway (opposite) in the Falealupo Rainforest Preserve offers accommodation in the top of a banyan tree. The tree house sleeps up to six people and mattresses and mosquito nets should be provided, as should shelter in bad weather (there's no roof). Breakfast and dinner are included in the price and are served down below, so banish any hopes of tree-top room service. But keep your liquid intake low, as it's a long climb down to the toilet. There's no telephone number for bookings but it's highly unlikely the tree house will be booked up.

Satuiatua Beach Fales (/fax 56026; Main South Coast Rd, Satuiatua; fale per person ST65) The beach here is good for snorkelling and surfing, and breakfast and dinner are part of the package. But this doesn't really justify the unusually high accommodation rate. *Fale* sleep two to eight people and some sport mattresses on a futon-style arrangement. The restaurant (lunch ST6-12, dinner ST25; lunch & dinner) is set up on a spacious outdoor deck and does good dinners, from chicken schnitzel to meat balls and fish curry.

There are several groupings of basic **fale** off the sandy track that runs around Falealupo Peninsula between Tufutafoe and Falealupo-tai. Most charge ST40 to ST50 per person for accommodation, breakfast and dinner. A few years back this area was subject to regular thefts and travellers have since tended to stay away. We couldn't confirm if these problems are ongoing or not. Talk to other travellers and to the Samoa Hotels Association in Apia (see p64) before sleeping beside the fabulously wild ocean here.

SOUTHERN SAVAI'I

Hidden off plantation tracks between the southern slopes of Tuasivi Ridge and Savai'i's southern coastline you'll find the ancient Polynesian marvel known as Pulemelei Mound and, nearby, Afu Aau Falls, one of the loveliest waterfall and swimming hole combinations you could hope for. As if to make up for the absolute serenity of these two sites, the south coast also yields the mighty gushing antics of the Alofaaga Blowholes.

AFU AAU FALLS

On the Letolo Plantation, once the biggest plantation on the island, is the utterly beautiful **Afu Aau Falls** (off Main South Coast Rd; person/car

ST2/10; ☻ 7am-5pm), one of the highlights of a visit to Savai'i. Also known as Olemoe Falls, this jungle waterfall plunges into the crystalline waters of a 3m-deep pool, which is marvellous for cooling off on a hot day. The waterfall is on the Falealila Stream, a small watercourse that frequently dries up. An underground spring feeds the pool, however, so the water level remains constant.

The plantation track to the falls leads off the main road about 300m west of the iron-girder bridge at the western edge of Vailoa village. The turn-off is marked by two tall iron poles and the track itself is bordered by low stone walls. Several hundred metres along the track is a *fale* where you pay admission to the falls; the fee also covers entry to Pulemelei Mound, accessed off the same track. From the *fale* you cross a rocky stream (which may not be passable after heavy rain) then continue for 500m to the waterfall sign. Leave your car here if you've driven and follow the side-trail across a small valley, usually occupied by grazing horses. After scaling the hill at the eastern end, you look down on an idyllic little chasm with the waterfall at one end. The path down to the waterhole is steep and slippery, with a makeshift ladder near the bottom.

You can normally negotiate the bumpy plantation track in a high-clearance 2WD, except after heavy rain when it becomes muddy.

PULEMELEI MOUND

Polynesia's largest ancient structure is **Pulemelei Mound** (off Main South Coast Rd; ☻ 7am-5pm), which is also known as Tia Seu Ancient Mound. It's on the Letolo Plantation, not far from Afu Aau Falls; the entry fee for the falls also covers admission to the mound. This large pyramid, measuring 61m by 50m at its base and rising in two tiers to a height of more than 12m, is almost squarely oriented with the compass directions. It's a wonderfully enigmatic place – standing on top of it, you can see south all the way to the ocean in one direction, while in the opposite direction trees are wrapped in enormous vines and other jungle foliage. On sunny days, butterflies of all colours swarm across the mound.

Samoan oral traditions imply that all ancient Polynesian monuments, such as

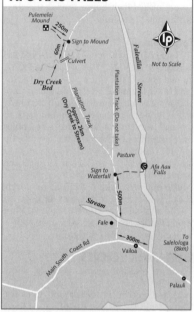

Pulemelei, were used for pigeon snaring. However, given its similarity to religious structures in Central America and midwestern USA, archaeologists have difficulty believing this. The complexity of its design and the effort expended in its construction leads them to believe that it may have had a religious purpose, perhaps even a strategic one considering the sightline to the coast.

Follow the directions given in the Afu Aau Falls section to reach the waterfall sign. Continue past the sign and follow the main track as it veers to the left (ignore the track that continues straight ahead). You'll soon reach the short signposted walking trail which leads to the mound. You can drive all the way to the start of this trail, but the walk through the lush heartland of Letolo Plantation is well worth it.

ALOFAAGA BLOWHOLES

The impressive **Alofaaga Blowholes** (Taga; adult/child ST5/2.50; ☻ 7am-6pm) are best seen at high tide, preferably when a storm is whipping up the ocean and white foam is soaring up over the black rocks along this stretch of coast. Pay the entry fee at the first *fale* and park your car at the second *fale*, near the main blowhole; if you drive into the accommodation compound you'll be charged ST5 to park there. Locals often demonstrate the power of the waves by tossing a coconut into the blowhole at just the right moment to send it flying up to 60m into the air. A word of warning – don't get too close to the edge of the blowhole or lava coast. Huge freak waves can appear from nowhere to wash you off your feet.

Keen walkers can follow an old track around the coast to the now deserted village of **Fagaloa** (three to four hours return).

SLEEPING & EATING

Alofaaga Beach Fales (☎ 594406; Taga; fale per person ST60) Located just opposite Alofaaga's main blowhole are five newish *fale*. The noise of surf hitting this rocky coastline may not suit light sleepers. The phone number belongs to the 3-Corner Store in Taga; ask for Juna. Price includes breakfast and dinner.

Meaole Beach Fales (Taga; fale per person ST70) These *fale* lie to the east of the Alofaaga Blowholes in a distinctive tropical setting, planted on black volcanic sand on the edge of a rough and rocky beach. Makeshift benches are arranged under leaning coconut palms. The price is high but includes all meals.

SAVAI'I

Tutuila

The serpentine island of Tutuila has some of the most dramatic scenery in the Samoan islands, if not the Pacific. It's impossible not to be impressed by the magnificent harbour at Pago Pago – a bowl of water dotted with supply ships and yachts, and surrounded by towering peaks and sheer cliffs. Many of the bays that indent the coastline make superb spectacles with their combinations of aquamarine water, bleached sand or rock-stubbled foreshores, nodding palms, and snoozing village houses and *fale* (traditional thatched houses). Forested mountains rise steeply up behind it all to converge on a jagged central ridge that gives willing hikers an inspiring perspective on the island's wild geography.

Don't believe all the bad press that the main island of American Samoa tends to attract. True, it does rain a lot, but there are also abundant blue-sky days when everyone makes a beeline for Alega Beach or one of the beachside parks around Utulei and Tafuna. Yes, much of the food is super-rich, meat-based fare that will scare the intestines out of anyone committed to healthy eating (or vegetables). But there are still plenty of good meals to be had, particularly if you are lucky enough to enjoy the hospitality of locals on a market day or when fresh seafood catches are around. And OK, the territory's capital and other urban areas can be infested with litter. But only a short drive away are bewitching switchbacks through mountain passes, pristine marine sanctuaries, and a small offshore island where rocky coves give way to quicksand lakes.

HIGHLIGHTS

- Hiking along a rocky ridge towards the summit of **Mount Alava** (p108) on a crisp, sunny morning
- Wading through knee-high grass to get a close-up of red quicksand on **Aunu'u** (p121)
- Motoring up the switchback to Rainmaker Pass and then winding down through the lovely **National Park of American Samoa** (p115) to friendly **Vatia** (p116) and the superb **Pola Tai** (p116)
- Swimming at gorgeous **Alega Beach** (p116), then being spoiled rotten at **Tisa's Barefoot Bar** (p117)
- Exploring coastal rainforest and snorkelling among the fish and coral at sublime **Fagatele Bay National Marine Sanctuary** (p118)

- POPULATION: 55,000
- AREA: 1813 SQ KM

TUTUILA

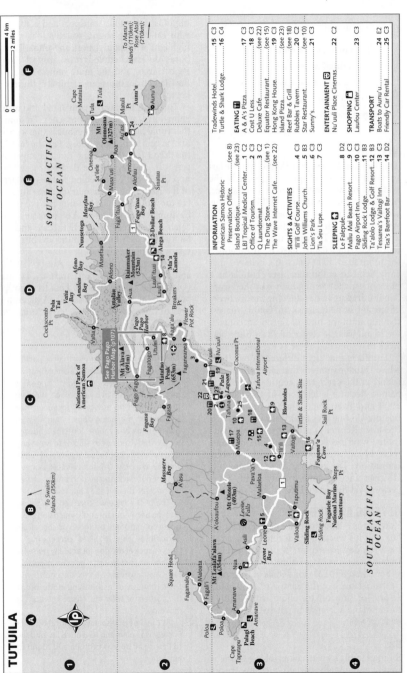

TUTUILA

HISTORY

The Samoans believe that Tutuila was the last island of the archipelago to be created by the god Tagaloa, and once it came into existence, he asked Tutu and Ila (the children of Fue, who was the son of Tagaloa) to populate it. Archaeological finds near the villages of Tula and Aoa, and at To'aga on the island of Ofu, reveal that the islands have been inhabited for more than 3000 years. It's believed that early Samoan authorities used Tutuila as a place of exile for wrongdoers banished from 'Upolu. Studies made following the discovery of ancient stone quarries on Tutuila suggest that, up until the time of European contact, the island was the centre of a vast trade network that stretched as far as the Solomons.

Tutuila is a far sight different today from when Dutch explorers first laid eyes on the island in the early 18th century. American Samoa became a territory of the USA in 1900 and Pago Pago Harbor found itself hosting US Marines for most of WWII. US President Kennedy decided the islands' traditional ways needed updating in 1960, and there began a period of intensive Americanisation. The reliance of the islands on US assistance became a daily reality after cyclone Val devastated the islands in 1991.

GETTING AROUND

You can get to most places on Tutuila by bus. But it's worth considering hiring a car for a few days to explore some of the more isolated sections of coastline.

See Aunu'u (p123) for details of transport to that island. See the Samoan Islands Directory for info on travelling from Tutuila to the Manu'a Islands by air (p147) and by boat (p148).

Bus

Riding Tutuila's squat, colourful 'aiga buses – small, individually owned pick-up trucks

modified for public transport and equipped with ear-busting sound systems – is a real highlight of a visit to American Samoa. These buses do unscheduled runs around Pago Pago Harbor and the more remote areas of the island from the main terminal at the market in Fagatogo.

To stop a bus, wave your hand and arm, palm down, as the bus approaches. To signal that you'd like to get off the bus, either knock on the ceiling or clap loudly. Pay the fare to the driver (try to have the exact change) or leave the money on the dashboard as you hop off. If you're travelling to the outskirts of the island, be at the market first thing in the morning and start heading back to town by 4pm at the very latest. You'll be lucky to catch a bus after 2pm on Saturday, and on Sunday the only buses running will be those taking people to church.

Buses regularly head east to Aua (US$0.75) and Tula (US$1.25), and west to Tafuna (US$1) and Leone (US$1). Less frequently, buses go to Fagasa (US$0.75), A'oloaufou over on the central ridge (US$1), Amanave

MAN'S BEST FRIEND?

Aggressive dogs are more than a passing nuisance on Tutuila. They are often frightening and sometimes downright dangerous, particularly when in a large pack. We were given conflicting advice by locals on how to deal with menacing dogs. When we were bailed up by two canines outside a house , we were advised not to stop or to wave anything at them, but to just slowly and calmly walk on our way. Other locals told us never to turn our back on any dog and to wave a big stick at them if they approached.

The best advice we received was to imitate the behaviour through which dogs have been conditioned by locals to be afraid. Sometimes this involves pretending to throw a rock at the dog (or actually throwing it if the animal doesn't get the message). Samoans also make a clucking noise with their tongues or a shhhhing noise out of the corners of their mouths to tell dogs to move on.

At the time of research, the local Humane Society was planning to launch an initiative to license all dogs on Tutuila and round up any strays.

(US$1.25), and Fagamalo in the far northwest (US$1.50); a trip to the northwest villages often means disembarking at Leone and catching another bus from there. Buses also head over Rainmaker Pass to Vatia; bus fares range from US$0.75 to US$1.50.

Car

Tutuila's one main road (signposted Route 1) follows the twisty coastline from Fagamalo in the northwest of the island to Onenoa in the far northeast, a distance of around 50km. Several narrower paved roads connect this road with outlying villages, particularly those along the heavily eroded north coast. The main road between Pago Pago and Tafuna has been shored up with a sea wall to protect it against the big waves generated during storms.

A 2WD is fine for motoring around Tutuila and petrol stations are scattered around the island. Car-hire agencies charge between US$60 and US$100 per day, with discounts offered for longer rentals; shop around for the best price.

Several local car-hire firms offered us contracts where there was no option of accepting a CDW (collision/damage waiver). Staff tried to reassure us that only a maximum excess of US$1000 would apply if there was an accident, and then only if it was our fault. But according to the fine print on these contracts, the lack of a CDW technically means that the car hirer is liable for *all* costs resulting from an accident, regardless of whose fault it is. Sign such contracts at your peril. You should insist on a CDW, for which you pay an extra fee of around US$8 to US$10 per day.

Some recommended companies:

Avis Car Rental (Map p103; ☎ 699 2746; res@avissamoa.com; Tafuna International Airport)
Friendly Car Rental (Map p107; ☎ 699 7186; Tafuna)
Kokonut Car Rentals (Map p107; ☎ 633 7855; kokonutrentals@yahoo.com; Pago Pago)
Sadie's Car Rentals (Map p107; ☎ 633 5981; sadies@samoatelco.com; Sadie Thompson Inn, Pago Pago)

Taxi

Taxis are plentiful in Pago Pago, Nu'uuli and Tafuna, but are prohibitively expensive for island touring if you're travelling alone. Just to get from Fagatogo to Tafuna can cost up to US$15, while a trip out to Leone will cost at least US$18.

PAGO PAGO

pop 5500

Pago Pago (it's pronounced pango pango; neighbouring Samoa refers to it as 'pungo pungo') is a place with a strong reputation for seediness, yet an equally strong reputation for beauty. When you arrive in town and see Pago Pago's ragged main street and its hulking tuna canneries framed by a rippling harbour and stunning jagged cliffs, you'll probably agree on both counts.

This truly is one of the most spectacular harbours in the world, all that remains of the volcanic crater that created Tutuila. There are times when it looks extraordinarily beautiful, such as when mist rolls across its steep forested peaks in a way that makes it look like it's seeping up from between the trees. The harbour waters used to be regarded as a cesspool, but have been dramatically cleaned up in recent years with the removal of shipwrecks and improved handling of cannery waste.

There is not much to the town itself, which has been subject to low standards of maintenance and at times appears to be populated by nothing but pick-up trucks. Also, on a 'bad tuna day', it won't just be the surrounding views that take your breath away. But look beyond the traffic and the monotony of the main strip (not to mention the abundant rain) to the serene summit of Mt Alava, the vitality of the Friday night market and the infectious indolence of the locals.

ORIENTATION

The several small villages around the harbour area that contain the territorial government and most of the industry and commerce in American Samoa are known collectively as Pago Pago, after the small settlement at the harbour's western end – the territory's actual capital is the village of Fagatogo, on the southern side of the harbour. Utulei is where the government offices are located, while Anua hosts the tuna canneries. Fagatogo contains the post office, central market and bus station, as well as the newish Fagatogo Sq shopping complex and the *Malae o Le Talu* (Town Square), a semi-circular slice of lawn with a *fale*-style bandstand at one end.

TUTUILA

Maps

The Office of Tourism distributes a small, fold-out *American Samoa* map (free) which has a plan of Pago Pago on one side. The map was last published in August 2004 and so is reasonably up-to-date.

INFORMATION

This section includes details of facilities located in nearby Nu'uuli and Tafuna.

Bookshops

Iupeli Siliva Wesley Bookshop (Map p107; ☎ 633 2201) Sells mainly Christian and educational books, but also has a small selection of Samoa history and culture titles, plus some mass-market paperbacks.

Transpac Store (Map p103; ☎ 699 9589; Nu'uuli) Stocks a decent range of Samoa-focused books, including some local publications.

Emergency

Ambulance (☎ 911)
Fire (☎ 911, 633 5000)
Police (☎ 911, 633 1111)

Internet Access

Internet access usually costs US$2 to US$3 per 15 minutes.

DDW (Don't Drink the Water; Map p107; ☎ 633 5297; ☾ 6.30am-2.30pm Mon-Fri, 6.30am-noon Sat)

Feleti Barstow Public Library (Map p107; ☎ 633 5816; ☾ 9am-5pm Mon, Wed & Fri, 9am-7pm Tue & Thu, 10am-2pm Sat) By obtaining a temporary library card (for details, see right) you can use this library's Internet-connected machines in the 2nd-floor Computer Lab. Alternatively, you can pay US$5 to access the computers for a single day.

Wave Internet Cafe (Map p103; ☎ 699 7077; Nu'uuli Place Shopping Center; ☾ 9am-9pm Mon-Sat) It's beside the cinemas.

Laundry

Laundries commonly charge US$0.75/1 to wash/dry one load.

Bayview Wash & Dry (Map p107; ☎ 633 4901; ☾ 8am-7pm Mon-Sat)

IBM Laundromat (☎ 633 5963; ☾ 5.30am-8pm)

Q Laundromat (Map p103; ☎ 699 4934; Nu'uuli; ☾ 9am-10pm)

Libraries

Feleti Barstow Public Library (Map p107; ☎ 633 5816; ☾ 9am-5pm Mon, Wed & Fri, 9am-7pm Tue & Thu, 10am-2pm Sat) This library has a good Pacific collection. Visitors can get a temporary library card – you need to produce a photo ID and pay US$25 (refundable) – which allows them to loan up to two books at one time.

Medical Services

Drug Store (Map p103; ☎ 633 4630; Faga'alu; ☾ 7.45am-5pm Mon-Fri, 7.45am-2pm Sat) This well-stocked pharmacy is on the road to the LBJ Tropical Medical Center.

Island Boutique (Map p103; ☎ 699 5335; Laufou Center, Nu'uuli; ☾ 8am-8pm Mon-Fri, 8am-6pm Sat) This generic gift store has a well-stocked pharmacy in one corner.

LBJ Tropical Medical Center (Map p103; ☎ 633 1222-29; Faga'alu; ☾ emergency 24hr) This centre can

---

PAGO PAGO IN...

One Day

Fuel up early in the morning with a big breakfast at **DDW** (p112) and then hike up along the ridge to the summit of **Mount Alava** (p108). For a full day of hiking, continue down the other side of the mountain to Vatia. Return to Pago Pago and wander through Fagatogo, stopping off at the **Jean P Haydon Museum** (p109) and the **Fono** (p110), then head east of town for an afternoon of swimming at **Alega Beach** (p116), followed by drinks and possibly an overnight stay at **Tisa's Barefoot Bar** (p117).

Two Days

You won't know you're really in American Samoa unless you eat Samoan pancakes, eggs and steak at **Mom's Place** (p112) for breakfast. If you haven't already organised a tour of the **Michael J Kirwan TV Studios** (p109), consider visiting the **old cable car terminal** (p108) on Solo Hill. Have an afternoon drink on the outside deck of the **Pago Pago Yacht Club** (p113). If it's a Friday evening, head to the **market** (p108) to soak up the social atmosphere. If it's a Thursday, catch the **fiafia** (time of celebration; p114) at Sadie Thompson Inn. On any other night, have a Mexican dinner at **Evie's Cantina** (p113).

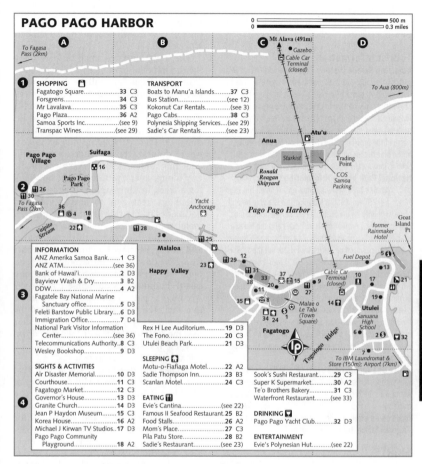

PAGO PAGO HARBOR

SHOPPING
Fagatogo Square...................33 C3
Forsgrens...........................34 C3
Mr Lavalava.......................35 C3
Pago Plaza.........................36 A2
Samoa Sports Inc................(see 9)
Transpac Wines.................(see 29)

TRANSPORT
Boats to Manu'a Islands........37 C3
Bus Station.........................(see 12)
Kokonut Car Rentals.............(see 3)
Pago Cabs...........................38 C3
Polynesia Shipping Services....(see 29)
Sadie's Car Rentals.............(see 23)

INFORMATION
ANZ Amerika Samoa Bank.......1 C3
ANZ ATM..........................(see 36)
Bank of Hawai'i....................2 D3
Bayview Wash & Dry.............3 B2
DDW..................................4 A2
Fagatele Bay National Marine
  Sanctuary office.................5 D3
Feleti Barstow Public Library....6 D3
Immigration Office.................7 D4
National Park Visitor Information
  Center............................(see 36)
Telecommunications Authority..8 C3
Wesley Bookshop...................9 D3

SIGHTS & ACTIVITIES
Air Disaster Memorial............10 D3
Courthouse.........................11 C3
Fagatogo Market..................12 C3
Governor's House.................13 D3
Granite Church....................14 D3
Jean P Haydon Museum.........15 C3
Korea House........................16 A2
Michael J Kirwan TV Studios...17 D3
Pago Pago Community
  Playground.......................18 A2

Rex H Lee Auditorium...........19 D3
The Fono...........................20 C3
Utulei Beach Park.................21 D3

SLEEPING
Motu-o-Fiafiaga Motel...........22 A2
Sadie Thompson Inn..............23 B3
Scanlan Motel.....................24 C3

EATING
Evie's Cantina.....................(see 22)
Famous II Seafood Restaurant.25 B2
Food Stalls.........................26 A2
Mom's Place.......................27 C3
Pila Patu Store....................28 B2
Sadie's Restaurant..............(see 23)

Sook's Sushi Restaurant.........29 C3
Super K Supermarket............30 A2
Te'o Brothers Bakery.............31 C3
Waterfront Restaurant........(see 33)

DRINKING
Pago Pago Yacht Club...........32 D3

ENTERTAINMENT
Evie's Polynesian Hut...........(see 22)

provide basic medical services, but anyone suffering serious medical problems is advised to go to Hawai'i or New Zealand.

Money

Note that there are no banks or money-changers at Tafuna International Airport, so bring some US dollars with you.

ANZ Amerika Samoa Bank (Map p107; ☎ 633 1151; 8.30am-3pm Mon-Fri, walk-up window 3-4.30pm Mon-Fri, 9am-noon Sat) Has an ATM. There are other ANZ ATMs at Pago Plaza and inside the Tradewinds Hotel (p120) and Cost U Less (p121).

Bank of Hawai'i (Map p107; ☎ 633 4226; Centennial Office Bldg; 9am-3pm Mon-Fri) This branch has an ATM. There's another Bank of Hawai'i ATM off the main road to the airport, about a 20-minute walk from the terminal.

Post

Post office (Map p107; 9am-3.30pm Mon-Fri, 9am-1pm Sat) Travellers should have mail addressed to themselves care of General Delivery, Pago Pago, American Samoa 96799.

Telephone

Telecommunications Authority (Map p107; ☎ 633 1121; 24hr) There's a choice of phonecard or operator-assisted calls for international connections. Phonecards are usually cheaper for short calls to Australia, New Zealand and the US.

Toilets

You'll find clean public toilets inside Pago Plaza, but these are locked away behind a security grill outside normal shopping hours. There's another toilet block at Utulei Beach Park.

Tourist Information

American Samoa Historic Preservation Office (Map p103; Ashpo; ☎ 633 2384; www.ashpo.org; Matafao) This is an excellent contact for history buffs and, given reasonable notice, may be able to take interested people on tours to isolated star mounds (p116); tours are free but you'll probably need your own vehicle. The office is about 400m north of the turn-off to the LBJ Tropical Medical Center, in the blue timber building opposite Matafao Elementary School; look for the black sign with gold lettering.

National Park Visitor Information Center (Map p107; ☎ 633 7082; www.nps.gov/npsa/home.htm; Pago Plaza; ⊙ 7.30am-4.30pm Mon-Fri) This is a very helpful place, with info on the National Park of American Samoa and the general environments of Tutuila and the Manu'a Islands, including walking trails. Pick up the free *National Park of American Samoa* leaflet, and check out the seashell exhibit. The National Park Service (NPS) runs a homestay programme (www.nps.gov/npsa/homestay/index.htm) where visitors are put in touch with villagers who offer accommodation and an opportunity to learn about local customs and crafts. Options have become much more limited in recent years, but at the time of research there were still a couple of possibilities around Vatia on Tutuila, and on Ofu and Ta'u. The cost averages around US$40 per day, including food.

Office of Tourism (Map p103; ☎ 699 9411; www.am samoa.com/tourism; Tafuna; ⊙ 7.30am-4pm Mon-Fri) Along with the brochures and maps the office can supply, make sure you pick up a copy of *A Walking Tour of Historic Fagatogo*, an excellent free booklet published by the American Samoa Historic Preservation Office.

SIGHTS

It's not hard to locate the attractions of Pago Pago as they're all either on or not far off the main road that loops around the harbour. The exception is the walking track to Mt Alava, which necessitates a trip up to Fagasa Pass to the west of town.

Mount Alava & Old Cable Car Terminals

Towering above Pago Pago Harbor is 491m Mt Alava, part of the mountain ridge marking the southern boundary of the Tutuila section of the National Park of American Samoa. The NPS maintains the 5.5km **trail** (1½ to two hours) that follows the ridge to the top of Mt Alava. It's an excellent walk, with spectacular views from the summit. You'll see birds and possibly bats, and may even be lucky enough to see whales out to sea to the northwest of the island (the best time of year for whale spotting is October/November).

The trail begins at a small car park (look for the national park sign) at Fagasa Pass, 2km from Pago Pago village. It's an often steep, rocky 4WD track (no unauthorised vehicles allowed) that has significant muddy stretches, even if it hasn't rained for a while. After the first section of the climb you look down on the lovely sweep of Fagasa Bay, where dolphins take shelter on their annual migrations. About two-thirds of the way along, after the track levels out, look for a track heading uphill to your right – a lookout treats you to terrific views on both sides of the ridge. On the summit, a metal stairway leads up to the rusted remains of a cable car terminal (see below) and a TV transmission tower. The views from here down over the harbour, reefs and open sea, west back down the ridge, and east to Rainmaker Mountain are awesome. A concrete path heads around the tower to a sheltered rest *fale*. Directly behind the *fale*, a newer, very steep trail (with ladders in some sections) leads a further 4km down to Vaita. It takes about an hour to descend, but at least twice that to return.

A **cable car** once ran 1.8km across Pago Pago Harbor from Solo Hill to the top of Mt Alava. It was constructed in 1965 as a service access to the TV transmission equipment on the mountain and was one of the world's longest single-span cable-car routes. Operations stopped many years ago, however, and the NPS trail became the access route to the TV antenna. The cable car terminals are still in place, as is a cable, which plunges dramatically towards the harbour.

During a Flag Day military demonstration in 1980, a US Navy plane hit the cables and crashed into the Rainmaker Hotel below. All six naval personnel aboard were killed, as were two hotel guests. A small white **monument** near the Solo Hill terminal commemorates those who died in the disaster. You can walk to it in 10 minutes by following the side road that branches off near the TV studios, but we came across a large pack of dogs on this road and recommend caution.

Market

For the majority of the week, the central market contains only a few scattered fruit stalls. But it comes to life on Friday night, when local growers sell bananas, coconuts, breadfruit and other fresh produce, and Tutuilans arrive to shop, socialise and scoff cheap meals. Sometimes it seems that half of Pago Pago is packed into the marketplace. Trading usually continues until early on Saturday morning – by the time the market reopens later that morning, all the best stuff is gone. On special occasions, such as national holidays, the market serves as a bingo hall and the turnout is phenomenal.

Michael J Kirwan TV Studios

The pioneer programme of broadcasting school lessons to elementary and secondary students began at the **Michael J Kirwan TV Studios** (☎ 633 4191) during the modernisation rush of the Governor Lee era. Nowadays, since schools started relying more on Web broadcasting, the facility's two studios are used exclusively to produce programmes for KVZK, the territory's government-run TV station.

Call to make an appointment if you'd like a free guided tour of the studio. The informal tours only take 20 to 30 minutes but are interesting, if only to see how a modern TV studio can be run on a shoestring. When you arrive for the tour, walk in through the doors facing the road and enter the first office on the right.

Jean P Haydon Museum

This interesting **museum** (☎ 633 4347; admission free; ⏲ 10am-3pm Mon-Fri) was named after its founder, the wife of Governor John Haydon. It is set in a building that was constructed in 1917 to house the original naval commissary, after which it served as the main post office.

The museum displays artefacts of early Samoa, including the *va'a* (bonito canoes) and *alia* (war canoes) that inspired the first European name for Samoa, the Navigator Islands. There are also other items that were in common use in early island life, such as coconut-shell combs, seashell and whales' teeth necklaces, fruit and seed jewellery, pigs' tusk armlets, fly whisks, bamboo panpipes, *siapo* (bark cloth made from the paper mulberry tree), stone tools and an impressive array of weapons. Especially fascinating is the display of native pharmacopoeia used by the early Polynesians, and the exhibit on traditional tattooing.

TUTUILA

SADIE THOMPSON

American Samoans will assure you that Sadie Thompson is a historical figure, and the account they provide of her antics is far more comprehensive than the one Somerset Maugham gave in his classic novel *Rain*.

The tale of Sadie Thompson was written after Maugham was delayed in rainy Pago Pago by an outbreak of measles while en route between Honolulu and Papeete on the steamship *Sonoma*. It is assumed that he stayed at the Rainmaker Boarding House with his US lover Gerald Haxton. There is some dispute over just where the boarding house was located, but it's generally agreed it stood on the main street in Fagatogo. Some locals believe it was the building currently housing the Sadie Thompson Inn – it would be nice to believe this, considering the building's style and atmosphere.

Samoans say that the historical Sadie Thompson, who lived upstairs in this building, was a laundress by day and practised her trade by night. We may never know her real name, but the woman Maugham called Sadie Thompson had been evicted from Honolulu's red-light district and travelled south in hope of finding a new market for her goods. While Maugham's ship and its passengers were detained in Pago Pago, the Reverend Davidson, a holier-than-thou missionary who also happened to be holed up in the same hotel, developed more than a passing concern for Miss Thompson's immortal soul. He set about changing her ways and persuaded her to repent. In the end, however, it was she who changed *his* ways (or at least brought out the human and humane in him).

Maugham's story more or less ends there, but Samoans go on to say that Sadie stayed on in Pago Pago and continued her chosen profession until one night she was found drunk in the rain somewhere in Fagatogo. A police officer allegedly gathered her up and placed her, unconscious, on an Australia-bound steamer.

'*Ava* (traditional, mildly intoxicating drink, also called *kava*) ceremonies and weaving and wood carving demonstrations sometimes take place in the *fale* beside the museum.

Fono

The Fono (legislature) comprises a large and impressive group of buildings down on the waterfront, and is where American Samoan law-makers convene and legislate during the months of January and July. Traditional Samoan architecture and building styles were integrated into the structure, built in 1973 at a cost of US$1 million, including the *fale afolau* style, which may be seen as the primary home design in Samoa, and the *fale tele* (meeting house) design.

Those interested in attending a session should drop by or call the **Office of the Senate Legislature** (☎ 633 5231) to confirm the date of the next sitting.

Governor's House

In 1903 a two-storey wooden colonial mansion was built atop *Mauga o Ali'i* (Chief's Hill). It served as the home for all of American Samoa's naval commanders until the Department of the Interior took control of it in 1951, after which it was used by territorial governors as their residence. When we visited the house, it looked like it had been hit by a cyclone and the governor was occupying a new residence at the foot of the hill. It turned out that the original building was being completely renovated, a process that may take several years. You can walk up to the site via the stone staircase that starts opposite the Fuel Dock.

Flower Pot Rock

Pretty Flower Pot Rock, or Fatumafuti, is planted in the sea near the village of Faga'alu. Legend says that Fatu and Futi were lovers living on the Manu'a Islands who wanted to marry but were forbidden to because they were members of the same '*aiga* (family). Fatu, the woman, built a coconut raft and set off for Tutuila. When Futi learned that she had gone, he was distraught and set out after her. Both their boats were destroyed by a tsunami as they approached Tutuila and the two lovers were stranded on the reef near Fatumafuti where they have remained to this day. The area near the rock is a good spot for picnics.

Tuna Canneries

American Samoa's two big tuna canneries are found in the kilometre-long industrial complex on the northern side of the harbour. One company is Starkist, the home of 'Charlie Tuna' and the largest tuna processing plant in the world. The other is COS Samoa Packing, which strangely markets tuna as 'Chicken of the Sea'. The olfactory assault of these canneries when you get near them is unbelievable. They also seem weirdly threatening at night when they're ablaze in spotlights and emitting the muffled drone of machinery.

Charlie probably wouldn't want to be 'Starkist' if he knew what went on at the cannery. It's estimated that US$250 million worth of tuna is processed each year in American Samoa, amounting to 9.7 million cases (at 48 cans to a case). Most of the workers relegated to the unpleasant task of cutting and cleaning the fish are Samoans and Tongans earning around US$3.30 per hour. Though the wage is meagre by American standards, it would be unheard of in the workers' home countries.

Both **Starkist** (☎ 644 4231) and **COS** (☎ 644 5272) conduct free guided tours lasting between 30 minutes and one hour. Tours need to be organised at least 48 hours in advance. You'll need to wear long trousers and enclosed shoes to take part.

WALKING TOUR

Start your tour in **Pago Pago village (1)**. The village that's given its name to the entire harbour area may be labelled 'low rent' by expats, but it looks no more dishevelled than the rest of town. At the head of the harbour is a large reclaimed area called **Pago Pago Park (2)**, where there's a football field and basketball and tennis courts. **Korea House (3)** was built as a social centre for Korean fishers but was gutted by fire in 1997 and is now just an eerie husk sitting beside the concrete skeleton of a derelict grandstand.

Double back around the head of the harbour and head down past the town's **yacht anchorage (4)** and into the heart of Fagatogo. The attractive two-storey, colonial-style **courthouse (5)** here was built at the minuscule cost of US$46,000 between 1900 and 1904 and now houses the territory's High Court. The featureless grey block next door is the new District Court building.

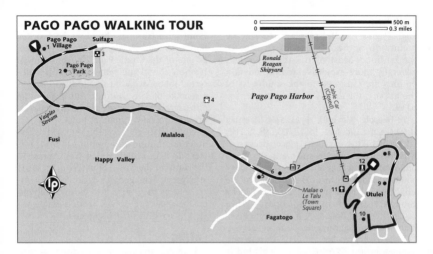

PAGO PAGO WALKING TOUR

TUTUILA

WALK FACTS

Start Pago Pago Village
Finish US Navy Plane Crash Monument
Distance 3km
Duration 1½ hours

Continue walking east past the **Fono** (**6**; opposite) and the **Jean P Haydon Museum** (**7**; p109) until you're almost opposite the old Rainmaker Hotel, where you can climb up a ragged stone staircase to see how work on the **Governor's House** (**8**; opposite) is progressing. Climb back down and continue around the point to the **Rex Lee Auditorium** (**9**), where concerts and other events are regularly held, and then poke your head into the **Feleti Barstow Public Library** (**10**; p106). If you want to take a closer look at the strikingly odd **granite church** (**11**) with the iron bell and cross that sits halfway up the hill behind the library, follow the road around the back of the Office of Samoan Affairs, climb up one of the stone stairs and wind your way up the narrow streets. The view down over Utulei from out the front of the church is impressive. Continue north along this road to the plane crash **monument** (**12**; p108) on Solo Hill.

PAGO PAGO FOR CHILDREN

The American Samoan capital is not exactly Eden for children, but it's not bereft of activities for youthful bodies and imaginations either. **Pago Pago Community Play-**

ground (6am-6pm Mon-Sat) is a small open-air compound with plenty of play equipment to keep kids occupied for an hour or two. It's only open to children between the ages of one and 10. When the urge for a picnic strikes, take the family down to **Utulei Beach Park** (6am-10pm), a pleasant strip of foreshore with several day-*fale* and nice views of the harbour mouth. Another good foreshore picnicking option is **Lion's Park** (6am-10pm) in Tafuna, which is dotted with tables and has some playground equipment at its southern end. The **Jean P Haydon Museum** (p109) reveals fascinating artefacts such as war canoes – call ahead to check if any demonstrations of traditional crafts (like weaving) are being held soon. Kids will also enjoy the **fiafia** (p114) put on by Sadie Thompson Inn. And don't forget that the sandy charms of **Alega Beach** (p116) are only a short drive or bus trip away.

TOURS

You'll find that organised tour offerings for American Samoa are extremely limited and fairly expensive.

Ecotour Samoa (Map pp62-3; ☎ 22144; www.eco toursamoa.com) This Samoa-based company does a seven-day guided tour of American Samoa – including all transfers, meals, accommodation and transport – that costs US$300 per person per day.

Oceania Travel & Tours (☎ 633 1172; oceania@blueskynet.as; 1st fl, Post Office Bldg) Conducts half/full-day tours (US$60/95) of Tutuila; itineraries are negotiable.

SLEEPING

Pago Pago's handful of places to stay lie mainly on or near the southern edge of the harbour. Most of the island's other, generally more-expensive accommodation options are clustered to the southwest of the airport; for details of these places, see p119.

Le Falepule (Map p103; ☎ 633 5264; lefalepule@ samoatelco.com; s/d from US$125/135, ste US$145; ⛌ 🖳 ⛌) This excellent place, decorated with lots of Samoan arts and crafts, sits atop a hill overlooking Faga'alu Bay – the driveway is about 200m north of the turn-off to the LBJ Tropical Medical Center. Guests lucky enough to install themselves in one of the five rooms here get breakfast, a complimentary laundry service and wireless Internet access.

Sadie Thompson Inn (☎ 633 5981; www.sadie thompsoninn.com; r US$95-150; ⛌ ⛌) This inn is set in an appealing timber villa backed by tree-cloaked cliffs. There are a dozen rooms and two self-contained apartments here, all modern, spacious and well-appointed. The more expensive rooms have a spa bath and face the harbour; one of these has wheelchair access. The inn has a good restaurant (Sadie's Restaurant; see opposite).

Scanlan Motel (☎ 633 4451; s & d US$30-60; ⛌) This dingy option for shoestringers is accessed via a rickety staircase to the left of the 'Golden Bell' sign. Rooms costing US$45 and higher come with air-con and a basic shower and toilet. Many rooms lack windows and are tainted by disrepair, so inspect them first.

THE AUTHOR'S CHOICE

Motu-o-Fiafiaga Motel (Evalani's; ☎ 633 7777; www.amsamoa.com/evie; r US$60; ⛌ 🖳 ⛌) Evalani's is the best value place in town. It offers clean, comfortable rooms with air-con, TV, a fridge and shared bathrooms; try for a room looking toward the harbour. There's also some merrily quirky décor – the hallway sports bright red carpet and prints devoted to old Hollywood icons, particularly Monroe – and a rather redundant sauna. Attached to the motel is Evie's Cantina (opposite), which doubles as a bar-nightclub called Evie's Polynesian Hut (p114). The overnight rate drops to US$50 if you stay for two nights or more.

The Rainmaker Hotel on Goat Island Point was a landmark building that worked hard over four decades to earn a reputation as one of the South Pacific's worst hotels. It's now closed and rather derelict (the deserted lobby wouldn't look out of place in a remake of *The Shining*). But at the time of research, half the site was being redeveloped into a new upmarket hotel.

Until relatively recently, one of the few other accommodation options in town was Herb & Sia's Motel, which was located to the south of the Town Square, but it closed after being damaged in a cyclone. The owners told us they were just about to rebuild on the same site, so ask around when you visit to see if this has happened.

EATING

Fortunately for visitors who don't want to chew spam and eggs, bacon and eggs, steak, hamburgers, fried chicken and pizza morning, noon and night, there are a couple of places in Pago Pago that don't specialise in US-style fast foods – only a couple though. The majority of eateries are in Fagatogo.

For details of eateries in nearby Nu'uuli and Tafuna, see p120.

Cafés & Quick Eats

DDW (Don't Drink the Water; ☎ 633 5297; meals US$7-14; ☪ breakfast & lunch Mon-Sat; 🖳 ⛌) This uncluttered café is kept cool by a flotilla of ceiling fans. It prepares quick and easy diner-style meals, including burgers, steaks, lasagne and the usual suspects for breakfast. It also does fantastic cakes and pies.

Pago Pago Yacht Club (☎ 633 2465; meals US$4-8; ☪ lunch) The town's convivial yacht club not only serves simple burgers and sandwiches at lunchtime, but also great-value meals of freshly caught fish (like yellowfin) accompanied with vegetables and rice.

Mom's Place (☎ 633 1414; meals US$4-7; ☪ breakfast & lunch Mon-Sat; ⛌) This friendly little diner whips up an assortment of breakfasts and fried foods, including Pago Pago's best burgers. If you're tired of starting your day staring at a plate of eggs, try the Samoan pancakes.

Te'o Brothers Bakery (☎ 633 2250; plates US$2-3.50; ☪ breakfast & lunch Mon-Sat) This is one of the cheap, canteen-style eateries on the eastern side of the market. It ladles out various curries and stews, and also sells sandwiches. For a cooler treat, head for the popular ice-cream shop on the western side of the market.

Waterfront Restaurant (☎ 633 1199; Fagatogo Sq; meals US$3-7; ☺ breakfast & lunch Mon-Sat; ✗) The Waterfront Restaurant is a garishly coloured fast-food place, specialising in anything fried in oil or smothered in cheese – namely foodstuffs such as burgers, nachos, fried chicken and hot dogs. It can be insanely busy at lunchtime.

At the western end of Pago Pago Park is a cluster of **food stalls** (meals US$1-3; ☺ breakfast & lunch Mon-Sat) selling all sorts of Korean, Chinese and pseudo-Samoan dishes. Dirt-cheap feeds available here include potato salad, *oka* (marinated raw fish) and fish patties.

Restaurants

Sook's Sushi Restaurant (☎ 633 5525; GHC Reid New Bldg; mains US$8-25; ☺ lunch & dinner Mon-Sat; ✗) Tucked away behind Transpac Wines is this humble Japanese restaurant. It serves up tasty sushi, sashimi and tempura dishes, plus Korean *kalbi* (ribs). It offers one of the few healthy eating options in this land of the deep-fried.

Famous II Seafood Restaurant (☎ 633 1159; meals US$8-17; ☺ lunch & dinner Mon-Sat; ✗) This is one of three Famous Seafood restaurants on Tutuila (the others are at Nu'uuli and Faga'alu). It prepares very good Chinese soups and seafood dishes, plus a variety of land-based meats and vegetarian options. There's a great-value seafood buffet on Saturday night (US$20). All meals are available for takeaway.

Evie's Cantina (☎ 633 4776; mains US$8-16; ☺ lunch & dinner Tue-Fri, dinner Sat & Sun) This restaurant is lined with snug booths and is a shrine to fairy lights and plastic foliage. The menu is divided between Mexican food and 'specialities', the latter devoted to carnivore delights like rib-eye steak and the eerie-sounding 'chicken fingers'.

Gourmet dinners can be organised for groups of six people or more at the hilltop Le Falepule (opposite) with at least 48 hours notice. Bookings are not possible on Thursday or Sunday.

Self-Catering

One of the town's better-stocked supermarkets is **Super K Supermarket** (☺ 7am-9pm Mon-Sat). The **Pila Patu Store** (☺ 24hr) sells a small

---

THE AUTHOR'S CHOICE

Sadie's Restaurant (☎ 633 5981; www.sadie thompsoninn.com; Sadie Thompson Inn; lunch US$11-20, dinner US$15-30; ☺ breakfast, lunch & dinner; ✗) Squeeze yourself into a comfy, burgundy-coloured booth in the cosy dining room of Sadie Thompson Inn. There's lots of space between tables and the décor is understated, except perhaps for the Samoan war clubs hanging on the walls. Catch-of-the-day specials are always worth trying, particularly the swordfish, and there's usually a vegetarian offering. The wine list is also reasonable.

---

range of canned goods, snacks and drinks (including beer), but its real selling point is that it's open around the clock – perfect for that 3am snack attack. Friday night and early Saturday morning are the only worthwhile times for browsing fresh produce at the market (p108) in Fagatogo.

DRINKING

There are only a couple of drinking options in town, all of which operate according to their own preferred opening hours.

Pago Pago Yacht Club (☎ 633 2465; ☺ from 11am) Expat yachties love to gather here and gab while clutching cold beers and cigarettes. From the outside deck there's a magnificent sea-level view of Rainmaker Mountain directly across the harbour. Closing times often depend on how keen patrons are to keep drinking.

Evie's Polynesian Hut (☎ 633 4776; ☺ noon-2.30pm & from 6pm Tue-Fri, from 6pm Sat & Sun) The bar at Evie's is a good place to relax over a drink. Night owls in particular will appreciate the fact that sunlight is not permitted to enter here. While sipping a cocktail (US$4), allow yourself to be regaled by the cheesy 'live band' (one guy playing guitar, another on a synthesiser) that plays from Thursday to Saturday nights.

Sadie Thompson Inn (☎ 633 5981; www.sadie thompsoninn.com; ☺ 2pm-midnight) The mellow though generic hotel bar at Sadie Thompson's is mostly frequented by expats and tourists. It has a well-polished counter running the length of the room and a TV that's almost always tuned to a football or baseball game.

TUTUILA

ENTERTAINMENT

Besides drinking, local entertainment is confined to a single nightclub, a night of traditional dancing and hit-and-miss movie screenings.

Nightclubs

Evie's Polynesian Hut (☎ 633 4776; admission before 10pm free, after 10pm US$3; ☼ 10pm-2am Fri & Sat) At one end of this long-standing restaurant-bar is a big-screen TV that blares sports early in the night, then screens video hits when the DJ gets fired up at the end of the week. It's sometimes booked out for functions.

The disreputable 'nightclubs' that used to exist on the northern bank of the harbour around the tuna canneries are apparently now a thing of the past, but you'll still find a ragtag collection of Chinese- and Korean-run bars and pool halls here.

Fiafia

Sadie Thompson Inn (☎ 633 5981; www.sadiethompsoninn.com; US$20) The town's one and only *fiafia* is held on Thursday night. It's very popular so you may want to book ahead for a place at the buffet.

Cinemas

Evie's Polynesian Hut (☎ 633 4776; admission free) It's not a cinema, but this place does screen a movie every Sunday night. The quality of the flick (and of the DVD player they use) is not always high.

The island's only fully fledged cinema is in Nu'uuli (p121).

SHOPPING

High-quality crafts are hard to come by in town, though there are plenty of *lava-lava* (wraparound sarongs) on offer. One of Pago Pago's newest developments is the Fagatogo Sq complex, which contains the local version of a department store, but it doesn't have much of interest to travellers.

Mr Lavalava (☎ 633 7061) This shop sells numerous handicrafts but is distinguished from other craft shops by its selection of Samoan CDs. Staff recommend the greatest hits of Aniseto (Seto) Falemoe.

Samoa Sports Inc (☎ 633 4075) You'll find a large selection of sporting goods here, including snorkel and mask packs (from US$25), fishing gear and golfing paraphernalia. It also sells reasonably priced T-shirts.

Forsgrens (☎ 633 5431) The cool interior of this big, white-washed barn of a place is filled with reasonably priced T-shirts, shirts, *lava-lava* and a small range of toiletries. In the late afternoon it's invariably overrun by Samoan shoppers.

Transpac Wines (☎ 633 2345; GHC Reid New Bldg) Transpac has a large selection of Australian, New Zealand and Californian wines, and plenty of spirits and liqueurs. Don't fret, beer swillers – you can stock up here too.

GETTING THERE & AWAY

For details of transport between Pago Pago and other parts of Tutuila, see the Getting Around section (p104) at the start of this chapter. For information on ferry services between Pago Pago and Apia (Samoa), see p294. Information on international flights to Pago Pago can be found on p290.

GETTING AROUND

International flights to American Samoa arrive at Tafuna International Airport, approximately 15km from Pago Pago Harbor. Buses between the harbour and here (marked 'Tafuna') are frequent during the day and cost US$1 one way. If arriving at night you'll probably need to get a cab into Pago Pago, which will cost between US$12 and US$15. There's a taxi stand just outside the entrance to the airport.

To travel from Pago Plaza to Utulei on one of the *'aiga* buses that constantly zip around the harbour will cost about US$0.50.

Taxis congregate at several points around the harbour, including opposite the market. **Pago Cabs** (☎ 633 5545) operates around the clock from a kiosk on the eastern side of the market.

EASTERN TUTUILA

The eastern district of Tutuila is dominated by the aptly named Rainmaker Mountain. The side road that skirts around the mountain to the west leads down into the beautiful valleys and bays of the National Park of American Samoa. Meanwhile, the main road that hugs Tutuila's southern shore heads east past the superb Alega Beach before curving around beneath Cape Matatula – along the way, it branches off towards remote, serene villages on the island's rugged north coast.

RAINMAKER MOUNTAIN

Also known as Mt Pioa, this 523m mountain is the culprit that traps rain clouds and gives Pago Pago Harbor the highest annual rainfall of any harbour in the world. It's Tutuila's best example of a volcanic plug associated with the major fissure zone that created the island. While it appears as one peak from below, the summit is actually three-pronged. The separate peaks are known as North Pioa, South Pioa and Sinapioa. Rainmaker Mountain and its base area has been designated a national landmark site due to the pristine tropical vegetation on the slopes.

The long rain shadow that the mountain casts over the harbour is best appreciated from the outside deck of the Pago Pago Yacht Club (p113). If you're seated out there just as water-swollen clouds blow in from the northeast, you'll actually see the rain drops marching across the surface of the harbour and climbing up the foreshore to smack down on the Yacht Club roof.

NATIONAL PARK OF AMERICAN SAMOA

On 1 November 1988, then US president Ronald Reagan signed a bill creating the National Park of American Samoa, which includes much of the island of Ta'u and part of Ofu, both in the Manu'a Group, along with a sizeable portion of the northern slopes of Tutuila. The park, which protects areas of coral reef as well as significant areas of mixed species old-world rainforest, offers spectacular snorkelling and some great hiking.

The Tutuila section of the national park is in the north-central part of the island between the villages of Fagasa to the west and Afono to the east, and is bounded by the Maugaloa Ridge to the south. It comprises 1000 hectares of land (most of which is covered in lowland and montane rainforest) as well as 480 hectares of offshore waters. Even though the NPS manages the land, it belongs to traditional Samoan landowners, who continue to grow subsistence crops around the villages of Vatia and Afono and in the Amalau Valley.

A 5.5km hiking trail leads from Fagasa Pass to Mt Alava. From the summit of Mt Alava, the trail continues another 2km along the crest of Maugaloa Ridge before working its way down over another 2km of steep terrain to the village of Vatia. For details of this walk, see p108.

Before exploring the national park, visit the helpful **National Park Visitor Information Center** (☎ 633 7082; www.nps.gov/npsa/home.htm; Pago Plaza, Pago Pago; ⏲ 7.30am-4.30pm Mon-Fri).

Amalau Valley

From the village of Aua on the northern side of the harbour, a surfaced road switchbacks steeply up to Rainmaker Pass and continues equally steeply down to Afono and beautiful Vatia. The views from the pass down to either side of the island are spectacular. Between Afono and Vatia is the secluded Amalau Valley, home to many forest bird species and to Samoa's two rare species of flying fox, or fruit bat. Look for

---

WINGED GUARDIANS OF THE FOREST

Flying foxes are the source of many traditional Samoan stories. In Samoan legends, flying foxes are regarded as guardians of the forest and rescuers of people in distress. Flying foxes also play an essential role as pollinators and seed dispersers of a significant portion of tropical forest plants.

There are two species of flying foxes in Samoa: *Pteropus samoensis*, known as *pe'a vao* in Samoan, and *Pteropus tonganus*, called *pe'a fanua*. The former translates as 'fruit bat of the forest' and the latter as 'fruit bat of settled lands'.

P. samoensis roosts alone or in small groups in the canopy of ridge-top trees. This species is unique in that it is active during the day, with two feeding peaks – one in the morning and the other in the late afternoon.

P. tonganus often roosts in groups of up to several hundred. Although found in the primary forest, it also exists in secondary forest growth, sometimes close to villages.

Adult members of both species have a wingspan of just under 1m and weigh about 500g. *P. samoensis* has a distinct light-coloured face, a brown body sprinkled with greyish white and broad wings. *P. tonganus* has a black face, a seal-brown body with a mantle that varies from buff to pale cream, and narrower wings.

flying foxes early in the morning or late in the afternoon.

The NPS has erected a *fale* at a lookout point just past the western side of Amalau Bay. Stop here for a wonderful view of Pola Tai (see below).

Vatia

Vaita is a peaceful village situated on the edge of a lovely, coral-fringed bay. From Vatia you can view **Pola Tai** (Cock's Comb), a tiny uninhabited island just offshore, whose magnificent sheer cliffs rise more than 120m straight out of the ocean. The craggy cliffs are home to numerous seabirds including frigates, boobies, white terns and noddy terns. To get there, drive through the village and park at the school, then walk 300m to reach a wonderfully isolated, rocky beach – you can also drive this last stretch and park just behind the beach. Walk to the end of the beach to see a small sea arch, and don't forget to look up to see all the birds wheeling overhead.

BEACHES

Just 10km east of Pago Pago is **Alega Beach**, one of Tutuila's finest beaches. It's not only a great place to swim and snorkel (check currents and conditions with locals first), but is also overlooked by Tisa's Barefoot Bar (opposite), the perfect spot for a cold beer or three. You can waive the access fee for the beach (US$5) by simply buying a

---

STAR MOUNDS

More than 140 distinctive earthen, and sometimes stone, mounds, dating back to late prehistoric times, have been found scattered across the Samoan archipelago. Dubbed star mounds, the structures range from 6m to 30m in length, are up to 3m high and have from one to 11 raylike projections radiating from their base. Forty of these star mounds have been discovered (though not yet excavated) on the road between Amouli and Aoa alone. Polynesian plainware (a type of undecorated pottery) dating from between 1000 BC and 500 BC has also been found in the Aoa area, though its exact origin is a mystery.

The main theory regarding the star mounds is that they were used for pigeon-catching, an extremely important sport of chiefs that was pursued from June through September. People would follow their *matai* (chiefs) into the forest to observe and support competitions.

In 1887 William B Churchward, the British Consul in Samoa, wrote:

Pigeon-snaring is the oldest and most cherished sport in all Samoa, and until lately, partook much more of the nature of a fixed ceremony than a mere amusement. It was made the occasion for feasting and junketing in a high degree, and whilst it lasted all sorts of irregularities could be indulged in without comment.

However, American archaeologists David Herdrich and Jeffrey Clark believe there is very strong evidence to suggest that star mounds also served a much more complex function in Samoan society. There is evidence that they were used as sites for ritual activity related to marriage, healing and warfare. The archaeologists also believe the star mounds came to reflect the position of the *matai* and the field in which personal ability and *mana* (supernatural power) could be expressed. Star mounds therefore would have become places of power in their own right.

In an interview with an American PhD student, C. Forsyth, in 1983, a Samoan *ali'i* (high chief) commented:

Do you know the star mounds? Well, they had to do with the *taulasea* (traditional healer) and energy and with special powers. The ancient Samoans did not build those just to catch pigeons. No Sir! They were part of our ancient religion, and so were the *taulasea* and the *taulaitu* (spirit medium). Look into the archaeology data on the mounds. The energy is still so strong on those mounds that it raises the hair on your body to visit them.

If you're interested in such a hair-raising experience, contact the **American Samoan Historic Preservation Office** (☎ 633 2384) to arrange a tour to any one of several star mounds on Tutuila.

drink at Tisa's. On the weekend this beach is inundated by day-tripping locals.

Just east of Alega Beach is **2-Dollar Beach**, which is shallow but also good for a swim. Guess what the access fee here is.

MASEFAU & SA'ILELE

A cross-island road leads from the village of Faga'itua up over a pass before winding slowly down to Masefau, which is one of those villages that looks too idyllic to really exist. It's nestled in the curve of a gorgeous little bay, the westernmost point of which reaches out towards a small island lodged in the bay's mouth.

Back at the pass, a turn-off to the right takes you down a narrow, potholed road to the town of Masa'usi, which is dominated by a beachside church fronted by colourful stained-glass windows. The road then leads through dense forest to Sai'ilele, which has one of the island's most lovely beaches – coconut palms are anchored in the sand by mounds of rocks and coral fragments, and the water is placid. The sandy area below the large rock outcrop at the beach's western end provides an excellent place for a picnic, but seek permission from a villager before unrolling the picnic blanket.

TULA & ONENOA

Tula, the easternmost village on Tutuila, is a quiet, laidback place with a pleasant white beach and apparently some good right and left reef breaks. It is the end of the bus line east, but you can continue driving or walking around the end of the island to Cape Matatula and Onenoa, a serene area of high cliffs, small plantations and forested slopes.

SLEEPING & EATING

Tisa's Barefoot Bar (☎ 622 7447; www.tisasbarefootbar.com; meals US$12-18; 11am-7pm, by reservation after 7pm) This wonderful, environmentally friendly place is run by Tisa and the 'Candyman'. It's not just a sleeping, eating and drinking option, but ranks as one of the highlights of a visit to Tutuila. The idiosyncratic driftwood bar is fronted by a deck that looks out over lovely Alega Beach. Just off the decking are two *fale* beach-huts (US$50 per person), each gazing toward the ocean and with super-comfortable beds; the price includes breakfast and dinner. More accommodation is being planned, including a place secreted in the nearby hills where you'll be dropped off with supplies. The food here is superb, with vegetarians easily catered for. You must book ahead for dinners (two days in advance to guarantee the freshest produce is used). On Wednesday night a mightily popular *umu* (feast cooked in a traditional underground oven) is held (US$30) where traditional Samoan fare is given an international twist. The Candyman can also take you on hikes that take full advantage of the unexplored nature of the surrounding property. Tisa's Tattoo Festival was held here in October 2005 and may become an annual event.

You may be able to arrange accommodation in Vatia through the National Park of American Samoa's homestay programme; for details, see p108.

WESTERN TUTUILA

Heading southwest from Pago Pago, you first reach Nu'uuli, a loosely defined commercial area along the main road between Coconut Point and the airport turn-offs. For information on facilities in this area and to the south near the airport in Tafuna, including details of American Samoa's Office of Tourism, see p106.

Beyond the low-profile strip malls and small local shops of Nu'uuli and Tafuna, the wild side of Tutuila takes over again. Spend at least a day or two listening to the surf at the Turtle & Shark Site, visiting star mounds, and weaving through remote, forested coastal valleys beyond Cape Taputapu. Those seeking true wilderness experiences can consider hiking down to Massacre Bay, climbing Matafao Peak, or exploring the remarkable Fagatele Bay.

MATAFAO PEAK

At 653m, Matafao Peak is the highest point on Tutuila. The peak itself, like Rainmaker Mountain across the harbour, is a remnant of the great volcanic plug. Above the 350m level, the peak area has been designated a national landmark site. A narrow, unrelentingly steep and very rough trail starts opposite the beginning of the Mt Alava walk (look for the metal ladder) and leads up the peak. The NPS estimates that the hike takes three to four hours one way, but can't vouch for its condition because it's on land owned by Fagasa village rather than lying within the national park. Only tackle this trail if you're a very experienced hiker/climber. It's strongly recommended that you organise a guide in Fagasa village.

TIA SEU LUPE

The **American Samoa Historic Preservation Office** (Ashpo; ☎ 633 2384; www.ashpo.org; Matafao) maintains a well-preserved ancient Polynesian star mound, *tia seu lupe* (literally 'earthen mound to catch pigeons'), near the Catholic cathedral at Tafuna. The mound has a unique connecting platform and fine views of Matafao Peak. Call Ashpo to ask about a personalised tour of the site.

Adjoining the site is a small rainforest reserve. The nearby cathedral contains some beautiful woodcarving and a fabulous photorealist painting of a traditional Samoan family by Duffy Sheridan.

TURTLE & SHARK SITE

The most famous of Tutuila's legends is set in the picturesque village of Vaitogi, along a scenic stretch of black lava coast. Confusingly, there are a myriad versions of this legend. The two that follow are the ones that most often surface, but you could ask five Samoans to relate the legend and get five completely different tales!

According to one explanation, a young husband on 'Upolu was selected as the 'guest of honour' at a cannibalistic feast to be given by Malietoa Faiga. He chose, understandably, to decline the invitation. The man and his wife set out in a canoe, but while attempting to escape there was a storm and they were blown to Tutuila, where they were put up by Letuli, the *pulenu'u* (village mayor) of 'Ili'ili. When the practice of cannibalism fell into disfavour, Letuli offered them a free trip home, but they refused. Instead, as repayment for his kindness, they jumped into the sea. The husband became a shark and his wife a turtle. The husband told the chief that any time a gathering of children sang from the shore at Vaitogi, a turtle and a shark would appear to greet them.

Another version relates that the turtle and shark are an old blind lady and her granddaughter who jumped into the sea after being turned out of their village on Savai'i.

It was during a time of famine and the two were incapable of providing for themselves. When their family learned what they'd done, they went to the shore, guilt-ridden, and called the pair by name. When the turtle and shark appeared, they knew that their family members were all right.

Even if the turtle and shark have taken the day off, you'll enjoy the solitude of the place, with its black lava cliffs, heavy surf, tide pools, blowholes and sandy beach. There's no swimming here though – the currents are treacherous, but more importantly this is a sacred site. There's a pleasant walk west along the road to Sail Rock Point, through pandanus and coconut groves.

FAGATELE BAY NATIONAL MARINE SANCTUARY

Fagatele Bay is a submerged volcanic crater surrounded by steep cliffs. The area contains the last remaining stretch of coastal rainforest on the island. In 1986 the fringing coral reef in the bay was designated a national marine sanctuary.

Nearly 200 species of coral are still recovering from a crown-of-thorns starfish attack in the late 1970s, which destroyed more than 90% of the coral. Scientists remain undecided as to whether the boom-and-bust cycle of the crown-of-thorns is natural or the outcome of human activity. It may be the result of increased erosion, which provides an unnaturally high volume of nutrients that nourish the plankton and, in turn, support the young starfish. however, the coral is slowly recovering and the fish population remains vibrant.

Southern humpback whales winter in the bay from August to November, while several varieties of porpoise and sperm whales have also been seen. Threatened and endangered species of marine turtles such as hawksbill and green sea turtles also use the bay. Other less frequent visitors include the leatherback, the loggerhead and the olive Ridley sea turtle. The rocky cliffs surrounding the bay are home to numerous seabirds.

All but traditional fishing methods are prohibited in the inner bay, the taking of invertebrates is prohibited (as is the removal of live coral) and historical artefacts found in the bay are protected.

It is permissible to dive, snorkel and swim in the bay, but it's very difficult to get out there – there's currently no dive operator on Tutuila, so your only option would be an expensive boat charter. Contact the **Fagatele Bay National Marine Sanctuary office** (☎ 633 7354; www.fbnms.nos.noaa.gov; ◷ 7.30am-4.30pm Mon-Fri) for the latest information on access to the bay. The office is wedged up against the western side of the old Rainmaker Hotel.

LEONE
pop 4000

The village of Leone is the second-largest settlement on Tutuila and once served as the Polynesian capital of the island. It was also the landing site of the first missionary, John Williams, who arrived on 18 October 1832 after spending two years in Samoa. One result of his work is an imposing **church**, the first in American Samoa (Leone actually has two imposing churches – head for the one with three towers and facing the sea). It's well maintained and has lovely stained-glass windows and some beautiful wood-work on the ceiling. There's a monument to Williams' efforts in front of the church.

When heading west from Leone, look for the tiny rocky islet across the bay that supports just a single coconut tree – the stuff of desert island cartoons!

MASSACRE BAY

A marvellous 4km hiking trail (four hours return) leads from the scenic village of A'oloaufou, high up on the rocky spine of Tutuila, down to A'asu on Massacre Bay. Massacre Bay is the site where, on 11 December 1787, 12 men from the crew of La Pérouse's ships *La Boussole* and *Astrolabe,* as well as 39 Samoans, were killed in a skirmish. There is an obscure **monument** in A'asu commemorating the European crew members who died there.

This track is apparently maintained (or not, as the case may be) by the sole family residing in A'asu. Needless to say, it's often overgrown, extremely muddy and difficult to navigate – getting down to A'asu isn't so bad, but a number of hikers have become disoriented climbing back up. It probably pays to hire a guide in A'oloaufou, which will cost between US$5 and US$10.

Across from the large park in A'oloaufou is a colourful garden that began life as an attempt by the Office of Tourism to create sites of interest on Tutuila. The trail to

A'asu takes off downhill just east of this garden. Once in A'asu, introduce yourself to the local family and ask for permission to use their beach. From Massacre Bay, you can also walk upstream for about 800m to a lovely waterfall, though note there's no real 'track' as such. The worn-out admonition not to go on Sunday holds. Wear long trousers since trail-side thorns and sharp grasses will slice unprotected skin.

If driving to A'oloaufou, take the turn-off in Pava'ia'i opposite the Gold Star Mart. To get to A'oloaufou by bus, take a Leone-bound vehicle from the market in Fagatogo to Pava'ia'i (US$0.75) and wait on the corner there for one headed up the hill.

CAPE TAPUTAPU

Cape Taputapu is Tutuila's most westerly point and a national natural landmark. The word *taputapu* means 'forbidden', and the cape was so named because it was the only source of paper mulberry trees on the island. The discoverers wanted to keep the bark for themselves in order to sell it to folks on other parts of the island. No doubt they related fearful tales and a taboo was placed on it.

Just shy of the cape, beyond the village of Amanave, is a lovely white-sand beach generally known as **Palagi Beach**. If you're in a rental vehicle, leave it by the Amanave store and ask for a guide to take you to the beach. Access is via the track above the shoreline, or by walking/wading along the reef at low tide. Allow about 10 or 15 minutes to get to the beach. You can paddle and snorkel in the small pool by the offshore island, on which sea birds nest, but be mindful of strong currents and a nearby *ava* (passage through the reef to the open ocean).

Beyond Amanave, the road climbs steeply and winds through valleys and over ridges to the small villages of Poloa, Fagali'i, Maloata and Fagamalo. There are some spectacular views of Tutuila's wild and trackless north coast along this stretch.

SLEEPING

Turtle & Shark Lodge (☎ 688 1212, 699 1212; www .turtleandshark.com; Vaitogi; r incl breakfast US$75-125; ⛄ ▯ ⛾ ⊠) This fine, secluded 10-room guesthouse is located at the end of the trail running west along the coast from Vaitogi. It's surrounded by a beautifully landscaped property overlooking Fogama'a Cove, and

TUTUILA

has tennis courts, a laundry and a BBQ area. Rates include continental breakfast, but guests also have access to a kitchen.

Ta'alolo Lodge & Golf Resort (☎ 699 7201; taalolo@samoatelco.com; 'Ili'ili; r incl breakfast & dinner US$80-135; 🔀 🖵 🖳 🗶) Golf aficionados will adore this lovely split-level home, located a mere chip shot from the 'Ili'ili Golf Course. It has five rooms, including a huge master bedroom, which all have en suites, DVD players, fridges and tasteful Samoan touches. The lodge is well off the main road, so there's nothing to disturb your dreams of a perfect round.

Sliding Rock Lodge (☎ 688 7553; www.slidingrockresort.com; Vailoa; r incl breakfast & dinner US$65-85; 🔀 🗶) This five-unit lodge is outstandingly positioned atop a hill overlooking a surf-pounded section of coast, including a feature called Sliding Rock where there's a sizeable tidal pool. The units are clean and comfortable and have windows looking to the sea. There's also an outside deck that's perfect for meals or drinks on sunny days.

Maliu Mai Beach Resort (☎ 699 7232; Tafuna; s/d US$65/85; 🔀 🗶) This low-key resort sits on a rough-and-tumble beach fringed by low cliffs. Upstairs in the main building are four large, private rooms, each with en suite, cable TV and access to a communal balcony. Several more rooms are available in a nearby house. There's an onsite restaurant. The bar can get busy at weekends (see opposite).

Tradewinds Hotel (☎ 699 1000; www.tradewinds.as; Tafuna; r & ste US$135-240; 🔀 🖵 🖳 🗶) The five-star Tradewinds is only a few years old and has over 100 rooms, half of them suites. Teak beds and furnishings lend the rooms a warm feel, but there's not much in the way of a view as the hotel is located well inland. It also lacks individual character outside the rooms – the only notable design feature is that the hallways are big enough to drive cars down them. The excellent facilities include the Equator Restaurant (opposite), an Internet café (guests only), wheelchair-accessible rooms and an ANZ ATM in the foyer. Baby cots are also available.

Tessarea's Vaitogi Inn (☎ 699 7793; tessarea99@yahoo.com; Vaitogi; r US$95; 🔀 🖳 🗶) Tessarea's is located off a paved road that runs between Vaitogi village and the road that skirts the nearby golf course. It offers guests decent-standard rooms and access to a kitchen. It can be tricky to find, so email or call ahead for directions.

Pago Airport Inn (☎ 699 6333; www.pagoairportinn.com; Tafuna; s/d US$75/100; 🔀 🗶) This place is conveniently near the airport and contains the interestingly designed Star Restaurant (opposite). But its rooms are overpriced considering the state of some furnishings and fittings: in ours the bed sagged dramatically and the TV was on the fritz.

EATING
Cafés & Quick Eats

Rubble's Tavern (☎ 699 4400; Nu'uuli; mains US$6-24; 🕑 lunch & dinner Mon-Sat, lunch Sun) Rubble's is an easygoing combination of American diner and sports bar that's dressed up in Polynesian decor. Its menu 'specialities' are things like hamburger steak, meatloaf and fried chicken – vegetarians will die of fright if they walk in here. True to its name, the 'U' in its signage has fallen off.

Good Food Bakery (☎ 699 6233; Nu'uuli; 🕑 6am-6pm Mon-Sat, 6am-3pm Sun) A few doors down from Rubble's is this basic little bakery selling bread, pies and sandwiches.

Deluxe Cafe (☎ 699 4000; Nu'uuli; meals US$6-13; 🕑 breakfast & lunch; 🗶) Set in a strange-looking green timber building, this cheerful café has plenty of tables and booths to accommodate hungry hordes. The menu is full of American Samoan favourites, from toasted sandwiches and burgers to steaks and chicken wings, plus several basic salads.

A & A's Pizza (☎ 699 9428; Nu'uuli; pizzas from US$12, meals US$2-5; 🕑 breakfast, lunch & dinner Mon-Sat) Such is the Samoan appetite that they don't bother serving 'small' or 'regular' pizzas here – sizes start at 'medium'. This business has merged with a Filipino eatery called Pinoy's, which is why some Asian noodle dishes and stews are also served at the front counter, as well as tacos and burgers. There's also a busy bakery. You'll find A & A's hidden behind the LYC Inc Store. It's near a colourful old playground that will keep kids occupied.

Island Pizza (☎ 699 1300; Laufo Center, Nu'uuli; meals US$5-18; 🕑 lunch & dinner Mon-Sat, closes 8pm) This speedy pizza dispenser is on the western side of the Laufo Center car park. It serves pizza by the slice and by the platter, and also produces hot dogs, BBQ chicken and other fast-food choices.

Restaurants

Reef Bar & Grill (☎ 699 7717; Tafuna; meals US$7-20; 🕑 lunch & dinner; 🗶) The Reef is a nice clean, bright, white-tiled place across the car park from Cost U Less. It cooks up lots of seafood, including Samoan *oka*, some pasta such as spaghetti and meatballs, burgers (including a strange-tasting vegetarian burger), and ribs and steak – try the New York strip steak, all 10oz of it.

Hong Kong House (☎ 699 8983; Nu'uuli; mains US$7-15; lunch & dinner Mon-Sat, lunch Sun;) Very good Chinese food is on offer in this open-plan restaurant (eat in or takeaway), including soups and beef, chicken and seafood dishes. There are several tofu-based choices and a small separate list of other vegetarian selections.

Sunny's (☎ 699 5238; mains US$6-13; lunch & dinner) A short distance west of Hong Kong House, this is another decent Chinese eatery with some good hot and spicy meals.

Equator Restaurant (☎ 699 1008; Tradewinds Hotel, Tafuna; meals US$6-22; breakfast, lunch & dinner;) This enormous restaurant, in a building adjacent to (and part of) the Tradewinds Hotel, has inherited the hotel's lack of character. But it's open all day and serves decent burgers, pasta, seafood and several vegetarian options. A house speciality is oven-roasted pig.

Star Restaurant (☎ 699 6333; Pago Airport Inn, Tafuna; meals US$8-18; breakfast & lunch Mon-Sat;) It's not worth coming out from Pago just to eat here, but this family restaurant is a good option for a hearty breakfast or lunch if you happen to be in the Tafuna area. It's set on an upstairs terrace at Pago Airport Inn and sports attractive tile-work and wrought-iron railings, and is encircled by glass shutters.

Self-Catering
Cost U Less (☎ 699 5975; Tafuna; 8am-8pm Mon-Fri, 10am-7pm Sat, 10am-6pm Sun) Self-caterers can stock up on imported groceries and some canned goodies in this enormous bulk-buying store. If you have enough money left over, pick up a spare DVD player while you're there.

DRINKING
Maliu Mai Beach Resort (☎ 699 7232; Tafuna; s/d US$65/85;   ) The bar at Maliu Mai is a good place for a drink. Drag a chair onto the sand and quench your thirst to the sound of the surf. On clear nights, look to the northeast to see Matafao Peak silhouetted by the glow of Pago Pago's lights.

Rubble's Tavern (☎ 699 4400; Nu'uuli; mains US$6-24; lunch & dinner Mon-Sat, lunch Sun) If you fancy a cold beer, perch yourself on one of the coconut tree stump bar stools here.

ENTERTAINMENT
Nu'uuli Place Cinemas (☎ 699 9334; Nu'uuli Place Shopping Center; adult/child US$6.50/4, adult US$4.50 for Tue & pre-6pm sessions) This two-screen cinema hosts the latest-release commercial movies, predominantly those from the US.

AUNU'U

area 3 sq km / pop 600

Tiny Aunu'u is a tranquil and pristine plot of nature. Its wild, thickly foliaged hinterland rises up the sides of an extinct volcano, and the surrounding waters are clear and blue. What's more, the lack of vehicles on the island means you can fully appreciate the silence and solitude. Since it's only a couple of kilometres from end to end, Aunu'u can easily be explored in a day, with plenty of time left over for a picnic at churning Ma'ama'a Cove.

Tracks on the island aren't always well maintained. They quickly become overgrown and sites may be difficult to find. It's worth asking around in the village for a guide; US$5 is a reasonable fee for a tour of the island. Wear full-length trousers and good walking shoes for your explorations.

PALA LAKE
After walking about 700m north from Aunu'u village, you'll arrive at the sizeable clearing in the undergrowth where the short side-trail to Pala Lake begins. The lake is a beautiful and deadly looking expanse of fiery red quicksand – its amazing colour is best appreciated at low tide. During the rainy season, the sand thins out and is inhabited by grey ducks. All birds and bats are now protected in American Samoa, but once upon a time locals would shoot the ducks and then swim out to retrieve the carcasses. To avoid being sucked down into sandy doom, swimmers had to remain horizontal at all times and propel themselves only using their arms.

RED LAKE
Red Lake lies in the middle of Fa'imulivai Marsh, which, in turn, lies in the middle of Aunu'u's volcanic crater. It is filled with eels and tilapia fish. They are sometimes

TUTUILA

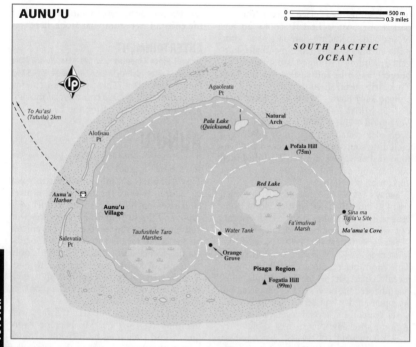

caught with a hook, but, thanks to the lake's frequent level changes, there's an easier method. When the water is high, the eels move to the lake's margins in search of food in the newly flooded areas. When the water drains, it does so quickly, leaving the eels stranded around the edges, so that all the villagers have to do is gather them up.

The water of Red Lake really is reddish, the colour of weak tea. To look at it and the eels, walk out to the edge on the sedges surrounding the marsh; just be careful not to go too far in or you'll sink. To get there, follow the track past Pala Lake and up the hill to the crater. There's usually a decent track around the crater, but access to the lake is tricky, since it will necessitate a bit of bushwhacking on the approach. The best place to try is from the western side of the crater north of the intersection of the village trails.

MA'AMA'A COVE

This is a less a cove, with its connotations of placidity, and more a cauldron of surf that pounds, sprays and boils over the surrounding rocks. Don't get too close to the intense

water action as large, unexpected waves can knock you off the rocks; a drowning occurred here only a few months before we visited. Check out the vertical ripples in the cliff face on the south side of the cove.

Legend says that this is the site of Sina ma Tigila'u (Sina and Tigila'u), two lovers who were shipwrecked here. You can make out bits of crossed 'rope' and broken 'planks' embedded in the rocks around the cove.

PISAGA

The Pisaga is a region near the crater, below Fogatia Hill, where people are forbidden to call out or make loud noises lest they disturb the *aitu* (spirits) that inhabit this place. When Gavin Bell (author of *In Search of Tusitala: Travels in the Pacific after Robert Louis Stevenson*) visited, he felt that all he needed was 'a bit of swirling mist to imagine that around the next corner I would find a wicked witch in a gingerbread house, with a soul as black as her cooking pot'. For a superb view over Red Lake, as well as Aunu'u village, climb up past the water tank on the slopes of Fogatia Hill.

OTHER SIGHTS & ACTIVITIES

The western slope of the crater is planted with an **orange grove**, a relatively new crop-diversification project in American Samoa. Below this are the **Taufusitele Taro Marshes**, which are planted Hawai'ian-style with swamp taro, a rarity in this part of Polynesia. The harbour in the village is safe, calm and great for a refreshing swim. There is also some good coral nearby and excellent underwater visibility, making for good **snorkelling**.

SLEEPING & EATING

There is no formal accommodation available on Aunu'u. If you'd like to stay with a family, you'll need to have a Tutuila connection beforehand – a 'sponsor' if you will – who can ensure that your activities on the island won't be disruptive. There is a bush store in the village where you can buy soft drinks and basic supplies.

GETTING THERE & AWAY

Small launches head over to Aunu'u from the dock at Au'asi. If you catch a boat with other villagers (these depart when enough people are on board), you should only have to pay US$1 each way. If you have to charter a boat – either because you're the only passenger or because you have specific drop-off/pick-up times in mind – then be prepared to pay around US$10 for the return trip. Boats don't run on Sunday. The crossing takes about 15 minutes and can get a little rough.

If there's no one at the dock, try asking at the store across the road, where you can also pick up drinks and snacks for your trip.

SWAINS ISLAND

Swains Island is not geologically part of the ridge that forms the other Samoan islands. Situated about 350km north-northwest of Tutuila, it consists of a 3.25 sq km ring of land surrounding a brackish lagoon with no entrance from the sea. Both culturally and geographically it belongs to Tokelau (a New Zealand territory north of the Samoas).

Swains Island was 'discovered' in 1841 by an American, WL Hudson, who learned of its existence from a whaler by the name of Swain. Soon afterwards it was settled by Tokelauans, who had long known it as Olohega, and some French entrepreneurs who

saw its potential as a copra plantation. The operation was taken over by Eli Jennings, an American, and his Samoan wife in 1856 and has been the private property of the Jennings family ever since. In 1925, the Jennings family persuaded the USA to annex the island as part of American Samoa. This became more official in 1983 with the Treaty of Tokehega, which gave sovereignty over the island to the USA in exchange for US recognition of Tokelauan fishing rights.

To visit Swains Island you need permission from the Jennings family – ask at the **National Park Visitor Information Center** (☎ 633 7082; www.nps.gov/npsa/home.htm; Pago Plaza, Pago Pago; ☺ 7:30am-4:30pm Mon-Fri) about how to go about contacting them. Unless you have your own boat, you'll need to prepare yourself for either a very short or very long stay – a supply ship only visits Swains once a month.

ROSE ATOLL

Rose Atoll, 100km east of the Manu'a Islands, is composed of two tiny specks of land and the surrounding reef. Rose Islet, only 3m above sea level at its highest point, has an area of 5 hectares. Sand Islet, soaring to an elevation of 5m, is only 2.5 hectares in area. The atoll is probably a shield volcano, but one that has been completely eroded since the Pleistocene era. Coral reefs have built up on the remnants, making the atoll visible today.

Rose Atoll is a designated US national wildlife refuge. The refuge exists primarily to protect the green turtle, which lays its eggs in the sand here, as well as the extremely rare hawksbill turtle. Numerous species of seabirds nest on the atoll, including the sooty tern (whose numbers on Rose Atoll represent 85% of the total seabird population of American Samoa), and a variety of other terns, tropicbirds, noddies and boobies. These bird populations were recently threatened by resident rats, but the rats have been removed and the birds are re-establishing themselves. Unfortunately, the atoll's coral has not been doing so well due to a shipwreck that, although removed, has left damaging levels of poisonous metals in the surrounding water. This is one of the reasons why visits are currently only allowed for scientific research purposes.

Manu'a Islands

The expression 'Getting away from it all' must have been invented to describe a trip out to the trio of fantastically remote outposts of land, sand and reef that comprise the Manu'a group. These three islands – Ofu, Olosega and Ta'u – lie only 100km east of Tutuila, but may as well exist in a different dimension. Barely populated and with a volcanic heritage that has bequeathed them high, sharply defined cliffs, these islands are the stuff of tropical daydreams. Wander along sparkling beaches almost entirely devoid of any sign of human visitation, paddle your way around serene lagoons crammed with every imaginable species of coral and a myriad species of fish and other marine life, and sit on end-of-the-earth spits of land and feel the immensity of the ocean rolling away beneath your suntanned feet.

Although the lack of transport will slow you down considerably, that's just what the Manu'a Islands do best. Every activity here is guilt- and expectation-free, be it spending entire days leafing through a book in the shade of a favourite palm tree, having long, rambling conversations with complete strangers in the small traditional villages, or staring out to sea with not a single coherent thought cluttering your mind. You'll know that these are paradisal places the moment you step off the plane or leave your sea legs behind on the boat, and you'll be hard-pressed to find a better spot to maroon yourself for a long, languid holiday.

HIGHLIGHTS

- Sinking into the coral garden that lies just a few lazy steps off sublime **Ofu Beach** (p127)
- Meditating on the extraordinary serenity of **Maga Point** (p128)
- Exploring the rainforests of Ta'u within the confines of the **National Park of American Samoa** (p129)
- Forgetting the 21st century in the place where Margaret Mead wrote her classic *Coming of Age in Samoa* – on Ta'u in the village of **Luma** (p130)
- Braving the jump into Asaga Strait off the **Ofu-Olosega Bridge** (p128)

Ofu-Olosega Bridge
Ofu Beach ★ Maga Point
National Park of American Samoa
Luma ★

- POPULATION OFU & OLOSEGA: 700; TA'U: 800 ■ AREA: 65 SQ KM

AND GOD CREATED SAMOA

Samoans accept the scientific theory that most Polynesians migrated to the Pacific islands from Southeast Asia. They believe this applies to Maoris, Hawai'ians, Tongans, Rarotongans, Easter Islanders and Tahitians…but not to themselves. Their land is the 'cradle of Polynesia'. Samoa, they say, was created by the god Tagaloa, and their story is remarkably similar to the account given in the Book of Genesis.

Before the sea, earth, sky, plants or people existed, Tagaloa lived in the expanse of empty space. He created a rock, commanding it to split into clay, coral, cliffs and stones. As the rock broke apart, the earth, sea and sky came into being. From a bit of the rock emerged a spring of fresh water.

Next, Tagaloa created man and woman, whom he named Fatu (Heart) and 'Ele'ele (Earth). He sent them to the region of fresh water and commanded them to people the area. He ordered the sky, which was called Tu'ite'elagito, to prop itself up above the earth. Using starch and *teve* (a bitter root plant) and the only vegetation then available, he made a post for it to rest upon.

The god then created Po (Night) and Ao (Day), which bore the 'eyes of the sky' – the sun and the moon. At the same time, Tagaloa made the nine regions of heaven, inhabited by various gods.

In the meantime, Fatu and 'Ele'ele were adding men and women to the area of fresh water. Tagaloa, reckoning that all these earthlings needed some form of government, sent Manu'a, a son of Po and Ao, to be the chief of the people. From that time on, Samoan *tupu* (kings) were called *Tu'i Manu'a tele ma Samoa atoa* (King of Manu'a and all of Samoa).

Next, the countries were divided into islands or groups of islands. The world now consisted of Manu'a, Fiji, Tonga and Savai'i. Tagaloa then went to Manu'a and noticed that a void existed between it and Savai'i. Up popped 'Upolu and then Tutuila.

Tagaloa's final command, before he returned to the expanse, was: 'Always respect Manu'a; anyone who fails to do so will be overtaken by catastrophe, but men are free to do as they please in their own lands.' Thus, Manu'a became the spiritual centre of the Samoan islands and, to some extent, of all Polynesia.

HISTORY

Many Samoans believe that Manu'a was the first creation – the first land to emerge at the hands of the god Tagaloa. With the islands so favoured by Tagaloa, the Tu'i Manu'a (the paramount chief of these islands) would certainly have been held in high esteem by the Samoans, and indeed, many supernatural powers have been ascribed to holders of the title down through history. Many believe that, directly and indirectly, the Tu'i Manu'a was revered as the sovereign of all Polynesia. Although wars and fragmentations had split the islands, he was still a proud and powerful figure at the time of cession to the USA.

The last Tu'i Manu'a ceded the islands in 1904, and in his will he stipulated that his title would die with him. By allowing themselves to come under the jurisdiction of a foreign power, the islanders at the centre of the Polynesian world lost much of the respect they had once been accorded, and the revered chief apparently decided that such a title would thereafter be su-perfluous. He died on 2 April 1909. Many American Samoans, however, whether they live on Tutuila or abroad (even those who have never set foot in the Manu'a Islands), give their official address as Manu'a out of respect for the place that Tagaloa created before all others.

In January 1987 Manu'a was hit by cyclone Tusi, one of the worst storms in its recorded history. Ofu and Olosega suffered badly and many buildings were destroyed, but Ta'u was the hardest hit. All three villages on the island were reduced to heaps of rubble, coconut trees were decapitated and crops ruined. To compound matters, cyclones Ofa and Val ploughed through the Manu'a Islands in early 1990 and late 1991. Then, in late 2005, the eye of the massive tropical storm Olaf passed right over the islands. In 1993, between these natural disasters, the Ofu and Ta'u sections of the National Park of American Samoa were officially established after the signing of a 50-year lease with traditional owners.

MANU'A ISLANDS

INFORMATION

Bring your own snorkelling gear, reading material and any particular foods you may need for your stay. There are no restaurants on the islands. Ofu has a bank near the wharf and a basic medical clinic. The only post office on Ofu–Olosega is in Olosega.

In the northeastern corner of Ta'u is the tiny, sleepy village of Fiti'uta. The airstrip is here, plus several stores selling basic supplies, a post office and a bank.

If you plan to go hiking anywhere in the Manu'a Islands, first contact the **National Park Visitor Information Center** (☎ 633 7082; www .nps.gov/npsa/home.htm; Pago Plaza) in Pago Pago for the latest information on walking trails and conditions.

GETTING AROUND
Air

Ofu's airstrip is a 500m runway at Va'oto on the south coast of the island, squeezed in between the sea and mountains. Fortunately for travellers heading for Ta'u, the old 400m nightmare airstrip there – which had a cliff at one end, a mountain at the other and lots of quirky air currents in between – was replaced several years ago by a flash facility in a more suitable location at Fiti'uta.

Inter-Island Airways (Pago Pago ☎ 699 7100; Ofu ☎ 655 7100; Ta'u ☎ 677 7100; www.interislandair.com) usually only flies between Pago Pago and Ofu, and Pago Pago and Ta'u. But when demand is high, shuttle flights between Ofu and Ta'u are sometimes organised. If you're planning to visit both islands, ask the airline about this possibility – the chances are slim but you may just save yourself those annoying extra flights back to and out of Tafuna International Airport.

For details of Inter-Island Airways flights to and from Pago Pago, see p147.

Boat

Both the **American Samoa Inter-Island Shipping Company** (☎ 633 4707) and the **MV Sili** (☎ 633 5532) service the route between Tutuila and the Manu'a Islands. You may be able to jump on one of the vessels while they are visiting Ofu or Ta'u and have them transport you to the neighbouring island, though we didn't hear of anyone doing this. Check with the companies involved to see if this is possible; see p148 for contact details.

Hitching

Getting around on the Manu'a Islands will involve sticking your thumb out more times than not. There are a few vehicles on the islands and few drivers will pass a walker without offering a lift.

OFU

The aerial introduction to the most beautiful of the Manu'a Islands couldn't be more dramatic if it was scripted. Buffeted by crosswinds, the plane drones towards a thin ribbon of flat land between the beach and

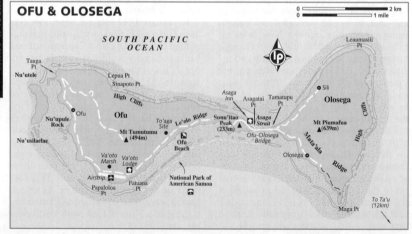

the southern slope of steep Mt Tumutumu. Its wings twitch frantically up and down a few times before the wheels finally hit dry land, and the plane scoots along tarmac bordered by a dazzling coral reef and a beach you immediately decide you want to kiss.

Ofu has lots in common with Olosega, the island to which it's joined by a short bridge. Both are made up of volcanic cones that have been buried by lava from two merging shield flows. During a long period of dormancy, deep valleys were carved out, leaving very high, sheer cliffs around the islands. The bight along the south coast of the islands was caused by the collapse of one wall of the caldera. The fringing coral reef here, part of the National Park of American Samoa, is one of the best-preserved reefs in the Samoas and offers sensational snorkelling.

OFU BEACH

Ofu's crown jewel is its south coast beach. It's surely one of the finest in the South Pacific: 4km of shining, palm-fringed white sand, and the only footprints to be seen other than your own are those of birds and crabs. This is the sort of place visitors to Waikiki and Surfers Paradise actually dream of.

The strip of beach stretching from 500m past Va'oto Lodge (p128) to the beginning of the Ofu-Olosega bridge, plus 140 hectares of offshore waters, comprise the Ofu section of the **National Park of American Samoa**. As you round a small point west of Vao'oto Lodge, you're confronted by a bewitching arc of sand sweeping around a glorious, coral-studded lagoon. At the far end, a magnificent backdrop is provided by the sharp summit of Olosega's highest peak, the 639m Mt Piumafua. Looking inland, sea birds drift across the sheer faces of immense cliffs. Best of all, you usually have the entire place to yourself.

Although the reef has suffered cyclone damage, attacks by crown-of-thorns starfish, and coral bleaching, it is considered to be one of the few healthy, intact reefs in all of the Samoan islands. Almost 300 species of fish and 150 species of coral have been identified here. Go out at low tide (at high tide, waves break over the reef and wash into the lagoon), and watch out for stinging flame coral.

The narrow strip of land that comprises the Ofu unit of the national park is an extremely important source of medicinal plants for the villages of Ofu and Olosega.

TO'AGA SITE

About 1km northeast of Va'oto Lodge, behind Ofu Beach, is the To'aga site, where in 1987 archaeologists found an unprecedented array of artefacts, ranging in age from the earliest times of Samoan prehistory to modern day. Pottery unearthed here has been dated to 1000 BC. Archaeologists reckon that virtually all the coastal flatlands and broad upland slopes of the Manu'a Islands are intensively covered in archaeological sites and features.

The To'aga excavations have been filled so there's nothing to actually see here, but the site also has legendary and spiritual significance for Samoans. In fact, the entire area of bush between the road and Ofu Beach is strongly believed to be infested with devilish *aitu* (spirits or ghosts). Wander down here alone in the dark and you're very likely to agree.

VA'OTO MARSH

This 2.3-hectare bog beside the airstrip is notable for a rare herb called *tamole vai*. The marsh also contains more common plants such as primrose willow and beach hibiscus. There's a small taro plantation at its western end. If you're here at dusk, you'll probably see flying foxes gliding around the airstrip.

OFU VILLAGE & SURROUNDS

Just 2km north of the airstrip is Ofu village, which was completely rebuilt after being devastated by cyclone Tusi. Along the shore is a calm lagoon for swimming (ask permission), but avoid the pass between Ofu and Nu'utele Island just offshore, as the currents are powerful and dangerous. You can also swim off the cyclone-proof wharf near Tauga Point, but again, don't venture out too far and don't swim alone. It is possible to walk along the shoreline beyond Tauga Point to the wild north coast, but the going is over huge volcanic boulders and it's a very rough proposition.

MOUNT TUMUTUMU

The 5.5km track (if you can call it that) to the summit of Mt Tumutumu (494m) begins just north of the Ofu village wharf and twists and climbs up to the TV relay tower atop the mountain. It's possible to climb this tower to get the full view, but a large rock on the summit is an equally handy viewpoint.

MANU'A ISLANDS

AUTHOR'S CHOICE

Va'oto Lodge (☎ 655 1120; vaoto@hotmail
.com; s/d US$35/70; 🖳 ✗) Besides being
exceptionally hospitable, this must be one
of the few places in the world where you
can watch planes take off through your
bedroom window. It's set off a paradisal
beach where you can lounge in a hammock
or go snorkelling for tiny electric-blue fish
and the resident moray eel in a coral lagoon undisturbed by rips. Hearty (nontrad-
itional Samoan) meals are prepared (US$15
for three meals) and beer and other drinks
are available. Laundry costs US$2 per load.
There are 10 big basic units facing the
ocean from across the airstrip, each with
en suites and firm beds. Bring plenty of insect repellent though, as the mosquitoes
here are vicious.

This trail is often overgrown but is usually
OK to tackle without a guide, and will take
you around five hours to get to the summit
and back. Wear long pants as some of the
local vegetation has cutting edges. The dogs
in Ofu village are a real problem so take a
big stick with you or consider getting a lift
to and from the start of the trail.

SLEEPING & EATING

Asaga Inn (☎ 655 1164, 655 1306; s/d US$40/60; 🔃)
Beside the Ofu-Olosega bridge, this inn was
damaged by hurricane Olaf at the beginning
of 2005 but was about to reopen when we
passed through. The guesthouse has four
comfy rooms and sits in its own compound,
which includes a small shop. It's a hot walk
from Ofu Beach, but you can always cool off
under the bridge. Meals are available.

You may be able to arrange accommodation on Ofu through the National Park of
American Samoa's homestay programme;
for details, see p108. There's a basic store
in Ofu village.

OLOSEGA

Olosega is virtually Ofu's twin island and
shares the same marvellous encircling reef
system. The two islands are separated by the
137m-wide Asaga Strait, which is crossed by
a cyclone-proof bridge. Strong winds and

water currents are funnelled through this
pass by steep cliffs on each island. Olosega
has a very nice beach along its southwest
coast between the pass and Olosega village.

There was another small settlement at
Sili on the northwestern side of the island,
in a location that was unfortunately fully
exposed to hurricanes and heavy seas. Now
only one determined family lives there.

MAGA POINT

The 1.5km walk from Olosega village up on
to Maga Point on the southern tip of the
island will give you an unforgettable experience in beautiful isolation. To avoid dealing
with local dogs, veer around Olosega village on the beach. After passing the rubbish tip, continue along the beach (which
is composed of husks of dead coral) and
look for the narrow trail that climbs steadily
along the side of the hill towards the point.
Bring a stick to clear the myriad spider webs
draped across this trail, and wear good walking shoes to keep your footing on the loose
rocks and soil. You'll eventually be abreast
of the point's rocky outcrop down below. Sit
down here to enjoy the magnificent view and
wondrous sense of remoteness. The white
bellies of boobies soar close overhead, rows
of coral march away from the jagged point,
and the southern shorelines of Olosega and
Ofu are laid out for your appreciation, while
to the southeast is the hulking outline of Ta'u
surrounded by empty, limitless ocean.

From here, the trail descends to a beach,
but few people head down there and we
couldn't ascertain the condition of this part
of the trail.

OFU-OLOSEGA BRIDGE

Local kids regularly jump off the Ofu-
Olosega bridge and into Asaga Strait, letting the current carry them to shore. If you
want to try this yourself, make sure you
assess the water's depth and the strength
of the current first. Looking down from
the bridge, the water in the strait is usually spectacularly clear, allowing you to see
large eels twisting near the shore.

SLEEPING & EATING

There is no official tourist accommodation
on Olosega. Basic, expensive supplies – soft
drinks and tinned food – are available at the
store in Olosega village.

TA'U

Remote Ta'u is a hulking shield volcano, half of which has fallen away in the south, leaving an island that really looks like half an island. On the dramatic south coast, some of the highest sea cliffs in the world rise 966m to Mt Lata, the highest point in American Samoa. Much of the island is covered in dense rainforest and dotted with inactive cones and craters. Ta'u feels seriously remote and sees few visitors: the place to go if you want to lose yourself in virtually unexplored terrain.

NATIONAL PARK OF AMERICAN SAMOA

The Ta'u unit of the national park occupies 2160 hectares of land, comprising most of the uninhabited southern half of Ta'u, and 400 hectares of offshore waters. As would be expected, the protected area takes in some of American Samoa's most fantastic scenery. Ta'u is a shield volcano that has undergone dramatic changes. The apocalyptic collapse of half its caldera left a spectacular escarpment along the southern side. On the northern slope, numerous craters and cones remained active after the big event, and continued to build that side of the island.

Ta'u's protected lowland and montane **rainforests** provide an excellent habitat for flying foxes and many native **birds**. Species include black noddies, white terns, white-tailed tropicbirds, Tahiti petrels, Audubon's shearwaters, Fiji shrikebills, friendly ground doves, multicoloured fruit doves, spotless crakes and the most important bird in Samoan culture – the *lupe* (Pacific pigeon).

Other native **wildlife** includes the Pacific boa, which lives only on Ta'u (in very small numbers); 13 species of amphibians and reptiles, most of which are geckos and skinks; and 20 species of land snail. It's believed that endangered sea turtles nest along the remote shorelines of Ta'u.

For more information on the national park, contact the **National Park Visitor Information Center** (☎ 633 7082; www.nps.gov/npsa/home .htm; Pago Plaza) in Pago Pago.

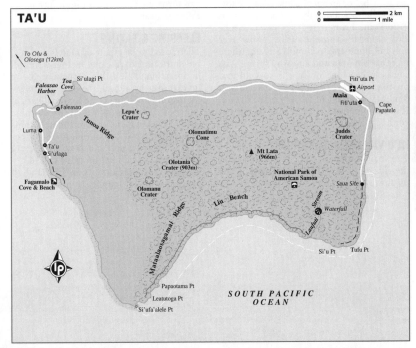

TA'U

0   2 km
0   1 mile

To Ofu &
Olosega (12km)

Faleasao Harbor
Toa Cove
Si'ulagi Pt
Faleasao
Fiti'uta Pt
Airport
Maia
Fiti'uta
Cape Papatele

Lepu'e Crater
Tunoa Ridge
Luma
Ta'u
Si'ufaga

Olomatimu Cone
Judds Crater

Mt Lata (966m)

Olotania Crater (903m)
National Park of American Samoa
Saua Site

Fagamalo Cove & Beach
Olomanu Crater
Mataalaosagamai Ridge
Liu Bench
Laufuti Stream
Waterfall

Papaotama Pt
Leatutoga Pt
Si'ufa'alele Pt
SOUTH PACIFIC OCEAN
Si'u Pt
Tufu Pt

MANU'A ISLANDS

Saua Site

Halfway down the east coast of the island (about 2.5km from Fiti'uta) is the legendary Samoan site of Saua. This is where the god Tagaloa is said to have created the first humans before sending them out to Polynesia (see And God Created Samoa, p125). Tagaloa also crowned the first Tu'i Manu'a here.

Only volcanic boulders, wild surf and a windswept beach mark this very sacred place. Archaeologists have located the remains of an ancient village near Saua, as well as numerous grave sites between Saua and Si'u Point. More intensive surveys are yet to be carried out. During calm seas (usually from October to March) the offshore waters near Saua are used by Fiti'uta residents for fishing and reef foraging. Coral reefs are only found along the eastern shoreline of Ta'u.

Judds Crater & Laufuti Stream

The three-hour climb to Judds Crater in the island's northeast is best done with a local guide, as it tends to get submerged in undergrowth. For an encore, hikers can follow the rough track along the east coast as far as Tufu Point. From here it's possible to hike 2km along the shoreline (slow going over volcanic boulders) to Laufuti Stream, where there's a waterfall and a nearby spring. The southern coastline of Ta'u is so wild and pristine that it's worth a look even if you don't want to walk all the way to the stream. It's recommended that anyone going beyond Si'u Point take a guide.

TA'U VILLAGE & SURROUNDS

The main settlement on Ta'u consists of the villages of **Ta'u**, **Luma** and **Si'ufaga** in the northwestern corner of the island. It was in Luma that the young Margaret Mead researched and wrote her classic anthropological work, *Coming of Age in Samoa*, in 1925. Also in Luma are the tombs of the last Tu'i Manu'a and several other early politicians. There are basic stores scattered around the villages, including a bakery in Ta'u. Further north at Faleasao is the harbour where the weekly cargo ship from Pago Pago drops off supplies (and the odd tourist). The waters off the northwest coast are treacherous. Three ancient **star mounds** have been discovered high on the ridges above Faleasao.

FAGAMALO COVE

The walk south from Ta'u village to the beach at secluded Fagamalo Cove is a pleasant way to pass a couple of hours. The track along the west coast can be muddy at times, but it offers some nice views of the cliffs above and pounding surf below. Mosquitoes, even at midday, are voracious, so don't forget to take repellent or you'll be miserable. The best time to go is in the cool of the morning, before the brilliant afternoon sun turns the white sand into a furnace of reflected heat.

SLEEPING & EATING

There used to be a pair of motels on Ta'u, but at the time of research neither were still in operation. Unless they reopen, or you're invited over by a local, the only possibility for overnight visitors is the National Park of American Samoa's homestay programme (p108). One of their recommended options is in Fiti'uta and costs around US$50 per night; breakfast and lunch cost an extra US$5 each, and dinner an extra US$10.

There are no restaurants on the island, so bring any special supplies from Tutuila.

MANU'A ISLANDS

Samoan Islands Directory

CONTENTS

PRACTICALITIES

■ Samoa's main newspaper is the *Samoa Observer* (ST2), published daily except Monday. In American Samoa, the *Samoa News* (US$0.50, Friday edition US$1) is published daily Monday to Saturday, while the *Samoa Post* (US$0.50) is published Tuesday, Thursday and Sunday.

■ The monthly magazine *Tapu* (ST5/US$3) declares itself the 'magazine from the Samoas, Niue and Tokelau' and has an interesting mix of current affairs, culture, sports and business. Another monthly is *Pacific Magazine* (US$3), though it spreads itself across all Pacific nations.

■ In Samoa, listen to popular music on Magik 98FM or the government-run AM station Radio 2AP. In American Samoa, the main stations are Radio KHJ 93FM and Radio KSBS (FM 92.1).

■ TV Samoa broadcasts mainly overseas programmes in Samoa. The American Samoan government-owned station, KVZK, is responsible for Channel 2 (local programmes, noncommercial US fare) and Channel 4 (commercial US programmes).

■ Use Australian-style three-blade plugs to access Samoan electricity (240V, 50Hz AC). USA-style plugs are used in American Samoa (110V, 60Hz AC).

■ The video format used in both Samoas is NTSC.

■ Samoa uses the standard metric system, while American Samoa uses the American version of the imperial system.

ACCOMMODATION

Compared to more developed Pacific islands such as Hawai'i and Fiji, accommodation options in the Samoas are fairly limited. Samoa offers a range to suit all pockets, but budget accommodation outside the ubiquitous *fale* (traditional thatched house) is not necessarily cheap. Also, though there are several expensive resorts to choose from, don't expect European pleasure palaces.

Good-value tourist accommodation in American Samoa is disappointingly scarce.

The accommodation options listed in this guidebook for Samoa and American Samoa are given in order of author preference – leading each section are the places our author recommends the most. In Samoa, we generally treat any place charging up to ST100 as budget accommodation.

Midrange places usually cost between
ST100 and ST250, while we regard anywhere charging over ST250 as top-end accommodation.

In American Samoa, budget accommodation peaks at US$50, midrange places charge
between US$50 and US$100, and top-end
facilities levy over US$100. Prices are fairly
consistent year-round in both countries.

An excellent source of information on
accommodation around 'Upolu and Savai'i
in Samoa is the **Samoa Hotels Association** (Map
pp62-3; ☎ 30160; Beach Rd, Apia).

Camping

It isn't really worth bringing camping gear
to the Samoan islands unless you intend,
for example, to hike up Mt Silisili on Savai'i,
spend a couple of days in the O Le Pupu-
Pu'e National Park on 'Upolu, or trek into
remote corners of Ta'u in the Manu'a Islands. More than 80% of land in the Samoas
is under customary ownership and if you
wish to camp on any of it – even a seemingly
secluded beach – you must ask permission
from the traditional owners.

Fale

Across Samoa, the cheapest and often the
best accommodation is in traditional thatch-
roofed shelters called *fale* – sometimes these
are enclosed but usually they're open-sided.
Fale are almost invariably planted on the
edge of a beach, where the occupants are
continually serenaded by the sounds of surf
and sea breezes, and where visions of tropical paradise start to become fully realised.
The downside to these idyllic settings is that
the incessant sound of wind and waves can
take a bit of getting used to, particularly
if you're tossing and turning inside your
mosquito net in the wee hours, and when a
storm blows in quickly you can sometimes
find yourself having a midnight bath.

Sleeping mats and mosquito nets are
supplied in all *fale*, which can cost anywhere from ST30 to ST90 per person. The
more expensive ones come with oil lamps
and occasionally electric lights, a table and
chairs, and sometimes a bed as opposed to
a mat. Bathroom facilities are usually pretty
basic, with cold water being the norm. The
fale price often includes at least breakfast
and dinner (eaten at communal dining
tables in the more social places), but self-
caterers may have the option of foregoing
meals and paying less; check this before you
commit to a place. *Fale* will be unattended
in more remote places, but if you hang
around someone will eventually come out
of a nearby residence to attend to you.

Theft from open *fale* can sometimes be a
problem. If you're worried about this, ask
the owners if they can provide a secure stor-
age area for valuables.

The only place that currently even approaches traditional *fale* accommodation
in American Samoa is Tisa's Barefoot Bar
(see p117).

Guesthouses

There is a handful of guesthouse options in
both Samoa and American Samoa. These
are often secluded, fairly luxurious modern homes with plenty of conveniences
on offer, though sometimes they involve
a more relaxed stay in a contemporary
dwelling in outer villages of main towns
like Apia. There used to be a lot of budget
guesthouses in Apia, but these have more
or less disappeared from the local accommodation scene. Breakfast is often included
in the price of a guesthouse stay.

Homestays

Samoan hospitality is legendary and sometime during their visit travellers may have
the opportunity to stay in the home of a
Samoan family. Not only will this provide
outsiders with invaluable insights into the
extremely complex culture of the islands,
it will reflect a degree of honour upon the
host in the eyes of other villagers.

No-one in the Samoas, foreigner or otherwise, will ever be required to spend a night
without a roof over his or her head. Those
who would choose to do so – to camp outside, for instance, especially within sight
of a village – might cast shame upon the

village for failing to invite the strangers in. Be warned, however, that the hospitality of the people should not be construed as a cheap means of 'doing' the islands. Even the most welcome guest will eventually become a strain on a family's resources. It would probably be best to move on after a few days, but of course that will depend upon the individual situation.

When it's time to leave, gather the family together and offer your sincerest thanks for their hospitality, then leave a *mea alofa* (gift) as a token of your esteem. Don't call it 'payment' or your hosts may be offended, thinking you may consider them guilty of selling their kindness and friendship.

Gifts most gratefully received include money and goods that can't normally be obtained without money (as a general rule, goods or money to the value of about ST30 will be adequate thanks if you're staying with a family for two or three days). Store-bought foodstuffs will always be appreciated, while clothing such as printed T-shirts will also be enthusiastically accepted, as will photographs of the family, picture books, musical instruments, simple toys for the children or any type of gadgetry unavailable or expensive in the islands.

In Samoa, more formal (and generally more expensive) village stays can be organised through **Safua Tours** (p90), based at the Safua Hotel on Savai'i. The **National Park of American Samoa** also operates a homestay programme; for details see p108.

Hotels, Motels & Resorts

There are quite a few smaller hotels, motels and bungalow-style resorts (in the Pacific, the term 'resort' can refer to any accommodation anywhere near the sea) that cater to the needs of budget and midrange travellers in both Samoas. These range from bare-bones accommodation in dilapidated buildings to reasonably well-maintained rooms with air-conditioning, a fridge, TV and an en suite. Occasionally there are tiny dorms and budget twin rooms on offer, and there's often access to a shared kitchen. The smaller resorts tend to offer self-contained accommodation in cabins located in a small grassy compound.

Big, upmarket resorts prefer to reside on 'Upolu, where swim-up cocktail bars, lavish meals, games rooms and virtually private

beaches can be indulged in. Note that in Samoa, a number of top-end hotels quote prices in US dollars. This is not always obvious, so it might pay to double-check whether a rate is being quoted in *tala* or US dollars.

ACTIVITIES

The Samoa islands have plenty of outdoor activities to offer visitors, but whatever you do – whether it's hiking up volcanoes, snorkelling in lagoons or even surfing offshore breaks – be sure to ask the local owners beforehand for permission to use their land/beach/lagoon.

Many beaches are subject to day access fees levied by the village that owns them. Sometimes a signpost will tell you how much this fee is and where to pay it. At other times there'll be someone waiting in a day *fale* or a nearby house to collect your cash. Don't pay the fee to anyone else (certainly not kids). Standard fees in Samoa are ST2 per person (on foot), and between ST5 and ST10 per car. In American Samoa, only a couple of beaches east of Pago Pago on Tutuila tend to charge access fees (between US$2 and US$5 per person).

Diving

SAMOA

Although diving in Samoa isn't as spectacular as in some other Pacific countries, it's still pretty good. Many of the popular dive sites are close to the villages of Maninoa and Si'umu on the south coast of 'Upolu; ask the local dive operators for more information. Some of the popular sites include:

Christmas Tree Rock This large boulder rises from a white sand bowl at 25m. A giant pink gorgonian sea fan with a sprinkling of black coral at its base perches on the boulder, and titan trigger fish and red snapper can be seen around the site.

Elephant's Arch The elephant-like rock formation that gives this site its name is actually onshore, out at the end of Cape Niuato'i. A narrow channel weaves gently through a long, sloping ledge of coral, home to a variety of smaller marine life. Depths are around 14m to 18m, but this site can be subject to swell.

Garden Wall Also at Nu'usafe'e, the Garden Wall is, as the name indicates, a solid and densely packed wall of colourful hard coral ranging from 6m down to 30m. Schooling fish and spotted eagle rays can be seen here.

Shark Plateau About 7km west of the south-coast resorts and then 4km offshore to the south, this site features a plateau rising from 30m to around 10m to 15m from the surface. This isolated outcrop, well out into the open sea, attracts a great number of pelagics, including the sharks which have given the site its name.

Sheer Wall Another 45 minutes past Nu'usafe'e and close to the eastern tip of 'Upolu is Sheer Wall, a lava-rock wall which drops away from 10m to over 35m. Small tropical reef fish are found here, along with larger trevally, tuna, snapper and sometimes reef sharks. Nearby is Namu'a, a popular turtle dive.

The Aquarium Anywhere in the diving world there's almost certain to be a dive site called 'The Aquarium'. Samoa's version is just offshore, close enough to snorkel out from the beach. A variety of outcrops and bommies at 10m to 15m depth are cloaked with a wide variety of lettuce, brain and other coral. There is lots of small marine life, including anemones and their colourful colonies of clown fish, while trevally, snapper and even turtles are sometimes seen.

The Terraces There are two popular dive sites about a 35-minute boat ride to the east of the south-coast resorts on the fringing reef of Nu'usafe'e. The Terraces are just offshore, where the lava cliffs drop into the ocean, and feature a shelf and terrace at around 5m depth and two sea mounds that drop down to the ocean floor at 30m. Large sea anemones with their attendant clown fish can be seen here, as well as schooling tropical fish and occasional dolphins and turtles.

Treasure Island Off the north coast of 'Upolu, Treasure Island is a submerged coral island with dense coverage of hard corals and many tropical reef fish. Large red snapper are sometimes seen here along with black-tip reef sharks. Five Mile Reef is another north-coast site, dived when weather conditions make the south coast unsuitable.

CORAL REEF – A BEAUTIFUL ANIMAL

Much of the coastline in the Samoan islands is fringed by coral reefs – fragile environments of calcareous deposits secreted by tiny marine animals known as coral polyps. The glorious white-sand beaches of the Pacific Ocean are often composed of dead coral, shells and marine algae.

Without the reefs, many of the beaches would eventually erode and disappear. The reefs also provide shelter and habitat for a variety of fish, shellfish, crustaceans, sea urchins and other marine life, which, in turn, provide a food source for larger fish (and, of course, for humans).

Coral is usually stationary and often looks decidedly flowery; until around 250 years ago it was generally considered to be a plant. In fact, it's an animal – a hungry carnivorous one.

Corals belong to the coelenterate class of animal, which also includes sea anemones and jelly-fish. The true reef-building coral, or *Scleractinia*, is distinguished by its lime skeletons, which are relatively indestructible and actually form the coral reef. As new coral continually builds on old, dead coral, the reef gradually builds up.

Coral takes a number of forms but all are distinguished by polyps, the tiny tube-like fleshy cylinders that resemble their close relation, the anemone. The top of the cylinder is open and ringed by waving tentacles that sting any passing prey and draw it into the polyp's stomach, the open space within the cylinder. Each polyp is an individual creature, but it can reproduce by splitting to form a coral colony of separate but closely related polyps. Although each polyp catches and digests its own food, the nutrition passes between the polyps to the whole colony. Most coral polyps only feed at night; during the daytime they withdraw into their hard, limestone skeleton, so it is only at night that a coral reef can be seen in its full, colourful glory.

Hard coral takes many forms. One of the most common and easiest to recognise is the stag-horn coral, which grows by budding off new branches from the tips. Brain coral is huge and round, with a surface that looks very much like a human brain. It grows by adding new base levels of skeletal matter and expanding outwards. Flat or sheet coral, like plate coral, expands from its outer edges. Many corals can take different shapes depending on their environment. Staghorn coral can branch out in all directions in deeper water or form flat tables when it grows in shallow water.

Like its reef-building relative, soft coral is made up of individual polyps, but they do not form a hard limestone skeleton. Lacking hard coral's protective skeleton, soft coral might be expected to fall prey to fish, but in fact it seems to remain relatively immune, either due to toxic substances in its tissue or to the presence of sharp limestone needles that protect the polyps. Soft coral can move around and will sometimes engulf and kill off hard coral.

Coral catches its prey by means of stinging nematocysts. Some corals can give humans a painful sting: the fern-like stinging hydroid, for example, should be given a wide berth.

On 'Upolu, try the recommended south-coast dive outfits Liquid Motion (p79), AquaSamoa (p79) and Moanalei Dive 'n' Surf (p83).

On Savai'i contact Dive Savai'i (p95).

AMERICAN SAMOA

There's plenty of good diving in American Samoa. At the northern and western ends of Tutuila, visibility is excellent and many places have walls of coral 18m deep or more. The Fagatele Bay National Marine Sanctuary on the south coast has some superb reefs. The problem is that at the time of research, there were no dive outfits operating in American Samoa. Get an update on this situation from the territory's **Office of Tourism** (Map p103; ☎ 699 9411; www.amsamoa.com; Tafuna, Tutuila).

Fishing

Samoan reefs and their fishing rights are owned by villagers, so you can't just drop a line anywhere; seek permission first. If you'd like to go fishing with the locals, inquire at your hotel or beach *fale,* or speak to the *pulenu'u* (mayor) of the village concerned.

Game fishing is becoming increasingly popular in the islands – in fact, Samoa has been rated one of the top 10 game fishing destinations in the world. The Samoa International Game Fishing Tournament, first held in 1996, takes place around 'Upolu usually during the second week of May and attracts competitors from all over the world. On 'Upolu you can organise fishing excursions through Sa'moana Resort (p82) and Boomerang Creek Resort (p83).

In American Samoa, the **Pago Pago Yacht Club** (Map p107; ☎ 633 2465; Utulei, Pago Pago) serves as the headquarters for the local game fishing association. Inquire here about fishing charters.

Golf

Golf lovers visiting 'Upolu in Samoa can play at the **Royal Samoa Country Club** (Map p75; ☎ 20120; off Main East Coast Rd), which has an 18-hole, par 72 course. Visitors are welcome and will pay ST10/20 to play nine/18 holes. Club hire is ST20 (with a ST50 deposit). There's also the **Faleata Golf Course** (Map pp58-9; ☎ 23964), located a few kilometres south of Vaitele. To play nine/18 holes here costs ST5/8. Only half-sets of clubs are available for hire (ST10).

In American Samoa, the **'Ili'ili Golf Course** (Map p103; ☎ 699 2995) on Tutuila is a 'very forgiving' par 70 course with dramatic mountain peaks overlooking it to the north and a view of the South Pacific to the east. The green fees for nine/18 holes are US\$3/4 on weekdays and US\$7/9 on weekends. Club hire costs US\$5. There is a country club here but it is a fairly ordinary place for a drink. Take care on the hellishly potholed access road.

Hiking

There are plenty of opportunities for hiking on all of the islands. Their rugged coastal areas, sandy beaches, lush rainforests and volcanoes all invite exploration on foot. The main challenge is that not all trails are well maintained, and can quickly become obscured with growth because of the lush tropical environment. Combine this with the effect heavy rain can have on tracks and there's a good chance of getting lost (or at least covering yourself in mud). So, for more remote treks, it might pay to organise a guide to go with you.

The cost of guiding can vary enormously. Sometimes villagers will be happy to accompany you for nothing and at other times they will be seeking goods as a reward (ie cigarettes), but mostly they'll be interested in cash. In remote places like Ta'u, you will probably have no choice but to pay a lot for a guide.

Even on short walks, the sun and the almost perpetually hot and humid conditions can take their toll. Be sure to carry insect repellent to ward off mosquitoes, antihistamines to counter wasp stings if you're allergic to them, sufficient water and salty snacks to replenish body elements lost to heavy sweating, and protect yourself from the sun with a hat and an effective sunblock cream. Good walking shoes are also essential.

SAMOA

Hiking possibilities on 'Upolu include the coastal and rainforest walks in O Le Pupu-Pu'e National Park (p80); the coastal route from Falefa Falls to Fagaloa Bay (p77); the short but rather taxing walk to see the graves of Robert Louis and Fanny Stevenson near the summit of Mt Vaea (p74); and the muddy but rewarding trek to Lake Lanoto'o (p77) in the central highlands.

On Savai'i, there is even more scope. Shorter possibilities include the hike to Afu Aau Falls (p99) and the mysterious Pulemelei Mound (p100), while longer day-hikes include exploration of the Mt Matavanu area (p95), the Tafua Peninsula Rainforest Preserve (p92) or the Falealupo Rainforest Preserve (p97) (with an overnight stop in a banyan tree). For more of an expedition, you can hire a guide and climb Mt Silisili (p97), the highest point in the Samoan islands.

A well established and reliable option in Samoa is Apia-based **SamoaOnFoot** (☎ 21529, 25416; samoaonfoot@hotmail.com), which can guide travellers to remote locations such as Lake Lanoto'o, Fagaloa Bay and Pe'ape'a Cave.

AMERICAN SAMOA
The **National Park Visitor Information Center** (Map p107; ☎ 633 7082; www.nps.gov/npsa/home.htm; Pago Plaza; ⏰ 7.30am-4.30pm Mon-Fri) in Pago Pago on Tutuila can tell you everything you need to know about hiking opportunities in the National Park of American Samoa. On Tutuila you can stride along a ridge to the summit of Mt Alava (p108) and continue down to the island's north coast, while on remote Ta'u you can take the lonely trail to places like Judds Crater (p130).

The other possibilities on Tutuila include tackling the overgrown trail to Massacre Bay (p119) and scaling the island's highest peak, Matafao Peak (p117). You can also take a slow walk around pristine Aunu'u (p121).

Kayaking & Canoeing
Sea-kayaking is an excellent way to explore the islands and one of the only ways to access some of the more remote parts of the coastline. A seven-day sea-kayaking tour is available with **EcoTour Samoa** (Map pp62-3; ☎ 22144; www.ecotoursamoa.com). On this tour you'll have the chance to see coral reefs just 4.5m below you, chat with local fishers in their *paopao* (canoes) and spot many dolphins. It costs US$190 per person per day, including most meals and village accommodation.

Island Explorer Sea Kayaking (☎ 22401; www .islandexplorer.ws) offers a range of guided tours for beginners to experienced paddlers. Day trips cost ST180 per person, while overnight two-day tours to Manono or the offshore islands at Aleipata are ST360 (you'll need to pay an extra ST50 to ST70 for accommodation and meals).

A number of places in Samoa offer outrigger canoe tours, including accommodation providers on Manono (p85) and the village of Sataoa (p80). If you want to see how the professionals do it, six-person outrigger canoe teams race across the harbour in Apia most evenings.

Snorkelling & Swimming
The Samoan islands offer abundant snorkelling and swimming opportunities, most of which involve walking into reef-sheltered waters straight from a beach and flopping face-first into a marvellous underwater world.

Always ask permission from local villagers before using their beach. Not many places hire out snorkelling gear, so it's well worth bringing your own mask and snorkel.

SAMOA
If you need to rent snorkelling equipment in Samoa, you can do so on 'Upolu at the Palolo Deep Marine Reserve (p64), Litia Sini's Beach Resort (p83) at Lalomanu, and Boomerang Creek Resort (p83) at Saleapaga. On Savai'i, you can hire gear at Lusia's Lagoon Chalets (p92) near Salelologa.

Although just about any stretch of reef in Samoa with more than a metre of water over it will qualify as a snorkelling site, one of the best areas for inexperienced snorkellers is in the Aleipata district (p83) at the eastern end of 'Upolu. Strong, experienced swimmers can tackle the turbulent waters en route to the excellent snorkelling around Nu'utele and Nu'ulua, and between Malaela village and Namu'a, but be extremely wary of the pounding surf and the overpowering current that sometimes ploughs through this area. Another excellent area for beginners is around Manono (p84).

There is less coral off Savai'i because recent volcanic flows have covered reef areas. The best snorkelling is in the northwest at Vaisala, where you can stay at the Vaisala Beach Hotel (p99), and on the east coast at Si'ufaga Beach (p92).

Some diving outfits (see Diving earlier in this chapter; p133) also offer organised snorkelling trips to sites around 'Upolu.

AMERICAN SAMOA
If you don't take your own gear to American Samoa, your best bet is to buy a snorkel

and mask at Samoa Sports Inc (p114) in Pago Pago.

Some of the best snorkelling in all of the Samoas is off Ofu Beach (p127) in the Manu'a Islands. There are some good spots for swimming and snorkelling along the south coast of Tutuila (though none as good as Ofu), including Alega Beach (p116), Fagatele Bay National Marine Sanctuary (p118), and off Aunu'u (p123). In Pago Pago itself, there is a beach at Utulei where the locals swim, however, although pollution levels have dropped in recent years, the harbour definitely isn't the cleanest swimming spot on the island. In general, snorkelling is safe on the north side of the island in winter when the trade winds blow in from the southeast, and on the southern coast in summer when winds come from the north.

It's worth remembering, too, that shallow reefs, pounding surf and the swift movement of water through *ava* (passages through reefs) make much of the coastline of American Samoa treacherous. Always seek local advice on the best places to swim, and never swim or snorkel alone.

Surfing

Powerful conditions, sharp reefs, and offshore breaks that are difficult to access mean that surfing in the Samoan islands is challenging, to say the very least, and probably one of the worst places in the world to learn how to surf! While the surf can be unbelievable at times, offering waves of a lifetime in glorious surroundings, conditions are generally difficult to assess, with some very dangerous situations awaiting the inexperienced or reckless. Despite all this, the islands have become an increasingly popular destination for experienced surfers. The wet season (November to April) brings swells from the north; the dry season (May to November) brings big swells from the south.

To really get the goods, it's best to go with an operator. They know all the best spots and provide boat transport to them, and, perhaps more importantly, they have established relationships with local villagers and understand the culture – they know where it is and isn't OK to surf. On occasion, independent surfers have caused great distress to locals by surfing in off-limit areas and not considering the local culture – stripping off into your board shorts in public as you might back home is likely to cause a great deal of upset in Samoa. This can also create difficulties for subsequent surfers.

Guest numbers at surf resorts are often limited to ensure the breaks don't get too crowded. For this reason, bookings are advisable, as most of the resorts get fully booked for the best part of the season.

SAMOA

Places on 'Upolu where guided surfing trips can be organised include Salani Surf Resort (p81), Sa'moana Resort (p82) and Maninoa Surf Camp (p82). Guided surfing is also conducted by Moanalei Dive 'n' Surf (p83). There's also an experienced surf-tour operator on the 'big island' – Savai'i Surfaris (p90).

Surfers planning to visit the big island should be aware of the Savai'i Education Fund. All surfers who visit Savai'i are asked to contribute ST10 per day to this fund, which was established to benefit the people of Savai'i, principally the local primary schools. This extra cost is included in all Savai'i Surfaris tours. Independent surfers will be asked by a village representative for their contribution (make sure you keep your receipt as confirmation).

Well-known surf spots on 'Upolu include Solosolo, 10km east of Apia; the break near the islet of Nu'usafe'e on the south coast; and Boulders (p79), off Cape Niuato'i. We have also heard that there's a decent surf break near Boomerang Creek Resort (p83). Two of the best spots on Savai'i are at Fagamalo (p95) on the north coast, and Satuiatua (p99) on the southwest coast.

AMERICAN SAMOA

According to those in the know, the surf in American Samoa is (or was) one of the best-kept secrets of the South Pacific. Powerful 2m waves breaking in very shallow water over very sharp coral, however, make it an activity only for the advanced. Tutuila is one of the few Pacific islands outside Hawai'i that has a high concentration of surf spots. Some of the best surfing is found just beyond the reef near Faganeanea (just south of Pago Pago), but if the trade winds are blowing and the tides aren't right, surfing will be impossible. The rest of the time, it is still very risky. Other breaks worth investigating include those at Poloa (p119),

Amanave (p119), Sliding Rock (where you will find the fine Sliding Rock Lodge; see p120), Nu'uuli, Lauli'ituai, Alofau and Tula (p117). There are currently no surf resorts or operators on Tutuila.

BUSINESS HOURS

Generally, banks in Samoa and American Samoa are open from 9am to 3pm Monday to Friday (some branches open on Saturday between 8.30am and 12.30pm). Shops usually operate from 8am to 4.30pm on weekdays and from 8am to noon on Saturday, though small kiosks and convenience stores keep longer hours. Restaurants and takeaway shops serve breakfast and lunch between 8am and 4pm, and dinner from 6pm to around 10pm. Bars in the main towns often open for drinking around lunchtime and point patrons to the front door at midnight.

In Samoa, government offices open from 8am to 4.30pm, while in American Samoa they're more likely to open at 9am and close at 5pm.

On Sunday, almost everything not directly related to the tourist industry is closed, although ripples of activity appear in the evening. Markets normally get under way by about 6am; the Maketi Fou in Apia (Samoa) is active more or less 24 hours a day.

We generally don't give opening hours for establishments mentioned in the text unless they differ greatly from the standard hours outlined above. Note, however, that time in the Samoan islands is tolerated rather than obeyed. Be prepared for prearranged meeting times and standard opening hours to regularly be ignored without a hint of remorse or social consequence.

CHILDREN

The Samoan islands' climate (except for long periods of heavy rain or the odd cyclone of course), warm waters and dearth of poisonous creatures make them a paradise for children. Samoans tend to lavish attention on very young children – this includes reprimands for bad behaviour – but are much more offhand with older children. This usually means that foreign toddlers will not be starved for attention or affection while visiting the islands.

Never leave your child unsupervised near beaches, reefs or on walking tracks, particularly those running along coastal cliffs

(these are never fenced). In the event of an emergency, be aware that medical facilities are limited in both Samoas. Lonely Planet's *Travel With Children* has useful advice on family travel. See also p53 in the Samoan Snapshots chapter for further information.

Practicalities

Bring your own baby carrier, as you won't find any for hire on the islands. Unfortunately, it's typically only the top-end hotels that are imaginative enough to provide cots for young children, and only the bigger car hire agencies can provide safety seats. When it comes to taxis or buses, you'll have no choice but to act the part of a safety seat yourself. Highchairs are also a rarity except in the restaurants of larger hotels and resorts. Formula and disposable nappies are available in Apia and Pago Pago, but we didn't come across any nappy-changing facilities. Breast-feeding in public is a definite no-no.

Professional baby sitters are as rare as vegetarian restaurants in the Samoan islands. Talk to your accommodation provider about the options if you want to have your child looked after.

Sights & Activities

All of the islands have natural attractions that will delight children. 'Upolu has arguably the safest beaches for swimming – head to the Aleipata district (p83) and to the beach further west at Matareva (p79). Also on 'Upolu is the marvellous Palolo Deep Marine Reserve (p64), Robert Louis Stevenson's charming old home (p74), Fatumea Pool (p78) and the cultural delights of peaceful Manono (p84). Savai'i offers numerous freshwater pools in which to take a dip, such as Mata'olealelo Spring (p96), as well as a walk through a rainforest canopy (see p98), a chance to swim with turtles (p95) and the opportunity to cheer on the oceanic power of the Alofaaga Blowholes (p100).

In American Samoa, children can watch traditional *fiafia* (singing and dancing presentations; p114), watch flying foxes swoop over Amalau Valley (p115), pretend they're stranded on wild Aunu'u (p121) and experience one of the best, most remote beaches in the world on Ofu (p127).

Concessions for children are only offered at a few attractions – we have indicated these in the text.

CLIMATE CHARTS

The equatorial Samoas enjoy a hot and humid climate for most of the year. The main climatic variation is in the amount of rainfall that washes over the islands during the wet season. See When to Go (p14) for more information on Samoan weather patterns.

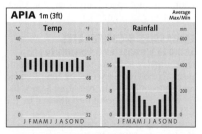

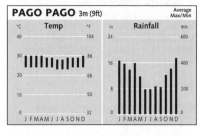

CUSTOMS

Visitors to Samoa can bring in a 1L bottle of spirits and up to 200 cigarettes duty free. You must declare all foodstuffs, flowers and items made of natural fibres (eg hats, mats) to officials of Samoa's **Quarantine Service** (☎ 20924; www.samoaquarantine.gov.ws) upon arrival in the country. Any sexually explicit publications or other material the officials consider objectionable will be confiscated.

Visitors to American Samoa can bring in one gallon of liquor and up to 200 cigarettes duty free. Items that must be declared are the same as for Samoa.

DANGERS & ANNOYANCES

The Samoan islands are not fundamentally dangerous destinations, unless you adopt Samoan eating habits (particularly those of fast food–loving American Samoans) or consider too much snorkelling to be deleterious to your health. But exploring the islands does mean having to be aware of some potential hazards and rip-offs.

See the Health chapter (p296) for warnings about sunburn and heat exhaustion, recommended vaccinations, the dangers of coral cuts, the importance of avoiding stepping on stonefish, and warnings about things that bite or sting. Issues that may affect solo women travellers are detailed on p146.

Custom Fees

Each village in the Samoan islands is separately governed by a village council (for an explanation of these institutions, see p34) responsible for the affairs of associated *'aiga* (families) and for furthering the cause of the village. Outsiders, both foreigners and residents of other communities, are often required to pay a fee to use resources, such as beaches, mountains and caves, belonging to one village or another. While this seems a fairly good way to supplement village coffers and is neither a 'danger' nor an 'annoyance', there can be a few scams involved.

Sometimes custom fees are prominently signposted, or a collection booth is set up near the entrance to the attraction. On other occasions, however, visitors will merely be approached and requested to pay. Sometimes this is legitimate, but often individuals who are in no way related to the village council get away with collecting money (sometimes in extortionate amounts) from unwary or foolish travellers.

Even authorised charges can sometimes be unrealistic. If you are in doubt about a particular fee, ask to see the *pulenu'u* before paying. As a rule, never pay children and never pay after the fact unless there was no-one around to collect a valid fee when you arrived. Standard custom fees range from ST2 to as high as ST10 per person. In many places, charges are made per vehicle.

Dogs

Dogs in the Samoas can be a real menace. Sometimes they'll run at you from their owner's house, while at other times you may encounter large groups of unfriendly strays while walking off the main road. Not all dogs are a threat of course, but it's better to treat them all with caution. For some advice on how to deal with being hounded, see the Man's Best Friend? boxed text (p104), which was written specifically about Tutuila, but applies just as much to the other islands.

Security

Theft is not a major problem across the Samoas, but it can happen. Avoid becoming suddenly destitute by keeping your money in inside pouches and secret stashes, and by not carrying your wallet in your back pocket. Also carry a combination of cash and credit cards, with maybe a few travellers cheques in small denominations as a back-up. When staying in beachside *fale*, particularly on the more isolated beaches, don't leave any valuables lying around.

Remember that it's not only honesty that's the issue here. Samoan society is traditionally communal, which means that an article belonging to one person also belongs to others who may need it. 'Borrowing' your possessions or absconding with them altogether (essentially the same thing) won't violate any real social protocols and won't cause severe strain on the Samoan conscience.

Violent crime and alcohol-related incidents do happen in the Samoan islands, but unless you hang around the rougher pool halls at closing time you're highly unlikely to be at risk.

Swimming

Many of Samoa's beaches aren't great for swimming as lagoons and reefs can become very shallow at low tide. Even in the protected waters of a lagoon, swimmers and snorkellers should be aware of currents and tidal changes, particularly the swift movement of water through *ava* into the open sea. An *ava* can usually be spotted from an elevated location onshore as a width of darker (deeper) water extending out through the reef. Avoid swimming or snorkelling alone and always seek local advice on conditions.

DISABLED TRAVELLERS

Unfortunately, travellers with restricted mobility will find little in the way of infrastructure designed to make it easier for them to get around in the Samoan islands. Almost all forms of transport and island activities are geared for the 'able-bodied', and only a handful of top-end hotels can accommodate disabled guests – the Aggie Grey hotels in Apia (p69) and near the airport (p79) on 'Upolu, Si'ufaga Beach Resort on Savai'i (p93), and Sadie Thompson Inn (p112) and the Tradewinds Hotel (p120) on Tutuila. However, this lack of infrastructure is made up for in some part by the helpful nature of most Samoans, who are more than likely to lend a hand if needed.

DISCOUNT CARDS

Card-carrying student, disabled and elderly travellers will unfortunately find that discounts are not specifically offered to them in the Samoan islands.

EMBASSIES & CONSULATES

Samoan Embassies & Consulates

In countries without Samoan diplomatic posts, Samoa is represented by New Zealand and British diplomatic missions. Samoa has its own diplomatic representation in the following countries:

Australia (☎ 02-6286 5505; fax 02-6286 5678; 13 Culgoa Circuit, O'Malley, ACT 2606)

Belgium (☎ /fax 322-675 0336; 123 Ave Franklin Roosevelt, 1050 Brussels)

New Zealand (High Commission; ☎ 04-472 0953; fax 04-471 2479; 1A Wesley Rd, Kelburn, PO Box 1430, Wellington)

USA (☎ /fax 212-599 0797; Suite 400D, 800 2nd Avenue, New York, NY 10017)

Embassies & Consulates in Samoa

Following is a list of countries with diplomatic missions based in Apia.

Australia (Map pp62-3; ☎ 23411; www.embassy.gov .au/ws.html; Beach Rd; ☿ 8.30am-4pm Mon-Fri) Canadian consular services are also provided here.

China (Map p75; ☎ 22474; Vailima)

New Zealand (Map pp62-3; ☎ 21711; Beach Rd; ☿ 8am-4.30pm Mon-Thu, 8am-1pm Fri)

USA (Map pp62-3; ☎ 21631; 5th fl, ACB Bldg; ☿ 8.30am-4.30pm Mon-Fri)

Embassies & Consulates in American Samoa

All American Samoan diplomatic affairs are handled by the USA. There are no consulates or embassies in American Samoa and currently no places that are able to issue visas for the USA.

FESTIVALS & EVENTS

Following are some of the main causes of celebrations across the islands, that is, aside from Sunday church services, Sunday feasts, extraordinarily lavish *fa'alavelave* (traditional gift-giving ceremonies), spontaneous singing sessions…you get the picture.

In August and September 2007, Apia will again host the **South Pacific Games** (www.internationalgames.net/southpac.htm), while the 10th **Festival of Pacific Arts** is slated to be held in American Samoa in 2008.

April

Flag Day Held on 17 April, this is American Samoa's territorial holiday. It commemorates the raising of the US flag over eastern Samoa on that day in 1900, and features an arts festival (in conjunction with long-winded speeches by political figures). Celebrations include *fautasi* (longboat) races, singing, dancing and traditional competitions such as coconut husking, basket weaving and fire building.

May

National Tourism Week American Samoa's rather lower-key version of Samoa's Teuila Festival takes place in early May.

June

Independence Celebrations Samoa celebrates its independence on the first three days of June with a number of well-attended events, including *fautasi* and outrigger races, horse races, dancing, feasting and more of the traditional competitions mentioned in the above discussion of Flag Day (yes, even the long-winded speeches by *tulafale*, the aptly named talking chiefs). Everything closes down for five days during this celebration, so don't expect to do any business during this time! (Samoa actually gained independence on 1 January 1962. However, as New Year's Day is already a cause for merriment, they decided to have another holiday in June.)

September

Teuila Festival (www.teuilafestival.ws) The main objective of this festival, based in Apia and named after red ginger, Samoa's national floral emblem, is to draw more tourists to the country, but locals have been quick to embrace the festival's celebratory spirit. The land behind the information centre is filled with food stalls, children's amusements and demonstrations of traditional crafts, including tattooing, while Beach Rd is strung up with coloured lights. There are also choir, dancing and brass band competitions, *paopao* (outrigger canoe) races and talent shows, with the pageantry culminating in the crowning of Miss Samoa. Accommodation is virtually booked out during the festival.

October

White Sunday Takes place in Samoa and American Samoa on the second Sunday in October and is dedicated to kids. They dress in their finest whites, parade to church and lead church services. Afterwards, the children are guests of honour at a feast that is prepared and served by adults.

Tisa's Tattoo Festival (www.tisasbarefootbar.com /eventstattoo.htm) The inauguration of this exuberant festival took place in October 2005 at Tisa's Barefoot Bar on Tutuila in American Samoa and looks set to become an annual event.

GAY & LESBIAN TRAVELLERS

Gays and lesbians will probably have to remain discreet in the Samoan islands. The obvious presence of the *fa'afafine* (effeminate Samoan men who sometimes dress as women and who are well integrated into society) belies the fact that homosexuality is not openly accepted in Samoan society – this is just one of many Samoan paradoxes. There is no 'gay scene' as such, and no specifically gay bars on the islands.

HOLIDAYS

Holidays celebrated only in Samoa are followed by an (S); those unique to American Samoa, an (AS).

New Year's Day 1 January (S & AS)
Day after New Year's Day 2 January (S)
Martin Luther King Day Third Monday in January (AS)
President's Day Third Monday in February (AS)
Flag Day 17 April (AS)
Anzac Day 25 April (S)
Good Friday & Easter April (S & AS)
Easter Monday April (S)
Aso o Tina or Mothers' Day First Monday in May (S)
Memorial Day Last Monday in May (AS)
Independence Celebrations 1 to 3 June (S)
Independence Day 4 July (AS)
Manu'a Day 16 July (AS)
Labor Day 4 August (S)
Labor Day First Monday in September (AS)
White Sunday Second Sunday in October (S & AS)
White Monday Second Monday in October (S)
Columbus Day Second Monday in October (AS)
Palolo Day October or November (S)
Arbor Day First week of November (AS)
Veterans' Day 11 November (AS)
Thanksgiving Third week of November (AS)
Christmas Day 25 December (S & AS)
Boxing Day 26 December (S)

INSURANCE

Don't underestimate the importance of a good travel-insurance policy that covers theft, loss and medical problems – nothing is guaranteed to ruin your holiday plans quicker than an accident or having that brand new digital camera stolen. Most policies offer lower and higher medical-expense options;

the higher ones are chiefly for countries that have extremely high medical costs, such as the USA. There is a wide variety of policies available, so compare the small print.

Some policies specifically exclude designated 'dangerous activities' such as scuba diving, surfing and even bushwalking. If you plan on doing any of these things, make sure the policy you choose fully covers you for your activity of choice.

You may prefer a policy that pays doctors or hospitals direct rather than you having to pay on the spot and claim later. If you have to claim later make sure you keep all documentation. Check that the policy covers ambulances and emergency medical evacuations by air.

See also Insurance (p296) in the Health chapter. For information on insurance matters relating to cars that are bought or hired, see p149.

Worldwide cover for travellers from over 44 countries is available at www.lonely planet.com/travel_services.

INTERNET ACCESS

It's usually only top-end hotels and resorts that can help those who have brought their own laptop or palmtop to the Samoan islands and want to connect to the Internet. Otherwise, your only option for accessing the Web (assuming your accommodation provider doesn't have any terminals for guest use) is an Internet café. Note that Web connections can drop out with frustrating frequency on these remote islands.

In Samoa, you'll find several Internet cafés scattered around Apia (for details, see p61). On Savai'i, you can get connected in Salelologa (p91) and Manase (p94). On 'Upolu, expect to pay up to ST4 per 15 minutes of access; on Savai'i you'll pay up to ST10 for the same amount of time.

American Samoa has several Internet café options in Pago Pago (p106), where you'll pay around US$3 per 15 minutes.

LEGAL MATTERS

It's fair to say that most travellers will have no formal contact with Samoan police, except perhaps when watching the Police Band do its early morning march along Apia's waterfront, or when asking a local American Samoan cop for directions to the taxi rank outside Tafuna International Airport.

Anyone caught carrying any amount of illegal drugs will face a potentially harsh penalty (particularly in American Samoa) so firmly resist the temptation to do this. Remaining in either of the Samoas beyond the life of your permit or visa is also not a good idea, as you risk deportation or other penalties. Remember that if you are arrested, your local consulate or embassy (assuming there is one) will not be able to help you if you are in any way at fault.

MAPS

The Tourism Authority in Apia distributes the free, super-basic Jasons *Samoa Visitor Map*. It also sells the much more detailed 1:200,000 *Samoa* map published by Hema (ST10), but it's woefully out of date.

The **Ministry of Natural Resources & Environment** (Map pp62-3; ☎ 23800; Beach Rd) in Apia sells 1:50,000 topographic sheet maps of 'Upolu (two sheets) and Savai'i (four sheets) for ST30 per sheet. Unfortunately these haven't been updated since 2000 and lack recent road system changes. You need to pay for the maps at the ministry office beside the New Zealand High Commission and then pick them up from a second office near the deep sea wharf.

The University of Hawai'i's *Islands of Samoa* map (US$4) contains topographic detail of both Samoa and American Samoa, comprehensive labelling of geographic names and a useful index. On the downside, it was last updated in 1990. In Apia the map is usually available from **Aggie Grey's Gift Shop** (Map pp62-3; ☎ 22880; Beach Rd). In Pago Pago it's available from the **Iupeli Siliva Wesley Bookshop** (p107; ☎ 633 2201).

The US National Park Service publishes a handy free map and guide to American Samoa. It's available from the **National Park Visitor Information Center** (Map p107; ☎ 633 7082; www.nps.gov/npsa/home.htm; Pago Plaza; ❂ 7.30am-4.30pm Mon-Fri).

Detailed topographic mapping for American Samoa is available through the **USGS** (US Geological Survey; www.usgs.gov), which has offices all over the USA.

MONEY

The *tala*, which is divided into 100 *sene*, is the unit of currency in use in Samoa. Because of Samoa's proximity to American Samoa, the most acceptable foreign currency is the

US dollar, which is normally negotiable in shops, restaurants and hotels. (Indeed, some hotels quote their rates in US dollars so they don't sound so expensive!) Banks will exchange just about any hard currency, but most preferable are US, New Zealand and Australian dollars, and pounds sterling.

The US dollar, divided into 100 cents, is the currency used in American Samoa.

See the Quick Reference listings on the inside front cover for a list of exchange rates. Hardly anyone uses travellers cheques in either Samoa because of the presence of internationally linked ATMs in main towns.

In this book, unless otherwise stated, all prices given in the Samoa chapters are in *tala*, and all prices in the American Samoa chapters are in US dollars. For an idea of local costs, see p15. For information on taxes, see p16.

ATMs & EFTPOS

Branches of the ANZ, Westpac and several local banks in the main towns of Samoa are equipped with ATMs. In American Samoa, ATMs are provided by the ANZ Amerika Samoa Bank and the Bank of Hawai'i. Be aware that ATMs don't always operate 24 hours, and that they can be prone to running out of bills at the start of the weekend. Take plenty of cash with you (in small denominations) when you're heading outside the bigger settlements.

Eftpos (Electronic Funds Transfer at Point of Sale) is a convenient service that allows you to use your bank card (credit or debit) to pay directly for services or purchases, and often withdraw cash as well. However, it's currently only available in some of the larger hotels and upmarket restaurants.

Credit & Debit Cards

A plastic card is arguably the best way of 'carrying' your money while travelling. Credit cards such as Visa and MasterCard are widely accepted by many hotels, restaurants and tour agencies, and are pretty much essential (in lieu of a large deposit) for hiring a car. They can also be used to get cash advances over the counter at banks and from many ATMs, depending on the card, though these transactions incur immediate interest.

Debit cards avoid the often steep interest charges associated with credit cards and let you draw money directly from your home bank account using ATMs and banks. Any card connected to the international banking network – Cirrus, Maestro, Plus and Eurocard – should work, provided you know your PIN. Fees for using your card at a foreign bank or ATM vary depending on your home bank; ask before you leave.

The most flexible option is to carry both a credit and a debit card.

Moneychangers

The three main banks in Samoa and those that change travellers cheques and foreign currency are the ANZ Bank, Westpac and the National Bank of Samoa. At Faleolo Airport there are currency-exchange branches that open to coincide with most incoming and outgoing flights. All the banks charge a small commission for changing travellers cheques.

In American Samoa you can exchange money in Pago Pago at the Bank of Hawai'i and the ANZ Amerika Samoa Bank. Both charge around 2% commission on travellers cheques. There is no exchange office or ATM at Tafuna International Airport, so make sure you have some US currency when you arrive.

Tipping

Tipping is not part of everyday life in Polynesia and is not expected or encouraged in the Samoas. It is, however, deemed acceptable for exceptional service at finer restaurants.

PHOTOGRAPHY & VIDEO
Equipment

Film is normally more expensive in the Samoan islands than it is in Europe, North America and Australasia, so stock up before you leave home. There are a couple of photographic and processing shops in the capitals, but memory cards and accessories for digital cameras are extremely thin on the ground – bring such items with you. Also bring spare batteries for cameras and flash units since they're quite expensive locally.

Photographing & Filming People

While many Samoans enjoy being photographed or videoed, others will be put off by it. The main point is to respect the wishes of the locals, however photogenic they may be. Ask permission to capture their image if a candid shot can't be made, and don't insist or snap a picture anyway if permission is denied.

Often, people will ask for a copy of the image for themselves, particularly if you've spent any time with them or their family. An excellent idea is to have prints laminated before sending them back.

Technical Tips

Points worth keeping in mind include the heat, humidity, very fine-grain sand, tropical sunlight, equatorial shadows and the great opportunities for underwater photography. The best times to take photographs on sunny days are the first two hours after sunrise and the last two before sunset. This brings out the best colours and takes advantage of the colour-enhancing long red rays cast by a low sun. At other times, colours will be washed out by harsh sunlight and glare, although it's possible to counter this by using a polarising filter.

If you're shooting on beaches, it's important to adjust for glare from water or sand, and to keep your photographic equipment well away from sand and salt water. When photographing out-of-doors, take light readings from the subject and not the brilliant background, or your subjects will turn out underexposed.

For more information, see Lonely Planet's *Travel Photography* by Richard I'Anson.

POST

Postal services in the Samoan islands are reasonably efficient. The main post offices in Apia and Pago Pago hold mail for visitors. You need to provide some form of identification (such as a passport) to collect mail.

Samoa

Samoa's postal service is run by SamoaTel. See its website (www.samoatel.ws/postal_mail_serv ices.asp) for further details.

American Samoa

The United States Postal Service is responsible for handling mail in American Samoa. To get an idea of the rates charged for sending envelopes and parcels of different sizes and weights from American Samoa, check out the organisation's postage calculator (http://postcalc.usps.gov/).

SHOPPING

Siapo, known elsewhere in the Pacific as *tapa*, is a type of cloth made from the pounded bark of the paper mulberry tree and is one of the most typically Polynesian souvenirs you can buy. Decorated with rich, earthy, natural dyes, *siapo* was originally used as clothing and covering. Its production declined rapidly when European cloth became available, but it is still produced for ceremonial use and collectors, and as artwork. Samoan *siapo* reach only a few square metres in size, making them fairly portable.

Baskets, bags and other articles of woven pandanus are beautiful, inexpensive and make excellent souvenirs. Woven mats of dried and treated pandanus are made by women in their spare time and serve as beds and carpeting in traditional *fale*. The *fala moe* (bedroll mats) are used for sleeping and the *papa laufala* (floor mats) cover the floors of Samoan dwellings. The much more intricate *ie toga* (fine mat) is made of pandanus leaves split into widths of just a couple of millimetres and, when completed, has the sheen and appearance of fine silk. An average one will take hundreds or even thousands of hours to weave, and the finest merit heirloom value.

Beautiful and finely made *'ava* bowls are popular with visitors and are actually used in the Samoan islands. These multilegged wooden bowls come in more imaginative shapes than their counterparts in other South Pacific countries, and all but the biggest bowls are reasonably priced.

Well-made wooden models of traditional outrigger canoes are another excellent souvenir. Carved wooden weapons can be found everywhere and there is plenty to choose from in the way of coconut-shell jewellery. In order to help protect endangered or threatened species, don't buy items made from coral or turtle shell.

Bargaining

The Pacific is not like Asia – bargaining isn't the norm on any of the islands and the price listed is the price you're expected to pay.

TELEPHONE

The telecommunications provider in Samoa is **SamoaTel** (Map pp62-3; www.samoatel.ws; Beach Rd, Apia). A three-minute local call will cost you ST0.50. International calls from Samoa to Australia or New Zealand cost around ST3 per minute and calls to the USA ST4.50 per minute. Collect and credit card international calls can be made from public phones by dialling ☎ 957.

The **Telecommunications Authority** (Map p107; ☎ 633 1121; Pago Pago) of American Samoa is open for both local and international calls. Local calls cost US$0.10. Station-to-station calls to the US mainland and Hawai'i cost US$6 for the first three minutes and US$0.40 for each minute thereafter, with evening and weekend discounts. To Australia, New Zealand and the Pacific, the charge is US$5.70 for the first three minutes and US$1.10 thereafter. Calls to Europe cost US$8 for the first three minutes and US$1.60 thereafter.

Mobile Phones

Samoa runs on an analogue system. You can organise for a local number to be allocated to your phone (if compatible) through **Telecom Samoa Cellular** (☎ 26081). Charges will be deducted from your credit card.

In American Samoa you can hire phones or buy SIM cards for GSM 900-compatible mobiles from **Blue Sky Communications** (Map p107; ☎ 699 2759; Pago Plaza, Pago Pago).

Phone Codes

The country code for Samoa is ☎ 685 and for American Samoa is ☎ 684. Neither nation uses area codes.

Phonecards

In Samoa, phonecards are available for ST5, ST10, ST20 and ST50, and can be used in around 75 card phones around 'Upolu and Savai'i. There's a similar choice of phonecards in American Samoa, though card phones are virtually nonexistent outside Pago Pago and the main commercial strips of Tafuna and Nu'uuli.

TIME

Time doesn't really move more slowly in the South Pacific, but it certainly seems that way. On Sunday in particular, it can even appear to grind to a halt. Visitors will need to get accustomed to an entirely different set of rules regarding punctuality. If a Samoan agrees to meet you at 9am, you may be waiting until noon, three hours being a perfectly acceptable margin of lateness in the islands.

Nothing is so pressing, they reason, that one should become flustered or inconvenienced. If it is worth doing, it can wait until later, or even until tomorrow. If not worth doing, it can be conveniently forgotten.

The Samoan islands lie just east of the International Dateline, which means their dates are the same as those of North America. The local time is GMT/UTC minus 11 hours. Therefore, when it's noon in the Samoas, it's 11pm the same day in London, 3pm the same day in Los Angeles, and 9am the following day in Sydney.

For more on international timing, see the map of world time zones (p319) at the back of the book.

TOILETS

The good news is that there are no fees for using public toilets in the Samoan islands. The bad news is that outside a couple of conveniences in Apia and Pago Pago, public toilets are few and far between. If you're travelling off the beaten track you may, on occasion, have to nip behind a banyan tree – coconut trees are potentially hazardous due to falling coconuts. Though all toilets are of the Western sit-down variety, many villages won't have flush toilets (water is supplied in a separate container). It's a good idea to always carry spare toilet paper with you.

TOURIST INFORMATION
Local Tourist Information

Office of Tourism (Map p103; ☎ 699 9411; www.am samoa.com; Tafuna, Tutuila; ⏱ 7.30am-4pm Mon-Fri) It may be inconveniently situated in a small prefab building to the northwest of the airport, but American Samoa's Office of Tourism does have very helpful staff. If they don't have the information at hand, they'll usually try to track it down for you. For other organisations that can be of assistance to travellers in American Samoa, see p108.
Samoa Tourism Authority (Map pp62-3; ☎ 63500; www.visitsamoa.ws; Beach Rd, Apia; ⏱ 8am-4.30pm Mon-Fri, 8am-noon Sat) Samoa's Tourism Authority inhabits a large *fale* on Apia's foreshore. We found them lacking in helpfulness during our research trip, but hopefully this was just a short-term experience and is not indicative of the country's willingness to assist visitors. Sharing the Tourism Authority *fale* is the highly efficient Samoa Hotels Association (p64).

Tourist Information Abroad

Samoa has Tourism Authority offices in the following countries:

Australia (☎ 02-9279 4808; samoa@ozemail.com.au;
Level 9, 99 York St, Sydney, NSW 2000)
New Zealand (☎ 09-379 6138; samoa@samoa.co.nz;
Level 1, Samoa House, 283 Karangahape Rd, Newton,
Auckland)

American Samoa has no official tourism
offices overseas.

VISAS

A free, 60-day visitor permit is granted to
all visitors on arrival in Samoa – except for
nationals of China who must obtain a visa
beforehand – provided you have an onward
ticket and a passport valid for at least another six months. You'll also be required to
provide a contact address within the country, so have the name of a hotel ready upon
arrival. A vaccination certificate for yellow
fever may be required if you are coming
from an infected area.

US citizens can visit American Samoa
visa-free if they have a valid passport and
an onward ticket. Nationals of the following
countries equipped with a valid passport and
an onward ticket receive a free one-month
visa on arrival in American Samoa: An-
dorra, Australia, Austria, Belgium, Canada,
Denmark, Federated States of Micronesia,
Finland, France, Germany, Iceland, Ireland,
Italy, Japan, Liechtenstein, Luxembourg, Mon-
aco, the Netherlands, New Zealand, Portugal,
San Marino, Spain, Sweden, Switzerland and
the UK. Nationals of all other countries must
apply in advance at any American embassy
for their one-month visa (US$40).

Visa Extensions

Samoan visitor permits may be extended by
several weeks at a time by the country's **Immigration Office** (Map pp62-3; ☎ 20291; www.samoa
immigration.gov.ws; Convent St; ⏰ 8am-3.30pm Mon-Fri)
in Apia. Take along your passport, wallet and
two passport-sized photos and don't make
any other plans for the rest of the day. You
may also need to have proof of hotel accommodation, onward transport and sufficient
funds for your requested period of stay. Your
application to extend your permit must be
made before the original permit expires.

American Samoa visa extensions are
handled by the **Immigration Office** (Map p107;
☎ 633 4203; www.asg-gov.net/LEGAL%20
AFFAIRS.htm; grd fl, Executive Office Bldg, Utulei;
⏰ 8am-2.30pm Mon-Fri). The office is located

within the Department of Legal Affairs in
Pago Pago. The office has no signage – it
has a long counter and is directly opposite
a (nonfunctioning) ANZ ATM. Visas can
only be extended by one month (US$50),
and you must be sponsored by a resident.

WOMEN TRAVELLERS

Thanks to Western and Asian videos, which
are extremely popular in the Samoan islands, foreign women have a reputation
for easy availability. Polite refusal of sexual
attention by a non-Samoan woman may
be taken to mean 'keep trying' by a hopeful Samoan man, who may have difficulty
imagining why you wouldn't be interested
given the promiscuity he sees portrayed on
the screen (a sort of Polynesian myth working in reverse). The Samoan word for 'no' is
leai (pronounced lay-*eye*) and it should be
used firmly (of course, only if that's what
you want to say). While frequent advances
may be annoying, sober Samoans are unlikely to physically force the issue.

To avoid the measure of attention that
a lone foreign woman is likely to attract,
modest dress is recommended. Don't turn
up at a pub or disco alone unless you're
expecting advances, and ignore the inane
remarks of adolescents who'll try to chat
you up. Samoan custom requires men to
ask permission of your male escort before
requesting a dance, so unwanted attention
can be screened that way.

Lone women may receive unwanted attention from men who offer to guide them
at more isolated locations around the islands. If you have any doubts about the
sincerity of the offer, try to make discreet
local inquiries before accepting.

Most of all, however, don't be paranoid –
you may miss out on some very pleasant
(and platonic) friendships.

TRANSPORT IN THE SAMOAN ISLANDS

This section is devoted to information
about travelling within Samoa and American Samoa. Information on travelling between the two nations, or to/from other
international destinations, is covered in
the Transport to & from Samoan Islands

& Tonga chapter (p290). There are also separate Getting Around sections at the beginning of the 'Upolu (p57), Savai'i (p90) and Tutuila (p104) chapters that deal with transport around each of these individual islands; a similar section appears at the beginning of The Manu'a Islands chapter (p126), summarising transport around this island group.

AIR
Samoa

The 15-minute flight between 'Upolu and Savai'i isn't as cheap as catching the ferry, and there'll be the hassle of organising another hire car in Salelologa if you want to do a driving tour, but you'll nonetheless get a great bird's-eye perspective of the islands. **Polynesian Airlines** (Map pp62-3; ☎ 21261; www.polynesianairlines.com; NPF Bldg, Beach Rd, Apia; ☽ 8am-4.45pm Mon-Fri, 8am-noon Sat) flies between Fagali'i Airport, just east of Apia on 'Upolu, and Ma'ota Airport, 5km west of Salelologa on Savai'i. There are usually two to three services a day and the fare is ST50/95 one way/return. There is another domestic airport on Savai'i – Asau Airport in the island's northwest – but at the time of writing there were no scheduled services using it.

American Samoa

Inter-Island Airways (Pago Pago ☎ 699 7100; Ofu ☎ 655 7100; Ta'u ☎ 677 7100; www.interislandair.com) services the 30-minute air route between Tutuila and the Manu'a Islands. It does flights between Tafuna International Airport on Tutuila and the tiny airstrip on Ofu (US$140 return), and between Tafuna and the airstrip on Ta'u (US$140 return). You'll need plenty of patience and flexibility when dealing with Inter-Island (their office at Tafuna Airport is signed 'Inter-Island Vacations') as it was still getting its act together when we used them: we were twice given incorrect departure times; it didn't accept credit card payments, only cash or cheques; and it was yet to offer direct flights between Ofu and Ta'u (to visit both islands requires flying to one, returning to Tafuna, then flying back out again to the other). At the time of writing, flights between Tutuila and either Ofu or Ta'u only took place on Tuesday and Thursday. Note that flight cancellations are regular occurrences, particularly in regard to Ofu because of the wind currents

that can cut across the airstrip and make landing impossible – prepare to be flexible with your Manu'a Islands itinerary.

BICYCLE

Touring 'Upolu and Savai'i by bicycle is a scenic, mostly relaxed option for fit, experienced cyclists – we say 'mostly' because aggressive dogs are a prevalent problem around the islands (p139). The roads are generally in good condition and traffic is minimal. The major roads encircling the islands are all sealed, but you'd need a sturdy mountain bike to tackle most of the trails to beaches and other coastal attractions. The longest stretch between accommodation options would be about 45km on Savai'i. You can transport a bike between Samoa's two main islands on the ferry that crosses Apolima Strait (p148).

Tutuila in American Samoa is much less suitable for cycling than the main islands of Samoa. Though smaller than 'Upolu and Savai'i, Tutuila is more mountainous, traffic is heavier and a complete circuit of the island is impossible since there are no roads across the rugged north coast. Dogs can be a major hassle here as well. You could conceivably take a bike over to the Manu'a Islands by boat, but the minimalist road networks of these islands would make this a rather dubious plan.

One of the biggest challenges for cyclists in the Samoas is the heat. Even during the coolest months (July, August and September), afternoon temperatures will still reach the high twenties. Plan your expedition carefully to avoid cycling long stretches in the heat of the day. Also bear in mind that buses are unlikely to be able to accommodate bicycles should you run out of leg power.

Bikes are a common form of local transport in the Samoan islands, so it shouldn't be hard to track down a bike repairer if you really need one. But it is obviously best to bring your own comprehensive bike repair kit, not to mention a decent lock and heavy-duty panniers. And don't expect high-quality parts to be available. Some accommodation providers rent bikes, but these are for day touring, not long-distance rides.

For information on the availability of topographic maps of the islands, see p142.

SAMOAN ISLANDS DIRECTORY

BOAT

Samoa

Ferries regularly plough the 22km across Apolima Strait between 'Upolu and Savai'i. Tickets cost ST9/65 per person/car. Large ferries officially depart the Mulifanua Wharf on 'Upolu and the Salelologa Wharf on Savai'i every two hours between 6am and 4pm Wednesday to Monday, while a smaller ferry services this route at less regular intervals on Tuesday. Sailing times are thrown into turmoil when big swells roll across the strait and slow the ferries down.

Vehicles should be pre-booked to ensure a place. Make reservations through the **Samoa Shipping Corporation** (Map pp62-3; Apia ☎ 20935; Salelologa ☎ 51477). Before putting your car on the ferry at Mulifanua Wharf, you must have its underside cleaned (free) at the spraying station 100m before the boat terminal. This is done to prevent the spread of the Giant African Snail. The spraying only takes a few minutes and you get a quarantine card to flash when driving on to the ferry.

American Samoa

The **American Samoa Inter-Island Shipping Company** (☎ 633 4707) operates a boat called the *Manu'a Tele*, which departs Pago Pago for the Manu'a Islands on Wednesday at 10pm; the trip takes about eight hours. Though primarily a cargo vessel, it does take passengers (US$35 one way, plus US$5 per piece of luggage). You can buy tickets and check in from 8am on the day of departure – the company's kiosk down at the waterfront is otherwise unattended. This boat is a good option for divers who want to transport their tanks to the Manu'a Islands, which they cannot do by plane.

You can also travel to the Manu'a Islands on board the **MV Sili** (☎ 633 5532), which departs Pago Pago every second Friday (coinciding with the Tutuila pay week) at 10pm. Tickets cost US$20 for a one-way trip (also around eight hours), plus US$1 per piece of luggage, and ticketing/check-in takes place between 8am and 4pm on the day of departure. This boat doesn't enter Manu'a harbours – rather, you transfer to a smaller boat at the harbour entrance.

Both the *Manu'a Tele* and MV *Sili* depart from the dock near the Fono in Pago Pago. Ask each company about pick-up times from Ofu and Ta'u.

BUS

Travelling by public bus is the most common method of getting around in the Samoan islands and is an experience that shouldn't be missed. The buses are vibrantly coloured, wooden-seated vehicles (prepare yourself for hard jolts) that blast music at volumes that, depending on your opinion of Samoan pop music, inspire you to either boogie while sitting down or become ill with a throbbing headache. In American Samoa, buses tend to be small *'aiga* (pick-up trucks with a bus frame attached at the back).

The biggest problem with bus travel is that services operate at the whim of the drivers. If a driver feels like knocking off at 1pm, they do, and passengers counting on the service are left stranded. Never, under any circumstances, rely on catching a bus after about 2pm. Buses are scarce on Saturday afternoon and often only cater to church services on Sunday.

Pay the fare to the driver or leave the money on the dash as you leave. Paying the fare will go more smoothly if you have as near to the exact change as possible. The buses make so many stops and starts that the going is slow anyway, but a driver having to dig for ST19.50 in change will hold things up considerably.

To stop a bus in either Samoa, wave your hand and arm, palm down, as the bus approaches. To signal that you'd like to get off the bus, either knock on the ceiling, clap loudly or, on the more 'modern' buses, pull the cord.

Although most visitors don't notice it at first, there is a seating hierarchy on Samoan buses, and a great deal of amusement can be derived from observing the manner in which Samoans seat and stack themselves. Unmarried women normally sit together. Foreigners and older people must have a seat and sit near the front of the bus. Don't worry about arranging this yourself – the Samoans will see to it that everything is sorted out. When all the seats are full (or a young woman boards and there is no other woman to sit with), people begin stacking up. Women sit on laps of women, men on men (although some mixed stacking occasionally happens) and sometimes they are stacked up to four high. When this system is exhausted, people sit on kero tins and sacks in the aisle. If someone in the rear of the bus is blocked by those seated, everyone systematically files off the bus, lets them off, and reboards without a word. You get the feeling they've been doing this for a long time.

Details about specific routes and fares are provided in the Getting Around sections at the beginning of chapters dealing with individual islands.

CAR & MOTORCYCLE

In either of the Samoan islands, hiring a car will give you the opportunity to see the sights around the main islands quickly and comfortably. It will also allow you to get to places that are not served by public transport. That said, a complete reliance on a hire car will rob you of some of the unique cultural experiences that can be gained on public transport.

At the time of writing, motorcycles were not available for hire in either Samoa.

Driving Licence

Visitors to Samoa need to obtain a temporary driving licence from the **Ministry of Works, Transport & Infrastructure** (Map pp62-3; ☎ 21611; Beach Rd; ☒ 8.30am-4pm Mon-Fri) in Apia. Bring your passport and driving licence with you when you apply. A licence valid for two/three months will cost ST10/50.

A valid foreign driving licence should allow you to drive in American Samoa, though you can always get yourself an international driving licence to be absolutely certain.

Fuel

In Samoa, petrol stations practically vanish once you get away from the north coast of 'Upolu but are more widely scattered on Savai'i (along the east and north coasts). In American Samoa, fuel is widely available around Tutuila.

Hire

There are lots of firms based in the capitals or at airports where you can hire vehicles. For details of car hire firms on 'Upolu, see p58. For details of outfits operating on Tutuila, see p105.

When hiring a vehicle, check for any damage or scratches before you get into the car and note everything on the rental agreement, lest you be held liable for dam-age when the car is returned. Furthermore, fend off requests to leave your passport or a cash deposit against possible damages.

Note that you can take hire cars from 'Upolu over to Savai'i and back, but cars hired on Savai'i cannot be taken over to 'Upolu.

Insurance

It's essential to have your hire car covered by insurance, as repair costs are extremely high in Samoa and American Samoa. Insurance costs aren't always included in the price of a quote, so make sure you always double-check this.

Hiring a car in Samoa means being subject to a ST2500 insurance excess (non-reduceable) in the event of any accident that's your fault. For information on the importance of being covered by a collision/damage waiver (CDW) when hiring a car in American Samoa, see p105.

Road Conditions & Hazards

The main roads that weave around 'Upolu, Savai'i and Tutuila are sealed and in fairly good condition. The same can't be said for all the side roads, which are often narrow, potholed and make for a rough drive.

The main hazard confronting drivers in the Samoan islands is streetlife – the pedestrians, dogs, chickens, pigs and other creatures that go about their daily business along the narrow verges. You need to be wary of what may lie around every corner, particularly in the cool of the late afternoon when people tend to go for walks, and on Sunday when villagers flock to local churches.

If you hit a domestic animal on the road, some travellers advise you to keep driving. If you stop, they say, you may experience the wrath of the offended village and possibly risk personal injury, or the destruction of your vehicle. Instead, you could note the name of the village and arrange to make fair restitution through the police.

Many Samoan drivers have lead feet and will attempt to pass you even if there's a vehicle approaching on the other side of the road. Bus drivers in particular seem to enjoy terrorising the rear ends of hire cars on the main coastal roads. Whatever happens, just let them do their thing, and if you're really worried, pull over.

Never park your car under a coconut palm unless you're interested in some natural panel beating.

Road Rules

Vehicles drive on the right-hand side of the road in both Samoa and American Samoa. The speed limit in Samoa within central Apia and through adjacent villages is 40km/h (25mph); outside populated areas it's 55km/h (35mph). In American Samoa, the limit is 32km/h (20mph) through villages and 55km/h (35mph) outside populated areas.

HITCHING

Hitching is never entirely safe in any country. Travellers who decide to hitch should understand that they are taking a small but potentially serious risk. People who do choose to hitch will be safer if they travel in pairs and let someone know where they plan to go.

The main difficulty with hitching in the Samoas is that rides won't generally be very long, perhaps only from one village to the next, so it could take you a good while to go a longer distance. Still, given the sorry state of the bus service on Savai'i, hitching is one way to see that island, and it will give you an out if you're caught in the nether lands of 'Upolu or Tutuila after the buses have stopped running for the day. You might be expected to pay a small fee for a ride, so offer what you think the ride is worth – a good rule of thumb (pun intentional) is to offer the bus fare equivalent for the distance travelled – although offers of payment will normally be refused.

TAXI

On 'Upolu in Samoa, taxis can be a useful transport option for day-tripping – see p59 for details of prices. The same can't be said for taxis on Savai'i, which are only convenient for short trips. Ditto Tutuila in American Samoa, where a cab ride can be an expensive venture.

Tonga

Tonga

The kingdom of Tonga is perched just east of the international date line: when it's a fun-packed Saturday at the beach in Samoa, it's already time for Sunday prayers in Tonga. Thus it's said, most often by the island's tourism industry, that Tonga is 'the place where time begins'. Others, perhaps observing the pace of local life, call it the place where time stands still. Both statements are true in a way, as Tonga is an eclectic country where ancient traditions sit alongside the latest offerings of modern life. Tongans avidly devour DVDs and download the latest hip-hop or international news and opinion from the Internet, but they also still resolve difficult issues the traditional way, around a bowl of *kava*, and many still weave, and wear, traditional mats.

For the traveller, Tonga offers a different experience to Samoa. The snorkelling and diving (p273) are far superior for one thing. And some travellers plan their entire trip around Tonga's marvellous whale-watching (p276). There's laid-back resort life if you want it, though without quite the same infrastructure that surrounds resorts in Samoa. There are many opportunities to get right off the beaten track in Tonga's 170-odd islands, with tiny forested islets calling your name left and right. For those seeking a genuine cultural experience, society in the Pacific's only remaining kingdom has remained more impervious to outside influences than Samoa (and it's certainly more traditional than American Samoa). You may find you have to work a little to get into the locals' confidence – Tongans are not as extroverted as Samoans – but it's worth the effort.

Tonga Snapshots

CURRENT EVENTS

Politically, Tonga is in the throes of change. Ruled by an absolute monarchy, recent wage strikes by the civil service led to unprecedented protest against the Tongan royal family. In July 2005, 3000 public servants went on strike. Schools closed and several incidents of vandalism occurred around the capital, including an arson attack on a disused royal residence. The vehemence of rallies in New Zealand and Tonga against the royal family resulted in an extraordinary address to demonstrators by Princess Pilolevu. On 6 September 2005, in the largest protest in Tonga's history, strikers called for the dismissal of Prime Minister Prince 'Ulukalala Lavaka Ata and his cabinet. After the six-week strike, wage increases of up to 80% were awarded to protestors. The fallout from these strikes continues, and on 11 February 2006, the Prime Minister resigned. People's Representative and Cabinet Minister, Dr Fred Sevele, was appointed acting Prime Minister, and many are hopeful that a more democratic Tonga is imminent.

The 2005 election also saw the re-election of seven candidates from the Tonga Human Rights and Democracy Movement (THRDM). Tonga's first incorporated political party, the Peoples' Democratic Party, was registered in July 2005, further adding to the voices of dissent. Though THRDM faces resistance from outside and division within, the Tongan Parliament agreed to the formation of a National Committee for Reform, which met in December 2005. This committee will consider submissions from the movement for political change, and key THRDM activists are preparing proposals for alternative models of governance.

Aviation controversies have also plagued Tonga in recent times. After discontinuing flights to the Niuas and 'Eua due to insufficient aircraft, Royal Tongan Airlines crashed financially midway through 2004. Two operators, Crown Prince–owned Air Peau Vava'u, and FlyNiu, emerged willing to take over domestic routes, but some heavy politicking served to keep FlyNiu out of the aviation equation. Struggling with only two DC3s, Air Peau Vava'u has been unable to fly to the Niuas or 'Eua. In light of this, the airline monopoly has been halted and a new carrier, Airlines Tonga, has reinstated services to the Niuas. It also hopes to extend their services to 'Eua, resources and pigs on the runway permitting.

Tonga's sporting future is a bright hope for the nation. Tongans were thrilled in 1996 when Paea Wolfgramm won Tonga's first Olympic medal in Atlanta, a silver for boxing. Unfortunately this Olympic success hasn't been repeated, but Tongans have been prominent in other sporting arenas, particularly rugby. Players of Tongan origin such as Steve and Toutai Kefu, Willie Ofahengaue, Finau Maka and All Blacks winger Jonah Lomu have dominated the rugby field. Tongan players have also joined forces with islanders from Samoa and Fiji to form the Pacific Island Rugby team, due to tour Europe in 2006. Surfing is becoming more high profile in Tonga, with the western coast of Nuku'alofa renowned for its breaks. Brother and sister Michael and 'Anau Burling won or were placed highly in a number of surfing events in 2005, including the Oceanic Cup. Amongst the world's first surfers, early Tongan islanders used the sides of canoes for surfing and body boarding, and the present king surfed in his youth. Today, surfing is growing in popularity and profile in Tonga.

FAST FACTS

GDP: T$296 million

Major exports: squash, pumpkin, vanilla, *kava* and other root crops

Population: 101,700

Population under the age of 25: 55%

Midnight: the hour nightclubs close on a Saturday night, in preparation for the Sabbath

Literacy rate: 99%

Total Tongan land area: 747 sq km

1806: the last year a missionary ended up in a Tongan cooking pot

HISTORY

MYTHOLOGY

Tonga has a rich mythological tradition. The main deities of this mythology were the male gods Tangaloa and Maui, rulers of the sky and the underworld respectively, and the female demigod Hikule'o who ruled Pulotu, Tongan paradise. Many ancient legends relate to the islands' creation. With characteristic humility, some say the Tongan islands were woodchips left over from the gods' workshop. In another tale, Tangaloa fished the islands from the sea with a tortoiseshell-and-whalebone hook. Perhaps not adept with the fishing rod, his line snagged on the island of Nuapapu, scattering into the sea the bits of land now known as the Vava'u Group.

Another story tells us that Tonga was the product of a successful fishing trip by Maui. Fishing with a hook borrowed from an old man called Tonga, Maui plucked all the islands from the ocean one by one, and called the largest Tonga to honour the old man and his miraculous hook.

> Natural disasters were always attributed to the gods. It was said that Maui carried the earth on his shoulder. When he switched shoulders or fell asleep, the land would shudder with an earthquake.

FIRST SETTLEMENT

In the 1940s, eccentric Norwegian scientist, explorer and archaeologist, Thor Heyerdahl, theorised that Polynesians first migrated from Peru and Easter Island on balsawood rafts. This hypothesis was based on the fact that currents and winds were easterly, and that sweet potato, or *kumala*, was historically found in South America and the Pacific, rather than Asia. To prove his point, Heyerdahl built a model of these rafts, and travelled from Peru to Polynesia in the famous Kon-Tiki expedition of 1947.

Heyerdahl convincingly demonstrated that early travel from the Americas to the Pacific was possible, but it is more widely accepted that the Lapita people were of Southeast Asian origin and that these Austronesians migrated westwards to become the ancestors of present-day Polynesians. Experts estimate that the Lapita people arrived in the region between 3100 and 3000 BC, but the earliest date confirmed by radiocarbon testing is around 1100 BC. These earlier dates are based on a series of archaeological discoveries, which unearthed similar examples of Lapita pottery in the Bismarck Archipelago, New Caledonia, Fiji, Tonga and Samoa.

> Tupou Posesi Fanua has published an excellent, bilingual collection of Tongan oral stories called *Po Fananga: Folk Tales of Tonga*. It includes the coconut-tree legend and stories of the gods, spirits and first islanders.

It's believed that when the Lapita people arrived in Tonga they founded the first in a series of capitals at Toloa, near present-day Fua'amotu International Airport. The second site for a capital was Heketa, on the northeastern tip of Tongatapu. Here, King Tu'itatui constructed the famous Ha'amonga 'a Maui Trilithon (p209), Tonga's very own Stonehenge.

Like at Toloa, the rugged coastline at Heketa offered no sea access or shelter for canoes, and finally the capital was moved to the more protected village of Mu'a (p199) by Tu'itatui's son Talatama. The pyramid tombs from this era have been excavated, and visitors to Tonga can now explore these significant archaeological sites.

EARLY ROYALTY

In between fishing trips, the god Tangaloa made a memorable expedition to Tonga that resulted in the birth of the first Tu'i Tonga (the royal title for Tongan rulers). He climbed down an ironwood tree from the sky to

3100–3000 BC	AD 950
Lapita people arrive in Polynesia	First Tu'i Tonga, 'Aho'eitu, believed to be the son of Tangaloa

> **CANNIBALISM**
>
> When the ample-bodied Queen Salote travelled in an open carriage through the streets of London for Queen Elizabeth's coronation with a diminutive sultan sitting next to her, Noel Coward famously quipped that this travelling companion was 'her lunch'.
>
> A few missionaries might have ended up in the Tongan *'umu* (underground earth oven) over the years but it's been a long time since the last guest of honour became the main course. Cannibalism was associated with absorbing the power of one's adversaries, and was not a remedy for a lack of protein!

the earth and had sexual intercourse with a beautiful local woman called 'Ilaheva. The product of their union was 'Aho'eitu, the first-born in a long line of Tongan royalty. According to oral history, this occurred around AD 950.

Early Tongan rulers sat at the top of a hierarchical pyramid similar to European feudalism. Strong distinctions were drawn between commoners, nobility and royalty, who were addressed with a deference otherwise reserved for the spiritual world. If chiefs became ill, commoners would self-mutilate and sacrifice fingers from one or both hands (an act known as *moimoi*) to ease the wrath of the gods.

Beneath commoners, Tongans also had a slave class called *popula*, many members of which were prisoners of war. Despite the existence of strong commercial and filial networks with Samoa and Fiji, the Tongans viciously pursued paramountcy in the region. They were great warriors, and, assisted by awe-inspiring war canoes *(kalia),* extended the Tu'i Tonga's empire so that it included part or all of Fiji, the Samoas, Niue and Tokelau at one point.

The Tu'i Tonga title passed down from father to eldest son, or to a brother if there was no heir. Interestingly, in the mid-17th century, the Tu'i Tonga created a political system with a conceptual basis akin to the present-day separation of powers doctrine. Authority was subsequently divided between the Tu'i Tonga, Tu'i Ha'atakalaua and Tu'i Kanokupolu.

EUROPEAN CONTACT

The first European arrivals in Tonga were the Dutch explorers Willem Schouten and Jacob le Maire in 1616. The duo navigated through the Niuas without landing, although they managed to squeeze in a sailboat altercation with a Tongan canoe.

The next visitor was also Dutch: Abel Janszoon Tasman passed through the southernmost Tongan islands in 1643 with his ships *Heemskerck* and *Zeehaen*. Tasman stopped for water and traded with communities on the islands of 'Ata, 'Eua and Tongatapu, which he renamed with European sensibility Pijlstaert, Middelburgh and Amsterdam. He then sailed northwards, stopping at Nomuka (renamed Rotterdam!) in Ha'apai, before heading towards Fiji.

Over a century later came English explorers Captain Samuel Wallis in 1767 and, most memorably, Captain James Cook who first visited Tongatapu and 'Eua in October 1773. Cook, not short of talent nor ego, famously

When Cook was in Nomuka, he dined on locally prepared fish cooked in coconut cream with the Ha'apai Chief Finau. Cook was so impressed with the food that he ordered his own chef to try and cook fish the Tongan way.

1616	1773
First Dutch explorers arrive in the Niuas	Cook arrives in Tonga for the first time

declared that '…ambition leads me not only farther than any other man has been before me, but as far as I think it is possible for me to go.'

Cook and his men traded metals and weapons for food, water, bark cloth and other 'primitive curiosities' which were later marvelled over in European society drawing rooms on his return. Cook tasted *kava* and witnessed many local rites.

Cook returned to Europe via Nomuka in 1774, and then on his third voyage spent April to July 1777 again in Tonga. Cook befriended Chief Finau in Ha'apai, who encouraged him to go to Lifuka island for supplies. Cook and his men had such a good time being feted by the locals that he magnanimously named the region the 'Friendly Islands'. Ironically, this Tongan friendliness masked a plan concocted by Ha'apai chiefs to kill Cook and his men. A combination of 'Tonga time' and miscommunication saved the guileless Cook, who set sail before this plot could come to fruition and the islanders' reputation for hospitality remained in tact. See the boxed text on p233 for more.

European discovery of the Vava'u Group was left to the Spanish explorer Don Francisco Antonio Mourelle of the ship *La Princesa*, who came across the islands en route to Spanish America in 1781. Mourelle was captivated by Vava'u Island, naming its harbour Puerto de Refugio (Port of Refuge) and claiming the group for Spain.

Tonga eluded the grasping reach of French imperialism. Antoine d'Entrecasteaux of France stopped briefly in Tongatapu in search of the missing explorer Jean-François de Galaup, comte de la Pérouse, who had been sailing from Siberia to Australia, but this was the extent of a French presence in Tonga.

Meanwhile, Mourelle's accounts of Vava'u had created some excitement in Spain. In 1793, Captain Alessandro Malaspina was sent around the Pacific to survey it and investigate the feasibility of establishing a colonial presence in Vava'u. Allegedly, Malaspina annexed Tonga for the Spanish crown by burying a decree on the main island, although this was never found. Distracted by interests in South America, the Spanish soon relinquished their colonial aspirations in the Pacific.

The first Europeans to settle permanently in Tonga were six deserters from the American ship *Otter* in 1796. The following year, 10 lay missionaries from the London Missionary Society (LMS) arrived in Tongatapu. This was a disaster: three were murdered soon after arrival and six others remained in hiding until they could be safely removed to Australia

> Captain Cook presented a Galapagos tortoise to the king of Tonga in exchange for *kava*. Named Tu'i Malila, the tortoise was a beloved royal pet for centuries until it died in 1965.

> Tonga is the only South Pacific nation that was never colonised.

MUTINY ON THE BOUNTY

In April 1789, Tonga became the setting for one of history's most famous mutinies. Off the volcanic island of Tofua in the Ha'apai Group, trouble was brewing on the HMS *Bounty* which was returning from Tahiti to England. Deteriorating relations on board saw Captain William Bligh and 18 crew men involuntarily relieved of their duties and set adrift in an open boat with minimal supples.

They landed at Tofua briefly, hoping to secure provisions, but local unrest forced them to cast off, having loaded only the most meagre rations. Quartermaster John Norton was attacked and killed by islanders and the other English sailors only narrowly escaped. They reached Timor in the Dutch East Indies on 14 June, having survived the longest-ever ocean voyage in an open boat.

1789	1806
Captain William Bligh and 18 crew men are set adrift off the volcanic island of Tofua after the crew of HMS *Bounty* mutiny	William Mariner is spared in the *Port-au-Prince* massacre

in 1800. The only one of the group able to survive in Tonga was George
Vason, who assimilated, renouncing Christianity and marrying a Tongan
woman. He was even tattooed in the Tongan way and was granted land
by a Tongan benefactor. Vason later wrote an account of his experience
that emphasised the lurid temptations present in the islands; he advised
that future missionaries be already married and with children!

Trade negotiations between European vessels and Tongans became
increasingly fraught and frequently ended in bloodshed. When the *Port-
au-Prince* landed in Lifuka on 29 November 1806, the ship was ransacked
and the crew massacred. The only one spared was the cabin boy, William
Mariner, who was taken under the wing of Finau. He went on to write
the now famous story of his four-year adventure in Tonga, *An Account
of the Natives of the Tonga Islands*. See the boxed text, p236, for more
information on William Mariner.

CHRISTIANITY

No-one visiting Tonga today could doubt the eventual efficacy of missionaries in the region. However, after the first, failed attempts of the
LMS, the kingdom was free of missionaries until a Wesleyan reverend,
Walter Lawry, arrived in Mu'a, Tongatapu. Lawry's stay was brief and
greatly protested by traditional Tongan priests. Successive missionaries
had more success, however, as a Tongan chief had become interested in
Christianity in the wake of Lawry's departure.

The most influential convert was Taufa'ahau, who went on to seize
control of Ha'apai from its rightful heir, Laufilitonga. Baptised in 1831,
Taufa'ahau took on the Christian name of Siaosi, or George, after the king
of England, and adopted the surname Tupou.

Under his influence, all of Ha'apai converted to Christianity. When
George's cousin, King 'Ulukalala III of Vava'u, followed suit, so did the
people of Vava'u. On Tongatapu, Wesleyan missionaries were gaining
momentum, and secured the conversion of George's great-uncle Tu'i
Kanokupolu. Upon his death, George Tupou assumed his title and became the sole king of a now united Tonga.

THE HOUSE OF TUPOU

Challenges for Tonga's King George did not end at the establishment of
centralised Tongan rule. Tension between Wesleyan and Catholic missionary presences was escalating, and many traditional chiefs and nobles
were still resistant to the new regime.

To address this problem, in the 1830s King George had started drafting uniform laws to govern the kingdom. The Vava'u Code was his first
effort; it forbade the worship of old gods and prevented those in power
acquiring property from the Tongan people by force. In 1853, King
George travelled to Australia. He was sufficiently impressed by Australian
governance arrangements to ask for assistance in revising his laws, and by
1862 he had developed a sophisticated new code that further consolidated
his power in Tonga.

Wesleyan missionary Shirley Baker played a significant part in the
drafting process, and was a trusted advisor to the king. Together they
formulated laws that abolished serfdom and the sale of Tongan land to

The Other Side of Heaven is a 2001 film based on the trials and tribulations of Mormon Elder John Groberg who was in Niuatoputapu during the 1950s. It's a convincing, if clichéd, portrait of missionary activity in Tonga.

1845	1900
King George Tupou I rules over a united Tonga	Tonga becomes a protectorate of the British Empire

foreigners. The revised code also mandated the distribution of land in the kingdom to male subjects over 16 years of age. Every man received a village lot and an *'api* (a plantation of 3.34 hectares) for an annual fee.

Baker and King George created a national flag, a state seal, a national anthem and a constitution, which mapped out legislative and judicial procedures and included a bill of rights and sections on land tenure and succession to the throne. This new constitution was passed on 4 November 1875.

In the book *Malo Tupou: An Oral History*, well-known Tongan personality Tupon Fanua Posesi recounts her first 21 years (1913–34) to Lois Wimberg Webster. This is a very readable account of her life and of many customs still seen in Tonga today.

Baker's royal patronage made him the object of jealousy in the Wesleyan missionary camp, which conspired to have him expelled from the church and Tonga on charges of adultery. This was unsuccessful, and Baker was unshakeable in his determination to shape the emerging Tongan kingdom. In 1876 he helped the King to conclude a treaty of friendship with Germany to deter French and British aspirations in the region.

In 1879, the church disassociated Baker from its mission and the king responded by cancelling Wesleyan leases; he appointed Baker prime minister of Tonga in 1880. Unheeding of criticism from various stakeholders, Baker created the Free Church of Tonga and the king urged all Tongan Wesleyans to abandon their church in favour of Baker's new one. Refusal was met with floggings, dispossession of property and dismissal from public office. Baker was nearly assassinated by the king's opponents, and six Wesleyans were executed in retribution while four others were sent into exile. Many remaining Wesleyans fled Tonga for Fiji.

This holy war of sorts attracted the attention of the British government, which had been keen to induct Tonga into its Pacific sphere of influence. Certain that Baker was exploiting his relationship with the King, the government sent an investigatory committee to assess the situation. Baker hit back and accused the British consul of having masterminded the assassination attempt. The British responded by convincing the aging king that religious freedom was necessary and that Baker had overstepped the boundaries of an advisor. After years of service to the king, Shirley Baker was deported. He eventually was allowed to return, and died in Ha'apai (p232).

In 1932 Tonga's reigning king achieved the national pole-vaulting record in his age group, unbroken until 1989.

King George died in 1893, and his great-grandson assumed the throne as George Tupou II. The new king lacked the charisma, character and fearlessness of his predecessor; he signed a Treaty of Friendship with Britain in 1900. This placed Tonga under British protection, and the British assumed control over Tonga's foreign affairs. Upon his death in 1918 King George Tupou II was succeeded by his 18-year-old daughter Salote.

Queen Salote was a passionate advocate of education, health care and the arts (p165). Of great stature, character and intelligence, she was well loved by subjects and foreigners alike. Her legendary attendance at Queen Elizabeth's coronation is one of the prevailing anecdotes of the occasion. On this rainy day in 1953, the queen proceeded through London in a covered carriage. Traditionally, Tongans show respect by remaining bareheaded in the presence of someone of higher rank. From her open carriage Queen Salote resolutely smiled at the crowds through the rain, paying homage to the newly crowned Queen of England. She won many hearts in the process, and the world mourned when she passed away in 1965.

1965	1996
Queen Salote dies, and King Taufa'ahau Tupou IV ascends the throne	*Taimi* editors and a prodemocracy activist are jailed for reporting on an impending government impeachment

KING TAUFA'AHAU TUPOU IV

The present king is Taufa'ahau Tupou IV, Queen Salote's son. He'll perhaps be best remembered for his involvement in costly get-rich-quick schemes, including selling Tongan passports, satellite slots and even flags of convenience. In 2002, the Tongan flag was spotted on the Red Sea, emblazoned on a ship transporting armaments to the Middle East. American businessman Jesse Bogdonoff, not so affectionately known as the court jester, persuaded the king to invest over T$50 million in offshore businesses; the money hasn't been seen since. In 2005, the king promised that millions of dollars would arrive in the Reserve Bank, courtesy of unknown foreign investors popularly suspected to be email fraudsters.

Still, King Taufa'ahau has been at the helm of Tonga's gradual modernisation. In 1970, Tonga recovered full sovereignty from Britain and was admitted to the Commonwealth of Nations soon after. Erratically forged diplomatic relationships with the Soviet Union, Taiwan and now China have kept this small Pacific nation in the regional spotlight. Chinese aid, trade and migration are having a profound influence on the kingdom, perhaps not least in encouraging Australia and New Zealand to step up their own Tongan aid programmes. Tonga joined the UN in 1999 and is presently negotiating membership to the World Trade Organization.

Unfortunately, King Taufa'ahau has been reluctant to embark on domestic political reform. The Crown Prince, Tupoutou'a, is the successor to the aging king, but is universally unpopular and considered to be pompous. The king's nephew, the reformist Prince Tu'ipelehake, is the people's favourite royal, well respected for his outspoken opinions and radical attitudes. The future of the royal family's rule in Tonga remains to be seen. With growing political unrest in 2005 and the resignation of Prime Minister Prince 'Ulukalala Lavaka Ata in February 2006, the royal family is under considerable pressure to abandon their political stranglehold and take on a ceremonial role instead.

Queen Salote of Tonga: The Story of an Era, 1900–65 by Elizabeth Wood-Ellem is an interesting written account of Tonga's most popular monarch, informed by the author's childhood experiences in the kingdom.

GOVERNMENT & ECONOMICS

Tonga is technically a constitutional monarchy, based on the British Westminster system of government. King Taufa'ahau Tupou IV has exercised absolute power, provided for by a constitution that has barely changed since 1875. The monarch is head of the nation and the government, which has a cabinet that consists of the prime minister and other ministers who are appointed for life. Until recently, cabinet comprised only nobles but in the 2005 election, two ministers were appointed from the popularly elected people's representatives. Significantly, one of these

---

THE PRO-DEMOCRACY MOVEMENT

The Tonga Pro-Democracy Movement began in the 1970s, initiated by a small group anxious to usher political reform into the kingdom. It advocated a constitutional monarchy without lifetime parliamentary appointments and absolute domination by the nobility. Since 1990, successive parliamentary elections have brought more supporters and a higher profile to the movement. In 1998, the group became the Tonga Human Rights and Democracy Movement (THRDM). Interested visitors will find its office on Fatafehi Rd in Nuku'alofa.

1999	2006
Tonga joins the UN	Prime Minister Prince 'Ulukalala Lavaka Ata resigns

ministers was appointed acting prime minister when Prime Minister 'Ulukalala Lavaka Ata resigned in early 2006.

The legislature is unicameral and is composed of an appointed speaker, the cabinet, nine nobles and nine elected people's representatives. The age of suffrage is 21, and elections are held every three years.

Tonga's highest judicial body is the Court of Appeal, composed of the Privy Council (king and cabinet) and the Chief Justice. Below this are the Supreme Court, the Land Court and the Magistrates Court. Local government consists of town and district officers who preside over villages and groups of villages.

Tonga tends to lurch from one economic crisis to another. GDP was T$2936 per capita in 2002 and imports ran at T$163 million, while inflation was around 11% in 2004. The national trade deficit figure for 2003 was T$10.5 million. In 2004, Tonga's Reserve Bank held foreign reserves of T$93.4 million, enough for just under six months' worth of imports.

Standards of living are generally dependent on remittances – money sent home from relatives living and working overseas. However, if family ties between Tongans at home and abroad become weaker and the money dries up, the Tongan economy will be in big trouble.

www.planet-tonga.com is a Tongan portal with everything from chat rooms to recipe-request services. It profiles a variety of inspirational Tongan community organisations, youth leaders and sport stars.

THE CULTURE

THE TONGAN PSYCHE

Tongan stereotypes are a mixture of truths, exaggerations, lies and statistics. Outside the kingdom, Tongans are perhaps most renowned for their girth, their musical talent and the nation's inimitable sense of hospitality.

Allusions to the larger-sized Tongan figure are founded in truth. While Tongan beauties are refreshingly voluptuous, along with fellow Pacific is-

---

TIPS ON MEETING LOCALS

- Ask permission. If you want to make sure that something is culturally appropriate, ask your hosts what they would do in the situation and act accordingly.

- Dress conservatively. This means sleeves, and shorts or skirts below the knee. Women in particular need to take care when sitting down to ensure that no-one can see up their skirts!

- Wear shorts and a T-shirt when swimming at a public beach. Skimpy swimwear is fine at the resorts, but most Tongans swim fully dressed.

- Take photos with the permission of the subject(s). Usually this won't be a problem; Tongan people (especially children) love being in photos and enjoy seeing the results, especially if you have a digital camera. If you promise to send photos, do so. They are enthusiastically received and placed in pride of place in people's homes.

- Be aware that solo women travellers can be vulnerable to excessive male attention. Caution at night-time is advised.

- Don't get impatient or try to cram too many activities into one day if you are spending time with locals. If things take a long time, meetings go for hours and feasts have an endless stream of speakers, you're getting a real insight into Tongan life.

- Don't refuse high table seats or front-row positions when offered. Again, this is a gesture of respect.

- Don't be surprised if you attract a fair bit of attention. Travellers are a novelty and your various habits and accessories will be foreign to many.

THE FAKALEITI

In a deeply Christian society like Tonga, there's not much tolerance for open displays of sexuality, rampant promiscuity or a tight pair of hot pants. Unless, of course, you are one of Tonga's *fakaleiti*. *Fakaleiti*, or *leiti* (ladies) as they call themselves, are men who dress and behave as women.

The most high-profile event in the *fakaleiti* calendar is the Miss Galaxy pageant. Taking place a week after the king's birthday celebrations, this is an outrageous display of pole dancing, high heels and costumes made out of everything from tulle to drinking straws. The participants display their talents, charms and dance moves to a highly appreciative audience, that always includes members of the royal family.

While most *fakaleiti* are probably gay, not all of them are; some are even married to women! Some *fakaleiti* grow up accepted, loved and without any experience of stigma. Others are not so lucky, and are cruelly persecuted as children and teenagers. Some church ministers are vehement critics, and Tongan fathers tend not to be particularly proud if one of their sons turns out to be a *leiti*.

However, the Tonga Leitis' Association is an active group, and Miss Galaxy attracts a huge amount of sponsorship. It's just unfortunate that Tonga's relative tolerance of transgendered creativity does not extend to gay men or lesbians.

land nation Nauru, the country recorded the greatest prevalence of obesity in a 2005 global study by the World Health Organization. An estimated nine out of 10 adults are said to be overweight. The Ministry of Health has responded with a public-health programme focusing on exercise, but as yet, few inroads have been made into promoting a leaner cuisine.

Having said that, Tongans are becoming more weight and health conscious. The king is renowned for having shed over 75 kilograms, and other members of the royal family have also become health role models, often spotted at the local gym. The annual Aerobics Extravaganza also attracts a huge number of entries from workplaces and community groups for its week-long programme.

The word taboo comes from the Tongan *tapu*, which means forbidden or sacred.

Visitors drawn to Tonga by the promise of beautiful singing will not be disappointed. Tongans are exceptionally musical and will harmonise perfectly at the drop of a hat. Music is usually church centred, with most people participating in choirs that are linked to their place of worship (see p166). Although American hip-hop, rap and R&B are increasingly imported into the country and embraced enthusiastically by young people, local music and musicians prevail as one of the most popular sources of entertainment. The local TV station devotes half an hour of airtime every week to homemade music videos produced by aspiring Tongan pop stars, crooners with ukuleles and enterprising choral groups.

Like most Pacific islanders, Tongans have a deep sense of hospitality, reciprocity and community. They are undeniably generous with food and belongings, and will welcome you into their homes. However, tourists are less usual here than in places like Fiji and Samoa; you may be greeted with some initial reserve before being embraced more wholeheartedly.

Anthropologist Helen Morton went to Tonga for one month in 1979, and ended up spending three years in the islands. *Becoming Tongan: An Ethnography of Childhood* gives an excellent insight into the 'Tongan way'.

This reserve is also related to ingrained traditions of respect and hierarchy. These customs and protocols can be difficult to negotiate and understand without spending a considerable amount of time in the country. Effectively, Tonga has three social tiers: royalty, nobility and commoners. Presently there are 33 noble families. Hierarchy is implicit even in the Tongan language, and the word for commoners, *me'a vale*, means 'the ignorant ones'. Commoners are required to address royalty in a special language and can only approach the monarch while crawling on their hands and knees. This deference is further evident in public life:

direct eye contact is disrespectful and people generally stoop or duck when passing a person of higher status.

Saving face is all-important, and Tongans do not like to disappoint or say no to anyone. Patience is a virtue and Tongan time is a flexible entity. Don't be surprised if you fail to receive straight answers, or are presented with directions and itineraries that go awry.

Much is unsaid in Tongan culture, and body language plays a huge part in day-to-day life. A common greeting is the raising of the eyebrows in passing. A more formal greeting involves shaking hands or an embrace, and the pressing of opposite facial cheeks while inhaling: it's meet- sniff-and-greet territory. While it's not uncommon to see same-sex friends holding hands or linking arms in the street, public displays of heterosexual affection are considered an affront to Tongan culture. Curiously, while you won't see couples holding hands or kissing in public, sexual innuendo plays a huge part in Tongan storytelling and the national sense of humour.

Following a traditional Tongan wedding, the bride's bloodstained sheets will be presented to the groom's family in a ceremony called 'api, as proof of her virginity.

LIFESTYLE

Family is the central unit of Tongan life. An average family unit may comprise adopted children, cousins and other distant relatives, alongside the usual smattering of siblings and grandparents. Everything is very communal, from food to sleeping arrangements, although brothers and sisters always sleep under separate roofs in accordance with the Tongan culture of sibling separation and respect.

Chores are distributed according to gender: men tend the 'umu (underground earth oven), grow and harvest food, collect and husk coconuts and perform all manual labour. The women clean, wash clothes, prepare and cook food, and take on the lion's share of child-minding responsibilities.

The patriarch is generally the head of the family, and land passes down from a father to his eldest son. However women possess high (even superior) status in other facets of family life. For example, a brother's *fahu* (oldest sister) will be accorded the highest level of respect at all formal and informal occasions, from funerals to weddings and births.

Most Tongans have their own homes and a family plot of land from which at least some of their livelihood is derived. Self-sufficiency is a necessity given low incomes and the high rate of unemployment. Most civil servants and teachers would be lucky to make more than T$70 a week, and the average salary is estimated to be less than T$2 an hour.

The book Voyages *by Cathy Small charts migration between Tonga and California. One striking image of cultural difference is the father who travels to Salt Lake City to buy a pony, and then, in front of the seller, kills it for his daughter's birthday celebrations.*

TONGAN FUNERALS

Funerals are of enormous cultural significance in Tonga. In contrast with the taboos regarding death and dying in Western society, death in Tonga is met with matter-of-fact acceptance and a highly ritualised grieving process.

Mourners are easy to spot: custom requires that Tongans dress in black and wear *ta'ovala* (waistmats). Visitors might observe some locals in particularly tattered *ta'ovala*, some of which almost reach the neck and face. These signify the death of an immediate family member, and are also worn in the case of a royal funeral. Certain female relatives also cut off their hair, while men grow their beards.

Funerals last up to 10 days, and require enormous preparation. Streets are cordoned off, choirs sing all night and neighbours and relatives all bring bark cloth, mats and quilts to present to the deceased's family, after which they are bestowed with the honour of kissing the dead body.

Funerals are a quintessential example of the extent of Tongan *fatongia* (duties and obligations). Families can spend thousands of dollars on catering, gifts and even filming the proceedings for family overseas.

Tongan society is devoid of materialism; personal possessions are shared communally and 'borrowing' is a way of life. Visitors staying with a Tongan family might expect some of their belongings to go astray. It's usually not malicious. Confrontation of the issue is best done with a sense of humour and the understanding that this is how Tongan society operates.

Substance abuse is a big problem in Tongan households. *Kava* is heavily used by most men, and alcoholism is increasingly widespread. Alcohol consumption is a major contributing factor to domestic violence in Tonga, which is rife but largely unreported. Use of substances like marijuana is not unheard of, but harder drugs are rarely encountered.

POPULATION

Tonga has a population of about 101,000. A little over a third of that number live in the capital, Nuku'alofa, while another third live in outer villages on Tongatapu. Vava'u is the kingdom's second-most populated region (20,000), followed by Ha'apai (10,000 approx), 'Eua and finally the Niuas.

Many young people are leaving the outer islands in search of better work and educational prospects and other opportunities. The destinations of choice are Tongatapu and overseas, where increasingly rigorous immigration laws in Australia, New Zealand and the US allow. Tongans are prolific travellers, and it is estimated that over 100,000 Tongans live overseas: more than 83,000 of these live in New Zealand, Australia and the US.

Tonga has the usual quota of temporary and permanent expat residents – often humorously dubbed 'misfits, mercenaries and missionaries' – who predominantly reside in Tongatapu and Vava'u. Australia, the US and Japan operate volunteer programmes throughout the Tongan islands, and Australia, China, Sweden, the UK and New Zealand all have a consular presence in the capital.

Other migrant communities (predominantly from China, although there are also smaller groups from India, Europe and Southeast Asia) are most prominent in Nuku'alofa and Neiafu. Generally, these groups live at arm's length from the Tongan population. While European migrants and visitors are usually accorded a high level of respect, racism towards those of Asian background is rife. While some Tongans tolerate the growing Asian presence, incidents and attacks stemming from racial hatred, financial insecurity and xenophobia are on the increase.

SPORT

Tongans are certainly avid spectators of sport. Rugby is the national favourite, and while the national team, Ikale Tahi, have experienced some spectacular defeats, they have been selected for every World Cup since 1999.

Touchingly, sports enthusiasm is extended equally to amateur and school sports, with village rugby tournaments and interschool sports days attracting huge turnouts. In terms of local male participation, rugby, soccer and even Australian Rules football are played. Sports options are limited for girls, but netball dominates in winter. The *fakaleiti* (men who dress as women; see boxed text, p161) community also has a netball competition, and even won a gold medal in the 2002 Gay Games in Sydney. Volleyball is played by both men and women, and competitions frequently take over the otherwise unused (and ubiquitous) Mormon school basketball courts.

MEDIA

Tonga is notorious for being the Pacific island with the most repressive approach to the media. The Government has waged a long battle against *Taimi 'o Tonga*, the often critical, biweekly newspaper published by

Tongans Overseas: Between Two Shores, written by Helen Morton Lee, is an extremely topical account of Tongan migration. The book has a special focus on youth identity and (now defunct) Internet forums like the Kava Bowl.

Kalafi Moala is one of Tonga's most outspoken journalists, and he has been jailed, censored and sued for his efforts. His book *Island Kingdom Strikes Back* outlines his experiences at the helm of Tonga's most controversial newspaper.

Kalafi Moala, which is often critical of the government. In 1996, its editors Moala and Filokalafi 'Akau'ola, and People's Representative 'Akilisi Pohiva, were jailed simply for reporting the impending impeachment of the Tongan Minister for Justice.

In 2003, the Government amended Clause 7 of the Constitution, effectively giving it the power to ban or restrict certain media outlets. Fortunately, this amendment was thrown out by the Supreme Court as unconstitutional. The worst affected publications, such as *Taimi 'o Tonga* and *Matangi Tonga,* are now back on Tongan shelves.

www.matangitonga.to provides excellent coverage of all Tongan happenings, from visiting Hollywood stars to political and social justice issues. It is widely read in Tonga and overseas.

Publisher of *Matangi,* Pesi Fonua, received a Pacific Island News Association Media Freedom Award in 2005 for his efforts in upholding freedom of speech and the media, and Kalafi Moala has previously been a recipient of this award. *Kalonikali* and the Tonga Broadcasting Commission (TV and radio station) are government-owned and -run, and tend to be very conservative, censored and self-censoring as a result. The Oceania Broadcasting network, *Tonga Star,* politically radical *Ko e kele'a* and a number of religious publications make up the remaining media outlets in Tonga.

RELIGION

Tongans are extremely religious, at least in theory. More than 99% of the country identifies as Christian; 41% of these ascribe to the Free Wesleyan Church, 16% are Roman Catholic, 14% belong to the Church of Jesus Christ of Latter-day Saints (Mormons) and 12% to the Free Church of Tonga. The remaining number of Tongans are Anglicans, Seventh-Day Adventists and Jehovah's Witnesses, and minority faiths include Baha'i, Islam and Hinduism. Missionaries in Tonga are prevalent and mostly well-respected, and local church delegates are frequently setting out or returning from missions in various parts of the Pacific, America, New Zealand and Australia.

Tongans invest great energy and creativity into decorating graves. Visitors passing cemeteries will spy embroidered quilts, beer bottles, plastic flowers, pictures of Jesus Christ, shells, rocks and soft toys marking burial sites.

The most prestigious local school is the government-run Tonga High School, but students who do not win a place here are dependent on the privately run church schools for their education. Of these, the Mormon schools are renowned for having the best-quality teachers and facilities, and many families convert to Mormonism in time for their children's education.

Faifekau (church ministers) are highly respected in Tonga, and are dutifully taken care of by their religious constituents. Churches rely on donations and fundraising both in Tonga and from overseas, and this often places a large burden on Tongan families who can ill afford to give more money. Many families end up taking out hefty loans or selling heirlooms in the markets around the time of annual church donations and church conferences.

Formal church occasions aside, all meetings and events in Tonga are opened with a prayer and or sermon, and religious iconography, memora-

---

CHURCH ON A SUNDAY

No visitor to Tonga should miss the cultural experience of attending church. Besides, on a Sunday, that's where all the action is. Outside of the churches, the streets are empty, all businesses bar those for tourists are closed, sports events are prohibited, planes don't fly, and people are fined for swimming or fishing, although this is slowly changing.

Whether you are religious or not, you'll find that Tongan church architecture is spectacular, the singing is world-class and it's a great opportunity to see the locals in their Sabbath finery.

Most Tongans attend two worship services: the main one begins at 10am, but others are also held at dawn and in the evening. It's important to dress respectfully and to remember that church is the one place in Tonga where punctuality is important!

bilia and billboards are everywhere. You'll see more than a few baseball caps with GAP on them (For 'God Answers Prayers', rather than an advertising slogan for the American clothing company) and biblical citations are the T-shirt slogans of choice.

Premissionary religions have a minimal public profile, but many superstitions still hold strong. *Tevolo* (devils) are feared and graveyard protocol retains the trace of ancient rituals. One such belief is that if a family member is suffering from a terminal or chronic illness, it is because the bones of their ancestors have been disturbed. Many will return to old family burial sites, dig up remains and rebury old relatives to remedy their own ill health. *Faito'o* (traditional Tongan medicine) is also practiced in every village, and for many it is the preferred alternative to Western medicine.

WOMEN IN TONGA

Tonga has a Government ministry devoted to women's affairs, and there is a healthy Nongovernmental Organization (NGO) presence that focuses on the advancement of women's rights. The Catholic Women's League has a particularly strong record, as does the Centre for Women and Children. While many women hold important roles in business, the public service and local NGOs, their representation in the political realm has been scant and women have significantly less legal and economic rights than their male counterparts, especially in relation to land. Despite growing public information campaigns, Tonga is yet to ratify the Cedaw (Convention on the Elimination of Discrimination Against Women). However, in the 2005 by-election, Lepolo Taunisila was elected People's Representative for the Niuas and became the first female Tongan parliamentarian for 10 years.

ARTS
Dance

Captain Cook was awed by the sight of Tongan dancing when he stopped in Ha'apai in 1777. On the request of the Tongan chief, Cook and his men had performed a poorly executed series of military exercises, which ended with gun fire. The Tongans responded with a considerably more polished traditional dance performance, and Cook noted in his diaries that this 'far exceeded anything we had done to amuse them'.

Dance in the Friendly Islands is still an impressive sight to behold, and is performed regularly: for tourists certainly, but also for special occasions, feasts and fund raisers.

Tongan dance is a fascinating step away from the swaying hips of the Hawaiian *hula* and the *kastom* dances of Melanesian nations like Vanuatu. While many of the male dancers possess the vibrant energy evident in other Pacific dances, female performers favour subtle movement, with an emphasis on the arms and hands.

Through songs and choreographed performances, Tongan dancers tell important cultural and historical stories. These movements are known as *haka*, and are choreographed and composed by a *punake* (the composers and choreographers of Tongan dance). *Punake* are highly regarded in Tongan society, and one of the most esteemed of these was the late Queen Salote, whose arrangements continue to shape the face of Tongan dance.

Most dances are performed in groups, like the *lakalaka*, a formal, standing dance which can require the participation of an entire village. Men and women perform together, although each performs different movements. The men and women placed in central positions are the highest-ranking villagers, known as *vahenga*. Their costumes are the most spectacular, but all the performers don impressive sheaths of *tapa* (mulberry bark cloth) or

Patricia Ledyard Matheson was one of Tonga's most famous foreign residents. She has written a brief but informative history of Tonga called *The Tongan Past*, as well as an entertaining autobiography called *'Utulei, My Tongan Home*.

finely woven pandanus, shells, flowers, leaves and feathered head dresses. Many of the outfits are heirlooms, passed down through the generations.

The *ma'ulu'ulu* is also performed for festive and state occasions. It is performed in three rows, and performers sit, kneel or stand accordingly.

Men also occasionally perform the *kailao*, or war dance. This is a dramatic display, with wooden clubs, rapid pacing, war cries and fierce drumming. Fire dancing is less common, but occasionally performed for visitors. It involves fire-stick juggling and vigorous movements to a drum beat.

The *tau'olunga* is predominantly a solo dance for young women. These dancers excel at the small, graceful movements synonymous with Tongan dance. They must keep their knees together and the lower half of the body still, unless they are moving around the dance space. The mark of a good *tau'olunga* is said to be in the dancer's smile and head tilt *(fakateki)*. Performers are usually accompanied by background singers and musicians playing the guitar and ukulele. The dancers are also doused in coconut oil, which must glisten and drip, or superstition holds that the young woman in question is not a virgin. Many chaperones and accompanying relatives swill the oil around their mouths before spitting it on the dancers to ensure that they are appropriately shiny!

Oiled skin also facilitates traditional tipping of Tongan dancers, known as *fakapale*. Spectators always slap one and two *pa'anga* notes on the bodies of performers to show respect and express gratitude. Visitors are expected to do the same. If you're attending a Tongan dance performance or cultural display, it's worth carrying a wad of smaller notes with you in preparation for the inevitable *tau'olunga*!

Enthusiastic about Tongan dance and its storytelling implications, Adrienne Kaeppler spent considerable time studying the technical and aesthetic elements of traditional dance for her book *Poetry in Motion*.

Literature

Epeli Hau'ofa's satirical *Tales of the Tikong* and *Kisses in the Nederends* are highly recommended for anyone travelling to Tonga. Renowned for his sharp wit and poignant Pacific commentary, Hau'ofa has written more than a dozen stories which unpack development, culture, foreign aid and other taboos in Tiko and Tipota, mythical nations that bear more than a passing resemblance to Tonga. Hau'ofa is also famous for his more academic essay 'Our Sea of Islands', a paper that challenges narrow constructions of the Pacific and its people. This can be read in *A New Oceania: Rediscovering Our Sea of Islands*.

Konai Helu Thaman is another highly respected Tongan writer and academic, and she has published many acclaimed books of poetry. The most famous of these is her first collection, *You, the Choice of My Parents*, but others include *Langakali*, *Hingano*, *Kakala* and *Songs of Love* (in English) and *Inselfeuer* (in German).

Pesi Fonua, award-winning Tongan journalist and editor, co-owner and publisher of Vava'u Press, has penned a collection of short stories called *Sun and Rain/La'a mo 'Uha*. These stories were written in Tongan and translated into English, and many of them explore the impact of migration, tourism and the English language on Tongan society.

Written for young adults, Brendan Murray's *Tev* is a coming-of-age story about a Tongan-Australian teenager who visits Tonga for the first time in fifteen years. He arrives just in time for Christmas with the cousins and cyclone season. It's a sensitive and appealing novel about Tongan families, customs and cross-cultural adjustment.

Music

Visitors in search of Tonga's famed a cappella music should go to the nearest church. Practice sessions are always held on Sunday evenings, and occasionally during the week. While the Pentecostal and Mormon churches increasingly incorporate electric guitars and brass bands into the proceedings, most church choirs and congregations sing unaccompanied. Church music protocol varies according to the denomination, but a soloist will usually sing the opening refrain, and then the choir or congregation will join in. Hymns translated from English into Tongan predominate, but there are also *hiva usi* – more traditional chants – which can be heard at the Free Church of Tonga and Free Wesleyan churches. The Royal Maopa choir based at the king's church (Centenary Chapel in Kolomotu'a, Nuku'alofa, p188) is well-respected, and often perform at state and royal occasions.

Apart from church music, string bands with guitars, ukuleles and sometimes a bass or banjo are well-loved, and often feature at parties, feasts, *kava* clubs and bars. Traditional instruments, such as the *fangufangu* (nose flute), *mimiha* (panpipes), *nafa* (skin drum) and *kele'a* (conch shell blown as a horn), are not often sighted, usually only on significant occasions.

Alongside local content, Tongan radio stations are dominated by the likes of UB40, 50 Cent, Bob Marley and Eminem, whose songs are often remixed with Pacific string-band melodies and reggae beats. Locally, DJ Darren produces the most popular remixes and mash ups of this ilk, and bootleg copies of his CDs can be found in most Tongan homes.

In terms of live contemporary music, rock concerts per se are rare, although reggae giants Lucky Dube, Maxi Priest and UB40 performed to sell-out crowds in 2005–6. Locally, the biannual hip-hop nights organised by Kool90FM are very popular. And no doubt inspired by the success of Islander contestants in international reality TV music shows, *Tongan Idol* has also taken off in Nuku'alofa. Due to budgetary constraints at the Tongan Broadcasting Commission (TBC), however, this is a live rather than televised spectacular.

Handicrafts

Tongan handicrafts are well respected in the Pacific for their use of patterns, textures and techniques. They also play an important cultural role in the community. Traditional Tongan wealth is measured in terms of *tapa*, pigs and mats. These items form *koloa*, offerings given out of respect and to mark important occasions like births, marriages and funerals.

TAPA

While *tapa* is the name commonly used overseas to describe Pacific bark cloth, in Tonga the elaborately decorated, finished product is actually called *ngatu*. The longest and most elaborate pieces of *ngatu* are reserved for the most important occasions. At the 2003 royal wedding of Princess Salote Lupepau'u Salamasina Purea Vahine Arii 'o e Hau Tuita to the more humbly titled Matai'ulua-'i-Fonuamotu Fusitu'a, some villages donated lengths of *ngatu* reaching over 100 metres in length.

Making *ngatu* is an extremely involved process. The cloth is made from the branches of Chinese paper mulberry trees, known as *hiapo*. *Hiapo* stems are cut before the tree has matured, usually about one year after planting. The rough, green outer is peeled off with a knife, leaving a smooth, white inner layer of bark. This is then twisted inside out and left to dry in the sun for one or two days, then wrapped into coils. Later, these dried strips are soaked in water and beaten with a flat wooden mallet *(ike)* over a long wooden anvil *(tutua)*. The narrow ends of the strips are overlapped and then beaten until the fibres merge. This creates a single length of cloth, called *feta'aki*. More and more *feta'aki* strips are then pieced together in layers with root vegetable glue.

Tonga's national anthem is called Koe Fasi Oe Tu'i Oe Otu Tonga, which is a prayer of thanks to God for watching over Tonga and its monarchy.

Pacific Pattern was put together by Susanne Küchler and Graeme Were, and is a beautiful photographic collection of textiles, textures and materials from all over the Pacific. It includes a detailed section on Tongan art techniques.

In *From the Stone Age to the Space Age in 200 Years*, well-respected anthropologist Adrienne Kaeppler reflects on Tongan art and its role in society. Of particular interest is the section on gender-based specialisation.

Designs are created using a *kupesi*, a stencil made out of local materials. Geometric patterns are common, as are animals, traditional flowers and the Tongan coat of arms. Some designs also commemorate historical events, like the installation of electricity and the passing of Halley's Comet. These are handpainted, using a dried piece of pandanus fruit as a paint brush. Paints tend to be earthy reds, browns and black. The inner bark of the mangrove tree *(tongo)* is used to make a glossy red-brown dye, and black dye is made from burnt candlenuts. Darker brown colours are also created by boiling up the dyes with pieces of scrap metal.

Ngatu is both decorative and functional. It can be worn, used to wrap corpses, sat upon, given, received, used as collateral for a bank loan and adorn walls in Tongan homes.

WEAVING

Pandanus mats are the most highly regarded examples of Tongan weaving, but weavers also make baskets *(kato)*, belts, hats, trays and other trinkets, toys and souvenirs. In times gone by, traditional Tongan boat sails were woven from pandanus leaves while ropes were made from the interwoven fibres of coconut husks.

Different varieties of pandanus plants are used for different colours and textures. The *kie* pandanus gives the finest mats, which are creamy white. White pandanus is also derived from the *tapahina, tofua* and *tutu'ila*. Off-white comes from *fa*, yellow from *totolo* and reddish brown from *paongo*. The leaves are buried in mud for several days to make black pandanus, while bronze colours require an involved process of smoking over a fire.

Pandanus requires considerable preparation before it can be used for weaving. The leaves must be cut and stripped of thorns, which are plentiful. The next stage of preparation depends on the type of pandanus. Cut *paongo* and *tapahina* leaves are placed under a mat for a few days and turned every day to allow air to circulate between them. These are then plaited into tight curls *(fakate'ete'epuaka)* and left to dry inside. *Tofua* leaves are boiled for an hour or two and then left in the sun to dry.

Preparing *kie* is more involved again. Established leaves are boiled, then the soft fibres are peeled from the coarse side, tied into bunches and left in carefully marked zones in the ocean for a fortnight to bleach and soften. They are retrieved and washed to remove the salt, then dried in the sun. When dry, women work each leaf between their finger tips and a piece of metal to make them more malleable, until they are cut into fine, threadlike strips and woven into the most valuable waistmats *(ta'ovala)*. These can take thousands of hours of weaving and are family heirlooms. For weddings, they are often embroidered with parrot feathers, wool and shells.

The Art of Tonga is an outstanding historical portrait of Tongan arts and material artefacts. After considerable travels through the Pacific, the author, Keith St Cartmail, became passionate about the longstanding Tongan culture of handicrafts.

Everyday mats *(fala)* are woven out of pandanus strips about 1cm to 1.5cm in width. Chiefly mats are known as *fala 'eiki*, and are double woven with one coarse and one fine side. The *fala tui* is also highly regarded and a specialty of weavers in Niuafo'ou. The base mat is made first from *tofua*, and then a finer layer of the darker coloured *paongo* is threaded through. Many floor mats are patterned with diamond or floral designs, which are embroidered on top rather than interwoven from the beginning.

CARVING

Carving and wood turning have a more functional than decorative purpose in traditional Tongan society. *Tufunga* (specialist carvers) were always men. They made neck rests *(kali)*, *kava* bowls *(kumete)*, canoe paddles, fly whisks *(fue)*, war clubs *(kolo; povai)* and, sometimes, figurative sculptures.

The most famous historical carvings are of female goddesses. Known artefacts have largely been attributed to artisans from the Ha'apai Group. Made from wood and ivory (more accurately, whale tooth), these carvings are eminently voluptuous with almost triangular features. Originally they would have been hanging from the rafters of religious houses, or worn by chiefs and others of high status.

Modern carving is less traditional and greatly influenced by the ubiquitous *tiki* motif. Although well made and often quite beautiful, they are designed with the tourist market in mind. Common carvings are of pigs, whales, turtles, masks and miniature war clubs.

ENVIRONMENT

THE LAND

Tonga is made up of 171 islands, scattered over 700,000 sq km of ocean. The kingdom lies where the Pacific tectonic plate slides underneath the Indo-Australian plate. Here, the continental crust forms and materials are melted and recycled into the earth's mantle. This occurs at the Tonga Trench, which is 1375km long, 80km wide and reaches a maximum depth of 10,882m. Plate convergence occurs at around 24cm a year, making Tonga a particularly volatile area renowned for volcanic and earthquake activity.

If Mt Everest was placed in the deepest part of the Tonga Trench, there would still be over 2km of water on top of it.

Geographically, the kingdom is divided into five island groups, which from south to north are 'Eua, Tongatapu, Ha'apai, Vava'u and the Niuas (Niuafo'ou and Niuatoputapu, which are closer to Samoa than Tongatapu). Minerva Reef, 350km southwest of Tongatapu, is Tonga's southernmost reach, and renowned for its wrecks and colourful snorkelling.

'Eua is the most dramatically different landscape of all the Tongan islands, with steep cliffs leading down to stunning beaches, and ancient forests. 'Eua receives a higher rainfall than the rest of Tonga, and significantly cooler temperatures all year round.

Tongatapu is the largest island in the country and is approximately 34km from east to west. Most of the land mass is less than 17m above sea level. The island peaks at 65m near the southern cliffs, between the villages of Fua'motu and Nakolo. Tongatapu's impressive geological features are well worth a visit, particularly the dramatic blowholes (p211) at Houma and the underground limestone caves.

Siosiane Fanua Bloomfield includes detailed information about traditional Tongan medicines and plant uses in her book, Illness and Cure in Tonga.

Ha'apai is a collection of low-lying coral atolls, renowned for beautiful beaches and postcard-perfect aquamarine waters. The reefs make for difficult sailing for novices, but the brave are rewarded with island paradise. Sparsely populated, Pangai on Lifuka provides the region with an administrative centre. To the east is the volcanic cone of Kao, Tonga's highest peak, reaching 1100m. Southeast of Kao and near the site of the *Bounty* mutiny

---

GLOBAL WARMING

Global warming promises dire environmental consequences for Pacific nations like Tonga. While conservative politicians reluctant to sign the Kyoto Protocol on Climate Change have seized on research that debunks the theory, it's widely accepted that the increased level of greenhouse gasses in the atmosphere are having a warming effect. The earth's temperature only needs to rise by a few degrees to affect the frequency and severity of droughts and storms, melt the polar ice caps and dangerously increase the volume of water on the planet.

The worst-case scenario forecast by the UN Intergovernmental Panel on Climate Change is that by 2070, Tonga, along with Kiribati, Tuvalu, the Cook Islands, Palau and French Polynesia could be under water. A 1m rise in sea level will result in the loss of over 10km of land on the island of Tongatapu alone. It is expected that at the current rate of temperature and sea-level increases, some Tongan communities will be forced to relocate, coastal erosion will dramatically increase and the warmer waters will result in widespread coral bleaching.

THE COCONUT TREE

Throughout the Pacific, the coconut tree is revered as a life-giving force. This is evident in Tongan mythology, and one of the legends goes something like this. Hina, one of the less committed virgins in oral folklore, was meeting her lover at the pool in which she bathed. They were interrupted midcopulation by her father, and the handsome man in question transformed into an eel and disappeared into the water. Her father ordered that the eel be killed. Just before it died, however, the eel spoke out and promised to provide for the community. He requested that his head be planted close to the surface. The villagers did as he asked, and the first coconut tree grew from this place.

And just as the eel promised, the coconut still sustains every part of Tongan life. The leaves are used for thatching in houses and to make baskets to carry food, and the husks are used as firewood. Green or new coconuts are punctured with a bush knife, and drunk straight away. When the coconut gets older and drops to the ground, it is split in two and the insides are scraped out. The shredded coconut meat is then squeezed to produce the coconut cream used in most Tongan food.

(p156) lies Tofua, the region's other volcano. A trip to Tofua can take up to eight hours by boat from Lifuka. Featuring a crater lake and a fascinating array of flora and fauna, Tofua is a must for intrepid travellers to Tonga.

Vava'u comprises over 50 islands, the largest of which is Vava'u Island which hosts the region's capital, Neiafu. The famous Port of Refuge features dramatic peaks rising straight out of the water, and is home to a significant number of yachts all year round.

Despite being grouped together, Niuafo'ou and Niuatoputapu are distinctly different landscapes. Despite its volcanic core, Niuatoputapu has many white, sandy beaches. Volcanic activity is more likely to occur at the neighbouring cone, Tafahi, which is about 656m above sea level.

Niuafo'ou is Tonga's most northerly island and it consists of a volcanic cone which erupted as recently as 1946. The beaches are black volcanic sand, and there is just one road that rings around this doughnut-shaped island. In the middle of the island are two spectacular crater lakes (p270).

WILDLIFE
Animals

The only land mammals native to Tonga are small, insect-eating bats and flying foxes (peka). The flying fox has a wing span of 1m and a large group of these can be easily spotted on the main road through Kolovai. The banded iguana (fokai) lives in Tongan bushland, but its green colouring makes it extremely difficult to spot. It is believed the iguana arrived in the Pacific from Central America some 1 million years ago.

The brightly coloured red and green parrot is found in 'Eua. The parrot's feathers have been used traditionally in ceremonial mats and clothing, but unfortunately the bird is increasingly rare. Other birds include the crowned lorikeet (henga) and the Tongan whistler. The Sopu mudflats in Tongatapu are good place to see the white-collared kingfisher and a variety of mangrove-dwelling birds. Niuafo'ou is also home to the rare Polynesian megapode (malau). A critically endangered species, the malau has recently doubled in numbers due to conservation efforts and the relocation of some eggs from Niuafo'ou to the uninhabited island of Fonualei.

Plants

Of course, the most prevalent plant in Tonga is the coconut tree (see the boxed text, above).

Dick Watling's Birds of Fiji, Tonga & Samoa is an excellent ornithological guide to this region. It features useful maps and identification guides.

The malau, Niuafo'ou's famous megapode, is unique in requiring hot volcanic ash to incubate its eggs.

Tuitui or candlenut can be used as a face or body cleanser. The nuts are chewed and then rubbed over the skin to form a lather. It is Tonga's favourite natural moisturiser.

Tonga's national flower is the *heilala*, a reddish flower that blooms with small balls of colour during the winter months. Highly prized, it is even more difficult to come by these days as it is thoroughly picked out during the Heilala festival for the king's birthday in July. Other flowers include several species of hibiscus, frangipanis and fabulous specimens of the bird of paradise flower. Most indigenous plants have cultural significance and are used in local medicines, but several introduced plants like *kava*, breadfruit, yam and *tuitui* (candlenut) also have uses in Tongan custom.

Under the Sea

Tonga's oceans abound with beautiful coral gardens, providing fantastic snorkelling. There are hard and soft corals with electric blue, red and green colourings. Endangered black coral is also found around Tonga.

Visitors will certainly sight a variety of colourful tropical fish and over 150 species have been identified in the area. Easy to spot are the black and yellow angelfish, the red-lipped clown fish and the apathetic sea slug. Tonga is also home to the banded sea snake, which fortunately is tolerant of curious snorkellers. Flying fish are frequently spotted from the beach, as are dolphins and porpoises. Less commonly sighted is the sea turtle, many of whom have ended up in Tongan cooking pots (p172).

Humpback whales arrive in Tonga between June and November and generally breed in Tongan waters. They are known as the 'singing whales' because the males sing during courtship, and their low notes reach a shattering 185 decibels and carry up to 100km.

Humpbacks are notoriously playful, and their antics are spectacular. They breach (throwing themselves out of water, landing with a huge splash), spyhop (stand vertically upright in the water), slap the water with their tail flukes or pectoral fins (flippers), and generally perform acrobatic feats.

A mature male adult is about 16m long and weighs about 40 to 45 tonnes. The calves are around 4m at birth and weigh up to 2.5 tonnes. They gain approximately 25kg a day – about a kilogram an hour – on their mother's milk. When the calves have put on about 10cm of blubber, the whales return to the Antarctic summer-feeding grounds, and calves stay with their mothers for two years.

Humpbacks feed by straining small fish and crustaceans through hundreds of keratin plates – keratin being what hair and fingernails are made of. Humpbacks live in several parts of the world, but their populations do not mix. Southern-hemisphere humpbacks are distinguished by a white belly, while the undersides of the northern-hemisphere humpbacks are dark. The two never cross paths.

During July and August, visitors can go whale-watching or even swimming with these magnificent creatures on an organised tour. See the Activities section in the destination chapters for more details. However,

The Tonga Visitors Bureau website (www.tonga holiday.com) is a little difficult to navigate, but click on 'things to do' on the home page, and there is an informative section devoted to bird-watching in Tonga. The section on whale-watching also has some good information.

Snorkelling enthusiasts will find *Reef Fish Identification: Tropical Pacific* by Gerald Allen, Roger Steene and Paul Humann to be a useful photographic guide.

WHALING POLITICS

Tongans have hunted whales for centuries, consuming whale meat and using whale bone in numerous traditional instruments and artefacts. Up until a royal decree in 1979, around 10 humpback whales were caught every year. Today, however, much of Tonga's tourist industry depends on the protected and migrating humpback whales. Although Tonga is not a member country of the IWC (International Whaling Commission), delegates have voiced their concern at Japan's attempts to reintroduce and increase commercial and scientific whaling. In June 2005, the bid by Japan and other countries to have the existing moratorium lifted was defeated by a narrow margin at the IWC.

RESPONSIBLE TRAVEL

■ Tonga has limited facilities for waste, so try to minimise the amount of packaging you consume.

■ Most land in Tonga belongs to someone, so ask permission before you create your own tracks.

■ Don't purchase items or souvenirs made of endangered resources like black coral or sandalwood.

■ Never fish, or collect shells or other specimens in any of Tonga's marine reserves or national parks.

some local providers still question whether this is safe or ecologically sound. Calving whales have been known to draw sharks and an attack on a Tongan guide swimming with whales has been recorded. While sharks are generally not abundant in Tonga, there have been attacks and snorkellers might well spot nonaggressive reef sharks and leopard sharks.

CONSERVATION AREAS

The Tongan Wildlife Centre operated a successful captive breeding programme for native birds. However, a misguided tourist recently ransacked the enclosure and set the birds free, undoing years of hard work. The centre is now closed.

Tonga currently has seven marine reserves and three national parks.

The marine reserves are mostly around Tongatapu island. Hakaumama'o Reef Reserve is situated 14km north of Nuku'alofa, while Pangaimotu Reef Reserve lies on the eastern edge of Nuku'alofa Harbour, and Monu'afe Island and Reef Reserve is just over 6km northeast of Nuku'alofa. Malinoa Island Park and Reef Reserve features numerous varieties of marine life, including octopuses, and is about 7km north of Nuku'alofa. For further details, see p213. Ha'atafu Beach Reserve, on the western tip of Tongatapu features a reef and 100 species of fish (p212). Other marine parks include Mounu Reef Giant Clam Reserve and Muihopohoponga Coastal Reserve. Ask at the Tongan Visitors Bureau for further details.

On the east coast of 'Eua is the 449-hectare 'Eua National Park (p220), a tract of untouched tropical rainforest. On northeastern Tongatapu is the Ha'amonga 'a Maui Trilithon National Historic Reserve (p209) while the Vava'u Group offers Mt Talau National Park (p252).

ENVIRONMENTAL ISSUES

Environmental activism has a long way to go in Tonga, although a newly established government ministry and an increasingly active NGO presence may go some way in improving this situation.

Deforestation is of high concern. Tongan agricultural lands are very fertile, but slash-and-burn farming and European-encouraged clearing has made lands vulnerable to erosion.

Visitors interested in assisting sustainable farming initiatives can contact the Tonga National Youth Congress in Fasi (☎ 25 474) or Tonga Trust in Kolofo'ou (☎ 23 478).

Waste management is also a high priority in the Tongan islands. Traditionally, locals have always burnt off excess rubbish, but the introduction of heavily packaged Western goods, technology and a culture of consumption has left the islands with ongoing problems of air and water pollution. Many beaches are heavily littered with household waste. Fortunately, beach clean ups are becoming more common, often taken on by youth, church and community groups.

Careless treatment of Tonga's reef has resulted to irreparable damage in some parts of the archipelago. Many sea creatures are becoming increasingly rare and endangered. It is prohibited to collect endangered giant clams and trident shells. Trident shells are the natural predator of the crown of thorns starfish, and their over-collection has made the reef vulnerable to extensive starfish damage. Also of concern to conservationists is that the ban on turtle killing has recently been lifted, allowing them to be hunted for food and shells between March and August.

FOOD & DRINK

At its best, Tongan food is superb. Visitors can expect a wide variety of fresh fish, coconut-based products, free-range chicken, pork, lobster, breadfruit, root vegetables such as yam, sweet potato and cassava, and seasonal tropical fruits like bananas, bush oranges and almonds, papaya, pineapple, guava, passionfruit and watermelon. Eating food fresh from the bush (albeit with local guidance), markets and with local families can be the highlight of a trip to Tonga.

However, some epicurean experiences in Tonga are less enticing. The ubiquitous tinned beef *(kapa pulu)* and the greasy mutton flaps *(sipi)* aren't to every visitor's taste. This national preference for fatty meat products over fresh produce, as well as the prevalence of soft drink, confectionary and fast food, has caused alarming rates of diabetes and obesity in the kingdom.

Markets can be found in Nuku'alofa, Pangai and Neiafu but in the outer islands the availability and diversity of fresh produce can be erratic. Most villages have *fale koloa* (corner shops) that are open all hours with milk, bread and other nonperishables. Major towns have supermarkets, but the quality and variety of goods varies from place to place. It's worth shopping around and checking the expiry dates on all food purchases!

> The American Peace Corps put out The Niu Idea Cookbook, which has a host of innovative recipes using local ingredients, and can be bought at the Friendly Islands bookshop.

STAPLES & SPECIALITIES

Without a doubt, Tonga is a nation of meat-eaters. The roosters you hear at the break of dawn, the chickens scratching across the road and the pigs snuffling in the bush may just be your next dinner. Roasted suckling pig is a national favourite, although it is usually reserved for important occasions. Local eggs are as freerange as the chickens, and are often boiled and sold as snacks from corner stores.

Not surprisingly, many of Tonga's other signature dishes come fresh from the sea. There's nothing quite like a whole, local lobster marinated in coconut cream, or lightly grilled snapper, tuna and mahimahi.

Raw fish salad *('ota ika)* is also a popular delicacy. Fish fillets are cubed, and then soaked for several hours in lime juice. The marinated fish is then combined with fresh coconut cream, chilli and chopped vegetables like cucumber and tomato. The resulting salad is served with plenty of root vegetables handy to soak up the juices.

DRINKS
Nonalcoholic Drinks

On a long walk or a day out in the sun, you can't go past a green coconut. You can often buy them from the roadside, but if you're feeling limber, try scaling a coconut tree to fetch your own. Always remember to ask permission from the local landowner first.

> When old coconuts are left on the ground for long enough, they sprout and grow a fungus on the inside known as *'uto*. This is a Tongan delicacy, and has a musky meringue flavour.

TONGA'S TOP FIVE RESTAURANTS

- Seaview Restaurant (p195)
- Mariners Café (p234)
- Mermaid Restaurant (p254)
- Akiko's (p194)
- Waterfront Café (p195)

Those addicted to their morning espresso might have some problems in Tonga, but places like Friend's Café do a mean cappuccino and even a chai latte! Ask for Royal Coffee – it's locally produced and tastes great.

Tongans make a great nonalcoholic cocktail called 'otai. Made from freshly made coconut milk, it's combined with a small amount of sugar and shredded watermelon or mango.

Alcoholic Drinks

In terms of locally brewed beverages, the Royal Beer is a tasty drop. The Royal Beer Company was initially formed in conjunction with AB Pripps Bryggerier in Sweden. You can choose between Premium, Draught and Ikale. You can tour the Royal brewery in Nuku'alofa, and on request they can also organise tasting sessions on site.

A limited range of imported beers, wines and spirits are available in bars, supermarkets and convenience stores. Some spirits are also being produced locally by the Billfish Spirits and Liqueurs Company.

While the relatively high price of alcohol means most Tongans stick to *kava*, alcohol has become increasingly popular. This has also led to a small but thriving (and illegal) home-brew market. Under-age and binge drinking is an increasingly big problem in Tonga; violent brawls and sexual harassment have become commonplace in night clubs and bars. The police do not use breathalysers and drink-driving is prevalent, so it's worth exercising extra caution if driving at night.

Tongans don't cook with a lot of spices. Chilli and garlic are both grown and sold locally, but are rarely used. Other spices and flavourings have to be imported, but curry powder is becoming more popular.

Kava, of course, is Tonga's most renowned drink. See the boxed text, p176.

CELEBRATIONS

Celebrations in Tonga revolve around food, and Tongan feasts *(kai pola)* are renowned throughout the Pacific. You're sure to spy or attend at least one during your time in the kingdom. Feasts are held for all occasions of note: weddings, funerals, church conferences, village clergy ordinations, first and 21st birthdays, Easter, Christmas, public holidays, arrivals and farewells. For noble and royal funerals, coronations and birthdays, villages will spend days and nights preparing food to feed a cast of thousands.

The Tongan feast itself is a marvel in terms of size and local protocol. Huge trestle tables will be set up in an assigned area under marquees, heaving with plates and plates of traditional food and whole roasted pigs.

SUNDAY LUNCH

Sundays have a more distinct culinary tradition. For nearly all Tongans, the Sabbath is a day of prayer, eating and sleeping. Most people attend church, but a few relatives will always be left at home to tend the *'umu* in preparation for Sunday lunch.

The *'umu* is an underground earth oven, similar to the Maori *hangi*. The traditional *'umu* dish is *lu*. Fresh from the *'umu*, *lu* is a tasty dish with an interesting, smoky flavour. It's made from taro leaves, which are wrapped around corned beef, mutton flaps *(sipi)*, fish or chicken mixed with coconut milk and onion. This is then wrapped in taro leaves or aluminium foil, and accompanied by whole root vegetables. Making an *'umu* is relatively simple. A hole about 25cm deep and 1m wide is dug in the ground, and a large fire is lit inside. Once the fire is ablaze, rocks are thrown on top and once they are hot enough, the remnants of burning wood are removed. The food is then placed on top of the rocks, with a layer of bark in between. Sticks, banana leaves and hessian sacks are placed over the top, and this is all covered with soil and left to cook for about two hours.

Tongan families will return from church, often with extended family, eat from the *'umu*, and then retire for a lazy afternoon sleep. Later in the afternoon, the village bakeries become the place to see and be seen. Loaves of bread, generously smeared with butter, usually suffice as the Sunday evening meal for most Tongan families.

TRAVEL YOUR TASTEBUDS

There are plenty of interesting foods to taste on your trip to Tonga. Some of these are:

- *feke* – octopus marinated in coconut cream
- *lomu* – pickled sea cucumber
- *nonu* – this fruit is eaten or juiced, and is said to be extremely beneficial to those suffering high blood pressure and digestive problems.

We Dare You

Shell fishing is an important local tradition. Just before sunset, visitors taking a leisurely walk along the waterfront in any part of Tonga will see families or lone divers collecting an assortment of crustaceans and molluscs for the dinner table. Buy or ask to try some of the shell fish.

If you're lucky, you may be able to join a fossicking expedition – just watch out for coral cuts, stings and things that bite!

Trays of fresh fruit, cans of soft drink and packets of chips and sweets then decorate the entire gastronomic affair.

Once everyone is seated, a minister will be called on to say grace and the eating begins. Like most events in Tonga, feasts are a hierarchical affair. The high table with nobles and most important guests is often decorated with *tapa,* and features the best of the available food. There are usually two sittings, and visitors, nobility and invited guests eat first.

WHERE TO EAT & DRINK

There's an ever-increasing number of Western-style cafés, restaurants and bars in Tongatapu and Vava'u, but options are limited or nonexistent on Ha'apai, 'Eua and the Niuas. While there are plenty of sticky tables and linoleum floors to be had, some of the country's upmarket restaurants boast amazing ocean views, tropical gardens and serve delicious and fresh produce at very reasonable prices.

European and Chinese influence is discernible in the limited international cuisine on offer. Several Italian residents have set up thriving pizza businesses and much of the Chinese food is well priced and tasty, if a little heavy on the MSG. There are also Indian, German, Japanese and modern cuisine options for restaurant goers.

Most Tongans cannot afford to go out for food. The result is a decided lack of restaurants selling traditional food, with the exception of the Tonga National Centre (p189) and the Good Samaritan Inn (p212) who put on Tongan feasts for visitors and locals.

Opening and closing times can be erratic in some establishments, but most advertise business hours and stick to them. Generally, solo travellers will feel safe and comfortable in cafés and restaurants in Tonga, although women travelling alone may receive some unwanted attention when dining in establishments that double as bars.

Tipping is not part of Tongan culture, but certain bars and restaurants will give you an opportunity to include a tip in the final bill.

Quick Eats

There's a variety of options for a comparatively quick bite to eat. For the health conscious or those on a budget, the markets are a virtual tropical fruit salad, with plenty of bananas, papaya and other seasonal fruits. Visitors with a sweet tooth can also purchase inexpensive bundles of *faikakai*

It's all about take-away. Tongans always leave feasts with containers of food, piles of fruit and cans of soft drinks for friends and family at home.

Tonga is one of the few countries in the world without a McDonald's or any other transglobal fast-food chain.

TONGAN KAVA CULTURE

There's nothing quite like the first spicy slurps of *kava* from a coconut shell. Your tongue and lips feel numb, the body relaxes and your mind feels hazy. It's certainly an acquired taste, and even local *kava* drinkers are known to follow a cup with a chaser of lollies, bananas or manioc chips. *Kava*'s denigrators liken it to dirty dishwashing water, but there's no doubt that this murky, peppery liquid is a central part of social and cultural life in Tonga.

Kava is made from the ground root of the *kava* plant *(Piper methysticum)*. The active ingredients in *kava* include 12 to 14 chemicals of an alkaloid nature. *Kava* is both anaesthetic and analgesic, high in fibre, low in calories, and serves as a mild tranquiliser, an antibacterial agent, a diuretic, an appetite suppressant and a soporific. Its more unfortunate side effects for committed drinkers are scaly and yellowing skin, excessive fatigue and a decreased blood-cell count. *Kava* is legal in North America, Europe and Australia, and frequently packaged and sent by Tongans to family living overseas.

Although widely consumed throughout the Pacific, the Tongans are extremely patriotic when it comes to *kava* and prefer to drink home grown Kava-Tonga. The best, most potent local *kava* is said to come from the volcanic islands of Tofua in Ha'apai and Tafahi in Niuatoputapu.

Traditionally, the ground-up root is mixed with water and then strained through coconut husks, although today muslin and other thin cloth are more commonly used. It is then served from a wooden *kava* bowl, which is placed at the head of the circle. Each man in turn claps and receives a coconut shell of *kava* from the server. He'll drink it, spit or pour the remaining dregs on the ground or in an ashtray, and scuttle the shell back to the server. Those in attendance will talk, tells stories and sing, often accompanied by a motley collection of guitars and ukuleles. A *kava* session can last from late afternoon until the early hours of the morning.

Drinking *kava* is extremely popular and a predominantly male activity, although it is traditionally served by young, unmarried women *(tou'a)*. This makes for a fascinating study of male-female interaction in Tonga. The *tou'a* is accorded great respect but there's always plenty of flirting, and sexual innuendo is flung wantonly around the circle causing much amusement.

Kava is used in both formal and informal settings. It is drunk before and after church on a Sunday, during the conferment of nobility, at village meetings and in the negotiations of contracts and other agreements. All villages have at least one *kava* club *(kava kulupu)* where some local men might be found every night of the week. Big, intervillage *kava* parties are also a popular and common fundraiser.

Kava is also an integral part of the courtship process in Tonga. A male suitor will ask the girl in question's family for permission to hold a *kava* circle in their house, where she will serve them. If the *kava* circle lasts until day break, the suitor and his friend must bring a roasted pig and other offerings of food to the girl's family. In a traditional Tongan wedding ceremony, it is also customary that the groom serves his bride half a coconut shell of *kava*. Once she drinks the cup, the couple are wed.

Male and female visitors are usually welcome at *kava* clubs. You may be formally invited, but otherwise just ask any local taxi driver to take you.

(pudding with a coconut syrup) or *keke* (deep fried cakes occasionally flavoured with banana). Makeshift stalls usually sell barbecue plates of meat (chicken, fish, *sipi* and sausages) served with a side of root vegetables.

Bakeries also stock a selection of breads, meat pies and cakes of varying quality. For those who like fast food, there's an array of establishments selling local versions of hamburgers, chips and fried chicken.

VEGETARIANS & VEGANS
Vegetarians may struggle with traditional Tongan food, where nearly every dish involves meat. Even if you request meat-free food from stalls, take-away stands and locally run restaurants, your food is likely to be cooked with other meat products. It's harder again for vegans.

Self-catering is probably the only option in many places, although most Western-style cafés and bars have a limited array of vegetarian options.

EATING WITH KIDS

Families dining out are unlikely to encounter any problems. Although accoutrements like highchairs and baby change rooms are rare, kids are likely to be affectionately greeted by owners and workers and often get free reign of the premises, much to the horror of their parents!

If you are going to a resort-operated or upmarket restaurant, however, it might be worth checking their policy on children.

One of the greatest insults in Tonga is to accuse someone of selfishly sneaking off and eating on their own (kaipo).

HABITS & CUSTOMS

Sharing food is one of Tonga's cultural cornerstones. While tolerated in foreigners, eating alone or failing to share is an affront to local custom. Visitors who offer and share food with Tongans in their midst will be heartily embraced by locals. The same hospitality is almost always returned and exceeded.

If you pass a Tongan house during meal time, don't be surprised if you are asked to come and eat! *(Ha'u kai!)* The invitation is genuine, so feel free to accept it. Eating with a local family will give you an amazing insight into family life and Tongan culture.

Tongans traditionally sit on the floor to eat, without cutlery. A member of the family always gives a prayer of thanks. Tongans are self-deprecating, and will probably offer an apology for the food you are about to eat, even it's a plate laden with lobster and other delicacies.

A common joke is that *palangi* (foreigners) eat until they are full, and that Tongans eat until they are tired!

FOOD GLOSSARY

faikakai – sticky dessert made from dough or sweet potato cooked with sugar and coconut
faina – pineapple
fingota – shellfish
fisi – spicy
ika – fish
inu – drink
kai – eat
kapa pulu – tinned corned beef
keke – deep-fried cake
kumala – sweet potato

DOS AND DON'TS

- Stand up and give a formal thank you to hosts for their hospitality.

- Bring a gift of food or other presents from home for your hosts. The culture embraces reciprocity, and Tongan people are often far more hospitable and generous than they can afford to be.

- Don't be offended if you are invited for a meal and not joined by the whole family. Chances are you will eat alone in the presence of a designated relative, while the rest of the family watch from a distance. This is a gesture of respect.

- Don't feel like you have to finish everything on your plate. Eat as much as you can, compliment those who have prepared the meal and explain that you are full.

- Don't get angry if service is slow in a café or restaurant. Everyone is on Tonga time after all, and you should be too! If you are in a hurry, simply smile at a waiter or waitress and ask politely about your food or drinks.

laise – rice
lu – taro leaves wrapped around meat cooked with coconut cream and onion
ma – bread
me'akai – food
meleni – watermelon
melie – sweet
moa – chicken
niu – coconut
niu fo'ou – new coconut
niu mata – old coconut
'ota – raw
'ota ika – raw fish salad
'otai – drink made of fruit and coconut milk
pia – beer
pulu – beef
siaine – bananas
sipi – mutton flaps
'ufi – yam
'uo – lobster

Tongatapu Group

On Tongatapu (meaning 'Sacred South'), old and new Tonga collide. Nuku'alofa (Abode of Love) will challenge your vision of a South Pacific idyll. The main island constitutes one third of the kingdom's land mass and a third of the island's population lives in Nuku'alofa, Tonga's 'big smoke'.

Outside Nuku'alofa most of the flat island's land is covered in a patchwork of plantations (coconuts, pumpkins, root crops), studded with sleepy villages that are home to roaming pigs and seemingly more churches than houses, and fringed with long stretches of white-sand beaches.

The first port of call for most visitors, due to its position at the hub of all activity within the kingdom of Tonga, it's hard to escape spending some time on Tongatapu. There's something to be seen and experienced here at every point of the compass. Head east and you'll stumble onto one of the densest concentrations of ancient structures in the Pacific, where you'll find the mysterious Ha'amonga 'a Maui trilithon, a sort of Stonehenge of the South Pacific. Explore the Lapaha area, riddled with *langi* (tiered tombs) and ringed with moats. Drop down south for the symphonic spurts at the blowholes, and wade in protected rock pools in sandy coves. Venture westward to the island's accessible surf breaks and beach resorts.

Still not enough for you? Then board a boat bound for the reefs and *motu* (coral islet) just north of the main island, where fine diving and snorkelling await and island resorts on Pangaimotu, 'Atata and Fafá will melt away your stress. An ecotourist's dream lies just a boat-ride south of Tongatapu on low-key 'Eua, with some of the best hiking in the Pacific.

HIGHLIGHTS

- Combining holiday with adventure by exploring 'Eua's trails, limestone caves and **natural wonders** (p215)

- Marvelling at the **ancient tombs** (p199) of Lapaha and the Ha'amonga 'a Maui **trilithon** (p209)

- Applauding the spectacle of the Mapu'a 'a Vaca **blowholes** (p211)

- Tucking into a sumptuous Tongan feast while watching a **traditional dance performance** (p196)

- Spending a Sunday snorkelling among Tongatapu's outlying **coral islands** (p213) and stretching out on a beach

---

- POPULATION: 66,979   - AREA: 261 SQ KM

HISTORY

The known history of Tongatapu is the result of oral tradition, dating from the middle of the 10th century when the first Tu'i Tonga, the son of the god Tangaloa and a beautiful Tongan maiden, came to power.

Around the year 1200, Tu'i Tonga Tu'itatui set about building the only trilithic gate in Oceania, the Ha'amonga 'a Maui (Maui's Burden), near the village of Niutoua. Legend has it that the Tu'i Tonga constructed the gate to remind two quarrelling sons that unity was better than division. After creating a wonderful future tourist attraction for Tonga, he moved his capital to Lapaha, on the calm lagoon near present-day Mu'a.

Over the following 100 years or so, war canoes full of Tongan raiding parties regularly set off for neighbouring islands. They created an empire ranging from the Lau Group in Fiji to the west, across to Niue in the east and northward to Futuna and Samoa, all of it ruled by the Tu'i Tonga from his capital on Tongatapu.

Tongatapu's first European visitor was Dutchman Abel Tasman, who spent a few days trading with islanders, and named the island Amsterdam. The next European contact came with Captain James Cook, who developed a close friendship with the 30th Tu'i Tonga, Fatafehi Paulaho, and presented him with Tu'i Malila, the tortoise that was treated as a chief and given the run of the palace for nearly 200 years (see p199).

ACTIVITIES

You'll find plenty of water-based action on Tongatapu and its nearby islands. Resort islands maintain water toys such as kayaks, boats and catamarans for their guests.

Diving & Snorkelling

Around the Tongatapu Group, subaquatic adventures range from snorkelling the wreck off Pangaimotu and the excellent Makaha'a Reef, to diving 'Eua's unique sea caves.

Water temperatures north of Nuku'alofa reach a comfortable 29°C in November and don't fall below 21°C in midwinter. Underwater visibility near the main island averages 15m but closer to the barrier reefs it increases to between 30m and 50m.

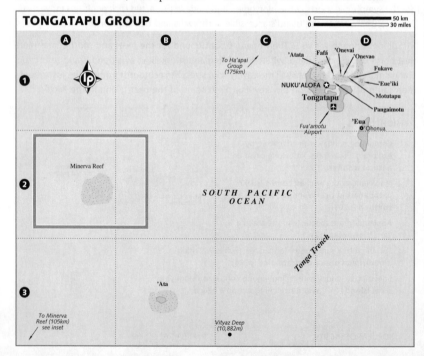

TONGATAPU GROUP

0 ——— 50 km
0 ——— 30 miles

To Ha'apai Group (175km)

'Atata Fafá 'Onevai 'Onevao

Fukave

NUKU'ALOFA

Tongatapu

'Eue'iki

Motutapu

Pangaimotu

Fua'amotu Airport

'Eua 'Ohonua

Minerva Reef

SOUTH PACIFIC OCEAN

Tonga Trench

'Ata

To Minerva Reef (105km) see inset

Vityaz Deep (10,882m)

TONGATAPU IN...

Two Days

Spend day one getting your bearings on a circumnavigational island tour, exploring archaeological marvels, caves and seaside cemeteries; witness the blowholes in action and get acquainted with Tongatapu's western beaches. Alight in Nuku'alofa to soak up the sunset tones over the waterfront and dine on the best seafood around at the **Pearl Inn** (p195). On day two, join the bustle and explore the wares at **Talamahu Market** (p188), take our **walking tour** (p189) of the capital's sights and get acquainted with traditional culture at the **Tongan National Centre** (p189).

Four Days

Follow the two-day itinerary and then catch a ferry to **'Eua** (p215) to bushwalk in its dramatic landscape and soak up impressive ocean views, particularly during whale season. Or head for Tongatapu's outer islands (p213) for beachside frolics and navel gazing. Join a **culture show** (p196) and do what the Tongans do so well – feast!

Save yourself potential grief by carefully inspecting all rental gear before heading out in a boat.

Deep Blue Diving Centre (Map pp184-5; ☎/fax 23379; www.deep-blue-diving.to; Vuna Rd, Nuku'alofa) One-/two-tank dives cost T$120 (including lunch and all gear), five-/10-day dive packages cost T$540/1060. Snorkellers can join trips for T$35; at least three people are required for most trips/dives. The major diving draws around Tongatapu are 'Eua's enormous sea caves (minimum of four people) and the beautiful, uninhabited island north of Tongatapu (T$100 for one dive, T$65 for nondivers, beach barbecue included).

Divers Lodge (Map pp184-5; ☎ 23379; fax 23576; www.deep-blue-diving.to; Funa Rd, Nuku'alofa) Extended dive charters and accommodation packages are available from Divers Lodge (p192) A two-tank dive with full equipment costs from US$98, and US$87 with tank, weights and a light lunch. Five-/10-day packages are available from US$400/755.

Royal Sunset Island Resort (Map p183; ☎/fax 21254; www.royalsunset.to; 'Atata) The 'Atata island resort (p214) is close to a host of dive sites, though you have to pay to get out there. One-/two-tank dives cost T$77/127, which includes a tank, weights, boat and guide. Full gear hire can mount up to an extra T$69/110. Divers need to show qualifications equivalent to the PADI open-water certification.

Fishing

Game fishing is excellent in Tonga (see p275) due to the incredible depth of the Tonga Trench, east of Tongatapu. Fish Aggregating Devices, located around the island, attract big game.

Precision Charters (☎ 24700; fax 24669; skipcust@kalianet.to) has a fully game-rigged 7m Buccaneer Billfisher, *Lady Di*, available for T$600/1000 per half/full day (including lunch) for a maximum of four people.

Royal Sunset Island Resort (Map p183; ☎/fax 21254; www.royalsunset.to; 'Atata) offers half-/full-day game fishing for T$550/850, including gear, with a maximum of four anglers.

Sea-Taxi (☎ 22797, 15723; http://kalianet.to/seataxi) has a fast 31ft fibreglass cruiser with many national records to its name, and offers full-day game fishing with full gear for T$1200.

Surfing

Tongatapu's northwest coast, off Ha'atafu Beach, is renowned for its surf. There's also a series of interesting-looking reef breaks between Fukave and 'Onevao.

The **Happy Hopa Surf School** (Map p183; ☎ 41088; fax 22970; www.surfingtonga.com; Ha'atafu Beach Resort, Ha'atafu) runs one-on-one surfing lessons (A$25 per hour) for beginners and reef novices.

Whale-Watching

Other than patiently scanning Tongatapu's watery horizons, the best bet for whale-watching in the Tongatapu Group is to ferry across to 'Eua. Whales are frequently seen en route. They can also be spotted cruising past Hideaway's whale-watching platform (p223) and boat trips can be organised from this resort for sole viewers and small groups.

LONELY PLANET INDEX

- **1L of unleaded petrol** T$1.80-2.30
- **1.5L of bottled water** T$1
- **355mL bottle of Ikale beer** T$3.50
- **Souvenir T-shirt** T$17-22
- **Street treat of sipi (mutton) curry** T$3.50

Game-fishing boats run whale-watching trips between June and December. **Deep Blue Diving** (Map pp184-5; ☎ /fax 23379; www.deep-blue-diving.to; Vuna Rd; Nuku'alofa) runs trips around 'Eua from July to November. **Royal Sunset Island Resort** (Map p183; ☎ /fax 21254; www.royalsunset.to; 'Atata) offers whale-watching boat trips to resort guests at a nominal fee depending on distance travelled. Charges on charter boats are also up for negotiation depending on how far from Nuku'alofa the charter boat travels.

You can charter **Sea-Taxi** (☎ 22797, 15723; http://kalianet.to/seataxi) for a full day of whale-watching for T$1000.

TONGATAPU ISLAND

NUKU'ALOFA

area 9.25 sq km / pop 22,162 (est)

Tonga's 'big smoke', Nuku'alofa, is the kingdom's seat of government and home of the royal family. While it may not fulfil a vision of Pacific paradise, Nuku'alofa still has a charm and a little promise when you blow the dust from its surface. Its broad waterfront strip provides magnificent views of the smaller islands in the Tongatapu Group, there's a thriving, friendly market, an enticing range of cuisines and quality dining options for a place this size, and you'll still find the odd chicken roaming the main street.

Nuku'alofa also has its issues to solve. Population migration from outer islands has caused the seams to burst on the outskirts of town; traffic clogs up the main street at peak hour and the market on bustling Saturday mornings. Blaring 'gangsta' rap and complex handshakes show the influence of American culture (especially on young people). But for the traveller, Nuku'alofa's few sights can be covered on foot and once the town has been explored, beautiful coral islands are just a pleasant boat ride across the bay.

History

Nuku'alofa began as a fortress for the western district of Tongatapu. Attacks on this fort appear to have been an annual jolly for Ha'apai raiders, who faithfully returned over at least an 11-year period. Will Mariner (see p236) recounted the sacking of the fort of 'Nioocalofa' in 1807 by Finau, the chief of Ha'apai. Finau and his men fired on the fort with cannons from the *Port-au-Prince* (the British privateer that had brought Mariner to Tonga and was subsequently destroyed), and then burnt it to the ground.

Following the destruction of the fort, the priests advised Finau that it would be necessary to reconstruct the fort in order to appease the gods, so the fortress was rebuilt and provided the Ha'apai warriors the opportunity to embark on their annual holiday of destruction the following year! However, Tarki, a rival chief, set fire to the fortress shortly afterwards, leaving Finau to watch the devastation from Pangaimotu, unable to stop it. Finau later learned that Tarki had destroyed the building just to irritate him.

Orientation

MAPS

The Tonga Visitors Bureau (p187) hands out simple hand-drawn maps of Tonga's major islands and island groups. For information on sea charts, see p280.

Information

Foto-Fix (☎ 23466; Taufa'ahau Rd) Stocks Fuji film, batteries and digital media cards, has digital photo–printing machines, processes film (not slides); takes passport photos and burns CDs (T$16).

Fung Shing Fast Photo (☎ 24787; Railway Rd) Sells batteries, Kodak and Fuji film, disposable cameras, and offers one-hour print processing. Also takes passport photos.

Tonga Meteorological Service (☎ 35123, satellite phone 00872 7629 41139; fax 31994; www.mca.gov.to /met/) Contact this service for tide times, marine and general weather forecasts, and satellite imagery of the region.

BOOKSHOPS

Most guesthouses have shelves of preloved paperbacks from which guests can borrow or exchange books.

Friendly Islands Bookshop (☎ 23787; Taufa'ahau Rd; ☽ 8.30am-5pm Mon, Tue & Fri, 8.45am-5pm Wed,

TONGATAPU ISLAND

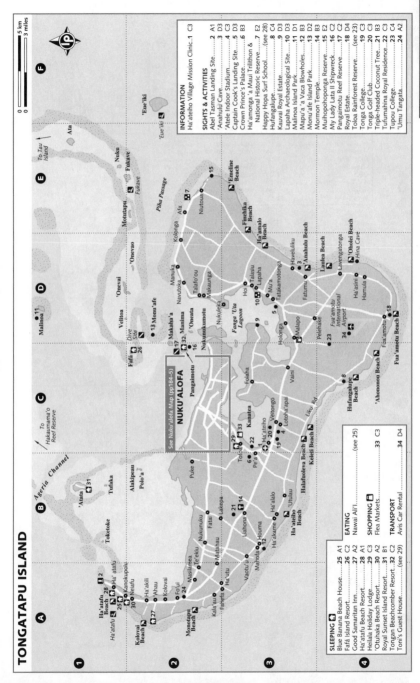

0   5 km
0   3 miles

'Eue'iki

'Eue'iki

Ata

Nuku
Fukave
Fukave

To Tau
Island

'Emeline
Beach

15

Piha Passage

Afa   7
Niutoua

Muihopohoponga Reserve

Motutapu
'Onevao
'Onevai

Manuka
Kolonga
Finehika
Beach
Ha'amalo
Beach
Kolonga

Malinoa 11
13 Monu'afe

Navutoka
Talafo'ou
Makaunga

Ha'amalo
Beach
Anahulu Beach

Velitoa

Makaha'a
17
32 Manima
16
'Oneata
Nukuleka
Nukunukumotu

Talasiu
Lapaha
Mua
Tatakamotonga

Hoi
10
5

Haveluliku

Laulea Beach
Lavengatonga
'Oholei Beach
Hina Cave

Fanga 'Uta Lagoon
9

Fatumu
Ha'asini
Hamula

Dive
Site
Fafá
26

NUKU'ALOFA

Pangaimotu

Folaha
Holonga
Malapo
Pelehake
Fua'amotu
International
Airport
Ha'asini
18
Fua'amotu Beach

See Nuku'alofa Map (pp184-5)

To
Hakaumama'o
Reef Reserve

Veitongo
Kanatea
Ha'ateiho
20
19
Lotoha'apai

Folaha
Vaini
Liku Rd
34
23

'Ahonoono Beach

Ageria Channel

31
'Atata

Alakipeau
Polo'a

Tufaka

Tokotoke

29
33
22
Tofoa
6   4
Pea
Puke

Halafuoleva Beach
Keleti Beach

Hufangalupe
Beach
8
Hufangalupe

Ha'atafu
Beach
25
28
Kanokupolu
Nelafu
Ha'akili
Kolovai
27
Ha'atafu
2

Monotapu
Beach
24

Kolovai
Beach

Masilamea
Te'ekiu
Nukunuku

Vaotu'u
Matahau
Matafonua
Houma
12
14
21
Fatai
Lakepa
Ha'utu

Liahona
Ha'alalo
'Utulau
Ha'akame
Ha'ateiho
Beach

Kala'au
Faheita

TONGATAPU GROUP

NUKU'ALOFA

INFORMATION
ANZ Bank (ATM).....................**1** G5	MBF...................................**11** F6	SOUTH PACIFIC
ANZ Bank (ATM)................(see 29)	Police Station.....................**12** G5	OCEAN
British High Commission...........**2** C3	Relax Café.........................**13** F5	
Chinese Traditional Medicine	Savoy Dry Cleaner...............**14** C4	
Centre................................**3** A6	TCC Shop......................(see 39)	
DataLine Internet Cafe............**4** G5	Teta Tours.........................**15** G5	
DHL...............................(see 79)	Tonga Communications	
FedEx............................(see 29)	Corporation (TCC)..............**16** E4	
Foto-Fix..........................(see 81)	Tonga Communications	
Friendly Island Medical Clinic.....**5** F4	Corporation (TCC)..............**17** F6	
Friendly Islands Bookshop........**6** F6	Tonga Visitors Bureau............**18** H5	
Friends Tourist Centre............**7** G5	Vaiola Hospital....................**19** B6	
Fung Shing Fast Photo............**8** G5	Village Mission Pharmacy.......**20** G6	
Game Stop......................(see 39)	Western Union (ATM)..........(see 29)	
GPO...................................**9** G5	Westpac Bank of Tonga..........**21** C4	
IOC Traffic Office................(see 12)	Westpac Bank of Tonga &	
Jetsave............................(see 29)	MoneyGram.....................**22** G4	
Jones Travel & Tours.............**10** F5	Westpac Bank of Tonga &	
	MoneyGram.....................**23** F6	

To German Dental Clinic;
Nukuma'anu Motel (200m);
Black Pearl Suites (500m);
Pearl Inn (500m)

Vuna Rd
Salote Rd

Mt Zion
Mala'e Pangai
Vuna Wharf
Yellow Pier

Wellington Rd

See Enlargement

Sumulakave Ka St
Alberti St
Sipu Rd
Salikotapu Rd
Tui Rd
Taufa'ahau Rd (One-Way Road)
Vuna Rd

Cemetery
Matelalona Rd

To Nukunuku
& Kolovai

Hihifo Rd

Vaha'akolo Rd
Taufa'ahau Rd
Railway Rd
Fatafehi Rd
Amaile Rd
Lavinia Rd
Kausela Rd
Laifone Rd
Tupoulahi Rd

Bypass Rd

Bypass Rd

Taufa'ahau Rd

To
Heilala Holiday
Lodge; Toni's
Guest House;
Tofoa & Pe'a

Vaiola Rd

To Tofoa
& Pe'a

Fanga 'Uta Lagoon

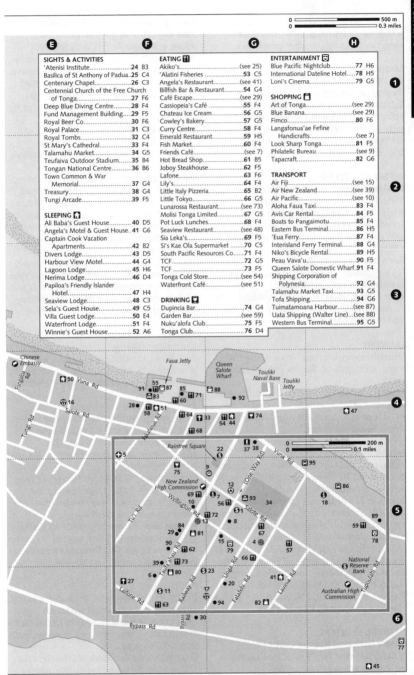

8.30am-12.30pm Sat) The only bookshop of any consequence in Tonga, with the best range of island-related titles anywhere, travel titles, novels, magazines and newspapers.

EMERGENCY
Fire (☎ 999)
Hospital (☎ 933, 23200)
National emergency number (☎ 911)
Police (☎ 922; cnr Railway & Salote Rds) Drivers licences are available from the OIC Traffic Office (open from 8.30am to 4.30pm Monday to Friday) situated within the Police Office. Enter on Railway Rd.

INTERNET ACCESS
DataLine Internet Cafe (☎ 27773; Royco Bldg, Fatafehi Rd; per hr T$2; ⏰ 8.30am-11pm Mon-Sat) Plenty of terminals, and blank CDs/DVDs available for T$1.30/5.
Friends Tourist Centre (☎ 26323; friends@tonfon.to; Taufa'ahau Rd; per 15min T$2; ⏰ 8am-10pm Mon-Fri, 8.30am-7.30pm Sat) Printing per page $1.
Game Stop (Tungi Arcade, Taufa'ahau Rd; per 12min/hr T$1/5; ⏰ 9am-8pm Mon-Fri, 9.30am-2pm Sat) In the arcade behind Friendly Islands Bookshop.
Relax Café (☎ 24444; cnr Taufa'ahau & Wellington Rds; per 20min/hr T$1/2; ⏰ 9am-2am Mon-Fri, 9am-late Sat) Blank CDs T$1.50, CD burning T$2.

LAUNDRY
Virtually every hotel and guesthouse makes some arrangement for its guests' laundry needs.
Savoy Dry Cleaner (☎ 23314; Fatafehi Rd) Nuku'alofa's only commercial laundry will wash and dry your laundry for T$2.50 per kg. It's a good idea to hand over a list of your clothes with your washing.

MEDIA
Tongatapu has two TV stations: a religious channel and TV Tonga, airing BBC News 24 at 8pm, weekdays. Sky Pacific TV satellite beams in 12 pay-to-view channels; Shoreline is a cable network with five channels including BBC World, children's programming, movies, sport and ABC (Australia).

Radio Tonga (90FM) and A3Z (1017AM) broadcast a mix of traditional Tongan and international rock music and worldwide news. Radio Nuku'alofa (88.6FM) is not bad, and Radio Australia's 103FM broadcasts Radio National programs 24 hours a day.

MEDICAL SERVICES
Chinese Traditional Medicine Centre (☎ 25178; Vaiola Rd) Just west of Vaiola Hospital. Chinese medicine and acupuncture treatments are available.

Friendly Island Medical Clinic & International Pharmacy (☎ 22736, after office hr 27021; jackis@kalianet.to; Wellington Rd; ⏰ 4.30-7.30pm Mon-Fri, 9am-noon Sat) Dr 'Ana 'Akau'ola charges T$20 for consultations; book for home visits while the clinic is open. There's a pharmacy and vaccinations are available by appointment.
German Dental Clinic (☎ 26797; Vuna Rd, Sopu; ⏰ 8.30am-noon & 3.30-8pm Mon-Thu, 8.30am-2pm Fri) Dental treatment available by appointment.
Ha'ateiho Village Mission Clinic (☎ 29052; off Taufa'ahau Rd, Ha'ateiho; ⏰ 8.30am-12.30pm & 2-4.30pm Mon & Fri) In a village 5km south of Nuku'alofa. Appointments are essential.
Vaiola Hospital (☎ 23200; Vaiola Rd) Recommended only for emergencies as no appointments are accepted. The dispensary is open 8.30am to 11pm weekdays and there's an on-site dentist. It's about 2km south of Nuku'alofa; take the Vaiola bus from the eastern bus terminal on Vuna Rd.
Village Mission Pharmacy (☎ 27522; 'Unga Rd; ⏰ 8.30am-5pm Mon-Fri, 9am-12.30pm Sat; medical clinic 2.30-5pm Tue, Thu & Fri) A medical clinic operates from this pharmacy, which is well stocked with sun screen, insect repellent, contact-lens solution, baby formula, oral rehydration salts, earplugs and the like. Fa's Beauty Spa offers waxing and beauty treatments here.

MONEY
Currency-exchange counters are open at Fua'amotu International Airport for all international flights. See p281 for further information about changing and transferring money.
ANZ (☎ 24944; www.anz.com/tonga; cnr Salote & Railway Rds; ⏰ 9am-4pm Mon-Thu, 9am-5pm Fri) ATM inside bank. There is another ATM situated outside the Fund Management Building on Taufa'ahau Rd.
MBF (☎ 24600; Taufa'ahau Rd; ⏰ 9am-4pm Mon-Fri) Near Hotel Nuku'alofa.
Western Union (☎ 24345; Fund Management Bldg, Taufa'ahau Rd; ⏰ 8.30am-4.30pm Mon-Fri, 8.30am-12.30pm Sat) International money transfers. Often has the shortest queues for currency exchange.
Westpac Bank of Tonga (☎ 23933; Taufa'ahau Rd; ⏰ 8.30am-5pm Mon-Fri, 8.30am-noon Sat) Two branches on Taufa'ahau Rd, with ATMs. The handiest is near the general post office, and also has a MoneyGram office.

POST
DHL (☎ 23617; Wellington Rd) Worldwide distributor of packages and documents, situated next to Loni's Cinema.
FedEx (☎ 28628; Fund Management Bldg, Taufa'ahau Rd) Packages and documents sent via airmail worldwide. Head to the back of the car park.
GPO (☎ 21700; cnr Taufa'ahau & Salote Rds; ⏰ 8.30am-12.30pm & 1.30-4pm Mon-Fri) Poste restante (addressed

to: Poste Restante, GPO, Nuku'alofa, Kingdom of Tonga) is collected from the window just outside the main entrance. Letters are filed alphabetically by surname or yacht name but you may need to check under Christian names to locate items. Ask specifically for any larger parcels you might be expecting. International post is cleared at 2pm on Monday and Friday. You'll also find the Philatelic Bureau here (p197).

TELEPHONE & FAX

Phonecards can be bought at Friends Tourist Centre on Taufa'ahau Rd, which has a blue TCC phone out the front (there are more outside the post office). Local calls are easily made from the place at which you are staying, though they may cost a little more than those from a public phone.

TCC Shop (☎ 080 0222; Tungi Arcade, Taufa'ahau Rd) Handy shop for mobile-phone and mobile-account needs.

Tonga Communications Corporation (TCC; ☎ 26700; www.tcc.to; Salote Rd; ⌚ 24hr) Offers international telephone and fax services. There's another office on 'Unga Rd.

TOILETS

Your best bet is to make use of café and restaurant toilet facilities when dining. Friends Tourist Centre has facilities for Internet users while the pool-side Splash Bar at the International Dateline Hotel also has facilities (including for nonguests who use the pool).

TOURIST INFORMATION

Friends Tourist Centre (☎ 26323; friends@tonfon.to; Taufa'ahau Rd; ⌚ 8am-10pm Mon-Fri, 8.30am-7.30pm Sat) This switched-on tour-booking office can tell you what you want to know about what's happening, and when, around the island.

Tonga Visitors Bureau (TVB; ☎ 25334; fax 23507; www.tongaholiday.com; Vuna Rd; ⌚ 8.30am-4.30pm Mon-Fri, 9am-12.30pm Sat & public holidays) TVB produces and stocks leaflets (which you can also pick up around town) on culture, language and historical sights. Inside the locally designed building are a couple of interesting display boards on marine ecology, while you can browse the board outside for lists of church services and 'island nights'. Staff can book accommodation for you if you can't manage it yourself, and will follow up on emailed queries.

TRAVEL AGENCIES

The following agencies make bookings for local tours in addition to selling international flights:

Jetsave (☎ 23052; www.taufonua.com; Fund Management Bldg, Taufa'ahau Rd) Books day tours and domestic package holidays to all island groups.

Jones Travel & Tours (☎ 23422/3; jonestrl@kalianet.to; cnr Taufa'ahau & Wellington Rds)

Teta Tours (☎ 23690; fax 23238; tetatour@kalianet.to; cnr Wellington & Railway Rds)

Dangers & Annoyances

As well as avoiding cranky dogs, you might want to steer clear of the boozed-up scuffles that tend to occur regularly in the waterfront car parks outside bars on Vuna Rd.

Sights

ROYAL PALACE

Amid sprawling lawns, behind a perimeter of Norfolk Island pines and barbed wire–topped cyclone mesh, sits the waterfront **Royal Palace**. The weathered, white Victorian timber, with its red corrugated-iron roof, has become a symbol of Tonga to the world. It was prefabricated in New Zealand in 1867. An upstairs veranda and the Royal Chapel, behind the palace, were built in 1882. The coronations of King George II, Queen Salote and King Taufa'ahau Tupou IV took place in the chapel in 1893, 1918 and 1967, respectively, and Sunday services were held there until the chapel was damaged in a hurricane. The coronation chair in the chapel is partially constructed from the wood of the *koka* tree from Lifuka (Ha'apai), under which King George I was invested with the title Tu'i Kanokupolu. The small octagonal gazebo in the gardens is called the Palesi and was used as a rest house for visiting chiefs.

The palace grounds are closed to visitors but you can get a good view of the palace from the waterfront on the west side.

The **Mala'e Pangai** area of the waterfront, beside the Royal Palace, is a public ground used for royal *kava* ceremonies, feasts, and football and cricket matches.

ROYAL TOMBS

The **Mala'ekula**, the spacious parklike area opposite the basilica, which serves as the royal tomb, was named after the Katoanga Kula festival, held here in the days of King George Tupou I (the *mala'e* part of the name refers to a sacred area). Since 1893 the graves of all the Tongan sovereigns as well as those of their husbands, wives and other close relatives, have been situated here. The large green is off limits to the public, though peering through the crested perimeter gates allows a fairly good view.

'ATENISI INSTITUTE

The **'Atenisi Institute** (☎ 24819; PO Box 90 or 200, Nuku'alofa) is a unique institution that operates without subsidy from either church or state and therefore without obligation to further the views of either. Classes in Tongan language and culture are taught, as well as philosophy, sciences and other disciplines. The institute was founded in 1967 by an extraordinary individual, 'I Futa Helu, to operate under a classic Western format in the tradition of the University of Oxford. He writes in the university syllabus:

...concern with the classical tradition means the keeping of a traditional core of studies. This is the academic equivalent of the English attitude that a university which does not teach philosophy as a discipline is a 'Mickey Mouse' university...all South Sea island communities have created beautiful cultures, but it must be pointed out that in all these cultures criticism as an institution is discouraged, and criticism is the very heart of education.

'Atenisi's graduation ceremony in November features dancing, entertainment, royal gifting and feasting, and a unique tradition called 'presentation of the *vala*' (traditional tunic); during this ceremony, the villages of 'Atenisi graduates present the university with gifts of elaborate mats and immense pieces of *tapa* (mulberry bark cloth). Visitors are welcome. Those spending some time in Tonga may want to check out the classes.

Polynesian Paradox, edited by Ian Campbell and Eve Coxon, is an insightful collection of essays in honour of 'I Futa Helu, written by distinguished scholars in commemoration of his 70th year.

TALAMAHU MARKET

A trip to Tongatapu would not be complete without immersing yourself in two-storey **Talamahu** (Salote Rd; ☺ early morning-4.30pm), the country's biggest market. Downstairs you'll find mostly root-crop produce in handmade woven-frond baskets, branches of bananas, colourful pyramids of weighed-out food stuffs, a few food stands, and second-hand clothing stalls surrounding the periphery.

The raw materials for Tonga's handicrafts are sold here, such as pandanus strips, white (unpainted) *tapa* (mulberry bark cloth) and *tapa* hammers, while excellent Tongan arts and crafts – including *tapa,* pandanus mats and weavings – are found on both floors. Upstairs, small stalls sell Polynesian-style wood carvings (from around T$20), wood-carved fishing lures, and jewellery and pendants carved from black oyster shell and ox bone (some in New Zealand Maori designs). You'll spot stylised fish hooks, infinity symbols, flowers, mermaids and geckos.

CHURCHES

Royal watchers and rubberneckers of all denominations head to the 1952 **Centenary Chapel** (Wellington Rd), behind Mt Zion, to catch a glimpse of members of the royal family at a Sunday service and to hear the magnificent, booming singing of the congregation. The

hymns may sound familiar – British hymns are sung in Tongan to the accompaniment of a brass band. Constructed mostly by volunteer labour, the chapel accommodates over 2000 people.

Nuku'alofa's most distinctive structure is the 1980 **Basilica of St Anthony of Padua** (cnr Taufa'ahau & Laifone Rds), opposite the Royal Tombs. The conical roof, draped like a circus tent over large ceiling beams, is quite something, especially during evening services when light pours through the stained glass. The sweeping staircase draws you into the beautiful interior, which features a handcrafted altar, lectern, baptistry, pews and tables, beam joints covered with *sennit* (coconut-husk string) mats, and Stations of the Cross made of coconut wood inlaid with mother-of-pearl. At Station XI, a tiny gold coconut tree that belonged to Queen Salote Tupou III is fitted into the hair of Christ.

Rose gardens surround **St Mary's Cathedral** (Vuna Rd), Nuku'alofa's other Catholic church. It's an odd mix of old and new styling and worth a look for its beautiful vaulted ceiling, stained glass and giant *kava*-bowl altar.

The imposing stone structure to the north of the Royal Tombs is the **Centennial Church of the Free Church of Tonga**. Built in 1983, it looks much older than its years.

For tips on church etiquette and choosing your Sabbath venue, see the boxed text, p164.

TONGAN NATIONAL CENTRE

It would be a major feat to spend any time in Tonga without having some kind of cultural experience, but a visit to the **Tongan National Centre** (☎ 23022; Taufa'ahau Rd, Vaiola; museum admission free; ☺ 9am-4pm Mon-Fri) is a good way to start. The museum contains historical artefacts – Lapita pottery, war clubs, headrests – and items still very much in use today, such as bark cloth and *kava* bowls.

Good-value **cultural tours** (adult/child T$15/8; ☺ 2pm Mon-Fri) take you through the phases of *tapa* (p167), weaving and basketry, traditional dancing, and carving, for which Tongans enjoy a fine reputation throughout the Pacific.

Tongans are as renowned for their feasting as for their monarch's former girth (the King has famously shed 75kg). The **dinner show** (adult/child T$25/13, show only T$5; ☺ 7.30pm Tue & Thu) starts with a *kava* ceremony, features traditional dishes cooked in an 'umu (underground oven), and has one of Tonga's best traditional dance and music shows. While the term **fashion show** (adult/child T$20/12; ☺ 12.30-1.45pm) might seem an odd one for a show featuring traditional costumes, you can view them all over a traditional lunch with music and dance performances.

A ride in a local bus to the Tongan National Centre offers an experience of Nuku'alofa's contemporary culture, so take the Vaiola bus (50 *seniti*) from the eastern

bus terminal on Vuna Rd for 2km to the centre. A taxi from town will cost about T$4. A shuttle bus (T$1) to and from town is available for the dinner show.

ROYAL BREWERY

The **Royal Beer Co** (☎ 25554; www.royalbeer.to; Small Industries Centre, Ma'ufanga; ☺ Mon-Sat), producer of Royal All Malt Premium Beer, Royal All Malt Draft Beer and the much-drunk Ikale, is quite small but tours can be arranged in advance.

Activities

Nuku'alofa provides easy access to activities such as diving, surfing, fishing and whale-watching; for details see p180.

You can tee off on the green of the nine-hole **Tonga Golf Club** (Map p183; Main Rd, Vietongo; green fees T$8), opposite 'Atele Indoor Stadium. The not-so-challenging course is open to visitors, and clubs can sometimes be hired.

Yoga and massage are both available in Nuku'alofa – check notice boards at Molisi Tonga Limited supermarket (p195) and Friends Tourist Centre (p187) for locations.

Local kids catapult themselves off the town's wharves on hot afternoons. A **swimming pool** was being constructed on the east side of Touliki Jetty in 2006, while the International Dateline Hotel lets nonguests use its pool (T$3) and the pool-side **Splash Bar** (☎ 23411; Vuna Rd).

Walking Tour

See the map on p190. Once you've completed a lap of **Talamahu Market** (**1**; opposite) and

---

IT'S SUNDAY IN NUKU'ALOFA

What to do, when nothing stirs on a Sunday and even mangy dogs have deserted the streets?

- Go to church – the magnificent singing lifts the soul and almost the roof. A favourite activity with visitors is to attend Centenary Chapel (opposite) to worship with the king and royal family, but there are rules of social etiquette to be followed (see p164).

- Take a round-the-island tour (p191) and explore Tongatapu's attractions: the Mapu'a 'a Vaca blowholes, the Ha'amonga 'a Maui trilithon, Mu'a's archaeological site and the beaches.

- Hire a bicycle (p198) and explore the island at your own pace.

- Visit your pick of the three offshore island resorts (p213) and enjoy the stunning white-sand beaches and good snorkelling, or join a boat trip to the more remote outer islands.

- Head for Ha'atafu Beach (p212).

- Lounge around the pool (above) at the International Dateline Hotel all day long for T$3.

- Sleep and eat – that's what most of the locals will be doing.

checked out its wares, watch the deft work of a *niu* (green drinking coconut) seller slicing the top off a husked coconut with a machete. Dunk a straw in one and take it with you on your way for a tour of the town.

On the market's west side, cross over **Railway Rd (2)**, along which a railway used to transport copra to Vuna Wharf, where it was loaded onto steamers for export. Continue west along Salote Rd and cross Taufa'ahau Rd to the GPO, where you'll find the **Philatelic Bureau (3**; p197) display of colourful first-day covers of stamps from Tonga and Nioafo'ou featuring historic moments, flora and fauna, and world monarchs.

Continue along Salote Rd, where towering Norfolk Island pines obscure the back

---

WALK FACTS

Start Talamahu Market
Finish Vuna Wharf
Distance 1.8km
Duration Allow two hours, which gives time for browsing and grazing

---

NUKU'ALOFA WALKING TOUR

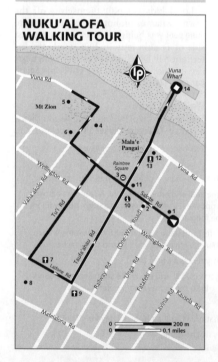

and sides of the **Royal Palace (4**; p187). Turn right onto Vaha'akolo Rd and head for the waterfront for the best palace views.

Head northwest along the grassy waterfront of Vuna Rd for around 100m until you come to the manicured grounds of the **British High Commissioner's Office and Residence (5)**. This beautiful building is the epitome of Pacific colonial architecture. The four cannons surrounding the flagpole on the front lawn are from the British privateer *Port-au-Prince* (p182).

Double back to the palace. Just beyond it, on the slopes of **Mt Zion (6)**, is the Sia Ko Veiongo, the 'royal estate'. The fortress of Nuku'alofa, with its ludicrous history of attacks and conflagrations, once stood here. The site is now occupied by a radio tower and the grave of Captain Croker of the HMS *Favourite*, who was killed attacking the fortress on 24 June 1840.

Continue back along Salote Rd and take the first right turn into Tu'i Rd, passing neat homes and the massive, stone **Centennial Church of the Free Church of Tonga (7**; p188) until you come to the end of Tu'i Rd. Here you can spy through the red metal fence with white crests into the **Royal Tombs (8**; p187), but entry is forbidden. Turn left onto Laifone Rd, following it for 50m to the distinctive **Basilica of St Anthony of Padua (9**; p188), perhaps stopping off for lunch at **Akiko's** (p194) in its basement.

Wander back towards the waterfront along Taufa'ahau Rd, checking out a few Tongan handicraft shops along the way (see p197). On the right-hand side, alongside Friend's Café, near the corner of Salote Rd, is the gingerbread-style **Langafonou Building (10)**, which houses Langafonua'ae Fefine Handicrafts (p197). It was originally built by a British expat for his five daughters who lived in New Zealand and spent winters in Tonga.

Across Salote Rd, you'll find the **Prime Minister's Office (11)**, containing numerous government offices said to be the source of much of the hot air blowing around Tonga. The tower was damaged in the 1977 earthquake but was rebuilt shortly afterwards. Opposite is a beautiful tree spanning Raintree Square.

The large lawn behind the **Treasury (12)** is the town common, which was the base for striking public servants during 2005. It has a small bandstand and the **Tongan War Memorial (13)**, which honours Tongans who served in the two world wars. On the waterfront opposite the treasury are a few monuments looking the worse for lack of upkeep, including a line-up of big guns and a flagpole used on ceremonial occasions. The (nonfunctioning) dolphin fountain was presented by the British government to commemorate the HMS *Dolphin*, the first British warship to land in Tonga. The floating soft-drink bottles were not part of the original monument.

Crumbling **Vuna Wharf (14)**, at the end of Taufa'ahau Rd, is a popular launching pad for overheated students looking for a refreshing dip. Local boats load and unload here and fresh fish is sold in the afternoon.

From here you can head back to inspect the market handicrafts again – and duck into Chateau Ice Creamery (p194) for a 'royal' scoop on the way – or continue along the waterfront.

Nuku'alofa for Children

There are no sights specifically for children but there are a few that they will particularly enjoy. The Tongan Cultural Centre offers engaging entertainment, and there are plenty of activities to wear out kids' limbs on outer-islands trips or on round-island tours, which allow them to climb, run, delve into caves and paddle in rock pools.

A park on Vuna Rd, opposite the waterfront, has playground equipment and plenty of grass. Some family accommodation has swimming pools; otherwise pay to use the pool at the International Dateline Hotel. A new outdoor pool was being constructed on the east side of the wharf in 2006.

Your accommodation may be able to arrange baby-sitting.

Tours

Boat tours can often be arranged through the place at which you are staying. Also try any of the game-fishing operators (p181) for fishing trips.

ISLAND TOURS

Tongatapu's main sights can be comfortably covered in a day tour of the island. Most tour operators require a minimum of four people per tour.

Toni's Tours (☎ 21049, 27068; tonigh@kalianet.to) Tongatapu's most popular full-day whole-island tours (T$30) offer exceptional value and run daily (minimum three people), including on Sunday. Toni usually winds up at Good Samaritan Inn (p212) for lunch – check first or bring your own, along with swimming gear, a torch and drinks. Other trips are negotiable.

Friendly Island Experience (☎ 29910; www.tonga experience.com) These tours (six to seven hours, T$45) cover the eastern half of the island and its archaeological sites, blowholes and flying foxes, and include fresh fruit. German and English are spoken.

Jones Travel & Tours (☎ 23422, 23423; jonestrl@ kalianet.to; cnr Taufa'ahau & Wellington Rds) The Whole Island Tour (T$70) visits all major sites and has an optional lunch stop at Good Samaritan Inn (p212) on the west coast. The half-day Historic East Side and Scenic West Side tours cost T$63 each.

Teta Tours (☎ 23690; fax 23238; tetatour@kalianet.to; cnr Wellington & Railway Rds) Half-island tours (T$55) cover Nuku'alofa's major sights and a little of eastern or western Tongatapu. Whole-island tours (T$70) include all of Tongatapu's major sights.

Festivals & Events

Nuku'alofa's biggest festival is the week-long **Heilala Festival**, which culminates in the King's Birthday on 4 July. Celebrations include a street parade with decorated floats, workshops, fashion shows, a beauty pageant, all manner of music, arts and sports competitions, feasting and general merriment.

Sleeping

If you're visiting Nuku'alofa during the Heilala Festival, be sure to book accommodation well in advance. All accommodation offers hot showers unless stated.

BUDGET

Refer to the Midrange section for excellent budget options in midrange establishments, specifically groovy Ali Baba's Guesthouse, Heilala Holiday Lodge and Papiloa's Friendly Islander Hotel. There are camping sites in Nuku'alofa and camping is possible at the Good Samaritan Inn (p212), on the Ha'atafu Beach and on Pangaimotu (p213), offshore from Nuku'alofa.

Toni's Guest House (Map p183; ☎ /fax 21049, ☎ 27 068; www.geocities.com/tmatthais2000; Tofoa; r per person T$10.75) Toni's is the ultrabudget favourite. It's renowned for regular all-inclusive *kava* sessions and the island's most popular tours (both peppered with the owner's dry English humour) as much as for its vivid green walls. The simple, laid-back place has basic, communal kitchen and bathroom facilities, and a small sitting area. The owners offer a shuttle service to and from town (which may incur a small fee); transfers to/from the airport cost T$10/6.

Sela's Guest House (☎ 25040; mettonga@kalianet .to; off Fatafehi Rd; dm/s/d/tr with shared facilities T$15/20/30/40, s/d with private bathroom T$50/60; breakfast T$8) In this lagoon-side place, stablelike rooms open off a central courtyard filled with tables. Guests have use of the kitchen and lavish cooked breakfasts with fruit are available. It's a 15-minute walk from town.

Divers Lodge (☎ 23379; fax 23576; www.deep-blue -diving.to; Funa Rd; s/d US$29/40) The local dive outfit has three clean and simple rooms on the 1st floor of a light and airy building, with a pleasant garden outlook from the balcony. It's mainly for organised dive groups, but individuals are welcome. There's a well-equipped kitchen and shared facilities. It's close to the lagoon and a T$3 taxi ride from Nuku'alofa town centre.

Winnie's Guest House (☎ 25215; winnies@kalianet .to; Vaha'akolo Rd; r per person incl breakfast T$40; 💻) This cosy, spacious house with homely décor has five fan-cooled rooms, a well-equipped guests' kitchen and a lounge with board games, a large DVD collection and a massive TV. It's very friendly and popular with international medical students, so book in advance. It's about 2km from town but you can take the Vaiola bus (50 *seniti*) from the eastern bus terminal on Vuna Rd. Lunch/dinner costs T$10/15.

Angela's Motel & Guest House (☎ 23930; fax 22149; cnr Wellington & Lavinia Rds; s/d with bathroom from T$25/35) The rooms are clean, though a bit grim and stuffy in summer, but Angela's is very conveniently located.

MIDRANGE

Nuku'alofa's hotels proper are in a shabby state and therefore cannot be recommended for any kind of value, so we have not listed them here.

Ali Baba's Guest House (☎ /fax 25154; www.ali babaguesthouse.com; off Tupoulahi Rd, Ngele'ia; s/d incl breakfast T$40/60, d & f incl bathroom & breakfast from T$80, extra person T$10; 💻) Funky floors in chequered gold and blue or green decorate the rooms, each with its own colour scheme and theme. Choose from four-poster beds with red candy-striped or blue-floral covers; the master suite has a zebra-print couch and a gilt-trimmed en suite with bath.

The facilities are ultraclean and festive; a friendly ambience prevails from the communal lounge to the pretty gardens. Meals (dinner T$15) here are plentiful and get rave reviews from guests. It's about a 15-minute walk from the GPO.

Heilala Holiday Lodge (Map p183; ☎ 29910; fax 29410; www.heilala-holiday-lodge.com; Tofoa; s/d T$40/60, s/d fale with bathroom T$60/80, s/d superior fale with bathroom T$90/115, extra bed T$25; 🌀 💷) A path winds through lovingly tended tropical gardens with labelled local plants, connecting very cute, *fale* (traditional thatched house) in this unlikely suburban location 3km south of Nuku'alofa. The spacious 'superior' *fale* have refrigerators. Request a *fale* with a hammock strung between its balcony beams. Sparse budget rooms in the house are clean but lack adequate ventilation and share one small bathroom. The above-ground, shaded pool is a lovely spot for an afternoon chill-out. Rates include breakfast of toast and tropical trims, and kitchen facilities are available. Dinner is available from T$17. Air-con is T$25. Catch a bus to Nuku'alofa (50 *seniti*, every few minutes) from Taufa'ahau Rd, a five-minute walk away.

Nukuma'anu Motel (☎ 22186; fax 24217; fml@ tonfon.to; Vuna Rd, Sopu; d T$104; 🌀) Readers have found these detached, solid Tongan *fale* amid palm trees and tropical blooms, opposite the waterfront, the perfect spot to retreat to. The airy, self-contained *fale* have queen-sized beds, cushioned cane furniture to sink into, solar hot water and plenty of comforts. Some of the capital's best restaurants are nearby and it's a short drive or good stroll from the GPO.

Harbour View Motel (☎ 25488; fax 25490; harb vmtl@kalianet.to; Vuna Rd; s/d T$58/81, deluxe s/d/f with private bathroom T$87/110/156, spa ste d/f T$196/207; P 🌀) Handily located near to Queen Salote Wharf, the Billfish and surrounding bars, this motel has comfortable beds and some of the best-pressure showers in Tonga. The tidy rooms have fans, telephones and tea/coffee facilities; deluxe rooms also offer air-conditioning, a fridge, TV and video. The continental breakfast (T$8) is ample.

Papiloa's Friendly Islander Hotel (☎ 23810; fax 24199; papiloa@tongatapu.to; Vuna Rd; dm T$20, d unit/fale with bathroom T$60/95, self-contained bungalow T$110; 🌀 💷) Like an uncle who found his look a couple of decades back – and stuck with it – this place is showing its age.

The multipastel-coloured *fale*, with chintzy bed covers, are pleasantly spread throughout the gardens, the lounge/bar is verging on retro. Budget accommodation is in drab units. A good spot for families, there's kids' play equipment (over concrete) next to the swimming pool. Continental/cooked breakfast costs T$7.50/12.

Nerima Lodge (☎ 25533; fax 25577; naoko@maca.to; 'Amaile Rd, off Fatafehi Rd; s/d/tr incl breakfast T$43/68/96; dinner by arrangement) There are no frills or blooms around the cyclone-fenced gardens, but the rooms (upstairs) in this large and secure lodge are comfortable enough, with duvet-covered futons and fans. You get a choice of cooked egg-and-bacon or Japanese breakfasts, and authentic Japanese banquets can be arranged with advance booking.

TOP END

Establishments in this category have some of Nuku'alofa's best restaurants attached to them; see right. While all of these options are on the waterfront, there is no real beach here.

Villa Guest Lodge (☎ /fax 24998; www.tongavilla.com; Vuna Rd; s/d/tr with bathroom & breakfast T$125/145/180; 🏊) For fans of an elegant and breezy, unfussed colonial style. Centrally located and nearby good restaurants (you can also eat in), this is one of the most attractive places to stay in Nuku'alofa. There's a huge lounge with cable TV and a broad balcony facing the waterfront – perfect for polishing off a novel or two.

Seaview Lodge (☎ 23709; fax 26906; seaview@kalianet.to; Vuna Rd; standard/garden/sea-view d with bathroom T$145/175/185; 🏊) Large balconied rooms are decorated with local crafts and offer phone, TV/video, refrigerator and tea and coffee facilities, as well as great showers. The lodge sits in immaculate gardens behind rave-worthy Seaview restaurant and is 10 minutes' walk west of the GPO. A reliable favourite.

Waterfront Lodge (☎ 25260; fax 24977; waterfro@kalianet.to; Vuna Rd; garden/sea-view d incl breakfast T$175/185, extra bed T$41; 🏊) The Waterfront's boutique-style elegance flows through its eight spacious rooms featuring Gauguin prints on antique-white walls, marine-blue bed covers and furniture in teak and cane. Luxurious trimmings include bathrobes, quality shampoos and complimentary toothbrushes, international direct dial (IDD) telephones and satellite TV. French

doors open onto the broad balcony with deck chairs; there are harbour views from 'sea-view' rooms. Children under 12 are not catered for. Airport transfers cost T$20.

Black Pearl Suites (☎ 28393; fax 28432; thepearl@kalianet.to; Vuna Rd, Sopu; ste T$180, executive ste T$345; 🏊) Friendly staff have their fingers on the pulse regarding guest comfort in this luxurious, quiet waterfront spot on the outskirts of town. The ski chalet–like interior is not necessarily what you'd expect of a Pacific destination – nor, perhaps, are the four-poster or sleigh beds with Versace-style covers in burgundy and emerald. Each room has a balcony, TV/DVD and telephone, while executive suites have azure tiled spa baths and fully equipped kitchens (with dishwashers). Baby-sitting can be arranged. Its restaurant, the Pearl Inn (p195), serves the best food in Nuku'alofa.

RENTAL ACCOMMODATION

Houses and flats for rent are listed at the Tonga Visitors Bureau and on the bulletin boards at Molisi Tonga Limited supermarket and Friends Tourist Centre. Prices for a furnished apartment/house start at around T$400/500 per month; elegance will set you back upwards of T$850 per month.

Marketonga (☎ 75623; www.marketonga.com; Taufa'ahau Rd) This place deals in furnished rental properties.

Captain Cook Vacation Apartments (☎ /fax 25 600; info@captaincook.to; Vuna Rd, PO Box 1959, Nuku'alofa; d apt T$144, over 5 nights T$133, extra person T$29; 🏊) West of the Royal Palace, these six self-contained, two-bed apartments with waterfront balconies have comfortable, if slightly grandma-esque, interiors. Two children under 12 stay free of charge. Long-term discounts are available.

Lagoon Lodge (☎ 26515; fax 24069; lagoon.lodge@kalianet.to; PO Box 51, 'Umusi; 1-/2-bed apt from T$170/195) Balconied, lagoon-side apartments with bright, white-tiled interiors are well decked out to suit daily living needs (particularly for those on longer stays). It's clean and tidy, with International Subscriber Dialling (ISD) telephone and laundry facilities on-site. You'll need to take a taxi or hire a car.

Eating

Nuku'alofa has surprising diversity and quality of food for a town centre its size. The decent spread of cafés and restaurants are stretched mostly along waterfront Vuna Rd and on, or nearby, Taufa'ahau Rd. Other options include resort restaurants around Tongatapu and its offshore islands, as well as island-style buffets or feasts (p196), where you can sample traditional Tongan cuisine.

CAFÉS & QUICK EATS

Akiko's (☎ 25339; Taufa'ahau Rd; snacks & meals T$1.80-6.60; 🕐 11am-3pm Mon-Fri) Duck under the basilica for excellent-value Chinese and curry dishes, mixed Tongan plates, 'ota ika (a Tongan raw fish dish) and mixed sandwiches in a clean and cool environment. The fruit juices and smoothies are excellent.

Friends Café (☎ 22390; Taufa'ahau Rd; breakfast T$4.50-13, mains T$9.50-20; 🕐 8am-10pm Mon-Fri, 8.30am-2pm Sat) With a breezy charm and dependably good food, Friends Café, at the centre of town, is deservedly popular. There's a dedicated breakfast menu, popular thick-cut panini, and a daily menu that may feature seafood chowder with garlic toast or lamb shanks in herbed tomato over kumala mash. Or choose the ever-popular stacked burgers or chunks of battered game fish, both served with chips and a crisp salad garnish. The impressive line-up of cakes and slices will give you a choice dilemma and there's dependably good Royal Coffee.

Café Escape (☎ 21212; Taufa'ahau Rd; breakfast T$3.50-16, mains T$8-16; 🕐 7.30am-9.30pm Mon-Thu, to 10.30pm Fri, to 4pm Sat) Slick little Café Escape could be anywhere but provides a refined, air-con oasis and infuses the tropics into its mixed menu of ample and tasty dishes. Choose from all-day breakfasts, including coconut bread (T$4) and baked egg with salmon, spinach and cream cheese (T$9); toasted sandwiches, panini and pies; Asian-style main dishes and sweet-tooth tempters. There are plenty of recent magazines to help you zone out, Internet access (T$2 for 15 minutes), good service and great coffee.

Cassiopeia's Café (☎ 11699; Queen Salote Domestic Wharf; takeaway T$1.20-7.50; 🕐 10am-4pm Mon-Fri, 10am-2pm Sat) Negotiate the 'witches hats' at Tonga's only drive-thru, or order Tongan takeaway (hamburgers or meal plates) from the window near the outdoor seating.

Chateau Ice Cream (cnr Salote & Railway Rds; cones T$1.50-4; 🕐 9am-11pm Mon-Sat) Creamy, delicious ice creams come in plain or 'royal' flavours, with the option of a waffle cone. Opposite Talamahu Market.

You'll find a few small stands selling drinking coconuts, peanuts, hot dogs (T$1.50) and seasonal snacks along Vuna Rd. Eating bain-marie chicken dishes in a tropical climate could be considered an extreme sport, but if you're game you can pick up a local chicken or sipi (mutton) curry at **Sia Leka's** (Taufa'ahau Rd; dishes T$4-6), or try **Lafone** (☎ 24744; Laifone Rd; curry T$3.50; 🕐 24hr Mon-Sat), opposite the basilica, or **Curry Centre** (curry T$3.50-4; 🕐 8am-7pm Mon-Sat), opposite Queen Salote Domestic Wharf.

RESTAURANTS

Budget

Pot Luck Lunches (☎ 25091; off Salote Rd; lunch T$4-6; 🕐 noon-1.30pm Mon-Fri, 6-9.30pm 2nd Mon of month during school terms) Become a guinea pig of the best kind, indulging in fine food and good service at the training restaurant of 'Ahopanilolo Technical College, behind St Mary's Cathedral. You take 'pot luck' on the one set meal prepared! BYO alcohol.

Lily's (☎ 24226; Vuna Rd; mains T$6.50-15.50; 🕐 10am-2pm Mon-Sat, 6-10pm daily) Opposite the wharf, Lily's has a stark and kitschy interior but clean food on its 101-item menu.

Angela's Restaurant (☎ 23930; cnr Wellington & Lavinia Rds; mains T$5.50-18; 🕐 lunch & dinner Mon-Sat, 8.30am-2pm Sun; 😋) Here you'll find yum cha breakfast and lunch on Sunday.

Emerald Restaurant (☎ 24619; Vuna Rd; mains T$5-18; 🕐 11.30am-2.30pm & 5.30-10.30pm) Mishmash of (slightly grotty) Tongan and Chinese décor may make you feel a bit iffy, but the locals (including the adventurous local-airline pilots) assure that the generously proportioned dishes are reliably good.

Midrange

Billfish Bar & Restaurant (☎ 24084; Vuna Rd; lunch & dinner T$10-32; 🕐 meals Mon-Sat) These are the closest you'll get to pub-style meals – and they're great. Beautifully presented and generous, the tasty meals include burgers, a mountainous chicken stir-fry, ultrafresh fish served as Thai fish curry or fish and chips, New Zealand steaks and garlic prawns. This is also a good place for a drink; see p196.

Joboy Steakhouse (☎ 27920; Taufa'ahau Rd; mains T$10-30; 🕐 lunch Mon-Fri, dinner daily) Popular with locals and visitors alike, Joboy's is named after rugby-playing son and sibling Joe Naufahu and this rugby-mad family tune into every international game on the big screen. Feast on seafood, top your prime

(New Zealand) beef with a choice of sauces or tuck into an all-homemade Joboy burger. Ikale beer flows on tap.

Little Tokyo (☎ 22474; Wellington Rd; mains T$7-17; ☺ lunch Mon-Fri, dinner Mon-Sat) This authentic Japanese *izakaya* (drinking restaurant) is consistently good and a local favourite. Wash down your sushi, sashimi or *don* (meat/fish on rice) dishes with some sake. Takeaway is also available.

Little Italy Pizzeria (☎ 25053; Vuna Rd; pizza & pasta T$14-20; ☺ lunch & dinner Mon-Sat) The Alps meet the Pacific in this Tongafied trattoria. Hit-and-miss pizzas feature smoked salmon or blue cheese and cream, and occasional oddities such as mushrooms in gravy or baked beans. Fish and steak dishes and homemade Italian desserts plump up the menu. The play equipment in the garden makes it a good family spot. Takeaway is available.

Top End

Lunarossa Restaurant (☎ 26324; Taufa'ahau Rd; mains T$18-36; ☺ from 7pm Mon-Sat; ☒) Sophisticates enjoy the intimate fine dining here, and the authentic Italian cuisine, with the added attraction of ultrafresh seafood. Italian staples are joined on the menu by dishes such as ravioli with lobster mornay or fresh salmon and tarragon sauce, and lobster Catalan (olive oil,

---

THE AUTHOR'S CHOICE

Pearl Inn (☎ 28393; thepearl@kalianet.to; Vuna Rd, Sopu; entrée salads T$16-21, mains T$25-40, desserts T$10-12; ☺ dinner Mon-Sun; ☒) This is where the foodies head for a fine-dining splurge (judged as 'five star by New Zealand standards' by an avid fan). Though the name may be reminiscent of a pirate's lair, the dining room resembles a ski chalet. Meals are cooked right in view. Prime rib, scotch- and eye-fillet steaks (sourced from Australia and New Zealand, along with the wines) are smothered in blue-cheese or avocado sauce, and accompanied by roast potatoes and fresh, lightly marinated vegetables. The best seafood, from 'Uiha in Ha'apai, includes huge grilled lobsters with mornay, avocado or whiskey sauce. Sunday's prime-rib-roast night is a regular favourite (bookings essential). Any room for a dessert of hot bananas in cinnamon coconut sauce?

---

garlic and chilli), which follow a cleansing, complimentary soup. The service is excellent and there's a good wine selection.

Seaview Restaurant (☎ 23709; Vuna Rd; starters T$12-23, mains T$31-43; ☺ dinner) With simple style and excellent service, and overlooking the waterfront just west of the Royal Palace, Seaview has long been on the lips of seafood-loving locals and expats. Order your lobster in the following permutations: natural, 'Seaview', *Thermidor*, Provençale, Polynesian or saffron, or try noncrustaceans such as red snapper and fillet steak. Bookings are recommended.

Waterfront Café (☎ 21004; Vuna Rd; breakfast T$11-18, snacks T$16, mains T$20-40; ☺ breakfast, lunch & dinner Mon-Sat) Opposite the waterfront, this relaxed wood and emerald green–trimmed place verges on the sophisticated; its glass louvre windows open onto the gardens and catch the breeze. Dine on reasonable dishes of pasta with truffle sauce, fish parcels, scotch-fillet steak, lobster and seafood among monochrome sailing prints and colourful Gauguin copies.

SELF-CATERING

Talamahu Market (Salote Rd; ☺ early morning-4.30pm) Here's the deal: fruit and vegetables are sold by the pyramid (around T$2 to T$3), or woven-frond basket (for root crops and coconuts) with prices generally marked. You may be able to negotiate a smaller portion.

Cowley's Bakery (Bread Bin; ☎ 26019; Salote Rd; baked goods 30 seniti-T$2; ☺ 6am-10pm Mon-Sat, noon-midnight Sun) This Sunday-afternoon social Mecca does a brisk trade in meat pies, sausage rolls, pull-apart savoury breads, muffins, doughnuts, lurid pineapple-iced cupcakes, half-metre Swiss rolls and birthday cakes, in addition to its breads.

Hot Bread Shop (☎ 21440; Taufa'ahau Rd; baked goods 30 seniti-T$2; ☺ 6am-10pm Mon-Sat, 2-10pm Sun) Here you can pick up grainy bread to get over the bleached-white blues; be tempted by choc-iced doughnuts, fruit pancakes, cakes and meat pies. It's 1km south of town.

Nuku'alofa has a number of supermarkets, that include the competitively priced branches of the **Tonga Cooperative Federation** (TCF; cnr Wellington & Taufa'ahau Rds; Taufa'ahau Rd) and the well-stocked **Molisi Tonga Limited** (Salote Rd), opposite Talamahu Market, which sells wine. **Si's Kae Ola Supermarket** (Taufa'ahau Rd) is by far the best-stocked supermarket, with a butcher and Eftpos facilities. You can find packaged meats, mince, beer and spirits at **Tonga Cold Store** (☎ 24084; Vuna Rd; 🕙 8am-5pm Mon-Fri, 8am-2pm Sat), next to Billfish Bar.

The fish market on Tuimatamoana Harbour starts when boats come in around 5am from Monday to Saturday. It's an interesting sight to see baskets of cockles, fresh and dried clams and dried octopus even if you're not buying. **South Pacific Resources Co** (☎ 26296; Tuimatamoana Harbour; 🕙 8am-5pm Mon-Sat), nearby, sells local fish and big game. Good-quality fish can also be bought at **'Alatini Fisheries** (☎ 24759; Small Industries Centre, Taufa'ahau Rd), along with imported meats, wine and gourmet goods, 2km southeast of central Nuku'alofa.

Drinking

Enquire locally about recommended *kava* circles (note that you'll need an invitation to join). Ordinarily a male-only affair, both men and women are welcome around the *kava* bowl at Toni's Guest House (p191).

Billfish Bar & Restaurant (☎ 24084; Vuna Rd; 🕙 9am-2am Mon-Thu, 9am-4am Fri, 5pm-12am Sat) Easily the most popular bar in town, this relaxed open-air place draped in flags and fishing trophies has a gravel floor and a great vibe. Ikale and Steinlager are on tap and there are plenty of other imported drinks in which to indulge, as well as good pub food (p194). Live music of varying quality is played for the dance floor on Wednesday and Friday night and karaoke is also popular.

Waterfront Café (☎ 21004; Vuna Rd) Sip on sundowners of champagne cocktails, margaritas and daiquiris, banana colada or a cool beer and sink into the Raffles-esque rattan chairs at this colonial-style bar/restaurant (see p195). It's one of the most popular waterfront bars and a good place for socialising.

Dupincia Bar (☎ 23598; Vuna Rd; 🕙 6pm-late Mon-Sat) Another waterfront nightspot, playing predominantly Tongan and Samoan love songs.

Tonga Club (☎ 22710; Tupoulahi Rd) For a cheap beer, head to this dingy, historic pub.

Garden Bar (☎ 22101; Vuna Rd) This lively place is behind the Emerald Restaurant.

Nuku'alofa Club (☎ 25160; cnr Salote & Tu'i Rds; 🕙 8am-close) Founded in 1914, this all-male, members-only relic is the oldest (and possibly last) club of its kind in the South Pacific. 'Old boys' (expats, Tongan nobles, yuppie politicians and businessmen) bond over billiards and beers. Technically, you must be the guest of a member. Tally-ho.

Entertainment
TONGAN FEASTS & TRADITIONAL DANCE

Feast – it's a cultural experience! At these showcases of traditional Tongan music and dance, including *kava* ceremonies and the accompanying island-style buffets, you'll often see just as many locals out for a good time as tourists. Bring along plenty of T$1 notes to stick onto the oiled skin of the dancers to show your appreciation – that's what the Tongans will be doing. The following cost T$25 (children generally half-price):

Tongan National Centre (☎ 23022; Taufa'ahau Rd, Vaiola; 🕙 7.30pm Tue & Thu) Indoor buffet and show featuring some of Tongatapu's best dancers.

International Dateline Hotel (☎ 23411; www.datelinehotel.com; Vuna Rd) Wednesday-night buffet and show from 7.30pm (show up around 8.30pm to drink at the bar and watch the show).

Good Samaritan Inn (Map p183; ☎ 41022; Kolovai; T$25, with Nuku'alofa transfer T$30) Buffet and show at 7.30pm on Friday, outdoors by the beach. Also has entertainment on Sunday with a barbecue and live music.

Kahana Lagoon Resort (☎ 24165; Bypass Rd) Polynesian floorshow and buffet at 8pm on Friday.

NIGHTCLUBS

Friday night is the big night for going out in Tonga but the pubs and clubs, mainly along Vuna Rd, swell with revellers from Thursday to Saturday. (On Saturday night, the partying is stifled at midnight to avoid revelry on Sunday.) Bars (left) in Nuku'alofa have dance floors and weekly live music. You'll need to be reasonably well dressed to get in; thongs (flip-flops) may be frowned on.

Blue Pacific Nightclub (☎ 25994; Bypass Rd; Fri/Sat T$6/3; 🕙 10pm-4am Tue-Fri, to midnight Sat) When other bars call for last drinks, night owls and those who 'just want to dance' head 3km southeast of central Nuku'alofa to Tonga's only real nightclub. It is packed on Friday night with people dancing, or swaying, to a mix of hip-hop, rap and reggae. It's quite likely someone else will commandeer your drink and that women – even those accompanied by husbands or male friends – will feel put upon to dance with local men.

CINEMA
Loni's Cinema (☎ 23617; Wellington Rd; admission T$5; 🕙 Thu-Sat, from midnight Sun) Nuku'alofa's only

cinema is a very basic affair screening recent Hollywood staples.

'Atenisi Institute (☎ 24819; www.atenisi.edu.to) Call or check notice boards around town for details on the International Film Society's open-air film screenings here. Beer, wine and popcorn are available.

SPORT

Tonga's favourite sport, rugby, is played at Teufaiva Outdoor Stadium off Taufa'ahau Rd, southwest of the city centre, from March to August. Games are played on Wednesday and back-to-back all day Saturday. Entry fees vary depending on which teams are playing; contact **Tonga Rugby Union** (☎ 26045) for match details and tickets.

Cricket (March to July) and football (soccer; March to November) are played at Mala'e Pangai, the lawn beside the Royal Palace, and at **Tonga College** (Map p183; Main Rd, Vietongo). There is rarely a charge.

'Atele Indoor Stadium (Main Rd, Vietongo) is the venue for tennis, as well as volleyball, badminton, table tennis, basketball, netball and boxing.

Shopping

While you won't find anything approaching high-end fashion (what a relief!), numerous variety shops along Taufa'ahau Rd sell sarongs and Polynesian-print clothing and fabrics.

Tongan arts, crafts and carvings are sold on both floors of the Talamahu Market (p188) and in various shops in town. Blow off the road dust in some Taufa'ahau Rd shops, and you'll find a vast range of Tongan handicrafts at very reasonable prices.

Art of Tonga (☎ 27667; Taufa'ahau Rd; ⏰ 9am-5pm Mon-Fri, 9am-1.30pm Sat) Master carvings in wood, bone and shell make up the centrepiece here. While you may find a better bargain searching through masses of carvings, jewellery and the like elsewhere, the refined collection of quality, well-displayed Tongan arts and crafts makes it easier to picture how they will look back home.

Langafonua'ae Fefine Handicrafts (☎ 21014; Taufa'ahau Rd; ⏰ 8.30am-5.30pm Mon-Fri, 8.30am-noon Sat) Founded by Queen Salote in 1953 to promote women's development and a continued interest in indigenous arts.

Friendly Islands Marketing Co-operative (Fimco; ☎ 23155; Taufa'ahau Rd; ⏰ 8am-6pm Mon-Fri, 8am-noon Sat) This is worth a browse. The Fimco fishing store, behind the craft shop, sells fishing gear.

Philatelic Bureau (☎ 21700; cnr Taufa'ahau & Salote Rds; ⏰ 8.30am-12.30pm & 1.30-4pm Mon-Fri) The displays of the beautiful coloured stamps of Tonga and Niuafo'ou (marking various moments in history) are interesting just to look at and also make good souvenirs.

Tapacraft (☎ 26760; Lavinia Rd; ⏰ 10am-4pm Tue-Sat) Worth perusing here are the detailed and purportedly original engravings from Captain Cook's three voyages, printed in England in 1777 and 1800.

Blue Banana (☎ 22662; Fund Management Bldg, Taufa'ahau Rd) Blue Banana prints bright, resort-style T-shirts and handmade sarongs with logos such as 'Kava-Cola'.

Look Sharp Tonga (☎ 26056; Taufa'ahau Rd) Sells souvenir T-shirts that are printed on quality cotton and feature plenty of hibiscus and Tongan *tapa* designs alongside obscure slogans. The signature range is dyed with *kava*. If you can't find your preferred style and design in a colour to suit, see if you can have one printed on-site.

Flea markets (Taufa'ahau & Vuna Rds; ⏰ Sat morning) Join the locals and riffle through the piles and racks at the flea market stalls to find bargains and something different from the traveller's wardrobe – second-hand clothes, presoftened Hawaiian shirts or a nice hot-pink latex animal-print miniskirt, perhaps? Among these items you'll find shoes, drinking coconuts and some old weavings and mats. Arrive early for the best selection.

Jones Travel & Tours (☎ 23422/3; cnr Taufa'ahau & Wellington Rds) Sells sports equipment, possibly including some snorkelling gear, though don't count on it.

Getting There & Away

See p290 for details of international flights, p294 for information on cargo-ship and yacht travel options to Tonga, and p285 for information on flights between Tongatapu and other parts of Tonga.

AIR

Fua'amotu International Airport is near the village of Fua'amotu, a 30-minute drive from Nuku'alofa. **Airlines Tonga Air Fiji** (Airlines Tonga; ☎ 23690; fax 23238; www.airlinestonga.com; Teta Tours cnr Railway & Wellinton Sts) services 'Eua, Ha'apai, Vava'u and the Niuas from the domestic terminal. **Peau Vava'u** (☎ 28326; Pacific Royal Hotel, Taufa'ahau Rd) services Ha'apai and Vava'u, also from the domestic terminal. Transfers between the terminals cost T$2.

Airline offices in Nuku'alofa connecting Tongatapu with other Pacific destinations include the following:

Air Fiji (☎ 23690; fax 23238; tetatour@kalianet.to; cnr Wellington & Railway Rds) Contact Teta Tours.

Air New Zealand (☎ 23192; fax 23447; www.airnz.co .nz; Tungi Arcade, Taufa'ahau Rd)

Air Pacific (☎ 23422/3; jonestrl@kalianet.to; cnr Taufa'ahau & Wellington Rds) Contact Jones Travel & Tours.

Pacific Blue (www.virginblue.com.au)

Polynesian Airlines (☎ 24566; fax 24225; www.poly nesianairlines.com; cnr Salote & Fatafehi Rds)

BOAT

The MV *'Olovaha*, and the MV *Pulupaki* connect Tongatapu with Ha'apai and Vava'u; the former also services the Niuas. Other vessels provide frequent services between Tongatapu and 'Eua. See p286 for details of schedules and fares.

Getting Around
TO/FROM THE AIRPORT

Taxis meet all incoming domestic and international flights. The standard fare for up to four passengers between the airport and Nuku'alofa is T$20 to T$25. Many hotels and guesthouses offer airport transport for guests if you let them know in advance.

Teta Tours (☎ 23690; tetatour@kalianet.to; cnr Wellington & Railway Rds) offers a shuttle bus service between Nuku'alofa and the airport (T$12 per person). It's **Toni's Tours** (☎ 21049; tonigh@kalianet.to) that provides the cheapest shuttle, charging T$10/6 to/from the airport, while **Friendly Island Experience** (☎ 29910; www .tongaexperience.com) offers transfers to/from the airport at T$8/9.50 per person.

BICYCLE

Tongatapu is flat and perfect for cycling. The island's major sites can be visited in three or four days, though Nuku'alofa's traffic is not exactly 'bike friendly' so take care. A couple of guesthouses hire bikes to guests.

Niko's Bicycle Rental (Vuna Rd; half-/full-day bicycle hire T$5/8; ⏰ 9am-5pm Mon, Tue & Thu-Sat) is run from a trailer roughly opposite the International Dateline Hotel. Test out a few. A special rate (and tool kit) can be negotiated for long-term rentals.

BOAT

The three offshore island resorts (p213) all provide boat transport and scheduled ferries connect Tongatapu to 'Eua (p286).

You can charter with **Sea-Taxi** (☎ 22795, 15723; http://kalianet.to/seataxi) for fishing, whale-watching and island trips around Tongatapu and as far afield as Tofua in Ha'apai.

BUS

Vuna Rd has two bus terminals. Buses to outlying areas of Tongatapu depart from the western terminal (close to Vuna Wharf), while buses to Nuku'alofa leave from the eastern terminal (opposite the TVB). One-way fares range from 50 *seniti* to T$1.

Bus services start around 6am, with the last departing about 4.30pm. There's no bus service on Sunday. Don't set off anywhere after noon unless you're planning to stay the night or are willing to take your chances hitching back.

In urban areas, bus stops are marked with a small sign reading *'Pasi'*. Elsewhere, flag down a bus by waving your outstretched arm. Passengers normally pay as they get off.

CAR & MINIBUS

Some hotels and guesthouses hire out vehicles to guests. Car and minibus rental companies include unlimited kilometres in rates and some offer special rates for weekends or long-term rental. Most companies offer seven days' rental for the price of six. Companies in Nuku'alofa include the following:

Avis Nuku'alofa (☎ 21179; Fund Management Bldg, Taufa'ahau Rd); Airport (☎ 35324) Cars from T$80 per day, less for multiple days; T$10 per day excess reduction. Chauffers can be arranged.

Fab Rentals (☎ 23077; fabsigns@kalianet.to; Salote Rd, Ma'ufanga) Automatic and manual cars and vans for T$50 to T$60 per day, including insurance. While there is no office as such, they do provide a door-to-door service.

Jones Rental Vehicles (☎ 23423; emjaut@kalianet .to; Taufa'ahau & Wellington Rds) Located at Jones Travel & Tours.

Marketonga Rental Cars (☎ 75623, 72623; www .marketonga.to; Taufa'ahau Rd, Havelu) Good cars for T$75 per day.

Sunshine Rental Cars (☎ /fax 23848; srental@yahoo .co.nz; Lopaukamea, Nuku'alofa) Cars from T$50.

TAXI

Within Nuku'alofa, taxis charge a standard T$3 fare; it's T$5 to T$6 to the outskirts of town. Check current taxi fares with the TVB and be sure to negotiate a price before setting off. Taxis do not run on Sunday; guesthouses may be able to help you with transport. Taxis are a good way to see the island quickly – all-day taxi tours of Tongatapu, including the traditional 'tourist' sites, are T$75 to T$100 for up to four people.

Taxi companies are numerous, and include the following:

Aloha Faua Taxi (☎ 22505) On the waterfront near the wharf.
Ngele'ia Taxi (☎ 24112)
Nuku'alofa Taxi (☎ 22910)
Talamahu Market Taxi (☎ 22713)
Wellington Taxi (☎ 24744)

AROUND THE ISLAND

Around Tongatapu's flat landscape are notable natural caves, blowholes, a natural limestone archway and impressive coral reefs, as well as some of the most extensive and well-excavated archaeological sites in the Pacific. Much of the island's interior is composed of agricultural land and rural villages, with a high church-to-home ratio.

The entire east coast, from the southern tip of the island right up to Niutoua, is fringed with lovely white-sand beaches; the west also has its share of white sandy beaches, as well as rock pools, spurting blowholes, sacred bats, a triple-headed mutant and the island's surf beach.

Sights are listed clockwise from Nuku'alofa around the island .

Royal Estates

As you round the lagoon between Tofoa and Pe'a, soon after leaving Nuku'alofa, you'll pass the Princess' **Tufumahina Royal Residence** (Map p183), with what appear to be white Bengal tigers guarding the entrance, and cannons pointed towards the Crown Prince's austere European-style hilltop **palace** opposite.

On the shore of picturesque Fanga 'Uta Lagoon, the **Kauvai Royal Estate** (Map p183) features lush vegetation, bizarre banyan trees and a secluded palace. It's reached via a long road through neatly ordered royal plantations and rows of coconut trees; the access road is open to the public during daytime. To get there without your own vehicle, take a bus to Vaini or Folaha, then walk 4km or 5km to the estate.

THE TU'I & THE TORTOISE

While visiting Tongatapu on his third Pacific voyage in 1777, Captain James Cook befriended Fatafehi Paulaho, the 30th Tu'i Tonga. Cook was amazed at the reverence and ceremony that surrounded this person: 'I was quite charmed at the decorum…had nowhere seen the like…not even amongst more civilised nations'.

Out of respect and affection, Cook presented the Tu'i Tonga with a fully grown tortoise. Later receiving the noble title Tu'i Malila, the creature lived nearly another 200 years. At the time of its death in 1966, Tu'i Malila enjoyed a seat at the royal *kava* circle and the run of the palace gardens.

When the beloved tortoise died – no-one knows at what age – its remains were sent to Auckland Museum to be studied and possibly preserved. It was determined that the noble tortoise was of a species originally found in the Seychelles, an island group in the Indian Ocean.

Tu'i Malila was so sorely missed at the palace that another tortoise was brought from Madagascar and named Tu'i Malila II.

Captain Cook's Landing Site

A **cairn** (Map p183) above a mangrove inlet near Holonga village marks the site where Captain Cook landed on Tongatapu on his final Pacific voyage in 1777. He took a nap under a banyan tree before moving on to Mu'a to visit his friend 'Pau', the reigning Tu'i Tonga.

Mu'a & the Lapaha Archaeological Site

The Mu'a area contains the richest concentration of archaeological remnants in Tonga. Sometime around 1200, the 11th Tu'i Tonga, Tu'itatui, moved the royal capital from Heketa (near present-day Niutoua) to Lapaha (p200), now known as Mu'a.

The *langi* (pyramidal stone tombs), constructed in ancient Tonga were traditionally used for royal burials. Commoners were buried in simpler heaps of sand lined with volcanic stones, much as they are today. There are 28 royal stone tombs at Mu'a, 15 of which are monumental. Most of the others are little more than conical mounds of stone.

A **moat** once surrounded the *kolo* (royal capital), just outside the site and is still

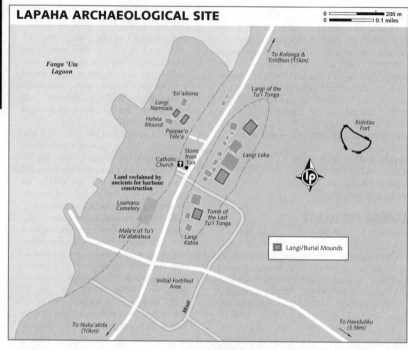

LAPAHA ARCHAEOLOGICAL SITE

To Kolonga & Trilithon (11km)

Fanga 'Uta Lagoon

'Esi'aikona

Langi Namoala

Hehea Mound

Paepae'o Tele'a

Langi of the Tu'i Tonga

Kolotau Fort

Stone from 'Eua

Catholic Church

Langi Leka

Land reclaimed by ancients for harbour construction

Loamanu Cemetery

Mala'e of Tu'i Ha'atakalaua

Tomb of the Last Tu'i Tonga

Langi Katoa

Langi/Burial Mounds

Initial Fortified Area

Moat

To Nuku'alofa (10km)

To Haveluliku (3.5km)

visible near Mu'a's southern edge – look for a prominent ditch a few metres deep bisecting the road.

All guided island tours stop briefly at Mu'a's principal archaeological sites, Paepae'o Tele'a and Langi Namoala, but you could easily spend a whole day here exploring the impressive excavated **pyramid tombs** and the host of smaller pyramids scattered through the village and bush across the road in **Langi Leka**. To explore the area independent of a tour, take the Mu'a bus (80 *seniti* one way) from the eastern bus terminal on Vuna Rd in Nuku'alofa and head back to Nuku'alofa by about 3.30pm to avoid getting stuck.

PAEPAE 'O TELE'A

Tonga's most imposing ancient burial site is the Paepae 'o Tele'a (Platform of Tele'a, Map p200), a pyramidlike stone structure north of the moat. It was long thought to have housed the remains of Tele'a, or 'Ulukimata I, a Tu'i Tonga who reigned during the 16th century. But his body may not be inside the tomb at all, since legend has it that he was drowned and his body lost. Tra-

ditional burial sites were topped by a vault (*fonualoto*), which was dug into the sand on top of the platform and lined with stones in preparation for the body. This platform, however, has no such vault, which supports the theory that the Paepae 'o Tele'a is not a tomb at all but, in fact, a memorial.

With the exception of the vault, this structure contains the best and most massive examples of all the early Tongan burial-tomb construction styles. The corner stones of the bottom tier on the eastern side of the monument are L-shaped. The upper surfaces of all the stones are bevelled, their bases firmly embedded in the earth and stabilised by the use of stone protrusions jutting out under the surface.

These and all the Lapaha construction stones are quarried limestone from dead coral reefs probably on Tongatapu and nearby Motutapu and Pangaimotu. They were transported using cradles slung between two *kalia* (seafaring canoes). (Some maintain that the stones were carried from

(Continued on page 209)

ERIC L WHEATER

Tropical palm trees line a beach in Samoa (p25)

JOHN BANAGAN

Banyan tree (p45), 'Upolu, Samoa

Local bus depot (p57) in Apia, 'Upolu, Samoa

JOHN BORTHWICK

Afu Aau Falls (p99), Savai'i, Samoa

Traditional *siapo* (bark cloth) painting (p42), Savai'i, Samoa

Footprints on a beach, Savai'i (p88), Samoa

Female dancers in traditional costume perform a *fiafia* (p41), Aggie Greys Hotel, Apia, 'Upolu, Samoa

Women outside a church (p65), Apia, 'Upolu, Samoa

Vendor, Salelologa market (p93), Savai'i, Samoa

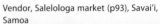

PETER HENDRIE

Waters off the coast of Olosega (p128), Manu'a Islands, American Samoa

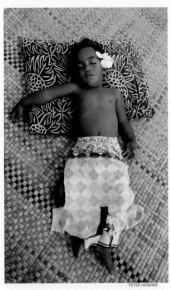

PETER HENDRIE

Child sleeping on woven mat, Ofu (p126),
Manu'a Islands, American Samoa

MICHELLE BENNETT

Colourful stained-glass window of Olosega
village Church, Olosega (p128), Manu'a
Islands, American Samoa

Cargo being unloaded, Manu'a Islands (p124), America Samoa

PETER HENDRIE

Tourists hitch a ride on the roof of a tour bus, Vava'u Island (p249), Vava'u Group, Tonga

Women wearing *ta'ovala* (p168), a pandanus leaf textile traditionally worn on formal occasions, Nuku'alofa, Tongatapu, Tonga

Artisan carving (p168) a traditional wooden mask, Tongatapu, Tonga

Vendor at Talamahu Market (p188), Nuku'alofa, Tongatapu, Tonga

PETER HENDRIE

PATRICK HORTON

Local girls, Lifuka Island (p228), Ha'apai Group, Tonga

Aerial view of Vava'u Group (p243), Tonga

PETER HENDRIE

208

The calm waters of Fafá Island resort (p214),
Tongatapu, Tonga

PETER HENDRIE

PETER HEN

Gathering shellfish off the coast of Tongatapu Island (p182), Tonga

Royal Palace (p187), Nuku'alofa, Tongatapu, Tonga

PETER HEN

(Continued from page 200)

the Ha'apai Group, or from Futuna or 'Uvea Island in the now-French territory of Wallis and Futuna, far to the northwest.) Oral history has handed down tales of the wooden rollers, *sennit* ropes and incredible leverage (and, of course, slave labour) required to move the enormous blocks – some weighing up to 12 tonnes – to the construction sites.

These days, the Paepae 'o Tele'a is suffering from age, weathering and other indignities, with houses almost at its base and pigs rooting on its mound, but the sheer bulk of it still conveys a sense of the mighty importance of the individual whose death prompted its construction.

LANGI NAMOALA

While the *fonualoto* is missing from the Paepae 'o Tele'a, the Langi Namoala tomb (Map p200), also at the Lapaha site, has a fine example of a *fonualoto* – but it's empty. Typical of such structures, it is covered with a stone slab and topped with *kilikili* (pumice-like volcanic gravel) that was collected from Kao and Tofua in the Ha'apai Group. *Kilikili* is still valuable as a decoration for graves.

If the Namoala tomb is indeed typical, a shelter of *tapa*, coconut fronds and fine mats to house the *matapule* (talking chief) would have rested on top of it. He would have lived on the *langi* and attended to the extensive funeral arrangements and ceremonies that followed a burial.

The Namoala *langi* is thought to have been the burial site of a female chief, but history supplies no further details. The stones used in this construction are much narrower than those in the adjacent pyramids. On the north side a stairway leads to the top.

To the north of the principal mounds rises the **'Esi'aikona**, an elevated platform used as a rest area by the chief and his family. Near the Namoala tomb is the **Hehea Mound**, which was originally believed to be a rubbish tip created during the construction of the *langi*. Two *fonualoto* were revealed amid haphazardly placed earth and rock when it was cleared of vegetation. Unlike the other structures, the Hehea was built on landfill. It's not known who engineered this incredible reclamation project or when it was done.

The large *langi* that now bears a cross on its top, across the road from the others in the modern cemetery, is the grave of **Laufilitonga**, the last Tu'i Tonga, who was deposed by King George Tupou I in 1826.

CATHOLIC CHURCH

The large, weathered stone **Catholic Church** (Map p200) here looks like it was shipped directly from the UK. There's an impressive traditional Polynesian podium, a few statues and some lovely stained-glass work inside. Near the main road is a statue of a particularly Anglo-looking slayer of the particularly islander-looking *tevolo* (devil).

Beside the main road, outside the gate of the church, is a rather ordinary 50cm-high boulder. Tradition has it that this stone was hurled by the demigod Maui from the island of 'Eua at a noisy rooster that had been keeping him awake at night. Visitors to Tonga will be particularly sympathetic to his reaction to such a situation.

The Fishing Pigs of Talafo'ou

While Talafo'ou (Map p183), north of the Mu'a area, is not the only place you'll find smart pigs in Tonga, here their low-tide ventures out on the tidal flat for shellfish are impressive.

Ha'amonga 'a Maui Trilithon

The South Pacific's Stonehenge, the Ha'amonga 'a Maui ('Maui's Burden') **trilithon** (Map p183), is one of ancient Polynesia's most intriguing monuments. According to legend this trilithon was carried by Maui from distant 'Uvea on a carrying yoke, but archaeologists and oral history credit its construction to the 11th Tu'i Tonga, Tu'itatui, who reigned at the turn of the 13th century. It's preserved in a National Historic Reserve (which unfortunately doesn't protect the site from graffiti and rooting pigs) at the northeastern end of Tongatapu, near Niutoua.

The structure consists of three large coralline stones, each weighing about 40 tonnes, arranged into a trilithic gate. The two uprights are about 5m high and just over 4m wide at their bases. The lintel, which rests in notched grooves in the uprights, is nearly 6m long, 1.5m wide and just over 50cm thick.

There was a theory that either the uprights represented the Tu'i's two competing sons or were the entrance to a royal compound when Heketa was Tonga's royal capital. It is now widely accepted that the structure had a similar function to Britain's Stonehenge: to determine the seasons. King Taufa'ahau Tupou IV theorised that an odd design on the lintel may have had something to do with determining seasons. He had the vegetation cleared in line with the arms of the double-V design between the trilithon and the sea, and on 21 June 1967 – the winter solstice – the sun was observed to rise and set in perfect alignment with the clearings. It was also noted that it rose and set in line with the other two arms on the longest day of the year.

For the ancient Tongans, the significance of the summer solstice probably related to the beginning of the *kahokaho* (yam) harvest, which was kicked off by the biggest annual festival held in ancient Tonga, the Katoanga 'Inasi. During this celebration, the year's finest yams were donated to the royal storehouses of the Tu'i Tonga.

A walking track winds north through the reserve, where fading interpretative signs make some sense of the remaining mounds of stones, which include **'Esi Makafakinanga**, supposedly used by Tu'itatui as a back rest to shield his back from surprise attack while he directed the construction work. It seems that Tu'itatui was more than a little paranoid. His name means 'leader who hits the knees', suggesting that he wielded a large stick at knee level to ward off potential aggressors.

The track passes several *langi* (known as the **Langi Heketa**), then enters the forest and continues for several hundred metres along a fence line to the shore.

Good-quality handicrafts, made by local artisans, are sold at the trilithon site.

To get to the Ha'amonga 'a Maui trilithon, hop off the (infrequent) Niutoua bus 1km short of Niutoua (T$1 one way); the driver can indicate the spot. Head out early and return in the early afternoon, or you may get stuck.

Muihopohoponga Reserve

The Muihopohoponga Reserve (Map p183) was set up in an effort to protect several species of native trees and some of the natural bush land that once covered the entire island. It incorporates a 2km stretch of white-sand beach at the easternmost extreme of Tongatapu and can be reached by a 2km walking track leading southeast from Niutoua.

'Anahulu Cave & Haveluliku

Tonga's most famous cave, 'Anahulu Cave (Map p183), is looking overloved, its stalactites and stalagmites blackened from the soot of flaming frond torches and too much foot traffic. In the first cavern is a freshwater pool, a popular swimming spot. It's unknown how far the caves go, but deeper caverns are more magical. The cave still retains an otherworldly, even eerie, atmosphere, in which the constant dripping of water combines with the screeching echolocation of white-rumped *pekepekatae* (swiftlets), which build nests on the cave's ceiling. You might notice a slightly musty smell caused by their deposits.

Solid walking shoes (or reef sandals) and a torch (flashlight) are essential for visiting 'Anahulu Cave – there's plenty of rubbish, including cans and the occasional bit of broken glass on the path. For serious exploration you'll need an underwater torch.

Opposite the cave's entrance, a path leads down to a beautiful sandy cove via a small cemetery.

Buses run to tidy Haveluliku, or to at least Fatumu just to the southwest, once or twice a day. Take the dirt road that runs to the ocean between the main part of Haveluliku village and the cream-and-blue Episcopalian Church to the south. From the grassy parking area, a set of steps leads to the cave and gives access to the beach. If you're already exploring Mu'a, you could walk from there (around 3km).

'Oholei Beach

The coastline around lovely and often deserted 'Oholei Beach is riddled with limestone caves. At the waterfront, turn right and wander past the eerily deserted remnants of a beach-resort venture, featuring a sweeping rock staircase to nowhere. Keep going until you reach **Hina Cave**. Soft light (and tree roots) filter through the open roof here. On the left, as you walk in, look for the rock resembling a 'sleeping goddess'.

The cave is about 4km south of Haveluliku; take the turn-off that's just north of Lavengatonga.

Fua'amotu Beach

Fua'amotu Beach is reached via the gates of the king's preferred **royal estate** (Map p183). A roller-coaster road dips towards a sandy beach and rock pools, protected from the surge. Behind the beach is an elaborate cemetery of sand-mound graves, elaborately decorated with rings of brown and green beer bottles, clam shells, stag-horn coral and lurid plastic flowers, and topped with *kilikili*.

Hufangalupe

On Tongatapu's south coast, plantations surround a large coralline limestone **archway** known as Hufangalupe (Pigeon's Gate; Map p183). The sea pounds through the opening and tears at the 30m walls of the bridge and adjacent pit. There's a good view into the pit from the bridge itself and it's possible to climb all the way down to the sea in the gully, but it's very steep and the coral rocks are razor sharp.

The sea churns at the base of the dramatic nearby cliffs, which make a good sea bird-watching spot. White-tailed tropical birds swoop past, trailing their long, graceful tail feathers, and lay their eggs on rocky ledges or even in the arch itself. You may also see sharks and turtles, and humpback whales between July and October, in the water below the cliffs.

It's a hard slog to get here by public transport. Catch a bus to Vaini, then follow the road opposite Vaini police station and walk south for almost 5km until you reach the coast. When you reach the cliffs you'll be on top of the bridge. Turn around and go back about 50m until you see a very faint track leading away to the east; follow it for a few metres and you'll soon see the archway.

Keleti Beach & Halafuoleva Beach

A series of coves divided by rocky outcrops slope gently into clear pools on the southern coast (Map p183), providing excellent spots for a swim at high tide and for observing the variety of marine life trapped at low tide. Plastic refuse mars the entrance to the beaches, which are otherwise clean, lovely and low in traffic. The reef consists of a line of terraces and **blowholes** that shoot like Yellowstone geysers when the waves hit them at high tide. Be cautious if you are swimming here and don't get too close to the blowholes or you may be dragged under by a powerful vortex and cut to shreds.

From Nuku'alofa, you can cycle, catch a taxi (around T$10), or take the Vaini or Mu'a bus to Veitongo village (T$1) and

then walk south for just over 2km to Liku Rd; then from there continue south for about 1km until you find a rough vehicle track that leads down to the sea.

Mapu'a 'a Vaca Blowholes

On an especially good day at Mapu'a 'a Vaca (Chief's Whistles; Map p183), hundreds of blowholes spurt at once. They are best viewed on a windy day with a strong swell, when the water, forced up through natural vents in the coralline limestone, can shoot up to 30m into the air. If the tide is too high, it will wash over the terraces containing the vents, 'extinguishing' the fountains. The blowholes stretch 5km along the southwest shore of Tongatapu, and are some of the most impressive in the South Pacific.

For an interesting sea-level view of the blowholes, turn westward just south of the church and school in Houma and follow the road to the shore. There's a wonderful snorkelling beach here at the right tide.

From Nuku'alofa catch the bus southwest to Houma (60 *seniti* one way) and then walk 1km south to the parking area above the blowholes. The *fale koloa* (grocery kiosk) at the turn-off on the main road sells delicious ice-cream cones.

Liahona

Yes, you are still in the Pacific, though you may be wondering whether you somehow stumbled into Midwestern USA. Amid uniform lawns that rival any pro-am golf course, stands Tongatapu's **Mormon temple** (Map p183), crowned with a golden angel. Other buildings in the 'English-speaking only' compound include the large Mormon high school. (Beulah College, which is the Seventh-Day Adventist counterpart to Liahona, is near the village of Vaini.)

Immediately west of Liahona, on the north side of the road, is a fascinating mutant – a **triple-headed coconut tree**! (Map p183).

Monotapu Beach

Beautiful Monotapu Beach (Map p183) nestles in a 1km-wide cove on the northwestern coast of Tongatapu. If you're marvelling that no savvy developers have nabbed this site, pay a few respects to Mother Nature – in 2003 Cyclone Eseta wreaked havoc on the western side of the island and destroyed the Princess Resort.

Fo'ui to Kolovai

A legend surrounds the site where the north-coast, south-coast and central roads converge just south of Fo'ui – that of the 'Umu Tangata (Man Oven; Map p183). There's no oven to be seen today, but the story goes that long ago a cannibal chef was preparing a feast here when he became distracted by an invasion. He left the meal unattended for so long that a tree grew out of each person. It's believed that descendants of these original trees remain to this day.

Most of the flying foxes that lived in a sanctuary at Kolovai, just north of Fo'ui, have left, but a number of these large, noisy, fruit-eating bats still roost in the odd tree in the village, dangling from branches like oversized tea bags.

Flying foxes have wing spans of up to 1m and are found all over the South Pacific (hunted for the pot in most places). In Tonga they are considered tapu (taboo/sacred), and officially only members of the royal family are permitted to hunt them for sport. In practice, well…

Taxis from Nuku'alofa (20 minutes) cost T$20, or take the Kolovai or Hihifo bus from the eastern bus terminal on Nuku'alofa's Vuna Rd (80 seniti one way).

Ha'atafu Beach Reserve

On the sunset side of the island, just 3km up the coast from Kolovai, the Ha'atafu Beach Reserve encompasses Ha'atafu's clean, white beach and the surrounding reef. There's safe swimming and reasonable snorkelling at high tide in the broad lagoon, but when the tide is low most of the reef lies just below the surface. Strong currents, extensive coral beds and breaking surf make it dangerous beyond the barrier reef. Due to the reserve's position at the juncture of both reef and deep-sea habitats, more than 100 species of fish can be observed here. It's regarded as Tongatapu's best surfing spot, but the all-reef breaks are suitable only for experienced surfers.

The Happy Hopa Surf School (at Ha'atafu Beach Resort, right), runs one-on-one surfing lessons (A$25 per hour) for beginners and reef novices.

Christian Missionary & Abel Tasman Landing Sites

At Tongatapu's extreme northwest, a dirt road leads north of Ha'atafu village to the Abel Tasman Landing Site monument (Map p183), where the Dutch explorer allegedly landed on 21 January 1643 (there's some controversy regarding the actual site). There's a fabulous viewpoint over fishing traps towards 'Atata and Hakaumama'o Reef. You'll pass the site where Christian missionaries first set foot on Tongatapu, and the site of Tonga's first Holy Communion.

Sleeping & Eating

The Hihifo bus passes the entrances to all the accommodations listed here other than the Good Samaritan Inn; one-way fares from Nuku'alofa cost T$1. A taxi costs T$20 to T$25.

Good Samaritan Inn (Map p183; ☎ 41022; fax 24102; fale with shared bathroom T$23, s/d/fale with private bathroom & breakfast from T$69/92/115, extra person T$23, camping per person T$10) Situated on Kolovai Beach amid a tropical assortment of crimson poinsettias, bougainvillea, palm trees and frangipani, you'll find a number of fale behind the ocean-view restaurant. Containing an islander-style mishmash of furniture and bright prints, the fale are clean and the mattresses firm. Each has a fan and small fridge. The family fale has million-pa'anga surf views from its balcony. Meals such as fish or teriyaki chicken and chips can be ordered throughout the week. Friday night's all-you-can-eat traditional Tongan meal, string band and rousing Tongan culture show (T$25), and Sunday's 'umu (T$15), are popular with locals and visitors alike. Sandwiches cost T$6.50 to T$7.50 and meals T$12 to T$14.50. The restaurant/bar is open 7am to 10pm. There's a small fale koloa nearby for supplies. The Inn is a good 2km walk (or hitch) from the bus stop on the main road. The resort runs airport/city transfers for T$40/10 for house and buffet guests.

Blue Banana Beach House (Map p183; ☎ 41575; bluebanana@kalianet.to; d & tw per night/week T$90/580, minimum 3 nights) If what you're looking for is a secluded, self-contained studio cabin nestled amongst trees on a beach you'll have all to yourself, you've found it. It's beautifully decorated in a beach-house style and has an outdoor shower. The toilet is a walk away at the main house. Surfers with their own gear will relish the position. You can dine at nearby Nawai Ali'i.

Ha'atafu Beach Resort (Map p183; ☎ 41088; fax 22970; www.surfingtonga.com; dm with half-board A$58, garden/beach-front fale per person with half-board A$64/75, child 2-12 A$40) Predominantly catering to all-inclusive surfing holidays, this family-run setup is as laid-back and peaceful as you'd expect. Paths of dark sand wind through foreshore growth, connecting comfortable thatched-roof bungalows to clean, shared facilities and the dining room (great reports on the meals, by the way!). Sandwiches cost A$2.50 to A$6. Good breaks are just a paddle across the lagoon, or Steve Burling (the Aussie surfie proprietor) can locate the best surf around by boat. Guests meet and mingle with local surfers here as it's the headquarters for the Tongan Surfriders' Association. Facilities including snorkelling gear and paddle skis are for guest use only.

'Otuhaka Beach Resort (Map p183; ☎ 41599; fax 24782; d fale T$50, d bungalow with bathroom T$85, ste T$250-270) The open-sided Tongan *fale* restaurant embraces an enviable slice of the beach front. Breakfast and lunch cost T$3.50 to T$12, mains T$15. It's very laid-back and rooms (with fans) are OK, but you wouldn't want to be stuck in one for consecutive rainy days. Choose a room with an updated bathroom – some are 'shower with thongs (flip-flops)' jobs.

Nawai Ali'i (Map p183; ☎ 41588; lunch & dinner T$12-18) You'll get the best traditional food in Tonga from the semiretired chef here – the buffet particularly is a Tongan-style gourmet gorge fest. The accommodation here isn't be recommended, but check for any sprucing up as the location is beautiful.

ISLANDS NORTH OF NUKU'ALOFA

You might almost hear a siren's call willing you across the water from Nuku'alofa's beach-front strip – particularly when yachts glide by under sail.

Four of Tonga's five marine reserves protect reefs immediately north of Tongatapu, including Hakaumama'o Reef Reserve, Monu'afe Island Park, the Pangaimotu Reef Reserve and the Malinoa Island Park, which features octopuses, gropers, damselfish and clown fish, amongst others, a nonfunctioning lighthouse, and the graves of six would-be assassins who attempted to kill Prime Minister Shirley Baker.

There are some great little dive sites in the shallows north of Tongatapu, while the reefs and shoals surrounding the maze of islands brim with all sorts of colourful marine life and coral.

Three island resorts lie within a boat ride north of Tongatapu, and a host of beautiful deserted islands await exploration.

PANGAIMOTU

Nuku'alofa's closest island resort makes for a popular day trip for locals and tourists alike, particularly on a Sunday. The resort's restaurant/bar is a great place to chill before a circumnavigational adventure (allow 30 minutes – longer if you want to claim one of the swinging chairs suspended from a tree branch). There's good snorkelling in the marine reserve off the island's northwest shore and around the half-submerged wreck of *My Lady Lata II* (Map p183) near the landing site (note: serious spinal injuries have befallen people diving from its bow). Another excellent spot is Makaha'a Reef, between Pangaimotu and Makaha'a, whose large coral heads serve as a breeding ground for an explosion of colourful fish.

With a slight castaway or pirates-lair feel, **Tongan Beachcomber Resort** (Map p183; ☎ 15762, 17257; www.pangaimotu.to; tent site/hire T$12/6, dm T$29, s/d with bath first night T$69/104, subsequent nights T$58/92) is an excellent spot overlooking the water and Nuku'alofa. It serves a range of tasty meals (snacks T$6 to T$8.50, mains T$11 to T$20) and the five rustic *fale* offer island charm with gas-lamp lighting and net-enclosed beds (yet no mozzies). Showers are served cold at this low-key resort and there's a 10-berth dorm. Snorkelling gear and fins (T$5 each) are available. No food or drink should be brought to the island.

From Monday to Saturday a boat leaves for Pangaimotu from Tuimatamoana Harbour in Nuku'alofa at 10am and 11am and returns from Pangaimotu at 4pm and 5pm. On Sunday the boat leaves Nuku'alofa at 10am, 11am, noon and 1pm and returns at 3pm, 4pm, 5pm and 6pm. Adult/child transfers cost T$15/7.50 return and take 10 minutes each way.

FAFÁ

From above, if you squint, Fafá Island (7km from Nuku'alofa) appears almost heart shaped, and Fafá Island Resort is its sole development. A leisurely loop of the island takes 30 minutes, though you'll want to dawdle on the signposted bushwalk through its lush centre, home to ground-dwelling *veka* (banded rails), purple *kalae* (swamp hens), a flutter of butterflies and the captive-bred *koki* (red shining parrot).

It is a tough life at **Fafá Island Resort** (Map p183; ☎ 22800; fax 23592; www.fafa.to; d & tw superior fale US$165, deluxe fale US$220, extra person US$44-55; half/full board US$51/60) – you can snorkel in tropical waters, beachcomb on a magnificent beach, read a book in a hammock, take a deserted-island trip or get an all-over tan in your private courtyard…choices present such a dilemma! This is the most elegant of Tongatapu's northern island resorts and one of the best places to stay in Tonga. Spaced through palm groves, the traditional-style *fale* are perfect in their simplicity, with tall wood-shingle roofs and walls of woven palm leaves, wooden floors, white mosquito-net canopies strung over beds and private garden bathrooms with solar hot water.

The restaurant, perched behind the beach on the sunny side of the island, serves beautiful Eurasian-Tongan dishes featuring plenty of local seafood, and hosts a weekly culture show and feast.

Water toys such as kayaks and boats are available free to guests, as is snorkelling gear (T$5.75 per day for day-trippers). On calm days snorkelling trips are run to Makaha'a Reef and Malinoa Island, and deserted-island picnics are also an option.

Nuku'alofa's dive operators (p180) will pick up divers here.

Day trips to Fafá (30 minutes; T$57.50) depart Faua Jetty, Nuku'alofa, at 11am and return at 4.30pm daily. Lunch is included, though readers have suggested it is not the best day-trip option.

One-way transfers from the airport and Nuku'alofa cost US$21 and US$10 respectively. Guests have access to complimentary twice-daily trips to Nuku'alofa.

'ATATA

'Atata has some spectacular beaches, and a small fishing village at its northern end, which can be visited on an organised tour. At 10km from the mainland, it's the most remote of the three island resorts.

At **Royal Sunset Island Resort** (☎ /fax 21254; www.royalsunset.to; PO Box 668, Nuku'alofa; s/d bungalow east side T$115/160, west side T$167/210, superior d T$250; half/full board T$75/86; 🖳) you can choose from the island's west-side (sheltered) beachfront bungalows with sunset views and the run-down east-side bungalows, which catch a few breezes. Bungalows feature hot-water bathrooms, ceiling fans, a fridge and tea- and coffee-making facilities. The resort's Polynesian-style restaurant/bar is an incredible structure supported by immense wooden beams. Snorkelling, diving (p180), kite-surfing and fishing are all possible from the resort. Standards have slipped a little at this once bright star and recent guests have been disappointed by tired facilities.

CALLING SHARKS

'Eue'iki (Little 'Eua) is the place where *kava* was famously given to Tonga and is also legendary for a long tradition of shark calling, an art practised on a few South Pacific islands for centuries. On 'Eue'iki a handful of shark callers remain, men who can summon these fearsome fish up from the depths by reciting ancient chants while shaking a giant necklace of coconut shells over and under the water. Once the shark is drawn close to the boat a rope is looped over its head and it is killed with a war club.

The origins of, and scientific basis for, shark calling are not easily explained. In local folklore, shark calling stems from a centuries-old tragedy when a young girl fell from a canoe and disappeared. The girl turned into a shark named Hina, and islanders have been calling her back home since. To aid in this quest the shark caller takes on the role of Hina's mythical lover, Sinilau.

During the week of the Tongan king's birthday, Sinilau will kill all the sharks he calls up from the deep and present them to the king. Although the sharks are the embodiment of the girl lost at sea, it doesn't matter that they are killed. Hina is reborn over and over again. In 1965, according to locals, 40 sharks were called and killed for the king.

'Eue'iki lies northeast of Tongatapu, just outside the barrier reef sheltering Tongatapu's lagoon.

Sunday day-trips to 'Atata including lunch and boat transfers (45 minutes) cost T$57.50. The boat departs from Tuimatamoana Harbour, Nuku'alofa, at 10am and returns at 4pm. Return boat transfers for guests cost T$34, or T$70 from the airport.

'EUA

area 87 sq km / pop 4934

You won't find many beaches to swim at that don't present the prospect of being cut to ribbons, but rugged 'Eua is a slice of paradise of its own, with a growing awareness of itself as an ecotourism destination.

It's no wonder travellers are inking it into their itinerary as an alternative to a simple sand-and-sea holiday. Adventures include hiking through the diverse plantation forest or rugged tropical rainforest, spotting soaring birds from sheer limestone cliffs, sating the thrill-seeker in you by delving into caves and massive sinkholes and climbing the Big 'Ovava, spotting whales and dolphins from the shore with an Ikale in hand, and seeing the light streaming in on a cathedral dive. It's all just a stone's throw southeast of Tongatapu (well, legend has it that Maui flung a stone from 'Eua to Tongatapu to quieten a rowdy rooster, but short of a demigod catapulting you, you'll probably have to catch the ferry).

History

When Abel Tasman, the first European to land on 'Eua, arrived in 1643 and named the island Middelburgh, little did he know that the demigod Maui had beaten him here and had stood on 'Eua to fish the islands of Tongatapu, Vava'u and Ha'apai out of the sea. In October 1773, Captain James Cook also stopped by, followed by several deserters from the US ship *Otter* who came ashore in 1796 and became the first 'European' residents of the Tongan islands.

In September 1946, the island of Niuafo'ou (in the Niuas) erupted for the 10th time in 100 years. Although no-one was killed, the Tongan government's concern about the potential danger saw the islanders evacuated and eventually resettled on 'Eua. The villages of central 'Eua are all named after the home villages of their inhabitants on faraway Niuafo'ou. Many people have now re-turned to Niuafo'ou, but a good proportion of 'Eua's population remains composed of evacuees and their descendants, amid 'Eua's original inhabitants and the descendants of those evacuated from 'Ata to protect them from slave traders (p222).

Climate

The combination of 'Eua's geography and a prevailing easterly trade wind means that despite 'Eua's close proximity to Tongatapu (you can see it clearly from Tongatapu's southeast shore), while the main island swelters in humid summer heat, 'Eua is perfectly pleasant, and even chilly in winter. 'Eua is long north-to-south and thin east-to-west, with a high volcanic ridge stretching north-to-south along the entire east side of the island. The ridge rises 312m above sea level at its highest point. The easterly wind hits the cliffs rising up out of the ocean on the east side, then the ridge, and is cooled as it's blown upwards. The cooled air then blows down from the ridge, across to the west side of the island and the villages.

Orientation

The western third of the island is a low coastal plain that merges into an area of forested hills, with north–south ridges forming the spine. The island's eastern edge consists of one- and two-tier cliffs up to 120m high. A road extends the length of 'Eua's western side, joining the villages in which most of the population lives. The island's services, including Nafanua Wharf (for the ferry) and a couple of supermarkets, are in 'Ohonua.

Basic maps of 'Eua are available from the Ministry of Agriculture and Forestry (MAF) office in Sapa'ata. If you can't rouse anyone here, the Hideaway (p223) usually has a good supply. You'll probably find the map in this book more detailed, but it's handy to mark up your intended trail on it before setting out.

Information

Niu'eiki Hospital (Map p216; Main Rd, Pangai) Very basic facilities.

Hofangahau College Internet Café (Map p216; Petania; access per hr T$6; ☾ 6-9pm) CD burning, colour printing and Skype are also available. Enter the college and follow the signs upstairs.

Westpac Bank of Tonga (Map p223; ☎ 50145; 'Ohonua; ☾ 9am-12.30pm & 1.30-3.30pm Mon-Fri)

TONGATAPU GROUP

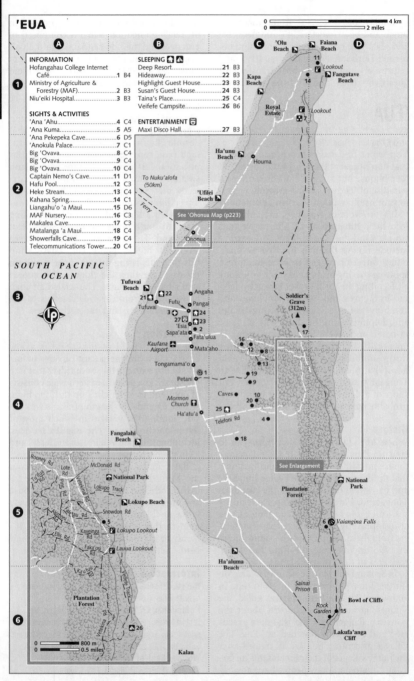

'EUA

0	4 km
0	2 miles

A

INFORMATION
Hofangahau College Internet
Café...1 B4
Ministry of Agriculture &
Forestry (MAF)........................2 B3
Niu'eiki Hospital.........................3 B3

SIGHTS & ACTIVITIES
'Ana 'Ahu..................................4 C4
'Ana Kuma.................................5 A5
'Ana Pekepeka Cave...................6 D5
'Anokula Palace..........................7 C1
Big 'Ovava................................8 C4
Big 'Ovava................................9 C4
Big 'Ovava...............................10 C4
Captain Nemo's Cave................11 D1
Hafu Pool................................12 C3
Heke Stream............................13 C4
Kahana Spring..........................14 C1
Liangahu'o 'a Maui...................15 D6
MAF Nursery............................16 C3
Makalea Cave...........................17 C3
Matalanga 'a Maui....................18 C4
Showerfalls Cave......................19 C4
Telecommunications Tower.......20 C4

B

SLEEPING
Deep Resort.............................21 B3
Hideaway.................................22 B3
Highlight Guest House...............23 B3
Susan's Guest House.................24 B3
Taina's Place............................25 C4
Veifefe Campsite.......................26 B6

ENTERTAINMENT
Maxi Disco Hall........................27 B3

C

'Olu
Beach

Faiana
Beach

11
Lookout
14

Fangutave
Beach

Kapa
Beach

Royal
Estate

Lookout
7

Ha'unu
Beach
Houma

To Nuku'alofa
(50km)

'Ufilei
Beach

See 'Ohonua Map (p223)

Ferry

'Ohonua

D

SOUTH PACIFIC
OCEAN

Tufuvai
Beach
21
22
Futu
Tufuvai
3
27
'Esia
Sapa'ata
Kaufana
Airport

Angaha
Pangai
24
23
2
Fata'ulua
Mata'aho

Soldier's
Grave
(312m)
17

16
12 8
13
Tongamama'o
Petani
@ 1
19
9
Mormon
Church
Ha'atu'a
Caves
25
10
20
4

Telefoni Rd
18

Fangalahi
Beach

Rooney Rd
McDonald Rd
National Park
Lote
Rd
Lokupo Track
Lokupo Beach
Snowdon Rd
Auhona
Rd
Teletau Rd
5
Lokupo Lookout
Kaveinga
Rd
Ellis Rd
Faka'osi
Rd
Lauua Lookout

Plantation
Forest

26

Plantation
Forest

National
Park

Vaiangina Falls
6

Ha'aluma
Beach

Sainai
Prison

Rock
Garden

Bowl of Cliffs
15

Lakufa'anga
Cliff

Kalau

0	800 m
0	0.5 miles

Changes all major currencies (travellers cheques or cash), offers cash advances on credit cards and handles Money-Gram cash transfers.

Friendly Islands Bookshop (Map p216; ☎ 50167; 'Ohonua; ☺ 8.30am-5pm Mon-Fri, 8.30am-1pm Sat) The limited book selection includes a few paperbacks, titles on Tonga and fairly recent gossip magazines (ask at the counter). Camera film and maps of 'Eua are sometimes available depending on stock.

Ministry of Agriculture and Forestry (MAF; Map p216; ☎ 50116; Sapa'ata; ☺ 8.30am-4.30pm Mon-Fri) A good source of information about the 'Eua Plantation Forest, 'Eua National Park and the island's trails and attractions. Bushwalkers should discuss their routes with the staff here before setting out.

Post office (Map p223; ☎ 50066; 'Ohonua; ☺ 8.30am-12.30pm & 1.30-4.30pm Mon-Fri) Fax facilities available.

Tonga Communications Corporation (TCC; Map p223; ☎ 50777; ☺ 8am-11pm Mon-Fri, 7am-2pm Sat) Has telephone cabins, sells phonecards and offers fax services.

Dangers & Annoyances

Normal hiking rules apply – take plenty of water, sunscreen, some food and warm clothing in case of changing weather. When heading out, always let someone know the vicinity to which you're heading and when you expect to be back. Due to the sinkholes and high cliffs, if you lose your way and it starts to get dark, it's advisable to stop for the night and carry on in the morning.

NORTHERN 'EUA

Some sights in 'Eua's northern half are accessible by taxi but the more remote can only be reached on foot. Guided day **bushwalks** (p273) and longer circuit expeditions are possible. If you're going without a guide, allow yourself lots of time to explore, wear sturdy shoes, carry plenty of water and take a map and compass.

Unfortunately, the beautiful beaches situated north of 'Ohonua are not suitable for swimming, though locals make good use of 'Ufilei Beach, a popular spot for picnics and afternoon lazing just a 20-minute walk north of Nafanua Wharf.

The northern end of the island can be reached from 'Ohonua by walking along the coastline for five or six hours, but it requires scrambling over high rocky outcrops.

Northern End

There are some magnificent **coastal viewpoints** over cliffs peppered with caves at the northern end of 'Eua, but the tracks can be difficult to find. Ask locals for directions before setting out and be very careful when walking off-track as the area is pockmarked with sinkholes.

From 'Ohonua, go over the bridge and continue 3km north to the small village of Houma. About 2km north of the village, the track forks (the left fork leads down to Kapa Beach) – continue to the right up the hill then, just after the sign to the Royal Estate, turn left down a rough 4WD track. This may be as far as a taxi will go.

This track rambles north through scrubby bush land and forest and past a couple of marginal plantations until, after about an hour, you'll enter a broad, open pasture with magnificent views across lower tiers of rainforest and a 270-degree view of the sea off the east coast.

To reach **Kahana Spring** (Map p216), follow the track all the way to the end, then it's a steep 150m descent northeast to the spring. Once an open pool, the spring now feeds from its source inside a cave into a white plastic pipe funnelling the water into huge, covered concrete water tanks.

From Kahana Spring you can bush whack about 200m north to an overgrown track heading through forest. This will bring you to a viewpoint above some dramatically high, sheer limestone cliffs. In the side of the cliff is the large limestone cave known as **Captain Nemo's Cave** (Map p216), one of around seven found in this rarely visited area. The secluded Fangutave Beach lies far below and it's perfectly possible (but very steep) to climb down to the beach at the northern end of the cove, though bear in mind the remoteness of this spot if you're going to attempt it. A whale-tailed tree trunk marks the track.

'Anokula Palace

Not much is left of the building that, if completed, would have been a royal palace atop 120m-high windswept cliffs. The views are spectacular, but there are even better viewpoints to the north of the ruins (from where you'll see the island of 'Eue'iki and part of Tongatapu) and on a rocky outcrop down to the east. Legend tells it that if you stand on this latter viewpoint at full moon and remain absolutely still you can see people swimming in the incredibly turbulent water below – lost spirits on an outing.

THE FLORA & FAUNA OF 'EUA

'Eua has the largest tract of primary rainforest in Tonga, considerable areas of regenerating rainforest and plantation forest, dramatic cliffs and a wonderful shoreline, which combined make it the most diverse landscape in which to experience the kingdom's flora and fauna.

'Eua's most famous wildlife species is the large 'Eua parrot or red shining parrot (koki or kaka). This spectacular bird was introduced to Tonga prior to European arrival and you'll most likely hear its raucous call in 'Eua's forests – the forest around Liangahu'o 'a Maui is a good place to look. 'Eua has Tonga's only stable koki population (about 1000 birds), but deforestation and the illegal collection of live birds remain problematic.

Sea-bird colonies nest on 'Eua's cliffs. The windy east coast is a good place to see brown and black ngongo (noddies) and white-tailed tavake (tropic birds), with their easily recognisable long tail streamers. Soaring great frigate birds, with their distinctive pointed wings and forked tails, are a hugely impressive sight – Lakufa'anga cliff is a good place to see them. White-rumped pekepekatae (swiftlets) nest in caves here and navigate to their nests in pitch black by echolocation.

'Eua has eight endemic species of flowering plant, and many medicinal and culturally important plants that are still collected for use. Much of the island is covered in plantations and grassland with small patches of coastal forest where at dusk you may see the cave-dwelling pekapeka (sheath-tailed bat) hunting for insects. The large peka (fruit bat or flying fox) roosts in tall forest or plantation trees.

In the primary rainforest on the island's steep eastern slopes, the unique 'Eua gecko is found. It was only recently spotted for the first time, an indication of just how much there's left to be discovered here.

The red lake after which 'Anokula Palace (Map p216) was named has become a dry, burnished-red sand trap.

In the scrubby grassland that is south of 'Anokula are plenty of potential camp sites, but bring your own water as no reliable supply is available.

In order to get to 'Anokula Palace via Houma, turn right when the road forks to Kapa Beach and continue past the pine and coffee plantations of the Royal Estate. Taxis are generally happy to go as far as the palace, but no further south. The road heading south from 'Anokula stays in good shape for 1km or so and then starts to break up, but it is possible to follow the faint 4WD track to the Soldier's Grave. Be sure to inquire locally as to the condition of the route.

CENTRAL 'EUA

'Eua Plantation Forest covers much of the slope that rises consistently east towards the island's 300m ridge, where lofty limestone cliffs plunge into 'Eua National Park. Plantations and villages dominate 'Eua's central western side.

There are a few good-looking, though rugged, beaches, and caves, sinkholes and waterfalls to explore.

Tufuvai Beach

Tufuvai Beach's lovely arc of white sand is the perfect spot to position yourself for sunset, if not half the day. A natural **swimming pool** forms in the reef at high tide and provides some good snorkelling, though it's too shallow for swimming at low tide. The channel here is suitable for strong swimmers, but only at low tide – whatever you do, don't swim in this channel when the tide is going out!

To get here, head south along the coastal road (about 2km) from 'Ohonua or turn west off the main road at Pangai. Midway through Tufuvai village, a road to the west leads to the beach and the Deep Resort.

'Eua Plantation Forest

Limestone caves, gaping sinkholes (with enormous banyan trees reaching out of them) and a rather weird mix of exotic plantation-timber species combine to give this Swiss-cheese landscape the air of a magical realm. The forest (Map p216) covers 'Eua's drinking-water catchment area and is dense and jungle-like with giant tree ferns, vines and high humidity in some areas, and in others, all straight lines of plantation pine, sandalwood, mahogany or red cedar.

Many of 'Eua's tourist highlights are found here and most can be visited in a long day's walk or on horseback. A 4WD could get you closer to many of them. One possible route you might take through the area (with a few detours) is listed here.

From the green MAF office in Sapa'ata, head east along a dirt road into the 'Eua Plantation Forest, towards the **MAF Nursery** (reached in about 35 minutes). Here the road forks. To the left, Rooney Rd leads up to Vetekina Rd (an overgrown and, in places, deeply rutted 4WD track) and on to the edge of the national park (2.6km). To the right, a track leads up to refreshing, fern-fringed **Hafu Pool** (250m), formed by the damming of a small stream that trickles through a slice of rainforest.

Cross over and continue along the old 4WD track. Ignore the first right turn and after about five minutes, the 4WD track levels off and a path breaks left (north) to a **Big 'Ovava** – a huge banyan tree growing out of a yawning sinkhole. Scramble down the path to the base of the sinkhole, which has a small stream running through it, then monkey-climb the roots to get out again. Continue straight ahead (east) on a thin track to **Heke Stream**, which courses down a long, smooth rock at about a 45-degree angle, creating a natural water slide *(heke)* in a beautiful, steep-sided gully covered in ferns and lichen. Further upstream is another slide above a larger pool.

Retrace your steps to the Big 'Ovava, then either backtrack to the MAF Nursery and head east along Rooney Rd (a good option in wet weather), or continue 900m up Tu'ifua Rd (a disused 4WD track) to the junction with Rooney Rd and then turn right. Either way, continue up to the end of Rooney Rd. One option from here is to continue along Lote Rd to Vetekina Rd, roughly 50 minutes from the Big 'Ovava, and turn left for Makalea and Soldier's Grave, which lie in plantations to the north. Otherwise, turn right into McDonald Rd and continue south, taking the fourth grassy 4WD track on the left and following it to the Lauua Lookout signpost off Vetekina Rd.

You'll need proper climbing gear to get down into the sinkhole that is **Makalea Cave**. It's reached after about eight minutes and lies about 100m north out of the forestry plantation boundary at an obscured sign under a small banyan tree due east (right) of the dirt road and a mango tree – you'll

have to travel through a plantation to get there. *Makalea* means 'speaking stone', and there is certainly an eerie echo in the cave, as well as some beautiful stalactites. Once you're facing its opening, head 15m or so to the left for the access point.

The right turn to **Soldier's Grave** lies about 250m after the turn-off to Makalea. A stand of pandanus is about the only marker of the overgrown path that leads uphill to 'Eua's highest point (312m) and the grave of AE Yealands, about whom there are a few versions of an apocryphal – or at least well-embellished – tale. See the boxed text, p220.

From the turn-off to Soldier's Grave it's about a two- to three-hour walk to the ruins of 'Anokula Palace at the northern end of 'Eua. Alternatively, after retracing your steps to the junction of Lote and Vetekina Rds, it's only an eight-minute walk south to the beginning of **Lokupo Track**, which leads down to **Lokupo Beach** (p220), and a further 15 minutes south to **'Ana Kuma** (Rats' Cave). Entering the cave via a hole in the rock and shuffling through the narrow passageway to a small ledge and a stunning view over the rainforest to the Pacific Ocean, is adrenaline-inducing. It's possible to climb down the left side of the overhanging ledge to another small cave cut into the cliff face about 2m below. It requires extreme care, as the cliff edge is very close when you drop down but the experience of perching here is well worth it.

South from 'Ana Kuma, signposts mark two vertiginous viewing platforms, **Lokupo Lookout** and **Lauua Lookout**, which cling to the cliff top and provide breathtaking views over the rainforest and the ocean pounding onto Lokupo Beach. It's always cool and windy here and if you're lucky you'll see red shining parrots and tropic birds gliding over the rainforest canopy below. The track to Lauua Lookout winds through the rainforest.

To make your way out of the forest from Lauua Lookout, retrace your steps to Vetekina Rd and then walk north to the junction of Vetekina and Faka'osi Rds. Turn left (west) down Faka'osi Rd and continue to McDonald Rd, which will lead you south to Telefoni Rd and the main road.

Southwest of the junction between Telefoni and McDonald Rds is **'Ana 'Ahu** (Smoking Cave), so called because of the mist that rises where a small stream plunges into the void. There is no set path; to get there head

SOLDIER'S GRAVE

WWII did not blight the kingdom of Tonga as it did other Pacific islands, though Tongans fought and died for the Allied cause. During the war, a group of New Zealand signalmen were stationed on 'Eua along with a group of Tongan comrades. One day in February 1943, a 24-year-old New Zealand soldier (AE Yealands) and a Tongan got drunk and decided to play a bizarre game of hide-and-seek. They asked a friend to hide a gun for them. It was decided that the one who first found the gun was to kill the other.

Unfortunately for Yealands, the Tongan won the game. The Tongans reportedly felt so bad about the incident that they erected a monument in the soldier's honour on the island's highest point.

west down Telefoni Rd, and, where it makes a sharp right turn, follow a line of pine trees to the entrance.

Other impressive caves in this area include the sinkhole below another **Big 'Ovava** roughly 50m northeast of the telecommunications tower on Telefoni Rd. This banyan *must* be the largest on 'Eua. The root network is truly amazing. To find this tree, continue down Telefoni Rd to the bottom of a steep slope where a dirt road on the right cuts back uphill. Follow this road to a dead end and then take the footpath on the left leading to a cave. From here it's a 30-minute walk west, downhill to 'Eua's main road.

'Eua National Park

There's something magical about this undisturbed ocean-side rainforest (Map p216) that makes the legend of Maui fishing the rest of Tonga out of the water from 'Eua seem totally believable.

'Eua National Park protects a tract of virgin tropical rainforest above the southeastern coast, which is bordered on the western side by the sheer cliffs that descend directly from the highest ridge on the island. The easiest access to the rainforest is down the ridge on one of two purpose-built tracks.

The first is **Lokupo Track**, which leads down to **Lokupo Beach**. Two cement clumps that once anchored the signpost mark the track, just north of the Vetekina and Snowdon

Rds junction. At a rock crevice around 80m down the track, you'll step down onto **Hina's Seat** (that's the imprint of her bottom you're looking at!), though the sign is misleading and says 'Maui's Footsteps'. The track then veers to the right around the rocky outcrop and in about 70m comes to **Maui's Footsteps** where, legend has it, cranky Maui took aim at a rowdy rooster on Tongatapu (see p199). Can't find them? The footsteps are on top of a 1.5-cu-metre rock to the left of the track, nearby a tree with 'Eloni' carved into it.

The second track is **Veifefe Track**, which leads off Veketina Rd (further south), gently winding down in a southeasterly direction past Veifefe Campsite to the south end of Lokupo Beach. In theory, at low tide it's possible to walk along the beach between these two trails, but finding the entrance to the second trail (which is not signposted) would be difficult. For a drama-free return, mark where you exit the forest onto the beach.

Veifefe Campsite (a patch of overgrown grass at present) is the only official camp site on 'Eua.

Matalanga 'a Maui

The story goes that the deep, dank and eerie sinkhole that is known as Matalanga 'a Maui (Maui's Fault; Map p216) was created when Maui buried the end of his planting stick in the earth and shook it back and forth, rocking the entire island and leaving it with a tilt that made the south end higher than the north. On bright days you'll see that the sinkhole is simply a huge hole whose walls are lined with tangled vegetation that disappears into the black void below. You'll get better views down into the cool, moist underworld with a torch. Climbing into the sinkhole and actually making it out again will require climbing gear and a climbing buddy.

To get there, head south from Ha'atu'a onto the dirt road, take the first left turn and continue for about 800m from the intersection, passing two vehicle tracks. The short walking track (currently signposted 'Maui's Fault') is on the right, about 70m from the second vehicle track, and leads about 30m through a vanilla plantation. Once you're in line with a row of pine trees to the right, turn left and you'll be on the edge of the abyss. Watch your step – you may not see the sinkhole until you almost fall into it!

Showerfalls Cave
The small Showerfalls Cave (Map p216) hides behind a steady stream of cool, fresh water which flows through a narrow, fern-covered limestone gorge. It's possible to walk right through this cave and come out the other end, though it gets narrow and requires some climbing, and the water can be at chest height. Slippery rocks make even the climb down the waterfall (about 2m) to the cave entrance a challenge, accompanied by a guaranteed soaking. Anything more than a cursory exploration requires ropes, waterproof torches and shoes with a good grip.

To reach Showerfalls Cave, follow the vehicle track heading east away from the tarmac road, along the southern boundary fence of Hofangahua College in Petani, and step over the gate. The track leads through plantations and up into the hills. A thin path crosses the track after about 20 minutes, but continue straight ahead up the increasingly overgrown track until reaching a junction. Fork left across flatter ground, then after a couple of minutes fork left again onto a 4WD track. Continue down the steep slope and past a cavelike rocky overhang before arriving at the small gorge a couple of minutes later. Some of 'Eua's water supply is drawn from this place through PVC pipes.

SOUTHERN 'EUA
Ve'ehula Estate
Much of the southern third of the island belongs to the large Ve'ehula Estate, in the heart of which is Sainai Prison (Map p216), Tonga's largest correctional facility. Some of the best tracts of original rainforest are found here and there are many meandering bush tracks to explore.

Ha'aluma Beach
'Eua's best beach is Ha'aluma (Map p216), a palm-fringed expanse of sand on the south coast, overlooking the small island of Kalau, 3km or so away. Deep rock pools (tide dependent) offer refreshing wading sites and there are good beach camping spots.

To get there, continue 4km south along the dirt road from Ha'atu'a until the road makes a sharp bend to the southeast (left) and turns into bitumen. At this intersection, take the steep 4WD track that veers slightly to the southwest (right) and continue for 1km or so.

Southern End
The southern tip of the island (Map p183), an area known as Lakufa'anga, contains some of 'Eua's finest geological treasures.

In dry weather a taxi can take you much of the way there, or you can see the southern portion of the island as part of a tour (p223). Head south from Ha'atu'a and continue along the road as it curves to the east and becomes bitumen (the 4WD track to the south leads to Ha'aluma Beach), passing a few plantations before it reaches a gate with a 'Jesus Loves You' reminder. Pass through (be sure to close the gate) onto the green pasture punctuated with the grey, tombstone-like outcrops of the **Rock Garden**. These large slabs of eroded, grotesquely shaped coral recall the time that this area served as 'Eua's continental shelf. The meadow is often full of nervous wild horses.

Two information signs in front of a large coral mass tell of the legends of the nearby features. The cliff to the southeast is **Lakufa'anga Cliff** (Calling Turtle Cliff). Women used to drop *fá* (pandanus fruit) into the sea from the cliff and sing, to call turtles into shore. Unfortunately, turtles are rarely seen here these days due to overfishing (despite bans on catching them). Inviting as the crumbly cliffs may seem to would-be explorers, be warned that climbers have recently lost their lives here.

The beautiful **Liangahu'o 'a Maui**, a giant limestone arch, lies about 400m northeast of here. Maui, the folk hero of epic stature, had a reputation for a volatile temper. This huge abyss and the natural bridge are said to have been formed when Maui angrily threw his spear across 'Eua, lodging it in the rock wall here. From the cliffs, walk northward along the 4WD track that leads into a patch of woodland (keep an eye out for vibrant red parrots). Pick up the marked trail on the left and follow it 50m or so up the hill, veering right before coming to a lookout perched on the edge of a gaping hole, with a spectacular view of the roaring sea surging towards the natural archway. This is a lovely spot, where haunting insect choruses intermingle with the sound of waves crashing on the rocks.

Complete the loop back to the 4WD track on the north side of the archway and continue to the Bowl of Cliffs, an impressive half-circle of cliffs in which the sea below churns like a flushing toilet bowl.

BLACKBIRDERS ON 'ATA

In May 1863 the Tasmanian whaling ship *Grecian,* under the command of Captain Thomas James McGrath, landed at 'Ata, an extinct volcanic island 136km southwest of Tongatapu. The details of what happened are hazy, but in 1929 two Tongans, who were 'Ata schoolchildren at the time, recalled that the ship was painted to resemble a man-of-war. The mayor of the island, Paul Vehi, boarded the ship and returned to report that the people of 'Ata were invited below the ship's deck to trade their wares for the ship's provisions. Once the islanders' goods were accepted, they were sent into cabins, ostensibly to select items they desired in exchange. The people remaining on shore never saw them again.

The *Grecian* was not licensed to land with slaves at Peruvian ports, where kidnapped Pacific islanders were normally taken. It seems that the cargo (including the Tongans) was sold to the *General Prim,* a slaver that crossed paths with the *Grecian* somewhere in the Cook Islands while searching for 'recruits' to carry back to Callao (Lima). When the *General Prim* arrived in South America, its captain reported that he carried 174 slaves from the island of 'Frinately' – obviously a mistranscription of Friendly Islands.

John Bryan, a crew member on the *Grecian,* reported that about 130 'Ata islanders had been taken on board. (It's also likely that the *Grecian* had been responsible for the kidnapping of 30 residents of Niuafo'ou, who had willingly left that island with the promise of lucrative jobs in Fiji.) The islanders blamed the mayor for arranging the blackbirding (kidnapping and slave trading) but it's unlikely that he knew anything about it beforehand. Concerned about blackbirding, King George Tupou I soon ordered the remaining 200 residents of 'Ata to resettle on 'Eua. 'Ata remains uninhabited to this day.

'Ata can only be accessed by private yacht, and finding a suitable, safe anchorage can be difficult.

From here, further exploration north into 'Eua National Park is possible, but to go any further you should plan to camp overnight. The pasture near the Bowl of Cliffs would make a fine, if exposed, camp site.

Rejoin the track heading north (which keeps to the easternmost ridge), cross the fence into a plantation and continue on the same track, following what remains of a white plastic water pipe. 'Ana Pekepeka (Swallows' Cave), named after the birds flitting in and out of the darkness, is a 25-minute walk from the fence. The dry floor of the large cave would make a decent camp site.

Vaiangina Falls is roughly a 15-minute walk past the cave. The remaining white pipe takes a sharp turn uphill just before Vaiangina Stream, but it's easier to walk ahead about 10m before rock climbing up to the tubing that leads to the stream. Vaiangina Stream emerges from between layers of limestone then disappears beneath an impassable thicket of vegetation before plunging more than 50m into the sea. The waterfall is only properly visible from the shoreline; though the stream is hardly impressive, it's one of the only freshwater sources in the area.

In some seasons it is possible to bushbash your way to Veifefe Campsite (p220) and then on to 'Anokula Palace. You'll be bashing most of the way along a track reclaimed by the jungle – allow several days.

Activities

'Eua has great bushwalking, ranging from day walks taking in many of 'Eua's highlights, to a complete 10-day-or-so loop of the island. You'll experience rugged coastal views from soaring cliffs, squawking parrots wheeling through the forest canopy, caves to discover and towering 'Faraway Tree'–like banyan trees that climb out of gaping sinkholes; unique adventures abound.

Ask MAF or your guesthouse hosts about routes, camp sites and the availability of drinking water. You'll need a tent, map, compass and plenty of water containers.

Rock-climbing sites and 'Eua's largely unexplored cave systems have exciting potential. The Lokupo Beach area (Map p216), which is backed by steep cliffs, has good climbing potential – favourite anchoring spots seem to be the Lokupo and Lauua Lookouts. Caving and rock climbing here are not for amateurs; come properly equipped.

Between June and December, pods of whales make their way through the channel between 'Eua and Tongatapu and can be viewed from the west coast. Ideal viewpoints from land are at the Hideaway (right), which also organises half-day whale-watching boat trips (one/two/three people T$150/125/100 per person), and at the Deep Resort (right).

Tonga's reportedly biggest sea caves are just off 'Eua, with the best ones found around the northern tip and down the eastern coast; one is likened to a cathedral. Visibility is upwards of 60m year-round. Contact the Deep Blue Diving Centre (p181).

Tours

Accommodation ventures (p191) on Tongatapu run 4WD tours that can be tailored to your interests.

Hideaway (Map p216; ☎ 50255; fax 50128; www.kalianet .to/hideawayeua; Tufuvai) Helps to plan unguided tours, and runs 4WD tours (T$45), and hiking tours (some including caves in the north; T$60), both including lunch. Horse riding/mountain bikes can be arranged for T$30/15.

Susan's Island Tours (Susan's Guest House; Map p216; ☎ 50088) Runs well-organised three-hour national park tours (T$40), three-hour Southern Legends tours (T$40) and two-hour 'Anokula Palace tours (T$25).

Taina's Place (Map p216; ☎ 50186; fax 50128; Telefoni Rd) Van tours are T$45 (children free). Bike or horse hire can be arranged for T$12.

Sleeping

'Eua's accommodation falls into the guesthouse or self-catering categories and can be

viewed at www.tongaholiday.com. If your plan is to stay just the one night and head back on the morning ferry, you could adopt 'Tongan style' by sleeping on the ferry's bench or floor space, sparing yourself the pre-4am wake-up call to head down to the ferry. Hosts generally offer wharf transfers for T$4.

Hideaway (☎ 50255; fax 50128; www.kalianet.to /hideawayeua; Tufuvai; camping T$12, s/d with bathroom & continental breakfast T$40/50) This is the first choice for most travellers to 'Eua and perhaps its trump card. A viewing platform built over the rocky shore makes for fantastic sunset- and whale-watching (June to December) and there is a *fale*-style bar and restaurant with ocean views (book by noon). The food is solid, with a choice of chicken, fish or pork à la garlic, sweet-and-sour or curry. Breakfast costs T$6 to T$8, dinner T$18 to T$20. The comfortable motel-style rooms have good, hot showers. Staff give sound walking advice and run a range of island tours.

Taina's Place (Map p216; ☎ 50186; fax 50128; Telefoni Rd; s/d/tr cabin T$20/30/40, camping per tent T$10, tent hire T$15, kitchen use per day T$5) Wood sprites can stay within a whisper of the forest's edge in one of five cute houses sprinkled through the gardens, with mosquito nets to keep stinging fairies at bay. The newly built family house has its own kitchen. Taina's five-dish dinner spread features chicken, rice and vegetables from the garden and for a few extra *pa'anga* she'll include Tongan specialties such as fish coconut cream curry and *'ota ika*. Breakfast costs T$6, dinner T$15 to T$18.

Susan's Guest House (Map p216; ☎ 50088; s/d T$20/30, extra person T$10) Rooms are basic (with fans on request) but clean in this friendly family home. There's a communal dining room and a lounge featuring funky red and green velour couches. Breakfast (T$7 to T$8), dinner (Tongan fish or chicken dishes, T$12) and a Sunday *'umu* (T$12) can be arranged.

Highlight Guest House (Map p216; ☎ 50143; fax 50128; Mata'aho; s/d T$25/40, kitchen use per day T$5) This is a spacious house with tiled floors, communal lounge and dining rooms, and comfortable beds in twin and double configurations. Cooked meals are available. Breakfast/lunch/dinner costs T$6/8/12.

Deep Resort (☎ 50421, 27406; moanas@kalianet.to; Tufuvai; dm T$25, s/d incl breakfast T$40/80) The inner real-estate agent in you will be crying out 'position, position, position' upon sighting the beautiful sweep of Tufuvai Beach (p218) onto which this place edges. Three roomy log-style cabins with terraces of whole tree branches have queen and single beds, a bathroom and screened windows. A downside is the weary linen. The Tongan-style bar and restaurant (open to guests and nonguests; meals T$7.50 to T$20) is a charming spot to soak up afternoon beverages and the symphony of surf crashing over the reef wall.

Consult **MAF** (☎ 50116) about any suitable camp sites in highland and beach areas.

Eating

The only restaurants in 'Eua are those attached to the island's places to stay; they welcome nonguests who book ahead. Self-caterers can get basic supplies in 'Ohonua. Pickings are slim so consider bringing a few items from Tongatapu. Small *fale koloa* are scattered up and down the main road between Houma and Ha'atu'a – one of the best stocked is in 'Ohonua on the way to the High School. In addition, there is a Saturday-morning fruit and veggie market at Nafanua Wharf and vegetables at roadside markets.

Ta'anga Supermarket & Bakery (Map p223; 'Ohonua; ✆ 8am-5pm Mon-Thu, to 9pm Fri, 8am-1pm Sat, bakery only from 4.30pm Sun) Here you'll find a fair range of goods and…refrigerated chocolate! White bread is the staple, though fruit bread, cream buns and occasionally fried dough may make a special appearance on Sunday. It's up the hill from Nafanua Wharf.

Tonga Cooperative Federation (TCF; Map p223; ☎ 50131; 'Ohonua; ✆ 8am-4.30pm Mon-Fri, 8am-noon & 6.30-8.30pm Sat) Alongside the post office, this supermarket south of Nafanua Wharf offers a limited choice including some meat.

Drinking & Entertainment

The restaurant/bars at the Hideaway (p223) and the Deep Resort (p223), both oriented to maximise sea views, are open to nonguests and form most of the social scene.

Maxi Disco Hall (Main Rd, 'Esia; men/women T$3/2; ✆ 8pm-2am Fri, 8pm-11.30pm Sat) The island's only dancing venue doesn't serve alcohol but the *fale koloa* next door to it does, and patrons get rowdy just the same. Go with a local or prepare to be harassed.

Getting There & Around

On a calm day there is nothing to the ferry trip between 'Eua and Tongatapu (p287), but when it gets rough…well, people have slid off the ferry roof into the trench. The return leg from 'Eua is generally a smoother ride.

At the time of writing, flights between Tongatapu and 'Eua's Kaufana Airport in Fata'ulua (10 minutes) had been suspended.

There is no bus service but you shouldn't have any problems hitching rides (note: palm down rather than thumb up) along the main road between Houma and Ha'atu'a. Normal safety precautions apply. Elsewhere you'll probably have to walk as there's very little traffic.

Your accommodation hosts will be able to assist with transportation to sights and trails, or you can call ☎ 50240 or ☎ 50320 for a taxi.

Most places to stay will organise horse hire (with blankets for padding rather than saddles) for T$30 per day, or mountain-bike hire (with pedal brakes) for T$15 per day. Both provide a bit of income for locals renting out their own horses and bikes.

Ha'apai Group

Sprinkled across the kingdom's central waters, the Ha'apai Group is an idyllic South Pacific paradise – low coral islands, vibrant reefs and kilometres of deserted white beaches fringed with coconut palms. Traditional culture is not something you pay an entry fee to experience in Ha'apai – it's all around, unexploited and alive. You won't find the distractions of shops, nightspots (or even running water at times) but those willing to forgo the trimmings reap the rewards. Even bare-brass budgeters can walk across a reef for a slice of paradise in a *fale* (traditional thatched house) on a large patch of sand. And only a scattering of tourists visit each year.

Of its 62 islands, 45 are uninhabited, including pyramidal Kao and its smoking partner, Tofua – venture to the remote shores of Tofua, hike up its Jurassic Park–cum–moonscape crater and peer into the glowing caldera. Lifuka's more accessible diving sites hold their own in the diversity stakes too. Divers enter a whole new realm exploring blackened walls laden with colourful corals, while pelagics rise from the depths nearby. Whale-watching is largely an incidental experience while travelling between islands, though low visitor numbers allow you to view the mammals without the crowds. A kayaking adventure through the islands is one of the most exhilarating adventures the world offers.

The languorous pace of life in Ha'apai has led many of its residents to relocate to Tongatapu or more distant shores in search of further opportunities, keeping the population of the island group low. People here largely subsist on agriculture and fishing: 'Uiha's fish and seafood ends up on the plates of the kingdom's finest restaurants.

HIGHLIGHTS

- Powering your own sea-kayak exploration to uninhabited **Nukunamo** (p237) or traditional **Ha'ano** (p237)
- **Diving** (p227) into Ha'apai's underwater world with massive coral heads, sea caves and a coral arch
- Peering into the glowing caldera and exploring the moonscape crater on the dramatic volcanic island of **Tofua** (p240)
- Walking on water (well…) between the islands of **Lifuka** and **Uoleva** (p238)
- Imagining yourself castaway, staying in a *tapa*-lined *fale* on an otherwise deserted tropical beach at **Uoleva** (p237)

Ha'ano

Tofua

Nukunamo

Uoleva Lifuka

| POPULATION: 8138 | AREA: 110 SQ KM |

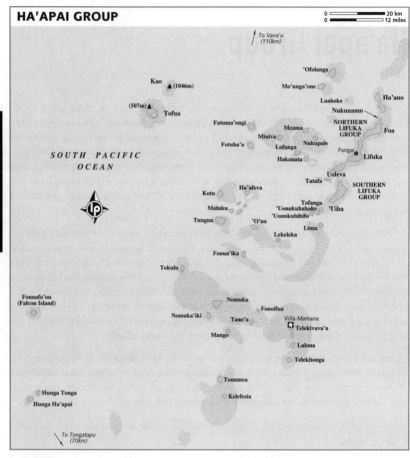

HA'APAI GROUP

0 [____] 20 km
0 [____] 12 miles

To Vava'u
(110km)

SOUTH PACIFIC
OCEAN

'Ofolanga

Kao ▲ (1046m)
Mo'unga'one
Luahoko
Ha'ano
Nukunamo

(507m) ▲
Tofua

Fatuma'ongi
Meama
Miniva
Fotuha'a
Lofanga
Nukupule
Hakauata

NORTHERN
LIFUKA
GROUP
Foa

Pangai
Lifuka

Uoleva

Tatafa
SOUTHERN
LIFUKA
GROUP

Kotu
Ha'afeva
Matuku
Tofanga
'Uonukuhahake
'Uiha
Tungua
'O'ua
'Uonukuhihifo
Limu
Lekeleka

Fonua'ika

Tokulu

Fonuafo'ou
(Falcon Island)
Nomuka
Fonoifua
Villa Mamana
Nomuka'iki
Tano'a
Telekivava'u
Mango
Lalona
Telekitonga

Tonumea
Hunga Tonga
Kelefesia
Hunga Ha'apai

To Tongatapu
(70km)

HISTORY
Archaeological excavations in the village of
Hihifo, in southern Pangai, revealed a settle-
ment dating back over 3000 years when
Lapita pottery (an early form of distinctive
Polynesian ware, named after the site in
New Caledonia where it was first found)
carbon dated to this period was unearthed.
Lifuka's other archaeological sights include
the Velata Mound Fortress (probably built
in the 15th century AD), several large burial
mounds, and an ancient stone quarry at
Holopeka Beach.

The first European to visit the Ha'apai
Group was Dutchman Abel Tasman, who
stopped at Nomuka in 1643 for fresh water.
Nomuka's sweet water springs were to be the

focus of many visits to the group throughout
the years of European Pacific exploration.

Subsequently, Ha'apai became the scene
of several notable events in Tongan history.
On Lifuka in 1777, Captain James Cook
and his men narrowly escaped unwittingly
becoming the main course at a cannibalistic feast they had been invited to attend, a
feast which resulted in Cook's christening
Tonga the 'Friendly Islands'. (See p233 for
more information on this encounter.) The
famous mutiny on the *Bounty* occurred in
Ha'apai in 1789.

Still later, in 1806, the British privateer
Port-au-Prince was ransacked off Lifuka's
north coast; survivor Will Mariner's tale
of his years spent in Tonga has become the

classic account of pre-Christian life on the islands (see p236).

Ha'apai was the first island group in the Tongan archipelago to convert to Christianity, due to the efforts of convert Taufa'ahau, who was baptised George in 1831 and became the first king of the House of Tupou. He set the stage for a united Tonga and established the royal line that remains in power to this day.

DANGERS & ANNOYANCES

Snappy, pack-forming dogs are occasionally hazardous here, as elsewhere in Tonga (see p278). Seek out tide charts and local knowledge on currents before slipping into the sea.

Ha'apai's brackish water should be used only for washing and bathing. Drinking water is collected in rainwater cisterns.

ACTIVITIES

Sandy, deserted beaches and uninhabited islands may be all you need for a perfect trip to Ha'apai, but cultural explorations, foot-powered reef crossings, cycling, horse riding, diving and whale-watching can be easily added to the mix.

To make the most of a trip to Ha'apai, including an exploration of its remote outer islands (including Ha'ano and 'Uiha), you'll need to plan in advance and have plenty of time to join local boats or the funds to privately charter them. Conditions can be fickle, so save that 1000-page novel and hammock-snoozing for the less idyllic days.

Those with a burning desire to visit volcanic Tofua (totally justified) to hike up onto the crater rim, or to dive Tofua's amazing watery surrounds, will need plenty of lead time to privately charter a boat (p241). You could also join a trip organised by Mariners Guided Camping Tours (see below), Happy Ha'apai Divers (p228) or foreign aid workers (for organisation contact details, see p284).

Camping & Hiking

Camping experiences on remote islands include fishing, possible whale sightings and the very cool experience of just being out there (especially climbing volcanic Tofua; see p240).

Mariners Guided Camping Tours (☎ 60374; fax 60504; www.tongacamping.com) has clever ways of tempting the intrepid out to Ha'apai's more

remote islands – some uninhabited, some offering a traditional cultural experience, one an active volcano. Two-/seven-day Tofua volcano tours (NZ$500/1050) and four-/seven-day island camping tours (NZ$400/1300) operate out of Pangai. The 13-day camping and volcano tour (NZ$1950) departs Nuku'alofa (Tongatapu), and ends in Pangai or Nuku'alofa. Tents, camp beds and fishing gear are supplied. You'll need to allow for a week in Ha'apai for the two-day Tofua trip to maximise the chances of good weather. Check the website for set tour departure dates or contact Trevor to organise a tour.

Diving & Snorkelling

Ha'apai has a dive site to suit every whim or fancy – caves, channels, tunnels, drifts, drop-offs, coral gardens, volcanic black walls framing an explosion of colour, and bommies and walls rising from the depths to bring large pelagics into view. In season (June to November), humpback whales add to the aquatic mix – their mesmerising singing can be heard when you dip your head below the surface. The reefs and shallows of the Ha'apai Group offer amazing underwater scenery, while outstanding visibility (from 25m to 30m in summer to over 50m in winter) and very comfortable water temperatures (23°C to 29°C) combine to create magnificent conditions for diving.

Impressive sites around the islands of 'Ofolanga, Mo'unga'one and Luahoko include huge sea caves and an incredible coral arch (one of only a few in the South Pacific) for experienced divers.

The remarkable seascapes around Tofua and Kao offer unique sites with pink soft corals set against black walls and visibility (50m plus) so clear 'it's like diving in gin'. There's incredible diversity, with lots of pelagics and turtles the size of tables. Getting there takes some advanced planning.

The exposed nature of the Ha'apai Group can make diving the outer sites (up to 45 minutes by boat from Foa) a weather-dependent event. Getting out to the best snorkelling spots requires a boat, but there are some lively coral heads off Houmale'eia Beach on Foa and throughout the island's reefs. The Tongan Visitors Bureau (TVB) has a display board listing some of Ha'apai's diverse mapped dive sights. Snorkellers can join dive groups or charter a local boat.

Happy Ha'apai Divers (☎ 60639; www.tonga-dive .com; PO Box 61, Pangai) focuses on long, slow dives. Based at Sandy Beach Resort on Foa, this reputable professional operator also runs NZ-based Ocean Blue Adventures. Diving tends to concentrate on the northern Lifuka Group and two-day diving trips to Tofua and Kao were set to commence in 2006. It offers one/two boat dives for US$65/90, six-/10-dive packages for US$255/400 and PADI Scuba Diver/Open Water courses (US$200/410, including gear). Dive Masters will take the time with less-experienced or rusty divers to ensure they feel comfortable. Discover Scuba 'try' dives cost US$75 and rental gear is available. Most dive sites are within 20 minutes of the dive base. Asthmatics require a specialist medical clearance to dive.

Snorkellers are welcome to join dive boats if there is room (US$65, including wetsuit and gear).

Horse Riding
Some guesthouses and the TVB can arrange horse hire (around T$30 per day), without saddles.

Sea-Kayaking
The seeming remoteness of this string of beautiful islands, with its ample deserted beaches, makes self-powered sea explorations an enticing option – from a short sea-kayak adventure to uninhabited Nukunamo (p237) or a longer stretch to traditional Ha'ano (p237), to a multiday organised expedition throughout the island group.

Happy Ha'apai Divers (above) rents sea kayaks with a spray skirt, vest and paddle for US$20 per day. Sandy Beach Resort has single and double kayaks for guest use.

Friendly Islands Kayak Company (☎ /fax 70173; www.fikco.com) supplies all the equipment for its 11-day kayak camping tour (US$2280) through Ha'apai's Lifuka archipelago – an amazing experience, especially when whales are visiting. The kayaking covers nine days, with an orientation in Pangai. Equipment is shipped from Vava'u, so prior booking is essential. See p227 for further details.

Mariners Guided Camping Tours (right) also run camping and kayaking adventures.

Whale-Watching
You don't have to leave the shores to whale-watch in season (mainly July to November,

with possible sightings in June) – just scan beyond reefs for breaching and spouts. Inter-island journeys, including the boat transfers between Pangai and the 'resorts' on Uoleva, are often accompanied by whale sightings.

Happy Ha'apai Divers (left) runs small-group whale-watching trips (half-/full-day US$45/70, including snorkelling gear) with environmental awareness and minimal impact to the animals.

Mariners Guided Camping Tours (☎ 60374; fax 60504; www.tongacamping.com) is able to organise whale-watching trips on demand between August and October.

FESTIVALS & EVENTS
The week-long **Ha'apai Festival** starts on the outer islands and concludes on Lifuka on Emancipation Day (4 June). Visitors are heartily welcomed to experience traditional culture.

LIFUKA GROUP

Most visitors to Ha'apai stay within the Lifuka group of islands, found along the eastern barrier reef of Ha'apai, including Ha'ano, Nukunamo, Foa, Lifuka, Uoleva, Tatafa and 'Uiha. Lifuka Island, with its main town Pangai (the island group's capital), is the centre of Ha'apai's limited activity, including the airport and main inter-island ferry port.

LIFUKA ISLAND
area 11 sq km / pop 2966

Lifuka's main town, Pangai, holds Lifuka's basic services (shops, post office, bank etc) and several guesthouses. There's little for the visitor to do (to the delight of many travellers) other than wander along the empty white beaches that nearly encircle the island, and swim and snorkel in the western shore's calm blue water or the wilder and more dramatic eastern coast.

Information
For weather forecasts, call ☎ 21555 or listen to 89.5FM.

BOOKSHOPS
Friendly Islands Bookshop (☎ 60198; Holopeka Rd; ◷ 8.30am-5pm Mon-Fri, 8.30am-noon Sat) Stocks some highly recommended and bestselling books on Tonga and the Pacific region (including *Tonga Islands: William*

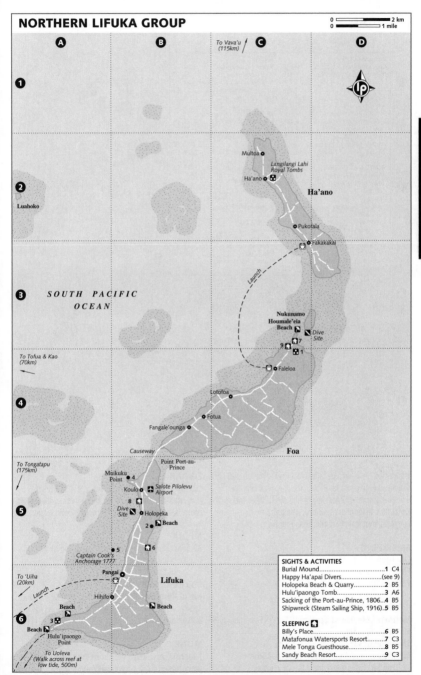

NORTHERN LIFUKA GROUP

0 ——— 2 km
0 ——— 1 mile

To Vava'u (115km)

Multoa

Langilangi Lahi Royal Tombs

Ha'ano

Ha'ano

Luahoko

Pukotala

Fakakakai

Launch

SOUTH PACIFIC OCEAN

Nukunamo
Houmale'eia Beach

Dive Site

To Tofua & Kao (70km)

Faleloa

Lofofoa

Fotua

Fangale'ounga

Foa

Causeway

Point Port-au-Prince

Muikuku Point

Koulo

Salote Pilolevu Airport

Dive Site

Holopeka

Beach

To Tongatapu (175km)

Captain Cook's Anchorage 1777

Pangai

Lifuka

Hihifo

Beach

To 'Uiha (20km)

Launch

Beach

Hulu'ipaongo Point

Beach

To Uoleva (Walk across reef at low tide, 500m)

SIGHTS & ACTIVITIES
Burial Mound...................................1 C4
Happy Ha'apai Divers.....................(see 9)
Holopeka Beach & Quarry................2 B5
Hulu'ipaongo Tomb.........................3 A6
Sacking of the Port-au-Prince, 1806..4 B5
Shipwreck (Steam Sailing Ship, 1916).5 B5

SLEEPING
Billy's Place.....................................6 B5
Matafonua Watersports Resort.........7 C3
Mele Tonga Guesthouse..................8 B5
Sandy Beach Resort.........................9 C3

HA'APAI GROUP

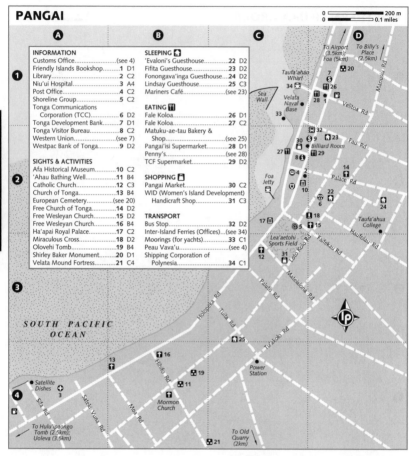

PANGAI

0 _____ 200 m
0 _____ 0.1 miles

INFORMATION
Customs Office......................(see 4)
Friendly Islands Bookshop.........1 D1
Library.................................2 C2
Niu'ui Hospital.....................3 A4
Post Office............................4 C2
Shoreline Group.....................5 C2
Tonga Communications
   Corporation (TCC)................6 D2
Tonga Development Bank.........7 D1
Tonga Visitor Bureau..............8 C2
Western Union......................(see 7)
Westpac Bank of Tonga.........9 D2

SIGHTS & ACTIVITIES
Afa Historical Museum..........10 C2
'Ahau Bathing Well..............11 B4
Catholic Church...................12 C3
Church of Tonga..................13 B4
European Cemetery............(see 20)
Free Church of Tonga...........14 D2
Free Wesleyan Church..........15 D2
Free Wesleyan Church..........16 B4
Ha'apai Royal Palace............17 C2
Miraculous Cross.................18 D2
Olovehi Tomb......................19 B4
Shirley Baker Monument.......20 D1
Velata Mound Fortress.........21 C4

SLEEPING
'Evaloni's Guesthouse............22 D2
Fifita Guesthouse..................23 D2
Fonongava'inga Guesthouse...24 D2
Lindsay Guesthouse..............25 C3
Mariners Café.....................(see 23)

EATING
Fale Koloa...........................26 D1
Fale Koloa...........................27 C2
Matuku-ae-tau Bakery &
   Shop..............................(see 25)
Pangai'isi Supermarket..........28 D1
Penny's.............................(see 28)
TCF Supermarket................29 D2

SHOPPING
Pangai Market......................30 C2
WID (Women's Island Development)
   Handicraft Shop...............31 C3

TRANSPORT
Bus Stop.............................32 D2
Inter-Island Ferries (Offices)...(see 34)
Moorings (for yachts)............33 C1
Peau Vava'u.......................(see 4)
Shipping Corporation of
   Polynesia.........................34 C1

To Airport (3.5km); Foa (5km)
To Billy's Place (2.5km)

Taufa'ahao Wharf
Sea Wall
Velata Naval Base

Foa Jetty

SOUTH PACIFIC OCEAN

Palace Rd
Taufa'ahua College
Haufolau Rd
Faifekau Rd
Fau Rd
Billiard Room
Velitoa Rd
Manusia Rd

Lea'aetohi Sports Field

Power Station

Holopeka Rd
Tuila Rd
Paluto Rd
Tufakolo Rd
Makalanga Rd
Loto Kolo Rd

Satellite Dishes
Sfa Rd
Sateki Vuna Rd
Mea Rd
Fihifo Rd

Mormon Church

To Hulu'ipaongo Tomb (2.5km); Uoleva (3.5km)

To Old Quarry (2km)

Mariner's Account and Epeli Hau'ofa's *Tales of the Tikongs*) among other paperbacks. Books take one week to arrive if ordered from the larger shop in Nuku'alofa. Also stocks Kodak film, magazines *(New Idea, Woman's Day)* from a range of dates, stationery and fishing supplies.

EMERGENCY
Emergency (☎ 911)
Fire (☎ 22222)
Police (☎ 21222)

INTERNET ACCESS
Mariners Café (Fau Rd; per 15min T$3; ◷ 9am-9pm Mon-Sat, 6-9pm Sun)
Shoreline Group (Faifekau Rd; per 15min/hr T$2.30/9.20; ◷ 8.30am-4.30pm Mon-Fri, 8.30am-12.30pm Sat) Easily found under the radio tower.

LIBRARIES
Library (cnr Holopeka & Palace Rds; ◷ 3.30-5.30pm Mon-Fri) A valuable resource run by volunteers with donated books. Become a member for T$5; donate books for free.

MEDIA
89.5FM (broadcasting ◷ 7am-11pm) English and Tongan broadcasts, including weather updates.

MEDICAL SERVICES
Niu'ui Hospital (☎ 60201; Hihifo) Pretty basic facilities. Appointments are necessary and the pharmacy is open 8.30am to 4.30pm.

MONEY
MasterCard and Visa can be used for larger purchases and payments at Mariner's Café,

Sandy Beach Resort and Happy Ha'apai Divers. Elsewhere, use cash.

Tonga Development Bank (Holopeka Rd; ✆ 9am-12.30pm & 1.30-3.30pm Mon-Fri) Offers Western Union money transfers.

Westpac Bank of Tonga (☎ 60933; Holopeka Rd; ✆ 9am-12.30pm & 1.30-3.30pm Mon-Fri) Exchanges foreign currencies (cash and travellers cheques), gives cash advances on Visa and MasterCard and also deals with MoneyGram cash transfers. Phonecards are sold here.

POST

Post office (cnr Waterfront & Palace Rds; ✆ 8.30am-12.30pm & 1.30-3.30pm Mon-Fri) Mail can be sent c/o Post Office, Pangai, Ha'apai. The Customs & Inland Revenue office is also based here.

TELEPHONE & FAX

Card-operated phones are located outside the Tonga Communications Corporation (TCC) office and at one of the *fale koloa* (small grocery kiosks) on Holopeka Rd in the centre of town. Purchase telephone cards at TCC, Westpac Bank of Tonga and Pangai'isi Supermarket, opposite the wharf.

Tonga Communications Corporation (TCC; ☎ 60255) On the road parallel to Holopeka Rd, between Palace and Faifekau Rds, in the centre of Pangai. Fax services are available.

TOURIST INFORMATION

Tonga Visitors Bureau (TVB; ☎ /fax 60733; www .tongaholiday.com; Holopeka Rd; ✆ 8.30am-12.30pm & 1.30-4.30pm Mon-Fri) On the corner opposite the Tonga Cooperative Federation (TCF) supermarket, the tourist office stocks some Ha'apai brochures, posts tide timetables and has some display information on dive sites. Depending upon the mood of the staff, you may get assistance with accommodation bookings, horse riding or boat charter queries, but don't count on it. You may also be told to 'go ask Mariner's Café'.

Sights

The ferry arrival from Tongatapu at the wharf, and its subsequent unpacking, is the peak of excitement for the week. A pretty section of the waterfront, south of the wharf and market, has picnic tables under pines with views of Tofua (and its puffing smoke) and Kao.

Lifuka's sights can be easily covered in about half a day by bike, by horse, by taxi or on foot. 'Evaloni's Guesthouse (p233) will negotiate to drive guests to sights of interest on request.

For details on diving, snorkelling, sea-kayaking and whale-watching around the Ha'apai islands, see p227.

On hot afternoons, the wharf is a writhing mass of drenched, cooling down kids. Feel free to join in (people here swim fully clothed). Visitors are welcome to join any game of basketball, volleyball, rugby or Aussie rules football going on.

PANGAI'S BUILDINGS

Pangai's colourful *fale koloa* and decaying old wooden warehouse buildings make for an atmospheric sight. The understated **Ha'apai Royal Palace** is the white weatherboard and red-roofed building close to the Catholic Church.

On the lawn of the **Free Wesleyan Church** is the concrete outline of a cross commemorating a 'miracle' that occurred there in 1975. Residents report that one night they saw a flame falling from the sky to land in front of the church. In the morning they found the outline of a cross burned into the grass. Cynics in the village attribute the whole 'miracle' to mischievous teenagers with kerosene tins and cigarette lighters.

The unusual-looking **Church of Tonga** (Holopeka Rd) at the southern end of Pangai has touches of Middle Eastern architecture.

AFA HISTORICAL MUSEUM

The interesting collection of **Afa Historical Museum** (Holopeka Rd; ✆ opening times vary) includes pieces of 3000-year-old Lapita pottery, traditional headrests, old photographs, rocks from Tofua and items used in the production of handicrafts, which the proprietor Virginia has lovingly collected. A folder of newspaper clippings sheds light on the history and geology of volcanic Tofua, but there is little other signage.

HIHIFO'S ARCHAEOLOGICAL SITES

Hihifo, the village at the south end of Pangai, hides some archaeological relics seemingly of more interest to pigs than anyone else.

Hidden behind a low wire fence in a grove of ironwood is **Olovehi Tomb** (Loto Kolo Rd). It's somewhat overgrown and neglected, but the upright memorial stone at the southwest corner and the large beach-rock slabs that make up the tired walls echo its former splendour. (There's an impressive banyan tree to climb behind it.)

The tomb was built in the late 1700s for Nanasipau'u, eldest sister of the reigning Tu'i Tonga. It's claimed that, as part of her funeral, those selected as her attendants in the afterlife were killed and buried around the outside of this tomb. Nanasipau'u's daughter, Latufuipeka, and her daughter's husband, Tuita Kahomovailahi, are also buried here. The modern extension to the south of the tomb is the burial ground for families holding the noble title of Tuita.

Freshwater bathing wells were owned by the highest chiefs and were *tapu* (taboo) to commoners. **'Ahau Bathing Well** (cnr Hihifo & Loto Kolo Rds) belonged to the chief Laufilitonga while he and his people were staying at the Fortress of Velata during the 1820s. Today it's nothing more than a muddy dip with garbage and a twisted palm growing out of it.

The 3000-year-old Lapita pottery was excavated a block south of here on the corner of Moa and Loto Kolo Rds, but there's nothing to see nowadays.

Just south of the bathing well, is the site of the circular **Velata Mound Fortress**, a type of ring ditch fortification found throughout Tonga, Fiji and Samoa. Today it's marked with an empty concrete plaque but the artificial ridges are virtually indistinguishable under the vegetation and strewn refuse.

Velata was remarkable in having the extra protection of a double ditch. A 2.5m- to 3m-high defensive wall would have been built on the inner ring that lies between 15m and 20m inside the outer ditch. Historians believe that Velata was first built in the 15th century. In the 1820s Laufilitonga, who later became the 39th and last Tu'i Tonga, restored the fort as a stronghold against the Taufa'ahau dynasty. In 1826 the fortress was burned when Laufilitonga was defeated in battle by Taufa'ahau, the future King George Tupou I.

SHIRLEY BAKER MONUMENT & EUROPEAN CEMETERY

In the European Cemetery 800m north of Pangai, the grave and monument of Rev Shirley Baker (Tonga's first prime minister and adviser to King George Tupou I) stands amid the graves of various 19th- and early-20th-century German and English traders and missionaries.

Following the former missionary and controversial politician's enforced exile in 1890, Baker returned in 1898 with the permission of King George Tupou II and lived out his days in Hihifo, just south of Pangai, where he died on 16 April 1903.

A Tongan cemetery, its sand and coral mounds decorated with colourful artificial floral tributes and handmade quilts, is directly opposite.

HOLOPEKA BEACH & OLD QUARRY

Sandy Holopeka Beach, east of Holopeka village, is a rarely visited spot with lovely rock pools set in natural stone terraces – similar to those on Tongatapu's south coast. At low tide the deep crevasses are full of coral and fish, though snorkelling is only recommended at low tide on a calm day as the sea surging into crevasses can make it dangerous.

At low tide you can see the remnants of an ancient beach-stone **quarry** and several stages of block removal. Quarries of this type supplied the large stone blocks found in the retaining walls of chiefly tombs from the 13th to 18th centuries.

SOUTHERN LIFUKA ISLAND

On the south side of Pangai is the village of Hihifo. From Hihifo, you can continue south along the dirt road all the way to **Hulu'ipaonga Point**, with its wide sweep of white beach (and a disappointing nonbiodegradable waste problem).

West of the road, about 200m short of the beach, is the **Hulu'ipaongo Tomb**. As described by Captain Cook, this is the highest burial mound in Lifuka and the Mata'uvave line of chiefs is buried here. The first Mata'uvave was sent to Ha'apai in the 15th century to establish political control over northern Ha'apai for Tu'i Tonga Kau'ulufonuafekai. His success resulted in his appointment as governor and Tu'i Ha'apai.

It's possible to walk between the southern tip of Lifuka and the northern tip of Uoleva at low tide (see p237).

Sleeping

All of Lifuka's accommodation is basic with cold showers unless otherwise stated. Most can make arrangements for boat trips and horse hire and offer free pick-up from the airport or wharf.

Camping on beaches or in undesignated areas is illegal throughout the Ha'apai Group unless you are on a guided trip (see p227) or have permission from the owners.

The tourist office or Mariners Café may have details on long-term accommodation rentals.

PANGAI

Fonongava'inga Guesthouse (Langilangi Guesthouse; ☎ 60038; fax 60200; vimahi@kalianet.to; Palace Rd; s/d/tr T$15/25/45) Sitting at the back of town in the middle of Lifuka, this place, also known as Langilangi Guesthouse, is a six-minute walk from the town, wharf and beach. There's a broad veranda, a homely light-filled communal lounge, and clean facilities. Fans are available and breakfast (T$6) and dinner (T$20 to T$30) can be arranged; kitchen use is T$3 per day. Langilangi enjoys teaching local crafts to guests, assisting them to create a small traditional weaving to take home.

'Evaloni's Guesthouse (☎ 60029; Loto Kolo Rd; s/d T$15/25, d with private bathroom T$45, ste d with private bathroom incl breakfast T$75) While guest room décor is hardly South Seas (the elaborate 'honeymoon suites' feature mirror-backed king-sized beds and private bathrooms), the rooms are comfortable and fan-cooled. You can shoot some pool on the long, *tapa*-lined veranda and dine there or in the sun-shaded garden *fale*. Guests can use the well-equipped kitchen (T$1.50 per day) or order meals; breakfast feasts include cheese omelettes, muffins, fruit pancakes and fruit (T$15). Discuss sightseeing options with the owners, who can arrange tours and transportation.

Fifita Guesthouse (☎ 60213; Fau Rd; s/d T$25/35, f with sitting room T$65) Fifita's central location behind Mariner's Café and just a short walk from the wharf makes it a popular place.

It's basic but friendly, with plenty of travel banter exchanged (sometimes loudly) in the communal kitchen. Toast and jam breakfasts are supplemented with some fruit, an egg or fried 'banana pancakes'. No communal lounge makes it a bit drab in rainy periods.

Lindsay Guesthouse (☎ /fax 60107; cnr Loto Kolo & Tuita Rds; s/d/f T$20/30/50, with bathroom T$45/55) The warm and irresistible scent of baking bread wafts across the lawn from the bakery – the attached grocery shop makes breakfast an easily self-catered affair, although the guesthouse can provide breakfast for T$6 to T$10. It's a clean and friendly spot, with a broad veranda and communal sitting room and kitchen, though you may have to beg for the one hot shower. The nearby town water pump is sometimes audible. Rental bikes (T$8 per day) are generally reserved for guests. Order evening meals (such as fish and chips, fresh seafood or salami pizza; T$15 to T$20) early in the day.

AROUND THE ISLAND

All beachside accommodation is located outside Pangai. The east side has big waves, while the west side is sheltered and offers magnificent sunsets and views of Kao.

Billy's Place (☎ 60336; s/d fale incl breakfast T$55/65, larger s/d fale T$65/75, self-contained fale T$100) Ropes of buoys in faded orange, white and yellow dangle from pandanus roots between Billy's open-sided dining terrace and views of breaking surf (and whales in season) beyond the quiet beach. Boardwalk paths wind through gardens, connecting secluded and well-presented bungalow-style rooms with

---

COOK'S 'FRIENDLY ISLANDS' NOT SO FRIENDLY?

On Captain James Cook's third Pacific voyage in 1777 he spent over two months in Tonga. At Nomuka, his first landfall, chief Finau of Ha'apai told him of a wealthier island, Lifuka, where supplies would be available.

While visiting Lifuka, Cook and his men were treated to lavish feasting and entertainment. Needless to say, the foreigners were impressed. Cook dubbed the Ha'apai Group the 'Friendly Islands' after the apparent disposition of its inhabitants.

Thirty years later it was learned that the entertainment had been part of a Tongan conspiracy to raid the ships *Resolution* and *Discovery* for their plainly visible wealth. The plan was to gather the Englishmen into a convenient place, so that they could be quickly killed and their ships looted. There was, however, a dispute between Finau and his nobles over whether the attack would occur by day or under cover of night. Having previously agreed to follow the chief's plan to take action during the afternoon, the nobles failed to do so at the appointed time. Finau was so incensed at such a defiance of his orders that the operation was abandoned altogether and the Englishmen never learned how narrowly they had escaped.

clean, shared facilities nearby; kitchen use per day is T$5. Nonguests can also enjoy the food here (lunch/dinner T$12/20), and a Sunday *'umu* (feast cooked in a stone underground oven) can be arranged. Situated 1.5km northeast of Pangai, lone travellers could relish the peace or feel a bit isolated. It's a 10-minute bike ride (free mountain bikes are available for guests) or a T$4 taxi ride. No children under 12 are allowed and it's a minimum two-night stay.

Mele Tonga Guesthouse (☎ 60042; Holopeka Rd, Holopeka; house d T$20, fale s/d T$20/30) The secluded *fale* just back from the western shore is a beachfront find for bargain hunters. Lantern-lit, it has a window overlooking the water, lacy overlays over the double bed, a table and two covered car bucket seats. There's a separate BBQ *fale* with a dining table and standard rooms in the house. Breakfast/lunch/dinner is available for T$8/10/12. About 100m south of the guesthouse a channel leads out from the beach and through the reef to a reasonable snorkelling spot.

From the airport turn left onto the main road, walk five minutes then turn right into a driveway on the north side of the Mormon school. Airport pick-ups and transfers to Pangai, 3km away, for shopping are free. A taxi to or from Pangai costs T$5.

Eating

There are few options to eat out in Pangai. 'Evaloni's and Fonongava'inga Guesthouses and Billy's Place may accept nonguests for dinner if you book in advance. Foa (p236) offers further options.

Mariners Café (☎ 60374; VHF Channel 16; Fau Rd; meals & snacks T$6.50-16.50; 9am-9pm Mon-Sat, 6-9pm Sun) You won't fully appreciate the lure of Mariners until you've spent some time on Ha'apai's shores. This relaxed social mecca is Lifuka's only real restaurant (and bar substitute) and has a good range of tasty and fresh dishes, including Thai green chicken curry, fresh tuna stir-fries and burgers. The high-crust pizzas rate highly and beer, wine and plunger coffee are served. It's a good place to come for local knowledge. (It's occasionally closed from 3pm to 5pm so the owner can go fishing.)

Penny's (Waterfront; breakfast, lunch & dinner) With a lovely view over the harbour from the first floor of the green waterfront building, Penny's was set to open its doors at the time of research and planned to serve meals and hire out bicycles (T$15).

Pangai Market (cnr Waterfront & Palace Rd; 9am-5pm Mon-Sat) Pangai's market opposite the waterfront is half fresh produce, half flea market. Pickings are often slim and you'll be lucky to find much more than root crops and bananas most of the time. Tomatoes, cucumbers and peppers are snapped up quickly. Saturday mornings are busiest.

Tonga Cooperative Federation (TCF; Holopeka Rd) The supermarket's limited choice includes racks of tinned meat, biscuits, tinned fruit and vegetables, two-minute noodles, UHT milk, formula milk and nappies (diapers), some refrigerated fruit and 18kg buckets of edible dripping.

Matuku-ae-tau Bakery (Lindsay Guesthouse; cnr Loto Kolo & Tuita Rds; 8am-5pm Mon-Sat, 5-8pm Sun) The bakery's two ovens keep the island well-stocked in bread, jam-filled rolls and *keki* (fried doughnut-like balls). There's a mad rush on Sunday afternoon.

The multicoloured *fale koloa* around the town sell their own selection of groceries, including two-minute noodles, tinned products, eggs, UHT milk and juice, frozen chicken, some fruit and vegetables and bread. One opposite Friendly Islands Bookshop at the corner of Holopeka and Velitoa Rds, sells some delicious homemade baked goods including cake (banana, chocolate and coconut). You can pick up a chocolate-coated creamy vanilla ice cream wherever you see a 'Topsy' sign. **Pangai'isi Supermarket** (7am-11pm) sells phonecards, while the *fale koloa* under the big tree opposite the market sells fish.

Drinking

Beer and wine is served at Mariner's Café (see left) but other than that you'll need to buy your own and consume it at your guesthouse. Bottles of (dubious heritage) rum and vodka (T$30) are sold in the *fale koloa* next to the TCF; beer is sold in the one opposite it.

Entertainment

On Friday nights, *kava* (intoxicating drink made from the root of the pepper shrub) clubs meet in several halls around Pangai. Ask someone to point you in the right direction – these are largely male affairs, though.

Other entertainment on the island generally revolves around church activities and includes dances.

Shopping

Women's Island Development Handicraft Shop (☎ 60478; Loto Kolo Rd) This women's handicraft cooperative sells *tapa* (mulberry bark cloth), cards and various woven items made from pandanus leaves.

Ha'apai is well known for its quality traditional *tapa*, which many expat Tongans purchase on order. Tupou at 'Evaloni's Guesthouse (see p233) may have some *tapa* for sale, while Langilangi at Fonongava'inga Guesthouse (see p233) can acquaint you with traditional weaving.

Coconut oil scented with candlenut or sandalwood can be purchased from several *fale koloa*.

Getting There & Away

AIR

The main Lifuka–Foa road bisects Ha'apai's Salote Pilolevu Airport, 3km north of Pangai. **Airlines Tonga Air Fiji** (Airlines Tonga; ☎ 23690; fax 23238; www.airlinestonga.com) and Peau Vava'u service the Ha'apai daily except Sunday. The round-trip flight services from Tongatapu alternate between stopping in Ha'apai then Vava'u or Vava'u then Ha'apai before returning to Tongatapu. See p285 for details.

The office of **Peau Vava'u** (☎ 60717; cnr Waterfront & Palace Rds) is next to the post office. Confirm flights 72 *and* 24 hours prior to departure.

BOAT

The MV *'Olovaha* and the MV *Pulupaki* stop twice weekly at Pangai on both their northbound and southbound runs between Tongatapu and Vava'u. The ships' offices beside the passenger shelter at Taufa'ahau Wharf only open on days when the ferries arrive. See p286 for ferry schedules and fares. The Church of Tonga's MV *Siu Pele* (see p288) runs from Nuku'alofa (Tongatapu) through the Ha'apai islands weekly.

The **Free Wesleyan Church** (☎ 60718, 60107, 60507) boat MV *Fetu Aho V* services Ha'apai's islands (irregularly and on demand) and may be available for charter.

Ha'apai is a port of entry into Tonga, but the immigration officer is not always in Ha'apai. If you're arriving in Ha'apai by yacht, you must check in with the **customs officer** (☎ 60608, 60666) upon arrival; the office is inside the post office. See also p295. Although the entrance to the harbour looks tricky on the sea chart the marker buoys are perfectly aligned.

There are marginally protected anchorages along the lee shores of the islands of Lifuka, Foa, Ha'ano, Uoleva, Ha'afeva, Nomuka and Nomuka'iki. Fuel will have to be transported in jerry cans from the 'service station' near the corner of Holopeka and Velitoa Rds, or nearby the hospital. Getting sufficient supplies of anything is sometimes difficult in Ha'apai.

Getting Around

TO/FROM THE AIRPORT

Most accommodation providers offer free airport pick-ups and drop-offs. Taxis charge T$5 between the airport and Pangai, while the sporadic bus service between Pangai and the airport turn-off costs T$1.

BICYCLE

Lifuka and neighbouring Foa, connected by a causeway, are both fairly flat and ideal for exploring by bicycle.

Bicycles (T$8 to T$15 per day) can be rented from Penny's (opposite). Sandy Beach Resort (p236), Billy's Place (p233) and Lindsay Guesthouse (p233) provide bicycles for guest use; the latter two may loan surplus bikes to nonguests.

BOAT

The TVB and guesthouses will generally assist in arranging boat transport around the island, or you can organise it directly with **Jim** (☎ 60612, 60292), 'the Boat Man'. Negotiate a price before heading out.

BUS

A sporadic bus service operates between Hihifo, south of Pangai, and Foa's northernmost village of Faleloa roughly between 8am and 4pm weekdays and 8am and noon Saturday. The trip from Pangai to Faleloa costs T$1. There's a bus stop on the corner of Holopeka and Fau Rds.

TAXI

Several taxis operate in Pangai – try **John** (☎ 60124), **Siaosi** (☎ 60072) or **Ioane** (☎ 60509). The fare around town costs T$2.

FOA

area 13 sq km / pop 1434

Houmale'eia Beach on the tip of Foa is the best beach on the 'mainland', with sandy water access, sublime views of Nukunamo and beautiful snorkelling (the best reef is opposite the Sandy Beach Resort). Connected by a causeway to Lifuka, the heavily wooded island boasts an ancient **burial mound** about 500m south of Houmale'eia Beach.

Sleeping & Eating

Matafonua Watersports Resort (contact Sandy Beach Resort; www.sandybeachresort.de; fale d & tw T$80) Look-

ing for water views over foreshore foliage from your private terrace? This place was purpose-built as a dive resort in 2006. The uncluttered, elevated *fale* have louvre windows and mosquito nets over beds. The freshwater supply here comes from underground tanks and provides good showers in well-designed shared facilities. Kids are welcome. A kiosk-style café-bar overlooks Nukunamo.

Sandy Beach Resort (☎ /fax 60600; www.sandy beachresort.de; d with bathroom US$140) This boutique-style labour of love, with beachfront bungalows on the magnificent white-sand beach at the northern end of Foa, is popular with

---

WILLIAM MARINER

Thanks to a series of serendipitous incidents, the world has an extensive account of the customs, language, religion and government of the Tongans before the arrival of Christianity.

In February 1805 William Charles Mariner, the well-educated 15-year-old son of an English sea captain, went to sea on the privateer *Port-au-Prince*. The voyage of plunder and pillage took the ship around the Americas and through the Pacific, finally anchoring at the northern end of Lifuka in the Ha'apai Group on 29 November 1806. The crew were immediately welcomed with yams and barbecued pork. The reception seemed friendly enough, but the following day, they became increasingly aware that some sort of plot was afoot and that appropriate caution should be exercised in dealing with the Tongans.

Captain Brown, the whaling master who had assumed command upon the death of the original skipper several months earlier, was convinced that the threat was imaginary and chose to ignore it. On 1 December the attack was launched while 300 hostile Tongans were aboard the ship. The British, sorely outnumbered, chose to destroy the ship, its crew and its attackers rather than allow it to be taken. Young Mariner had gone to procure the explosives when he met with several locals, who escorted him ashore past the fallen bodies of his shipmates.

Mariner was persecuted by the Tongans until he was summoned by Finau 'Ulukalala I, the reigning chief of Ha'apai. The king assumed that Mariner was the captain's son, or at least a young chief in his own country, and ordered that his life be preserved.

Meanwhile, the *Port-au-Prince*, which hadn't been destroyed, was dragged ashore, raided and burned. The conflagration heated the cannons sufficiently to cause them to fire, creating a general panic among the Tongans. Calmly accepting his fate, Mariner pantomimed an explanation of the phenomenon and initiated a sort of rapport with the Tongans that would carry him through the following four years.

Although a few other crew members of the *Port-au-Prince* were spared, Mariner was the only one taken so completely under the wing of Finau and he was therefore privy to most of the goings-on in Tongan politics. He learned the language well and travelled about the island groups with the chief, observing and absorbing the finer points of ceremony and protocol among the people. He was given the name Toki 'Ukamea (Iron Axe). In a moment of compassion Finau appointed one of his royal wives, Mafi Hape, to be Mariner's adoptive mother, as he was sure the young man's real mother at home must have been extremely worried about him.

After the death of Finau, the king's son permitted William to leave Tonga on a passing English vessel. Anticlimactically, back in England, Will Mariner married, fathered 12 children and had an unremarkable career as a stockbroker. Were it not for a chance meeting in a London restaurant with an amateur anthropologist, Dr John Martin, his unique Tongan experiences might forever have been lost to the world. Martin, fascinated with Mariner's tale, suggested collaboration on a book and the result, *An Account of the Natives of the Tonga Islands*, is a masterpiece of Pacific literature. William Mariner drowned in a canal in southern England in 1853.

European holiday-makers and honeymoon-ers. The modern bungalows are comfortable though plain – offering no distraction from the beautiful surrounds – and are oriented for privacy and sunset terrace views (crack open the duty-free, ice is provided!). Large water tanks and solar panels guarantee warm, freshwater showers (a rarity in Ha'apai). In-cluded in the price are bicycles, snorkelling gear, kayaks, airport and town (bank) trans-fers, laundry service and borrowing rights to the English/German library. Horse riding (T$30) can be organised. No children under 12. Breakfast/dinner is US$9/29. Depend-ing on guest numbers, nonguests can book for three-course dinners (call before noon), which have a main-course choice of lobster, fresh fish or a meat dish. Snacks (sandwiches, burgers; T$7 to T$15), pizza (T$22) and cocktails are served at the terrace bar.

Getting There & Away

There's a sporadic bus service between Pan-gai and Faleloa, Foa's northernmost village, which generally serves students between about 8am and 4pm weekdays and 8am and noon Saturday (T$1 one way).

The 15km of mostly flat and reasonable road from Pangai to Sandy Beach Resort and Houmale'eia Beach takes around one hour to cycle; the taxi fare is about T$15. It's 1.5km north of Faleloa (a 15-minute walk from the village).

NUKUNAMO

The picture-postcard island viewed from the tip of Foa is Nukunamo, an uninhabited island with a shining white beach covered with beautiful shells. You can walk around and through the island (take thongs or san-dals – the harsh rock and coral is a killer on the feet); the mound here was built as a platform, used by members of the royal family for hunting pigeons. Coral heads in the reef between the two islands make for some beautiful easy-access snorkelling. You'll need a strong swimming ability and awareness of tide tables as currents through the pass are powerful. You can also cross by kayak (see p227).

HA'ANO

area 6.6 sq km / pop 773
Cultural travellers will get a good dose of traditional Tongan life on the strikingly clean and friendly island of Ha'ano. You may even be able to cruise its lovely beaches and four pleasant villages by horse and cart (contact the TVB or call ☎ 60374).

Getting to Ha'ano requires the finances to charter a boat (T$50 one way) or the time to wait for the water taxis that leave from Faleloa jetty, on Foa, early morning and midafternoon (around T$5 one way). You could turn your Ha'ano visit into an adven-turous day by taking a double kayak (p228) across from the tip of Foa in the morning and returning in the early afternoon. Check tides and weather reports wherever you get your kayak from and let them know where you're going. Bank on between one and two hours paddling each way.

UOLEVA

area 3.5 sq km
If you're looking for paradise on a budget, Uoleva is the place to come for it. With some of the finest, most peaceful white-sand beaches imaginable and little to do other than swim, snorkel and fish, those that can withstand the lack of creature comforts reap the natural rewards. A few people cross over from Lifuka to tend their livestock, but the island is basically unin-habited except for the penned pigs and the 'resort' (a loose term!) owners and guests. Yachts moor off the sandy cove.

There's some superb snorkelling around the reefs at the western end of Uoleva the broad bays on the island's sheltered north-ern shore and the protected Community Clam Circle. The 16th-century **burial mounds** at the centre are difficult to find without a guide.

Sleeping & Eating

Uoleva's (very basic) accommodation has unbeatable, absolute beachfront positions on a broad, white-sand beach on the north-west coast. Bring your own drinks, some food and mosquito repellent for your stay, which can be booked directly or through the TVB. The only trouble with this para-dise is that there's no love lost between Uol-eva's 'resort' owners.

Daiana Resort (☎ 60612; s/d/f fale T$18/25/45) This is an absolute beach-bum paradise and a great place to stay, where you can ponder the stars and lapping waves over the nightly beach bonfire. Set in a coconut plantation, just metres from the beach, the *tapa*-lined *fale* have mats over sandy floors and enclosed sitting areas. There's no denying the bathroom facilities are rudimentary (water is pumped from the well for a shower), but that contributes to its charm. The owners go fishing every night and cook the catch (which may include lobster) to serve in the mosquito-mesh enclosed kitchen-dining *fale*. Breakfast/dinner is T$5/12; book meals ahead. On Sunday, guests can assist in the preparation of the *'umu*, then feast on it an hour later (T$12).

Captain Cook Resort (☎ 77106, 60014; s/d cabins T$18/25) Dappled sunlight streams through shade-giving trees onto the attractive, sandy grounds around these basic wood-panelled cabins. Each contains good beds, mosquito nets and a funky hurricane lamp, and shares the basic bathroom facilities. The blue, absolute beachfront cabin is the pick of the bunch. Dinner (T$12; book ahead) includes a generous spread of four tasty Tongan dishes. Breakfast is T$6 and kitchen use per day is T$4.50. Handlines, snorkelling gear (T$4) and a single kayak (T$15) are available. Lone travellers (particularly women) have found this environment, at times edgy, uncomfortably isolated.

Getting There & Away
You can walk or wade (there is one deep channel to cross) the 1.5km south from Lifuka to Uoleva on the right tide. It takes around 40 minutes to walk from Pangai to Hulu'ipaongo Point on the southern tip of Lifuka (taxi T$5), around 20 minutes to cross between the islands, and a further hour or so to reach Uoleva's resorts. Get local advice and only cross at low tide, or an hour or so either side of low tide (it can be dangerous – locals have drowned crossing here). Do not cross on a windy day, if the sea is high or if the current is too strong as there is the danger of being swept away. Check tide charts at the TVB or Mariner's Café.

Both resorts offer transfers for guests from Pangai (T$15 one way), providing a free airport-to-wharf service. Alternatively, catch a ride on a 'Uiha-bound boat (see opposite) and ask to be dropped at Uoleva.

To charter a small boat for a full day (around T$50) contact the TVB, the resorts themselves or Pangai guesthouses.

'UIHA
The conservative and traditional island of 'Uiha is a friendly place with two villages: 'Uiha, with a wharf, and Felemea, about 1.5km south. 'Uiha's community nursery propagates endangered fruit trees, and rare and medicinal plants from various islands. Its fish and seafood stocks end up in Tongatapu's best restaurants.

Sights & Activities
A large, elevated burial ground in the centre of 'Uiha village contains **royal tombs**. Accompanied by much pomp and ceremony in 1988, the tombs of three relatively obscure members of the royal family were shifted here, two from Pangai and one from

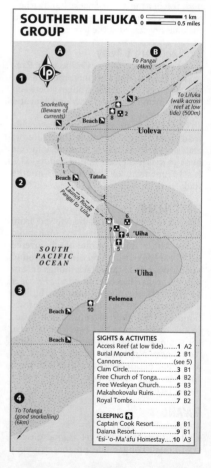

SOUTHERN LIFUKA GROUP

SIGHTS & ACTIVITIES	
Access Reef (at low tide)	1 A2
Burial Mound	2 B1
Cannons	(see 5)
Clam Circle	3 B1
Free Church of Tonga	4 B2
Free Wesleyan Church	5 B3
Makahokovalu Ruins	6 B2
Royal Tombs	7 B2

SLEEPING	
Captain Cook Resort	8 B1
Daiana Resort	9 B1
'Esi-'o-Ma'afu Homestay	10 A3

THE MARGARITA

On 26 January 1863 the Peruvian black-birder (slave ship) *Margarita* left Callao (Lima) and was never seen again. According to a preacher on 'Uiha at the time, a ship called in and lured several islanders aboard. When their families on shore realised what had happened, they banged iron pots, hoping to deceive the slavers into returning to shore to pick up more people who'd decided to go along.

The ploy worked, the ship was seized, the Tongans were released and then the ship, which was probably the *Margarita*, was subsequently destroyed.

Tongatapu. Ostensibly the project was to consolidate the tombs of the royal family, but rumours of treasure in the cemetery compound prompted the king to look for an excuse to excavate the otherwise *tapu* area. Nothing of importance was unearthed during the excavation.

Walking beyond the royal tombs, you can't miss 'Uiha's fascinating **Free Wesleyan Church**. As evidence of the sinking of the *Margarita*, the 'Uihans display two cannons, one planted in the ground outside the church in 'Uiha village and the other in front of the altar inside – the latter is used as a baptismal font!

A pleasant 10-minute walk north from 'Uiha village leads to the **Makahokovalu Ruins**. There hasn't been much theorising as to the purpose or origin of the complex, which features nine stones standing on end in an L-shape (though the name means 'Eight Joined Stones') and a few similar stones lying about the site, reportedly scattered by a cyclone.

You can gain a fairly good insight into the preparation and production of village handicrafts here by looking on as the locals do their nimble work. Horse riding or boat trips to other islands for picnics, swimming, snorkelling and fishing can be arranged through 'Esi-'o-Ma'afu Homestay.

Sleeping & Eating

'Esi-'o-Ma'afu Homestay (☎ 60605, 60438; VHF Channel 16; fale s/d T$20/25) You'll get a good introduction to village life (and will probably be woken in the early hours by enthusiastic singing and church bells) at this friendly, welcoming place right on the beach at Felemea. Snooze in a thatch-and-fibro *fale* by night and swing in a hammock by day. Shared facilities are clean and there's a small kitchen (use per day T$3), or with notice the owners will prepare delicious Tongan food (breakfast T$6, dinner T$12 to T$15). You can also book through the TVB.

Getting There & Away

Boats to 'Uiha depart from Pangai most days (most dependably on Saturday and Monday) and can be arranged at the TVB or the waterfront kiosk opposite the market. It costs around T$10 per person one way. The 'Esi-'o-Ma'afu Homestay provides transfers for T$25/30 for one/two people, one way.

TATAFA

The uninhabited island of Tatafa is just a short, low-tide walk across the reef from northern 'Uiha. It has a lovely surrounding beach, good snorkelling and a large colony of flying foxes. There's a rainwater cistern on the island but it's still wise to carry some water or to ask permission (on 'Uiha or Lifuka) to drink coconuts.

OTHER HA'APAI GROUP ISLANDS

TOFUA & KAO

From practically any west-facing shore in the Ha'apai group of islands the pyramid-like cone of Kao (Tonga's highest mountain) and the smouldering, volcanic Tofua (site of the mutiny on the *Bounty*) dominate the scene, and entice you to come a bit closer. Game fishing and diving around Kao and Tofua are excellent.

MUTINY ON THE BOUNTY BEACH

On Tofua's southwestern beach, on 28 April 1789, Captain Bligh of HMS *Bounty* and 18 loyals landed after the famous mutiny. Islanders clubbed quartermaster John Norton to death. Bligh and the rest of the men escaped and embarked on a 6500km journey to Timor in an open boat, with minimal rations and short of water, having not discovered Tofua's large freshwater lake.

HA'APAI GROUP

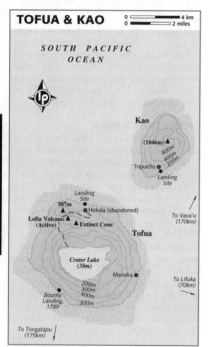

TOFUA & KAO

SOUTH PACIFIC OCEAN

Kao
(1046m)▲
800m
400m
200m
Topuefio
Landing Site

Landing Site
507m▲ ●Hokala (abandoned)
Lofia Volcano ▲
(Active) ▲Extinct Cone
Tofua
To Vava'u (170km)

Crater Lake (38m)
Manaka ●
To Lifuka (70km)

200m
300m
400m
Bounty Landing, 1789
300m

To Tongatapu (175km)

Tofua

area 55 sq km / pop 5

Lofia, Tonga's most active volcano, constantly smokes, steams, belches and rumbles near the crater's 507m-high northern rim. In 1874 the king evacuated the island due to excessive volcanic activity. People returned to live here, but the population remains tiny. This is increased as farmers return periodically to tend and harvest *kava,* which cover much of the island's outer slopes. Tofua also produces *tamanu* trees for canoes and *toa* (ironwood) in small noncommercial quantities. The *kilikili* (black volcanic slag pebbles used to decorate grave mounds throughout Tonga) come mostly from Kao and Tofua.

There's a reasonable campsite just above the landing site at Hokala on the northern shore, and fresh water may be available in a rainwater tank at the old school, along a path roughly 450m away. The track to the crater heads uphill from the school.

TOFUA'S CRATER

Climbing to the edge of Tofua's crater rim can be easily managed in a day and affords spectacular views of nearby Kao, Tofua's crater lake and the smouldering Lofia Volcano. It's a physically demanding trip. Be sure to carry plenty of water and wear sturdy, enclosed footwear and preferably long trousers. If you plan to climb down to the lake or to Lofia it's worth taking your time and camping on the old crater rim – it's mosquito-free but there's very little shade and no water.

The crater rim is a tough one-hour climb from the old school at Hokala. To find the track, look up towards the ridge; it's 50m due south from the old school. Once you've found the track, it's fairly easy to follow and heads south to southeast up the ridge, the vegetation gradually getting shorter as you climb. Look out for the beautiful orchids.

Much of the inner slopes of the crater are covered in tropical rainforest. At the crater rim is a campsite, and a series of small cairns marks a trail heading northwest. After about 30 minutes (before the vegetation finishes and the ash fields begin) a route leads down to Lofia Volcano and the Crater Lake. The difficult scramble down from the old crater rim, across the barren ash fields and up to the rim of Lofia takes about an hour. Take the direct route to Lofia then pass around its right side to get to the crater lake. (Steer clear of the volcano's noxious fumes.) At the bottom of the circular crater is a beautiful, crystal-clear 250m-deep lake, 38m above sea level (and, to complete the stats, covering 7 sq km). From the crater rim to the lake is about 45 minutes and there's no trail through the virgin rainforest that encircles the lake.

Kao

area 11.6 sq km / pop 0

On clear days, the immense and frighteningly beautiful volcanic cone of Kao is visible from Lifuka and the other main islands. Kao's 1046m summit is frequently shrouded in cloud. Rainforest skirts the bottom third of the mountain and the upper slopes are covered with dense ferns. The island is uninhabited, though farmers harvest *kava* here.

The tough four-hour climb to the summit, usually following one of the southern ridges, is not recommended without a guide as there is no marked trail, and the vegetation is very dense in places. Weather conditions rapidly change for the worse on the summit. When the cloud blows in, visibility can drop below 50m in a few minutes – and half-way up you'll be in the clouds and scrambling over mossy rocks on your hands and knees. Freshwater sources are unreliable; take plenty with you, along with warm, waterproof clothing. Good walking boots and trousers will make the trek much more enjoyable.

Strong swimmers will enjoy the dramatic snorkelling off Topuefio, Kao's southern landing site. There are plenty of large fish and a few coral heads cling to the volcanic rock, which suddenly drops off into the deep blue about 20m offshore.

Getting There & Away

Forest-covered red and black lava cliffs rise directly out of the surf and make landing at either island difficult, especially in a strong swell. You'll need a small dinghy to reach the shore and be careful of the slippery rocks when landing. On Tofua there's a landing site below the disused village of Hokala. The landing site on Kao is at Topuefio, which is marked by a couple of *fale*.

Tongans believe that the shark god, Tu'i Tofua, protects the passengers of any boat in the vicinity of Tofua. Should a boat sink, the vessel and its passengers will be carried to shore by benevolent sharks!

Reaching Tofua or Kao is not easy. Few boats are prepared to make the journey and if they are it will be expensive. If you can get a large group together in Lifuka you may be able to charter the Ministry of Education's launch MV *Pako* (T$1700 with crew for five days, plus T$10 per hour waiting time) which is a suitable boat for the trip. Happy Ha'apai Divers (p228) and Mariner's Guided Camping Tours (p227) both organise diving and camping/tramping trips to the islands. Another option is to hook up with one of the aid organisations, who organise trips out to Tofua a few times a year so their workers can experience it. They're happy to have any other travellers along and just divide expenses (it saves them some money too) for transport there and back. Any tourist would need to have camping gear and provisions.

It's essential to carry plenty of food and water.

LUAHOKO

The island of Luahoko is known for the many sea birds and sea turtles that call it home. The island has protected status to conserve the birds and turtles, but some

Tongans still occasionally come here to (illegally) collect eggs. It's about 10km or 15km northwest of Pangai.

HA'AFEVA

From Ha'afeva, around 40km southwest of Lifuka, you'll get beautiful views of Tofua and Kao and great sunsets. The island's small land area and relatively high population make it a crowded place with plantations occupying all uninhabited land outside the village, but it has a friendly nature. On a reef northwest of the island, the sunken fishing boat *Eki'aki* makes for good diving.

Ha'afeva is accessed most easily on the MV *'Olovaha*, which stops or hovers here on its weekly trips between Tongatapu and Lifuka. See p286 for schedules. Small local boats go from Ha'afeva to the tiny outer islands of Matuku, Kotu and Tungua, all of which offer excellent snorkelling.

NOMUKA & NOMUKA'IKI

Petite Nomuka (population 550) was historically important because of its freshwater springs. The first European to arrive on the

HA'APAI GROUP

FONUAFO'OU...NO FONUAFO'OU

From 1781 to 1865 there were repeated reports of a shoal 60km west of Nomuka. In 1877 smoke was seen rising from that spot and by 1885 a cinder, scoria and pumice island 50m high and 2km long had risen from the sea, spewed up in a violent sub-marine eruption.

In recognition of its birth, Tonga planted its flag on the island and claimed it for the king. It was named Fonuafo'ou – meaning 'New Land' (or Falcon Island as it was referred to by Europeans).

Then in 1894 Fonuafo'ou went missing. Less than two years later there appeared an island 320m high, which subsequently also disappeared. In 1927 it emerged again and by 1930 had risen in a series of fiery eruptions to 130m in height and 2.5km in length. By 1949 there was again no trace of Fonuafo'ou, which had once more been eroded by the sea.

Unless you're on a private yacht, the only way to catch a glimpse of Fonuafo'ou (if it's around when you're there!) is to ride one of the ferries returning to Tongatapu from Niuafo'ou, which normally pass within a few kilometres of it.

---

island was the Dutchman Abel Tasman, who named it Rotterdam while picking up water there. Subsequent well-known visitors included Captain James Cook, Captain William Bligh and William Mariner.

A large, brackish lake dominates much of Nomuka's hilly interior and the island is surrounded by raised coral formations up to 45m high. There are two smaller lakes near the island's northern end, one of which appears reddish orange from the air during dry periods, due to algae concentration. Nomuka's only accommodation is 'Eseta's Guesthouse (contact the Tongatapu TVB).

Numaka'iki, the companion island to Nomuka, has an old prison ruin and shipwreck to explore.

See p227 for details on organised kayaking and camping trips to the islands.

Access is normally by small boat from either Lifuka or Ha'afeva. However, the Free

Church of Tonga operates a boat that travels between Tongatapu, Nomuka and Lifuka (see p288). Sometimes it runs weekly, sometimes monthly.

Though it's not on their schedule, the inter-island ferries may occasionally stop in midwater near here, a fascinating sight when smaller boats come out to meet it.

TELEKIVAVA'U

If you've dreamed of having your own island paradise, this tiny island has the key ingredients – exclusivity, solitude, seclusion… and lots of languid luxury. Surrounded by a beautiful reef, **Villa Mamana** (toll free ☎ 86-VM-TONGA; www.villamamana.com; villa US$1060) exclusively hosts one party of four adults at a time (children under 12 are free) on otherwise uninhabited Telekivava'u. Rates include boat transfers (from Tongatapu), meals, beverages and excursions, and satellite phone access.

Vava'u Group

To really experience Vava'u, you have to get out on the water. Picturesque at every turn, stunning, uncrowded stretches of white sand appear like the swathe of an artist's brush skimming through an aquamarine palette before plunging into an inky blue abyss.

Regarded as one of the world's great sailing locations, this tranquil island group is fringed with vibrant coral reefs, offering myriad channels, deep waterways and secluded anchorages, along with one of the South Pacific's most protected harbours, the Port of Refuge. On other islands, sheer basalt cliffs drop 30m into the water, some pock-marked by caves accessible only via boat, or in the case of concealed Mariner's Cave, by diving beneath the water's surface.

The many protected coves and caverns provide exquisite diving sites, and there are plenty of vibrant heads of coral immersed in a tropical fish soup to explore. Sea-kayaking, mountain biking, bushwalking, impressive game-fishing, surfing and even abseiling into caves are possible here. Uniqueness joins beauty in the humpback breeding season, when dedicated whale-watching outfits organise swims with these awe-inspiring giants.

Neiafu is home to a third of Vava'u's people – along with restaurants, bars and a Friday yacht race – and is the only place with any bustle. On Sundays the town is empty and quiet, aside from the uplifting singing emanating from churches. Outside Neiafu, the rest of the population live among emerald hills in villages scattered across 50-odd thickly wooded islands.

Of course, if all the available activities sound a bit too energetic, there are always the beaches at various eclectic island resorts, perfect for lazing in the sun, dabbling in a bit of snorkelling and soaking up the sublime views.

VAVA'U GROUP

HIGHLIGHTS

- Snorkelling and kayaking with **humpback whales** (p248), and scanning the horizon for breaches over breakfast at island resorts
- Getting the **wind in your sails** (p246) between beautiful islands, beaches and coves
- **Diving and snorkelling** (p246) in a clear fish soup above stunning coral gardens and geological marvels
- Delving underwater into wondrous **Mariner's Cave** (p262)
- Feasting on paella and revelling at rustic **La Paella** (p260) on Tapana

- POPULATION: 15,715
- AREA: 119 SQ KM

VAVA'U GROUP

VAVA'U GROUP

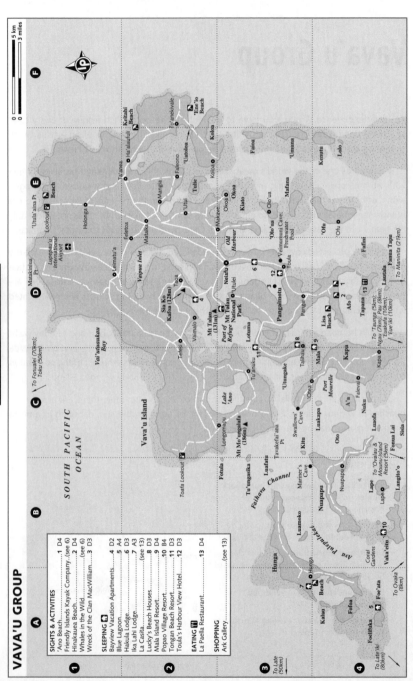

SIGHTS & ACTIVITIES
'Ano Beach..1 D4
Friendly Islands Kayak Company..(see 6)
Hinakauea Beach...............................2 D4
Whales in the Wild..........................(see 6)
Wreck of the Clan MacWilliam.......3 D3

SLEEPING
Bayview Vacation Apartments........4 D2
Blue Lagoon.....................................5 A4
Hakula Lodge..................................6 D3
Ika Lahi Lodge.................................7 A3
La Casita.......................................(see 13)
Lucky's Beach Houses...................(see 13)
Mala Island Resort..........................8 D3
Popao Village Resort........................9 D4
Tongan Beach Resort......................10 B4
Toula's Harbour View Hotel...........11 D3
                                          12 D3

EATING
La Paella Restaurant.......................13 D4

SHOPPING
Ark Gallery...................................(see 13)

0 _____ 5 km
0 _____ 3 miles

HISTORY

Vava'u is believed to have been settled for around 2000 years. Its first European visitor was Don Francisco Antonio Mourelle of Spain. His ship, the *Princesa,* ran short of supplies while sailing from the Philippines to Spanish America, and after a fruitless visit to the volcanic island Fonualei (which they named Amargura, meaning 'bitterness'), they sighted Vava'u Island on 4 March 1781. Mourelle named Neiafu's harbour Puerto de Refugio or 'Port of Refuge', though Tongans knew it as Lolo 'a Halaevalu, or 'Oil of the Princess Halaevalu', because of the smooth, natural sheen that appears on the water's surface on calm days. Mourelle claimed the new-found paradise for Spain and named it Islas de Don Martin de Mayorga after the viceroy of Mexico. The islanders welcomed the Spaniards and stocked their ship before they departed.

In 1793, Spain sent Captain Alessandro Malaspina to Vava'u to survey the new territory and inform the inhabitants of the Spanish claim – allegedly somewhere in Vava'u a decree of Spanish sovereignty is buried – but the captain didn't stay on Vava'u for long. Other than dominating diners with paella on Tapana Island, the Spanish have not pursued their claim.

William Mariner also spent a great deal of time here (see the boxed text, p236), during which he was involved in Finau 'Ulukalala I's conquest of Vava'u. When the English brig *Favourite* landed on Vava'u Island in November 1810, the then king of Vava'u and son of 'Ulukalala I, Finau 'Ulukalala II, permitted Mariner to return home with it.

But when he saw the marvels on board the ship, the Tongan king begged to be permitted to accompany Mariner. He said he was willing to forsake his princely life in the islands for even a lowly station in England. He wanted to learn to read, write and operate mechanical wonders.

Captain Fisk of the *Favourite* refused young Finau's entreaties, whereupon the Tongan made Mariner swear that he would some day return and carry the king back to England. Unfortunately, Mariner never returned to Tonga.

'Ulukalala II's tomb (p258) can be seen in the village of Feletoa on Vava'u Island. His son was converted to Christianity by King George Tupou I of Ha'apai. When 'Ulukalala III died, George was entrusted to look after the throne of Vava'u for the boy king 'Ulukalala IV. But George seized the opportunity to add the group to his own realm and in 1845 he formed a united Tonga.

CLIMATE

Vava'u has Tonga's wettest climate, with most rain falling in occasional tropical storms between late November and April, which is also the cyclone season. March is the wettest month, but gentle warm rains and occasional downpours occur at any time of year. Vava'u is generally warmer than Tongatapu, and although it can be particularly hot and sticky during the cyclone season, this can be a great time to visit, with fine days if you can stand the humidity. See p285 for information on air travel during the cyclone season.

The prevailing easterly and southeasterly trade winds blow at an average of 15 knots. Between November and April, both northerly and northwesterly winds can occur, usually accompanied by more unsettled seas which can impact on activities, such as sailing, diving and fishing on the western side of the group.

See p277 for more information.

ACTIVITIES

Vava'u is the kingdom's adventure playground, geared towards activity-based tourism, with plenty of locations (and smooth,

---

WRECK OF THE CLAN MACWILLIAM

The wreck of the copra steamer *Clan Mac-William* lies in 37m of water in the southern arm of the Port of Refuge. Built in 1918, this 127m, 6000-tonne Clan Shipping Line freighter steamed into Neiafu Harbour in December 1927 with a smouldering fire in the No 3 copra hold. The forward holds collapsed, cracking open the steamer's plates. One story has it that the captain and first engineer refused to abandon ship and went down with it; another relates that the captain locked the first engineer into the engine room to prevent him from abandoning the effort to save the ship!

The wreck is now teeming with marine life, and is a popular dive site.

VAVA'U GROUP

clued-in operations) to dive, snorkel, sail, whale-watch, surf, fish, kayak, mountain bike and hike. See p273 for further details. Many businesses and activity operators still communicate over VHF radio and most will be happy to assist you in making contact.

Diving & Snorkelling

Vava'u's impressive dive sites range from hard and soft coral gardens and encrusted wrecks (see the boxed text, p245) to vast sea caves and other geological marvels. Contact Vava'u's two dive operators for full details on dive sites.

Dolphin Pacific Diving (☎ /fax 70292; VHF Channel 71; www.dolphinpacificdiving.com; PO Box 131, Neiafu) is a friendly operation based alongside Puataukanave Hotel on the waterfront. It offers two-/three-tank boat dives (T$140/200), snorkelling trips (T$60) and runs PADI/IDEA Open Water (T$550/500), advanced (T$500/450), rescue diver (T$550) and Divemaster (T$1050) courses. The 'dive and whale-watch combination' is great value at just T$180, including two-tank dives. Sunset cruises (T$40) and sole boat charters (T$800) are also options. Air refills cost T$9 and snorkelling gear is available for hire.

Beluga Diving (☎ /fax 70327; VHF Channel 16; www.belugadivingvavau.com; PO Box 70, Neiafu), along the waterfront at Fangafoa Marina in Neiafu, offers one-/two-tank dives (at two different sites) from US$35/65, and PADI courses from Open Water (US$230) to Divemaster (US$750). Full gear is included in course rates and is available for hire, but remember to check it all over before heading out on a boat. You can hire a mask, snorkel and fins here for US$12 or take a guided boat-based snorkelling trip for US$25 (including gear, minimum four snorkellers).

Most boat tours and some of the whale-watching trips include a little snorkelling, such as into Mariner's and Swallows' Caves or over coral gardens. Diving, fishing and whale-watching operators will run snorkelling trips along with their regular excursions for around T$80. Joining a diving trip as a snorkeller is usually no problem, though some sites lie at reasonably deep depths, over 5m.

For a good snorkelling day trip, head out to Mala Island Resort (p260) for lunch and snorkel from its beach to the beautiful Japanese Gardens nearby.

Fishing

Regarded as one of the best game-fishing destinations in the Pacific, Vava'u is a prime site for catching marlin and has a few resorts catering primarily to anglers. Almost all fishing is concentrated in the area west of Vava'u where the ocean is over 1000m deep. See p275 for general fishing information.

The Ikapuna Store (see p256) in Neiafu is stocked with lures and other fishing commodities, and sometimes has fishing gear available to hire.

Low-season (January to April) price reductions may be possible and most fishing charters listed here can be contacted on VHF Channel 71.

Dora Malia (☎ 70698; ikapuna@kalianet.to; Ikapuna Store, PO Box 106, Neiafu) Fully equipped game boat with light and heavy trolling gear. Charters are T$600/800 per day for two/four anglers.

Hakula Sport Fishing Charters (☎ 70872, 71381; www.fishtonga.com; PO Box 23, Neiafu) Fully equipped game-fishing boat (A$900, maximum six anglers). Trips to the exciting fishing grounds around Tofua and Koa in the Ha'apai Group are a possibility.

Ika Lahi Lodge (☎ /fax 70611; www.tongafishing.com; PO Box 24, Neiafu) Based on the island of Hunga, operates charters on fully rigged game boats with Shimano tackle (NZ$800/1400 per half/full day, maximum four anglers).

Mounu Island Resort (☎ 70747; VHF Channel 77; www.mounuisland.com) Can arrange game-fishing charters (maximum four anglers).

Target One (☎ /fax 70647; www.visitvavau.com/target1; Private Bag 3, Neiafu) Game fishing on a fully equipped fast boat for US$500/600/700 for two/three/four anglers.

Sailing & Boating

This is the perfect way to experience Vava'u – cruising the islands and stopping to snorkel and wander beaches at will.

Moorings (☎ 70016; fax 70428; VHF Channel 72; www.tongasailing.com; PO Box 119, Neiafu) charters out catamarans and monohulls ranging from 12m to 15m, sleeping up to 10 passengers. Prices vary according to the season, but range from NZ$480 to NZ$1450 for bare-boat charters during high season. Additional costs for a skipper/cook/guide are NZ$170/140/140 per day plus food. Check its website for details and book direct.

Melinda Sea Adventures (☎ 70975, 70861; VHF Channel 16; www.sailtonga.com) operates the traditionally rigged gaff ketch, *Melinda*, a beautiful sight under sail in Vava'u. You can do as much (or as little) sailing as you want on the fully crewed charters on this 13m, smooth-sailing craft which sleeps two to four guests. Minimum three-day charters cost US$175 per person per day. Day trips (whole-boat charter US$350) and whale-watching are also available. Contact the operators for further details and off-season rates.

SY Impetuous (www.sailingtonga.com) is a fully crewed 51ft Beneteau available for day sails around Vava'u (up to 10 people) and flexible longer charters. You can choose how hands-on you want to be. If you want to feel the wind in the sails, join the yacht in Vava'u and sail to Ha'apai or Nuku'alofa (or vice versa), or alight in Fiji or Samoa. Fully catered charters cost US$190 per day per person for a maximum of six people in three double cabins. There's a dive compressor on board.

Sailing Safaris (☎ 70650; VHF Channel 68; sailing safaris@kalianetvav.to; PO Box 46, Neiafu) hires out a 26ft yacht (bare-boat/skippered from US$150/250 per day) and also runs five-day live-aboard sailing courses for US$1500 (up to two people). Skippered speedboats are available for US$300 per day.

Sailing dinghies can be hired from **Aquarium Adventures** (☎ 70493; aquariumadventures@yahoo.com) for T$25/125 per hour/day.

A number of the Neiafu fishing, diving, whale-watching and sailing operators run day boat excursions that typically include Swallows' and Mariner's Caves, picnicking on an uninhabited island and snorkelling at an offshore reef, but they'll also cater to individual whims. The presence of humpback whales (July to November) is a special bonus. Check at the Tonga Visitors Bureau (TVB) for seasonal operators.

Soki's Island Tours (contact the TVB) runs boat tours (T$50, minimum three people) guided by a born-and-bred local, Soki, that are tailored to your interests, such as snorkelling over coral reefs and into Swallows' Cave, and fishing trips.

Hakula Lodge (☎ 70872, 71381; www.fishtonga.com) boat tours (T$65, lunch T$15) depart Neiafu at 10am for snorkelling, exploration of Nuku Island, Swallows' and Mariner's Caves and the Japanese Gardens, lunch at Mala Island and return at 4pm.

Coconet Café (☎ 71311), on the waterfront nearby the market, hires out small power boats for T$70/80 per half/full day, plus petrol.

MAPS

A condensed version of the sea chart covering Vava'u (and showing all decent anchorages) is available from the Moorings (opposite). The Moorings charter yachts have their own sea charts, though you can pick up a laminated colour version in their office. Alternatively, pick one up before you arrive in Vava'u (see p280). Yachties should be aware that these charts are not accurate enough for GPS navigation.

Sea-Kayaking

Island resorts and beachside accommodations invariably all have a kayak or two for guests to paddle to caves, nearby islands and good snorkelling spots. Between July and November paddling alongside humpback whales is possible.

Beluga Diving (opposite) rents single/double sea kayaks with dry bags for US$20/30 per day, and Adventure Backpackers (p253) hires out kayaks (nonocean-going) with jackets for T$30 per day.

Friendly Islands Kayak Company (☎ /fax 70173; VHF Channel 71; www.fikco.com; Private Bag 10, Neiafu; ☷ Jun-Dec) has been revealing some of Tonga's magic to kayaking adventurers on their camping and paddling expeditions around Vava'u (and Ha'apai) since 1991. This environmentally conscious company provides truly unique experiences (and supplies excellent equipment) on five-/nine-/eleven-day packages (with four/six/eight days of guided kayaking) for US$900/1790/2130. No experience is required, but all trips require a minimum of four people (and a maximum of 10). Tents, camping mats and snorkelling equipment are provided for a fee. Routes are strongly influenced by weather and tide patterns. Other multiadventure tours include whale-watching, diving, sailing and mountain-biking as well as kayaking.

Surfing

Vava'u's surf breaks around the three- to five-foot range, and you'll need a boat to access it. Booties are almost as imperative as a surfboard and though the water's warm, pack a wetsuit to counter the chill factor.

Vava'u Surf & Adventure Tours (☎ 71283, 12515; http://groups.msn.com/cafetropicanavavautonga/; Private Bag 34, Neiafu) has received glowing reports from surf travellers for its well-organised yet laid-back guided boat trips (half-/full-day per person T$75/105) that drop surfers on tried and tested uncrowded reef breaks depending on daily conditions. Nonsurfing partners are well looked after (dropped off at snorkelling spots and on uninhabited islands for explorations), extra sights such as Mariner's Cave and Swallows' Cave can be included, and surf/accommodation packages can be arranged.

Whale-Watching

If you're staying on an island resort or sailing through Vava'u's waters between July and November, you only need to patiently keep an eye seaward to whale-watch. Vava'u has fast become the world's top whale-watching destination.

Whales Alive (www.whalesalive.org.au) is a non-government organisation devoted to the protection of whales. Concern for their welfare (particularly in relation to swimming 'with' them) has seen industry standards implemented to limit the negative impact and possible stress to breeding whales.

Operators (p246) fit whale-watching between dives and run specific whale-watching trips. Sometimes videographers accompany whale-watching charters and sell DVDs spliced with footage from your whale encounter. At the time of writing, uniform rates for the following companies (generally with a minimum of four people) were T$150.

Melinda Sea Adventures (☎ 70975, 70861; VHF Channel 16; www.sailtonga.com) Sailing, snorkelling and whale-watching are often combined in day trips (including lunch; minimum two people) on *Melinda*.

Sailing Safaris (☎ /fax 70650; VHF Channel 68; www .sailingsafaris.com; PO Box 153, Neiafu) Full-day whale-watching trips on hydrophone-equipped *Whale Song*. Snorkel gear and refreshments available (lunch T$15).

Whale Discoveries (☎ /fax 70173; VHF Channel 71; www.whalediscoveries.com; Private Bag 10, Neiafu) Informative, ecologically sensitive whale-watching trips (US$82 including lunch and drinks) aboard a 14-passenger rigid inflatable with sun canopy and toilet. Snorkelling gear provided. Note: no swimming with whales.

Whale Watch Vava'u (☎ 70747; VHF Channel 77; www .mounuisland.com) A long-time operator with a purpose-built vessel for small-group trips and an enviable reputation and uncanny knack for finding whales. Lunch can be arranged.

Whales in the Wild (☎ 71381, 70872; VHF Channel 71; www.whales-in-the-wild.com) A friendly operation with a shaded boat for up to 12 passengers. Free hotel pick-up and special family rates available. Swimmers/non-swimmers T$150/120.

WhaleSwim Adventures (☎ 71266; www.whale swim.com) Multiday swim with the whales expeditions and organised holidays.

Other Activities

Bird-watchers can peruse the local avian scene in Mt Talau National Park (p252) and visit the island breeding site of Maninita (p263).

You can peddle around on your own mountain-bike exploration of the islands connected to Vava'u Island (p257) or take a guided mountain-biking trip. The Friendly Islands Kayak Company (p247) runs half-/full-day mountain-biking trips (T$30/50), in addition to their action-packed Adventure Week (US$1570 including food and accommodation) between May and February which includes sea-kayaking, whale-watching, mountain biking and sailing or diving.

Few people rock climb in Vava'u, but the short (around 50m) sea cliffs of Tu'ungasika and Luafatu (among others) look promising. Logistics could be tricky and you would need your own climbing gear. Vava'u Surf & Adventure Tours (p247) compiles adventure tours between July and October, one incorporating walking on Kapa Island, abseiling into a sinkhole and swimming out of Swallows' Cave (T$130, or T$150 including a swim into Mariner's Cave). Small-group snorkelling and island-hopping boat trips, including Swallows' Cave and Mariner's Cave (half-/full-day T$50/80) are also possible.

FESTIVALS & EVENTS

The Vava'u Festival, the biggest festival of the year, takes place during the week leading up to 4 May, the crown prince's birthday. This week-long party includes a variety of events, from processions to weaving, dance and song, sports matches, drinking bashes and feasts. It now incorporates the Vava'u Tuna Fest. Other fishing tournaments are held throughout the year. Fishing tournaments take place in the deep waters of Vava'u (to the west of Hunga etc), but fisher folk congregate around Neiafu for meetings, awards and so on. They often include other meals and events on Mala and other islands, while fishing guests will stay at fishing-focused islands and in Neiafu. Contact Hakula Sport Fishing Charters (p246) for further information.

VAVA'U ISLAND

area 90 sq km / pop 12,418
The hilly island of Vava'u is the main island
in the Vava'u Group, with nearby islands
linked to it by causeways. Outside of Neiafu
are quiet villages and *'api* (plantations).

NEIAFU
pop 5650
Nestled between several low hills in the Port
of Refuge, Neiafu is Tonga's most picturesque harbour town and the Vava'u Group's
administrative capital. It's the only town
with any sort of bustle, particularly around
the market on Saturday, and has a good selection of restaurants and upbeat bars.

History
Prior to European contact, Neiafu was a sacred burial ground of the indigenous people,
and political unrest and tribal skirmishes
were forbidden. Every person entering the
village was required to wear a *ta'ovala* (pandanus mat tied around the waist and worn
on formal occasions) as a symbol of esteem
for the chiefs entombed there.

The waterfront area around the Halaevalu Wharf is called Matangimalie (Pleasant Winds). Formerly it was the site of a
palace built by Finau 'Ulukalala II. In 1808
Finau built a fortification on slightly higher
ground at Pou'ono. The fort was called
Vaha'akeli (Between Trenches), a reference
to the moats surrounding it.

Information
Many businesses in Vava'u communicate
by VHF radio and a yachties' information
net is held on VHF Channel 6 at 8.30am
Monday to Saturday.

Film is sold at several shops around Neiafu,
though the best retailer is **Pacific Timber & Hardware** (☎ 70500; Fatafehi Rd). It sells slide, black-
and-white and colour print film, as well as
waterproof disposable cameras.

BOOKSHOPS
Most places to stay have libraries and/or
book exchanges for guests. Tropical Tease
(p256) has a selection of titles for exchange.
Friendly Islands Bookshop (☎ 70505; Fatafehi Rd)
Limited stock, but with a few excellent titles on Tonga and
some children's books, magazines and film.

EMERGENCY
Fire (☎ 933, 70233; Tu'i Rd)
Medical emergencies (☎ 933)
Police (☎ 922, 70236; Tu'i Rd) Clerical division (for driving
licences) is open from 8.30am to 4.30pm Monday and Tues-
day, and 8.30am to 12.30pm Wednesday to Friday.

INTERNET ACCESS
Aquarium Adventures (☎ 70493; per hr T$12) Also
burns CDs.
Café Tropicana (☎ 71322; Fatafehi Rd; per 15min T$3)
Also burns CDs.
Coconet Café (☎ 71311; VHF 16; per 5min T$1;
🕒 8.30am-5.30pm Mon-Sat) Waterfront, below Tongan
Bob's. Printing and faxes from T$1 per page.
Maamamo'onia Hall (☎ 70570; Tu'i Rd; per 15/30/60min
T$1.50/3/5; 🕒 8.30am-11pm Mon-Sat) In the high school.

LAUNDRY
Most places to stay offer laundry service or
washing facilities for guests.
Adventure Backpackers (☎ /fax 70955; www.visit
vavau.com/backpackers; Fatafehi Rd) Per load T$6.
Coconet Café (☎ 71311) Waterfront, below Tongan
Bob's. Wash/dry/fold T$5/5/1.

LIBRARIES
Vava'u Library (Fatafehi Rd; 🕒 noon-5pm Tue-Fri, 9am-
1pm Sat) Opposite the post office. Annual membership costs
T$3. Computer usage (no Internet) per hour T$2.40.

MEDIA
Vava'u FM1 is found at 89.3FM, and satellite TV can be accessed at some of the available accommodation. The Friendly Island
Bookshop has some Tongan newspapers
which sometimes have a bit of information
in English.

MEDICAL SERVICES
Italian Clinic and Pharmacy (☎ /fax 70607;
i_clinic@kalianetvav.to; Main Wharf; 🕒 clinic 8.30am-
12.30pm Mon-Fri, 8.30-10.30am Sat; pharmacy 8.30am-
2.30pm Mon-Sat) Consultations with Dr Alfredo Carafa
cost T$25 to T$35; dive health certification is T$25. Stocks
antibiotics and can have prescription medicines within 24
hours if not stocked.
Prince Wellington Ngu Hospital (☎ 70201, 70204;
🕒 24hr, pharmacy 8.30am-12.30pm, 1.30-4.30pm &
6-11pm Mon-Fri) Outpatient and dental clinics (rudimentary equipment) also available. For emergencies.

MONEY
ANZ (Fatafehi Rd; 🕒 9am-4pm Mon-Fri) Has ATM inside
bank. Provides cash advances on Visa, MasterCard and JCB.

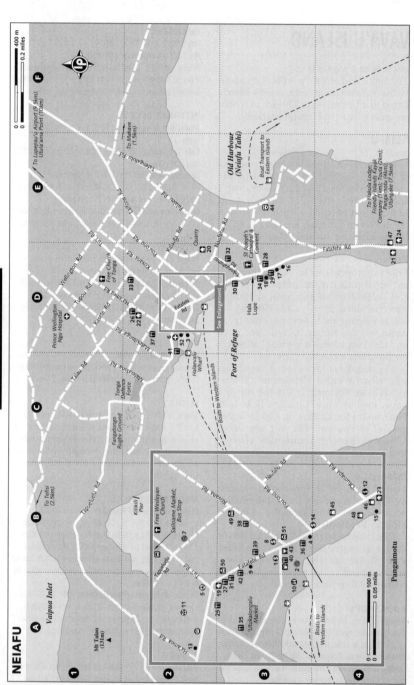

NEIAFU

VAVA'U GROUP

MBF (Fatafehi Rd; 9am-4pm Mon-Fri, 9am-11.30am Sat)

Western Union (70888; Fatafehi Rd; 8.30am-4.30pm Mon-Fri, 8.30am-noon Sat)

Westpac Bank of Tonga (70168; Fatafehi Rd; 9am-4pm Mon-Fri, 8.30am-11.30am Sat) Has an ATM, provides cash advances on Visa and MasterCard and offers MoneyGram money transfer services.

POST
Post office (70002; Fatafehi Rd; 8.30am-4pm) North of 'Utukalongalu market. Poste restante mail (c/o General Delivery, Post Office, Neiafu, Vava'u, Tonga).

TELEPHONE & FAX
Public phones are available outside the TCC office and Adventure Backpackers.

Tonga Communications Corporation (TCC; 70101; Fatafehi Rd, behind post office; 8am-11pm Mon-Fri, 7am-2pm Sat) Offers fax services and sells phonecards and SIM cards.

TOURIST INFORMATION
Tonga Visitors Bureau (TVB; 70115; fax 70666; VHF Channel 16; Fatafehi Rd; 8.30am-4.30pm Mon-Fri) A well-stocked office with visitor information brochures (including one on Talau National Park) and tourist maps of Neiafu and Vava'u (T$1). Helpful, well-informed staff happily assist with bookings and accommodation reservations.

Sights & Activities
Taking in the Port of Refuge view of yachts bobbing on their moorings from a café or bar, with a cool drink in hand, may be the only sight you need to see in Neiafu, but there are a few reasons to take a wander.

Standing high above the Port of Refuge, on Fatafehi Rd, **St Joseph's Cathedral** is the most prominent structure and acts as a beacon for arriving yachties. Attempts to establish a Catholic mission in Vava'u began in 1837, but it wasn't until over a century later that construction of the wonderful cathedral began; it was to take nine years to complete. The white and red façade survived the strong cyclone in 1961 and is a classic example of Catholic colonial architecture. Within the light interior is a considerably Tongan-looking Jesus.

Hala Lupe (Way of Doves) is the stretch of road along the waterfront clifftop between St Joseph's Cathedral and the Moorings office. The road was constructed by female prisoners convicted of adultery by the church. Their mournful singing was likened to the sound of cooing doves.

Below Hala Lupe is the **IFAW Marine Awareness Centre** (www.ifaw.org), an excellent place to learn more about humpback whales and their conservation. Head down the stairs and follow the pathway towards the Mermaid Restaurant.

NEIAFU TAHI (OLD HARBOUR)
Neiafu's Old Harbour is much shallower than the Port of Refuge – so shallow that you'll see pigs dining on the mudflats here at low tide. It served as Vava'u's main landing site until the arrival of relatively large European ships, and has its own colourful past. Around 1808, Finau 'Ulukalala II, during the conquest of

VAVA'U GROUP

Vava'u, bound several resisting chiefs into decomposing canoes and set them adrift on Neiafu Tahi to drown.

Hala Tafengatoto (Tafengatoto Road; Road where Blood Flows) meets the Old Harbour, and is part of a network of sunken clay pathways found around the main island of Vava'u. Tradition has it that this sunken trail, the route to the village of Feletoa, ran with the blood of warriors killed during the conquest of Vava'u by Finau 'Ulukalala II.

Near the entrance to Hala Tafengatoto are several **freshwater springs** bubbling into the Neiafu Tahi. The most reliable is **Matalave**, around the harbour to the east. Nearby is the rocky outcrop that is said to have been the primary Vava'u landing site of the *kalia* (double-hulled canoes) used in ancient times.

KILIKILI PIER
At the far western end of Neiafu, Kilikili Pier once served as a British coal station. It was so named because the coal loaded there by the foreigners resembled, to the Tongans, the familiar *kilikili* (black volcanic slag pebbles used to decorate grave mounds throughout Tonga).

MOUNT TALAU NATIONAL PARK
Mt Talau (131m), the flat-topped mountain dominating the Port of Refuge, is protected in the Mt Talau National Park. The marked trail through the park (45-minute circuit) leads steeply over slippery rocks to the summit, linking four viewpoints from which you can get your bearings while scanning stunning views of Neiafu, the Port of Refuge, the Vaipua causeway and the 128m-high Sia Ko Kafoa across Vaipua Inlet. The truncated mountain off in the distance is 186m-high Mo'ungalafa, rising above the freshwater Lake 'Ano at the west end of Vava'u Island. Mt Talau is a good place for contemplative sundowners, though pack a torch.

To get to the trailhead, head west along Tapueluelu Rd for about 2km from the centre of Neiafu until you reach a small car park.

Walking here you may see the rare *fokai* (banded lizard); *hengehenga* (Tongan whistler), a rare and distinctive bird – males have bright yellow chests; and, at dusk, *peka* (flying fox). Pick up the map and guide to the park from the TVB for details of other flora and

> ### MT TALAU LOSES ITS PEAK
> A popular Tongan legend explaining how Mt Talau came to lose its peak suggests that a mischievous Samoan *tevolo*, or devil spirit, decided to filch the attractive peak and carry it away to his homeland. There is some disagreement as to what happened next; some maintain that a patriotic Tongan *tevolo* caught the offender and forced him to drop the peak by convincing him of the imminent arrival of daylight, the time for all devils to be back under cover. Another source claims that the mountain simply became too heavy and the thief dropped it. Whatever the case, the mountain top splash-landed in the middle of the Port of Refuge. It is now called Lotuma and is used as the Vava'u naval base of the Tongan Defence Forces.

fauna in the park. The legend of the mountain is revealed in the boxed text, above.

YACHT RACES
On a balmy Friday afternoon you can't beat knocking back an Ikale on the bow in a relaxed yacht race around the Port of Refuge. If you want to become 'rail meat' (crew), turn up to the Port of Refuge Yacht Club (at the Mermaid) when the skippers meet around 4pm between May and December. Spectators can watch from the bar at the 5pm race start. The only requirement for membership of the yacht club is arrival in Tonga on a yacht or launch (the *'Olovaha* doesn't count!).

RUGBY & FOOTBALL
Rugby and football games are held year-round at church school pitches and Fangatongo Rugby Field (on Saturday games are held all day). Ask locals for details.

Tours
Tour companies on Vava'u Island come and go, so contact the TVB for further information. Hiring a taxi with or without driver (see p257) is another option. Be aware that after heavy rain some roads become deeply rutted and impassable to anything but 4WD vehicles.

Most organised boat tours include a range of sights throughout Vava'u's islands. See p245 for details.

Sleeping

Neiafu has a good range of accommodation, while other options soak up quiet beach- or harbour-side positions around Vava'u Island, its causeway-connected islands and on outer-island resorts. Boat tour operators (see p246) happily collect guests from the jetties and beaches of their accommodation around the Vava'u group of islands.

Bookings are advised between April and December.

BUDGET

Port Wine Guest House (☎ 70479; portwine@kalianet .to; Ha'amea Rd; s/d T$15/25) You'll feel like you're staying with your dear Tongan grandmother (who in fact lives next door) in this clean, four-room guesthouse with a breezy lounge and soft couch to sink into (beneath lots of family photos and a cat disguising itself as a mantelpiece ornament). The only downside is that you will have to take a cold shower. Cook your meals in the good kitchen, fill water bottles from the tank and dine on Port Wine's veranda. It's in a quiet spot, just a few minutes' stroll from the centre of town.

Adventure Backpackers (☎ /fax 70955; www.visit vavau.com/backpackers; Fatafehi Rd; dm T$24, s/d from T$48/78, d with bathroom T$88) This modern hostel in the centre of town makes a handy base to spring into the activities and nightlife of Vava'u. Fan-cooled rooms are bright, clean and secure (if a bit sterile), there is an excellent shared kitchen and communal area, and a terrace to sun yourself on. Hot showers in winter only. Book ahead.

Vava'u Guest House (☎ 70300; Fatafehi Rd; r per person T$15, bungalow s/d with bathroom T$35/45) At the time of research, this unkempt and shabby option was barely an option; check with the TVB for updates. It's 1.2km south of the town centre, opposite Paradise International Hotel.

MIDRANGE

Hill Top Hotel (☎ /fax 70209; sunset@kalianet.to; Holopeka Hill; garden/harbour-view d with bathroom from T$75/115) The main balcony of this small hotel takes in 180-degree views over town, the Port of Refuge, the Old Harbour and neighbouring islands, and harbour-view rooms have an outlook almost as sublime. Spacious, tiled rooms are fan-cooled and have good beds (but thin, scratchy sheets). Arm yourself with a torch and antidog mis-

siles for the night-time walk up Holopeka Hill (Place of Gathering Bats).

Toula's Harbour View Motel (☎ 70687, fax 70846; marcella@kalianet.to; s/d/tr with bathroom & breakfast T$75/100/125) The old Marcella Resort is set in tropical gardens south of Neiafu, with a magnificent fan palm and tennis court. Each of the nine detached cabins comes with a veranda and quality linen. Opening off the motel's guest lounge is a bar/restaurant (see p254) with a pleasant view of the Port of Refuge. You can swim off the wharf below the resort, or walk for 15 minutes to a beach (see p259). Taxis from Neiafu cost T$4.

Puataukanave Motel (☎ 74000; fax 70080; puas hotel@kalianetvav.to; Fatafehi Rd; s/d with bathroom & fan T$85/110, with air-con from T$100/120; waterfront deluxe/ super deluxe d T$170/205; ☒ ☒) Oddly furnished rooms seem to get more austere with size, but the 'super deluxe' waterfront rooms have kitchens as well as balconies. Negotiate for budget rooms.

TOP END

Hakula Lodge (☎ 70872; VHF Channel 71; www.fish tonga.com, s/d/tr with bathroom A$150/175/210; ☒) The most attractive and atmospheric of Neiafu's accommodations, Hakula Lodge consists of two units opening onto a full-length veranda overlooking the Port of Refuge, complete with a barbecue and dining table. The spacious, tiled units also have well-equipped kitchens and lounge chairs which can be transformed into extra beds. Guests can head down the tropical garden path to swim off the private jetty, from where the owners' whale-watching and fishing trips depart on MV *Hakula* (see p246). Substantial low-season discounts and high-season 'standby' specials are available. The owners will book and confirm domestic flights to ensure smooth travel. It's 2km south of Neiafu.

Paradise International Hotel (☎ 70211; fax 70184; www.tongahost.com; Fatafehi Rd; island-/garden-/harbour-view d with bathroom US$70/95/115; ☒ ☒) A sprawling place with heavy furniture and 'ma and pa' velour armchairs in tired but clean interiors. A valuable feature is the large, clean pool (T$5 for nonguests), where you can flake on a sun lounge and sip on a 'Vava'u breeze' (dark rum, pineapple, coconut cream and ice cream), served from the nearby restaurant/bar (open from 6.30am to 10pm; breakfast T$7 to T$13, lunch T$8 to T$23, dinner T$30 to T$45).

VAVA'U GROUP

RENTAL ACCOMMODATION

Guesthouses allow guests to use their kitchen facilities, while Hakula Lodge and Puatakanave offer self-contained accommodation. Check the notice boards of Adventure Backpackers and the Mermaid (or contact both places) for details on rental houses – some with stunning water views.

Bayview Vacation Apartments (☎ 70724; 1-bedroom apt per week T$400) Well-furnished apartments are available for weekly or long-term rental and boast elevated views across Vaipau Inlet. Book through Adventure Backpackers.

Eating

Neiafu has access to the widest variety of fresh produce outside of Nuku'alofa, ultra-fresh local seafood and restaurant cuisine from every continent.

CAFÉS & QUICK EATS

Café Tropicana (☎ 71322; Fatafehi Rd; breakfast T$4-16, meals T$11-16; ⏲ 6.30am-6pm Mon-Sat; 🖳) Pass the cabinet stuffed with pies, cookies and cakes, if you can, and nab a table in the cool interior or slouch into a deckchair on the harbour-view terrace. The tasty, mixed cuisine ranges from sandwiches (around T$6) and burgers to Thai chicken laksa and a few Tongan dishes, such as *ota ika* (Tongan raw fish salad) and *otai*, a rich, smoothie-like melange of tropical fruits and coconut cream. Such a shame it's not open for dinner too – you'll just have to wait until breakfast.

Lighthouse Café (Tokangahahau Rd; ⏲ 7.30am-4.30pm Mon-Sat) Munch on danishes and other pastries in thatched *fale* (thatched house) in the bakery's garden, just off the main street.

Neiafu Market Kiosks ('Utukalongalu Market; snacks T$2-5; ⏲ 8.30am-4.30pm Mon-Thu, 8.30am-midnight Fri, 7am-noon Sat) You can buy *ota ika* and *sipi* (mutton flap) curry here along with sausages and two-minute noodles. The bright liquid in bags is cordial.

RESTAURANTS

Tongan Bob's (Kovana Rd; mains T$16-20; ⏲ noon-late Mon-Fri) A sand floor to sink your toes into and tasty Mexican staples to sink your teeth into. *Tostadas*, enchiladas, tacos and burritos come packed with fresh pickings and you can stoke the fire with extra hot chilli sauce, or head straight for the cinnamon and sugar-rolled banana *tostada* dessert.

Ciao Italian Restaurant (☎ 71030; Fatafehi Rd; pasta & pizza T$10-18, mains T$23-30; ⏲ lunch & dinner) Near the cathedral, this provincial-style Italian bistro serves authentic Italian cuisine, including pizza. Couple your meal with an Italian wine and finish it off with tiramisu, homemade gelato and espresso coffee.

Compass Rose (☎ 71167; VHF Channel 16; Fatafehi Rd; lunch T$8-15, mains T$18-30; ⏲ lunch & dinner Mon-Sat) Perched on the edge of Hala Lupe, with elevated views over the Port of Refuge, this small restaurant offers relaxed elegance and good food. Dishes include curries, marinated kebabs, barbecued lamb chops on mash, and lobster tails.

Dancing Rooster (☎ 70886; Fatafehi Rd; mains T$24-42; ⏲ lunch & dinner Mon-Sat) Descend the stairs from the main road to this relaxed, tropical garden setting and dine on dishes served with finesse from the Swiss chef. Generously proportioned options include rich local fish soup, blue-cheese ravioli in homemade Provençal sauce and lobster any which way. Service is attentive and meals are accompanied by Australian and Californian wines…or Swiss schnapps.

Pierre's Table (☎ 70687; Toula's Harbour View Resort, Toula; 5-course meals T$27-68; ⏲ dinner) Just out of Neiafu, Pierre's offers intimate dining on European-style dishes. Its Quebecoise owners speak English and French and provide a relaxed family atmosphere. Five-course meals start with lobster-topped hors d'oeuvres and finish with rich desserts and coffee. Price is determined by your choice of main course: rib eye steak with peppercorn sauce, lobster tail or garlic-butter surf and turf.

THE AUTHOR'S CHOICE

Mermaid Restaurant (☎ 70730; VHF Channel 16; breakfast & light meals T$4-16, mains T$25-36) Yachties tie up tenders to the pontoon while others wind down a pirate-like lair from Hala Lupe to the most popular spot in town. Flags and yacht T-shirts, signed by their crews, hang from the thatch-fringed ceiling and flap in the breeze at Mermaid's, where a relaxed atmosphere and good cheer pervade. The extensive menu (including bulging tortillas, juicy grills and the popular pizzas and seafood dishes) attracts plenty of repeat diners. Saturday's barbecue includes fish and octopus.

Bounty Bar (☎ 70576; VHF Channel 16; Fatafehi Rd; snacks & mains T$6.50-19; ✆ lunch & dinner Mon-Sat) Near Tongan Bob's, this small bar with an open side onto the Port of Refuge also serves meals.

In addition to the options given above, try La Paella (p260) on Tapana Island and Mala Island Resort (p260), which is a good option on a Sunday. The restaurants of the Puataukanave and Paradise International Hotels serve all meals daily.

TONGAN FEASTS

Joining in on a Tongan feast is the best way to experience Tongan food (much of which is cooked in an *'umu*, or pit oven), and get a good dose of traditional Tongan music and dance. Most can be booked through the TVB. Take plenty of smaller denomination *pa'anga* with you.

Hinakauea/'Ano Beach (☎ 71135; VHF Channel 16; feast & transfers T$30; ✆ 6pm Thu) A fine Tongan feast on Pangaimotu, with dancing by village children, weaving demonstrations and crafts to buy.

Mala Island Resort (☎ 71304; ✆ Sat) Dinner and a unique floor show put on by the staff. Also has a popular Sunday barbecue, see p260.

Tongan Beach Resort (☎ 70380; ✆ 7pm Wed) Book ahead for the Tongan feast at this resort on 'Utungake.

Barnacle Beach (✆ Sat) Traditional feast at Port Mourelle on Kapa island, accessed by boat. Contact the TVB.

SELF-CATERING

The *fale koloa* (corner shop) around Fatafehi and Tu'i Rds stay open until around 11pm Monday to Saturday. **Royal Beer Shop** (Fatafehi Rd; ✆ 8.30am-11pm Mon-Thu & Sat, 8.30am-2am Fri) sells beer, wine, vodka, gin and rum.

The best-stocked supermarket is **Puataukanave Supermarket** (☎ 70644; Fatafehi Rd), affectionately known as 'Pua', which has refrigerated chocolate as well as wine, beer and spirits. **Tonga Cooperative Federation** (TCF; Fatafehi Rd) and **Vava'u Trading Centre** (Fatafehi Rd) supermarkets stock a good range of imported grocery products and staples.

'Utukalongalu Market (✆ 8.30am-4.30pm Mon-Thu, 8.30am-midnight Fri, 7am-noon Sat), close to Halaevalu Wharf, is the best place to get fruit and vegetables – stacked in pyramids or frond baskets – and eggs.

The freshest fish (around T$5 to T$7 per kilogram) can be found at the **Vava'u Fish Market** (Halaevalu Wharf; ✆ 8.30am-4.30pm Mon-Fri, 8.30am-noon or 1pm Sat) or early in the morn-

ing on the waterfront near 'Utukalongalu Market. For fresh lobster (around T$18 per kilogram), head to **Ikapuna Store** (p256) or **'Alatini Fisheries** (☎ 70939), behind 'Utukalongalu Market, which also sells ice, imported gourmet goods and deli foods (think soft and hard cheeses, salami, olives, yoghurt and chocolate biscuits – but perhaps not mixed together), wine and beer.

On Sunday afternoon, just follow your nose through town to the bakeries – the places to be. **Tangitau & Sons Bakery** (Kovana Rd) and **Siaosi Fainga'a Bakery** (George's Bakery; Tapueluelu Rd) sell basic bread and rolls, while the latter also has muffins and *keki* (a sort of Tongan donut). The **bakery** (cnr Ha'amea & Talau Rds) produces a continuous stream of excellent scrolls, cinnamon buns, chocolate and fruit muffins, and pull-apart savoury breads good enough for a meal. **Lighthouse Café** (Tokangahahau Rd; ✆ 7.30am-4.30pm Mon-Sat) bakes European-style breads and Danish pastries.

Drinking & Entertainment

Most night entertainment centres around the waterfront bars. When the town's bars call last drinks, **Motele Nightclub** (Old Harbour; admission T$3; ✆ Fri & Sat), Neiafu's only nightclub, swells with the young and drunk. It's a bit rough – go in a group for more fun.

The home of the Port of Refuge Yacht Club and the first port of call for many – yachtie or land-lubber – the **Mermaid** (☎ 70730; VHF Channel 16) is always casual but picks up its party cheer in the evening. The food is good and happy hour flows from 4pm to 6pm, while the changing nightly entertainment includes darts competitions, quiz nights and Friday's yacht race (see p252), which is followed by live Tongan music and dancing. Hats off unless you want to shout the bar a drink.

This jovial restaurant bar with a great vibe is as laid back as a Mexican after siesta early in the evening and festive as the night wears on. Nightly happenings at **Tongan Bob's** (Kovana Rd; ✆ noon-late Mon-Fri) include Monday's live Tongan string and ukulele band accompanied by a *kava* ceremony (*kava* T$1; open to all), T$1 tacos on Tuesday, and dancing when the tables are slid aside later in the week. Knock back an Ikale or margarita at happy hour (5pm to 7pm).

Bounty Bar (☎ 70576; Fatafehi Rd; ✆ Mon-Sat) is a lively, very local place with karaoke on Tuesday night and live music.

The waterside decking at Puataukanave Motel (p253) is a good spot for afternoon drinks.

KAVA CLUBS
For information about *kava* clubs in Neiafu (men only), ask any local man to steer you in the right direction. Tongan Bob's (p255) has an all-inclusive *kava* session.

Shopping
'Utukalongalu Market (p255) has many craft stalls to cruise, with some beautiful carvings and jewellery in bone, black coral, shells and wood. Commissions are possible. Good handicrafts can also be found in the shops lining Fatafehi Rd. **Fata Fata Mafana** (☾ 8.30am-4.30pm Mon-Sat), next to the TVB, sells a range of items and many local weavings. In addition to stocking local art and quality crafts you may not find elsewhere, **Hibiscus Hut** (☎ 70381; Fatafehi Rd) sells coconut oils, sarongs, shorts and T-shirts. A small selection of nautical wear is sold at the Moorings office (see p246).

Quality surf-brand T-shirts (T$45) featuring local artwork in *kupesi* (mulberry bark designs), and Vava'u 'dirt shirts', dyed (or stained) with Vava'u's soil, are printed onsite at **Tropical Tease** (☎ 71271; tropical@kalianet .to; enter off Fatafehi Rd). If you can't find your favourite design in your size and colour, get it printed. Stubby holders and sun visors are stocked here; there's a small book exchange.

Opposite Paradise International Hotel, **Look Sharp Shop** (☎ 70757; Fatafehi Rd) sells quality Tongan printed T-shirts, including its signature *kava*-dyed range.

For fishing supplies head to the **Ikapuna Store** (☎ /fax 70174; VHF Channel 69; Fatafehi Rd). It's one of the best-stocked shops in the Pacific, with a good range of lures, as well as tackle, ropes and basic trawling rods and reels.

You can purchase duty free on the first day of arrival from a foreign port and on the last day before departure to a foreign port. **Leiola Duty Free Shop** (☎ 70748; Fatafehi Rd; ☾ 9am-12.30pm & 2-4.30pm Mon-Fri) sells alcohol, cigarettes, watches, jewellery and perfume.

There's a Saturday-morning **flea market** at Sailoame Market on Tu'i Rd.

Getting There & Away
See p290 for details on international transport to and from Vava'u. See p285 for information on transport between Vava'u and other parts of Tonga.

AIR
Lupepau'u Airport is on the northern side of Vava'u Island, about a 15-minute drive from Neiafu. **Airlines Tonga Air Fiji** (www.airlines tonga.com) and **Peau Vava'u** (Neiafu ☎ 71480; Fatafehi Rd; Airport ☎ 71403) fly between Vava'u, Tongatapu and Ha'apai daily except Sunday. The former also services the Niuas from Vava'u twice weekly. See p285 for details.

See p285 for details on weekly flights between Samoa and Vava'u on **Polynesian Airlines** (☎ 70644; in Puataukanave Supermarket; Fatafehi Rd).

BOAT
Two ferries travel weekly between Tongatapu and Vava'u via Ha'apai. The offices of **'Uata (Walter Line) Shipping** (☎ 70490), for MV *Pulupaki*, and **Shipping Corporation of Polynesia** (☎ 70128), for MV *'Olovaha*, are at Neiafu's main wharf and open the day before the ferry arrives and the day of the ferry. See p286 for ferry schedules and fares and contact the shipping company for MV *'Olovaha*'s scheduled trips to the Niuas from Vava'u.

Arriving by yacht in Vava'u is reasonably straightforward, if a little time-consuming (see p295). For details on customs see p278. Moorings can be hired from Beluga Diving (p246) for US$9 per night, or the Moorings and Sailing Safaris (p246) for T$15.

Sailing Safaris Marine Centre (☎ 70650; sailing safaris@kalianetvav.to; VHF Channel 68; PO Box 46, Neiafu), near the Mermaid, looks after yachtie needs including various sorts of fuel, engineering services and repairs, water, ice, laundry facilities and yacht slipway for boats up to 30 tonnes. It also offers poste restante.

See p294 for details on opportunities for cargo ship passage to and from Vava'u. If you're looking to crew, check out the notice boards at the Mermaid, the Bounty Bar and Adventure Backpackers.

Getting Around
TO/FROM THE AIRPORT
Some accommodations, including island resorts, offer airport transfers. The Paradise International Hotel bus meets all incoming flights and is free for guests, T$5 for nonguests. Taxis charge T$12 for the airport to Neiafu trip.

BICYCLE
Vava'u is hilly, but fairly manageable by bicycle. Adventure Backpackers hires out good bikes (half/full day T$13/20) and the Friendly Islands Kayak Company runs mountain-bike tours (see p248).

BOAT
For passenger transport to outer islands in the Vava'u Group, ask around close to 'Utukalongalu Market and at the jetty on the Old Harbour. You'll probably be able to strike a bargain with someone who's going your way. All offshore island resorts will provide boat transport for a fee.

Tide timetables and daily weather reports are posted at the Mermaid and Moorings. For information on hiring boats see (p246).

BUS
Buses run from Sailoame and 'Utakalongalu Markets to most parts of Vava'u and connected islands, leaving when full. They usually make the run into town in the morning and return in the afternoon, so they're not very convenient for day trips from town.

CAR
Tongan driving licences are available from the Police Station (p249). For details of what is required to obtain a license, see p288. Taxi drivers will often hire out their vehicles for a negotiable fee of around T$55 to T$65 per day (advice from experience: check the brakes!).

JL Rental Car (☎ 71128; Kovana Rd) has a few rental cars for T$65 per day.

TAXI
You'll find that taxi drivers often declare they have absolutely no change, so be sure to ensure you have enough *pa'anga* in smaller denominations (there's little likelihood the driver will return with your change). Taxis charge anywhere up to T$3 around Neiafu, T$10 to 'Ano and Hinakauea Beaches, T$12 to the airport, T$12 to Keitahi Beach and 'Utula'aina Point, and T$14 for a fare to Talihau village.

Taxi companies in Neiafu:
Issac (☎ 12261) Minibus.
JV Taxi & Rental Cars (☎ 70136, 71136; Fafafehi Rd)
Liviela (☎ 70240; Fafafehi Rd)

AROUND THE ISLAND
Vava'u Island is a different world once you're outside Neiafu. Not that Neiafu is bustling, but the rest of the island is just a tranquil jumble of small villages, plantations and bush, and is full of beautiful and interesting features.

The easiest way to get around is by taxi or guided tour but, with a bit of effort, you could cover good ground by bicycle, public transport or on foot.

You'll need the best part of a day to see either side of the island. The TVB has a map with information on sights of interest but many of the road cairns are now missing.

Western Vava'u Island
SIA KO KAFOA
Vava'u Island is nearly bisected by the **Vaipua Inlet**, which separates the Neiafu area from western Vava'u. The inlet was used by ancient Polynesian canoes en route to the fort complex at the village of Feletoa.

The two sides of the island are connected by a causeway. On the western shore are the twin hills of Lei'ulu and Sia Ko Kafoa. Historically, this area has served as a burial ground, an *'esi* (resting site), a lookout and a fortification.

From Neiafu, follow the road north past the hospital and cross over the causeway spanning Vaipua Inlet. The road turns right as it climbs up to the village of Taoa (meaning 'spear').

Lei'ulu, the hill behind Taoa, is used as a burial ground. Walk downhill along the coral road behind Lei'ulu hill; when the road begins to angle right on an uphill slope, about 10 minutes from the village, you'll see the track to Sia Ko Kafoa (128m) turning uphill to the left. On the summit is an *'esi*, a mound used as a rest area by chiefs and nobles and a place where young virgins were presented to amorous chiefs.

The village of Tefisi has impressive views from its prominent, coloured church.

LAKE 'ANO
This freshwater lake at the extreme western end of the island is an eerie sort of place. It's accessible only by a steep, muddy climb down from Longomapu village. If approaching it via the main road from the north, turn left at the intersection in the village and follow that road for several hundred metres.

VAVA'U GROUP

Look carefully for a track turning off to the right and leading downhill – access is difficult after heavy rain. You can fish for edible *lapila* (telapia) fish in the lake.

MOUNT MO'UNGALAFA

With a little effort you can climb Mt Mo'ungalafa (186m), the highest point on Vava'u Island, via a track just south of Longomapu. The spectacular view from the top takes in all of Vava'u and is well worth the effort.

TOAFA LOOKOUT

On a clear day, the Toafa Lookout cliff, to the northwest of Longomapu, affords an expansive ocean view all the way to the volcanic islands of Late and Fonualei.

Northern Central Vava'u Island

FELETOA

The small village of Feletoa (which means 'many brave warriors'), between Neiafu and Holonga, is the site of a fortification constructed in 1808 to resist the conquest of Vava'u by Finau 'Ulukalala II. At the time, Feletoa was the centre of government for Vava'u, thanks to easy canoe access up Vaipua Inlet. The fortification is surrounded by trenches, which you may be able to make running perpendicular to the road.

On the south side of the road between Feletoa and the nearby village of Mataika is a **burial site** containing the *langi* (pyramidal stone) tomb of the ubiquitous Finau 'Ulu-

kalala II. Finau died of what appears to have been internal haemorrhaging after an animated wrestling contest in Neiafu – in spite of the sacrifice of a young Neiafuan child in an attempt to appease the greater powers of the day.

'UTULA'AINA POINT

'Utula'aina Point provides what is perhaps the most spectacular view on Vava'u Island and should not be missed. A couple of beautiful sandy coves can be reached from here also. To get to the trailhead, you may need to walk north from Holonga village (depending on the state of the track) to get to a track that forms a fork. Head straight ahead from the intersection and continue along the path as it curves to the left and emerges onto a grassy open area after about 15 minutes. Bear right through the bushes, climb the grassy knoll and you'll emerge on 'Utula'aina Point, surrounded by cliffs above a turbulent sea. On exceptionally clear days the volcanic outlines of Toku and Fonualei are visible. Look out for whales between July and November.

Fifty metres before arriving back at the trailhead, as the track bends right, a narrow path on the left leads (almost north at first) down to a beautiful secluded beach. It's a steep climb, but you're likely to have the place to yourself (keep an eye on your belongings though). A shallow coral shelf restricts swimming, but snorkelling at high tide is possible.

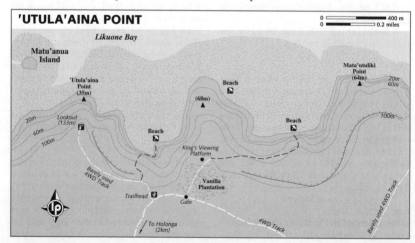

'UTULA'AINA POINT

To get to the second beach, walk east from the trailhead along the 4WD track. Head north straight through the vanilla plantation (as long as you counter no objections) and follow the narrowing path to a copse and earth mound (once possibly a viewing platform for ancient Tongan kings). From the mound a path leads (in about 10 minutes) northeast down through forest and kava plantations to a beach. It's just as beautiful as the one close to the point and just as dramatic, guarded on each side by towering sentinels of rock.

There's no drinking water available on the coast.

Eastern Vava'u Island
MAKAVE

One of the most interesting beaches on the island, Makave is easily accessed on foot from Neiafu along the shore from the Old Harbour. Walk past the entrance to Hala Tafengatoto (p252) and follow the shore east towards Makave village, the legendary home of a mysterious, dark, giant people.

An hour from Neiafu, on the beach below Makave village, you'll find an ancient **canoe mooring** beside an obtrusive rock and cave. Further east are the refreshing **freshwater springs** of Matalave.

The name Makave (Take a Stone) refers to the ancient custom of piling a stone on Kilikilitefua Wall upon the birth of a child. To visit this wall, follow the faint track leading back to the road from the end of the beach. Turn south here and continue along the peninsula until you reach a small rise. At this point the remains of the stone wall, now less than 1m high, can be seen stretching nearly 100m across the peninsula. It once reached a height of 1.5m, but bits of it were removed for use in concrete cisterns.

TOULA & VEIMUMUNI CAVE

The freshwater spring and swimming hole of Veimumuni Cave is carved into the rock east of Toula village, 3km south of Neiafu. From Toula, turn left (east) following the path uphill past a cemetery. As you descend to the beach, you'll see Veimumuni Cave in the bluff.

Several legends tell of a beautiful spirit maiden who appeared on the rock before the cave and teased mortal men with her beauty, tempting every passing soul with

the contents of the mysterious cave. One version has her finally being outwitted by a *tea* (albino) woman, who became the first mortal to taste the water inside the cave before being tickled into submission by a pair of *tevolo* (devil spirits). In reference to this story, the wells around Toula are called *vai 'ene* (tickling water). Another version of the tale has her being tricked into the clutches of an amorous young gardener. Watch the effect as you throw a stone into the water here.

From the cave, walk north along the shore to a series of further caves, once used by Toula villagers to bury enemies from other villages. At low tide there's plenty of marine life in the rock pools.

ENE'IO & KEITAHI BEACHES

At the easternmost end of the island, near the village of Tu'anekivale, are a couple of seldom-visited, rugged beaches, better for strolling or sunbathing than for swimming or snorkelling.

At **Keitahi Beach**, strong snorkellers will find some interesting things to look at in the large tide pools about 100m offshore (be careful as the currents are dangerous at high tide) or you can wander out across the reef with proper footwear at low tide. It's reached via a dirt road to the east between Ha'alaufuli and Tu'anekivale.

'Ene'io Beach is signposted from Neiafu and reached via a turnoff from Tu'anekivale. With pounding offshore surf and soaring cliffs, it's a secluded and stunning area to explore on foot but not good for swimming.

Further south, across the causeways to 'Uataloa and Koloa Islands, mangroves grow in an eerily still swamp area.

OTHER VAVA'U GROUP ISLANDS

Pangaimotu and 'Utungake are connected to Vava'u Island by causeways, while other islands are reached by boat. Mala Island Resort and La Paella restaurant on Tapana Island welcome diners. Other island resorts primarily cater for their house guests, but may accept meal bookings made in advance (and may not be too welcoming if you just show up).

PATRICIA LEDYARD MATHESON

One of Tonga's most famous *palangi* (foreign) authors, Patricia Ledyard Matheson lived at 'Utulei (Vava'u) for 51 years until her death in October 2000. During that time she wrote three books: *Friendly Isles: A Tale of Tonga; 'Utulei, My Tongan Home;* and *The Tongan Past,* revolving around her life in Tonga, its people and traditions.

Patricia was born in San Francisco in 1913 and served in the Pacific during WWII, during which she volunteered for front-line duty. Feeling drawn to Tonga, Pat arrived in Vava'u during 1949 to take up a position as principal of Siu'ilikutapu College. She soon married and set up home at the entrance to the Port of Refuge. Known for her hospitality, sharp wit and sharper sense of humour, she established a fine academic library. Pat was still crossing the harbour to Neiafu in a small boat with a dodgy outboard motor weeks before she died. She is buried in the village cemetery on 'Utulei.

PANGAIMOTU

area 8.86 sq km / pop 1298

Just across the scenic causeway from Toula village is Pangai (Royal Island), so called because it belongs to the royal estate.

'Ano and Hinakauea Beaches, near the south end of Pangaimotu, are actually two different parts of the same beautiful beach, with sheltered turquoise water, emerald vegetation, good snorkelling and a safe anchorage. 'Ano Beach Feast (see p255) is held here weekly or you can catch a dinghy across to the island of Tapana for La Paella restaurant (see right).

The village of 'Utulei lies across the Port of Refuge from Neiafu's Kilikili Pier. You can kayak or catch a boat across the harbour from Neiafu, or drive round, park on the hill and walk down to the village. Writer and long-time resident Patricia Ledyard Matheson set her autobiographical accounts of island life here (see the boxed text above).

Tavalau Beach is a five-minute scenic walk north from the eastern end of the 'Utungake causeway.

TAPANA

Tapana has a few beaches, is a popular island with yachties and has a number of moorings. At the Ark Gallery (☎ 12673; VHF Channel 10; Anchorage 11), located on a house boat, expat Sheri sells her paintings and other artworks inspired by her surroundings and the Tongan way of life.

The island's La Paella (☎ 16310; VHF Channel 10; dinner & entertainment T$50) gets rave reviews for its plentiful paella and lively entertainment. Go there if you can. Land-lubbers can get a boat pick-up from 'Ano Beach; taxis from Neiafu cost T$10. You can stay in La Casita (d T$100) here.

'UTUNGAKE

The long, thin island of 'Utungake is connected by a causeway to Pangaimotu and has a pleasant beach near its southern tip.

Set in immaculate gardens, Lucky's Beach Houses (☎ /fax 71075; luckysbeach@yahoo.com; Talihau; tent site for 2 T$25; fale s/d incl breakfast T$35/60, beachhouse T$58/80, extra person T$25) has a king-sized bed downstairs and a day-bed upstairs, overlooking the water at the tip of 'Utungake. Rustic romantics will love the traditional thatched *fale*, with shuttered windows onto the beach, nets and hurricane-lamp lighting. The tent site includes a tent and has its own sparkling bathroom facilities. Guests can launch a kayak off the beach to explore the islands and paddle over to nearby Mala. It's the only accommodation in an otherwise quiet village. Dinner costs from T$20.

Primarily aimed at the 'baby-boomer' market on prebooked packages, the three-star Tongan Beach Resort (☎ /fax 70380; www.the tongan.com; VHF Channel 71; high season d & tw with bathroom US$160, extra bed US$50; half-/full-board US$48/60) on Hikutamole Beach, has standard rooms, a lovely sand-floor *fale* bar and a restaurant. Bring reef shoes. Children under 10 stay for free and pay 50% for meals.

MALA

Just south of 'Utungake, the small island of Mala has a sandy swimming beach and a welcoming resort. The Japanese Gardens is a beautiful snorkelling spot between Mala and Kapa, though a strong current flows between these two islands and 'Utungake. Beware of a legendary cannibal god who reputedly lives on Mala and is said to capture and devour passing boaters.

Mala Island Resort (☎ 71304; VHF Channel 16; mala@kalianet.to; dm T$50, s/d bungalow with bathroom T$125/150; meal plan T$55; 🛇) is an upbeat, welcoming place where some wild stories get exchanged (you may want to reach for the occasional grain of salt). The *tapa*-lined bungalows have creaky wooden floors, beautiful views and plenty of charm (though remodelling is planned in the near future). There's dinner and dancing on Friday, a Tongan feast on Saturday, and a Sunday barbecue. Plenty of yachties file into the broad restaurant (open to nonguests) and join guests for sundowners (happy hour 4pm to 7pm), often staying on for dinner and extra nights at Anchorage 6. Transfers from the airport and town cost T$25 per person, or a water taxi can meet you at Talihau Beach. Low-season rates available.

SOUTHERN VAVA'U GROUP ISLANDS
Hunga & Fofoa
At the centre of the westernmost cluster of the Vava'u group of islands is a large, placid lagoon formed by Hunga, Kalau and Fofoa. It looks like a volcanic crater lake with three small openings to the sea and offers superb anchorage – although entering can be tricky – and impressive snorkelling.

Meaning 'big fish, many fish', **Ika Lahi Lodge** (☎ /fax 70611; ikalahi@tongafishing.com; www .tongafishing.com; PO Box 24, Neiafu; tw/tr/q NZ$295/ 285/280; meals per day per person US$60) is just what you want a fishing-focused resort to aspire to. On the Hunga shore of the beautiful

sheltered lagoon, it's handily close to the deep ocean and has four guest units with balconies (fans work when the generator runs from 6.30am to midnight) and plenty of interest for nonfishing partners.

On the cliffs behind the resort is a lookout from where humpback whales can be seen between July and November.

Foe'ata & Foelifuka
Immediately south of Hunga, Foe'ata offers glorious white beaches (sometimes diminished by tides) and good snorkelling. At low tide you can walk across the sand bar to Foelifuka, which has an anchorage on its north side.

This ecolodge-cum-eccentric dream resort has an idyllic beach position on Foe'ata. Each of the six large *fale* at **Blue Lagoon** (☎ /fax 70247; VHF Channel 16; www.foiata-island.com; standard fale d T$160, superior fale for up to 4 people T$280, extra bed T$40; half/full board T$90/100) is uniquely constructed in its immediate environment from materials sourced on and around Foe'ata and Foelifuka – one even has an open-air, mosquito-netted bed on the balcony – and include private bathrooms with hot showers. The German chef/owner serves some of Vava'u's best food and may be willing to cater for yachties (tip: organise *before* landing!). Language sometimes verges on the colourful. Transfers cost T$130.

MARINER'S MYSTERIOUS CAVE

Will Mariner was shown this cave hidden below the water's surface by Finau 'Ulukalala II. Puzzled that several chiefs he'd seen dive into the water had failed to return to the surface, he was instructed to follow their example and was guided into the dim cathedral-like cavern. He observed that the cave was about 14m high and 14m wide, with narrow channels branching off all around. As they drank *kava* on a rock platform inside, one of the chiefs related this story:

A tyrannical governor of Vava'u learned of a conspiracy against him and ordered the primary conspirator drowned and all his family killed. The conspirator's beautiful daughter, betrothed to a young chief, was rescued by another chief, who also had amorous intentions. To prevent her imminent demise, he spirited her away into a secret cavern and visited her daily, bringing gifts of food, clothing, coconuts and oils for her skin. His ministrations were so sincere that, eventually, he won her heart as well as her gratitude.

Realising that he couldn't just bring her out of the cavern, he formulated an elaborate plan, which involved a secret voyage to Fiji with some underling chiefs and their wives. When they inquired why he would attempt such a trip without a Tongan wife, he replied that he would probably find one along the way. True to his word, he stopped the canoes before the bare rock above the cave entrance, dived into the water and emerged a few minutes later with the girl, whom his companions surmised to be a goddess until they recognised her striking resemblance to the daughter of the condemned conspirator. They all went off to Fiji, only returning to Vava'u two years later after hearing of the death of the tyrant governor.

Nuapapu

Nuapapu is best known for the hidden cave at its northern end known as **Mariner's Cave** (see the boxed text, p261) after Will Mariner, who was the first European to see it.

A strange atmospheric phenomenon occurs inside the cave. Pacific swells surging through the entrance compress trapped air and when the sea recedes every few seconds, the moisture condenses into a heavy fog, the result of water vapour cooling as it expands. As soon as another wave enters the opening, the fog instantly vanishes. To enter the cave, snorkelling gear is recommended. You need to be a confident swimmer to try this and don't go in if the swell is strong. Enter the cave when the swell pulls you towards it, exit when the swell pushes you out, and be sure to look up before surfacing. The main entrance is a couple of metres below the surface and the tunnel is about 4m long. Divers can access a second exit at 15m depth.

Between the southern end of Nuapapu and the adjoining island of Vaka'eitu are the Coral Gardens, which offered some of the best snorkelling in Vava'u before sustaining damage from a cyclone.

Vaka'eitu

The small, hilly island of Vaka'eitu has secluded beaches on each side, a secure overnight anchorage and some of Vava'u's best snorkelling in the nearby coral gardens. Check with the TVB for details about the island's **Popao Village Resort** (☎ 70308; info@popao .org), which has stunning views over the islands from its hilltop position (a bit of a walk up from the beach).

Kapa

Beautiful **Swallows' Cave** ('Anapekepeka) cuts into a cliff on the west side of the northern end of Kapa Island. Despite its name, it's actually inhabited by hundreds of white-rumped swiftlets (*Collocalia spodiopygia*) that flit about in the dim light and nest in the darkness. In the late afternoon, the slanting sunlight lights up the water.

The water is crystal clear despite the floor of the cave being 18m below the surface and the only access is by boat (unless you want to abseil in, see p248). On entering the cave, you'll see Bell Rock hanging down on your left (along with graffiti dated from 1886 and 1891). When struck with a solid object, it emits melodic vibrations. Deeper in the cave, you'll see a shaft of light shining through a hole in the ceiling; from there, you can follow a rocky trail into the adjoining dry cave.

Organise to snorkel in the cave on your tour (or you may just get a quick boat view) but be aware of the current that sweeps past the entrance and may cause problems for weak swimmers.

Some excellent snorkelling can be had off **Port Mourelle**, on the protected western bay of Kapa Island, which was the original landing site of the Spaniard Don Francisco Antonio Mourelle, the first European to visit Vava'u. It was here that he took on water from the springs of the swamp near Falevai (House of Water). A track from Port Mourelle leads north and south along the spine of the island. If you would like to camp, ask for permission in the island's villages, Kapa, 'Otea and Falevai. The **Barnacle Beach Feast** (contact the TVB) is held at Port Mourelle.

Nuku

A magical white sand spit runs off the tiny, uninhabited island of Nuku, into gradients of turquoise and azure water. It's a favoured spot for numerous official functions, celebrations and private parties and locals often paddle over from Kapa to collect a small fee from anyone who stops here. Watch the current at the western tip of the island.

Taunga, Ngau & Pau

Just south of Kapa, the inviting and sporadically inhabited islands of Ngau and Taunga boast idyllic beaches with fine snorkelling and four good anchorages. At low tide, Ngau and Taunga are connected by a fine sandy beach. Ngau is in turn connected to the uninhabited island of Pau by a slender ribbon of sand that is exposed except at the turn of high tide. There's a superb anchorage in the bight of Ngau on the eastern shore.

'Eue'iki

The raised island of 'Eue'iki has easy boat access to the stunning white beach, and a coral garden off the southern shore. You can circumnavigate the island in around 45 minutes at low tide, and explore the caves at the far side of the resort.

The Australian reality-TV series *Treasure Island* was filmed on 'Eue'iki, hence the name of the resort.

Treasure Island Resort (☎ 12935; treasure@kalianet .to; 'Eue'iki; d fale with bathroom T$150; meal package T$90) Located in a magical setting on the north side of the island, the resort's thatched bar/restaurant perches on a white, coral-free sandy beach which descends to 70m, making it ideal for swimming and simply watching whales pass by (in season). Solid *fale* with water-view balconies are spaced along the beachfront and feature firm beds, private bathrooms (check if hot water is now available), clam-shell soap holders and hibiscus flower adornments. Two family *fale* also have bunk beds. Guests can make use of the kayaks to explore nearby 'Euakafa or possibly fish with the English- and German-speaking owners, but bring your own snorkelling gear. The European cuisine generally features fish (the day's catch) or meat, and may be available to yachties if booked ahead. Return boat transfers cost T$60.

'Euakafa

A sandy beach rings this relatively small, uninhabited island's north side. From its eastern end a trail leads through the forest and mango trees to the summit (100m), containing the overgrown tomb of Talafaiva, a queen of Tonga (see the boxed text, below). On the way up you can peer through the trees to stunning vistas of the islands to the northeast. 'Euakafa is a good spot for swimming and snorkelling – there's a coral garden south of the island.

Mounu & 'Ovalau

Just southeast of Vaka'eitu are two more of those idyllic sunning, snorkelling, swimming and lazing-on-the-beach islands, Mounu and 'Ovalau. You can walk completely around Mounu in a few minutes and there's good snorkelling.

Vava'u's most elegant accommodation for those wanting privacy and their own space for contemplation, **Mounu Island Resort** (☎ 70747; VHF Channel 77; www.mounuisland.com; d fale with bathroom US$175, honeymoon fale with bathroom US$200; meals per day US$70) consists of a few ecofriendly wooden *fale*, linked by coconut palm–lined sandy paths. Each has its own balcony, and hammocks to mooch in are slung between trees nearby. Pass through a humpback whale's jaw bones to the breezy restaurant and well-stocked bar. Island-to-airport transfers cost US$60 and excellent whale-watching tours are run by the owners. Three nights minimum (unless agreed in advance); children under 12 not accepted.

Maninita

Located in the remote, extreme south of the Vava'u Group is the tiny wooded island of Maninita. The terraced coral reef on the approach forms lovely tide pools and the island is an important breeding ground for birds. There's an anchorage on the island's western side. Contact Mounu Island Resort (above) to organise bird-watching trips.

'THE FO'UI DID IT'

Back in the mists of time, a Tongan chief called Tele'a came to live on 'Euakafa because he considered Vava'u the most beautiful part of the kingdom. He took a lovely girl, Talafaiva, as his third wife and accepted her dowry, which consisted of 100 other attractive girls. The whole family set up house on the plateau of little 'Euakafa.

Outside the royal residence grew a *fo'ui* tree, which Talafaiva wanted chopped down. But Tele'a refused to do so. One day, while Tele'a was out fishing, Lepuha, one of Tonga's irresistible 'handsome men', arrived to 'conquer' the king's bride. By climbing the *fo'ui* tree, he was able to avoid the royal guard and enter the castle in order to seduce the queen. All would have been well had he not tattooed his signature mark on her belly.

When Tele'a saw the mark he was outraged, but all the queen could do was blame the tree that she'd wanted to destroy in the first place. 'The *fo'ui* did it,' she said, and the *fo'ui* has served as a Tongan scapegoat ever since.

Tele'a ordered his wife beaten for her indiscretion, but in doing so his servant inadvertently killed her. The chief built her a tomb on the summit of 'Euakafa, which can still be visited, although a body has never been found. Some claim that it was stolen by Lepuha. The *fo'ui*, by the way, has gone as well.

VAVA'U'S OUTLYING VOLCANIC ISLANDS

On clear days, the distinctive silhouette of **Late** is visible to the west from the mainland. When King George I realised that some of the outer areas of his kingdom were being ravaged by blackbirders (South American slave traders, see p222), he evacuated Late and resettled its people in Hunga, beside the lagoon.

The heavily forested island is dominated by a 555m-high volcanic crater (dormant since 1854) and remained uninhabited until breeding pairs of the endangered Niuafo'ou megapode were installed there in the 1990s in an attempt to protect it from extinction. For further information, see the boxed text, p267.

Between Late and the immense cone of Kao (Ha'apai), far to the south, enigmatic **Late'iki** first broke the surface in 1858, but was gone by 1898. On 12 December 1967, it made a 'pulsing glow on the horizon' during a particularly violent eruption, had reached an altitude of 18m within a week, and subsequently went down again. In May 1979 the island, which locals nicknamed Metis Shoal, began spewing and erupting and the king decided to check it out. On 7 July 1979 the king sailed to the site and looked on as his son planted the Tongan flag on the new land, christening it Late'iki ('Little Late').

On a clear day, **Fonualei** can be seen from Vava'u's northern cliffs, 64km to its northwest. In 1846 the island erupted, covering parts of the main island with volcanic ash. This is the island Mourelle named Amargura (Bitterness) when he discovered it was barren and wouldn't provide him and his crew with much-needed and long-awaited supplies. The ferry passes within a couple of kilometres of its eastern coast en route to the Niuas from Neiafu.

Fonualei's old and worn volcanic neighbour, **Toku**, remains uninhabited since its evacuation during the blackbirding scare of the 1860s. Its inhabitants resettled in 'Utulei village on Pangaimotu. There's a freshwater lake near its summit and it's possible to climb, but difficult as there are no tracks.

EASTERN VAVA'U GROUP ISLANDS

Transport to the eastern islands is much shorter and easier if you start from Neiafu's Old Harbour rather than the Port of Refuge.

'Ofu

The waters near 'Ofu are the primary habitat of the prized but endangered *'ofu* shell – so discourage their collection by resisting the temptation to buy them. The island is friendly and well worth a day's exploration.

Kenutu, Lolo & 'Umuna

The small uninhabited island of Kenutu, just east of 'Ofu, has superb beaches, and coral patches south of the island. The land itself is heavily wooded but there's a well-defined trail across it to steep cliffs on the eastern coast.

The reef between Kenutu and Lolo, immediately south, is very dramatic. On the eastern side the waves crash and boil, while the crystalline waters on the western shore are calm.

'Umuna is another uninhabited island just north of Kenutu. At its centre is a large cave containing a freshwater pool. Both Lolo and 'Umuna are accessible from Kenutu by crossing over the reef on foot at low tide.

The Niuas

The closest most people will ever get to the remote Niuas (meaning Rich in Coconuts), in Tonga's extreme northern reaches, is picking up a first-day cover of Niuafo'ou's decorative postage stamps. Tongan tradition remains very much alive on these three small volcanic islands. The highest-quality white mats are made in Niuatoputapu and Niuafo'ou, while Tafahi *kava* (an intoxicating drink made from the root of the pepper shrub) is renowned as the best in the island kingdom. The solitude of the environment has given the people a decidedly mellow attitude towards their world and visitors, and those venturing this far will have a truly rewarding cultural experience without distractions.

To most Tongans, Niuafo'ou is an enigma. They may have a vague idea of where it is but psychologically it is unimaginably far away. Perhaps for this reason, Niuafo'ou's inhabitants are credited with fortitude and often regarded with reverence by other Tongans. The people of Niuafo'ou are largely self-sufficient and fiercely proud of their lonely, comparatively sterile island with no harbour or landing place and a generally very turbulent sea. Many vow they will never leave – even if Niuafo'ou erupts again – 'because our fathers lived here before us and here they are buried'. Niuafo'ou is the only island in Tonga with a notably different dialect, closer to Samoan than Tongan, and very little English is spoken here. Despite a sultry climate the highly traditional and conservative culture requires modest dress (no short shorts or skirts above the knee, and baggy clothes for swimming) and minimal exposed skin.

THE NIUAS

HIGHLIGHTS

- Exploring Niuafo'ou's lava fields, freshwater lakes and walking trails, and catching a glimpse of the **megapode** (p267)
- Cooling off in the fresh waters of **Niutoua Spring** (p267)
- Watching the precarious loading and unloading of supplies at **harbourless Niuafo'ou** (p270)
- Walking Niuatoputapu's inland **ridges** (p267) and combing its **beaches and water channels** (p267)
- Sighting Samoa from the cone-shaped peak of **Tafahi** (p268)

★ Niuafo'ou

Tafahi's Peak
★
Niutoua Spring ★
Niuatoputapu ★

| ▪ POPULATION: 2168 | ▪ AREA: 72 SQ KM |

www.lonelyplanet.com

GETTING THERE & AWAY

Any trip to the Niuas should be approached with flexibility, as weather conditions often cause delays and cancellations of services. **Airlines Tonga Air Fiji** (Airlines Tonga; ☎ 23690; fax 23238; www.airlinestonga.com) flies from Tongatapu via Vava'u for Niutoputapu's Mata'aho Airport (one-way fare from Tongatapu/Vava'u T$390/245) and Niuafo'ou's Queen Lavinia Airport (T$430/285).

The MV *'Olovaha* travels the 240km distance north from Vava'u to Niuatoputapu roughly once every six weeks (depending on government subsidies). It continues to Niuafo'ou (640km north and slightly west of Tongatapu), returning a couple of days later on the long (2½-day) return journey to Tongatapu. Getting to Niuafo'ou by boat is a fraught business as the island lacks a decent anchorage or landing site, leaving access to the mercy of wind and waves (see the boxed text, p270). And if the weather isn't at its best, the boat must turn around and leave without stopping. Always check the *'Olovaha's* schedule in Nuku'alofa before you make any plans to visit the Niuas by sea. See p286 for more information.

Most visitors to the Niuas arrive on the 100-odd cruisers that pass through en route to Samoa, Fiji and Tonga's Vava'u Group, generally between the months of June and September. During this season you may be able to join a crew on a yacht deapting from 'Apia (Samoa) or from Pago Pago (American Samoa) for Niuatoputapu.

NIUATOPUTAPU

area 18 sq km / pop 1283

The squashed sombrero shape of Niuatoputapu (meaning 'Very Sacred Coconut') is made up of a steep and narrow central ridge 130m high, and surrounding coastal plains. Much of this is plantation land, with many archaeological sites hidden in the undergrowth waiting to be explored.

The north coast is bounded by a series of reefs, but there is a passage through to Falehau Wharf; yachts anchor just northwest of here.

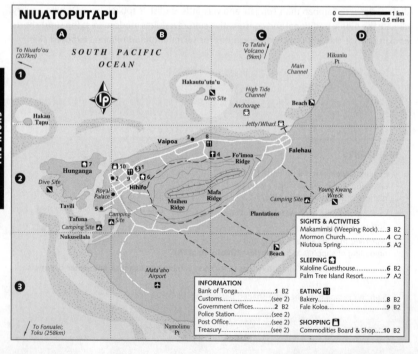

THE NIUAFO'OU MEGAPODE

Niuafo'ou's fascinating brown and grey Niuafo'ou megapode *(Megapodius pritchardii)*, locally known as *malau*, spends the day on the forest floor, subsisting on seeds, insects, worms, fruit and even small geckos, and roosts in the treetops.

Megapode pairs inhabit the shores of Niuafo'ou's crater lakes, keeping track of each other with a sort of mating duet. When it's time to lay an egg, a megapode hen digs a burrow 1m to 2m deep in the loose volcanic soil near active steam vents (usually in the same place where she herself hatched). She deposits a disproportionately large egg and covers it with earth, leaving it to incubate unattended in the naturally heated volcanic environment. A hen may lay up to 10 eggs, normally at intervals of about two weeks.

The chicks hatch after around four weeks and are forced to make their own way to the surface over a couple of days, at risk from the long-legged ants that head for their eyes. When they finally emerge from this gruelling 'birth', they bear a full coat of feathers and are able to fly and fend for themselves.

Owls and domestic cats prey on adult megapodes, but the greatest threat is from humans. Habitat destruction and the local predilection for eggs and flesh are driving this incredible bird to extinction. A recent experiment saw the transplanting of chicks to the uninhabited volcanic island of Late, in the Vava'u Group.

INFORMATION

Sleepy Hihifo is the Niuas' 'capital' and boasts a police station, a post office and a couple of small stores.

Change cash and travellers cheques at the Treasury, though it sometimes runs out of cash so bring *pa'anga* (Tongan currency) from Tongatapu. You'll find the police station, post office and customs office all situated in the Government Offices.

SIGHTS & ACTIVITIES

Niuatoputapu's most interesting sights can be covered over a couple of days' pleasurable walking; you'll be greeted by smiles and a 'What is your name?' from every child you meet (exhausting their English vocabulary in the process).

The island is surrounded by magnificent white beaches of remarkable diversity and is easily circumnavigated in seven to eight hours (an 11km round trip).

There's good diving outside the **reef**, and plenty of lobster, but no diving equipment is available on the island. Boat trips can be arranged with local fishermen for around T$30 per hour.

Niutoua Spring

The cool, sparkling pool of Niutoua Spring flows through a crack in the rock just west of Hihifo. It's full of fish, though fishing here is banned (for reasons why, listen to one of the four versions of the spring's le-

gend). A swim here will take the bite out of a typically sticky Niuas day. The spectacle of *palangi* (foreigners) swimming will quickly draw an audience. Kids appear to ditch school and adults abandon their work, just to attend the free entertainment.

Beaches & Swimming

The most beautiful beaches are on the northwest side of the island and on Hunganga, an offshore islet. Near Hihifo, a maze of shallow waterways winds between the islets of Nukuseilala, Tafuna, Tavili and Hunganga. At low tide, they form vast expanses of sand and leaning palms, and you can walk anywhere in the area by wading through a few centimetres of water. At high tide the passages (especially between Niuatoputapu and Hunganga) are excellent for swimming.

Makamimisi (Weeping Rock), right on the coast in Vaipoa, is the outlet to the sea for a spring that's a little way inland; when it's dry, you can pound on this rock with another rock to bring up fresh water.

Ridge Walk

The central ridge, comprising three smaller ridges, affords a grand view of the coastal plain and the multicoloured reefs of the lagoon. Reaching it requires a bit of effort. From the village of Vaipoa, take the route past the bakery and Mormon church, then continue upwards through the maze of trails until you reach a very steep taro plantation. Once you've scrambled about 20m above the highest taro plant, you're on the ridge.

You can follow the ridge in either direction. The eastern route entails a near-vertical rock climb of about 10m but it's easy to do, with clear footholds.

SLEEPING & EATING
There are excellent camp sites to the west of Hihifo and on the beach along the island's south coast, though you need to get permission before camping (p271).

Fale (traditional thatched houses) on Hunganga beach front feature comforts such as baths, hot water and electricity, and provide a comfortable base for exploration or navel gazing. Meals at **Palm Tree Island Resort** (☎ 85090; fax 85123; palmtreeislandtonga@yahoo.it; s/d fale T$180/220, half/full board T$35/50) contain lots of fresh fish and organic fruit and vegetables, and the owners even bake muffins and cakes. There's a dinghy shuttle to Hihifo or you can walk across at low tide. Snorkelling, fishing and walking trips can be arranged.

Warm hospitality awaits in this Hihifo village home. **Kaloline Guesthouse** (☎ 85021; s/d T$20/25) has a spacious lounge and neat rooms with mosquito nets over chintzy bed covers. Guests can use the kitchen or book meals in advance.

Take your own food to the island. Limited groceries may be purchased at *fale koloa* (small grocery kiosks) and bread is available at the bakeries in Hihifo and Vaipoa after about noon every day, including Sunday.

TAFAHI

area 3.4 sq km / pop 150
Looming like the mythical Bali Hai (the island created by James A Michener in his 1946 short-story collection *Tales of the South Pacific*), the perfect cone of extinct volcano Tafahi dominates the view from Niuatoputapu's north coast.

On the right tide, you can cross to Tafahi (9km and 40 minutes north of Niuatoputapu by boat) in the morning and return in the afternoon. A 3½-hour return walk to the summit (656m) takes an intermittent trail, leading up the gradual northern slope and connecting the two landing sites on the island. At the crater on a clear day you can

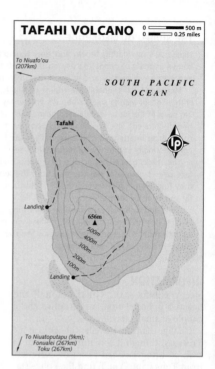

TAFAHI VOLCANO

see the 1866m peak of Savai'i's Mt Silisili (Samoa), over 200km away.

Vanilla and some of Tonga's best *kava* are grown in small quantities on Tafahi.

The northern landing is the one to use, though you can only come in or out on a wave, and only at high tide. Arrange a price for boat transfers with local fishermen before departure (up to T$80), or ask around for local boats heading out there. Carry food and plenty of water.

A similar legend to the one relating to Mt Talau in the Vava'u Group (p252) tells that the island of Tafahi is the mountain that was stolen from Niuafo'ou by ghosts who tried to pull it to Samoa.

NIUAFO'OU

area 49 sq km / pop 735
Remote Niuafo'ou resembles a doughnut floating in the sea, its water-filled caldera encircled by new lava flows. Its pseudonym, 'Tin Can Island', derives from the island's unusual previous postal service. Since there

was no anchorage or landing site, mail and supplies for residents were sealed up in a biscuit tin and tossed overboard from a passing supply ship, then a strong swimmer would retrieve the parcel. Outbound mail was tied to the end of metre-long sticks, and the swimmer would carry them balanced overhead, out to the waiting ship. This method persisted until 1931, when the mail swimmer was taken by a shark.

HISTORY

Niuafo'ou's hot and shaky past 150 years have included 10 major volcanic eruptions and the destruction of three villages. Lava oozed over the villages of 'Ahau and Futu in the eruptions of 1853 and 1929, respec-

tively, burying them completely. In 1943 a particularly violent eruption caused a general famine, destroying plantations and decimating natural vegetation.

Earthquakes and lava flows on the northern slope destroyed the erstwhile wharf and capital village, 'Angaha, in September 1946. Although a quick evacuation prevented injuries, Queen Salote decided to evacuate the island as future eruptions could render the place uninhabitable. Beginning in late October, the reluctant islanders were shuttled by boat to Tongatapu, then resettled on 'Eua. The 22 recalcitrant inhabitants who refused to leave during the general evacuation were forcibly collected in October 1947, leaving the island uninhabited.

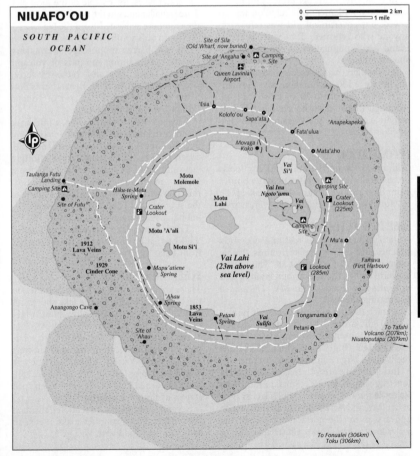

NIUAFO'OU

LANDING AT NIUAFO'OU

Niuafo'ou has no anchorage and no wharf, and the entire island is exposed to the full wrath of the sea. Ships stop about 150m offshore; the crew drops two lines into the water, which are retrieved by swimmers and carried to the cement platform that serves as the landing site. Passengers, luggage and cargo are literally dropped or thrown into a wooden dory at an opportune moment and ferried ashore, where hulking Tongans wait to pluck them out of the rolling and pitching craft.

Returning craft are filled nearly to the gunwales with copra. Oil drums and pens of squealing pigs are thrown (again, literally) on top of the sacks, and assorted produce is tucked in wherever there's space. Finally, passengers are balanced on top. When only a few centimetres of freeboard remain and the centre of gravity of the whole mess hovers at least 1m above the gunwales the boats are shoved off through the surf. Passengers must constantly lean in one direction or another to prevent what would appear to be the imminent capsizal of the vessel. On arrival at the ship, all cargo is rolled, herded and pitched aboard.

In 1958, after many petitions by homesick islanders, resettlement of Niuafo'ou was allowed, but government aid was refused to anyone who returned. Two years later the island had a population of 345, which has since doubled.

It is thought that the volcano once reached an altitude of 1300m, but these days the highest point is only about 285m above sea level. Although there's been no obvious volcanic activity since 1946, the volcano is still classified as active.

INFORMATION

Boil all lake water before drinking; locals are generally happy to fill your water bottles from their rainwater tanks when asked.

Money can be changed at the Treasury.

SIGHTS & ACTIVITIES

Niuafo'ou has no coral reef and no sandy beaches, just open ocean surrounds. People swim only in the lake, if at all. The lack of a wharf makes the precarious loading and unloading of goods from MV 'Olovaha a fascinating spectacle.

A track (taking approximately six hours) leads right around the doughnut-shaped volcanic cone and its splendid freshwater lake, **Vai Lahi** (Big Lake), which nearly fills the island's large and mysterious crater.

Inside the lake are four major islands: **Motu Lahi** (Big Island), **Motu Si'i** (Small Island), **Motu Molemole** (Smooth Island), which has its own crater lake, and **Motu 'A'ali** (Low Island), which appears above the surface only when the water level is low. The *lapila* (telapia) fish of

the crater lakes are a staple of the local diet. Three smaller lakes in the northeast corner of the crater are separated from the big lake.

Niuafo'ou's southern and western shores are a vast, barren moonscape of **lava flows**. On the north shore, mounds of volcanic slag, lava tubes, vents and craters are accessible from the main road. Beneath this flow is the village of 'Angaha, a sort of Tongan Pompeii without the bodies.

Between Mu'a and Mata'aho, a trail leads up to a magnificent **viewpoint** looking out over Vai Si'i, Vai Lahi and the islands. Between Futu and 'Esia, another trail affords a view of the entire expanse of Vai Lahi. From Mu'a, a rough road crosses the sandy isthmus between the two major lakes, leading to the shore of Vai Lahi. Other trails lead to a bubbling sulphur spring and lava vents.

The sulphur lake, **Vai Sulifa** (also called Vai Kona, or Poison Water), is best reached from Petani village.

SLEEPING & EATING

There are numerous excellent camp sites on the crater (especially on the lake shores). A handful of village houses offer guestrooms; contact the Tonga Visitors Bureau (p187) in Tongatapu for details. Expect to have solar-powered lighting, communal cold showers and no refrigeration. Many local people would be happy to take you in for a night; a gift of corned beef or the like – even such staples as flour – is appropriate.

Several small shops are scattered through the villages. Scant supplies make it wise to bring all your food with you.

THE NIUAS

Tongan Directory

ACCOMMODATION

Unless you're on a package holiday, don't trust accommodation bookings made by airlines or travel agents, since there are often weak or missing links in the system. You may like to confirm the booking directly with the hotel. Many hotels and guesthouses now have email, so make bookings yourself,

> **BOOK ACCOMMODATION ONLINE**
>
> For more accommodation reviews and recommendations by Lonely Planet authors, check out the online booking service at www.lonelyplanet.com. You'll find the true, insider lowdown on the best places to stay. Reviews are thorough and independent. Best of all, you can book online.

particularly between May and September and over Christmas. You can often just turn up to places of accommodation without a booking, particularly guesthouses on outer islands, but then you may run the risk of there being no bed. Room rates generally stay the same throughout the year.

The accommodation options listed in this guidebook are given in order of author preference – leading each section are the places our author recommends the most. We generally treat any place that charges up to T$80 as budget accommodation. Mid-range places usually cost between T$80 and T$120, while we regard anywhere charging over T$120 as top-end accommodation.

Most accommodation options offer laundry service or a place to wash your own clothes (generally cold water). Nuku'alofa (Tongatapu) and Neiafu (Vava'u) have commercial laundries.

Camping

Camping is often discouraged in Tonga and is illegal in both the Ha'apai and Vava'u Groups, unless as part of a guided trip. In practice, seeking permission from the landowner or local community will suffice or check in with the main police station for the island.

It's possible to 'bush camp' on 'Eua, and a few accommodation places on 'Eua and Tongatapu will allow you to pitch a tent.

Camping next to a village, though, may be seen as an impolite rejection of Tongan hospitality.

Guesthouses

Guesthouses are found throughout the islands and take the place of hostels (of which

PRACTICALITIES

■ The *Tonga Chronicle* is the official paper of the Tongan government and runs a couple of articles and job ads in English.

■ The only English-language newspaper for sale is the *New Zealander*, a weekly published in Australia for New Zealanders. Other English-language periodicals include gossip magazines, the *Economist* (a weekly international business magazine) and the international edition of *Time*.

■ The English-language *Matangi Tonga* (Wind of Tonga; www.matangitonga.to) website has the best coverage of Tongan issues at home and abroad and addresses some sensitive topics.

■ Tune into Radio New Zealand International (www.rnzi.com; 15720kHz, 9885kHz, 9870kHz and 17675kHz); Radio Australia (www.abc.net.au/ra; shortwave frequencies include 5995kHz, 12080kHz, 15515kHz), broadcast at Nuku'alofa 103FM and 101.7FM; and BBC World Service (www.bbc.co.uk/worldservice; no direct service, refer to the East Asia schedule online). See each website for details on shortwave and satellite radio frequencies and listening via the Internet.

■ Tonga has both the PAL video format system, used in Australasia and most of Western Europe, and the NTSC system, used in North America and Japan.

■ Power in Tonga is 240V, 50Hz AC. Three-pronged plugs used in New Zealand and Australia are OK here. European appliances require a plug adaptor. US appliances require a plug adaptor plus a voltage converter. Bring a 'surge breaker' or 'spike buster' to protect sensitive appliances from Tonga's erratic power supply.

■ Tonga uses the standard metric system for everything except land area, which is mostly measured in acres. See the table inside the front cover of this book for metric and imperial unit conversions.

there is only one, Adventure Backpackers on Vava'u). They usually have large, homey communal lounge areas with plenty of islander style – an explosion of colour, doilies, fluoro plastic flowers and beads.

Most guesthouses are clean, can provide good-value home-cooked meals and allow guests to use the cooking facilities for a few extra *pa'anga*. Nightly rates range from T$11 to T$25 per person. Bathroom facilities are generally communal and outside Tongatapu often have only cold showers.

Homestays

Frequently, foreigners will be invited by Tongans to stay in their homes. There could be no better way to learn about the culture and lifestyle of the country, and the hospitality of the Tongan people is abundant and genuine. Keep in mind, though, that their means are limited and although they might proudly refuse any monetary compensation, simple gifts such as *kava* (an intoxicating drink made from the root of the pepper shrub) or tinned corned beef will be greatly appreciated.

Bear in mind that 'borrowing' may occur (see Security, p278). Look after your valuables and don't leave anything of obvious value lying around within view.

Hotels & Resorts

Tonga is not a destination for the precious traveller seeking pampering, but will reward the more adventurous soul with unique experiences and plenty of comforts. 'Resort' is a loose term here and seems to apply more to location – generally on an idyllic, uninhabited coral island or strip of perfect beach – than particular services or facilities offered. Larger hotels often disappoint, while a handful of boutique-style hotels in Nuku'alofa and Vava'u, and resorts on the outer islands, offer the most atmospheric and luxurious accommodation in unique surrounds. If all you want is a good bed in an eclectic bungalow with million-dollar beach views, fresh food plucked from the sea, a decent coffee and water to slip into a few steps away, you'll love what's on offer.

Rental Accommodation

Self-contained, furnished apartments are available in Nuku'alofa and some long-term residents may rent out their private homes in Vava'u. Refer to the Sleeping sections in individual chapters for details.

ACTIVITIES

You could easily pass a couple of weeks on the beach or in a hammock, but Tonga is also an excellent active holiday destination, with a diverse range of activities – both organised and self-propelled. The website www.tongaholiday.com has links to operators of diving, surfing, sailing, kayaking, cruising, fishing and whale-watching trips.

Vava'u reigns supreme as activity king of the island groups, but don't overlook the charms of other island groups. Tongatapu Island offers easily accessible snorkelling; 'Eua is the spot for rock climbing, bird-watching, bushwalking and caving; and Ha'apai has heaps of sand, some incredible diving and the volcanic island of Tofua for adventurous exploring.

Horse-riding is an option throughout the islands. There are no ranches (and very few saddles – blanket padding is often supplied), so horse hire will need to be arranged directly with the horse's owner. Guesthouse owners will generally help out.

See each destination chapter for details of local operators.

Bird-Watching

Tonga is not renowned for its birdlife, but there are sea-bird colonies of noddies, terns, great frigate birds and tropic birds (white-tailed and the rare red-tailed variety) on all of the main islands. Possible twitching spots include Hufangalupe on Tongatapu, Maninita in Vava'u, Luahoko in Ha'apai and Lakufa'anga on 'Eua, along with its entire forest and cliff-top viewpoints.

The purple-crowned and many-coloured fruit doves are the most exotic species found on Tongatapu. The red shining parrot can be seen in the 'Eua Plantation Forest and National Park. Mt Talau (p252) on Vava'u is home to a number of bird species and boat trips can be arranged to the breeding grounds on remote Maninita. Most twitchers will be more interested in seeing the Niuafo'ou megapode around Niuafo'ou's central lakes, though the logistics of this are problematic (see p270).

For further reference, pick up a copy of *Field Guide to Landbirds of Tonga* by Claudia Matavalea.

Bushwalking

And beach walking! With hundreds of kilometres of sandy beaches (especially in Ha'apai and on Niuatoputapu) it would almost be a sin not to circle at least a few islands. The only potentially hazardous creepy-crawlies you might meet on land are centipedes.

'Eua offers the best, most accessible areas for bushwalking (mostly over forested terrain), while the Niuas (p265) and Tofua in Ha'apai (p240) both have a combination of volcanic landscapes, ash fields and dense forest. Kao (p240, 1046m), Tonga's highest peak, can also be climbed. Vava'u Island (p248) is a maze of trails and 4WD tracks, while its uninhabited islands offer peaceful explorations.

Trails in Tonga quickly become overgrown, replacing bushwalking with bushwhacking in many areas (particularly 'Eua's rainforest, see p220), and signs and markers tend to disappear – making bushwalking here all the more tempting to trailblazers.

To get the most out of extended bushwalking in Tonga bring a tent, good strong boots, tough trousers, mosquito repellent, cooking equipment (camping gas is not available), a compass and plenty of water containers – finding fresh water can be a problem and sometimes several days' supply must be carried. See the boxed text Responsible Walking, p274. In Vava'u and Ha'apai camping is illegal, but in practice as long as you have permission from the property owner you should have no problems. See p271 for further details.

Caving

With dozens of limestone caves, caverns and tunnels, 'Eua (p218) is the best place for caving in Tonga, though it's a do-it-yourself affair for those already experienced underground and totally self-sufficient in terms of equipment and emergency support.

Smaller land caves can be explored on other islands, while scuba diving outfits continue to discover amazing sea caves, caverns and 'cathedrals' off 'Eua, Vava'u and the Ha'apai Group that experienced divers can explore.

Diving & Snorkelling

Tonga's reefs are among the richest and most diverse ecosystems in the world. Many can be accessed straight from the shore, but

RESPONSIBLE WALKING

Rubbish

■ If you've carried it in, you can carry it back out – everything, including empty packaging, citrus peel and cigarette butts, can be stowed in a dedicated rubbish bag. Make an effort to pick up rubbish left by others.

■ Sanitary napkins, tampons and condoms don't burn or decompose readily, so carry them out, whatever the inconvenience.

■ Burying rubbish disturbs soil and ground cover and encourages erosion and weed growth. Buried rubbish takes years to decompose and will probably be dug up by wild animals who may be injured or poisoned by it.

■ Before you go on your walk remove all surplus food packaging and put small-portion packages in a single container to minimise waste.

Human Waste Disposal

■ If a toilet is provided at a campsite, please use it.

■ Where there isn't one, bury your waste. Dig a small hole 15cm deep and at least 30m from any stream, 50m from paths and 200m from any buildings. Take a lightweight trowel or a large tent peg for the purpose. Cover the waste with a good layer of soil. Toilet paper should be burnt, although this is not recommended in a forest, above the tree line or in dry grassland; otherwise, carry it out – burying is a last resort. Ideally, use biodegradable paper.

■ Contamination of water sources by human faeces can lead to the transmission of giardia, a human bacterial parasite.

Camping

■ In remote areas, use a recognised site rather than creating a new one. Keep at least 30m away from watercourses and paths. Move on after a night or two.

■ Pitch your tent away from hollows where water is likely to accumulate so that it won't be necessary to dig damaging trenches if it rains heavily.

■ Leave your site as you found it – with minimal or no trace of your use.

Washing

■ Don't use detergents or toothpaste in or near streams or lakes; even if they are biodegradable they can harm fish and wildlife.

■ To wash yourself, use biodegradable soap and a water container at least 50m from the watercourse. Disperse the waste water widely so it filters through the soil before returning to the stream.

■ Wash cooking utensils 50m from watercourses using a scourer or gritty sand instead of detergent.

Fires

■ Use a safe existing fireplace rather than making a new one. Don't surround it with rocks – they're just another visual scar – but clear away all flammable material within at least 2m. Keep the fire small (under 1 sq metre) and use a minimum of dead, fallen wood.

■ Be absolutely certain the fire is extinguished. Spread the embers and drown them with water. Turn the embers over to check the fire is extinguished throughout. Scatter the charcoal and cover the fire site with soil and leaves.

Access

■ Many of the walks in this book pass through private property, although it may not be obvious at the time, along recognised routes where access is freely permitted. If there seems to be some doubt about this, ask someone nearby if it's OK to walk through.

TONGAN DIRECTORY

reef quality generally improves the further you are from a population centre, and you may need a boat to see the best reefs. Tonga has a great variety of scuba dive sites – soft and hard coral teeming with tropical fish, vertigo-inducing drop-offs, huge caverns (some tunnelling into islands of the Vava'u Group!), channels, magnificent geological formations (some volcanic), tunnels and wrecks are all found in Tonga's waters.

Between June and November dives are accompanied by the mesmerising murmur of humpback whalesong. Dolphins, sea turtles and rays are present year-round.

Visibility is outstanding and averages 30m to 50m on the barrier reefs around Tongatapu and Vava'u, reaching up to 70m in winter. Visibility is slightly lower in Ha'apai during summer as the island group is more exposed. Water temperatures range between 23°C and 29°C, with the sheltered waters of Vava'u' seeming to stay warmer longer. Still, a 3mm wet suit is still a good idea.

Snorkellers can often tag along with a dive group in order to access coral gardens off the beaten track. A collection of marine reserves and beautiful reefs provide accessible snorkelling north of Tongatapu (p213). In Ha'apai (p227) you're never too far from a reef with excellent coral gardens, and in Vava'u (p246) most boat/snorkelling trips visit beautiful coral gardens.

You'll need diving certification to dive in Tonga. Make sure you explain your level of experience before planning any dive and don't be tempted to dive beyond your ability. Carefully inspect all rental gear before heading out for a dive, as we have received reports that some divers have found these not up to scratch. Tonga's dive operators are affiliated either with PADI, NAUI, SSI or CMAS. Expect to pay between US$65 and US$90 for a two-tank dive (that's two separate dives on a single trip) inclusive of equipment. Booking packages will get you a discount.

There is no decompression chamber in Tonga – Suva (Fiji) has one, but patients are usually transferred to New Zealand. See p301 for details regarding the bends.

Fishing

Anglers are lured to Tonga from around the world for its sport fishing and big game fishing, thanks to the plummeting depths of the Tongan Trench not far offshore. The main game includes yellowfin and skipjack tuna, wahoo, barracuda, sailfish, mahi mahi and blue, black and striped marlin. Marlin can be caught year-round, though most are caught between July and November (August and September are the peak months).

Vava'u (p246) is the base of much game fishing in Tonga, but there are a number of fine boats available for charter in Tongatapu (p181).

Trawling (towing a number of lures on long lines behind a boat) takes place in the very deep waters surrounding Tonga. Some of it – in Vava'u and Tongatapu – is focused around Fish Aggregating Devices (FADs). Bottom fishing and salt-water fly fishing can be catered for and equipment is usually provided, though quality is variable. Salt-water fly fisherfolk should bring their own tackle.

Tonga International Game Fishing Association (Tigfa) holds an international competition in Vava'u in September – temporary membership allows you to enter competitions. Tag and release earns higher points.

For Tongan-style fishing trips (with hand lines) ask around at the various wharfs in Tonga or at the place you're staying. In the more remote areas, you may even see octopus ensnared by locals using intriguing cowry shell lures.

Rock Climbing

The sheer, 150m limestone cliffs on the east coast of 'Eua and caves running off sinkholes offer Tonga's best climbing. There are some great, largely unclimbed routes, though there's always a strong easterly wind off the ocean. The rock is pretty sharp, but there are plenty of holds. The best places to anchor off are around or on Lokupo and Lauua lookouts. Bring all your own gear.

Many of the islands in Vava'u have squat but promising 40m sea cliffs, most of them untried and untested. Vava'u Surf & Adventure Tours (p247) takes people abseiling into Swallow's Cave.

See also Caving on p273.

Sailing

Tonga is well known for some of the best sailing in the South Pacific. Yacht charter activity in the kingdom is based in Vava'u (p246). Easterly trade winds blow at a steady 15 to 18 knots across this group of idyllic, sheltered islands between May and

November (the most popular sailing time), and there are many excellent anchorages and a couple of island resorts that welcome yachties into their restaurants. During the cyclone season – you'll be warned in plenty of time – cheap charters are sometimes available.

Ha'apai is just as picturesque, though you'll probably need your own vessel, as Vava'u-based charter companies don't allow their boats out of Vava'u. Ha'apai's anchorages offer protection from rough seas, but not from unexpected gales. Tongatapu is more limited for cruising yachts, but 'Eua, 'Ata and the beautiful coral islands north of Tongatapu can be explored.

Sailors should be aware that Tongan sea charts are not 100% accurate and are thus inappropriate for GPS navigation. However, due to the great visibility, navigating around Tonga's reef systems is not difficult – though a moderate level of experience is required. See p294 for more information on sailing to and from Tonga.

See p295 for listings of cruising guides.

Sea-Kayaking

Sea-kayaking in Tonga was recently voted amongst the top 50 adventure activities in the world. With its myriad islands, lagoons and beaches, Tonga offers great scope for sea kayakers – including the clear, sheltered waters of the Vava'u Group and the remote, traditional (and sometimes uninhabited) islands of the Ha'apai Group. Island resorts generally have a few kayaks for guest use. See p228 and p247 for details on rental gear and companies offering 'trip of a lifetime' kayaking/camping paddles through the islands in Ha'apai and Vava'u, respectively.

The islands and reefs north and northeast of Nuku'alofa (see p213) have good potential for sea-kayaking and the island resorts have some equipment for guest use, though there's no equipment available for hire in Nuku'alofa.

A 3mm wet suit is a good idea. If you bring your own kayak to Tonga you'll have to transport it around the islands by ferry.

Surfing

Tonga's winter south swell season runs from April to October when surfing is reliant on storm activity around Australia and New Zealand. The summer north swell season runs from November to March, with prevailing swells originating both in the North Pacific (the same swells that hit Hawai'i) and from cyclones in the South Pacific.

There are no beach breaks in Tonga. All surf is over shallow coral reefs, demanding an intermediate to advanced skill level. You'll definitely need booties, and you may want to consider a helmet and a basic first-aid kit – to deal with the inevitable cuts and grazes.

Great surf can be found throughout Tonga, but accessibility is the key. On Tongatapu, namely at Ha'atafu Beach, a number of surf spots are only a short paddle (100m) across the lagoon. Other breaks around Tongatapu and Vava'u are reached via boat.

Check the website of **Tonga Surfriders Association** (www.surfingtonga.com), which operates from Ha'atafu Beach Resort (see p212). It features a sample of Tongatapu's breaks and lists recommended travel agencies to book surfing holidays through. Lessons for beginners and reef novices are available.

Vava'u Surf & Adventure Tours (☎ 71283, 12515; http://groups.msn.com/cafetropicanavavautonga/; Private Bag 34, Neiafu) drops surfers on Vava'u's best breaks and organises trips. Surf information on Ha'apai is hard to get. No doubt good waves await, but they take some finding.

Whale-Watching

Nothing compares with the experience of dangling midwater, staring into an azure abyss, with a massive humpback whale nearby – a mother keeping a watchful eye and fin over its playful and curious calf, or a lone singing male sending vibrating soundwaves through your chest… Some get very 'hippy' about it, with exclamations of 'it changed my life…it looked right into my eye…it looked into my soul'. Others grow very quiet. Many men even shed tears. It's mesmerising, it's exhilarating, and to be honest, it's a bit scary too.

Tonga is an important breeding ground for humpback whales, and one of the best places in the world to see these magnificent creatures. They can be seen bearing young in the calm reef-protected ocean, caring for new calves (conceived here 11 months earlier), and engaging in elaborate mating rituals.

The whale-watching season is from June to November in Tongatapu and Ha'apai (p228), and July to November in Vava'u, which is the centre for whale-watching in Tonga (p248).

Whales can also be spotted in the deep-water channel between Tongatapu and 'Eua – often on the crossing to/from 'Eua (p222), and often so close to 'Eua they can be seen from the shore. This short trip from Tongatapu offers the most economical means of an encounter; small boat trips can be organised here also.

Tonga is one of the few places in the world where swimming with whales is possible. Most whale-watching trips provide snorkelling gear so you can swim with the whales, and some provide underwater microphones and DVD footage of your encounter (at an extra cost, of course).

Subsistence whaling in Tonga (where perhaps 10 whales were taken per year by primitive methods) occurred until 1979 when the king banned all whaling. Pressure from Japan for permission to begin whaling 'for scientific purposes' has been resisted, but 2006 will be a defining year.

See the boxed text on p171 for further information.

BUSINESS HOURS

Business hours are flexible, but are usually from 9am until 4.30pm, with most shops open from 8.30am to 5pm on weekdays (some close for an hour at lunch), and 9am to noon on Saturday. *Fale koloa* (small grocery kiosks) have the longest hours, from around 6am to 10pm Monday to Saturday.

Restaurants usually operate from 8am to 10am for breakfast, noon to 2pm for lunch, and 6pm to 10pm if they serve evening meals. Larger hotels and a few Chinese restaurants open to the public on Sunday, but most restaurants are closed. Produce markets generally operate from 6am to 4pm on weekdays and are busiest from 6am to noon on Saturday.

Bakeries become the social hub on Sunday afternoon, with wafts of freshly baked bread, pastries and pies drawing customers in. They open from about noon (around 4pm on smaller islands) to anywhere between 8pm and 11pm. Note, however, that time in Tonga is tolerated rather than obeyed. Be prepared for prearranged meeting times and standard opening hours to regularly be ignored without a hint of remorse or social consequence.

CHILDREN

Some hotels in Tonga allow children to stay free of charge, others have a reduced children's rate, and a few do not accept children at all.

Lonely Planet's *Travel with Children* is a useful resource with plenty of pre-trip and on-the-road tips.

Practicalities

Children aged under two travel for 10% of the standard fare (or free) on airlines; however, they don't get a seat or baggage allowance. Children aged between two and 12 can usually occupy a seat for half to two-thirds of the full fare and will be eligible for a baggage allowance.

Hire cars rarely have child seats, so you'll need to bring your own and check that it clips into seat belts.

The larger supermarkets in Nuku'alofa and Neiafu are well stocked and will probably have everything you need, but at a price. Bring as much as possible from home, including any special foods required. Disposable nappies (diapers), cartons of fruit juice, and UHT and powdered milk are widely available, but out of Nuku'alofa, sunscreen and insect repellent can be hard, if not impossible, to find.

See p177 for tips on dining.

Sights & Activities

Tonga is a great place to travel with children and there's plenty to keep them happy – swimming, snorkelling, beachcombing, bicycling, kayaking, short boat trips, visits to interesting places and cultural events (especially the Tongan feasts). Other travellers with children can be an excellent resource for local information.

Accommodation with a beach or swimming pool may be all the entertainment you need. Nuku'alofa has a couple of fenced-off parks with children's playground equipment and 'pay for use' pools.

It's worth picking up some children's snorkelling gear before arriving in Tonga in order to get a good, leak-free fit. The range in Tonga is very limited.

CLIMATE CHARTS

Despite its great latitudinal range, Tonga does not experience dramatically diverse climatic conditions. Vava'u and the Niuas

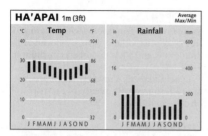

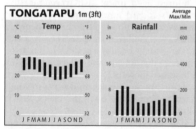

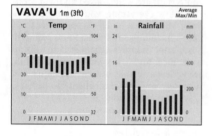

are noticeably warmer than Tongatapu, and 'Eua is noticeably cooler.

CUSTOMS

Travellers aged 18 and older may import up to 500 cigarettes, 2.25L of spirits and 4.5L of wine duty-free. Animals, fruit and plant products require a quarantine certificate. The import of firearms, ammunition, drugs and pornographic material is prohibited.

DANGERS & ANNOYANCES
Animals

There are a lot of dogs roaming around Tonga. Most are either friendly or will keep their distance, but a few (especially when they're in packs) are aggressive. Pretending to throw a stone often discourages them.

Sea Creatures

Tonga is surrounded by a lot of open ocean inhabited by an impressive range of marine species, from colourful, tropical coral dwellers to large pelagics. Tropical marine creatures encountered can sting, bite or stun, including jellyfish, cone shells, stinging corals or cone fish – see Venomous Marine Life boxed text, p301. Shark incidents rarely occur, though they are known to hang around the calving humpback whales, for obvious reasons. If you're concerned, seek local advice.

Security

Tonga is one of the safest destinations in the South Pacific and theft from the individual is rarely a problem; however, items left lying around can wander.

'Borrowing' is rife. By Tongan reckoning, all property is effectively communal. If one person has something another needs, the latter either asks for it or surreptitiously 'borrows' it. Of course, it can be 'borrowed' back if needed, but it will otherwise never again see its rightful owner. Unattended items are considered ripe for 'borrowing', so watch your possessions. Unfortunately most long-term residents experience a 'break and enter' and theft of property.

The threat of rape does exist, but you can easily protect yourself by using common sense and avoiding drinking alcohol alone with Tongan men (see p284).

Travellers cheques are one of the safest ways to carry money (be sure to keep the receipts separate). Keep a handful of small denomination notes handy for day-to-day transactions but put the rest in a moneybelt or another safe place.

DISABLED TRAVELLERS

Tonga is not out of bounds for those with a physical disability and a sense of adventure despite its lack of suitable facilities. Tongans are friendly and helpful people who will do their best to accommodate you. Places of accommodation with the easiest access (though no purpose-built facilities) include The Villa Guest Lodge, The Black Pearl Suites, Papiloa's Friendly Islander Hotel and Seaview Lodge in Nuku'alofa (p191); Fonongava'inga Guesthouse in Ha'apai (p232) and Sandy Beach Resort in Foa (p236); Adventure Backpackers and Paradise International Hotel in Vava'u (p253); and The Hideaway on 'Eua (p223).

Get in touch with your national support organisation before leaving home for recommendations on travel literature and specialist travel agents to help with holiday planning.

Warn airlines at the time of booking if you require special arrangements for wheelchair assistance at airports, visual or audio notification of airport announcements or special meals on the flight. Disability-friendly website **Allgohere** (www.everybody.co.uk) has an invaluable airline accessibility guide.

EMBASSIES & CONSULATES
Tongan Embassies & Consulates
Tonga has diplomatic representatives in the following countries:

UK (☎ 020-7724 5828; fax 020-7723 9074; 36 Molyneux St, London W1H 6AB)

USA Hawai'i (☎ 808-953 2449; fax 808-955 1447; Suite 306B, 738 Kaheka St, Honolulu, HI 96814); CA (☎ 415-781 0365; www.tongaconsulate.us; Suite 604, 360 Post St, San Francisco, CA 94108)

Embassies & Consulates in Tonga
It's important to realise what your own embassy – the embassy of the country of which you are a citizen – can and can't do to help you if you get into trouble. Generally speaking, it won't be much help in emergencies if the trouble you're in is remotely your own fault. Remember that while in Tonga you are bound by Tongan laws. Your embassy won't be sympathetic if you end up in jail after committing an offence locally, even if such an action is legal in your own country.

The following foreign diplomatic representatives are found in Nuku'alofa:

Australia (☎ 23244; fax 23243; www.embassy.gov .au/to.html; Salote Rd; ⏰ 8.30am-12.30pm & 1.30-5pm Mon-Fri) High Commission. Limited Canadian consular services available here.

China (☎ 24554; fax 24596; Vuna Rd) Embassy.

European Union (☎ 23820; eutonga@kalianet.to; Taufa'ahau Rd) European Commission.

Germany (☎ 23477; fax 23154; Taufa'ahau Rd) Honorary Consulate.

New Zealand (☎ 23122; nzhcnuk@kalianet.to; Taufa'ahau Rd; ⏰ 8.30am-12.30pm & 1-4pm Mon-Fri) High Commission.

UK (☎ 24395; fax 24109; Vuna Rd) High Commission.

USA (Peace Corps; ☎ 25466; Ministry of Foreign Affairs 23600) National Reserve Bank.

FESTIVALS & EVENTS
Tongan families need little excuse for a feast: a birthday, a visitor, an academic accomplishment, a birth, a marriage or just a sunny Sunday are all good reasons. University graduations, religious holidays, children's first birthdays and royal birthdays invite celebration on an even larger scale, often with several days of feasting, dancing and organised entertainment. Instead of fireworks, youngsters detonate homemade bamboo and kerosene bazookas that explode with the same impact as heavy artillery.

Some of Tonga's organised annual festivals are listed below.

February
Vava'u Tuna Fest A one-week tuna festival with plenty of cultural land action too.

March/April
Easter Festival A week-long festival featuring youth choirs, passion plays, band concerts and cultural performances.

May
Vava'u Festival The Crown Prince's birthday sets the stage for the Vava'u Festival, a popular week of partying.
'Eua Festival Starting on 28 May this is a two-week festival based around the national park.
Red Cross Festival A major event in Tonga which is capped off with the Red Cross Grand Ball in Nuku'alofa.

June
Ha'apai Festival The most prominent annual event in the Ha'apai Group, this week-long festival in early June precedes Emancipation Day festivities.

July
Heilala Festival The king's birthday is celebrated on Tongatapu with this festival named after the country's national flower. It's a week-long bash featuring parades and processions, music festivals and competitions, cultural events and dance, art, craft, beauty and sports competitions. Coinciding with this festival is the torch-lighting ceremony *Tupakapakanava* in which people line the northern coastline of Tongatapu carrying flaming torches of dry reeds.
Miss Galaxy Pageant Held in Nuku'alofa, this international *fakaleiti* (see the boxed text, p161) competition is always sold out. It's great fun.
Kalia Cup Regatta A 10-day event around Vava'u's islands with plenty of onshore revelling at the end of each race.

August-October
Agricultural Fairs Derived from the ancient *'inasi* festivals, agricultural fairs take place in all the major island groups and are presided over by the king. The first is normally on Vava'u, followed by Ha'apai, Tongatapu and 'Eua.

September

Tonga International Billfish Tournament Local and international anglers are lured to Vava'u in late September to compete in this fishing tournament. Fish tagged and released get higher points.

GAY & LESBIAN TRAVELLERS

Homosexuality is an accepted fact of life in Tonga and you'll see plenty of gay men around. There are also *fakaleiti* – men who dress and behave as women. Whatever lesbian population exists is much more undercover and not at all vocal.

While there's no need for gay or lesbian travellers to hide their sexuality in Tonga, public displays of sexual affection are frowned upon, whether gay or straight.

HOLIDAYS

Primary and secondary school holidays include two weeks beginning the second week of May, two weeks beginning the third week of August and six weeks beginning the first week of December. You may get the feeling that '4' is the royal lucky number for public holidays.

New Year's Day 1 January
Good Friday, Easter Sunday & Easter Monday March/April
Anzac Day 25 April
HRH Crown Prince Tupouto'a's Birthday 4 May
Emancipation Day 4 June
King Taufa'ahau Tupou IV's Birthday 4 July
Constitution Day 4 November
King George I's Birthday 4 December
Christmas Day 25 December
Boxing Day 26 December

INSURANCE

Always take out travel insurance. You should be covered for the worst-case scenario (eg an accident that requires medical evacuation and repatriation). Check the small print to ensure the policy you take out covers the endeavours you intend to partake in, which may be deemed 'dangerous activities', such as diving and even trekking.

If you are planning long-term travel, insurance may seem very expensive – but if you can't afford it, you certainly won't be able to afford a serious medical emergency overseas.

Worldwide cover for travellers from more than 44 countries is available online at www .lonelyplanet.com/travel_services.

INTERNET ACCESS

Internet access is expensive (expect to pay T$6 to T$8 per hour, though some will try to slug you for more) anywhere except Tongatapu, where you can find places charging T$2 per hour. Outside Nuku'alofa, the best value access is through high schools, which also offer the only access on 'Eua and Niuatoputapu.

LEGAL MATTERS

Police and government officials in Tonga seem friendly, helpful and straightforward, but don't overstay your visa, get caught with illegal substances or offend a member of the nobility. For legal information or representation, see 'Law Practitioners' in the Yellow Pages of the *Tonga Telephone Directory*.

MAPS

Maps in this guidebook are ample for a traveller's needs, and give the most detail you will find on maps generally available.

The Tonga Visitors Bureau dispenses a simple map of Tonga's major islands and island groups, plus street maps of Nuku'alofa (Tongatapu) and Neiafu (Vava'u), while a sketchy map of the island groups is available at the Friendly Islands Bookshop. It's handy to mark up an 'Eua map (small and lacking much detail) with greater detail before heading out for a hike.

The **Ministry of Lands, Survey & Natural Resources** (Map pp184-5; ☎ 23611; www.lands.gov.to; PO Box 5, Vuna Rd, Nuku'alofa) sells topographic dyeline prints (most scaled 1:50,000) of individual island groups. Unfortunately, however they don't give much detail or labelling. Download them at www.lands.gov.to/tiki /tiki-index.php.

The **Hydrographic Unit** (☎ 24696; fax 23150; PO Box 72, Touliki Naval Base, Nuku'alofa) has navigational sea charts of individual island groups and their harbours. At 1:72,600, these charts aren't accurate enough for GPS navigation.

New Zealand–based **Trans Pacific Marine** (www.transpacific.co.nz) sells a chart folio called *Tonga and the Niue Islands* (NZ$250) including charts, approaches, landings and anchorages, and also sells them separately for NZ$22.

A reduced-size sea chart of the Vava'u Group (around T$16) is available from various places in Neiafu.

MONEY

Tongan banknotes come in denominations of one, two, five, 10, 20 and 50 *pa'anga* (written T$1, T$2 etc). One hundred *seniti* make up T$1 and these coins come in denominations of one, five, 10, 20 and 50 *seniti.*

The banks are open from at least 9am to 3.30pm or 4pm weekdays; in Nuku'alofa and Neiafu some open from 8.30am to noon on Saturday as well. Money can be changed at the Treasury offices on the more remote islands of Niuatoputapu and Niuafo'ou.

A currency exchange window at the airport on Tongatapu is open for all international arrivals and departures.

For information about taxes in Tonga, see p16.

ATMs

Both ANZ and Westpac Bank of Tonga have ATMs in Nuku'alofa which accept credit and debit cards from Visa, MasterCard and Cirrus. ANZ's Neiafu branch has an ATM inside the bank, available during business hours. Don't leave it until your last *seniti* to access money – ATMs can be fickle.

Cash

Currency exchange is relatively straightforward. Australian, Fijian, New Zealand and US dollars and pounds sterling are the most easily exchanged currencies (both cash and travellers cheques), but euros and yen are also widely accepted in Tonga. Surprisingly few businesses accept payment in anything but Tongan *pa'anga.*

Credit Cards

Credit cards are accepted at many tourist facilities (attracting a 5% fee), with MasterCard, Visa and American Express the most common; JCB is also accepted. There are ATMs with Visa, MasterCard and Cirrus facilities in Nuku'alofa (Tongatapu) and Neiafu (Vava'u).

Cash advances using MasterCard and Visa can be obtained at the Westpac Bank of Tonga in Nuku'alofa, 'Ohonua ('Eua), Pangai (Ha'apai) and Neiafu. In Neiafu and Nuku'alofa you can also get cash advances at the ANZ bank should you not be able to use the ATM. MBF only gives advances on MasterCard.

EFTPOS (Electronic Funds Transfer at Point Of Sale) credit/debit is less widespread in Tonga.

International Transfers

Given the amount of money sent home by Tongans overseas, it's no surprise that two

---

MONEY IN TONGA

In the early 1800s, when the young William Mariner explained the monetary system used by Europeans to the Tongan chief Finau, the chief immediately grasped its advantages over Tonga's traditional barter system. He also perceived a potential drawback of such a system and deemed it unsuitable for Tonga. From Mariner's book:

If money were made of iron and could be converted into knives, axes and chisels there would be some sense in placing a value on it; but as it is, I see none. If a man has more yams than he wants, let him exchange some of them away for pork... Certainly money is much handier and more convenient but then, as it will not spoil by being kept, people will store it up instead of sharing it out as a chief ought to do, and thus become selfish... I understand now very well what it is that makes the *papalangis* (foreigners) so selfish – it is this money!

Chief Finau had been disappointed to find so little of value to him on the Port-au-Prince. Unlike Captain Cook's ships, which had carried all sorts of valuables, the ship Mariner had travelled in contained only whale oil, bits of iron and 10,000 pieces of metal resembling *pa'anga* (bean-shaped playing pieces used in the game called *lafo*).

Finau had taken the pieces of metal to be worthless and assumed that the ship belonged to a very poor man indeed (King George's cook, perhaps – a cook being the lowest rank in Tongan society at the time). Having ordered the ship to be burned, the chief later realised with regret that he had burned the ship of an extremely rich man without first securing its *pa'anga*. Not surprisingly, the Tongan unit of currency is now called the *pa'anga*.

multinational money-transfer companies are heavily represented in Tonga. **Western Union** (www.westernunion.com) has dozens of offices, while **MoneyGram** (www.moneygram.com) is represented by the Bank of Tonga. Check their websites for contact details in your home country. Services are quick (a matter of minutes) and straightforward.

Tipping

Tipping and bargaining are not the usual custom in Tonga, though in some tourist facilities they do occur. Dances (see p165) are an exception; take plenty of T$1 and T$2 notes to stick on the oiled arms of dancers. While tipping is an excellent way to show your appreciation (many Tongans put tips towards paying school fees), a few *palangi*-run businesses attempt to guilt-trip tourists into tipping staff to supplement measly wages, while the management charges top dollar for services.

Travellers Cheques

Travellers cheques are the best way to carry your travel funds in Tonga. They fetch 4% to 5% more than cash, with a nominal transaction charge of only 10 *seniti* per cheque (compared to the 4% to 5% charged for credit card transactions). All brands of travellers cheques are acceptable.

PHOTOGRAPHY

Film is expensive and limited in range and good quality camera equipment is very difficult to get in Tonga, so bring everything from home. In the shops of Nuku'alofa the average cost of 100ASA 35mm colour print film is T$11/15 for a roll of 24/36 exposures (200ASA and 400ASA film is also available). APS film is available in Nuku'alofa and Neiafu. Colour slide film is harder to find. Film in Vava'u and Ha'apai is more expensive and the range is smaller.

Colour print processing can be done in Nuku'alofa (T$7/8 to T$16/24 for 24/36 prints). CD burning is available in Vava'u and Nuku'alofa, which also has a digital imaging centre.

If you think that the quest for the perfect 'people shot' is a photographer's greatest challenge, go to Tonga; it would be safe to say that nowhere else in the world will you find so many willing and photogenic subjects. In fact, if you're not quick about it, your perfect 'people shot' could easily turn into a crowd scene featuring plenty of complicated (rap-style) hand gestures! Having said that, ask permission before photographing anyone and always respect their wishes if they decline. If you agree to send people a copy of the photo you've taken of them, do so.

Lonely Planet's *Travel Photography* includes plenty of professional tips to make the most of your holiday snaps.

POST

Every major island has a post office, generally open from 8.30am or 9am to 12.30pm, and from 1.30pm to 4pm weekdays, except holidays.

Postage rates for letters up to 200g are 90 *seniti* to the South Pacific region (including New Zealand), T$1 to Australia, T$1.20 to the Americas and Southeast Asia, and T$1.40 to the rest of the world. Postcard stamps cost 70 *seniti* to anywhere in the world. Postal services are sometimes slow, but usually reliable, though if possible, avoid posting anything from the Niuas, particularly Niuafo'ou, since communications are limited and weeks can go by without mail service.

Parcels posted to you in Tonga may, upon collection, incur import duty to the value of the goods enclosed. See individual island information sections for poste restante addresses.

International freighting companies have representations in Nuku'alofa (see p186).

First-day covers of Tonga's collectible postage stamps depict colourful shells and birds or commemorate such events as royal birthdays, exhibitions and visits by foreign heads of state; the island of Niuafo'ou has its own unique stamps. The **Philatelic Bureau** (Map pp184-5; ☎ 22455; GPO, Nuku'alofa) displays and sells old and unusual stamps.

SHOPPING

You won't find much by way of tourist tat and tacky-placky souvenirs in Tonga. Even finding a postcard can be difficult. With the exception of Polynesian carvings, Tongans themselves use the products they design and make. Perhaps the most distinctive of Tongan handicrafts are the *tapa* (mulberry bark cloths; see p167), which you can pick up in markets, craft cooperatives and through some guesthouses (ask your host). Despite the skill, care and time required to create the expert carvings, woven baskets, carved jewellery and *tapa*, Tongan handicrafts are quite reasonably priced.

The methods used in producing handicrafts are the same today as they were in ancient times and only natural materials are used, including bone, *ahi* (sandalwood), *pueki* (shells), mulberry bark, pandanus fronds and coral. Some of these materials are protected or restricted overseas (including black coral, which most countries prohibit the importation of, sandalwood, whalebone and tortoiseshell) and the purchase of products made from them is discouraged for ecological reasons.

Locally grown vanilla pods, Royal Coffee and coconut oils – scented with *ahi* and *tuitui* (candlenut), which is great for the skin and hair – are also worth buying. Tongan *kava* is highly regarded (particularly that produced on Tafahi in the Niuas) and nono juice (bottled in Vava'u) is believed to be a panacea to many ills.

Quality hand-designed T-shirts available in Tongatapu and Vava'u feature stylised Tongan designs, *kava-* and 'Vava'u mud–' dyes, and logos such as 'Kava-Cola' and 'Tongan Surfrider's Association'.

For local details, see the shopping sections in each chapter.

TELEPHONE & FAX

A rather unorthodox, yet surprisingly effective means of communication used throughout the islands is the 'coconut wireless'. All over Tonga, especially in Tongatapu, people somehow know what's going on in government, what each foreigner is up to (they're watching you), who is sleeping with whom, what the king is doing at the moment and so on – while it's happening or immediately thereafter.

Tonga Communications Corporation (TCC; www.tcc.to) has offices in Nuku'alofa (Tongatapu), 'Ohonua ('Eua), Pangai (Ha'apai), Neiafu (Vava'u), Hihifo (Niuatoputapu) and also on Niuafo'ou. International telephone and fax services are available. Prepaid phonecards, which can be used in both public and private telephones, are also available.

Calls to remote islands with radio or community telephones can be booked through **National Directory Assistance** (☎ 915). Give the operator the name of the required person, and the telephone number and island, in addition to your name and contact number. The operator will contact you regarding your telephone booking.

In order to make an international call from Tonga, dial 00, your destination country code, the area code and phone number.

For directory information, refer to the *Tongan White Pages* (www.tcc.to/directory.htm). Useful (free) service numbers:

Directory Enquiry ☎ 910
Emergency Number ☎ 911
International Directory Assistance ☎ 913

Fax

Facsimile services are available at post offices and the TCC (T$1.50/3 per sent page to the South Pacific/elsewhere; 50 *seniti* per page received). Many private businesses have fax machines and some will fax documents for a fee.

Mobile Phones

Simcards are available through **UCall** (☎ 0800 222; www.tcc.to/ucall_main.htm) or through **Tonfön** (☎ 875 1000; www.tonfon.to). UCall's service is more reliable and has simcards for T$45 including T$10 credit, and a minimum recharge of T$10; Tonfön has simcards for T$10 including T$5 credit, and a minimum recharge of T$5. Mobiles need to be GSM 900 compatible and must be unlocked from your local operator.

Phone Codes

Tonga's international telephone code is ☎ 676; there are no local area codes.

Phonecards

TCC's Malo e Lelei cards, available at TCC shops, some banks and *fale koloa,* come in denominations of T$5, T$10, T$20 and T$50. Visa and MasterCard are accepted at all TCC offices. Check the compatibility of telephone calling cards from international systems before leaving home.

TIME

Your whole concept of time will be given a good shaking in Tonga. The kingdom promotes itself as the 'land where time begins'; along with the Chukotka Peninsula in far eastern Russia, Tonga is the first place to see a new day. Though it could also be said that it is the 'land where time has stood still'.

Due to an odd kink in the International Date Line, Tonga is 20 minutes east of the 180th meridian, placing it 13 hours ahead of Greenwich Mean Time. Noon in Tonga is 3pm the previous day in Los Angeles, 11pm the previous day in London and 9am the same day in Sydney. In the Samoan islands, north of Tonga, the time would be noon the previous day! When New Zealand is on summer daylight-saving time, Tonga and New Zealand share the same time; the rest of the year New Zealand is one hour behind. Refer to the World Time Zones map on p319.

TOILETS

Tonga has flush toilets, though in remote areas pit toilets are used. Very few public toilets exist.

TOURIST INFORMATION
Local Tourist Information

Tonga Visitors Bureau Nuku'alofa (TVB; Map pp184-5; ☎ 25334; www.tongaholiday.com; PO Box 37, Nuku'alofa); Pangai (Map p230; ☎ /fax 60733; www.tongaholiday.com; Holopeka Rd; ☼ 8.30am-12.30pm & 1.30-4.30pm Mon-Fri); Neiafu (Map p250; ☎ 70115; fax 70666; VHF Channel 16; Fatafehi Rd; ☼ 8.30am-4.30pm Mon-Fri)

Tourist Information Abroad

For advance information and pre-trip planning, a web trawl of the listings in this guide will net the most up-to-date results. PDF brochures can be downloaded from the **Tonga Visitors Bureau** website (www.tongaholiday .com); if you email them a query you've probably got more chance of winning the lottery before getting a response.

VISAS

Most country's citizens are granted a 31-day visitor's visa on arrival upon presentation of a passport with at least six months' validity and an onward ticket. Those intending to fly in and depart Tongan waters by yacht require a letter of authority from one of Tonga's diplomatic missions overseas or the Immigration Division (see below).

For information on arriving in Tonga by yacht, see p295.

You can extend your stay for up to six months at any immigration office; each island group has one, usually located next to the police station in the main town. In Nuku'alofa, this is handled by the visa and naturalisation section of the **Immigration Division** (☎ 26969; fax 26971; Salote Rd; ☼ 9am-12.30pm Mon-Fri, 1.30-3pm Mon, Tue, Thu & Fri), opposite Cowley's Bakery. You'll need one passport photo for each extension (T$46) and a photocopy of your onward ticket. You'll need to show evidence of sufficient funds for your stay in Tonga, though a credit card is often enough.

WOMEN TRAVELLERS

Most of the time women travellers have no special problems in Tonga, but the closer you are to the culture and people, the more aware you'll need to be of Tongan traditional values.

Don't be paranoid about relating to people of the opposite sex but keep in mind that in traditional Tongan culture, women aren't permitted to freely associate with men on their own – they must be chaperoned. In Nuku'alofa and other large towns, being a solo woman traveller will scarcely be an issue. Elsewhere you may feel more comfortable with other travellers or a child of the family you're staying with. If, for example, you go to an isolated place alone with a man, or have a drink with him, you are giving him the signal that you are available for sex.

The way you dress will have a lot to do with how people perceive and treat you in Tonga. This is a deeply Christian culture (see p164) and Tongans expect both women and men to dress modestly – despite what you might see in Nuku'alofa.

Alcohol is an important issue and if you drink with Tongan men, you may be putting yourself at risk. Don't expect much peace when visiting nightclubs even when you're accompanied by your partner/husband – Tongan men can be incredibly persistent in their requests that you dance with them. Use common sense when going out at night and head for a larger hotel or tourist place rather than a small male-dominated bar, and consider arranging a taxi rather than walking.

As a general rule, avoid walking alone on a deserted beach, bush track or back road, but enquire about this on individual islands. While hitchhiking is fairly common on the islands, be careful and try to have somebody with you. See p289.

WORK

Tourist permits specifically prohibit working in Tonga. Many foreigners have set up small businesses considered beneficial for

Tonga, such as tourist resorts, though before you snap up that slice of paradise on the Internet, it pays to get sound local advice. It has been said that 'for every beach in Tonga, a *palangi's* dreams lay buried in the sand'.

Officially, you must get a work permit from the immigration office. This requires a specific offer of employment, filing an application with the immigration office (see opposite) and a lengthy wait for processing.

Volunteering is a great way of gaining a rare and privileged insight into another world, one beyond the irresistible lure of unspoilt beaches, palm trees and balmy evenings. It's not, though, an option for the casual tourist: volunteer programmes require a serious and long-term commitment. Most organisations require volunteers to have tertiary qualifications or work experience in their particular field, and to hold residency in the organisation's base country. Foreign aid organisations operating in Tonga:

AusAID (www.ausaid.gov.au)

Japanese Overseas Cooperation Volunteers (www.jica.go.jp)

US Peace Corps (☎ 25467; www.peacecorps.gov)

Long-Term Residency

Unless you possess highly transferable and beneficial skills or marry a Tongan citizen, nonbusiness immigration is difficult. Business immigrants are normally permitted to remain, but only as long as they retain their jobs. Those intent upon setting up a business will be required to place controlling interest in the hands of a Tongan partner.

For more information on business investments in Tonga, contact the **Ministry of Labour, Commerce & Industries** (☎ 23365; fax 23887; PO Box 110, Nuku'alofa).

TRANSPORT IN TONGA

All travel through Tonga's islands requires a degree of faith and fluidity, and comes with a dose of uncertainty and unreliability, dependent on tides, strong winds, holidays, church events, weddings, funerals, or a late-night *kava* drinking session.

AIR

Flying is the easiest and fastest way to get around Tonga, and the good news is that there are now two options: Airlines Tonga Air Fiji and Peau Vava'u. Unreliability is still a problem and flights are cancelled or rescheduled at short notice, making delays and missed connections common. Get used to it now and it won't ruin your holiday.

Flights can be delayed or cancelled in extreme weather; this is more common in the cyclone season. There are good lead warnings for cyclones and severe storm activity; your best bet is to be aware of the possibility and stay informed.

Reconfirm your flight 72 hours before departure (leaving a contact phone number) and then reconfirm again 24 hours before flying. If you have an international connection you *must* catch, return to Tongatapu two days beforehand, to be safe.

Airlines in Tonga

One-way fares and flight durations are given in the following table, though check the website for updates. There are no flights in Tonga on Sunday. Flights are valid for 12 months from the date of issue and demand no restrictions on changes, though a T$20 fee is charged for reimbursement. Children under

---

DOMESTIC FLIGHTS & FARES

Flight	Peau Vava'u Adult/Child	Airlines Tonga Adult	Duration
Tongatapu–'Eua	T$45/30	T$45	10min
Tongatapu–Ha'apai	T$154/122	T$87	50min
Tongatapu–Vava'u	T$209/153	T$145	1¼hr
Ha'apai–Vava'u	T$99/71		40min
Vava'u–Ha'apai	T$99/71	T$77	40min
Vava'u–Niuatoputapu	T$166/121	T$244	1¼hr
Vava'u–Niuafo'ou	$207/152	T$284	1½hr

* Daily flights Monday to Saturday with second services daily on demand only

two are charged 10% of the full fare; children aged two to 11 pay 50%.

Bookings are confirmed only upon full payment (cash, Visa, Mastercard or Amex). Check-in time at the terminal is 1¼ hours prior to departure.

Airlines Tonga Air Fiji (Airlines Tonga; ☎ 23690; www .airlinestonga.com; Teta Tours, cnr Railway & Wellington Rds, Nuku'alofa) flies between Tongatapu, Ha'apai and Vava'u daily, between Tongatapu and 'Eua twice daily, and from Tongatapu to the Niuas via Vava'u twice weekly. The baggage allowance is 10kg, with a per kilo excess charge of T$0.70 to 'Eua, T$1.35/2.20 to Ha'apai/Vava'u, and up to T$6.45 per kilo to the Niuas.

Peau Vava'u (www.peauvavau.to) flights from Tongatapu follow a circular route via Vava'u and Ha'apai, alternating in order of first stops. Normal fares have a baggage allowance of 20kg, while a slightly discounted resident's fare (often granted on request where possible and if the staff decide they like you) allows 10kg. Excess baggage is theoretically charged at T$6 for the first kilogram and then T$3 for every extra kilogram.

BICYCLE

Cycling is a great way to get around the kingdom. Distances aren't great, the islands are reasonably flat (though Vava'u and 'Eua are hilly in places) and a bike allows you to see the islands at island pace.

Transporting your own bike into Tonga should be no problem (check carriage details with the airline before purchasing your ticket). You can transport your bike on inter-island ferries, or internal flights (see p285 for details of baggage allowances), though you'll need to deflate the tyres.

A few notes of caution: before you leave home, go over your bike with a fine-tooth comb and fill your repair kit with every imaginable spare as they may be difficult to find in Tonga. Care should be taken around towns (Nuku'alofa especially) where vehicle numbers are high and driving skills poor. And watch out for crazed canines and wandering pigs.

Hire

Bicycles are available for hire on all major islands (T$8 to T$15 per day; see specific chapters for details), mostly of the foot-brake variety as there's a lot less that can go wrong with them.

Purchase

A couple of department/variety stores near Talamahu Market in Nuku'alofa sell bicycles of Chinese descent, and of varying quality and price – you're unlikely to find them boasting 'Shimano' anything.

BOAT
Inter-Island Ferry

Islands near Tongatapu can be reached by small boats which generally depart from Queen Salote Domestic Wharf. See p213 for details on boat transfers run by island resorts for their guests and day visitors. A couple of passenger ferries operate services between the main island groups, in addition to church-run boats.

Ferry rides in Tonga range from almost pleasurable cruising with sightseeing and whale-watching (in season), to barfing hell-rides kept afloat with midnight prayers. In either event, taking one is a major cultural experience, particularly while witnessing a ferry hovering mid-sea off an outer island as a flotilla of boats descends on it to load myriad cargo, including livestock and fish.

INTER-ISLAND FARES		
Route	**MV 'Olovaha**	**MV Pulupaki**
Tongatapu–Ha'apai (Lifuka)	T$43	T$45
Tongatapu–Vava'u	T$63	T$60
Tongatapu–Niuas	T$93	
Ha'apai–Vava'u	T$39	T$38
Vava'u–Niuas	T$55	
Niuatoputapu–Niuafo'ou	T$40	

Fares listed are one-way

INTER-ISLAND FERRY TIMETABLE

	Port	MV 'Olovaha	MV Pulupaki
Dep	Nuku'alofa	noon Tue	6pm Tue
Arr	Ha'afeva (Ha'apai)	9pm Tue	-
Dep	Ha'afeva	9.30pm Tue	-
Arr	Lifuka (Ha'apai)	11.30pm Tue	11.59pm Tue
Dep	Lifuka	2am Wed	2.30am Wed
Arr	Neiafu (Vava'u)	10am Wed	9am Wed
Dep	Neiafu	2pm Wed	10.30pm Wed
Arr	Lifuka	10pm Wed	4.30am Thur
Dep	Lifuka	1am Thu	6.30am Thu
Arr	Ha'afeva	3.30am Thu	-
Dep	Ha'afeva	4am Thu	-
Arr	Nuku'alofa	noon Thu	12.30pm Thu

Most passengers travel deck class as indoor spaces are stuffy, cramped and claustrophobic, while outdoor spaces can be wet and/or cold and difficult to find sleeping space. There's no denying the toilets are truly awful – overflowing and sloshing around – and vomiting fellow passengers don't enhance the experience either. Though a seafaring people, Tongans tend to get seasick as soon as the boat leaves the harbour if the sea is rough. Also, the boats are always running late.

NORTHERN ISLAND GROUPS

Both inter-island ferries (see following) depart from Queen Salote Wharf in Nuku'alofa. Their schedules are very prone to delay and change, so must be checked prior to intended travel, though we have included an inter-island ferry timetable (above) to provide an idea of travel times. It's possible to arrange a cabin (sometimes the captain's quarters) though most people travel deck class.

MV 'Olovaha is a squat, German-built flat-bottomed boat (which tends to bob like a cork in rough seas). It's operated by the **Shipping Corporation of Polynesia** (Nuku'alofa Map pp184–5; ☎ 23853; scp@tonfon.to; Queen Salote Wharf; Vava'u Map p250; ☎ 70128; Ha'apai Map p230; ☎ 60699) and runs weekly between Tongatapu (Nuku'alofa), Ha'apai (Ha'afeva and Lifuka Islands) and Vava'u (Neiafu).

MV 'Olovaha currently services the Niuas every two months (or so) – as it relies on government subsidies for the trip, it may run more or less frequently to these remote islands. From Vava'u to Niuatoputapu it takes about 24 hours, then 12 to 15 hours to Niuafo'ou. Occasionally rough conditions make it impossible to unload or load cargo (and passengers) at Niuafo'ou.

MV Pulupaki, operated by **Uata Shipping Line** (Walter Line; Map pp184–5; ☎ 23855; uataline@kalianet.to; Queen Salote Wharf), does the inter-island run between Tongatapu and Vava'u. It was the preferred ferry at the time of writing and has a keel, which some travellers maintain gives a smoother journey. Economy (deck class) fares are listed in the table on p286 (children aged under 12 pay about 50%).

'EUA

The trip across to 'Eua is generally a simple crossing, though usually choppy when the ferries pass out into the open sea. The journey takes two to three hours. The return leg from 'Eua to Nuku'alofa is usually a little quicker and smoother as the boat travels with the prevailing swell, not against it. Locals travelling to/from 'Eua are generally more used to sea travel, so there's less seasickness. Ferrying to 'Eua can be quicker than flying (when this is actually an option) when you add on taking a taxi to the airport, check in, delays etc. The one-way fare is T$20; tickets are sold on board the ferries.

Uata Shipping Line (Walter Line; Map pp184–5; ☎ 23855; uataline@kalianet.to; Queen Salote Wharf, Nuku'alofa) operates the MV Ikale, the quickest ferry between Tongatapu and 'Eua. The ferry leaves Nuku'alofa at 12.30pm, returning from 'Eua's Nafanua Wharf about 5am the next morning. There's one service every day except Sunday.

MV *'Otu Tonga,* run by **Tofa Shipping** (Map pp184-5; ☎ 21326), also does the Nuku'alofa to 'Eua run, departing around noon on Monday, Tuesday and Wednesday. It is sometimes replaced by MV *'Alaimoana.*

Yacht

October and November are the best months for yacht hitchhiking around Tonga, though once yachties have arrived here they're usually content to cruise around the islands leisurely and don't need extra crew. Details of yachting, crewing, permits and charges are on p294. Yacht and sailing charters are available in Tongatapu and Vava'u.

Minerva Reef, which is awash most of the time, is at Tonga's southernmost extreme, 350km (about two days' sailing) southwest of Tongatapu. With breaking waves in the vast ocean at high tide and two feet of reef at low tide, Minerva Reef serves as a rest point for yachts waiting for clearer conditions on the five-day (or so) crossing to New Zealand.

Other Vessels

Most island resorts offer boat transfers to their overnight guests and day visitors. The most economical way to get around is on local boats, but you'll be at the mercy of a very fluid schedule which requires time and flexibility. If you've got the cash, skippered boats can be organised on just about any island, while aluminium boats can be hired in Neiafu. Bear in mind the high fuel costs when quoted a price. See p246 for details.

The Church of Tonga's boat, **MV Siu Pele** (☎ contact Tiukala 25555; one-way fare T$42) departs from Nuku'alofa's Domestic Wharf at 9pm Monday for Pangai (in the Ha'apai Group) via Nomuka, Ha'afeva and 'Uiha, returning from 'Uiha some time on Thursday.

You could try your luck hitchhiking on fishing boats, freighters and launches. Ask around port and landing areas and contact the shipping companies.

BUS

Culture vultures hear this: travelling on a local bus on Tongatapu is a must – at least once. As passengers squeeze into painted mini-buses and catch the breeze while dangling out of the open doorway, you'll marvel at how much volume the driver can get out of such tiny speakers. Tongatapu's fairly decent bus network covers the island. Else-

where, transport is limited to Lifuka and Foa in Ha'apai, and Vava'u Island, with services running infrequently or only if enough passengers accumulate for a trip; some buses in outlying districts exist only to ferry students and villagers to and from town in the morning and afternoon. Don't rely on catching a bus after about 3pm.

In the urban areas of Tongatapu, the bus stops are marked with a sign reading *'Pasi'.* Elsewhere, flag down buses by waving your outstretched arm.

Costs

Fares range from 50 *seniti* to T$2 depending upon the island and the distance travelled. Pay the fare on exiting the bus.

CAR

In Tonga, traffic moves on the left. Tonga is a harsh environment for cars, with little protection from the salt-laden elements and scant preventative servicing. Some vehicles are only held together by the sheer will of the occupants, though the ubiquitous 'Western Union' stickers seem to help.

On Tongatapu, if you see a motorcade flanked by police motorcyclists and containing a large blue Dodge van with blacked-out windows, pull off the road and wait for it to pass. It's the king. Smaller motorcades containing the queen, the princess or one of the princes occasionally crawl through town and demand similar respect.

Driving Licence

International and home country driving licences are not valid in Tonga. You need a Tongan driving licence from the police station in Nuku'alofa or Neiafu, for which your only test will be to simultaneously produce your home driving licence, your passport and T$17 cash.

Fuel & Spare Parts

Petrol stations are easy to locate. They're fully serviced on Tongatapu and in Neiafu, though filling up often requires hand siphoning from 40-gallon drums on other islands. Fuel prices were pushing T$2.20 per litre on outer islands in 2005. The slim availability of spare parts may explain the seeming trend to go without them – particularly away from Tongatapu, where most spare parts need to be sourced, if not imported into Tonga.

Hire

Hire cars – ranging from the zippy with remnants of suspension to the completely 'Tonganified' and probably unroadworthy – are available on both Tongatapu and Vava'u, and can be arranged with private owners on other islands (this author hired the taxi, while the taxi driver happily slept the day away in the cab rank). Alternately, negotiate hiring a taxi with its driver for the day. Those choosing to drive will need to buy a Tongan driving licence (opposite).

Insurance

Insurance is only available in Nuku'alofa, see p198.

Road Conditions

The sealing of main roads, a project recently funded by the EU, will no doubt extend the lives of Tonga's rattled cars along with their occupants' teeth. Tongan driving skills are not the sharpest in the world (you only need to pass a simple theory test to get a licence), and many people drive everywhere at under 40km/h. Expect the unexpected.

Road Rules

Drinking and driving is strictly forbidden in Tonga, even though it's apparent that the practice is widespread. If there's an accident and you have alcohol on your breath, you'll be sent to prison whether or not you were at fault.

Drivers should keep their speed down to 40km/h in villages and towns and 65km/h elsewhere, especially now that the police have radar guns. If you're caught speeding, you'll have to pay a fine (T$2 for each kilometre per hour you're over the limit).

HITCHING

Hitching is never entirely safe in any country and we don't recommend it. Travellers who decide to hitch should understand that they are taking a small but potentially serious risk. People who do choose to hitch will be safer if they travel in pairs and let someone know where they are planning to go.

However, hitching is fairly common in Tonga, especially where public transport is rare. Flag down vehicles by waving palm down rather than sticking out your thumb. Only occasionally will you be asked to pay.

HORSE

Horses can be hired on all inhabited islands directly from their owners. Expect to pay around T$30 per day. Horses rarely have saddles (a few blankets for padding, maybe) but generally have bridles and reins, and stirrups aren't totally out of the question. Tongan horses seem adept at shedding unwanted objects from their backs!

TAXI

Taxis throughout Tonga can be recognised by a 'T' at the beginning of the vehicle's licence plate (if it has a licence plate). There are plenty of taxis on Tongatapu, Vava'u and Lifuka (Ha'apai), and one on 'Eua. Though the taxis are not metered, government maximum rates are vaguely followed. Always agree on the fare before you climb in. The Tonga Visitors Bureau representative at Fua'amotu International Airport can give you an indication of current taxi prices. Taxis in Ha'apai have a printed rate card priced by destination.

Some taxis charge according to the destination, and allow you to make a couple of stops and do some shopping without additional waiting fees.

Taxi drivers will often claim to be out of change, so either have a fistful of dollars or be prepared to change larger notes at your destination.

If your airport taxi driver insists that your selected hotel is closed, fully booked or no good, don't take it too seriously. Chances are you've chosen an establishment that doesn't pay commission to taxi drivers.

TOURS

Organised tours can give a good introduction to an island and offer an easy way to visit major sights. Commercial tour operators circle Tongatapu and its sights in little over half a day while minibus tours cover a selection of land sights in Vava'u. Small-group 4WD tours with a combination of walking, exploring, caving and sightseeing can be arranged on 'Eua, while boat tours to outer islands can be negotiated in Ha'apai, Vava'u and the Niuas. Whale-watching and fishing tours operate from each island group, while organised diving excursions are possible in all groups bar the Niuas. Vava'u also boasts guided 'surfaris', where surfers are dropped on breaks by boat.

TONGAN DIRECTORY

Transport

CONTENTS

THINGS CHANGE ...

The information in this chapter is particularly vulnerable to change. Check directly with the airline or a travel agent to make sure you understand how a fare (and ticket you may buy) works and to be aware of the security requirements for international travel. Shop carefully. The details given in this chapter should be regarded as pointers and are not a substitute for your own careful, up-to-date research.

The physical isolation of the Samoan islands and Tonga means you need to give careful consideration to the best way of getting out there. Flying direct to/from each island grouping, for instance, probably won't represent the greatest value for money. It might make more sense to engage in some careful route planning that may enable further exploration of the South Pacific or even Australasia.

For information on travelling within either Samoa or American Samoa, see p146. For information on travelling within Tonga, see p285.

Flights and tours can be booked online at www.lonelyplanet.com/travel_services.

ENTRY REQUIREMENTS
Entering Samoa

To be issued a visa on arrival in Samoa, you must have an onward ticket, a passport valid for at least another six months, and a contact address within the country (have the name of a hotel handy). An international yellow fever vaccination certificate will also be required if you've visited a high-risk country in the six days prior to your arrival in Samoa (see p296).

Entering American Samoa

A passport valid for at least six months beyond your arrival date and an onward ticket will allow nationals of 25 countries to obtain a visa on arrival. Nationals of other countries will need to apply for a visa in advance. For full details, see p146.

The yellow fever regulations that apply to Samoa also apply to American Samoa.

Entering Tonga

Citizens of most countries are granted a 31-day visitors visa on arrival in Tonga upon presentation of a passport with at least six months' validity and an onward ticket. An international yellow fever vaccination certificate will be necessary if you've been to a high-risk area in the past six days.

AIR

While the Samoan islands and Tonga aren't exactly as remote or obscure a destination as Tuvalu or Kiribati, they are not as popular as Fiji or Tahiti either (not yet anyway), and airfares often reflect this. Access to either island group is fairly straightforward from New Zealand, Australia, Fiji, Hawai'i or Los Angeles. From anywhere else, however, travelling there will almost always entail reaching one of these connecting points first. Auckland and Nadi/Suva are the most convenient and best-served runs, and there are often some good discount fares on these routes. Tonga and the Samoas are also popular as a stopover or cheap 'optional extra' on some tickets and round-the-world fares between Europe or North America and New Zealand.

Visitors to Samoa will arrive near Apia on 'Upolu, those visiting American Samoa will arrive near Pago Pago on Tutuila, and the majority of those visiting Tonga will arrive at Nuku'alofa.

Airlines

Airlines that service the region include the following (note all phone numbers mentioned here are for dialling from within Samoa, American Samoa and Tonga):

Air New Zealand (airline code NZ; Apia ☎ 20825, Nuku'alofa 23192; www.airnz.com; hub Auckland International Airport)

Air Pacific (airline code FJ; Apia ☎ 22738, Nuku'alofa 23422; www.airpacific.com; hub Nadi International Airport)
Hawaiian Airlines (airline code HA; www.hawaiianair lines.com; hub Honolulu International Airport, Hawai'i)
Inter-Island Airways (Pago Pago ☎ 699 7100; www.in terislandair.com; hub Tafuna International Airport, Tutuila)
Pacific Blue (airline code DJ; www.flypacificblue.com; hub Brisbane International Airport)
Polynesian Airlines (airline code PH; Apia ☎ 22737, Pago Pago 699 9126, Nuku'alofa 24566, Neiafu 70644; www .polynesianairlines.com; hub Faleolo Airport, 'Upolu)
Polynesian Blue (airline code DJ; www.polynesianblue .com; hub Brisbane International Airport)
Qantas (airline code QF; Apia ☎ 21261; www.qantas .com.au; hub Kingsford-Smith Airport, Sydney)
Royal Tongan Airlines (airline code WR; Nuku'alofa ☎ 23414; www.tongatapu.net.to/tonga/islands /royalt/default.htm; hub Fua'amotu International Airport, Tongatapu)

Tickets

Automated online ticket sales work well if you're doing a simple one-way or return trip on specified dates, but are no substitute for a travel agent with the lowdown on special deals, strategies for avoiding stopovers and other useful advice.

Paying by credit card offers some protection if you unwittingly end up dealing with a rogue fly-by-night agency, as most card issuers provide refunds if you can prove you didn't get what you paid for. Alternatively, buy a ticket from a bonded agent, such as one covered by the **Air Travel Organiser's Licence** (ATOL; www.atol.org.uk) scheme in the UK. If you have doubts about the service provider, at the very least call the airline and confirm that your booking has been made.

INTERCONTINENTAL (RTW) TICKETS
Round-the-world (RTW) tickets are generally put together by the three biggest airline alliances – **Star Alliance** (www.staralliance.com), **Oneworld** (www.oneworldalliance.com) and **Skyteam** (www.skyteam.com). They give you a limited time (usually a year) in which to circumnavigate the globe. You can go anywhere the participating airlines go, as long as you stay within the prescribed kilometre extents or number of stops and don't backtrack when flying between continents. Backtracking is generally permitted within a single continent, though with certain restrictions; see the relevant websites for details.

An alternative type of RTW ticket is one put together by a travel agent. These are usually more expensive than airline RTW fares but allow you to devise your own itinerary.

RTW tickets start at around UK£900 from the UK and US$1800 from the USA.

CIRCLE PACIFIC TICKETS
A Circle Pacific ticket is similar to a RTW ticket but covers a more limited region, using a combination of airlines to connect Australia, New Zealand, North America and Asia, with stopover options in the Pacific Islands. As with RTW tickets, there are restrictions and limits as to how many stopovers you can take.

INTERNATIONAL AIR PASSES
Polynesian Airlines' Polypass is good for 45 days (excluding the Christmas holiday period) and allows five stops in the Pacific, which may include Tonga, Samoa, American Samoa and Fiji. In the USA, this is sometimes called the Pacific Explorer Air Pass and costs from US$1100. The airline also offers various Polypacks, where travellers have up to two months to complete an itinerary that includes several Pacific destinations (these cost from NZ$1400); see the Polynesian Airlines website for details. Note, however, that at the time of writing the future of these passes was in doubt due to the launch of the Polynesian Blue airline (a joint venture between Virgin Blue and the Samoan government), which is slated to take over most of Polynesian Airlines' international routes.

The Visit South Pacific Pass offers discounted airfares on a variety of South Pacific routes. The options are many and varied – altogether the pass covers 45 possible routes and involves nine Pacific carriers. The pass must be purchased in conjunction with an international air ticket from outside the Pacific region, but can offer fare savings of up to 50%. All passes are basically tailor-made; discuss the options with a travel agent.

ONLINE TICKET SITES
For online ticket bookings, including RTW fares, start with the following websites:
Air Brokers (www.airbrokers.com) This US company specialises in cheap tickets.
Cheap Flights (www.cheapflight.com) Informative site with specials, airline information and flight searches from the USA, the UK and other regions.

TRANSPORT

FLYING WITHIN THE REGION

You can fly direct between Samoa and American Samoa with Inter-Island Airways and Polynesian Airlines for about US$180 one way.

The principal airlines that fly between Samoa and Tonga are Air New Zealand (from NZ$250 one way) and Polynesian Airlines (from ST1000 one way). At the time of research, the only airline between Tonga and American Samoa was Polynesian Airlines (T$470 one way); in Tonga, you embark or disembark in Vava'u, not Tongatapu.

For more info on travel within the South Pacific region, see opposite.

Flight Centre International (www.flightcentre.com) Respected operator handling direct flights.

Flights.com (www.tiss.com) International site for flight tickets; offers cheap fares and an easy-to-search database.

Roundtheworld.com (www.roundtheworldflights.com) This excellent site allows you to build your own trips from the UK with up to six stops.

STA (www.statravel.com) Prominent in international student travel but you don't have to be a student; site linked to worldwide STA sites.

Travelocity (www.travelocity.com) US site that allows you to search fares (in US$) from/to practically anywhere.

Travel Online (www.travelonline.co.nz) Good place to check worldwide flights from New Zealand.

Asia

Air Pacific has direct flights from Tokyo to Nadi, which connect with flights to Samoa (Apia) and Tonga (Nuku'alofa). Air New Zealand has a number of flights from Tokyo, Nagoya and Osaka to Auckland, where there are many onward flights to the Samoas. Most flights from other parts of Asia are also routed through Auckland and Nadi.

Qantas flights from countries in the Asian region touch down in Brisbane, Sydney and Melbourne before flying towards South Pacific islands via Nadi. The exception is the direct flight to Apia from Sydney.

Excellent bargains are often available in Hong Kong. Recommended local agents in Southeast Asia:

Phoenix Services Hong Kong (☎ 852-2722 7378)

STA Travel Bangkok (☎ 02-236 0262; www.statravel .co.th); Singapore (☎ 65-6737 7188; www.statravel.com .sg); Tokyo (☎ 03-5391 2922; www.statravel.co.jp)

Australia

From Australia, flights to Samoa and Tonga are available from Sydney with new carrier Polynesian Blue and with Qantas. Pacific Blue also flies to both Samoa and Tonga from Brisbane as well as Sydney. Flights are often routed through Nadi or Auckland.

Polynesian Blue fares to Apia from Sydney start at around A$450, though keep in mind that this was an introductory fare at the time of writing and prices may rise (probably not by much though) if the route proves popular. The average fare from Sydney to Nuku'alofa is around A$650, although we did come across promotional fares as low as A$300.

There are no direct flights to Pago Pago in American Samoa from Australia. You need to get to Apia (Samoa) first to hook up with a regional route.

Bear in mind that the Australian Christmas holiday season (December to January) is the busiest and most expensive time to fly. Standard fares increase by up to 25%, though 'holiday specials' are occasionally offered. Travellers should also be aware that ever-increasing code-share agreements mean that it should be easy to arrange a through-ticket from destinations across Australia.

STA Travel (☎ 1300 360 960; www.statravel.com.au) and **Flight Centre** (☎ 133 133; www.flightcentre.com .au) have offices throughout Australia. **Hideaway Holidays** (☎ 02-8799 2500; www.hideawayholi days.com.au) is a South Pacific specialist offering a range of flight/accommodation deals to the Samoan islands. Packages start at approximately A$1300 (for five nights) and, once your five nights are up, there's nothing to stop you moving somewhere else and staying on a bit longer.

New Zealand

From New Zealand there are a number of flight options to Samoa and Tonga with Air New Zealand, Qantas, Royal Tongan Airlines, Polynesian Blue and Pacific Blue. One-way fares from Auckland to Apia start at NZ$570; one-way fares for the 2½- to three-hour flight from Auckland to Nuku'alofa start around NZ$450.

Flight/accommodation packages from New Zealand can be excellent value; such packages can sometimes work out cheaper than the flight alone. Air New Zealand is a good starting point for such deals.

For reasonably priced fares, try one of the numerous branches of **STA Travel** (☎ 0508 782 872; www.statravel.co.nz). Another good option is **House of Travel** (www.houseoftravel.co.nz); see its website for contact telephone numbers for its dozens of New Zealand offices.

South Pacific

While island-hopping around the Pacific isn't difficult, some flights operate only once or twice per week from the Samoan islands and Tonga and you might face more than a few scheduling problems on some routes. There are direct flights from both of the island groups to Fiji and Hawai'i, but if you are travelling on to other Pacific islands you'll probably need to either fly back to New Zealand to make connections, or travel via Fiji. Check out one of the regional air passes (see p291) if you want to see a host of other Pacific islands.

Air Pacific and Royal Tongan Airlines both fly between Nuku'alofa (Tonga) and Nadi (Fiji) three times a week. Air Pacific also flies between Nadi and Apia (Samoa), as does Polynesian Airlines. One-way fares from Fiji to Apia usually start at F$300, while fares to Nuku'alofa cost from F$220.

Royal Tongan Airlines also puts on a weekly Tongatapu to Niue flight via Vava'u (a two-hour trip). Royal Tongan is the only international airline serving Niue.

UK & Continental Europe

An Air New Zealand flight from London to Apia (Samoa), via Los Angeles, is the most straightforward option for travel from Europe to the Samoan islands. High-season return fares from London start at UK£1500. There are also a number of flights from Frankfurt to Los Angeles, where passengers can connect with onward flights to the Samoas or other South Pacific countries. Other cheap fares from Europe generally go via Sydney, Australia.

The best fares from Europe to Nuku'alofa (Tonga) are generally with Air New Zealand from London via Los Angeles, then Auckland or Nadi. However, various code-sharing agreements mean that other stopovers and routings through the South Pacific are possible. Air New Zealand's return fares from London to Tonga, via Los Angeles and Auckland, start from UK£1100. You are usually allowed one free stopover in each

direction. Air New Zealand's flights via Fiji are often at least 10% more expensive.

Popular agencies in the UK include the ubiquitous **STA Travel** (☎ 0870-1630 026; www .statravel.co.uk), **Trailfinders** (☎ 020-7938 3939; www .trailfinders.co.uk) and **Flight Centre** (☎ 0870-499 0040; www.flightcentre.co.uk).

A good option in the Dutch travel industry is **Holland International** (☎ 0900-8858; www .hollandinternational.nl). From Amsterdam, return fares start at around €1500. Another recommended agency in the Netherlands is **NBBS Reizen** (☎ 0900-102 0300; www.nbbs.nl). Recommended German agencies include the Berlin branch of **STA Travel** (☎ 069-743 032 92; www .statravel.de).

In France (more specifically, Paris), try **Odysia** (☎ 01 43 29 69 50; www.odysia.fr) or **OTU Voyages** (☎ 01 40 29 12 22; www.otu.fr) – both are student/youth specialists and have offices in many French cities. Other recommendations include **Voyageurs du Monde** (☎ 01 40 15 11 15; www.vdm.com/vdm) and **Nouvelles Frontiéres** (☎ 08 25 00 08 25; www.nouvelles-frontieres.fr/nf); the details given are for offices in Paris, but again both companies have branches elsewhere.

USA & Canada

Los Angeles and Honolulu are the two main gateway cities for travel between North America and the South Pacific. Although a huge amount of Pacific traffic passes through Los Angeles, there are also direct flights to Honolulu from nearly every major city in the USA. In Honolulu you can connect with Air New Zealand flights going direct to Samoa and Tonga.

Air New Zealand operates direct Los Angeles–Apia flights (about US$620 one way) and direct Los Angeles–Nuku'alofa flights (around US$650 one way). Return flights to Pago Pago start from about US$580 from Honolulu with Hawaiian Airlines.

Discount travel agents in the USA are known as consolidators (though you won't see a sign on the door saying 'Consolidator'). San Francisco is the ticket consolidator capital of America, although some good deals can be found in Los Angeles, New York and other big cities.

STA Travel (☎ 800-781 4040; www.statravel.com) has offices all over the USA.

Canadians will find the best South Pacific deals are via Honolulu. Like travellers from the USA, you'll probably fly with at least two different code-sharing carriers. From Canada, flights to the Samoas are through Los Angeles/San Francisco and Honolulu. Return fares from Vancouver to Apia are around C$2220, while return flights from Vancouver to Nuku'alofa are about C$2500.

The airfares sold by Canadian discount air ticket sellers (consolidators) tend to be about 10% higher than those sold in the USA. **Travel Cuts** (☎ 866-246 9762; www.travelcuts.com) is Canada's national student travel agency and has offices in all major cities.

SEA
Cargo Ships
As a transport option, cargo ships are not opportunities for stowaways or free berths, but involve paid tickets to ride aboard willing supply vessels. If you're interested in this unusual option, check out the website of California-based **Freighterworld** (☎ 800-531 7774; www.freighterworld.com), which has lots of relatively up-to-date information on container ships that offer berths on trips through the South Pacific. Prices obviously vary considerably according to the itinerary, but US$2000 for two weeks of travel is not uncommon.

Three cargo ships sail between Apia in Samoa and the remote Tokelau Islands. Bookings for the 20-hour trip can be made in Apia at the **Tokelau Apia Liaison Office** (Map pp62-3; ☎ 20822; Fugalei St; ⏱ 8am-5pm Mon-Fri). You must obtain a permit to visit Tokelau before booking. Sailings are usually fortnightly but occasionally more frequent. Return deck fares are NZ$290/145 per adult/child; return cabin fares are NZ$530/270.

Cruise Ships
A number of cruise ships make their way (very slowly) into the ports at Apia (Samoa), Pago Pago (American Samoa) and Nuku'alofa (Tonga), disgorging passengers keen to have a fully catered and organised South Pacific experience. Itineraries vary from two weeks to a month, and the routes are limited only by the imaginations of the tour providers. While Tahiti is the favoured main destination for such cruises, the Samoan islands and Tonga tend to be included in many such leisurely South Pacific voyages.

A good place to start your research into what sort of cruise suits you is the website of **Travel Wizard** (www.travelwizard.com), which provides oodles of information on international cruise lines and options. Also have a look at the website of the **Cruise Lines International Association** (www.cruising.org) – it focuses on North American–based lines, but this is where most Pacific cruises will be coming from.

Fares vary widely depending on the length of the trip, the luxuriousness of the boat and its facilities, the number of stopovers, and the embarkation/disembarkation points. A typical itinerary for a one-month voyage starting from Los Angeles takes in Hawai'i, Tahiti, Samoa, Tonga, Fiji and New Zealand. Fares for such a voyage often hover around US$3500 per person (double occupancy).

Ferries
Samoa Shipping Corporation (Map pp62-3; ☎ 20935/6; reservations@samoashipping.com; Beach Rd, Apia) runs a car ferry called *Lady Naomi* between Apia and Pago Pago once a week. It departs Apia on Wednesday at midnight and returns on Thursday at 4.30pm. The trip takes seven hours each way. The return deck/cabin fare from Apia to Pago Pago is ST100/140. Note that American passport holders can only buy one-way tickets from Apia.

In Pago Pago, the ferry runs every Thursday at 3.30pm and tickets must be purchased at least one day in advance from **Polynesia Shipping Services** (Map p107; ☎ 633 1211). The return deck/cabin fare from American Samoa is US$75/100.

Yachts
Yacht charters are practically impossible to track down in the Samoan islands, whereas the myriad scattered islands and enigmatic sailing passages of Tonga seem to have been custom-designed for those wanting to undertake a lengthy island-hop.

Between May and October (outside the cyclone season) the harbours of the South Pacific swarm with cruising yachts from around the world, many following the favourable winds west from the Americas, while others come north from New Zealand.

The yachting community is quite friendly, especially towards those who display an interest in yachts and other things nautical. Sometimes they are looking for crew, and for those who'd like a bit of low-key adventure, this can be the way to go. Most of the time, crew members will only be asked to take a turn on watch – that is, scan the horizon for cargo ships, hazardous objects and the odd reef – and possibly to cook or clean. In port, crew may be required to dive and scrape the bottom, paint or make repairs. Sailing experience is usually not necessary; 'green' crew members learn as they go. Most yachties charge crew upwards of US$15 per day for food and supplies.

All that aside, bear in mind that the conditions of a long ocean voyage greatly magnify rivalries and petty concerns. Only set out on a long passage with someone with whom you feel relatively compatible and remember that, on board, skipper's rule is law.

INFORMATION

Private yacht owners who intend to visit Samoa's islands aer required to apply for clearance from the **Prime Minister's Department** (Map pp62-3; ☎ 21339; 5th fl, Government Office Bldg, Beach Rd) in Apia – bear left as you exit the elevator and take the unmarked door straight through the archway. The captain will need to present crew passports and the boat's registration papers.

On Tongatapu in Tonga, the boarding officers are in the **One Stop Shop** (☎ 23967; Queen Salote Wharf; ◷ 8.30am-12.30pm & 1.30-4.30pm Mon-Fri) in Nuku'alofa. Check-in is possible on weekends but will incur a fee. There's a charge for anchoring anywhere in Tongan waters, payable upon departure at the **Ports Authority** (Map pp184-5; ☎ 23168; marports@kalianet.to; Queen Salote Wharf; ◷ 8.30am-12.30pm & 1.30-4.30pm Mon-Fri) in Nuku'alofa, or whichever port you're using. Anchoring fees/charges in Tongatapu are calculated by multiplying T$1.80 by gross tonnage of the yacht. Pay the harbour dues and then take the receipt to Customs.

In Vava'u, pull up at the southern end of Neiafu Wharf and contact the **boarding officers** (☎ 70053; ◷ 8.30am-12.30pm & 1.30-4.30pm Mon-Fri).

To summon the harbour master and for emergencies in Tonga use VHF channel 16. However, there's only a slight chance that any Tongan government or navy vessel will come to your assistance (they rarely have fuel); your best bet is the local sailing and fishing community. If you're in VHF range of Vava'u, contact the charter yacht company The Moorings (VHF channel 72) which can coordinate rescue efforts. Any response to a triggered EPERB (an emergency beacon that sends SOS messages via satellite) will come from, or be coordinated by, the New Zealand navy. It may take days before help arrives.

BOOKS

If you're travelling by yacht in Tonga or elsewhere in the Pacific, *Landfalls of Paradise: Cruising Guide to the Pacific Islands* by Earl R Hinz is highly recommended. The experienced Pacific yachtie author provides all the nitty-gritty on anchorages, navigation, marinas, fees and officialdom throughout the South and central Pacific region. *Sailingbird's Guide to the Kingdom of Tonga*, by Charles Paul and Katherine Pham-Paul, is a staple cruising guide that doubles as a coffee table book and also includes plenty of land sights. *Cruising Guide for the Kingdom of Tonga* by Ken Hellewell, is a comprehensive, spiral-bound guide covering the entire kingdom, including charts, over 90 anchorages, GPS waypoints and port practicalities. If you're planning to charter a yacht in Vava'u and cruise around its islands, *A Cruising Guide to the Kingdom of Tonga*, produced by charter company The Moorings, is probably ample.

CHARTER VESSELS

To begin getting your mind around the possibility of chartering a yacht, see p275. To charter a vessel for a leisurely exploration of South Pacific waterways can roughly cost anywhere between US$280 and US$450 per person per night for two people; between US$250 and US$300 per person per night for three people; and around US$240 per person per night for four people. One such option is **Impetuous** (www.sailingtonga.com), a fully crewed charter yacht operating mostly around Vava'u (Tonga), but which may be willing to pick up/drop off guests in Ha'apai, Nuku'alofa, Fiji or even Samoa. Another option worth checking out is chartering a yacht called **Melinda** (www.sailtonga.com).

SAMOAN PORTS

Apia in Samoa and Pago Pago in American Samoa are the main ports in these countries, and serve as the official entry points for private yacht owners. On Savai'i (Samoa), there are also anchorages at Fagamalo, Salelologa Wharf and Asau Harbour.

TONGAN PORTS

Ports of entry for cruising yachts in Tonga are Nuku'alofa (Tongatapu), Pangai on Lifuka (Ha'apai), Neiafu (Vava'u), Falehau (Niuatoputapu) and Futu (Niuafo'ou).

Health Dr Michael Sorokin

Fortunately for visitors to the Samoan islands and Tonga, there is no malaria in the region. Nor is rabies a danger in any of the islands. And there are no crocodiles. Mosquitoes do exist, however, and the main danger from them is dengue fever. Health facilities vary from good in American Samoa to reasonable in Samoa and Tonga. These are all small governments with limited budgets so even 'good' does not necessarily equate with the facilities you could expect in a well-developed country.

BEFORE YOU GO

Prevention is the key to staying healthy while abroad. A little planning before departure, particularly for pre-existing illnesses, will save trouble later. See your dentist before a long trip, carry a spare pair of contact lenses and glasses, and take your optical prescription with you. Bring medications in their original, clearly labelled, containers. A signed and dated letter from your physician describing your medical conditions and medications, including generic names, is also a good idea. If carrying syringes or needles, be sure to have a physician's letter documenting their medical necessity.

INSURANCE

If your health insurance does not cover you for medical expenses abroad, consider supplemental insurance. (Check the Travel Links section of the Lonely Planet website at www.lonelyplanet.com.au/travel_links for more information.) Find out in advance if your insurance plan will make payments directly to providers or reimburse you later for overseas health expenditures. (In many countries doctors expect payment in cash.)

For Americans, be sure to check whether your health plan covers expenses in American Samoa. Serious illness or injury may

---

REQUIRED & RECOMMENDED VACCINATIONS

If you have been in a designated yellow fever country within the previous six days, you need an International Certificate of Vaccination against yellow fever for entry into American Samoa, Samoa and Tonga. For all countries in the region, vaccinations are recommended for hepatitis A, hepatitis B and typhoid fever.

Side-Effects of Vaccinations

All injected vaccinations can produce slight soreness and redness at the inoculation site, and a mild fever with muscle aches over the first 24 hours. These are least likely with hepatitis A and a little more common with hepatitis B and typhoid inoculations. Typhoid inoculation can cause a sensation of nausea within 24 hours and hepatitis B vaccine can produce temporary joint pains.

Allergy to eggs or poultry is a condition that makes the yellow fever vaccination inadvisable; an exemption certificate can be issued. Very rarely an acute allergic (anaphylactic shock) reaction can occur within minutes of vaccination. More commonly a flu-like illness of varying severity may occur at any time up to 10 days from vaccination. In the elderly, encephalitis has been recorded.

require an evacuation, eg to Apia or Pago Pago, or even to a major regional centre such as Los Angeles or Auckland; make sure that health insurance has provision for evacuation. Under these circumstances hospitals will accept direct payment from major international insurers but for all other health costs cash up front is the usual requirement.

RECOMMENDED VACCINATIONS

The World Health Organization (WHO) recommends that all travellers be covered for diphtheria, tetanus, measles, mumps, rubella and polio, regardless of their destination. Since most vaccines don't produce immunity until at least two weeks after they're given, you will need to visit a physician approximately six weeks before departure. A recent influenza vaccination is always a good idea when travelling. If you have not had chicken pox (varicella), consider being vaccinated.

MEDICAL CHECKLIST

It is a very good idea to carry a medical and first-aid kit with you, to help yourself in the case of minor illness or injury. Following is a list of items you should consider packing.

- acetaminophen (paracetamol) or aspirin
- adhesive or paper tape
- antibacterial ointment, eg Bactroban for cuts and abrasions (prescription only)
- antibiotics (by prescription only), eg ciprofloxacin (Ciproxin) or norfloxacin (Utinor; Noroxin)
- antibiotic as well as steroid eardrops (by prescription only), eg Sofradex, Kenacort Otic
- antidiarrhoeal drugs, eg loperamide
- anti-inflammatory drugs, eg ibuprofen
- antihistamines (for hay fever and allergic reactions)
- antigiardia tablets, eg tinidazole (by prescription only)
- bandages, gauze, gauze rolls, waterproof dressings
- DEET-containing insect repellent for the skin
- iodine tablets (for water purification)
- oral rehydration salts, eg Gastrolyte, Diarolyte, Replyte
- Permethrin-containing insect spray for clothing, tents, and bed nets

- pocket knife
- scissors, safety pins, tweezers
- steroid cream or hydrocortisone cream (for allergic rashes)
- sun block (30+)
- syringes and sterile needles, and intravenous fluids if travelling in very remote areas
- thermometer (digital)

Note that aspirin should not be used for fever – it can cause bleeding in dengue fever. Remember, don't take your scissors, tweezers or pocket knife in your carry-on luggage.

INTERNET RESOURCES

There is a wealth of travel health advice on the Internet. For further information, the Lonely Planet website (www.lonelyplanet .com) is a good place to start. The WHO produces a superb text entitled *International Travel and Health,* which is revised annually. It is no longer published in book form but is available online at no cost at www.who.int/ith/. Other websites of general interest are MD Travel Health at www .mdtravelhealth.com, which provides complete travel health recommendations for every country, updated daily and also at no cost; the Centers for Disease Control and Prevention at www.cdc.gov; Fit for Travel at www.fitfortravel.scot.nhs.uk, which has up-to-date information about outbreaks and is very user-friendly; and www.travel doctor.com.au, a similar Australasian site.

It's also a good idea to consult your government's travel health website before departure:

Australia (www.dfat.gov.au/travel/)
Canada (www.hc-sc.gc.ca/hl-vs/travel-voyage/index _e.html)
New Zealand (www.mfat.govt.nz/travel)
UK (www.dh.gov.uk/PolicyAndGuidance/HealthAdvice ForTravellers/fs/en)
USA (www.cdc.gov/travel/)

FURTHER READING

Good options for further reading include *Travel with Children* by Cathy Lanigan; *Healthy Travel Australia, New Zealand and the Pacific* by Dr Isabelle Young; and, *Your Child's Health Abroad: A Manual for Travelling Parents* by Dr Jane Wilson-Howarth and Matthew Ellis.

HEALTH

IN TRANSIT

DEEP VEIN THROMBOSIS (DVT)

Blood clots may form in the legs during plane flights, chiefly because of prolonged immobility. The longer the flight, the greater the risk. The chief symptom of DVT is swelling or pain of the foot, ankle or calf, usually but not always on just one side. When a blood clot travels to the lungs, it may cause chest pain and breathing difficulties. Travellers with any of these symptoms should immediately seek medical attention.

To prevent the development of DVT on long flights you should walk about the cabin, contract the leg muscles while sitting, drink plenty of fluids and avoid alcohol and tobacco.

JET LAG & MOTION SICKNESS

To avoid jet lag (common when crossing more than five time zones) try drinking plenty of nonalcoholic fluids and eating light meals. Upon arrival, get exposure to natural sunlight and readjust your schedule (for meals, sleep and so on) as soon as possible.

Antihistamines such as dimenhydrinate (Dramamine) and meclizine (Antivert, Bonine) are usually the first choice for treating motion sickness. A herbal alternative is ginger.

IN THE SAMOAN ISLANDS & TONGA

AVAILABILITY & COST OF HEALTH CARE

American Samoa has readily available doctors in private practice, and standard hospital and laboratory facilities with consultants in the major specialties – internal medicine, obstetrics/gynaecology, orthopaedics, ophthalmology, paediatrics, pathology, psychiatry and general surgery. Private dentists, opticians and pharmacies are also available.

In Samoa and Tonga, specialised services may be limited or available periodically, but private general practitioners, dentists and pharmacies are present.

Not surprisingly, the further you get from main centres, the more basic are the services.

Private consultation and private hospital fees are approximately equivalent to Australian costs, and particularly less expensive in Tonga. Government-provided service fees vary from modest to negligible but waiting times can be very long. Direct payment is required everywhere except where a specific arrangement is made, eg in the case of evacuation or where prolonged hospital stay is necessary; your insurer will need to be contacted by you. Although large hospitals are coming into line in accepting credit cards, there will be difficulty with the more remote, small hospitals and most private practitioners are reluctant to accept this form of payment except for the larger private doctor groups in American Samoa. Even they still prefer cash and not all credit cards are acceptable – check with the relevant company beforehand. If a credit card is not accepted you should be able to arrange cash on credit through the local banking system.

Most commonly used medications are available in countries with good or reasonable health care. Where only basic care is available, even aspirin and antiseptics may be hard to come by. Private pharmacies are not allowed by law to dispense listed drugs without prescription from a locally registered practitioner, but many will do so for travellers if shown the container. While the container should preferably specify the generic name of the drug, this has become much less of a problem with the use of Internet search engines. Asthma inhalers and most anti-inflammatories are over-the-counter preparations in the Samoan islands. It is best to have a sufficient supply of a regularly taken drug as a particular brand may not be available and sometimes quantities can be limited. This applies particularly to psychotropic drugs like antidepressants, antipsychotics, anti-epileptics or mood elevators. Insulin is available even in smaller centres, but you cannot guarantee getting a particular brand, combination or preferred administration method. If you have been prescribed 'the very latest' oral antidiabetic or antihypertensive, make sure you have enough for the duration of your travel.

Except in the remote, poorly staffed clinics, the standard of medical and dental care is generally quite good even if facilities are not sophisticated. The overall risk of illness for a normally healthy person is low, the most common problems being diarrhoeal upsets, viral sore throats, and ear and skin infections, all of which can mostly be treated with self-medication. For serious symptoms, eg sustained fever, or chest or abdominal pains, it is best to go to the nearest clinic or private practitioner in the first instance.

Tampons and pads are readily available in main centres. Dengue fever, especially in the first three months of pregnancy, poses a hazard because of fever but otherwise there is no reason why a normal pregnancy should prevent travel to the region. However, on general principles immunisation in the first three months of pregnancy is not recommended and yellow fever vaccines should not be given.

For young children, it is again dengue fever that could be a problem. The disease tends to come in epidemics mainly in the hotter, wetter months so it should be possible to plan holidays accordingly.

INFECTIOUS DISEASES

Despite the long list, the realistic risks to visitors to the region from infectious diseases are very low with the exception of dengue fever.

Dengue
Risk All countries
Dengue fever is a virus disease spread by the bite of a day-biting mosquito. It causes a feverish illness with headache and severe muscle pains similar to those experienced with a bad, prolonged attack of influenza. Another name is 'break bone fever' and that's what it feels like. Danger signs include prolonged vomiting, blood in the vomit and a blotchy rash. There is no preventive vaccine and mosquito bites should be avoided whenever possible. Self-treatment involves paracetamol, fluids and rest. Do not use aspirin, as this can cause bleeding. Haemorrhagic dengue has been reported only occasionally, manifested by signs of bleeding and shock and requires medical care.

Eosinophilic Meningitis
Risk Tonga
This is a strange illness manifested by scattered abnormal skin sensations, fever and sometimes by the meningitis (headache, vomiting, confusion, neck and spine stiffness), which gives it its name. Eosinophilic

meningitis is caused by a microscopic-size parasite – the rat lungworm – which contaminates raw food. There is no proven specific treatment, but symptoms may require hospitalisation. For prevention pay strict attention to advice on food and drink.

Filiriasis
Risks All countries
Also known as elephantiasis, this disease is spread by mosquitoes. It can cause a fever with lymph gland enlargement and later chronic leg swelling. It is now rare and requires prolonged exposure. Antimosquito precautions are essential. Specific treatment is available.

Hepatitis A
Risk All countries
Hepatitis A is a virus disease causing liver inflammation and is spread by contaminated food or water. Fever, nausea, debility and jaundice (yellow colouration of the skin, eyes and urine) occur and recovery is slow. Most people recover completely but it can be dangerous to people with other forms of liver disease, the elderly and sometimes to pregnant women towards the end of pregnancy. Food is easily contaminated by food preparers, handlers or servers, and by flies. There is no specific treatment. The vaccine is close to 100% protective.

Hepatitis B
Risk All countries
This virus disease causes liver inflammation but the problem is much more serious than hepatitis A and frequently goes on to cause chronic liver disease and even cancer. It is spread, like HIV, by mixing body fluids, ie sexual intercourse, contaminated needles and accidental blood contamination. Treatment is complex and specialised but vaccination is highly effective.

Hepatitis C
Risk Incidence is uncertain within the region but must be assumed to be present
This virus disease is similar to hepatitis B, causing liver inflammation which can go on to chronic liver disease or result in a symptomless carrier state. It's spread almost entirely by blood contamination from shared needles or contaminated needles used for tattooing or body piercing. Treatment is

HEALTH

complex and specialised. There is no vaccine available.

HIV/AIDS
Risk All countries

The incidence of HIV infection is on the rise in the whole region. Safe sex practices are essential at all times. If an injection is needed in a smaller clinic it is best to provide your own needles. Blood transfusion laboratories do tests for HIV.

Japanese B Encephalitis
Reported outbreaks No outbreaks in region, but potential exists for this to happen

This is a serious, but quite rare, virus disease spread by mosquitoes. It can cause brain fever (encephalitis) with an approximate death rate of 30%. There is no specific treatment. An effective vaccine is available but is expensive and involves a course of three injections over a month. Allergic reactions to the vaccine, though rare, can occur. Vaccination is only recommended for anyone staying more than a month and going to work in village situations, and certainly if there has been a reported recent outbreak.

Leptospirosis
Risk American Samoa

Also known as Weil's disease, leptospirosis produces fever, headache, jaundice and, later, kidney failure. It is caused by a spirochaete organism found in water contaminated by rat urine. The organism penetrates skin, so swimming in flooded areas is a risk practice. If diagnosed early it is cured with penicillin.

Typhoid fever
Risk All countries

This is a bacterial infection acquired from contaminated food or water. The germ can be transmitted by food handlers or flies, and can be present in inadequately cooked shellfish. It causes fever, debility and late onset diarrhoea. Untreated it can produce delirium and is occasionally fatal, but the infection is curable with antibiotics. Vaccination is moderately effective, but care with eating and drinking is equally important.

TRAVELLER'S DIARRHOEA

Diarrhoea is caused by viruses, bacteria or parasites present in contaminated food or water. In temperate climates the cause is usually viral, but in the tropics bacteria or parasites are more usual. If you develop diarrhoea, be sure to drink plenty of fluids, preferably an oral rehydration solution (eg Diarolyte, Gastrolyte, Replyte). A few loose stools don't require treatment, but if you start having more than four or five stools a day, you should start taking an antibiotic (usually a quinolone drug) and an antidiarrhoeal agent (such as Loperamide). If diarrhoea is bloody, persists for more than 72 hours or is accompanied by fever, shaking, chills or severe abdominal pain you should seek medical attention. Giardiasis is a particular form of persistent, although not 'explosive', diarrhoea caused by a parasite present in contaminated water. One dose (four tablets) of tinidazole usually cures the infection.

To prevent diarrhoea pay strict attention to the precautions regarding food and water as described in the section on environmental hazards.

ENVIRONMENTAL HAZARDS

Threats to health from animals and insects (including wasps) are rare indeed but you need to be aware of them.

Bites & Stings
JELLYFISH

The notorious box jellyfish (seawasp) has not been recorded in these waters, but the blue-coloured Indo-Pacific 'Man o' War' is found in all waters. If you see these floating in the water or stranded on the beach it is wiser not to go in. The sting is very painful. Treatment involves ice packs and vinegar; do not use alcohol. Smaller cubo-medusae are abundant and are found particularly on still, overcast days. They usually produce only uncomfortably irritating stings but can cause generalised symptoms (although this is rare), especially in someone with poorly controlled heart disease.

POISONOUS CONE SHELLS

Poisonous cone shells abound along shallow coral reefs. Stings mainly cause local reactions but nausea, faintness, palpitations or difficulty in breathing are signs flagging the need for medical attention.

SEA SNAKES

As in all tropical waters, sea snakes may be seen around coral reefs. Unprovoked, sea

---

VENOMOUS MARINE LIFE

Various fish and other sea creatures can sting or bite dangerously, or are dangerous to eat. Listen to local advice on how to avoid them.

Certain cone shells found in the Pacific can sting dangerously or even fatally. Do not touch any cone-shaped shell.

Several species of jellyfish are found in these waters (blue-bottle jellyfish are the most common) and can deliver a painful sting. Dousing in vinegar will deactivate any stingers which have not 'fired', while calamine lotion, antihistamines and analgesics may reduce the reaction and relieve the pain.

Stonefish have poisonous dorsal spines which deliver a very painful sting requiring medical treatment. As the name suggests, they are very well camouflaged and inhabit coral or rocky areas. You'll also need medical treatment if you get stung by lionfish or stingrays.

As a rule, don't touch anything unfamiliar while snorkelling or diving and wear reef sandals, wet-boots or old trainers while paddling or exploring rock pools.

More commonly encountered is stinging coral – it's the bright, sulphur-yellow-coloured coral with a smooth surface. The sting is only bothersome, not dangerous, and can be neutralised by applying vinegar or fresh urine.

---

snakes are extremely unlikely to attack and their fangs will not penetrate a wet suit. First-aid treatment consists of compression bandaging and splinting of the affected limb. Antivenin is effective, but may have to be flown in. Only about 10% of sea snake bites cause serious poisoning.

Coral Cuts

Cuts and abrasions from dead coral cause no more trouble than similar injuries from any other sort of rock, but live coral can cause prolonged infection. If you injure yourself on live coral don't wait until later to treat it. Get out of the water as soon as possible, cleanse the wound thoroughly (getting out all the little bits of coral), apply an antiseptic and cover with a waterproof dressing. Then get back in the water if you want to.

Coral Ear

This is a commonly used name for inflammation of the ear canal. It has nothing to do with coral but is caused by water entering the canal, activating fungal spores resulting in secondary bacterial infection and inflammation. It usually starts after swimming, but can be reactivated by water dripping into the ear canal after a shower, especially if long, wet hair lies over the ear opening. Apparently trivial, it can be very, very painful and can spoil a holiday. Apart from diarrhoea it is the most common reason for tourists to consult a doctor. Self-treatment using an antibiotic-plus-steroid eardrop

preparation (eg Sofradex, Kenacort Otic) is very effective. Stay out of the water until the pain and itch have gone.

Diving Hazards

Because the region has wonderful opportunities for scuba diving, it is easy to get overexcited and neglect strict depth and time precautions. Diving on old shipwrecks is fascinating and some of these dives can be up to or beyond 30m. Coral-viewing dives are not so deep but the temptation to spend longer than safe times at relatively shallow depths is great and is probably the main cause of decompression illness (the 'bends') in the region. Early pains may not be severe and attributed to other causes but any muscle or joint pain after scuba diving must be suspect. There are no compression chambers in the Samoan islands or Tonga. Even experienced divers should check with organisations like DAN (Divers' Alert Network) about the current site and status of compression chambers in the region, and insurance to cover costs both for local treatment and evacuation. Novice divers must be especially careful. If you have not taken out insurance before leaving home you may be able to do so online with DAN.

Food & Water

The municipal water supply in Apia, Pago Pago and Nuku'alofa can be trusted, but elsewhere avoid untreated tap water. In some areas the only fresh water available

HEALTH

may be rain water collected in tanks, and this should be boiled. Steer clear of ice. Only eat fresh fruits or vegetables if cooked or peeled; be wary of dairy products that might contain unpasteurised milk. Eat food which is hot right through and avoid buffet-style meals. Food in restaurants frequented by locals is not necessarily safe, but most resort hotels have good standards of hygiene, although individual food-handlers can carry infection. Food which comes to you piping hot is likely to be safe. Be wary of salads. If you are preparing your own salads from market produce, make sure that each piece and leaf is thoroughly washed with water that is safe. Be adventurous by all means but expect to suffer the consequences if you succumb to adventurous temptation by trying raw fish or crustaceans as eaten by some locals.

FISH POISONING

Ciguatera is a form of poisoning that affects otherwise safe and edible fish unpredictably. Poisoning is characterised by stomach upsets, itching, faintness, slow pulse and bizarre inverted sensations, eg cold feeling hot and vice versa. Ciguatera has been reported in many carnivorous reef fish, especially barracuda but also red snapper, Spanish mackerel and moray eels. There is no safe test to determine whether a fish is poisonous or not. Although local knowledge is not entirely reliable, it is reasonable to eat what the locals are eating. However, fish caught after times of reef destruction, eg after a major hurricane, are more likely to be poisonous. Treatment consists of rehydration and if the pulse is very slow, medication may be needed. Healthy adults will make a complete recovery, although disturbed sensation may persist for some weeks.

Heat Exhaustion

The region lies within the tropics so it is hot and frequently humid. Heat exhaustion is actually a state of dehydration associated to a greater or lesser extent with salt loss. Nat-

ural heat loss is through sweating, making it easy to become dehydrated without realising it. Thirst is a late sign. Small children and old people are especially vulnerable. For adults, heat exhaustion is prevented by drinking at least 3L of water per day and more if actively exercising. Children need about 1½L to 2½L per day. Salt replacement solutions are useful since muscle weakness and cramps are due to salt as well as water loss and can be made worse by drinking water alone. The powders used for treating dehydration due to diarrhoea are just as effective when it is due to heat exhaustion. Apart from commercial solutions, a reasonable drink consists of a good pinch of salt to a pint (½L) of water. Salt tablets can result in too much salt being taken in, causing headaches and confusion.

Heatstroke

When the cooling effect of sweating fails, heat stroke ensues. This is a dangerous and emergency condition characterised not only by muscle weakness and exhaustion, but by mental confusion. Skin will be hot and dry. If this occurs 'put the fire out' by cooling the body with water on the outside and if possible with cold drinks for the inside. Seek medical help as a follow-up anyway, but urgently if the person can't drink.

Sunburn

It should go without saying that exposure to the ultraviolet (UV) rays of the sun causes burning of the skin with accompanying pain, dehydration and misery (together with the long-term danger of skin cancer) but experience shows that reminders are necessary. The time of highest risk is between 11am and 3pm and remember that cloud cover does not block out UV rays. The Australian *Slip, slop, slap* slogan is a useful 'mantra' – slip on a T-shirt or blouse, slop on a sunscreen lotion of at least 15+ rating, and slap on a hat. Treat sunburn like any other burn – cool, wet dressings are best. Severe swelling may respond to a cortisone cream.

Language

CONTENTS

SAMOAN

The main language spoken in the Samoan islands is Samoan, a Polynesian language similar to Maori, Tongan, Hawaiian and Tahitian. All of these belong to the Austronesian family of languages, which also includes Malay, Malagasy and Melanesian languages. The similarity between Samoan and Malay reflects ancient migrations to Polynesia from southeast Asia.

Nearly everyone in Samoa speaks English as a second language, so unless you're travelling to some of the more remote villages on Savai'i, you're not likely to have any major communication problems.

Having said that, it's worth the effort to try and speak a little Samoan and people are delighted when foreigners make any attempt to use it – whether it's a simple *malo* (hello) in greeting or *tasi pia fa'amolemole* when you're asking for a beer.

Pacific languages do not use an 's' to denote plurals (as the English language does). Although this rule is happily broken almost everywhere – a Samoan hotel owner will offer to show you around their *fales* (huts). We have stuck to the rules in this book and relied on the context to make the meaning clear.

There are a few shops in Apia and Pago Pago that sell Samoan dictionaries. The Wesley Bookshop in Pago Pago carries a good one, compiled by GB Milner and published by Polynesian Press; a less comprehensive publication is available at the la Malamalama Bookshop in Apia.

PRONUNCIATION

The Samoan alphabet consists of only 14 letters – five vowels and nine consonants. Stress is normally placed on the next-to-last syllable.

Vowels

The five vowels may be long or short, depending on whether or not they are stressed, but the actual difference in sound between them is very slight to the untrained ear. A long vowel is conventionally indicated by a line above it (a macron) and is pronounced as a long version of its short counterpart.

Diphthongs (combinations of vowels) are also common in Samoan, and are pronounced as they would be in English (eg in the word 'ear').

The main thing to remember is that all vowels are pronounced (you'd be amazed how many travellers pronounce *fale* as the English word 'fail' rather than the correct 'fa-leh').

a   as in 'father'
e   as in 'set'
i   as in 'sit'
o   as in 'hot'
u   as in 'full'

Consonants

Most consonants are pronounced the same as their English counterparts. The letter **g** is pronounced as a soft 'ng' – so that *palagi* is pronounced 'pa-lung-i'. The glottal stop (represented by an apostrophe) is the sound you hear between the vowels in the expression 'oh-oh' – it's produced by a momentary closing of the throat. In Samoan. the glottal stop replaces the 'k' of other Polynesian languages.

CONVERSATION & ESSENTIALS

Hello/Hi.	*Malo.*
Goodbye.	*Tofa.*
Bye. (informal)	*Fa.*
Goodbye/Farewell.	*Tofa soifua.*

Good morning.	*Talofa.*
Good evening.	*Talofa.*
Good night.	*Manuia le po.*
Yes.	*Ioe.*
No.	*Leai.*
Maybe.	*Masalo.*
Please.	*Fa'amolemole.*
Thank you (very much).	*Fa'afetai (tele).*
Welcome.	*Afio mai.*
Excuse me.	*Tulou.*
I'm sorry.	*Ua ou sese.*
Forgive me.	*Malie.*
How are you?	*O a mai 'oe?*
I'm fine, thanks.	*Manuia, faafetai.*
What's your name?	*O ai lou igoa?*
My name is ...	*O lo'u igoa o ...*
Where are you from?	*Fea lou atunu'u?*
Where are you going?	*Alu i fea? (often used as a pleasantry)*
Are you married?	*Ua fai se aiga?*
How many children do you have?	*E to'afia tama'iti?*
How old are you?	*Fia ou tausaga?*
I'm ... years old.	*Ua ... o'u tausaga.*
Do you like ...?	*E te manao i le ...?*
I like it very much.	*O lo'u vaisu.*
May I?	*E mafai?*
It's all right/No problem.	*Ua lelei.*

girl	*teine*
little girl	*teine'iti'iti*
woman	*fafine*
mother	*tina*
boy	*tama*
little boy	*tama'iti'iti*
man	*tamaloa*
father	*tama*
family	*'aiga*
boyfriend	*uo tama*
girlfriend	*uo teine*
white person	*palagi*

bad	*leaga*
beautiful	*manaia*
fine	*manuia*
good	*lelei*
happy	*fiafia*
journey	*malaga*
love	*alofa*
How much is it?	*E fia le ta'u?*
I'd like to buy it.	*Ou te fia fa'atauina.*
It's too expensive.	*Taugata mo a'u.*

LANGUAGE DIFFICULTIES

I understand.	*Ua ou Malamalama.*
I don't understand.	*Ou te le mala-malama.*
I don't speak ...	*Ou te le tautala ...*
Do you speak English?	*Ete iloa Nanu?*
How do you say ...?	*E faapefea ona ...?*
Please write it down.	*Fa'amolemole tusi i lalo.*

OUT & ABOUT

Where is (the/a) ...?	*O fea (le/se) ...?*
church	*falesa*
city centre	*nofoaga autu o le a'ai*
hospital	*falemai*
market	*maketi*
store	*faleoloa*

beach	*matafaga*
bird	*manulele*
chicken	*moa*
entrance/exit	*ulufale/ulufafo*
fish	*i'a*
flower	*fuamatala*
house	*fale*
island	*motu*
lake	*vaituloto*
mosquito	*namu*
pig	*pua'a*
rain	*timu*
sea	*sami*
sun	*la*
village	*nu'u*
wind	*savili*

TONGAN

Tongan is a Polynesian language belonging to the Austronesian language family. Its closest relatives are the other Polynesian languages like Samoan, Hawaiian, Maori and Tahitian. More distant cousins are Malay, Malagasy and Melanesian languages, a connection that adds weight to the widely accepted theory that the Polynesian peoples originated in South-East Asia.

The same Tongan language is spoken on all the islands in Tonga, with the exception of Niuafo'ou, the most north-westerly island, where a dialect that's closer to Samoan is spoken.

Both Tongan and English are used in the schools throughout Tonga, so you shouldn't encounter any problems communicating in

English. On major islands (Tongatapu, Vava'u), almost everyone speaks English as a second language. On smaller, more remote islands people may speak less English, but communication can always be achieved somehow. Tongans are often surprised when foreigners make an attempt to speak their language, and will be very helpful and encouraging.

PRONUNCIATION

The Tongan alphabet has only 16 letters, with five vowels and 11 consonants.

It's worth listening to the way native speakers pronounce vowels because vowel length can affect the meaning of some words. You may see vowels written with a macron or *toloi* (eg **ā**), which indicates that they are long. The long sound is simply an extended and accented (stressed) version of the short vowel. Stress is placed on the next to last syllable in most Tongan words, unless there's a long vowel, in which case that syllable receives the stress.

Another important element of Tongan language is the glottal stop, represented by an apostrophe ('). It signals a momentary halt in the flow of air through the vocal cords, similar to the non-voice between the syllables of 'oh-oh'.

Diphthongs, or combinations of vowels, are pronounced by enunciating each of the component sounds individually. When a glottal stop is inserted between two vowels, a stop must be made in the pronunciation. This, too, is a significant element of Tongan language that changes not only the pronunciation but also the meaning of words: for example, *tae* means 'cough', but *ta'e* means 'faeces'! The word *hau* means 'earring', but *ha'u* means 'come here'.

Even if you do make mistakes with the pronunciation of glottal stops, and long and short vowels, Tongan people are usually very helpful, and they'll still try to understand what you're saying.

The letters used in the Tongan alphabet are pronounced more or less as follows:

Vowels

a	as in 'far' or as in 'ball'
e	as in 'end'
i	as in 'Fifi'
o	as in 'go'
u	as in 'tune'

Consonants

f	as in 'far'
h	as in 'here'
k	as the 'c' in 'curd'
l	as in 'love', with a slap of the tongue
m	as in 'me'
n	as in 'no'
ng	as in 'singer', not as in 'finger'
p	midway between the 'p' in 'park' and the 'b' in 'bark'
s	as in 'sand'
t	midway between the 't' in 'tip' and the 'd' in 'dip'
v	as in 'very'

CONVERSATION & ESSENTIALS

Hello.	*Malo e lelei.*
Goodbye.	*'Alu a.* (to someone leaving)
	Nofo a. (response to someone staying)
Good morning.	*Malo e lelei ki he pongipongini.*
Good evening.	*Malo e lelei ki he efiafini.*
Yes.	*'Io.*
No.	*'Ikai.*
Maybe.	*Mahalo pe.*
Please.	*Faka molemole.*
Thank you (very much).	*Malo ('aupito).*
You're welcome.	*'Io malo.*
Welcome.	*Talitali fiefia.*
Excuse me.	*Kataki.*
I'm sorry.	*Faka molemole'iau.*
How are you?	*Fefe hake?*
Fine, thank you.	*Sai pe, malo.*
What's your name?	*Ko hai ho hingoa?*
My name is ...	*Ko hoku hingoa ko ...*
Where are you from?	*Ko ho'o ha'u mei fe fonua?*
I'm from ...	*Ko 'eku ha'u mei ...*
Are you married?	*Kuo ke'osi mali?*
How old are you?	*Koe ha ho ta'u motua?*
I'm ... years old.	*'Oku 'ou ta'u ... ta'u motua.*
I'm a tourist/student.	*Ko 'eku ha'u (eve'eva/taha ako).*
Do you like ...?	*'Oku ke sai'ia 'ihe ...?*
I like it very much.	*'Oku 'ou sai'ia 'aupito.*
I don't like ...	*'Oku ikai teu sai'ia ...*
Just a minute.	*Tali si'i.*
May I?	*Faka molemole kau?*
It's all right/no problem.	*'Io 'oku sai/sai pe ia.*

girl	*ta'ahine*
woman	*fefine*
boy	*tamasi'i*

man	tangata
big/bigger	lahi/lahi ange
small/smaller	si'i si'i/si'i si'i ange
more	lahi
less	si'i
expensive	mamafa
cheap/cheaper	ma'ama'a/ma'a ma'a ange
good	lelei
bad	kovi
pretty	faka 'ofa 'ofa

Where is ...?	Ko fe'ia a'e ...?
How much is it?	Fiha hono totongi?
I'd like to buy it.	'Oku ou fie fakatau ia.
It's too expensive for me.	Fu'u mamafa kiate au.

LANGUAGE DIFFICULTIES

I understand.	'Oku mahino kiate 'au.
I don't understand.	'Oku ikai ke mahino kiate 'au.
Do you speak English?	'Oku ke lava 'o lea faka palangi?
Does anyone speak English?	'Oku 'iai ha taha'oku lea faka palangi?
How do you say ...?	Koe ha ho lea ...?
What is this called?	Ko 'e ha hono hingoa 'o 'e me'a ko 'eni?

OUT & ABOUT

bank	pangike
beach	matatahi
bridge	hala kavakava
church	fale lotu
city centre	i loto kolo
embassy	'api 'oe 'amipasitoa
hospital	fale mahaki
island	motu
lake	ano vai
market	maketi
ocean (deep)	moana
palace	palasi
post office	positi 'ofisi
rain	'uha
restaurant	fale kai
ruins	maumau
sea	tahi
street/road	hala
suburb	lotokolo
sun	la'a
telephone office	fale telefoni
tourist office	'ofisi taki mamata
tower	taua
village	kolo si'i si'i
wind	matangi

LANGUAGE

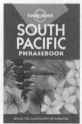

Also available from Lonely Planet:
South Pacific Phrasebook

Glossary

SAMOAN ISLANDS

'aiga – family, descent group
aitu – spirit, ghost
alia – war canoe
ali'i – one of two orders of high chief *(matai)*
alofa – love
aoa – banyan tree
ava – passage through a reef
'ava – traditional, mildly intoxicating drink (also called *kava*) produced from the root of the *Piper methysticum* (pepper plant)

esi – papaya, pawpaw

fa'aaloalo – respect for elders
fa'afafine – effeminate men who sometimes dress as a woman
fa'afetai – thank you
fa'alavelave – occasion, such as a wedding or funeral, when family assistance should be given; literally, 'distraction from normal life'
fa'a Samoa – according to Samoan customs and tradition
fai – banana
fale – a traditional thatched house
fale talimalo – traditional Samoan guesthouse or hotel
faleaitu – traditional entertainment by Samoan youth
faletua – wife of the high chief or *ali'i*
fautasi – Samoan longboat, made from the *fau* tree
fiafia – time of celebration; presentation of singing and dancing
fofo – traditional Samoan healer
fono – governing council of a village made up of its *matai*
Fono, the – the national parliament

ie faitaga – man's undecorated formal *lava-lava*
ie toga – finely woven mat made from pandanus fibres
ifilele – large tree used for timber and *'ava* bowls
ifoga – traditional apology

kava – see *'ava*
kirikiti – Samoan cricket
koko Samoa – drink made with locally grown roasted cocoa beans, sugar and water

lalaga – weaving
laumei – sea turtle
lava-lava – wraparound sarong
lotu – religious observance

malae – village green; sacred site in pre-Christian times
malu – female tattoo
mana – supernatural power
matai – chief of an *'aiga*
mea alofa – gift
mo'o – gecko
musu – moodiness, silence as form of protest

oka – Samoan dish of marinated raw fish

palagi – white-skinned person; literally, 'those who burst from the sky' (*pa* = burst; *lagi* = sky)
paopao – traditional outrigger canoe
pe'a – male tattoo
pili – skink
pisupo – corned beef
pola – coconut-leaf blinds
popo – mature coconut; also a spongy, white substance in a sprouting coconut known as Samoan ice cream
puaa – pig
pulenu'u – village mayor
puletasi – long skirt and tunic worn by Samoan women

sa – sacred, forbidden; time set aside for prayer
sene – currency unit; 100 *sene* equals ST1
siapo – bark cloth made from the paper mulberry tree

ta'amu – large edible tuber, 'big taro'
tala – Samoan unit of currency (ST)
talking chief – see *tulafale*
tamaiti – children
tanoa – *'ava* bowl
taulaitu – spirit medium
taulasea – traditional healer
taupou – title of office bestowed by high-ranking *ali'i* upon a young (virgin) woman of his *'aiga*
teuila – red ginger; Samoa's national floral emblem
to'ona'i – Sunday lunch
tufuga – tattoo artist
tulafale – an orator who liaises between the *ali'i* (high chief) and outside entities, carries out ceremonial duties, engages in ritual debates and, traditionally, protects the *ali'i*

u'a – mulberry tree
ula – flower garland; also lobster
umu – traditional underground oven
umukuka – cooking house

vai Samoa – traditional medicines

TONGA

ahi – sandalwood
'api – plantation of 3.34 hectares

'esi – resting site or mound

faikakai – breadfruit pudding
faito'o – traditional Tongan medicine
faka Tonga – the 'Tongan way'
fakaleiti – men who dress and behave as women
fakapale – custom of rewarding Tongan dancer with money; literally 'to award a prize'
fala – everyday mats
fale koloa – small grocery kiosks
falekai – restaurant
fatongia – duties and obligations
feke – octopus
feta'aki – single piece of *tapa* cloth
fihu – valuable, silk-like pandanus mat
fingota – shellfish

hala – road
heilala – Tonga's national flower

'ika – fish
'inasi – traditional Tongan agricultural fair or festival

kailao – war dance
kalia – large seafaring canoes, also war canoes
kapa pulu – tinned beef
kava – intoxicating drink made from the root of the pepper shrub; also see *'ava*
kava kalapu – *kava* club
kilikili – pumice-like volcanic gravel
koloa – wealth; offerings given out of respect and to mark important occasions
kumala – sweet potato
kupesi – relief of *tapa* pattern

lafo – Tongan game played with pieces called *pa'anga*
lakalaka – a traditional dance
langanga – strips of tapa
langi – pyramidal stone tomb

mala'e – sacred area/field
malau – local name for the Niuafo'ou megapode, a bird native only to Niuafo'ou
mali – spouse
malo – thank you
matapule – 'talking chief' involved in ceremonies and burial rituals of the nobility
Maui – demigod who, according to one myth, fished Tonga out of the sea
ma'ulu'ulu – dance performed at feasts and on public holidays
motu – coral islet

ngatu – decorated/finished *tapa* product

pa'anga – Tongan unit of currency (T$)
palangi – foreigner (originally *papalangi*)
pasi – bus stop
peka – flying fox or fruit bat
pekepekatae – white-rumped swiftlets
popao – outrigger canoe

RTA – Royal Tongan Airlines

seniti – currency unit; 100 *seniti* equals T$1
sipi – mutton flaps

ta'ovala – pandanus mat tied around the waist; worn on formal occasions
tapa – mulberry bark cloth
tapu – sacred
tau'olunga – graceful traditional dance performed by a solo woman at ceremonies
TCC – Tonga Communications Corporation
TCF – Tonga Cooperative Federation (supermarket)
tevolo – devil spirit
tiki – wooden statue representing old Polynesian god
toa – ironwood tree
Tu'i Tonga – royal title
tuitui – candlenut
tupenu – men's wraparound skirt
TVB – Tongan Visitors Bureau

u'a – inside bark of the mulberry tree, used for making *siapo*
'umu – stone oven in the ground

Behind the Scenes

THIS BOOK

Lonely Planet's first guide to the lovely Samoan islands (including both Samoa, then called 'Western' Samoa, and American Samoa) was published in 1990. Our first guide to the delightful kingdom of Tonga was published that same year. The intrepid Deanna Swaney researched and wrote both books.

This edition of the guidebook combines all three political entities (Samoa, American Samoa and Tonga) in one handy package, reflecting the close cultural ties between the islands and to better cater for travellers taking advantage of air passes to visit both island groups in one trip. Paul Smitz was the book's coordinating author, and researched and wrote all Samoan and American Samoan chapters. Susannah Farfor did all on-the-ground research and writeup in Tonga. Ex-Samoan resident Martin Robinson wrote the expert Samoan Snapshots while ex-Tongan resident Miranda Tetlow wrote Tongan Snapshots. The Health chapter was written by Fiji-based Pacific-health expert Dr Michael Sorokin. Zayne D'Crus wrote the boxed text 'When It's Raining Cats and Dogs'. *Samoan Islands & Tonga* was commissioned in Lonely Planet's Melbourne office, and produced by the following:

Commissioning Editors Errol Hunt
Coordinating Editor Jeanette Wall
Coordinating Cartographer Jolyon Philcox
Coordinating Layout Designer Wibowo Rusli
Managing Cartographer Corinne Waddell
Managing Editors Imogen Bannister, Carolyn Boicos, Suzannah Schwer

Assisting Editors Michelle Bennett, Yvonne Byron, Gennifer Ciavarra, Barbara Delissen, Liz Heynes, Dianne Schallmeiner, Louisa Syme
Assisting Cartographers Simon Tillema, Ross Butler
Cover Designer Sonya Brooke
Colour Designer Liz White
Project Managers John Shippick, Nancy Ianni, Eoin Dunlevy
Language Content Coordinator Quentin Frayne

Fa'afetai and malo 'aupito to Pete Cruttenden, Sally Darmody, Anna Demant, Laura Gibb, Darren O'Connell, Malisa Plesa, Marg Toohey, Jane Thompson, Meagan Williams and Gabrielle Wilson

THANKS
PAUL SMITZ

Thank you to everyone who made me feel welcome and helped me out with information across Samoa, American Samoa and – while my tan was fading in spectacular fashion – back home. In particular, thanks to Anita and Josh for surfing tips and reminding me just how small 'Upolu is; Fune, for postdinner company and conversation; Daniel for making the Rosa sound like such an appealing place ('People die!') and for the tipple; everyone I met on Ofu for the all-round good feelings and the beachside bonfire, including world travellers Barbara and Boštjan Lozar; Fipi, Puluseu, So'o, Apolima-tai and Seni for allowing me to play volleyball badly and to consume more food than I thought was humanly possible on Apolima; Jason, Tisa and the Candyman for nurturing me back to health; Adam for the walking tips for Tutuila; Errol

---

for just being Errol; Susannah for writing half this book, but mainly for promises of authentic *kava;* and Marcelle for a big dose of true on-the-road friendship. Special thanks to the enigmatic woman who looks to her Eskimo friend.

SUSANNAH FARFOR
Huge thanks to Ian Malcolm for sharing the Tonga highlights and 'living the Tongan dream', and to family forever in the Pacific. Thanks to the many Tongans and semilocals (particularly the Peace Corp and AusAID workers) who answered so many questions and queries, and to the TVB for their assistance.

A warm and tropical thanks to Tenzin Tsering; Lhamo Tsering; Trevor, Fusi and Steve in Ha'apai; Dave and Renee; companion hikers on 'Eua; Paul and Brianna for coaxing me through Mariner's Cave; adventurous Edward McCowan, Nicholas Car, Pip Coen, the German dental students and British medical students (Lucy Crosland, Neil Brierley, Alison Cran, Stephanie H and Rob Greville) for the great enthusiasm in providing tips and feedback, and particularly for making rainy days in Ha'apai fun. Corina, hope you're feeling better! Thanks to Lincoln Flynn and all the travellers who offered their valuable tips and feedback – both on the road/ferry in Tonga and through reader's letters. Paul Smitz, you are the best coordinating author ever!

OUR READERS
Many thanks to the travellers who used the last edition and wrote to us with helpful hints, useful advice and interesting anecdotes:

A Sarah Acland, Joe Altham, Nir Altman, Paula Antony **B** Shirley Bador, Edward Baral, Robert Barash, Brian & Belinda Barton, Tina Bartys, Rainer Beck, Tonya Beck, Allison Bernard, Marie Bell, Kirsty Blair, Jennifer Bond, Shelley Bourke, Victor Brumby **C** Mark Challis, Richard Cleaver, Kevin Cromwell **D** Géza Dámosy, Sabine Delrue, Luis Di Criscio, Julie DiCataldo, Aurora Dowling **E** Humphry Esser, Caroline Ewing **F** Katharina Faleovalu, Renee Farrar, Jim Flewelling, Pamela Flick, Michele & Richie Fox, Daniela Friedrich, David Friend **G** John Garratt, Dan Gaughan, Line Glemmestad, Sandra Gros **H** Jacqueline Harris, Lucy Harris, Jennifer Heebink, Rob Hendrikx, Hjoerdis Hentschel, Earl Hinz, Evan Hunter **J** Paul Jackson, Ben Jansen, Trevor Jefferson, Graham Jenner, Sian Jones **K** Jennifer Kavanagh, Paul & Becki Kimber **L** Chris Lange,

Gerhard Lammel, Paul Lassman, Fabien Lebon, Mike Lebson, Paul Lenz, Raimar Lenz, Caroline Lofthouse, Jürgen Lottermoser **M** Rowena Macgill, Monica Mackaness, Hitesh Makwana, Michael Marquardt, Matteo Marsilio, Neil Mattey, Liam McGowan, Angela McKay, Angela McWhirter, Markella Mikkelsen, Stuart & Vine Molony, Hamish Monro, Peter Morton, Jen Murray **N** Vanessa Nitsos **O** Kate O'Reilly **P** Elizabeth Parker, Keith Parsons, Henning Petersen, Mahannah Pike, Stephanie Briana Poyer **R** Thomas Rau, Sally Raudon, Christine Riches, Graham Ritchie, David Roberts, Andrea Rogge, Alan Ruben **S** Sara Sande, Casey Smith, Josh Smith, Cassilda Soeiro, Karin Steinkamp, Kathleen Stewart, Scott Sutton **T** George Talbot, Belinda Tate, Paul Taumoepeau, Donald Telfer, Giuliana Torta **U** Catherine Urbani **V** Eric Vaandering, Maurice van Liempd, Chris von Saarn **W** Reto Wagner, Darren Walmsley, Bayley Webster, Birgit Weischedel, Catrin Williams, Kylie Willows

ACKNOWLEDGMENTS
Many thanks to the following for the use of their content:

Globe on back cover ©Mountain High Maps 1993 Digital Wisdom, Inc.

Index

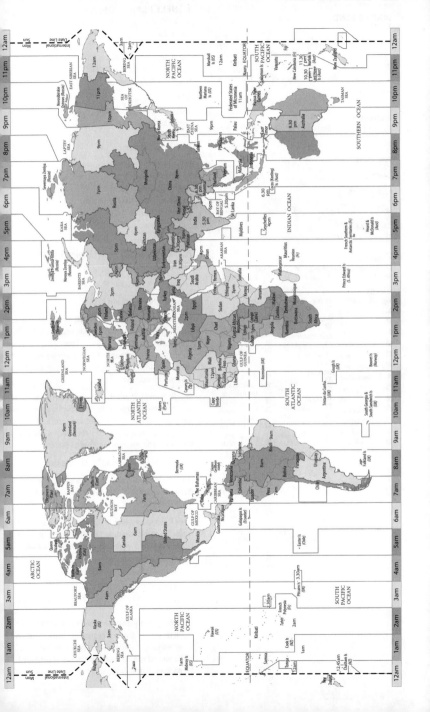

320

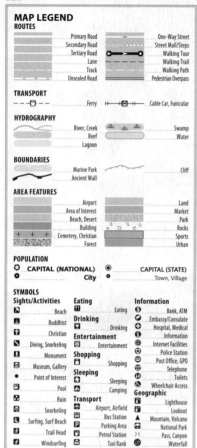

MAP LEGEND

LONELY PLANET OFFICES

Australia
Head Office
Locked Bag 1, Footscray, Victoria 3011
☎ 03 8379 8000, fax 03 8379 8111
talk2us@lonelyplanet.com.au

USA
150 Linden St, Oakland, CA 94607
☎ 510 893 8555, toll free 800 275 8555
fax 510 893 8572
info@lonelyplanet.com

UK
72–82 Rosebery Ave,
Clerkenwell, London EC1R 4RW
☎ 020 7841 9000, fax 020 7841 9001
go@lonelyplanet.co.uk

Published by Lonely Planet Publications Pty Ltd
ABN 36 005 607 983

© Lonely Planet Publications Pty Ltd 2006

© photographers as indicated 2006

Cover photographs: Local youngsters play on the beach at a youth camp, Randy Olson/National Geographic Image Collection (front); Lalomanu Beach on the eastern end of 'Upolu Island, Samoa, Peter Hendrie/Lonely Planet Images (back). Many of the images in this guide are available for licensing from Lonely Planet Images: www.lonelyplanetimages.com.

All rights reserved. No part of this publication may be copied, stored in a retrieval system, or transmitted in any form by any means, electronic, mechanical, recording or otherwise, except brief extracts for the purpose of review, and no part of this publication may be sold or hired, without the written permission of the publisher.

Printed by SNP Security Printing Pte Ltd, Singapore

Lonely Planet and the Lonely Planet logo are trademarks of Lonely Planet and are registered in the US Patent and Trademark Office and in other countries.

Lonely Planet does not allow its name or logo to be appropriated by commercial establishments, such as retailers, restaurants or hotels. Please let us know of any misuses: www.lonelyplanet.com/ip.

Although the authors and Lonely Planet have taken all reasonable care in preparing this book, we make no warranty about the accuracy or completeness of its content and, to the maximum extent permitted, disclaim all liability arising from its use.